MDX Solutions
Second Edition

With Microsoft® SQL Server™ Analysis Services 2005 and Hyperion® Essbase

George Spofford
Sivakumar Harinath
Christopher Webb
Dylan Hai Huang
Francesco Civardi

Wiley Publishing, Inc.

MDX Solutions, Second Edition: With Microsoft® SQL Server™ Analysis Services 2005 and Hyperion® Essbase
Published by
Wiley Publishing, Inc.
10475 Crosspoint Boulevard
Indianapolis, IN 46256
www.wiley.com

ISBN-13: 978-0-471-74808-3

ISBN-10: 0-471-74808-0

Manufactured in the United States of America

10 9 8 7 6 5 4 3

2MA/RX/QS/QW/IN

For general information on our other products and services or to obtain technical support, please contact our Customer Care Department within the U.S. at (800) 762-2974, outside the U.S. at (317) 572-3993 or fax (317) 572-4002.

Library of Congress Catalog Nmuber: 2005032778

About the Authors

George Spofford is a Distinguished Engineer at Hyperion Solutions, Inc. He has been developing OLAP server and client software since 1998, when he led the development of FreeThink, one of the first desktop multidimensional modelling and analysis tools provided by Power Thinking tools, Inc. Upon its acquisition by Computer Corporation of America, he became product architect for their integrated OLAP/data warehouse server. Subsequently, he co-founded the consulting firms Dimensional systems and DSS Lab, where he provided technology consulting, benchmark development and auditing, and development services to vendors and users alike of decision-support technology, including organizations such as AC Nielsen, IMS Health, Intel, Oracle, and Microsoft. He has written numerous articles for trade journals, spoken at trade shows, co-authored the book *Microsoft OLAP Solutions*, and authored the first edition of *MDX Solutions*. george@dsslab.com.

Sivakumar Harinath was born in Chennai, India. Siva has a Ph.D. in Computer Science from the University of Illinois at Chicago. His thesis title was: "Data Management Support for Distributed Data Mining of Large Datasets over High Speed Wide Area Networks." Siva has worked for Newgen Software Technologies (P) Ltd., IBM Toronto Labs, Canada, and has been at Microsoft since February of 2002. Siva started as a Software Design Engineer in Test (SDET) in the Analysis Services Performance Team and is currently an SDET Lead for Analysis Services 2005. Siva's other interests include high performance computing, distributed systems and high-speed networking. Siva is married to Shreepriya and had twins Praveen and Divya during the course of writing this book. His personal interests include travel, games/sports (in particular, Chess, Carrom, Racquet Ball, Board games) and Cooking. You can reach Siva at sivakumar. harinath@microsoft.com.

Christopher Webb (cwebb_olap@hotmail.com) has worked with Microsoft Analysis/OLAP Services since 1998 in a variety of roles, including three years spent with Microsoft Consulting Services. He is a regular contributor to the microsoft.public.sqlserver.olap newsgroup and his blog can be found at http://spaces.msn.com/members/cwebbbi/.

Dylan Hai Huang (Dylanh@microsoft.com) is currently working as a program manager in Microsoft Office Business Application Team. Before joining the current team, he had been working in Microsoft Analysis Service Performance Team. His main interests are business intelligence, high performance computation and data mining.

Francesco Civardi (fcivardi@daisylabs.com, fcivardi@hotmail.com) is Chief Scientist at DaisyLabs, a Business Intelligence Company. He has been working with Microsoft Analysis/OLAP Services since 1999, in the financial, industrial and retail sectors. His main interests are mathematical and financial modelling and Data Mining. He is Professor of Data Analysis Tools and Techniques at the Catholic University of Brescia and Cremona.

Credits

Executive Editor
Robert M. Elliott

Development Editor
Ed Connor

Technical Editor
Deepak Puri

Production Editor
Angela Smith

Copy Editor
Foxxe Editorial Services

Editorial Manager
Mary Beth Wakefield

Production Manager
Tim Tate

**Vice President and
Executive Group Publisher**
Richard Swadley

**Vice President and Executive
Publisher**
Joseph B. Wikert

Project Coordinator
Ryan Steffen

Graphics and Production Specialists
Denny Hager
Joyce Haughey
Jennifer Heleine
Stephanie D. Jumper
Alicia South

Quality Control Technicians
John Greenough
Charles Spencer
Brian Walls

Proofreading
TECHBOOKS Production Services

Indexing
Sherry Massey

Contents

Acknowledgments

This book would not be possible without the assistance of a large number of people providing several kinds of support, especially editing of prose, clarifying explanations, verifying the content of the material, hoisting of slack in workloads, and tolerating the long and persistent retreats into the home offices that enabled the authors to get the work done. George Chow and Richard Mao at Simba Technologies get special recognition for authoring chapter 15 (Client Programming Basics). Deepak Puri provided technical review during book development. The authors would like to thank the following individuals or organizations for their assistance during this effort:

Matt Abrams, Steve Allen, Luca Allieri, T.K. Anand, Teresa Andena, Dario Appini, Jon Axon, Graeme Axworthy, Nenshad Bardoliwalla, Marin Bezic, Veronica Biagi, Peter Bull, Matt Carroll, the Computer Café, Marcella Caviola, Saugata Chowdhury, Chiara Civardi, Claudio Civetta, Valerio Caloni, Marina Costa, Andrea Cozzoli, Thierry D'Hers, Marius Dumitru, Darryl Eckstein, Leah Etienne, Willfried Faerber, Hanying Feng, Curt Fish, Lon Fisher, Carlo Gerelli, Robert Gersten, Stefania Ghiretti, Alessandro Giancane, Sergei Gringauze, Colin Hardie, Alice Hu, Alessandro Huber, Graham Hunter, Andrea Improta, Gonsalvo Isaza, Thomas Ivarsson, Eric Jacobsen, Bruce Johnson, Yan Li, Ben van Lierop, Domiziana Luddi, John Lynn, Dermot MacCarthy, Aldo Manzetti, Al Marciante, Stefan Marin, Teodoro Marinucci, Frank McGuff, Krishna Meduri, Sreekumar Menon, Akshai Mirchandani, Michael Nader, Amir Netz, Ariel Netz, the Office Business Application team, Mimi Olivier, Marco Olivieri, Paul Olsen, Domenico Orofino, Massimo Pasqualetti, Mosha Pasumansky, Franco Perduca, Tim Peterson, Ernesto Pezzulla, Simona Poggi, John Poole,

Amynmohamed Rahan, Giuseppe Romanini, Marco Russo, Carlo Emilio Salaroglio, Lisa Santoro, Vaishnavi Sashikanth, Rick Sawa, John Shiangoli, Eric Smadja, Paolo Tenti, Alaric Thomas, Erik Thomsen, Richard Tkatchuk, Fabrizio Tosca, Piero Venturi, Massimo Villa, Mark Yang, Jeffrey Wang, Barry Ward, Robert Zare, and Tonglian Zheng. Ed Connor helped form this work into a coherent book, and Robert Elliott kept it on track.

Introduction

Dimensional applications are best and most easily built using a dimensional language. These dimensional applications are typified by the related notions of OLAP and dimensional data warehouses and marts. MDX (for *MultiDimensional eXpressions*) is the most widely accepted software language used for these applications. The book you read here, *MDX Solutions*, is the second edition of a guide to learning and using MDX. Since the first edition of *MDX Solutions*, the number of analytical applications that use MDX has grown very large, and several more servers and many third-party and homegrown client tools now allow you to use MDX to express the logic you use to calculate and to retrieve your information.

As a language, MDX is rather different in style and feel from SQL, and quite different from other programming languages like C++, C#, Lisp, Fortran, and so on. You can think of the formula language of a spreadsheet like Excel as another programming language, and while it is different than Excel, characterizing MDX as a sort of Excel-like SQL or a SQL-like Excel seems more apt than any other analogy. (If you're familiar with other OLAP query or calculation languages, it has more in common with them, but many readers will not be.)

In particular, compared to the first edition, this edition incorporates both a new version of a product and a product that has added support for MDX since then. Microsoft has released Microsoft® SQL Server 2005™ Analysis Services, which changes its use of MDX from the product's prior version. Hyperion Solutions has released Hyperion® System™ 9 BI+™ Analytic Services™, which builds on the Essbase functionality that introduced the term OLAP to the industry. (Since this book will refer to these products many times, we will refer to them with names that are informally shortened from the vendor's designations: *Analysis Services 2005*, *Analysis Services 2000*, and *Essbase 9*.)

Overview of the Book and Technology

The dimensional language works with a (multi-) dimensional data model. There are no formal or detailed standards of data model in the OLAP industry, and the number of details that would need to be worked out is quite large. However, there are a good number of aspects that are common by convention to different products. MDX has a standard syntax that handles the constructs and capabilities of many servers quite well. Vendors with additional capabilities extend MDX to provide access to them.

MDX originated as part of Microsoft's OLE DB for OLAP specification, and while the language was controlled by Microsoft, it sought input from several OLAP vendors and industry participants to help ensure that the language would be useful to multiple vendors. Microsoft has committed to transfer control of the specification to the XMLA Council (http://www.xmla.org), a consortium committed to coordinating and promoting a standard XML for Analysis specification. XML for Analysis is a web services API, spearheaded and supported by Microsoft, Hyperion and SAS Institute.

This book attempts to guide a pragmatic course between learning the language, and learning how to use it for the three product versions that we emphasize:

- Microsoft Analysis Services 2005
- Essbase 9
- Microsoft Analysis Services 2000

Microsoft has made a number of changes to its underlying data model with the 2005 release, and also a number of changes to how things built in MDX work with each other. This book devotes significant attention to using both of these kinds of changes. The Hyperion Essbase model has had a number of additional capabilities as well.

Other vendors or projects whose server products support MDX include: Applix, Microstrategy, MIS AG, Mondrian, SAP, and SAS Institute. Other companies, like Simba and Digital Aspects, provide tools and SDKs to assist construction of servers and clients that use MDX and related APIs. A large number of client tools use MDX to provide end users the ability to access sophisticated applications using MDX.

In order to fully wield MDX, you will need to really master how the server supports OLAP and how MDX behaves, since the two sides impact each other. Awesome MDX can make up for or extend the capabilities of a dimensional design; an awesome server design can eliminate the need to devote much MDX to solving the problem. This being a book on MDX, we won't spend much time telling you how not to use MDX, but we will point out some cases where you're better off using some other aspect of your application environment.

How This Book Is Organized

If you are new to MDX, welcome! The chapters are sequenced to introduce you to the syntax, capabilities and use of MDX. Chapters 1, 2 and 3 introduce the basics of MDX and use. Chapter 4 discusses the logic of actually executing MDX in some depth, and although it is sort of a large chapter, there is a lot to know across the three product versions to actually understand in some detail how your MDX actually works. Chapters 5, 6, and 7 then build on using the details of how it works. Chapters 8 and on begin to cover product-specific aspects. So the first half of the book forms a background in capabilities and technique, and the second half introduces a range of possibilities specific to Microsoft and Hyperion.

Appendix A is a reference to all of the functions and operators of standard MDX and the extensions provided by the product versions covered. These functions are a big part of the language, and combining them in the right ways allows you to solve many different problems. They are a big part of the vocabulary for MDX, so the more of them you familiarize yourself with, the better. If the reference weren't so large, it would probably be a chapter in between Chapters 3 and 4, so that after learning the basics of MDX use you would immediately progress to the range of functions available. In several places within the chapters, you are specifically encouraged to look in Appendix A, and here in the introduction we will also encourage you to go through it. We won't be able to cover the use of every single function within the chapters otherwise, so you will pick up some useful nuggets by reviewing it on its own.

You will pick up a lot of technique and a number of tricks from the first seven chapters. These techniques will all be amplified by the contents of later chapters, or will be applicable to them. Unfortunately, we won't be able to give you every solution to every problem that you will have, but we hope to give you all you need to know about putting it together for yourself.

MDX is suited for a large number of applications. In order to simplify examples and explanations, this book includes only a few and really focuses on two. The Waremart 2005 database provides a common frame of reference between Hyperion and Microsoft products across many features and techniques, although it provides only a simple cube to work with. Chapters that deal largely with Analysis Services 2005 capabilities (including Chapters 8, 10, 13, and 14) will also refer to the Adventure Works database that ships with that product. Chapter 13 also includes a series of simple but incrementally more sophisticated databases.

What's Not in This Book

This book does not really cover the non-MDX aspects of building an analytical application, nor does it cover OLAP concepts and principles. For a comprehensive treatment of OLAP, you may wish to read *OLAP Solutions, 2nd Edition* by Erik Thomsen. For developers targeting the Microsoft tool set, you may wish to refer to *Professional SQL Server Analysis Services 2005 with MDX* by Sivakumar Harinath, and Stephen R. Quinn, or *The Microsoft Data Warehouse Toolkit : With SQL Server 2005 and the Microsoft Business Intelligence Toolset* by Joy Mundy and Warren Thornthwaite.

Who Should Read This Book

This book is for any developer, consultant, or manager that needs to build and maintain a proficiency in MDX. MDX, dealing with calculations and selections, can be used for a large part of an overall application, so your concern may be as a front-end developer tasked with matching gestures or other specifications into MDX that retrieves a modified query. You may be an ASP or JSP developer, or developing reports in SQL Server's Reporting Services, and need to be able to translate simple and complex report requests. You may also be developing server-side calculation and modeling logic or security filters. Each of these may boil down to MDX that you write or MDX that you form in some helpful GUI. While the GUI may completely address your concerns, the code it generates will interact with other definitions and you are much better off having a good idea of what is going on and what the limits are.

Tools You Will Need

In order to run queries from the book, you will need a front end or API that you can send MDX in through and receive results back. Microsoft SQL Server 2005 ships with the SQL Server Management Studio, which can be used to run MDX queries. If yoiu have upgraded from Analysis Services 2000, you may still use the MDX Sample application from that product edition against Analysis Services 2005. Hyperion Essbase incudes the Analytic Administration Services console and the Essmsh command shell. Other tools are available as well; see the following on the related Web Site.

What's on the Web Site

The web site contains a collection of sample databases and code for use in Analysis Services and Essbase, and an MDX query interface for Essbase.

Summary

MDX is its own language, similar in some ways to languages you are familiar with and different in other ways. Even if you are familiar with OLAP concepts from one of the covered products, and especially if you are new to them, you may find it helpful to approach the language on its own terms. We don't assume that you know any of the language at the beginning, but if you do then we hope you will learn useful details that you didn't know at the outset. And we hope that you enjoy both learning and using it.

A First Introduction to MDX

This first chapter introduces the syntax and semantics of the MDX (*MultiDimensional eXpressions*) language, looking at basic queries and the language's modular nature. We will assume that you have a basic understanding of the multidimensional structures and metadata supported by the server(s) that you work with, but we won't assume that you've ever seen MDX before. This chapter introduces most of the major aspects of an MDX query and builds an important foundation for the subsequent chapters. It also introduces you to many important parts of the language. This material may bear reading slowly and perhaps more than once if you are new to the language.

What Is MDX?

MDX is a language that expresses selections, calculations, and some metadata definitions against an Online Analytical Processing (OLAP) database, and provides some capabilities for specifying how query results are to be represented. Unlike some other OLAP languages, it is not a full report-formatting language, though. The results of an MDX query come back to a client program as data structures that must be processed in some way to look like a spreadsheet, a chart, or some other form of output. This is quite similar to how SQL works with relational databases and how its related application programming interfaces (APIs) behave. As of this writing, there are several different APIs that support MDX, including Object Linking and Embedding Data Base for Online Analytical Processing (OLE DB for OLAP), ADO MD, ADOMD.Net, XMLA (*XML for Analysis*), the Hyperion Essbase C and Java APIs, and the Hyperion ADM API.

The specification for OLE DB for OLAP describes the full relationship between MDX queries and the data structures that convey the queried information back to the client program. This chapter focuses more on the more logic-related side-what queries are asking for-rather than the programming-oriented aspect of how the results are returned.

Query Basics

We will start by looking at simple MDX queries and build on them in small steps. Throughout this chapter, we will mix descriptions of the abstract properties of a query in with concrete examples to build up a more comprehensive picture of MDX.

Imagine a very simple cube, with dimensions of time, sales geography, and measures. The cube is called Sales. Let's say we want to look at a grid of numbers that has the Massachusetts sales and costs for the first two quarters of 2005. MDX queries result in grids of cells holding data values. The grid can have two dimensions, like a spreadsheet or table, but it can also have one, three, or more. (It can also have zero; we'll talk about that in the section "Queries.") The grid we want to see is shown in Figure 1-1.

The MDX query in the following example would specify the cells we want to see in Figure 1-1:

```
SELECT
{ [Measures].[Dollar Sales], [Measures].[Unit Sales] }
on columns,
{ [Time].[Q1, 2005], [Time].[Q2, 2005] }
on rows
FROM [Sales]
WHERE ([Customer].[MA])
```

	Dollar Sales	Unit Sales
Q1, 2005	96,949.10	3,866
Q2, 2005	104,510.20	4,125

Figure 1-1   A very simple data grid to retrieve.

In the query, SELECT, FROM, and WHERE are keywords that denote different parts of the query. The result of an MDX query is itself a grid, essentially another cube. You lay out the dimensions of the cube you are querying onto the *axes* of the result; this query refers to two of them by the names *rows* and *columns*. In MDX terminology, an *axis* is an edge or dimension of the query result. Referring to "axis" rather than "dimension" makes it simpler to distinguish the dimensions of the cube being queried from the dimensions of the results. Furthermore, each axis can hold a combination of multiple cube dimensions.

You may guess some generalizations immediately from this example. Let's break this simple query down into pieces:

1. The SELECT keyword starts the clause that specifies what you want to retrieve.

2. The ON keyword is used with an axis name to specify where dimensions from your database are displayed. This example query puts measures on the columns axis and time periods on the row axis.

3. MDX uses curly braces, { and }, to enclose a set of elements from a particular dimension or set of dimensions. Our simple query has only one dimension on each of the two axes of the query (the measures dimension and the time dimension). We can separate different elements with commas (,). Element names may be enclosed by [ ] characters, and may have multiple parts separated by dot (.) characters.

4. In an MDX query, you specify how dimensions from your database lay out onto axes of your result. This query lays out measures on columns and time periods on rows. Each query may have a different number of result axes. The first three axes have the names "columns," "rows," and "pages" to conceptually match a typical printed report. (You can refer to them in other ways, as you will see in the "Axis Numbering and Ordering" section.) Although this simple query does not show more than one dimension on a result axis, when more than one dimension maps to a result axis, each cell slot on the axis is related to a combination of one member from each of the mapped dimensions.

5. The FROM clause in an MDX query names the cube from which the data is being queried. This is similar to the FROM clause of Structured Query Language (SQL) that specifies the tables from which data is being queried.

6. The WHERE clause provides a place to specify members for other cube dimensions that don't appear in the columns or rows (or other axes). If you don't specify a member for some dimension, then MDX will make use of some default. (We will ignore the parentheses in this query until later on when we discuss tuples.) The use of WHERE is optional.

Once the database has determined the cells of the query result, it fills them with data from the cube being queried.

MDX shares the keywords SELECT, FROM, and WHERE with SQL. Based on substantial experience teaching MDX, please take this advice: If you are familiar with SQL and its use of SELECT, FROM, and WHERE, do your best to forget about SQL when learning MDX. The meanings and semantics are quite different, and trying to apply SQL concepts to MDX will most likely create confusion.

Let's look at another example. As far as MDX is concerned, every dimension is like every other dimension, even the measures dimension. To generate the result grid shown in Figure 1-2, with sales shown over all three quarters across the columns and for two states down the rows, we can use the following query:

```
SELECT
{ [Time].[Q1, 2005], [Time].[Q2, 2005], [Time].[Q3, 2005] }
on columns,
{ [Customer].[MA], [Customer].[CT] }
on rows
FROM Sales
WHERE ( [Measures].[Dollar Sales] )
```

As you can see, the orientation of time, location, and measures has been switched just by listing time on columns, customers on rows, and measures in the WHERE section.

MDX has a number of other relevant aspects that the remainder of this chapter will describe:

- The MDX data model
- Simple MDX query construction
- Parts of MDX queries

You can skip ahead to the section "Simple MDX Construction," later in this chapter, if you want to jump right into learning more MDX vocabulary. In the discussion of the first two topics-the MDX data model and how metadata entities are named-we will present a lot of detail that may seem mundane or boring. However, the details are important for almost every query, and gaining a deep understanding of MDX demands mastery of the basics. If you do jump ahead and later find yourself getting lost in the syntax, come back to this chapter and get a refresher on the basics before moving on to the next level.

	Q1, 2005	Q2, 2005	Q3, 2005
MA	96,949.10	104,510.20	91,025.00
CT	12,688.40	24,660.70	16,643.90

Figure 1-2   A second simple result grid.

Axis Framework: Names and Numbering

You signify that you are putting members onto columns or rows or other axes of a query result by using the "on columns/rows/pages/etc" syntax. The axis designations can come in any order; the last query would have been just as valid and would mean exactly the same if it had been phrased as follows:

```
SELECT
{[Customer].[MA], [Customer].[CT] }
on rows,
{ [Time].[Q1, 2005], [Time].[Q2, 2005], [Time].[Q3, 2005] }
on columns
FROM Sales
WHERE ( [Measures].[Dollar Sales] )
```

You can also use axis numbers to specify the axis in the query, by stating, for example:

```
{ [Time].[Q1, 2005], [Time].[Q2, 2005], [Time].[Q3, 2005] }
on axis(0),
{[Customer].[MA], [Customer].[CT] }
on axis(1)
```

The phrase on axis(n) indicates that those members should be put on the axis numbered n. The names used so far are synonyms for these numbers:

0	Columns
1	Rows
2	Pages
3	Chapters
4	Sections

For axes beyond axis(4), you must use the numbers, because there are no names for them. You can also mix and match names and numbers in a query:

```
SELECT
{[Customer].[MA], [Customer].[CT] }
on rows,
{ [Time].[Q1, 2005], [Time].[Q2, 2005], [Time].[Q3, 2005] }
on axis(0)
FROM Sales
WHERE ( [Measures].[Dollar Sales] )
```

However, a query that uses axis 1 must also use axis 0, and a query that uses axis 2 must also use axes 1 and 0. You cannot skip an axis in a query-you'll get an error. The following won't work because it skips axis 1:

```
SELECT
{[Customer].[MA], [Customer].CT] }
on axis(2),
{ [Time].[Q1, 2005], [Time].[Q2, 2005], [Time].[Q3, 2005] }
on axis(0)
FROM Sales
WHERE ( [Measures].[Dollar Sales] )
```

If you think of the result of an MDX query as a hypercube (or subcube), and each axis as a dimension of that hypercube, then you can see that skipping an axis would be problematic.

Case Sensitivity and Layout

MDX is neither case-sensitive nor line-oriented. For example, both of the following fragments are equally valid:

```
SELECT
{ [Time].[Q1, 2005], [Time].[Q2, 2005], [Time].[Q3, 2005] }
ON COLUMNS, ...
```

```
select
{ [Time].[Q1, 2005], [Time].[Q2, 2005], [Time].[Q3, 2005] }
on columns, ...
```

You can mix capitalization of letters as you want. For language keywords, capitalization doesn't matter. For names, capitalization may or may not matter to the MDX provider-it usually doesn't for Analysis Services or Essbase, although there are some cases that we will cover later where Essbase does care about capitalization. It also doesn't matter where you put spaces and line ends. You can rewrite the prior fragments as the following:

```
SELECT {
  [Time].[Q1, 2005]
, [Time].[Q2, 2005]
, [Time].[Q3, 2005]
}
ON
COLUMNS,
```

This gives you some flexibility when you are generating MDX by code as well as when you want to arrange it for readability. We strongly recommend using plenty of indenting when writing MDX queries, for both you and anyone else who has to understand your work.

TIP In this book, we will frequently use white space and an outline-like style in MDX examples. Our experience is that this helps make code more readable and much easier to edit, debug, and evolve. This follows the same principles as development in any other programming language. In order to conserve page space, however, we will sometimes compress the examples a bit more than we would prefer.

Additionally, MDX makes heavy use of parentheses, brackets, and braces. These can look fairly similar in common fonts like Arial. In whatever environment you write MDX, if you can use a monospace font such as Lucida Console or Courier, you will have an easier time reviewing the MDX you have written.

Simple MDX Construction

Let's build up a little vocabulary and look at some of the very simplest and most frequently used operators and functions. We will introduce them here and describe how they are often used. (More complete and detailed descriptions can be found in Appendix A, which is a reference on MDX functions and operators.) The ones we will look at here are

- Comma (,) and colon (:)
- .Members
- .Children and Descendants()

We will use the term *set* when discussing these functions and operators. A set is a rather important concept in MDX, and will be described in detail in the section "The MDX Data Model: Tuples and Sets." Until then, we will be a little informal with our use.

Comma (,) and Colon (:)

We have already seen the comma operator used to construct sets; let's talk about this more here. We can assemble a set by enumerating its components and separating them with commas, as in:

```
{ [Time].[January 2005], [Time].[February 2005],
  [Time].[March 2005] }
```

This expression results in a set that holds the first three months of 2005.

EXPRESSIONS: THE "X" IN MDX

MDX has a lot of little primitive "moving parts" that can be put together in many ways. Mastering MDX requires building up both your vocabulary of parts and techniques for assembling them. In this discussion (and in many to follow), we will show the operators in use both within whole queries and as fragments of MDX. We encourage you to begin trying to understand what MDX provides in terms of building blocks as well as finished products.

At every level in every dimension, the members of that level are arranged in a particular order (usually by member key or by name). When it makes sense, you can specify a set as a range of members in that order by listing two members from the same level as endpoints and putting a colon between them to mean "These members and every member between them." (This is similar to the syntax used to specify ranges of cells in spreadsheets like Excel.) For example, the following query, whose results are shown in Figure 1-3, selects the months from September 2004 through March 2005 and the product categories from Tools through Home Audio for customers in Lubbock, and Unit Sales:

```
SELECT
{ [Time].[Sep,2004] : [Time].[Mar,2005] } on columns,
{ [Product].[Tools] : [Product].[Home Audio] } on rows
FROM [Sales]
WHERE ([Customer].[Lubbock, TX], [Measures].[Unit Sales])
```

Sets are usually built like this when the database-defined ordering corresponds to a useful real-world ordering, such as with time. The colon takes two members on the same level as its endpoints. It is not an error to put the same member on both sides of the colon; you will just get a range of one member.

The comma operator can be used anywhere within a set specification to add subsets to an overall set. For example, the following creates a set of the first three and last three months of 2001:

```
{ { [Time].[January-2001] : [Time].[March-2001] } ,
  { [Time].[October-2001] : [Time].[December-2001] } }
```

whereas the following creates a set of 2001 and its first three months:

```
{ [Time].[2001], { [Time].[January-2001] : [Time].[March-2001] } }
```

	Sep, 2004	Oct, 2004	Nov, 2004	Dec, 2004	Jan, 2002	Feb, 2005	Mar, 2005
Tools		79	120	236			62
Toys	28	44	159	292	48	51	35
Auto Electronics		54		47			
Computers, Peripherals	48	72	204	325	67	74	53
Digital Photography							
Home Audio							

Figure 1-3   Result of query using the colon (:) operator.

When subsets are concatenated by commas, the order in which the commas join them is the order in which they are returned.

PRODUCT DIFFERENCES

ANALYSIS SERVICES

In Analysis Services, regardless of whether the member on the left of the colon is before or after the member on the right in terms of database ordering, the set that results will have all members between the two in database ordering. That is, the following two return exactly the same set:

```
{[Time].[April-2001] : [Time].[January-2001]}
{[Time].[January-2001] : [Time].[April-2001]}
```

ESSBASE

In Essbase, the set starts with the left member and runs through the right member. The following returns the ordering April, March, February, January:

```
{[Time].[April-2001] : [Time].[January-2001]}
```

The members must also be at the same level; you can use the `MemberRange()` function to get a range from a common generation.

.Members

Getting the set of members for a dimension, hierarchy, or level is very common both for retrievals and as a starting point for further operations. The .Members operator takes a dimension, hierarchy, or level on its left-hand side, and returns a set of all members associated with that metadata scope. For example, [Customer].Members results in the set of all customers, whereas [Product].[Product Category].Members returns all members of the Product Category level in the Product dimension. For example, the query

```
SELECT
{ [Scenario].Members } on columns,
{ [Store].Members } on rows
FROM Budgeting
```

lays out all members of the scenario dimension across the columns and all members of the store dimension down the rows.

When a client uses .Members (or other metadata functions that return the set of members associated with some metadata element), neither Analysis Services nor Essbase will include any calculated members in the returned set. (Calculated members are a means for introducing calculations onto other data in the database, and are discussed starting in Chapter 2.) This means that the preceding request for [Scenario].Members, as written, will not return any calculated members in the scenario dimension. We can always ask for them by name, however, and Analysis Services provides the AddCalculatedMembers() and .AllMembers functions to add them into a set. See Appendix A for details on these functions.

Getting the Children of a Member with .Children

Another kind of selection that is very frequent is to get the children of a member. We may want to do this to implement a drill-down operation, or simply to conveniently obtain a range of members based on a common parent. MDX provides a .Children function that will do this for us. The following query selects both the [Product].[Tools] member and its children on the rows of a report, which is shown in Figure 1-4:

```
SELECT
{ [Time].[Q3, 2005].Children }
on columns,
{ [Product].[Tools], [Product].[Tools].Children }
on rows
FROM Sales
WHERE ([Customer].[TX], [Measures].[Unit Sales])
```

You can get the children of any member that has children using this function. If you request the children of a leaf-level member, you'll get an empty set of members back. We'll talk more about what this means later on.

PRODUCT-SPECIFIC ASPECTS OF .MEMBERS

ANALYSIS SERVICES 2000 AND 2005

In Analysis Services, hierarchies behave like dimensions, and multiple dimensions have different sets of members. As a result, in an Analysis Services dimension that contains multiple hierarchies, you cannot simply request `[Dimension].Members`. **If you do, it will complain of an unknown dimension. For example, given a logical** `[Time]` **dimension that contains two hierarchies,** `[Time].[Fiscal]` **and** `[Time].[Calendar]`, **a client taking metadata from OLE DB for OLAP will see one time dimension. However, the expression** `[Time].Members` **will result in an error rather than result in all members on all time hierarchies. To obtain a set of members, the client must request either** `[Time].[Fiscal].Members` **or** `[Time].[Calendar].Members`. **If the dimension has only one hierarchy and that hierarchy does not have an explicit name, then** `[Dimension].Members` **will work. For example, if time has only one hierarchy, then [Time].Members will work.**

ESSBASE

In Essbase 9, when you request all members of some scope with `.Members`, **all copies of shared members are returned in the result set. There is no way to strip shared members from a set. Therefore, you may need to build awareness of where shared members exist into your MDX, for example using** `Descendants()` **(described later) instead of** `.Members`.

	July, 2005	Aug, 2005	Sep, 2005
Tools	484	554	319
Bench Power Tools	42	133	94
Compressors, Air Tools			51
Electrical Shop	107	118	33
Garage Door Openers	57	46	53
Hand Tools, Carpentry		55	
Hand Tools, General Purpo	138	164	31
Mechanics Tools	88	38	57
Portable Power Tools	52		
Power Tool Accessories			

Figure 1-4   Result of query using .Children.

Getting the Descendants of a Member with Descendants()

To request members further away than immediate children, or for a more generalized search below in the hierarchy, you use `Descendants()`. We will skim the surface of this function because it has too many options to go into here; you can refer to a complete reference for it in Appendix A.

Syntax:

```
Descendants (member [, [ level ] [, flag]] )
```

Descendants() returns the members below *member* related to the *level* or generation, with a number of selection options based on the optional *flag*. The choices for *flag* are

```
SELF
BEFORE
AFTER
SELF_AND_BEFORE
SELF_AND_AFTER
SELF_BEFORE_AFTER
LEAVES
```

SELF refers just to the members at *level*, and this is the most frequent option. For example, the following selects the months of 2005, which is shown in Figure 1-5:

```
SELECT
{ [Product].[Tools], [Product].[Toys] }  ON COLUMNS,
Descendants (
  [Time].[2005],
  [Time].[Month],
  SELF
)
ON ROWS
FROM Sales
WHERE [Measures].[Dollar Sales]
```

Since SELF is so frequently used, it is the default option if you omit the flag from your code. For example, Descendants ([Time].[2005], [Time].[Month]) will also return the list of months in 2005 even though SELF is not explicitly included in the query.

The other flags that include SELF refer to levels around the level you reference. SELF_AND_BEFORE means to return all members between the SELF and "before" that level, which means all of them up to and including the starting member. For example, the following picks out [2005] and all quarters and months within it, and the results are shown in Figure 1-6:

```
SELECT
{ [Product].[Tools], [Product].[Toys] }  ON COLUMNS,
Descendants (
  [Time].[2005],
  [Time].[Month],
  SELF_AND_BEFORE
)
ON ROWS
FROM Sales
WHERE  [Measures].[Dollar Sales]
```

	Tools	Toys
Jan, 2005	59,722.40	49,948.20
Feb, 2005	65,604.10	42,885.40
Mar, 2005	57,715.50	56,601.70
Apr, 2005	64,179.90	51,794.40
May, 2005	68,152.60	62,135.70
Jun, 2005	67,476.70	55,582.90
Jul, 2005	71,997.90	50,111.80
Aug, 2005	71,411.90	48,965.30
Sep, 2005	58,979.60	52,532.90
Oct, 2005	77,720.10	58,969.60
Nov, 2005	196,946.70	147,854.50
Dec, 2005	223,948.60	171,600.20

Figure 1-5   Result of using Descendants(, , SELF).

	Tools	Toys
2005	1,083,855.90	848,982.70
Q1, 2005	183,042.90	149,435.30
Jan, 2005	59,722.40	49,948.20
Feb, 2005	65,604.10	42,885.40
Mar, 2005	57,715.50	56,601.70
Q2, 2005	199,809.20	169,513.10
Apr, 2005	64,179.90	51,794.40
May, 2005	68,152.60	62,135.70
Jun, 2005	67,476.70	55,582.90
Q3, 2005	202,389.30	151,610.00
Jul, 2005	71,997.90	50,111.80
Aug, 2005	71,411.90	48,965.30
Sep, 2005	58,979.60	52,632.90

Figure 1-6   Result of using Descendants (, , SELF_AND_BEFORE).

SELF_AND_AFTER means to return all members from the level referenced down to the leaf level. SELF_BEFORE_AFTER means to return the entire subtree of the hierarchy down to the leaf level, starting with the given *member*. Note that this is the same as just saying Descendants ([Time].[2005]), since leaving off both the flag and the level means to take all descendants.

Note also that you can refer to descendants relative to a specific level, or you can refer to descendants relative to some depth away from the given member by using a number instead of a reference to a level. There are several more useful options; once again, you might be well served by looking at the reference in Appendix A.

NOTE In Essbase, you can refer to either generations or levels in the *level* argument.

Removing Empty Slices from Query Results

In a multidimensional space, data is frequently sparse. For example, not all products are sold in all stores at all times to all customers, so a query for some particular set of products, time periods, and customers may return some slices along one or more axes that are entirely empty. You can be pretty sure that any large retailer won't be selling snow shovels in Hawaii in December but will have a hard time keeping them in stock in Chicago. A user may want to see the empty slices, because the empty slice may tell him or her about a complete absence of activity, but the user may also just want the empty slices treated as irrelevant and have them removed from the report. Let's take as an example the following query, the results of which are shown in Figure 1-7:

```
SELECT
{ [Time].[Jan,2005], [Time].[Feb,2005] }
ON COLUMNS ,
{ [Product].[Toys],
  [Product].[Toys].Children
}
ON ROWS
FROM Sales
WHERE ([Measures].[Dollar Sales], [Customer].[TX])
```

For some reason, we haven't sold any Dolls, Electronics, Games, or Musical toys during these two months anywhere in Texas. If we only want to see the products that we did sell within the report's time frame, MDX provides a way to remove the entirely empty slices from the query result, by using the NON EMPTY keywords. You can see it in use in the following query, whose results are shown in Figure 1-8:

```
SELECT
{ [Time].[Jan, 2005], [Time].[Feb, 2005] }
ON COLUMNS,
NON EMPTY
{ [Product].[Toys],
  [Product].[Toys].Children
}
ON ROWS
FROM Sales
WHERE ([Measures].[Dollar Sales], [Customer].[TX])
```

All we need to do is to add the NON EMPTY keywords at the beginning of our request for the axis. In this case, it is after the comma that comes after ON COLUMNS, and before the { that starts our request for products. The query is evaluated and after all the data for the columns is known, the rows where at least one column has data in it are returned.

	Jan, 2005	Feb, 2005
Toys	6,950.00	7,666.20
Action Figures	747.20	421.50
Arts & Crafts	2,499.80	2,135.90
Cars & Trucks		1,078.40
Construction	3,002.90	982.00
Dolls		
Educational	700.10	597.10
Electronics		
Games		
Musical		
Radio Controlled		2,451.30

Figure 1-7   Query with empty slices on rows.

	Jan, 2005	Feb, 2005
Toys	6,950.00	7,666.20
Action Figures	747.20	421.50
Arts & Crafts	2,499.80	2,135.90
Cars & Trucks		1,078.40
Construction	3,002.90	982.00
Educational	700.10	597.10
Radio Controlled		2,451.30

Figure 1-8   Empty slices removed with NON EMPTY.

NON EMPTY works on any axis, and with any dimensions and tuples. The query can be flipped around so that you can see this:

```
SELECT
{ [Time].[Jan, 2005], [Time].[Feb, 2005] }
ON ROWS ,
NON EMPTY
{ [Product].[Toys],
  [Product].[Toys].Children
} ON COLUMNS
FROM Sales
WHERE [Customer].[TX]
```

There are other functions that you can make use of to remove members with empty data from your results, but NON EMPTY is perfectly suited for this.

NOTE Analysis Services 2005 introduces a HAVING clause to queries, which is similar in effect to NON EMPTY but is more flexible. It is discussed in Chapter 4.

Comments in MDX

To facilitate documentation, three variations of comment syntax are allowed in MDX, which should suit a variety of styles. (As with other programming, comments can also be used to exclude sections of code for debugging, too.)

The first style uses the symbols /* and */ to delimit a comment. All characters between the /* and the */ are ignored by the MDX parsing machinery. This enables comments to be placed within a line and for the comment to span lines. The following is an example of this style of comment:

```
SELECT /* Put products
on columns */ [Product].Members
on columns FROM Cube
```

The second style uses the // symbol to begin a comment, and the comment will extend to the end of the line. The following is an example:

```
SELECT // Put products on columns
[Product].Members
on columns FROM Cube
```

The third style is like the second style but uses a pair of dashes (–) to begin a comment. The following is an example:

```
SELECT — Put products on columns
[Product].Members
on columns FROM Cube
```

Comments can be placed anywhere white space could be used. For example, `[Product]./* whole dimension */ Members` will work just fine. Comments can be used in queries or expressions. Make sure that you don't use them directly inside a member name, though!

If you use comments to selectively include and exclude portions of a query or expression (for example, while debugging it), keep in mind that the `/* */` comments cannot be nested. That is,

```
/* /* comment */ */
```

is not a valid comment, whereas

```
/* /* comment */
```

is a valid comment. In the first of these two examples, the first `*/` ends the overall comment, so the second `*/` is a token that the MDX parser will try to parse (and fail on).

The MDX Data Model: Tuples and Sets

MDX uses a data model that starts with cubes, dimensions, and members, but it is richer and somewhat more complex. Understanding this data model is the key to moving beyond the basics and unlocking powerful analyses. In this section, we will explore the key elements of this model: *tuples* and *sets*. Tuples and sets are very similar to members and dimensions, but are more generalized and more flexible.

TIP Understanding tuples and how to use them in the various components of MDX is sometimes the most difficult part of learning MDX. You may want to revisit this section again before proceeding with the more advanced content later in this book.

Tuples

A *tuple* is a combination of members from one or more dimensions. It is essentially a multidimensional member. A single member is a simple tuple (for example, [Time].[Jun, 2005]). When a tuple has more than one dimension, it has only one member from each dimension. To compose a tuple with more than one dimension, you must wrap the members in parentheses, for example:

```
([Customer].[Chicago, IL], [Time].[Jan, 2005])
```

A tuple can stand for a slice of a cube, where the cube is sliced by each member in the tuple. A tuple can also be a data object that you can manipulate on its own in MDX.

We can involve tuples that we build using this syntax directly in queries. For example, consider the following, the results of which are shown in Figure 1-9:

```
SELECT
{  ( [Time].[2005], [Measures].[Dollar Sales] ),
   ( [Time].[Feb, 2005], [Measures].[Unit Sales] )
}
ON COLUMNS ,
{ [Product].[Tools], [Product].[Toys]} ON ROWS
FROM [Sales]
```

Our result was asymmetric as far as the combinations of time and measures that get returned. This gives us a great deal of fine control over the combinations of members and cells that will come back from a query.

You can always put a single member within parentheses, but it's not required if the tuple is defined by just that member. However, the following is not valid because it has two time members in it:

```
([Customer].[Chicago, IL], [Time].[Jan, 2005], [Time].[Feb, 2005])
```

Also, you can't compose an empty tuple. () is not a valid tuple. (Analysis Services 2005 has the concept of a null member that you can specify using null, so you can create a tuple by writing (null) or (null, null), but this appears to be mostly useful when using stored procedures as discussed in Chapter 10.)

In addition to composing tuples by explicitly creating them in code, a number of functions will return tuples.

The "dimensionality" of a tuple refers to the set of dimensions whose members compose it. The order in which dimensions appear in a tuple is an important part of a tuple's dimensionality. Any and all dimensions can be part of a tuple, including members of the measures dimension.

	2005	Feb, 2005
	Dollar Sales	Unit Sales
Tools	1,083,855.90	2,621
Toys	848,982.70	1,695

Figure 1-9   Simple example of tuples on columns.

Although you can compose a tuple from members wrapped by ( ), you cannot use syntax to compose a tuple from tuples. That is, you can build up a tuple by saying:

```
(
  [Time].[2004],
  [Customer].[Chicago, IL],
  [Product].[Tools]
)
```

but not:

```
(
   [Time].[2004],
   (
   [Customer].[Chicago, IL],
   [Product].[Tools]
   )
)
```

(Using functions that let you compose tuples in other ways, you can build tuples from other tuples. We'll talk about that later. But not by putting their names together like this.)

In calculations and queries, MDX identifies cells based on tuples. Conceptually, each cell value is identified by a tuple composed of one member from each dimension in the cube. (This is sort of like a spreadsheet, in which Sheet 1, Column B, Row 22 identifies a cell.) In a query, some of these members' dimensions may be placed on rows, others on columns, others on pages, and yet others on the query slicer. However, the intersection of two or more tuples is yet another tuple, so combining them all together yields a cell in the end. The tuple ([Product].[Leather Jackets], [Time].[June-2005], [Store].[Fifth Avenue NYC], [Measures].[Dollar Sales]) may completely define a cell with a value of $13,000.

Although a tuple either refers to a combination of members, when it is used in an expression where a number or string might be used, the default behavior is to reference the value in the cell that the tuple specifies. This is a little point that makes a big difference when trying to understand what some of the MDX functions do. How these references play out is the subject of Chapter 4.

In addition to creating tuples by explicitly coding them, a few functions also return tuples. We will describe them later in this book.

Sets

A set is simply an ordered collection of tuples. A set may have more than one tuple, have only one tuple, or be empty. Unlike a mathematical set, an MDX set may contain the same tuple more than once, and ordering is significant in an MDX set. Although sets might be better called "collections" or "sequences," we are stuck with "set" for now. Depending on the context in which a set is used, it either refers to that set of tuples or to the value(s) in the cell(s) that its tuples specify.

Syntactically, a set may be specified in a number of ways. Perhaps the most common is to list the tuples within { }. The following query uses two sets, where the rows use a set of one dimension and the columns a set of two dimensions:

```
SELECT
{  ( [Time].[2005], [Measures].[Dollar Sales] ),
   ( [Time].[Feb, 2005], [Measures].[Unit Sales] )
}
ON COLUMNS ,
{ [Product].[Tools], [Product].[Toys] } ON ROWS
FROM [Sales]
```

Whenever one or more tuples are explicitly listed, you will need to enclose them within braces. Some MDX operators and functions also return sets. The expressions that use them do not need to be enclosed in braces if the set is not being combined with more tuples, but we will usually enclose set expressions in braces for the sake of style.

Although a single member is by default a tuple of one dimension, a set that has only one tuple is not equivalent to a tuple. As far as standard MDX is concerned, the following two examples are quite different:

```
([Time].[2001 Week 1], [Product].[HyperGizmos])
{ ([Time].[2001 Week 1], [Product].[HyperGizmos]) }
```

The first of these is a tuple, and the second is a set containing that tuple. You might think it reasonable that wherever a set is called for, you can use a single tuple and it will be interpreted as a set of one. Analysis Services 2005 can make use of tuples or members in some contexts that otherwise ask for a set. For other servers, you will need to wrap the tuple in curly braces as in the second sample just given. Hence, the following is a valid query only for Analysis Services 2005 (it needs braces around the tuple to be valid otherwise):

```
SELECT
([Time].[Jun, 2005], [Geography].[Chicago, IL]) on columns
FROM [Sales]
WHERE ([Measures].[Dollar Costs])
```

The following is valid across all MDX providers:

```
SELECT
{ ([Time].[Jun, 2005], [Geography].[Chicago, IL]) } on columns
FROM [Sales]
WHERE ([Measures].[Dollar Costs])
```

Similarly, a set that happens to contain only one tuple is still considered to be a set. To use it in a context that calls for a tuple (for example, in a WHERE clause), even if you have guaranteed that it only contains one tuple, you must still employ an MDX function (such as .Item()) that takes a tuple from a set.

A set can also be empty, both explicitly (for example, {}) and because a function returns a set that is empty for some reason.

Every tuple in a set must have the same dimensionality (that is, the dimensions represented and their order within each tuple). The following would result in an error, because the order of the dimensions changes:

```
{  ( [Time].[2005], [Measures].[Dollar Sales] ),
   ( [Measures].[Unit Sales], [Time].[Feb, 2005] )
}
```

However, different sets can have whatever differing dimensionality and dimension order they need in order to serve your purposes. An empty set has no dimensionality.

In addition to creating sets by explicitly coding them, a large number of functions return sets. We will explore many of them in the following chapters.

Queries

An MDX query result is just another cube that is a transformation of the cube that is being queried. This is analogous to a standard SQL query result, which is essentially another table. The result cube can have one, two, three, four, or more axes (up to 128 in Analysis Services 2005, and up to 64 in Analysis Services 2000 and Essbase). It is also technically possible for a query to have zero axes, but it will still return a single-cell value. Each tuple in a result axis is essentially a member of the result cube.

As described earlier, each axis of the query result is composed of a set of tuples, each of which can have one or more dimensions. When multidimensional tuples end up on the axis of a query, the order in which the dimensions appear in the tuples affects the nesting order in the axis. The first dimension listed becomes the outermost dimension, the second becomes the next outermost, and so on. The last dimension is the innermost. For example, suppose that the following set was placed on the "rows" axis in a query:

```
SELECT
...
  { ([Time].[2001], [Product].[Leather Jackets]),
    ([Time].[2001], [Product].[Silk Scarves]),
    ([Time].[1997], [Product].[Leather Jackets]),
    ([Time].[1997], [Product].[Silk Scarves])
  } ON ROWS
...
```

In this case, the expected presentation for data brought back to a client through OLE DB for OLAP or ADO is shown in Figure 1-10. Note that the layout shown in Figure 1-10 is simply conventional; your applications may do something different with the results.

Queries with Zero Axes

We have mentioned twice that a query may have zero axes without really describing what that means. Two examples of zero-axis queries are

```
SELECT FROM SalesCube
```

and

```
SELECT FROM SalesCube
WHERE ([Time].[2004], [Geography].[Quebec],
       [Product].[Snorkels], [Channel].[Superstores])
```

Because no members were assigned to any (non-slicer) axis in either query, the results are considered to have zero axes and by convention would be single unlabeled cells, or at least cells with no distinct row or column headers. In all APIs that currently support MDX, the slicer information is returned as part of the query result. Whether you consider the results here to be zero-dimensional depends on whether or not you choose to ignore the dimensional information conveyed in the slicer information returned with the cell.

2001	Leather Jackets
2001	Silk Scarves
1997	Leather Jackets
1997	Silk Scarves

Figure 1-10   Typical expected client data layout.

Axis-Only Queries

Note that all MDX queries return cells. However, many useful queries ask "What members belong in this set?" where the result that is of real interest is not cell data, but the members that are associated with cell data or member property values. A query of this form, such as "Show me the customers that make up the top 10 percent of our revenue," will at least implicitly prepare a set of cell values as well. (It may not actually retrieve their values due to internal optimizations, though.)

This is in contrast to SQL, which will return only the columns that you request. There are uses for queries that have no interest in cells; we will look at an example of this in Chapter 7.

More Basic Vocabulary

Now that we have introduced tuples and sets and the earlier bits of vocabulary, we can introduce three more functions that are extremely common in the MDX you will write:

- CrossJoin()
- Filter()
- Order()

CrossJoin()

In many cases, you will want to take the cross-product of members (or tuples) in two different sets (that is, specify all of their possible combinations). The CrossJoin() function is the most direct way of combining the two sets in this way.

The syntax is as follows:

```
CrossJoin (set1, set2)
```

For example, you may want to lay out on the columns of a query the first two quarters of 2005 and the two measures Dollar Sales and Unit Sales. You would generate this set with the following expression:

```
CrossJoin (
  { [Time].[Q1, 2005], [Time].[Q2, 2005] },
  { [Measures].[Dollar Sales], [Measures].[Unit Sales] }
)
```

You would use it in this way; the results are shown in Figure 1-11:

```
SELECT
CrossJoin (
  { [Time].[Q1, 2005], [Time].[Q2, 2005]},
  { [Measures].[Dollar Sales], [Measures].[Unit Sales] }
)
ON COLUMNS ,
{ [Product].[Tools], [Product].[Toys] } ON ROWS
FROM Sales
```

CrossJoin() only takes two sets as inputs. If you want to take the CrossJoin() of three or more sets, such as times, scenarios, and products, you can do it by nesting calls to CrossJoin(), like the following:

```
CrossJoin (
  [Time].Members,
  CrossJoin (
    [Scenario].Members,
    [Product].Members
  )
)

CrossJoin (
  CrossJoin(
    [Time].Members,
    [Scenario].Members
  ),
  [Product].Members
)
```

Notice that each of these results in a set whose dimensionality is, in order: time, scenario, product. While you may have a personal preference for one method or another, when the sets are large, you may want to look out for performance differences between them in your MDX provider.

	Q1, 2005	Q1, 2005	Q2, 2005	Q2, 2005
	Dollar Sales	Unit Sales	Dollar Sales	Unit Sales
Tools	183,042.00	7,179	199,809.20	7,912
Toys	149,435.30	5,878	169,513.10	6,476

Figure 1-11   CrossJoined dimensions on columns.

CrossJoin() is standard MDX. Microsoft Analysis Services also provides an extension to express this as "set multiplication" by using * (asterisk):

```
{ [Time].Members } * { [Scenario].Members } * { [Product].Members }
```

This performs the same operation as CrossJoin(), and may be easier for you to read and write when you are not concerned with portability.

A common use for CrossJoin() is to combine a single member of one dimension with a set of members on another dimension, such as creating a set in which a particular measure is referred to over a set of tuples from other dimensions. When the formula of one calculated measure involves the count of nonempty cells for another measure, this construct is required. Although it might seem preferable, you cannot construct tuples on multiple dimensions by using range operators. For example, to express the range "toothpaste in stores 1 through 10," you might want to write something like the following:

```
([Product].[Toothpaste],
 {[Geography].[Store 1] : [Geography].[Store 10] })
```

Instead, you will need to use CrossJoin() (or the * variant), such as in the following:

```
CrossJoin (
  { [Product].[Toothpaste] },
  [Geography].[Store 1] : [Geography].[Store 10]
)
```

In the phrasing in the CrossJoin() example, we did not use curly braces around the set; they were not needed there. However, since the function requires a set, we did use them around the single member [Toothpaste], so we could convert the tuple to a set.

NOTE In Analysis Services 2005, CrossJoin() **doesn't always create a full Cartesian product. See Chapter 4 for more details.**

Filter()

Operators like CrossJoin() and : help you construct sets. In contrast, Filter() lets you reduce a set by including in the resulting set only those elements that meet some criteria. Filter() takes one set and one Boolean expression as its arguments and returns that subset where the Boolean expression is true.

The syntax for Filter() is:

```
Filter (set, boolean-expression)
```

For example, the expression

```
Filter (
  { [Product].[Product Category].Members },
  [Measures].[Dollar Sales] >= 500
)
```

will return a set of all product category members in which the associated Dollar Sales value was at least 500. This is the first time we have used comparisons. Any Boolean expression may be used to filter the set. As a more complex example, the expression

```
Filter (
  { [Product].[Product Category].Members },
  ([Measures].[Dollar Sales] >= 1.2 * [Measures].[Dollar Costs])
    AND [Measures].[Dollar Sales] >= 150
)
```

will return a set of all product category members in which the associated sales measure value was at least 1.2 times the associated cost measure value and the sales value was at least 150. How do you specify the associated values? The answer to that has important details, which we will address in Chapter 4. For the moment, rely on your intuition.

Filter() works on general sets of tuples, not just on sets of one dimension's members. The following expression returns the set of all (product category, city) tuples in which the associated sales value was at least 500:

```
Filter (
  CrossJoin (
    [Product].[Product Category].Members,
    [Store].[City].Members
  ),
  [Measures].[Dollar Sales] >= 500
)
```

In determining the value of sales associated with each product category, or each (product category, city) tuple, you must take into account the other dimensions that are associated with sales values. For example, the first two Filter() expressions and the last one did not account for the time or times with which the sales values were associated. You can specify any additional dimensions' members that you need to in either the Boolean condition or in the set. For example, if you wanted to filter based on 2000's sales in Baton Rouge, you would simply say:

```
Filter (
  [Product].[Product Category].Members,
  ([Measures].[Dollar Sales], [Time].[2000],
    [Store].[Baton Rouge, LA]) >= 500
)
```

Within the filtering operation, the cell value will be taken from the 2000 Baton Rouge sales at each product category. The result is a set of product category members.

On the more advanced side, you can also specify more members in the set. For example, the preceding operation could be specified as follows:

```
Filter (
  CrossJoin (
    {(([Time].[2000], [Store].[Baton Rouge, LA]) },
    [Product].[Product Category].Members
  ),
  [Measures].[Dollar Sales] >= 500
)
```

This expression filters a set of tuples that all include 2000 and Baton Rouge, thus fixing on the correct time and store. However, the set returned would consist of tuples with dimensionality:

```
([Time], [Store], [Product]).
```

These `Filter()` expressions have introduced the concept of query context (the relevant members for the dimensions that are not part of the filter condition or the set being filtered). Every MDX expression ultimately operates in a context that is set up outside it. Nested MDX operations are resolved within the context of the operation that invokes the nested operation. We'll defer discussion of contexts here; Chapter 4 explains query evaluation and context in far more detail.

POWER OF TUPLES

The expression `([Measures].[Dollar Sales], [Time].[2000], [Store].[Baton Rouge, LA]) >= 500` **is the first use of the power of tuple references to precisely refer to cells holding data values of interest. We will show how to exploit this many times; it is one of the powerful aspects of MDX.**

Order()

To put the tuples in a set into a sequence based on associated data values, we need to use the `Order()` function.

The syntax for the `Order()` function is:

```
Order (set1, expression [, ASC | DESC | BASC | BDESC])
```

`Order()` takes a set, a criterion for ordering the set, and, optionally, a flag that indicates what sorting principle to use (ascending or descending, including or ignoring hierarchical relationships between the tuples). `Order()` returns a set that consists of the original set's tuples placed in the new order. The precise operations of the orderings that include hierarchical relationships are fairly complex. Appendix A includes a complete description. Here, we will use simpler examples that don't show as much complexity.

For example, given the set of product categories in our database, we may want to sort them in descending order by sales. A very simple query for this may look like the following; its results are shown in Figure 1-12:

```
SELECT
{ [Measures].[Dollar Sales] } on columns,
Order (
  [Product].[Product Category].Members,
  [Measures].[Dollar Sales],
  BDESC
)
on rows
FROM [Sales]
WHERE [Time].[2004]
```

Often, you will want to use particular tuples to precisely specify the sort criteria. For example, let's say that you want to sort specifically by the profit realized in 2005 by all customers. This would be expressed by the following:

```
Order (
  [Product].[Product Category].Members,
  ([Measures].[Profit], [Time].[2005], [Customer].[All Customers]),
  BDESC
)
```

For example, the following query (whose results are shown in Figure 1-13) provides multiple time periods, customers, and measures, so you would want to use a tuple to pick out which ones to sort on:

```
SELECT
CrossJoin (
  {[Time].[2004], [Time].[2005]},
  CrossJoin (
    { [Customer].[Northeast], [Customer].[West] },
    { ([Measures].[Dollar Sales], [Measures].[Unit Sales] }
  )
) on columns,
Order (
  [Product].[Product Category].Members,
  ([Measures].[Unit Sales], [Time].[2005],
   [Customer].[All Customers]),
  BDESC
) on rows
FROM [Sales]
```

As you can see, the rows are sorted by the values related to the (2005, West, Dollar Sales) tuple, which corresponds to the next-to-last column.

Because `Order()` works on tuples, you can also sort the interesting (product and store) combinations by their unit sales. For example, the following expression filters (product and promotion) tuples by Dollar Sales, then orders each resulting (product and promotion) tuple according to its unit sales in 2005, and returns them; Figure 1-14 shows the resulting order.

```
Order (
  Filter(
    CrossJoin(
      [Product].[Product Category].Members
      ,[Promotion].[Media].Members
    )
    , [Measures].[Dollar Sales] >= 500
  )
  , ([Measures].[Unit Sales], [Time].[2005])
  , BDESC
)
```

	Dollar Sales
Tools	894,495.80
Computers, Peripherals	847,595.00
Toys	768,126.20
Camping, Hiking	646,902.40
Phones	640,023.80
Outdoor Gear	572,151.00
Sports Equipment	541,098.50
Exercise, Fitness	534,700.60
TV, DVD, Video	500,910.80

Figure 1-12   Result of query using Order().

| | 2004 | 2004 | 2004 | 2004 | 2005 | 2005 | 2005 | 2005 |
| | Northeast | Northeast | West | West | Northeast | Northeast | West | West |
	Dollar Sales	Unit Sales	Dollar Sales	Unit Sales	Dollar Sales	Unit Sales	Dollar Sales	Unit Sales
Computers, Peripheral	118,438.80	4,612	147,504.80	5,791	148,902.90	5,695	196,868.70	7,318
Tools	132,914.20	5,282	125,364.10	5,269	152,571.30	5,916	176,282.70	6,850
Toys	103,469.60	4,220	108,991.00	4,454	106,096.30	4,233	141,530.10	5,370
Phones	120,098.40	4,913	98,190.80	3,871	125,115.60	4,787	131,831.80	4,869
Outdoor Gear	73,977.90	3,185	75,927.10	2,962	84,289.00	3,193	128,668.20	4,892
Camping, Hiking	147,407.10	5,863	69,414.90	2,819	170,091.00	6,467	123,632.60	4,727
Personal Care	31,457.50	1,312	85,282.60	3,328	53,120.30	2,083	117,788.00	4,371

Figure 1-13   Result of more complex Order() query.

Electronics	Radio
Outdoor & Sporting	Radio
Electronics	Boat
Electronics	newsp
Electronics	email
Outdoor & Sporting	newsp
Electronics	Personal

Figure 1-14   Result of sorting tuples.

Note that the BDESC variant breaks (that is, ignores) the hierarchy. You'd get back a more complex and possibly more interesting ordered set if you instead chose DESC, which respects the hierarchy and the dimensional components of tuples. See the section "Ordering Sets" in the description of Order() in Appendix A for a full description of ordering sets.

Querying for Member Properties

An MDX query can also retrieve member properties defined for members in a cube along the query's axes using the DIMENSION PROPERTIES clause. For example, the following will query for the zip code and hair color of customers returned in the query:

```
SELECT
  { [Customer].[Akron, OH].Children }
DIMENSION PROPERTIES [Customer].[Zip Code],
        [Customer].[Individual].[Hair Color]
on columns,
  { [Product].[Category].Members } on rows
FROM Sales
WHERE ([Measures].[Units Sold], [Time].[July 3, 2005])
```

The DIMENSION PROPERTIES clause comes between the set for the axis and the ON AXIS(n) clause. The DIMENSION keyword is optional; you could also write:

```
SELECT
  { [Customer].[Akron, OH].Children }
PROPERTIES [Customer].[Zip Code],
           [Customer].[Individual].[Hair Color]
ON COLUMNS,
...
```

Member properties can be requested on any axis but not on the slicer in standard MDX. (Essbase 9 extends MDX to allow a DIMENSION PROPERTIES clause on the slicer.)

If a member property is defined for only a single level of a dimension, and the query axis includes multiple levels, the query will succeed and you will just not get values for members at the inapplicable levels. If a member is repeated in a result axis, its related member property value will be repeated too.

Properties can be identified either by using the name of the dimension and the name of the property, as with the zip code property just given, or by using the unique name of the dimension's level and the name of the property, as with the hair color property.

NOTE While the values of properties requested with the PROPERTIES statement in an MDX query are returned, along with all other result information, in the result data structures, it is up to the client application to retrieve and utilize this information.

Both intrinsic and database-defined member properties can be queried. Analysis Services defines intrinsic properties named KEY, NAME, and ID, and every level of every dimension has them. (These, and other kinds of properties for Analysis Services, are described in Appendix C.) For example, the KEY property of a Product dimension's SKU level is named [Product].[SKU].[KEY]. The member key property contains the values of the member keys as represented in the dimension table. The member name property contains the values of the member names as represented in the dimension table. The ID property contains the internal member number of that member in the dimension-wide database ordering. (Since these properties are maintained internally, your application should not use them to avoid problems with ambiguous names.) Essbase 9 defines intrinsic properties named MEMBER_NAME, MEMBER_ALIAS, GEN_NUMBER, LEVEL_NUMBER, MEMBER_UNIQUE_NAME, IS_EXPENSE, COMMENTS, and RELATIONAL_DESCENDANTS. These are the names for which Essbase is case-sensitive: if you enclose these names in [], they should be in all caps (for example, [MEMBER_NAME]).

When property names between levels of a dimension are ambiguous, you can get ambiguous results if you query for member properties on the axis of a query. For example, every layer of an organizational dimension may have a `Manager` property for each member above the leaf. Consider the following query fragment:

```
SELECT { Descendants ([Organization].[All Organization],
[Organization].[Junior Staff], SELF_AND_ABOVE }
PROPERTIES [Organization].[Manager] on columns
 . . .
```

When the query is executed, it will return the specific `Manager` property for only one level. It is not a good idea to rely on whatever level that would happen to be. (In our experience, it would be the lowest level in the query, or the Junior Staff level in this case.) Members belonging to that level will have a valid `[Manager]` value; members belonging to other levels won't. Suppose that, instead, you queried for each level's properties independently, as with the following:

```
SELECT { Descendants ([Organization].[All Organization],
          [Organization].[Junior Staff], SELF_AND_ABOVE }
PROPERTIES
[Organization].[Executive Suites].[Manager],
[Organization].[Middle Managers].[Manager],
[Organization].[Junior Staff].[Manager] on columns
 . . .
```

In this case, the property for each level at each level's member will arrive appropriately filled in (and be empty at members of the other levels). However, when you access properties in member calculations, there won't be any ambiguity. Suppose, for example, that some calculated member referred to (in Microsoft syntax) `[Organization] .CurrentMember.Properties ("Manager")`. (Appendix A provides a detailed reference to this function, and we also use it in the "Using Member Properties in MDX Expressions" section of Chapter 3.) The lookup of this value is done on a cell-by-cell basis, and at each cell the particular manager is unambiguous (though the level of manager to which it refers may change). For this case, you can easily and simply reference member properties on multiple levels that share the same name.

Querying Cell Properties

Querying for specific cell properties is fairly tightly bound to the programming layer that retrieves results from a query. In keeping with the nonprogramming focus of this book, we won't cover all of the programming details here. (We do introduce client programming in Chapter 15.) However, we will explain the basic model that querying for specific cell properties supports and how an application might use it. This explanation is relevant to OLE DB for OLAP, ADO MD and ADO MD.Net, and XMLA.

Every query is a specification of one or more result cells. Much as each member is able to have one or more related properties, each result cell also has more than one possible result property. If a query specifies no cell properties, then three properties are returned by default: an ordinal number that represents the index of the cell in the result set, the raw value for the cell in whatever data type is appropriate, and the formatted textual value for the cell. If the query specifies particular cell properties, then only those are returned to the client. We discuss formatting the raw value into text in the section "Precedence of Display Formatting" in Chapter 4. The ordinal cell index value is germane to client tools that are querying the data that has been generated through OLE DB for OLAP or XMLA. Other cell properties can be queried for, which can be specified for any measure or calculated member in the cube. The full list of cell properties and how they are used in OLE DB for OLAP and ADO MD/.Net is found in Appendix C.

The way to specify cell properties in a query is to follow the slicer (if any) with the CELL PROPERTIES keywords and the names of the cell properties. For example, the following query

```
SELECT
{ [Measures].[Units Returned], [Measures].[Value Returned] } on columns,
{ [Time].[2000], [Time].[2001] } on rows
FROM InventoryCube
CELL PROPERTIES FORMATTED_VALUE
```

returns to the client only the formatted text strings that correspond to the query results. Generally speaking, clients that render their results as text strings (such as spreadsheet-style report grids in ASP pages) will be most interested in the formatted values. Clients that render their results graphically (such as in bar charts where each height of each bar represents the value of the measure at that intersection) will be most interested in the raw values. An Excel-based client will benefit from retrieving the raw value and the format string together. Other OLE DB for OLAP standard properties available in Analysis Services enable string formatting, font, and color information to be stored and retrieved for measures and calculated members. This gives you server-side control over useful client rendering operations. Analysis Services adds more cell properties covering cell calculation specifics.

Our discussion of CREATE MEMBER in Chapter 12 describes how to specify the various cell properties that should be associated with calculated members. In Chapter 4, we describe how calculated members influence cell properties in queries.

TIP Some development teams avoid using formatted values, claiming that it is preferable to separate formatting from the database. However, that requires mid-tier or front-end code to be conscious of the meanings of individual members and tuples, making generic display code quite complicated, while not delivering one jot of different capability. You can also think of that as breaking encapsulation. In our experience, they are extremely helpful, and can always be overridden by client code anyway if you really want to.

Client Result Data Layout

Although the result of an MDX query is a data structure, it is typically converted to some human-accessible rendering. When more than one dimension is on an axis, there is a convention that you should be aware of for how clients use the results. Recall that the order of dimensions in a tuple is important in MDX. Consider, again, the sample query involving CrossJoin():

```
SELECT
CrossJoin (
  { [Time].[Q1, 2005], [Time].[Q2, 2005] },
  { [Measures].[Dollar Sales], [Measures].[Unit Sales] }
)
ON COLUMNS ,
{ [Product].[Tools], [Product].[Toys] } ON ROWS
FROM Sales
```

The Measures dimension is the second dimension in each of the tuples, and the Time dimension the first. The first dimension in a tuple is the one at the outermost level of nesting as it comes out of the CrossJoin(), and it is also the outermost one in a client's rendering of the results. The last dimension in a tuple is the innermost, both from CrossJoin() and in client's rendering.

The order of dimensions in tuples, when they show up in an axis, is reflected in the order of the dimensions in the returned data structures.

	Q1, 2005	Q1, 2005	Q2, 2005	Q2, 2005
	Dollar Sales	Unit Sales	Dollar Sales	Unit Sales
Tools	183,042.00	7,179	199,809.20	7,912
Toys	149,435.30	5,878	169,513.10	6,476

Figure 1-15 Typical client rendering of rows and columns.

Summary

While we have covered only the basics of MDX queries, we really have covered quite a lot, and fairly quickly. Let's summarize what we have gone over:

- The SELECT . . . FROM . . . WHERE framework of a query
- Axis names and numbering, and the slicer
- The tuple and set data model
- The most basic and frequent functions and operators: braces ({ }), commas (,), parentheses for tuple construction (( )), and the colon (:) for range construction; .Members, .Children, Descendants(), CrossJoin(), Filter(), and Order()
- Referencing member properties as additional query results
- Referencing cell properties
- Including comments
- Removing empty slices with NON EMPTY

We have also tried to emphasize the modular nature of MDX and explain expressions as an independent concept from queries. Whew! You might want to take a break before plunging on to the next chapter. In the next chapter, we will build on this understanding to start performing calculations.

CHAPTER 2

Introduction to MDX Calculated Members and Named Sets

In addition to selecting data, MDX provides the ability to define new calculations, and to define named sets of tuples that can be referred to in other selections and functions. These can be done within a query, which frees the database developer from needing to account for all applications of the database, and it frees the users and/or applications from relying on the database for all calculations and set or filter definitions. In this chapter, we introduce you to creating calculations using the MDX construct called "calculated members." Calculated members are a form of DDL (*data definition language*) that servers such as Analysis Services and Essbase allow to be defined as part of the database as well as part of a query. The way they behave is the same in either case, so we will look at how they behave from the point of view of queries. We will also introduce you to creating named sets.

Servers such as Analysis Services and Essbase also allow MDX-based calculations to be defined at the database, and Analysis Services allows them to be defined within a client session as well. Analysis Services also allows named sets to be defined at the server. Essbase 9 provides an alternate technique to accomplish the same result within MDX queries, which will be discussed in that section.

Dimensional Calculations As Calculated Members

If you have some experience with SQL, you will find that the numerical calculations that are straightforward in SQL are also straightforward in MDX. However, a great many calculations that are very difficult in SQL are also straightforward in MDX. If you have experience with spreadsheet formulas (with their absolute and relative cell references in two or three dimensions), then you are already familiar with some of the basic concepts of dimensional calculations. MDX provides a much clearer language in which to create calculations, however, and you don't have to put a formula into each cell to calculate the cell. Rather, you can specify a formula and control the range of cells that all share that formula.

Not all calculations need to be put into calculated members. Only those whose results you wish to return as values for cells to a client application need to be put in calculated members. When a calculation is needed somewhere else (for example, as a basis for selecting or sorting members), an arithmetic expression will do just as well. However, you may wish to use a calculated member to package the logic of the calculation if you are going to use it more than once.

The simplest form of a calculated member is a named member in some dimension, and a formula with which to calculate cells related to that member. Calculated members exist to provide a place to put the results of calculations. Every query to a cube results in a collection of cells, where every cell is identified by one member from each dimension of the cube. There are no members without names, and there are no areas of the query that fall outside the cube. Therefore, we add a member to add a slot to a dimension that will hold the results.

> **TIP** Whenever you are trying to perform a calculation in MDX, you need to define a calculated member (or perhaps some other calculated entity in Analysis Services) to contain it and then reference this entity in a query.

Under the hood of the Analysis Services 2005 BI Development Studio and the Analysis Services 2000 Analysis Manager, the user interface generates exactly the same MDX statements that create the calculated members that will be discussed in the remainder of this chapter. So, although the calculated members are metadata entities, they are also MDX language constructs. Two of the purposes of this chapter are to give you an understanding of MDX queries and of how to create calculated members for cubes in databases.

> **CALCULATIONS IN ANALYSIS SERVICES**
>
> Calculated members are only one of six different ways to compute the value of a cell in Microsoft Analysis Services 2000, and four of those ways involve MDX. Analysis Services 2005 adds yet another MDX-based way. This section focuses on calculated members because they are a workhorse, and one of only two ways that an OLAP client can define without special permissions. The concepts you gain in understanding how calculated members work go a long way towards helping you understand how to use the other techniques.

Calculated Member Scopes

The MDX specification allows three different lifetime scopes for calculated members:

- Within the duration of a query ("query scope")
- Within the duration of a user session ("session scope")
- Persistent within a cube until the calculated member is dropped ("global scope")

Analysis Services supports the first two of these scopes. Essbase supports the first one in the syntax we discuss in this chapter; calculated members defined at the server are neither created nor dropped with DDL but rather via outline editors and API calls.

Calculated Members and WITH Sections in Queries

In order to introduce calculated members, we also need to introduce a new and optional part of a query. As this section begins with the keyword WITH, we will refer to this part of the query as the "WITH section."

The WITH section of a query comes before the SELECT keyword and forms a section where the definitions private to the query are made. Calculated members and named sets (described later on) are the only two standard things that may be specified in the WITH section. (In Analysis Server, declaring a cell calculation and a cache of data to be loaded would be the other two things. We will cover cell calculations in Chapter 12. Caches are purely a physical optimization, which we will discuss in Chapter 14.)

For example, the following query whose results are shown in Figure 2-1 will augment the database measures of Unit Sales and Dollar Sales with a measure named [Avg Sales Price]:

```
WITH
MEMBER [Measures].[Avg Sales Price] AS
'[Measures].[Dollar Sales] / [Measures].[Unit Sales]'
SELECT
{ [Measures].[Dollar Sales], [Measures].[Unit Sales],
  [Measures].[Avg Sales Price]
}
on columns,
{ [Time].[Q1, 2005], [Time].[Q2, 2005] }
on rows
FROM Sales
WHERE ([Customer].[MA])
```

As you can see, the Avg Sales Price calculation is carried out across each of the time members, for the stated customer (and all other dimensions as well).

Let's step back from this example and identify some general features. The core syntax for defining a calculated member on a dimension is

```
MEMBER MemberIdentifier AS 'member-formula' [, properties...]
```

The three main parts are

- Member identifier, which specifies the name, dimension and hierarchical positioning of the calculated member.

- Formula, which specifies how the calculated member's results are derived.

- Optional properties, which can provide additional calculation, display, and other kinds of information.

The member must be associated with a dimension of a cube, so `Member Identifier` must contain a dimension name as a component. If the calculated member is to appear as the child of another member, that parent member's name must also appear as part of the member identifier. For example, the name `[Measures].[Ratios].[Avg Sales Price]` would make the name appear to be a child of the Ratios member in the measures dimension (although, as we mentioned in Chapter 1, you would need to use the `.AllMembers` or `AddCalculatedMembers()` functions to see the member appear in the list of children). Note that neither Analysis Services or Essbase allows calculated members to be the children of other calculated members.

WHY DEFINE A CALCULATED MEMBER ONLY WITHIN A QUERY?

Some kinds of calculations can only be performed by calculated members in a WITH clause. In particular, any calculation on members that are picked by a user in the course of a session cannot be stored in the database. We'll see examples of this later on.

	Dollar Sales	Unit Sales	Avg Sales Price
Q1, 2005	96,949.10	3,866	25.1
Q2, 2005	104,510.20	4,125	25.3

Figure 2-1   Result of query with calculated member.

The formula is an expression that results in numbers or strings. The MDX standard does not include the quotes around the expression. To conform to the standard, the query should read:

```
WITH
MEMBER [Measures].[Avg Sales Price] AS
[Measures].[Dollar Sales] / [Measures].[Unit Sales]
SELECT ...
```

Since the first two versions of Microsoft's server required quotes around the expression, most vendors support it. At the time of this writing, only Analysis Services 2005 supports the standard, but we hope that other servers do shortly as well.

MDX provides two variations on this core syntax to define calculated members. If you put this definition in a WITH section, the calculated member is part of the query but not available in any other query. The other variation defines a calculated member that will be available to more than one query; we will discuss that one later on.

Calculated members can be on any dimension, so you can also query for the growth in dollar and unit sales between Q1 and Q2 of 2005 with the following query (its results are shown in Figure 2-2 with the growth calculation shaded in):

```
WITH
MEMBER [Time].[Q1 to Q2 Growth] AS
'[Time].[Q2, 2005] - [Time].[Q1, 2005]'
SELECT
{ [Measures].[Dollar Sales], [Measures].[Unit Sales] }
on columns,
```

```
{ [Time].[Q1, 2005], [Time].[Q2, 2005], [Time].[Q1 to Q2 Growth] }
on rows
FROM Sales
WHERE ([Customer].[MA])
```

Two things stand out here: First, it is just as easy to calculate new rows as it is new columns. If you are familiar with SQL, you may appreciate the uniformity of the syntax for this. Second, we have the same syntax for measures, time, and any other dimensions that you want to define a calculation in.

Formula Precedence (Solve Order)

So far, we have only considered formulas for members of one dimension. You will very likely have formulas on members of more than one dimension, which raises the issue of what you should do when these formulas intersect. For example, consider the set of base and calculated cells shown in Figure 2-3. They are combined from the queries for Figures 2-1 and 2-2, where each calculated slice has numbers in italics.

In the example in Figure 2-3, there are formulas in two different dimensions; the cell in which they overlap shows two possible values. This cell has two possible formulas: (Q2 Avg Sales Price – Q1 Avg Sales Price) or (Difference in Sales / Difference in Units).

	Dollar Sales	Unit Sales
Q1, 2005	96,949.10	3,866
Q2, 2005	104,510.20	4,125
Q1 to Q2 Growth	7,561.10	259

Figure 2-2   Query result with calculated time growth member.

	Dollar Sales	Unit Sales	Avg Sales Price
Q1, 2005	96949.1	3866	25.1
Q2, 2005	104510.2	4125	25.3
Q1 to Q2 Growth	7561.1	259	0.3 or 29.19

Figure 2-3   3 x 3 cells with formulas: a ratio and a sum.

How do you control the ordering of calculations among dimensions? This issue is sometimes called dimensional precedence, or formula overlap.

The mechanism that standard MDX uses for dealing with dimensional formula precedence is called *solve order*. Every calculated member has an associated solve order number, which is an integer that says what the calculation priority of the member is. When calculated members overlap on a cell, the member with the highest solve order number "wins" and is used to calculate the cell. For example, the following query uses solve order numbers to make sure that the difference of average sales prices is defined as the difference of the ratios, not the ratio of the differences (resulting in the value 0.3 in the intersecting cell):

```
WITH
MEMBER [Measures].[Avg Sales Price] AS
 '[Measures].[Dollar Sales] / [Measures].[Unit Sales]',
SOLVE_ORDER = 0
MEMBER [Time].[Q1 to Q2 Growth] AS
 '[Time].[Q2, 2005] - [Time].[Q1, 2005]',
SOLVE_ORDER = 1
SELECT
{ [Measures].[Dollar Sales], [Measures].[Unit Sales],
   [Measures].[Avg Sales Price]
}
on columns,
{ [Time].[Q1, 2005], [Time].[Q2, 2005], [Time].[Q1 to Q2 Growth] }
on rows
FROM [Sales]
WHERE ([Customer].[MA])
```

The standard behavior is that if you don't specify a number when you specify the formula for the member, it defaults to 0. The number is fixed when you create the calculation and cannot be changed without dropping and recreating it. The numbers are simply relative precedence numbers, so there is no real requirement that the smallest number you use be 0. Nor is there any requirement that you use 2 or 1 if the highest number in use is 3 and the lowest is 0. See Chapter 4 for a detailed discussion on solve orders.

Note that you don't need to care about solve order when it doesn't make a difference which dimension wins. If one dimension's formula specifies a sum or a difference and another dimension's also specifies a sum or a difference, a solve order tie between them won't change the results. Similarly, multiplication and pure division will be indifferent to solve orders.

SOLVE ORDERS

ANALYSIS SERVICES

Analysis Services supports solve order numbers down to -8191 and up to 2,415,919,103. Some of these solve order numbers are reserved for particular kinds of calculations. Although Microsoft states that the concept of solve order is deprecated for Analysis Services 2005, this can only be true for server-defined calculated members; it cannot really be deprecated for calculated members defined in a session or a `WITH` clause.

ESSBASE

Essbase 7.1.3 and later supports default solve orders on a dimension-wide basis (defined at the server). Specifying a solve order of 0 actually means to use the dimension-wide solve order, which is 0 by default but could be different.

A few paragraphs ago we referred to other parts of a calculated member that we can specify in the member definition. The solve order property shown in the preceding query is one of them.

Note the following syntactic point about defining multiple calculated members in the `WITH` section of the query. Each member definition is simply followed by the next one. A comma is used to separate the formula definition from the solve order definition, but no punctuation, such as a comma, semicolon, or other device, is used to separate the end of one from the beginning of the next. Instead, they are separated by the `MEMBER` keyword.

You should keep two other points in mind regarding solve orders. First, if members on two different dimensions have the same priority, it's up to the server to decide which one goes first, and they generally use some list ordering of dimensions in the cube as the basis. If the DBA rearranges the ordering, the MDX may behave differently.

You should only let formulas on different dimensions have the same solve order number when the formulas are commutative (either when they all involve only addition and subtraction or when they all involve only multiplication and division). Second, the solve order only affects the priority of calculation between dimensions. The database still uses actual formula dependencies to determine what to calculate first. For example, consider the following four formulas. Figure 2-4 shows these four formulas and their inputs laid out on a grid, together with the formula that is actually in use for any given cell.

SOLVE ORDER TIES

ANALYSIS SERVICES

A calculated member solve order tie in Analysis Services is won by the dimension that appears later in the server's list of dimensions. Measures is always the last dimension in the list, so it always effectively wins. Note there are other kinds of definitions that also have solve order and may win the tie instead-see Chapter 4 for details.

ESSBASE

Winning a solve order tie in Essbase is different between BSO and ASO applications. In a block-storage cube, and in ASO cubes prior to version 7.1.2, it is won by the dimension that appears earlier in the server's list of dimensions (which is generally compatible with precedence in Essbase's other languages). In 7.1.2 and after, a tie is won by the dimension that appears *later* in the list of dimensions.

```
[Measures].[Profit]
  AS '[Measures].[Sale Amount] - [Measures].[Total Cost]',
  SOLVE_ORDER = 0
[Scenario].[Amount of Variance]
  AS '[Scenario].[Actual] - [Scenario].[Planned]',
  SOLVE_ORDER = 1
[Measures].[Percentage Margin]
  AS '[Measures].[Profit] / [Measures].[Sale Amount]',
  SOLVE_ORDER = 2
[Scenario].[Percentage Variance]
  AS '[Scenario].[Amount of Variance] / [Scenario].[Planned]',
  SOLVE_ORDER = 3
```

Calculated members for a cube's dimension may be defined at the server or at the client. Calculated members defined at the server will be visible to all client sessions that can query the cube and can be used in any number of queries. A client can also define such calculated members as well. Clients and servers do this by using the second variation of the syntax for creating calculated members: the CREATE MEMBER command.

NOTE Essbase 9 does not support creating calculated members in a client session with CREATE MEMBER.

	Sale Amount	Total Cost	Profit	Percentage Margin
Actual			▓▓▓	╱╱╱
Planned			▓▓▓	╱╱╱
Amount of Variance	≡≡≡	≡≡≡	≡≡≡	╱╱╱
Percentage of Variance	╲╲╲	╲╲╲	╲╲╲	╲╲╲

Figure 2-4   Map of calculated member definitions and overlap on a grid.

Calculated members defined with the CREATE MEMBER command must be named with the cube as well as the dimension that they are to be a part of. The CREATE MEMBER command is not part of a query that uses SELECT, but is its own statement. Other than that, the core syntax for naming the member and defining its formula and other properties is basically the same as a WITH-defined member. For example, the following MDX statement will create [Scenario].[Amount of Variance] on the Scenario dimension used by the [Sales Cube] cube:

```
CREATE MEMBER [Sales Cube].[Scenario].[Amount of Variance] AS
'[Scenario].[Actual] - [Scenario].[Planned]', SOLVE_ORDER = 1
```

This calculated member will only be visible to queries on the [Sales Cube] cube. Queries to other cubes, even if they also use the scenario dimension, will not be able to see this calculated member, just like they cannot see any other information about another cube. The CREATE MEMBER statement defines a calculated member for a dimension that can be used by any query (until the member is dropped or the client exits), and additionally in Analysis Services will exist in the dimension's metadata visible through OLE DB for OLAP. (In Analysis Services, this metadata will only be visible on that client; that metadata will not be visible at the server or at any other client attached to that server.)

Note that the name of the cube was part of the specifications of the member to create. This is necessary because of OLAP providers such as Analysis Services 2005, a session isn't ordinarily associated with any particular cube. However, in Analysis Services 2005, you can include a cube name in the connection string or connection parameters, which you use to establish a session (see Appendix B for details). In that case, you can omit the cube name portion of a named set definition.

When a query uses calculated members in Essbase and in Analysis Services 2000, all solve order numbers from all the calculated members in the query are thrown together regardless of their source. A formula defined in the WITH section of a query as having solve order = 2 will lose to a server-defined formula or a formula defined in a CREATE MEMBER statement as having solve order = 3. This allows for very graceful interaction of definitions. For example, key ratios can be defined at the server, such as Average Sales Price and Period-to-Period % Growth, clients can create calculations such as totals across custom sets of members (one of the many uses for named sets), and a query can take the correct ratio of sums.

NOTE Analysis Services 2005 behaves somewhat differently than this. How it handles solve orders is treated in depth in Chapter 4.

At the time a query is constructed, you can know the solve orders for all calculated members included in the cube definition on the server. However, when a database is constructed, you obviously cannot know the formulas used in queries and their solve orders. Furthermore, since solve orders are integer numbers, you cannot slip a calculated member into a query between two members whose solve orders are 1 and 2 by giving the new member a solve order of 1.5.

For these reasons, you may want to leave gaps in the solve order numbers that are used for calculated members created as part of a cube's definition (through the GUI or through ASO if you are creating them through your own code). For example, the lowest-precedence number at the server might be 10, the next one 20, and so on. If you ever programmed in classic BASIC, this procedure should be familiar (remember line numbers running 10, 20, 30, and so on?). Analysis Services' solve order numbers can run up to 2,147,483,647, so you have plenty of headroom here. While the Essbase maximum solve order number of 127 may seem limiting, you still have lots of room if you leave gaps of 5.

NOTE As of Essbase 7.1.2, when you define a calculated member, its solve order must be at least as large as the largest solve order of one of its inputs, or you will get an error message (instead of perhaps wrong results) calculating affected cells when the query is run. When you are building queries, you may need to be aware of the solve orders in use at the server.

The solve order of calculated members is one facet of the concept of formula application ranges. Basically, every formula that you will create will apply to some set of locations in your database. As far as MDX semantics are concerned, the formula that you define for a calculated member will be calculated over every cell in the database that intersects that member. This may or may not be what you want, depending on your circumstances. You may, at times, want some formulas to calculate differently, depending on what level they are at in a dimension. Profitability may be calculated differently in different countries, for example. A formula to compute GNP will not apply to a subnational level of data. We will explore techniques for controlling application ranges in Chapter 7. Also, Analysis Services 2005's MDX Scripts provide a different way to approach the problem, and we discuss them in depth in Chapter 13.

Basic Calculation Functions

MDX includes a collection of functions with which to calculate numbers, which is rather small, so both Microsoft and Hyperion have added a number of useful extensions. Now that we have looked at the outline of how to define a calculation, let's examine some of the functions available.

Arithmetic Operators

As you might expect, MDX provides support for the most common arithmetic operators:

FUNCTION OR OPERATOR	CALCULATES:
+ - * /	Addition, subtraction, multiplication, and division
-	For unary negation
()	Parentheses for grouping operations
^	For "raised-to-the-power-of" (Microsoft-only)

Addition, subtraction, multiplication, and division are expressed as usual, with the usual order of operations. You can apply grouping parentheses as well to specify the order of operations. Note that parentheses are used for constructing tuples as well, but there should be no cases where the use of the parentheses is ambiguous.

Summary Statistical Operators

MDX also provides a collection of summary statistical operators, including:

FUNCTION OR OPERATOR	CALCULATES:	EXTENSION
Avg()	Average (mean) of values	
Aggregate()	Aggregate of values based on server definition of aggregation function	
Count()	Count of values or tuples	
DistinctCount()	Distinct count of values or tuples	Microsoft
Sum()	Sum of values	
Max()	Maximum of values	
Median()	Median value from a set	
Min()	Minimum of values	
NonEmptyCount()	Count of values or tuples	Hyperion
Stdev()	Sample standard deviation across values	
StdevP()	Population standard deviation across values	Microsoft
Var()	Sample variance across values	
VarP()	Population variance across values	Microsoft

With the exception of Count() and NonEmptyCount(), these functions all aggregate across a set of numbers and return a single number. Count() and NonEmptyCount() look at the presence of data values in cells rather than the values themselves.

The syntax and usage for each of these aggregation functions is described in the following sections.

Avg()

The Avg() function takes a set of tuples and an optional numeric expression, and returns the average (mean) value of the expression over the set. By default, empty cells aren't counted, so its result is the sum across the set divided by the count of nonempty values for the expression across the set. Essbase extends the standard function with an optional INCLUDEEMPTY flag; when it is provided, the function returns the sum across the set divided by the number of tuples in the set. If the numeric expression isn't provided, it will take the average value over the cells related to the set in the current context.

Standard syntax:

```
Avg (set [, numeric_value_expression])
```

Hyperion syntax:

```
Avg (set [, numeric_value_expression] [,INCLUDEEMPTY] )
```

Example:

```
Avg (
  {[Product].[Tools],
   [Product].[Toys],
   [Product].[Indoor, Outdoor Games] },
   [Measures].[Dollar Sales]
)
```

Count(), .Count

The Count() function takes a set of tuples and an optional flag to signal including or excluding tuples with empty related data values. In Analysis Services, the default behavior is to count all tuples in the set (as though INCLUDEEMPTY had been specified). If EXCLUDEEMPTY is specified, the related cells are evaluated and only the count of tuples with nonempty cells is returned. In Essbase, if the INCLUDEEMPTY flag is included, the function returns the count of tuples in the set, otherwise it defaults to excluding tuples related to empty data values.

Note that this function behaves differently from the other aggregating functions, in that it does not take an expression for which to count the values. This makes use of it a bit tricky. Its typical use involves CrossJoin()ing the measure whose values might be empty in with the set. Otherwise (as will be explained in Chapter 4), you may get an infinite recursion error.

Standard syntax:

```
Count (set [,INCLUDEEMPTY] )
```

Microsoft syntax:

```
Count (set [,EXCLUDEEMPTY | INCLUDEEMPTY] )
```

Example:

```
Count (
   CrossJoin (
      { [Measures].[Unit Sales] },
      [Product].[Tools].Children
   )
)
```

To simplify programming, Microsoft also accepts the `.Count` syntax that is familiar to VB programmers as a variation on `Count ( ... INCLUDEEMPTY)`, which makes it more clear that it is counting tuples rather than cell values:

```
{[Product].[Tools].Children}.Count
```

or

```
[Product].[Tools].Children.Count
```

DistinctCount() (Microsoft extension)

The `DistinctCount()` function takes a set of tuples and returns the count of distinct, nonempty tuples in the set. Note that only a calculated measure may use this function. It is equivalent to `Count ( Distinct (set), EXCLUDEEMPTY)` when the set includes a measure (as shown in the example, which is similar to the correct usage for `Count()`). When the set does not include a measure, the difference is that `Count()` will return an infinite recursion error, while `DistinctCount()` will return the full number of tuples in *set*. (See Chapter 4 for an explanation of the infinite recursion.)

Syntax:

```
DistinctCount (set)
```

Example:

```
DistinctCount (
   [Measures].[Dollar Sales] *
   {[Product].[Tools], [Product].[Toys],
    [Product].[Indoor, Outdoor Games]
   }
)
```

Sum()

The Sum() function takes a set of tuples and an optional numeric expression, and returns the sum of the expression over the set. If the numeric expression isn't provided, it will sum over the cells related to the set in the current context. (We haven't talked about the current context yet-we will talk about it in detail later.)

Syntax:

```
Sum (set [, numeric_value_expression])
```

Example:

```
Sum (
   {[Product].[Tools],
    [Product].[Toys],
    [Product].[Indoor, Outdoor Games] },
   [Measures].[Dollar Sales]
)
```

Max()

The Max() function takes a set of tuples and an optional numeric expression, and returns the maximum value of the expression over the set. If the numeric expression isn't provided, it will take the maximum value over the cells related to the set in the current context.

Syntax:

```
Max (set [, numeric_value_expression])
```

Example:

```
Max (
   {[Product].[Tools],
    [Product].[Toys],
    [Product].[Indoor, Outdoor Games] },
   [Measures].[Dollar Sales]
)
```

Median()

The Median() function takes a set of tuples and an optional numeric expression, and returns the median value found (the one for which an equal number of values in the set were larger than as smaller than). If the numeric expression isn't provided, it will take the median value over the cells related to the set in the current context.

Syntax:

```
Median (set [, numeric_value_expression])
```

Example:

```
Median (
    [Product].[Tools].Children,
    [Measures].[Dollar Sales]
)
```

NOTE Essbase does not implement this function.

Min()

The `Min()` function takes a set of tuples and an optional numeric expression, and returns the minimum value of the expression over the set. If the numeric expression isn't provided, it will take the minimum value over the cells related to the set in the current context.

Syntax:

```
Min (set [, numeric_value_expression])
```

Example:

```
Min (
    [Product].[Tools].Children,
    [Measures].[Dollar Sales]
)
```

NonEmptyCount() (Hyperion extension)

To make the task of counting nonempty cells more like the other aggregation functions, Hyperion provides the `NonEmptyCount()` function, which takes a set of tuples and an optional numeric expression and returns the number of tuples in the set for which the expression is not empty. If the numeric expression isn't provided, it will take the count of nonempty tuples over the cells related to the set in the current context.

Syntax:

```
NonEmptyCount (set [, numeric_value_expression])
```

Example:

```
NonEmptyCount (
    [Product].[Tools].Children,
    [Measures].[Unit Sales]
)
```

Stdev(), Stddev()

The Stdev() function takes a set of tuples and an optional numeric expression, and returns the sample standard deviation across the values found. If the numeric expression isn't provided, it will take the sample standard deviation over the cells related to the set in the current context. Analysis Services accepts Stddev() as a synonym for Stdev().

Syntax:

```
Stdev (set [, numeric_value_expression])
```

Example:

```
Stdev (
   [Product].[Tools].Children,
   [Measures].[Dollar Sales]
   )
```

NOTE Essbase does not implement this function.

StdevP(), StddevP() (Microsoft Extension)

The StdevP() function takes a set of tuples and an optional numeric expression, and returns the population standard deviation across the values found. If the numeric expression isn't provided, it will take the population standard deviation over the cells related to the set in the current context. Analysis Services accepts StddevP() as a synonym for StdevP().

Syntax:

```
StdevP (set [, numeric_value_expression])
```

Example:

```
StdevP (
   [Product].[Tools].Children,
   [Measures].[Dollar Sales]
   )
```

Var(), Variance()

The Var() function takes a set of tuples and an optional numeric expression, and returns the sample variance across the values found. If the numeric expression isn't provided, it will take the sample variance over the cells related to the set in the current context. Analysis Services accepts Variance() as a synonym for Var().

Syntax:

```
Var (set [, numeric_value_expression])
```

Example:

```
Var (
   [Product].[Tools].Children,
   [Measures].[Dollar Sales]
)
```

NOTE Essbase does not implement this function.

VarP(), VarianceP() (Microsoft Extension)

The VarP() function takes a set of tuples and an optional numeric expression, and returns the population variance across the values found. If the numeric expression isn't provided, it will take the population variance over the cells related to the set in the current context. Analysis Services accepts VarianceP() as a synonym for VarP().

Syntax:

```
VarP (set [, numeric_value_expression])
```

Example:

```
VarP (
   [Product].[Tools].Children,
   [Measures].[Dollar Sales]
)
```

Additional Functions

There are more standard and extension statistical aggregation functions that we will list only briefly here:

FUNCTION	CALCULATES:
Correlation ()	Correlation coefficient of two data series over a set
Covariance ()	Covariance of two data series over a set
CovarianceN ()	(Microsoft) Sample covariance of two data series over a set
LinRegIntercept ()	Linear regression intercept

(continued)

(continued)

FUNCTION	CALCULATES:
LinRegPoint ()	Point on linear regression line
LinRegR2 ()	Linear regression coefficient
LinRegSlope ()	Slope of linear regression line
LinRegVariance ()	Variance of set from linear regression line

You are encouraged to peruse Appendix A for the details on these functions (and many more). Note that Essbase 9 does not support this set of statistical functions. Besides these functions, there are a great many more that you will want to use. Before you move on to the next chapter, you may find it most useful to at least skim Appendix A to see what is there.

Analysis Services provides access to many of the string and numeric functions of the VBA and Excel object libraries, and you can use the functions from these libraries as though they were built into your server. In Analysis Services 2005, it does so through the stored procedure mechanism, whereas in Analysis Services 2000, it does so through the external function (or "UDF"-*user-defined function*) mechanism. These are described more fully in Chapter 10. For example, logarithms, exponentiation, substring searches, combinatorial functions, percentiles, time conversions, duration calculations, and the like are all provided through the libraries.

Essbase provides an additional set of numeric calculation functions built-in. They include the following:

FUNCTION OR OPERATOR	CALCULATES:
Abs (num)	Absolute value of *num*
Exp (N)	E *raised to the power* N
Factorial(N)	Factorial of *N*
Int (num)	Number rounded down to the next lowest integer
Ln (num)	Natural logarithm
Log (num)	Logarithm, base *N*
Log10 (num)	Logarithm, base 10
Mod (num, M)	Modulus *M* (remainder from *num* divided by *M*)
Power (num, M)	Number *num* raised to power *M*
Remainder (num)	Number left over after removing integer portion from *num*
Round (num, M)	*Number* num *rounded to* M *places*
Truncate (num)	Number *num* with fractional part removed

Introduction to Named Sets

Building and using sets is an important part of MDX. Sometimes, it is most convenient to attach a name to a set that you've defined so you can reference it later. Standard MDX provides *named sets* to do just that. Both Analysis Services and Essbase extend the standard with set aliases to provide names for sets in additional contexts. (Essbase further provides tuple aliases as well.) These are easy to use and frequently used. The second half of this chapter has some rather involved query requirements that get solved with only a small number of features and functions working together. It both explains how some sophisticated user requests are handled and also continues to work through constructing MDX as assemblies of small simple expressions, so it may bear reading slowly and more than once.

Named sets are just names for a particular set. They can hold any kind of members or tuples so long as the set is valid; anywhere that you can use a set in MDX, you can reference a named set.

For example, the following shows the definition of a named set and its use in two places: in a calculated member and in forming the set of an axis. The result is shown in Figure 2-5.

```
WITH SET [User Selection] AS
'{ [Product].[Action Figures], [Product].[Dolls] }'
MEMBER [Product].[UserTotal] AS
'Sum ( [User Selection] )'
SELECT
{ [Time].[Jan, 2005],
  [Time].[Feb, 2005]
}
ON COLUMNS,
{ [Product].[Toys],
  [User Selection],
  [Product].[UserTotal]
}
ON ROWS
FROM Sales
WHERE ([Measures].[Unit Sales])
```

	Jan, 2005	Feb, 2005
Toys	1,989	1,695
Action Figures	405	352
Dolls	28	30
UserTotal	433	382

Figure 2-5   A query result incorporating a named set.

The basic syntax for defining a named set that is supported by most vendors is as follows:

```
SET Set-Identifier AS 'set-formula'
```

The syntax defined by the standard is similar, just without the single quotes around the set formula. As of this writing, Analysis Services 2005 is the only product that supports this syntax, but we hope more vendors do in the near future:

```
SET Set-Identifier AS set-formula
```

Essbase 9 supports a variation on the first version of the syntax, which we will discuss in Chapter 5, after discussing context in query execution in Chapter 4.

A named set name is just a name, and is not prefixed with any dimension. A set may contain tuples for more than one dimension, and if it's empty it won't appear to have any dimensions. There are no additional properties that you can specify for it.

Once it is defined and evaluated, its collection of tuples is fixed throughout its life.

Named Set Scopes

Named sets are scoped just like calculated members. If you create a named set in the WITH part of a query, it is not visible outside of the query. If you create a named set using CREATE SET (as with the following), then it will be available to more than one query and you can drop it with the DROP SET command. The following shows examples of the standard MDX for CREATE SET and DROP SET, available in Analysis Services.

```
CREATE SET [SalesCube].[User Selection] AS
'{ [Product].[Action Figures], [Product].[Dolls] }'

DROP SET [SalesCube].[User Selection]
```

Note that the name of the set is prefixed with the name of the cube. In Analysis Services, a session isn't ordinarily associated with any particular cube. However, in Analysis Services 2005, you can include a cube name in the connection string or connection parameters that you use to establish a session (see Appendix B for details). In that case, you can omit the cube name portion of a named set definition.

In a context like an MDX script, a local cube file, or in a DSO command in Analysis Services 2000, you can also use the token CURRENTCUBE instead of the cube name, since the cube context is clear.

Essbase does not follow the standard, but rather uses an optional FROM clause to name the cube in which to create the set. For example, the following statements would be equivalent to the foregoing examples of CREATE and DROP:

```
CREATE SET [User Selection] AS
'{ [Product].[Action Figures], [Product].[Dolls] }'
FROM [Sales]

DROP SET [User Selection]
FROM [Sales]
```

Note that the FROM clause is optional in the same way that it is in Essbase queries. For APIs that connect to an application and cube, if the FROM clause is omitted, then the cube is inferred from that. (In the MAXL and AAS interfaces, you must use the FROM clause, because they do not have a connection to a cube.)

Although the official MDX specification says that such sets are not visible to metadata, Analysis Services will surface them to client applications (which is much more helpful than hiding them).

NOTE Essbase also supports an optional WHERE clause; we will see what it is used for in Chapter 5, after we have covered query evaluation context in Chapter 4.

ESSBASE SUBSTITUTION VARIABLES AND NAMED SETS

Although Essbase does not support named sets as such at the server, it does support "substitution variables," which are named snippets of arbitrary text that can be substituted in and are treated as part of the MDX expression at the point it is parsed. (They have broader application than just as a proxy for named sets, but are especially relevant in this context.) For example, in Analysis Services, you might define the following at the server:

```
CREATE SET [SalesCube].[East Region Promotion Products] AS
'{ [Product].[Action Figures], [Product].[Dolls] }'
```

In Essbase, you might define a substitution variable named "East_Region_Products" with the contents:

```
{ [Product].[Action Figures], [Product].[Dolls] }
```

You could then execute any of the following:

```
CREATE SET [East Region Promotion Products] AS
'&East_Region_Products'

WITH SET [East Region Promotion Products] AS
'&East_Region_Products'
SELECT &East_Region_Products on axis(1) ...
```

Named sets can be defined anywhere within a WITH section. If a named set references a calculated member or another named set, it needs to appear after the things it references. Conversely, any calculated member that references a named set needs to appear after the definition of the set.

As with calculated members, multiple named sets can be defined in a WITH section. Each set definition appears in sequence, as follows:

```
WITH
SET [User Selection 1] AS '...'
SET [User Selection 2] AS '...'
```

In general, named sets and calculated members can be interspersed as necessary. There are no commas between the definitions; the MEMBER and SET keywords are enough to signal the start of a definition.

```
WITH
SET [User Selection 1] AS '...'
SET [User Selection 2] AS '...'
MEMBER [Measures].[M1] AS '...'
SET [User Selection 3] AS '...'
MEMBER [Product].[P1]  AS '...'
```

As you can see, named sets are simple to create and use. In Chapter 5, we will cover them more, and look at their cousins, named set aliases.

Summary

You have looked at the basics of creating calculated members and named sets. We introduced the WITH section, how calculated members are made members of some dimension, and described calculated member formulas and solve orders. We also introduced some of the many functions that can be used to calculate the results that a calculated member can provide. However, all of this was really describing simple mechanics. Much of the real power of MDX comes from specifying how to get the input values to these functions (the various functions that return sets, tuples, and members). In the next chapter, you start to look at how to express many kinds of common calculations used in many kinds of applications, and spend more attention to the thought process of arriving at the right expression to calculate what you want.

CHAPTER 3

Common Calculations and Selections in MDX

Having had a brief introduction to queries, and to how calculations are formed, you are ready to look at how a variety of common calculations and selections are expressed in MDX. Some will be trivial and amount to using one of the many MDX functions. Some will be less simple but composed of just a few of the functions working together. This chapter is an introduction to a vocabulary of the most commonly used functions. Here is where you start to actually see examples of composing MDX as small assemblies of "moving parts." Chapter 7 will put the vocabulary and techniques introduced here to more use.

This chapter will provide a fairly broad, technical introduction. Although we can make suggestions for how the techniques can be applied to different domains, such as analyzing trends in manufacturing quality, insurance claims, analyzing cross-sectional drug prescription behavior, or consumer purchasing patterns, most applications of MDX for analysis and reporting draw on the same collection of techniques tied together in only slightly differing ways. The rest of this book attempts to provide examples in terms of the Waremart 2005 application available on this book's web site. However, in order to provide techniques for domains not covered in that database, this chapter will provide illustrative MDX that does not correspond to any sample database.

Different application domains may use different terminology for the same technique. For example, analyses of insurance claims, production quality control, and customers' shopping preferences may all require the calculation of an item's percentage contribution to an aggregated item. In an insurance claim analysis, this calculation may be required to see which claimants, treatments, or plans consume the largest proportion of resources. In a production quality control analysis, this calculation may be used to see which products or production steps produce the greatest proportion of defects. In a customer shopping preference analysis, this calculation may be used to see which products contribute the highest proportion of profits for a customer or set of customers, or which customers are the proportionately highest-volume shoppers for a store. However, these analyses all use the same basic dimensional calculation (namely, a ratio between different levels in a hierarchy).

Wherever possible, we will lean on the sample database provided with this book. However, because it does not provide all kinds of data for all kinds of applications, we will stray from it wherever necessary (with apologies).

NOTE We will use MDX functions and operators in this chapter without describing them in detail. Their details appear in Appendix A (the operator and function reference). You are encouraged to start reading the function reference right now just to get an idea of what is available.

If you want to find a way to solve a calculation problem immediately, here is an outline of the topics in this chapter:

- Many kinds of ratios, averages, percentages, and allocations
- Simple ratios between levels in a hierarchy
- Ratio to parent
- Ratio to ancestor
- Ratio to [All]
- Percentage contribution to parent/ancestor/All
- Handling divide-by-zero
- Basic allocations
- Proportional allocation of one quantity based on the ratios of another
- Unweighted allocations down the hierarchy
- Averages
- Simple averages
- Weighted averages
- Time-based references and time-series calculations
- Period-to-period references and calculations
- Year-ago references and calculations
- Year-to-date (period-to-date) aggregations
- Rolling averages

- 52-week high/low
- Mixing aggregations: sum across non-time, average/min/max along time
- Mixing aggregations: sum across non-time, opening/closing balance along time
- Using member properties in MDX expressions (calculations and sorting)
- Filling in blanks
- Carryover of balances for slowly changing values
- Reporting of last entered balance (as opposed to balance for last time descendant)
- Finding the last time member for which any data has been entered

Each of these calculations is a fairly generic operation that many applications require, regardless of their analytical domain (finance, manufacturing, quality, shipping, consumer behavior). Some of them may have specialized support in the database (particularly the aggregation-related ones), but the calculations sometimes need to be run in MDX nonetheless. There are also more expressions and types of calculations than there are whole analytical queries. We discuss more sophisticated analytical queries in the next chapter.

Along the way, we will introduce the functions and operators in the following table, and see how they can be used on their own and in combination with others.

NAME	EXTENSION
`.CurrentMember`	No
`.Parent`	No
`Ancestor()`	No
`.PrevMember, .NextMember`	No
`.Lag(), .Lead()`	No
`PeriodsToDate()`	No
`ParallelPeriod()`	No
`LastPeriods()`	No
`OpeningPeriod()`	No
`ClosingPeriod()`	No
`Iif()`	No
`IS`	Microsoft, Hyperion

(continued)

(continued)

NAME	EXTENSION
IsGeneration()	Microsoft, Hyperion
IsLevel()	Hyperion
IsValid()	Hyperion

We will also introduce the concept of a recursive calculated member in this chapter, when discussing the problem of carrying over the last reported value into cells that otherwise don't have data values reported.

Metadata Referencing Functions in MDX

One of the most important aspects of an OLAP model for information is the number of ways that pieces of information can be related to each other. In a relational query, you can relate columns that are on the same row. Quite a bit of an SQL query involves joining, subquerying, and otherwise lining up fields to be on the same row. In an Excel spreadsheet, you can reference cells by row, by column, and by page, and you have some flexibility in terms of relative and absolute referencing for each of those. In an OLAP model, you can refer to pieces of information by absolute and relative references on any dimension (not just row or column), and you can involve more kinds of relationships. Most importantly, you have relationships up and down the hierarchy as well as within a level of the hierarchy. In order to make use of these relationships, you need functions that work with them. Figure 3-1 shows some of the basic relationships that can be exploited.

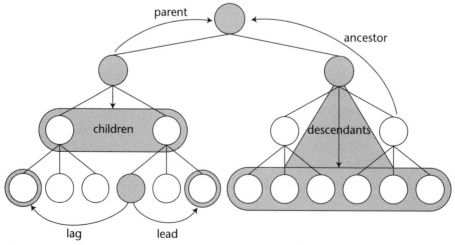

Figure 3-1   Illustrating hierarchy-based referencing.

> **METADATA REFERENCING AND .CURRENTMEMBER**
>
> Many of the metadata reference functions take as an argument a member that is the starting point for the reference. For example, the `.Parent` function takes a member and returns the parent member of the starting member. All of these functions can take a particular member as the input member. They can also take the "current" member, which is identified by a function like `.CurrentMember`. (We won't cover the full detail about how the "current" member becomes current here, but intuitively it's set to the appropriate member for each cell in which the calculation is invoked.) *Metadata references that involve* `.CurrentMember` *are probably the single most important thing (out of a large number of important things) to master to become an expert in MDX.*

MDX has a largish set of functions that refer to related metadata (particularly members and sets of members) in various ways. These functions form a very important portion of the vocabulary that you want to master to become an expert in MDX construction. Referring to related data usually involves combining a metadata reference with a reference to a measure in a tuple, which we will see over and over.

Many Kinds of Ratios, Averages, Percentages, and Allocations

Ratios are one of the most common calculation requirements in an OLAP system, after sums and differences. Percentages, averages, and allocations are all either alternate names for ratios, alternate representations of a ratio, or based on ratios. We devote this section to a variety of common ratios. We won't deal with the most common ratio (taking the ratio of two measures for some location), because we've already done that in earlier chapters.

Percent Contribution (Simple Ratios between Levels in a Hierarchy)

A very common business request is to calculate the percent contribution of values to some totals or set of totals. When those totals are found at higher levels in the hierarchy than the values contributing to them, you translate the business need into a calculation of the ratio of data at some member to an aggregate based on that member. This calculation has several permutations. If the total is found at some member of the hierarchy, then the ratio is very simple and can be put into any calculated member. We'll discuss that case here. If the total is found by aggregating some user-defined selection, then you need to do that work in a query. That case is discussed in Chapter 7. The following is a list of the generic types of these ratios within a hierarchy:

- Ratio of value to value at the [All] or dimension total member
- Ratio of value to value at a parent
- Ratio of value to value at an ancestor higher than the parent

Each of these types of calculations involves taking the ratio of some measure at one level to the measure's aggregate at a higher level and returning the result to a different measure (or different tuple) at the lower-level location.

Percent Contribution to Total

The following expression calculates the [Unit Sales] percent share of total for product members:

```
[Measures].[Unit Sales] / ([Measures].[Unit Sales], [All Product])
```

Note that you simply form a tuple of [Unit Sales] and [All Product] to refer to the data value there. In this context, the tuple identifies where the data value for the denominator comes from.

In order to build the other kind of ratios, we will introduce three functions quickly, as follows.

Using the .CurrentMember function

Syntax:

Dimension.CurrentMember	
CurrentMember (*Dimension*)	**Hyperion extension**

The .CurrentMember function returns a reference to the current member (in calculation or query context) for that dimension. The usual reason to obtain a reference to this member is as a starting point to refer to a related member, for example the parent using the .Parent function described next.

Using the .Parent function

Syntax:

Member.Parent	
Parent (*Member*)	**Hyperion extension**

The .Parent function returns a reference to the parent member of the given member.

Taking the Share-of-Parent Using .CurrentMember and .Parent

The expression to calculate the ratio of a Unit Sales measure to that measure at a product member's parent is

```
[Measures].[Unit Sales] /
([Measures].[Unit Sales], [Product].CurrentMember.Parent)
```

In this case, there is a ratio between two tuples: the unit sales (at some product, which is implied) and the tuple of unit sales at the current product member's parent member. You can explicitly reference the current member of a dimension with the .CurrentMember function. The usual reason to do this is to then modify its reference somehow. In this case, we do it so we can refer to its parent member. If the query is for a set of product subcategories, then the ratio calculated is "share of category"; if the query is for product categories, then the ratio calculated is "share of family," and so on.

If you want to take a consistent "share of family" so that you get share of family regardless of whether you are querying categories, subcategories, brands, or SKUs, then you need to use the Ancestor() function, as described next.

Using the Ancestor() function

Syntax:

Ancestor (*member*, *level*)	
Ancestor (*member*, *index*)	*Microsoft & Hyperion extension*

The Ancestor() function returns a reference to the Ancestor member of the given member either at the specified *level* or up *index* steps in the hierarchy. In Essbase, *level* can be either a level or a generation reference.

Calculating the Share-of-Ancestor using .CurrentMember and Ancestor()

You can calculate the share to ancestor ratio using the following expression. Note that the Ancestor() function is employed in a similar way to the .Parent function in the core expression:

```
[Measures].[Unit Sales] /
([Measures].[Unit Sales],
  Ancestor (
    [Product].CurrentMember,
    [Product].[Family]
  )
)
```

(Notice that the expression is indented to highlight nesting levels. This is a very helpful style when you are responsible for a lot of MDX, and it will be used heavily.)

Ratio to ancestor:

```
[Measures].[Payroll Total] /
([Measures].[Payroll Total],
   Ancestor ([Geography].CurrentMember, [Geography].[State]))
```

Ratio to [All] (in Analysis Services):

```
[Measures].[Payroll Total] /
([Measures].[Payroll Total], [Geography].[All Geography])
```

Ratio to [All] (in Essbase):

```
[Measures].[Payroll Total] /
([Measures].[Payroll Total], [Geography])
```

(Note that the difference between the ratio to all in Analysis Services and Essbase is that in Analysis Services, the dimension is called [Geography] with a root member named [All Geography], while in Essbase, the name of the dimension is the name of the root member in that dimension.)

A calculated measure that uses the appropriate formula will specifically name the measure it is taking the ratio of. For example, the ratio-to-ancestor expression appears in the following query, which requests the payroll proportions and total payroll for each store in Texas and Louisiana, and the results shown in Figure 3-2:

```
WITH MEMBER [Measures].[State Payroll Proportion] AS
'[Measures].[Payroll Total] / ([Measures].[Payroll Total],
   Ancestor ([Geography].CurrentMember, [Geography].[State]))',
SOLVE_ORDER = 5, FORMAT_STRING = '0%'
SELECT
{ [Measures].[Payroll Total], [Measures].[State Payroll Proportion] } on
columns,
{ Descendants ([Geography].[State].[TX], [Geography].[Store],
               SELF_AND_BEFORE),
   Descendants ([Geography].[State].[LA], [Geography].[Store],
               SELF_AND_BEFORE)
} on rows
FROM [Overhead]
WHERE [Time].[Year].[2004]
```

This calculation could also be put into a calculated member defined at the server, in which case the WITH MEMBER section of the query would be unnecessary. Note that the calculated member uses a format string property that causes the cells to be shown as percentages. Use of format strings is described more fully in Chapters 4 and 12 and in Appendix D.

	Payroll Total	State Payroll Proportion
TX	**110**	**100%**
Laredo	65	59%
Store_TX001	30	27%
Store_TX002	20	18%
Store_TX003	15	14%
Dallas	45	41%
Store_TX004	25	23%
Store_TX005	20	18%
LA	**125**	**100%**
Baton Rouge	30	24%
Store_LA001	20	16%
Store_LA002	10	8%
Shreveport	95	76%
Store_LA003	15	12%
Store_LA004	50	40%
Store_LA005	30	24%

Figure 3-2 Results of ratio-to-ancestor query.

You will want to keep in mind where these ratios can be calculated. A calculated member that uses the ratio-to-parent pattern will be valid at every level except the top level in the dimension, because there is no parent for the member(s) there. The ratio to ancestor will be valid at every level from the ancestor's level (where the ratio's value will simply be 1, unless the total is 0) down to the leaf level. The ratio to [All] will be valid everywhere in the dimension. It is a special case of ratio to ancestor, but it will be slightly more efficient to phrase this special case as the "ratio to the [All]" member than as the "ancestor of the current member at the All level."

Handling Division by Zero

One issue that almost always pops up when taking ratios is how to handle division by zero. Different OLAP providers return different results for division by zero. The typical approach is to compare the denominator to zero and return NULL, if it is. For example, the preceding Payroll Proportion calculation would be rephrased as the following to handle zeros:

```
'iif (
  ([Measures].[Payroll Total],
    Ancestor ([Geography].CurrentMember, [Geography].[State])) = 0,
```

```
    NULL,
    [Measures].[Payroll Total] / ([Measures].[Payroll Total],
     Ancestor ([Geography].CurrentMember, [Geography].[State]))
  )'
```

Essbase automatically makes the result of division by zero an empty cell value, so you don't need to worry about this. (We talk more about handling invalid data in Chapter 4.)

Basic Allocations

One use of ratios between levels within a hierarchy is to allocate higher-level values, such as total overhead or sales, to lower levels, such as individual business units or products. Here, we will discuss two basic types of allocations: allocation of a measure weighted by some proportion of another, and unweighted allocation. You might use these allocations in queries; in Analysis Services, you might use these in an UPDATE CUBE statement, which is covered in Chapter 11.

Proportional Allocation of One Quantity Based on Ratios of Another

Given a ratio between a measure and its value at some ancestor, you can perform a proportional allocation of any other measure based on that ratio. The measure being allocated is likely to come from a higher level than the target locations, although it could come from the same level. For example, budgeting models frequently allocate costs from a higher level down, based on head count or anticipated sales. Suppose that you need to allocate an advertising budget to arrive at a calculated budget per store, given your anticipated sales aggregated up a geography dimension. The following calculation would perform the allocation of advertising budget based on sales:

```
([Measures].[Advertising], [Geography].[All Geography]) *
[Measures].[Sales] / ([Measures].[Sales], [All Geography])
```

At the [All Geography] member, the allocated advertising budget should be equal to the total advertising budget. Assuming that sales have summed evenly up all levels, at each state in the Geography.State level, the allocated advertising budget should be proportional to that state's sales compared to the total organization's sales. At each city, the allocated ad budget should be proportional to that city's sales compared with the cities in that state. That budget should also be proportional to the city's sales compared with the total organization's sales.

Unweighted Allocations down the Hierarchy

You may also need to allocate values for some measure down a hierarchy, but in proportion to the number of children under a parent, rather than in proportion to some other measure's values. For example, measures that were input by quarter may need to be spread out to days. In this case, the ratio is simply going to be the reciprocal of the number of days in each quarter. In general, to get the ratio, you simply divide 1 by the number of descendants under the ancestor of the current member in that dimension. For example, to allocate from the quarter level of the time dimension down to a lower time level, the ratio would be expressed as:

```
1.0 / Count (
    Descendants (
      Ancestor (
        [Time].CurrentMember,
        [Time].[Quarter]
      ),
      [Time].CurrentMember.Level,
      SELF
    ),
    INCLUDEEMPTY
  )
```

In Analysis Services, you can simplify the syntax for this a bit using the `.Count` function instead of `Count ()`:

```
1.0 / Descendants (
      Ancestor (
        [Time].CurrentMember,
        [Time].[Quarter]
      ),
      [Time].CurrentMember.Level,
      SELF
    ).Count
```

Notice that you use the `Member.Level` operator to get the level of the current member in the time dimension, so that we make sure to take the descendants at the level for which we are calculating this ratio. This is a different kind of metadata reference than referencing members. For clarity, we also explicitly list the default `SELF` option for `Descendants ()`.

Averages

Another very frequent task in OLAP applications is calculating averages. There are a number of types of averages to calculate; we'll look at the simpler ones here. Rolling averages will be treated in their own section later.

Simple Averages

Because neither Microsoft Analysis Services nor Essbase ASO provides the capability to preaggregate data by averaging, you will frequently calculate an average by taking the ratio of a measure that represents a sum of input values with a measure that represents a count of input values. Because the measures often represent the same concept aggregated two different ways, their names will often be related, as in the following expression, which you might well use as the formula for a Sales Average calculated measure:

```
[Measures].[Sales Sum] / [Measures].[Item Count]
```

If you need to take a simple average of values associated with a set of cells, you can use the MDX Avg() function, as in the following example:

```
WITH
SET [My States] AS
'{ [Customer].[MA], [Customer].[ME], [Customer].[MI], [Customer].[MO] }'
MEMBER [Customer].[Avg Over States] AS 'Avg ([My States])'
SELECT
{ [Measures].[Dollar Sales], [Measures].[Unit Sales] } on columns,
{ [Products].[Family].Members } on rows
FROM Sales
WHERE ([Customer].[Avg Over States])
```

This query returns a grid of three measures by *N* product families. The sales, units, and profit measures are each averaged over the five best customers in terms of total profit. Notice that the expression to be averaged by the Avg() function has been left unspecified in the [Avg Over States] calculation. Leaving it unspecified is the equivalent of saying:

```
([Measures].CurrentMember, [Products].CurrentMember , . . . )
```

	Dollar Sales	Unit Sales
Doing	84,019.50	3,251.80
Electronics	157,241.40	6,356.50
Health & Fitness	71,890.60	2,770.00
Outdoor & Sporting	114,714.10	4,532.00

Figure 3-3   Calculated average results, with averaging member as a slicer.

Weighted Averages

When you calculate weighted averages, you are usually trying to take the average of some ratio (such as the price per share of stock) weighted by some quantity of the quotient (such as the number of shares traded). What you want to calculate is the average of the product of these two things. As far as the aggregate calculation architecture of Analysis Services and Essbase is concerned, the most efficient overall way to calculate the average of the product is by performing the multiplication into yet another measure in the fact table, and then summing it and counting it through the implicit aggregations. Assuming that this was not done for you (for example, because part of the quotient was itself derived), you can still do it effectively. For example, the expression

```
Sum (
  CrossJoin(
    Descendants ([Industry].CurrentMember, [Industry].[Company],
               SELF),
    Descendants ([Time].CurrentMember, [Time].[Day], SELF)
  )
  ,([Measures].[Share Price] * [Measures].[Units Sold])
) / [Measures].[Units Sold]
```

will calculate this weighted average.

A difficulty lurks in formulating the query this way, however. The greater the number of dimensions you are including in the average, the larger the size of the cross-joined set. You can run into performance problems (as well as intelligibility problems) if the number of dimensions being combined is large and the server actually builds the cross-joined set in memory while executing this. Moreover, you should account for all dimensions in the cube or you may accidentally involve aggregate [Share Price] values in a multiplication, which will probably be an error. In Analysis Services 2005, you can improve this by using NonEmpty() around a cross-join, as follows:

```
NonEmpty (
  { [Measures].[Share Price], [Measures].[Units Sold])}
  * Descendants ([Industry].CurrentMember,
               [Industry].[Company], SELF)
  * Descendants ([Time].CurrentMember, [Time].[Day], SELF)
  * Descendants ([Customer].CurrentMember, [Time].[Day], SELF)
)
```

In Analysis Services 2000, you can improve the performance by using its `NonEmptyCrossJoin()` function instead of `CrossJoin()`. For example:

```
NonEmptyCrossJoin(
  Descendants ([Industry].CurrentMember, [Industry].[Company],
           SELF),
  Descendants ([Time].CurrentMember, [Time].[Day], SELF),
  Descendants ([Customer].CurrentMember, [Time].[Day], SELF),
  { [Measures].[Share Price] },
  3
)
```

These will be faster but still somewhat awkward, because you need to account for all dimensions. Another way to handle this in Analysis Services is to use cell calculations or an MDX Script, which introduces some additional considerations and restrictions. We cover those techniques in later chapters.

> **TIP** This is an example of a calculation that you can do in MDX if necessary, but which you should try to leverage your server's aggregation facility if possible. If the product of share price and units is summed, and the units are summed, then the MDX involved only needs to be a simple ratio.

Time-Based References and Time-Series Calculations

A great many OLAP reports and analyses revolve around time, as do selections for purposes like specification of secured cell ranges. They can involve selecting data or cells relative to a particular time, and/or creating time-related calculations. In this section, you will take a look at the basics of working with the time dimension in terms of referencing members and cells based on time and in terms of time-series calculations. The examples in this section perform selections and create calculated measures that define time-series calculations. In Chapter 7, you will take a brief look at database options and MDX constructs for making time-based calculations even more powerful.

> **NOTE** In all of these examples, we are assuming that time is a single-hierarchy dimension. Many time dimensions will have multiple hierarchies. Multiple time hierarchies will add a layer of complexity that will not be addressed here.

Period-to-Period References and Calculations

One typical query requirement is to return or use data from a prior period. The `.PrevMember` function is the simplest way to obtain that prior period's member. (For symmetry, the `.NextMember` function obtains the following period's member.) For example, the following query includes a calculated measure that returns the period-to-period difference in expenses, and returns them relative to a time period and its previous time period:

```
WITH MEMBER [Measures].[Unit Sales Increase] AS
'[Measures].[Unit Sales]
- ([Measures].[Unit Sales], [Time].CurrentMember.PrevMember)'
SELECT
{ [Time].[Oct, 2005].PrevMember, [Time].[Oct, 2005] } on columns,
{ [Measures].[Unit Sales], [Measures].[Unit Sales Increase] } on rows
FROM Sales
```

The way that the calculation is phrased, it does not matter what level the time members in the query belong to—the previous member to a month should be a month; the previous member to a quarter should be another quarter. The following is equally valid, and its results are shown in Figure 3-4. Note that the Q4 difference is based on Q3 and Q4 expenses, whereas each month's difference is based on its expenses and the prior month's expenses.

```
WITH MEMBER [Measures].[Unit Sales Increase] AS
'[Measures].[Unit Sales]
- ([Measures].[Unit Sales], [Time].CurrentMember.PrevMember)'
SELECT
{ [Time].[Q4, 2005], [Time].[Q4, 2005].Children } on columns,
{ [Measures].[Unit Sales], [Measures].[Unit Sales Increase] }
on rows
FROM Sales
```

	Q4, 2005	Oct, 2005	Nov, 2005	Dec, 2005
Unit Sales	256,753	34,804	97,918	123,851
Unit Sales Increase	160,140	6,989	63,114	25,933

Figure 3-4   Result from multilevel prior-period calculation.

(Note that this calculation will also will return a period-to-period difference for the first period at each level of the time dimension, which is probably a bogus value. Later in the chapter we discuss how to avoid seeing these numbers.)

Same-Period-Last-Year References and Calculations

Another very common request is for the same period one year ago, and less commonly the same period last quarter or same day last week. They are all very easy to phrase in MDX and use the same MDX function. Although it is most useful for the year-ago case, the query can be run for any time level at or below the year (such as months, quarters, weeks, or days), so you can just have a simple generic "year-ago" calculation. The following query demonstrates the use of the `ParallelPeriod()` function for just this purpose:

```
WITH MEMBER [Measures].[Unit Sales YAgo Increase] AS
'[Measures].[Unit Sales]
- ([Measures].[Unit Sales],
   ParallelPeriod ([Time].[Year], 1, [Time].CurrentMember))'
SELECT
{ [Time].[Quarter].[Q1, 2005],
   [Time].[Quarter].[Q1, 2005].Children} on columns,
{ [Measures].[Unit Sales], [Measures].[Unit Sales YAgo Increase] } on
rows
FROM Sakes
```

Note that the [Unit Sales YAgo Increase] for Q1, 2005 is the difference in first-quarter sales, whereas the [Unit Sales YAgo Increase] for Jan, 2005 is the difference in January sales.

What if Jan, 2005 is the first month in the time dimension (and Q1, 2005 is the first quarter)? What should the year-ago or period-ago value be when we do a period-to-period difference (or ratio) for January 2005 or Q1 2005? Our users would probably rather see an empty difference than a shockingly high one. If you don't account for this in the calculated member expression, you'll get a misleading result from both Analysis Services and Essbase because the missing/nonexistent value gets treated as a zero. This is covered later in the chapter.

Year-to-Date (Period-to-Date) Aggregations

The calculation of year-to-date totals (or averages) is also a frequent requirement. The examples you have just looked at involved referencing individual members. Year-to-date or period-to-date aggregations are formed by using an aggregate function such as Sum() or Avg() with an input set that corresponds to the time periods forming the periods to date. The `PeriodsToDate()` function makes that most convenient. You can go about constructing these sets in a couple of different ways.

The `PeriodsToDate()` function provides a direct way of building the set. (You might wish to refer to its detailed documentation in Appendix A.) To calculate a year-to-date total, such as year-to-date expenses, you can create and use the calculated member in the following query:

```
WITH MEMBER [Measures].[YTD Dollar Sales] AS
'Sum (
  PeriodsToDate ( [Time].[Year], [Time].CurrentMember ),
  [Measures].[Dollar Sales]
)'
SELECT
{ [Time].[Quarter].[Q3, 2000], [Time].[Quarter].[Q4, 2000],
  [Time].[Quarter].[Q1, 2001]
} on columns,
{ [Measures].[Expenses], [Measures].[YTD Expenses] } on rows
FROM Costing
```

If the time dimension is tagged as being of `Time` type and the year level within it is tagged as being of type `Year`, then you could also use the shorthand:

```
'Sum (
  YTD ([Time].CurrentMember),
  [Measures].[Expenses]
)'
```

or even:

```
'Sum (
  YTD (),
  [Measures].[Expenses]
)'
```

One requirement that comes up for some applications is calculating a running total for all periods to date in the database. That is, instead of year to date, the request is for all times to date. This is pretty straightforward, although there is no direct MDX primitive for it. In AS2005, you can rely on the fact that a range from a "null" member to some member causes the range to go from one end of the level to the named member. For example, the following returns all months from the first month in the time dimension to July, 2005:

```
{ NULL : [Time].[Jul, 2005] }
```

In a more standard way, you can reference the first member at the current level of the time dimension with one of the following expressions:

```
[Time].CurrentMember.Level.Members.Item(0)
OpeningPeriod ([Time].[All Time], [Time].CurrentMember.Level)
OpeningPeriod ([Time], [Time].CurrentMember.Level)
```

The first way takes the level of the current time member, gets its members, and selects the first member in it, whereas the second one simply asks for the opening period at the current member's level across all times. The third way reflects Essbase dimensions, in which a dimension always has a single root member. The second way also requires an All level in the time dimension, which may or may not be defined. Using the second approach, you could specify:

```
WITH MEMBER [Measures].[All Accumulated Unit Sales] AS
'Sum (
   { OpeningPeriod ([Time].CurrentMember.Level, [Time].[All Time])
     : [Time].CurrentMember },
   [Measures].[Expenses]
)'
SELECT
{ [Time].[Quarter].[Q3, 2005], [Time].[Quarter].[Q4, 2005]
} on columns,
{ [Measures].[Unit Sales], [Measures].[All Accumulated Unit Sales] } on
rows
FROM Sales
```

The most direct way, if the time dimension has an All level, is simply to use `PeriodsToDate()` with the `[Time].[(All)]` level:

```
WITH MEMBER [Measures].[All Accumulated Expenses] AS
'Sum (
   PeriodsToDate ( [Time].[(All)], [Time].CurrentMember ),
   [Measures].[Expenses]
)'
SELECT
...
```

If you have no All level in the time dimension, then you must use one of the following to define the set over which you are aggregating (Essbase databases always have a dimension tip member):

```
{ NULL : [Time].CurrentMember }
{ [Time].CurrentMember.Level.Members.Item(0)
   : [Time].CurrentMember }
```

> **NOTE** Analysis Services 2000 and 2005 allow NULL to be used as a means of specifying no-member. Analysis Services 2005 allows tuples to be composed such as (null) and (null, null). These will simply disappear from sets if included in one.

Rolling Averages and 52-week High/Low

These two calculations are part of a general class of calculations that are called moving aggregates, in which a measure is aggregated over a sliding window of members within a level. (A Pareto, or 80/20, analysis is related to moving aggregates, but in Pareto, the window is fixed at one end and grows toward the other. We will talk about the techniques for related calculations in the "Pareto Analysis and Cumulative Sums" section of Chapter 7.)

In a moving aggregation, the important technique is to construct a range within the level using endpoints that are relative to the current member. The LastPeriods() function is a bit easier to use than .Lag() for this purpose. MDX gives you several other functions and operators to construct these with: Dimension.CurrentMember lets you reference the current member, the colon (:) implies a range between two endpoints, and .Lag(), .Lead(), PrevMember(), NextMember(), Cousin(), and ParallelPeriod() all let you reference members that are related to the current member. Note that to use these MDX member-referencing operators and functions, you must assume that the ordering of members within the hierarchy corresponds with the ordering the sliding window will follow. For the time dimension, this ought to be true.

Let's go through some examples. Consider the following two expressions:

```
Avg ( { [Time].CurrentMember.Lag(5) : [Time].CurrentMember },
      Measures.[Volume Traded])
Avg (LastPeriods (6, [Time].CurrentMember),
      [Measures].[Volume Traded])
```

These expressions easily take the rolling average over a six-period time range: from the current time through the time five units back (0, 1, 2, 3, 4, and 5 units away makes six periods altogether). The expression

```
Avg( {[Time].CurrentMember.PrevMember, [Time].CurrentMember},
      [Measures].[Volume Traded])
```

takes the average of the current period and the prior period.

Notice that each of these three expressions is taking either a six-period or two-period average, not a six-month or two-day average. The level at which these averages are being calculated is determined by the context they are being evaluated in. If the first expression is being calculated for a month-level cell, then the process will create a six-month average, and if it is being calculated for a year-level cell, the process will create a six-year average.

You can control that behavior in a couple of ways. If the measure being calculated truly needs to be a six-month average, you can control the function so that it is only evaluated at the month level. MDX Scripts in AS2005 provide one way to control the scope for a calculation, as described in Chapter 13. You can also use the techniques described in the "Handling Boundary Conditions" section later in this chapter to just return NULL if the calculation is requested at the wrong level(s). If the measure really means "Average over the last half-year's worth of data at this level," then you can use the ParallelPeriod() or Cousin() functions to set this up for multiple levels at the same time.

If you have a half-year level in the database, you can be direct, as in the following two expressions:

```
Avg( { ParallelPeriod ([Time].[HalfYear], 1,
                       [Time].CurrentMember).MextNember
     : [Time].CurrentMember }, [Measures].[Volume Traded])
Avg( {ParallelPeriod ( [Time].[HalfYear]).NextMember
     : [Time].CurrentMember }, [Measures].[Volume Traded])
```

The second of these examples is terse but adequate, in that the 1 and Time.CurrentMember are the default arguments for ParallelPeriod. If you don't have a half-year level, but you do have quarters, then you can be a little less direct:

```
Avg( { ParallelPeriod ([Time].[Quarter], 2, [Time].CurrentMember) :
Time.CurrentMember }, [Measures].[Volume Traded])
```

This works as well because two quarters create the same distance as one half-year. (Note that this is one reason to take a parallel period more than one ancestor level away.) A 52-period high can be computed at the week level with the following:

```
Max ({ [Time].Lag(51) : [Time] }, [Measures].[Share Price])
Max ({ LastPeriods (52, [Time]) }, [Measures].[Share Price])
```

If your calendar uses years and weeks, you may have some 53-week years to deal with inconsistencies between weeks and years. `ParallelPeriod()` will not work when you are looking for the 53rd week of one year in a parallel year that has only 52 weeks, so you wouldn't want to use it for that purpose.

Note as well, as explained in the "Invalid Locations" discussion of Chapter 4, that when there is no time period 52 weeks ago or two quarters ago, you will get ranges of time members in your sets that may or may not be what you want.

Using LastPeriods() to Select Time Ranges Based on a Target Member

Because `LastPeriods()` is a set function, you can also use it to specify a range of time periods for an axis (or for any other set). For example, to request Unit Sales for a four-month span *starting* in March 2005, you can simply use the following query, whose results are shown in Figure 3-5:

```
SELECT
{ LastPeriods ( -4, [Time].[Mar, 2005] ) }
on columns,
{ [Product].[Toys],
  [Product].[Toys].Children
}
on rows
FROM Sales
WHERE [Measures].[Unit Sales]
```

	Mar, 2005	Apr, 2005	May, 2005	Jun, 2005
Toys	2,236	1,988	2,100	2,350
Action Figures	572	351	248	289
Arts, Crafts	173	281	324	252
Cars, Trucks	131	270	194	286
...	...	...	...	...

Figure 3-5   Result of LastPeriods() using a negative count of members.

Different Aggregations along Different Dimensions (Semi-Additive Measures Using MDX)

In this section, we will discuss aggregating along the time dimension using a different function than along the other dimensions. We will discuss two basic cases: taking the average, minimum, or maximum along time, and taking the opening or closing balance along time. In the data-warehousing community, the term semi-additive measure refers to a measure that sums along one set of dimensions, but not along others.

> **NOTE** Analysis Services 2005 introduces support for semi-additive measures into the cube definitions, so that some of the aggregations here can transparently be calculated. When possible, you should use that capability, because it will perform much faster than the equivalent MDX. However, the techniques described here will still be available, for example if you need to perform calculations using calculated member results, or you have multiple time dimensions. Also, some more ways of thinking about MDX will be discussed here, which may be useful to your general technical toolchest.

Mixing Aggregations: Sum across Non-Time, Average/Min/Max along Time

Depending on the data you are aggregating, cases may arise when you want the measures to aggregate according to different techniques in different dimensions. For example, measures that represent populations, including both people and inventory, will typically sum in all dimensions except time, and they will aggregate across time by average, MIN, or MAX.

Analysis Services's built-in SUM, COUNT, MIN, and MAX aggregations for base measures aggregate along all dimensions equally. To take an average over the time dimension of sums over the non-time dimensions, you take the average of the precalculated sums over the averaging period. You must be careful to define the averaging period as being the span of time members from the time level at which the data entered the cube. Otherwise, you will be dividing by either too many time periods or too few. To take the MIN or MAX over the time of sums over non-times, you simply need to take the MIN or MAX over the time period. You can do each of these by using the Descendants() function, which will return the appropriate set.

For many applications, you will discover that the measure that you want to sum and then average will already be implicitly summed up to the current level. In this case, you can simply divide the sum you find by the number of time periods over which the data entered the cube. For example, in a human resources–related cube, the `Headcount` measure represents a population. Assuming that the head count number is input at the week level of time, in order to calculate the average and maximum aggregate head counts for the enterprise, you would need to use the following query:

```
WITH
MEMBER [Measures].[Aggregated Headcount] AS
'[Measures].[Headcount] / Count (Descendants ([Time].CurrentMember,
[Time].[Week], SELF)'))
MEMBER [Measures].[Max Headcount] AS
'Max (Descendants ([Time].CurrentMember, [Time].[Week], SELF),
[Measures].[HeadCount])'
  . . .
```

Mixing Aggregations: Sum across Non-time, Opening/Closing Balance along Time

For inventory balances, we are frequently also interested in opening and closing amounts in any time period. This can be expressed straightforwardly in MDX. The `OpeningPeriod()` and `ClosingPeriod()` functions give us direct references to the appropriate members. For example, the following defines a measure that represents the closing inventory balance for any time period:

```
CREATE MEMBER [InventoryCube].[Measures].[Closing Balance] AS
'([Measures].[Inventory],
  ClosingPeriod ([Time].[Day], [Time].CurrentMember)
)'
```

From whatever time member you are at in any time level, you can find the last day-level member that corresponds to that time in the hierarchy, and the value is taken from that member. Because this is not really an aggregation function (it selects from a single member, not over a range), it executes quickly, even though it is not preaggregated. (Note that Analysis Services provides a `LastChild` aggregation method to allow this to be performed as a database aggregation, as described in Chapter 12.)

If you are looking to calculate the last balance found in a time range in which not all of the data has been filled in (that is, the last balance so far in the quarter because there is only data for October and November), look ahead to the section "Carryover of Balances for Slowly Changing Values and Reporting of Last Entered Balance" for techniques for accomplishing this.

Carryover of Balances for Slowly Changing Values and Reporting of Last Entered Balance

Sometimes, records in a fact table represent the attainment of a certain state, such as an account balance or a salary level. Rather than posting these records every time period, these records will only appear when the state is attained. Your application would like to use the value that is relevant for the time period of evaluation, yet the last record for that kind of balance may have been posted that month, one time period ago, two time periods ago, or more.

You can get around this problem within Analysis Services or Essbase. The LastNonEmpty aggregation method in Analysis Services 2005 fits the bill perfectly. For Essbase ASO cubes, it may be worth your time to perform the logic in SQL so a value actually exists for each month. This is so because whenever the slowly changing value is used as the input for a calculation (especially one that is then aggregated), the calculations will be performed in a cache at run time. When the calculation is then aggregated, as a calculation involving a tax rate, price, or salary would be, the performance of the query may be fairly bad unless the data set size is reasonably small.

Two very different methods can be used to perform the reference for balance carryover for slowly changing values: by using a recursive calculated member function and by using set expressions. The most practical method in terms of calculation speed is the recursive function. (Recursive functions can rely on a large stack in Analysis Services 2005, and the stack in Essbase is also quite capable.) The set expression technique is instructive for examining issues in expression construction, however, but let's look at the recursive calculation first.

The goal is to find the most recent value for a cell if one is not available in the current cell. This means you need to test whether the current cell is empty or not, and if it is empty, you need to check the previous cell. To efficiently reference the previous cell, you should put this calculation into its own calculated measure that searches the last found value of the measure you are interested in. A calculated member that almost does this to our liking is

```
WITH MEMBER [Measures].[Last Update of Price] AS
'iif (NOT IsEmpty ([Measures].[Price]),
  [Measures].[Price],
  ([Measures].[Last Update of Price], [Time].PrevMember)
)'
  . . .
```

The reason that this calculated member is almost but not quite adequate is that if the value for [Price] at the first time member along this level was itself empty, the formula would reference the value for a nonexistent member. This would make the cell reference for [Measures].[Price] empty and trigger a recursive reference for another nonexistent cell from another nonexistent member. Since MDX does not intrinsically distinguish between invalid locations and empty cells, you need to wire the appropriate logic into the expression. In Analysis Services, you can do this by testing whether the time member itself exists using the `IS` operator, as in the following expression:

```
WITH MEMBER [Measures].[Last Update of Price] AS
'iif ( NOT IsEmpty ([Measures].[Price]),
  [Measures].[Price],
  iif ( [Time].PrevMember IS NULL,
    NULL,
    ([Measures].[Last Update of Price], [Time].PrevMember)
  )
)'
   . . .
```

In Essbase, we can use the `IsValid()` function, as in the following expression:

```
WITH MEMBER [Measures].[Last Update of Price] AS
'iif ( NOT IsEmpty ([Measures].[Price]),
  [Measures].[Price],
  iif ( Not IsValid ([Time].PrevMember),
    NULL,
    ([Measures].[Last Update of Price], [Time].PrevMember)
  )
)'
   . . .
```

(For each of these, you could use the CASE construct too; see Appendix A.)

Because you expect that some value will usually be found before the searching operation runs off the edge of the dimension, you place the clause that tests for the edge of the dimension after the test for a valid cell value. Either way, `[Last Update of Price]` now returns values corresponding to the most recent change of price at the level which the measure is requested.

Now, let us see how you would express this using set expressions. A set-based strategy would be to: (1) filter out all empty cells and then (2) isolate the last one. The following is a search expression that makes no assumptions about where data can be found and performs those two steps, using the `Tail(set, count)` function that returns the last *count* tuples in the *set*:

```
Tail (
  Filter( PeriodsToDate([Time].[All]),
    NOT IsEmpty ([Measures].[Price])
  )
  , 1
)
```

If you are assured that every *N* time period will contain one record, then you can search through that many periods with `.Lag()` or `LastPeriods()`, like this:

```
Tail(
  Filter( LastPeriods (12, [Time].CurrentMember),
    NOT IsEmpty([Measures].[Price])
  )
  , 1
)
```

Because each of these options returns a set of one tuple, you will need to do something to turn it into a single value. The .Item() function will extract this one tuple, which expands the expression. The full member definition for [Last Update of Price] becomes the following:

```
WITH MEMBER [Measures].[Last Update of Price] AS
'Tail(
  Filter( PeriodsToDate([Time].[All]),
    NOT IsEmpty([Measures].[Price])
  )
  , 1
).Item (0)'
  . . .
```

Regardless of how it was defined, using the last found value in queries is straightforward. Using it to calculate further values is also straightforward, but possibly costly. Assume that you have an adequate [Last Update of Price] measure. Using it to compute, say, [Dollars Sold] AS '[Units Sold] * [Last Update of Price]' will almost certainly require that you aggregate it. Performing aggregations of leaf-level cells in MDX also can be expensive if the number of leaf-level cells being aggregated to solve the query is high. The aggregation function will need to incorporate potentially all leaf-level cells, which will be expensive with one or more large dimensions:

```
WITH MEMBER [Measures].[Dollars Sold] AS
'Sum (
  CrossJoin (
    Descendants ([Time].CurrentMember, [Time].[Month],
    CrossJoin (
      Descendants ([Geography].CurrentMember, [Geography].[Store]),
      Descendants ([Products].CurrentMember, [Products].[SKU])
    )
  ),
  ([Measures][Units Sold] * [Measures][Last Update of Price])
)'
  . . .
```

This assumes that sales only vary by time, geography, and product. If sales vary by other dimensions, then those dimensions must all have aggregations in the formula for Dollars Sold as well.

In Analysis Services, there are a couple of ways to solve the performance and complexity issues. Refer to Chapters 12 and 13 for how to declare these kinds of ranges with Microsoft's cell calculations and MDX scripts. The performance can be greatly improved by use of Microsoft's NonEmpty() or NonEmptyCrossJoin() functions; the last calculation will be much faster if it is written like this:

```
WITH MEMBER [Measures].[Dollars Sold] AS
'Sum (
  NonEmptyCrossJoin (
    Descendants ([Time].CurrentMember, [Time].[Month]),
    Descendants ([Geography].CurrentMember, [Geography].[Store]),
    Descendants ([Products].CurrentMember, [Products].[SKU]),
    {[Measures][Units Sold]},
    3
  ),
  ([Measures][Units Sold] * [Measures][Last Update of Price])
)'
. . .
```

(Refer to Appendix A for detailed descriptions of NonEmpty() and NonEmptyCrossJoin().)

Note that the difficulty with these carryover calculations is more in tractability than logic. Analysis Services provides a much more convenient environment for expressing the logic of [Last update of price] than SQL. And in your specific environment, the system that feeds you transaction data may currently only track changes to price (or salary, tax rate, and so on). However, the larger the number of dimensions involved in calculations that use this value and the larger the number of members in these dimensions, the greater the challenge of maintaining them and the greater the resources required to calculate them. Furthermore, other applications in your overall decision-support environment may well benefit from having these values explicitly maintained at every time period. For example, many data mining tools have very weak dimensional logic, and their capability to discover patterns based on rates or balances over time will be enhanced if the rates or balances are explicit in the database.

Finding the Last Child/Descendant with Data

The .LastChild and ClosingPeriod() functions let us directly access the last time period under some time period and can be used to implement closing-balance operations. Often, you will want to report the last value that is available, instead of the value at the last time period itself. This could arise because the higher-level time period is under way. For example, a closing balance for Q4, reported in the month of November, would be more helpful if it reported November or October's value instead of NULL for December's value that hasn't been calculated yet.

There are at least two ways to handle this, depending on your style and your requirements for generic or highly tailored MDX. You can tweak the `Tail(` `Filter( ... ))` pattern provided earlier, like this:

```
Tail (
  Filter( [Time].CurrentMember.Children,
    NOT IsEmpty ([Measures].[Price])
  )
  , 1
)
```

Alternatively, you can just use `CoalesceEmpty()` to return the data value, although this tailors the MDX substantially, as it embeds the number of time periods:

```
CoalesceEmpty (
  ([Measures].[Price], [Time].CurrentMember).LastChild),
  ([Measures].[Price], [Time].CurrentMember.LastChild.Lag(1)),
  ([Measures].[Price], [Time].CurrentMember.LastChild.Lag(2)),
)
```

The general syntax of CoalesceEmpty() is as follows:

```
CoalesceEmpty (expr1, expr2 [... , exprN ])
```

It evaluates each of the expressions in order until it finds one that returns a nonempty result, and returns that result. It saves you from writing a number of tests based on emptiness, and is well-suited for this purpose.

Finding the Last Time Member for Which Any Data Has Been Entered

An issue related to reporting the last entered balance is determining the last time period for which data is actually available. A cube may use a time dimension with months for the entire year for budgeting purposes, but while the year is in progress, the last month for which data is available will not be the last month for the year. One solution for this is to use an external function to retrieve the last time period for which that data was stored from an external source. (We discuss this use for an external function in Chapter 10.)

Another plausible solution, entirely in MDX, would be to scan the leaf level of the time dimension for the last nonempty time member at the All level of every other dimension. Once the cube has been processed, at every time member for which data has been entered, there will exist an aggregate value at the intersection of that time member with the All member for every other dimension. So, requesting the last time member for which there is an all-product, all-store, all-customer (and so on) sales value present would give you the last time member for which you have data. An expression that returned that time member could be used in a query, in a CREATE SET or WITH SET statement, or as the expression for a default member in an Analysis Services time dimension.

The following CREATE SET expression will capture the last day member for which any data exists:

```
CREATE SET [Cube1].[Last Day Periods] AS
'Tail (
  Filter (
    [Time].[Day].Members,
    Not IsEmpty ([Measures].[Sales])
  ),
  1
)'
```

Using Member Properties in MDX Expressions (Calculations and Sorting)

Member properties in a dimension are often used as the basis for selecting members and sorting them in queries, as well as for simply displaying them alongside query results. You may be interested in sorting a set of customers by the date they first placed orders, or sorting stores by their associated zip/postal code rather than their name.

NOTE This section specifically describes the use of member property values in Analysis Services 2005. Chapter 9 describes the use of Essbase attributes and UDAs for these purposes.

In order to reference member properties in an Analysis Services MDX expression, for filtering and sorting, as well as for other cell calculations, you can make use of two different functions. The member.Properties() function allows you to access member property values related to the member in question. If the member is itself an attribute member (represents an attribute value), you can use the member.MemberValue function to retrieve its value as a value usable in an expression (as opposed to as a member identifier).

For example, if store square footage is a numerical member property and sales is a measure in a cube, the expression that calculates sales per square foot is

```
[Measures].[Dollar Sales]
/ [Store].CurrentMember.Properties ("Store Sq Ft", TYPED)
```

We might also sort our stores by square footage in a query; the following query uses the same member property to sort on:

```
SELECT
{ [Measures].[Dollar Sales], Measures.[Sales per Square Foot] } on
columns,
{ Order (
  [Store].[Store].Members,
  [Store].CurrentMember.Properties ("Store Sq Ft", TYPED)),
  BDESC
) } DIMENSION PROPERTIES [Store].[Store].[Store Sq Ft] on rows
FROM Sales
```

In regular Analysis Services dimensions, member properties are defined for a single level. This makes them unavailable for members at other levels (unless the dimension is a parent-child dimension, in which case they will be available at all levels except for a database-defined ALL level). Analysis Services 2005 improves on Analysis Services 2000's handling of requests for member properties at levels for which they are *not* defined. In Analysis Services 2005, a request for a member property where it is not defined results in an empty value. In Analysis Services 2000, it results in an error condition, and this causes cell retrievals to return an error code for cells returned to the client, and causes query execution to stop with an error if these cells were returned to a function like Filter(). For example, in Analysis Services 2000, you would have needed to include a test using iif(), as shown, to make the following query work:

```
SELECT
{ [Measures].[Sales], [Measures].[Sales per Square Foot] } on columns,
{ Filter (
  /* this is just an example to guarantee members from more than one
level */
  Descendants (
    [Store].[City].[Dallas, TX],
    [Store].[Store],
    SELF_AND_BEFORE
  ),
  iif (
    [Store].CurrentMember.Level IS [Store].[Store],
    Val([Store].CurrentMember.Properties ("Store Sq Ft")),
    NULL
  ) > 500,
  DESC
) } on rows
FROM Sales
```

TYPED: A MICROSOFT EXTENSION

The *member*.Properties (*name*, TYPED) **syntax is a Microsoft extension to the MDX standard** *member*.Properties() **function. Without the** TYPED **flag, the property value is returned as a string (converted if necessary from the internal data type), and you would need to use an external function like** Val() **or** CDate() **to convert it into an appropriate value. This may be exactly what you want to do on occasion, but most often you will want to use the value directly.**

Also, you should be aware that in Analysis Services, member properties cannot be defined for a server-defined All level, so accessing a property there will fail too. (This is one reason to provide an explicit All level in your database.)

TIP The [All] **member defined by Microsoft Analysis Server never has database member properties associated with it. For correct queries, you either need to include MDX logic that handles a reference to the** [All] **member, or you need to define an All member in your dimension table(s) or data source views with which you can associate member properties.**

The .MemberValue function, available in Analysis Services 2005, is quite handy for at least a couple of different contexts. One is that you can manipulate sets of members derived from attributes more directly. For example, if you have a ShipWeight level in a product hierarchy, getting all of your shipping weight values that are between 1 and 5 pounds would be as simple as (assuming that the hierarchy is called ShipWeight):

```
Filter (
  [Product].[ShipWeight].[ShipWeight].Members,
  [Product].[ShipWeight].CurrentMember.MemberValue
    >= 1
  AND
    [Product].[ShipWeight].CurrentMember.MemberValue
    <= 5
)
```

Returning them in reverse order is also easy, as shown in the following:

```
Order (
  Filter (
    [Product].[ShipWeight].[ShipWeight].Members,
    [Product].[ShipWeight].CurrentMember.MemberValue
      >= 1
    AND
      [Product].[ShipWeight].CurrentMember.MemberValue
```

```
      <= 5
  ),
  [Product].[ShipWeight].CurrentMember.MemberValue,
  BDESC
)
```

Another use is for filtering related base or key dimension members. Chapter 4 explains the mechanics in more detail, but in Analysis Services 2005, attribute members are tightly linked to base dimension members, so that the current member of the base dimension influences the current member of the attribute member. So we could filter product SKUs by their ship weight with the following as well:

```
Filter (
  [Product].[ByCategory].[SKU].Members,
  [Product].[ShipWeight].CurrentMember.MemberValue
    >= 1
  AND
    [Product].[ShipWeight].CurrentMember.MemberValue
    <= 5
)
```

Remember that member properties are defined for a particular level, but when you reference them through the .Properties() function, only the name is of interest, not the unique name. This means that if the same property name is in two or more levels, all of them will return a result when referenced through the .Properties() function. In the case of parent-child dimensions, a member property is defined for every apparent level (except perhaps the All level, depending on the dimension definition), because internally, all parent-child members are stored in one database level.

Handling Boundary Conditions (Members out of Range, Division by Zero, and More)

There are a variety of boundary conditions that can exist, where either data is not valid or out of range, or else your MDX may reference nonexistent parts of your cube or dimension space. Earlier in this chapter, we identified some conditions. Now, we will address them and provide some techniques for dealing with them.

This section will discuss approaches for both Analysis Services and Essbase. The issues are mostly the same for both products, with some differences in the technique to use for each product because their exact semantics and functions differ.

Handling Insufficient Range Size

Time-series and other types of calculations use relative member references. Because the dimension is bounded, a previous member or a parent member may not exist. In MDX, you handle this by using the iif() function along with an appropriate test to determine whether an input to the calculation is out of range.

For all manner of lags and leads, and complex lags like those specified by ParallelPeriod(), you need to handle this by seeing if the range is valid.

In Analysis Services, you can accomplish this by testing whether the furthest member you want is equivalent to NULL. (Analysis Services provides a concept of a NULL member, which was introduced earlier.) The IS operator is used to test whether two members are the same or not. (The = and <> operators are used to test whether values related to members are the same, which is a bit different.) For example, to verify that a six-period rolling average contains all-valid members and returns NULL if you're in one of the first five months in the time dimension, you would write the formula as follows:

```
Iif (
  Time.CurrentMember.Lag(5) IS NULL
  NULL,
  Avg (
    LastPeriods (6, Time.CurrentMember),
    [Measures].[Dollar Sales]
  )
)
```

In Essbase, although the IS operator functions the same way for members, there is no NULL member, so you use the IsValid() function, which accomplishes the same essential test. The following is the same formula written using IsValid:

```
Iif (
  Not IsValid (Time.CurrentMember.Lag(5))
  MISSING,
  Avg (
    LastPeriods (6, Time.CurrentMember),
    [Measures].[Dollar Sales]
  )
)
```

Handling Insufficient Hierarchical Depth

Share-to-parent calculations require that there be a parent member available. However, there is no parent for the top member in a dimension. The same issue arises when you want to handle share-to-ancestor and the ancestor is specified by number of steps up, or might be below in the course of the query.

The techniques for testing whether a target member exists, which are described for handling insufficient range size, are also suitable for this test. You simply test for the ancestor's existence, as opposed to the lagged member.

Handling a Wrong-Level Reference

Sometimes, data is only valid at one level, or a small set of levels. This occurs, for example, when referencing member properties, which are defined for specific levels for both Essbase and Analysis Services.

For Analysis Services, we discussed the handling of these earlier while describing how to use member properties in expressions. This would also occur if, for example, you wanted a rolling six-period average to only be calculated at the month level. (This assumes that you are calculating this in a calculated member and not an MDX script.) You can test what level a member is in with:

```
Iif (
   Dimension.CurrentMember.Level IS Dimension.Level_Identifer,
   ...
)
```

The complete rolling average expression would look like the following:

```
Iif (
   [Time].CurrentMember.Level IS [Time].[Month],
   Avg (
     LastPeriods (6, [Time].CurrentMember),
     [Measures].[Dollar Sales]
   ),
   NULL
)
```

For Essbase, the simplest way to handle the test for a valid use of a member property is, once again, to use the `IsValid()` function. To restrict the range of the rolling average formula, you can also test for a particular level or generation number with the `IsLevel(member, number)` and `IsGeneration(member, number)` functions. These use the number of the level (starting at 0) or the number of the generation (starting at 1) to identify the layer the member is in, and not the outline name of the level or generation, so you need to keep these numbers in mind. The complete rolling average expression, assuming that months are the first level up from the leaf level, would look like the following:

```
Iif (
  IsLevel (
    [Time].CurrentMember,
    1
  ),
  Avg (
    LastPeriods (6, [Time].CurrentMember),
    [Measures].[Dollar Sales]
  ),
  MISSING
)
```

Handling Division by Zero

In Analysis Services, the result of division by zero is a special infinity code that shows up in a report as something like 1.#INF. Often you would rather show a blank to a user. You might be able to get away with showing a blank by using a special format string (see Appendix D for format string codes), but more likely you will want to just return an empty (NULL) value. Among other reasons for this is that you then automatically have those values stripped out by NON EMPTY.

To handle this, you need to test for zero as the divisor, and return NULL when the test is true, as in the following:

```
Iif (
  [Measures].[Unit Sales] = 0,
  NULL,
  [Measures].[Dollar Sales] / [Measures].[Unit Sales]
)
```

In Essbase, division by zero automatically results in a NULL/MISSING result.

Summary

In this chapter, although you have only scratched the surface, you have explored the most frequent types of calculations and uses for MDX. It has introduced the most frequently used functions for metadata referencing, and you have seen how combinations of metadata referencing and cell- and property-based formulas produce extremely common business calculations. These functions and operators introduced so far (building on Chapter 1 and 2) are the primary cogs for the MDX "assemblies of moving parts." Perhaps between a third and a half of all the MDX you will ever write will be various combinations of the components discussed so far. We were informal in the use of the .CurrentMember function, which is the source of a great deal of power. In the next chapter, you will delve into the details of execution context, and you will see how CurrentMember comes to be. That provides the driving motion for MDX, and when you have mastered that, you will be well positioned to fully leverage MDX.

MDX Query Context and Execution

Having explored the basics of MDX queries, and expanded our vocabulary of functions and useful expressions, we need to turn our attention to the way that queries and statements are actually evaluated. Context and interpretation are the two major themes of this chapter. As we examine them, we will look at how MDX is supposed to function in any vendor's implementation and point out a number of important concrete aspects of Microsoft's and Hyperion's implementations. In particular, Analysis Services 2005 adds a couple of very important ways to manipulate cube context, and modifies some of the implicit behavior of its earlier versions.

Execution and session context isn't everything, but it is very important. Every portion of every query and action has a particular context within a cube's space. Part of what makes MDX powerful and useful is how the explicit parts (what you say) combine with the implicit parts (what you leave out). For example, when an expression only mentions one or two dimensions and it is used in a cube with more dimensions, the others still play a role and combine with the dimensions you do mention to produce a result. This impacts how you compose queries and calculations in MDX. The interpretation of invalid data, missing data (NULLs), and invalid members is another important area that we will cover in this chapter. Cubes that you build will usually have many cells that contain no data, and your queries will need to deal with both invalid data and invalid members.

Every cell that is obtained from a query has a set of properties associated with it. The data value you calculate is just one of the properties. Another one, tightly related, is the type of that data, and another is the formatted string version of that value as well as rendering information like the name of the font in which to display it. In this chapter, we will take a look at how the context of calculated members affects these cell properties.

So far, we have hardly discussed the concept of data types in MDX expressions at all, apart from the distinction between numbers, strings, Boolean conditions, and empty cells. In this chapter, we will discuss the specific data types that MDX calculations take on in Analysis Services. The relevance of the data types used in calculations depends on your application, in that you can readily put cells into a calculation and report values out of them and usually get a suitable answer. However, depending on your application, you may need to precisely control the data types that are used. For example, external functions may need to deal with the exact data types of the values passed to them. (Considerations to be taken into account when using external functions are described in Chapter 10.)

We won't deal with context in Microsoft's MDX Scripts here. Whether or not you ever write a script, you will write queries. (We will cover context in script execution in Chapter 13.)

Cell Context and Resolution Order in Queries

The process of answering a query involves resolving the sets that compose each of the axes and the members (or set, in Analysis Services 2005 and Essbase) of the slicer, then filling in the cells at each intersection of members from each axis and the slicer. Resolving the sets that make up each axis will very often require calculations against cells that are formed from base or calculated members. At every point in the preparation of the set of result cells, a context for calculations determines what you need to say to reference the cell data you are interested in using.

> **WARNING** Although there is nothing inherently tricky about how queries are resolved and calculations are performed, in my experience training numerous groups on MDX, this is the section of knowledge that causes the most brains to hurt. Much of what happens is rather intuitive to people who have prior OLAP or BI experience, but it seems that making it all explicit ends up being a largish bundle of knowledge. Taking it slow, reading this chapter twice, and running the related example queries are the best way to leave this chapter with a strong sense of "I get it."*

* As always, it's my fault if you don't.

Analysis Services 2000 introduced calculation passes for cell calculations and a collection of ways to calculate cells (custom members and custom rollups), which make for a complex set of possibilities. Because these are part of query execution, we'll examine them in depth in Chapter 12, but will start here with the basics. Analysis Services 2005 changes the context and implicit semantics that Analysis 2000 and Essbase share, and you should be aware of the changes because any applications you have already built may break in AS2005. This is particularly true for the handling of solve orders between calculated members defined at the server and defined in queries and sessions.

The Execution Stages of a Query

Recall that the outline of a query is as follows (with the introduction here of HAVING, which is specific to AS2005):

```
WITH ...
SELECT [NON EMPTY] ... [HAVING ...] on axis(0),
   ... on axis(1), ...
FROM ...
WHERE ...
```

Every query passes through five main execution stages after the query is successfully parsed. The stages, in order, are

1. Resolving the FROM clause (if any—it is optional in Essbase)

2. Resolving the WHERE clause, if any

3. Resolving named sets in the WITH clause

4. Resolving the tuples on each axis

5. Calculating the cells brought back in the axis intersections

   a. Resolving NON EMPTY intersections

   b. (AS2005) Resolving the HAVING clause on each axis

Physically, there is no requirement that this is the required order, but logically this is the sequence. Figure 4-1 provides a conceptual flowchart of the process.

In Analysis Services 2005, the FROM clause may be a nested SELECT statement itself. If this is the case, it will logically fit into these execution stages. We will first discuss the behavior of a query that has just a cube as its FROM clause.

In Essbase, the FROM clause is optional; if you use an API that is connected to a particular cube, you don't need to include it. You can also specify a substitution variable (such as FROM &UseThis), in which case it's essentially the same as a literal cube name.

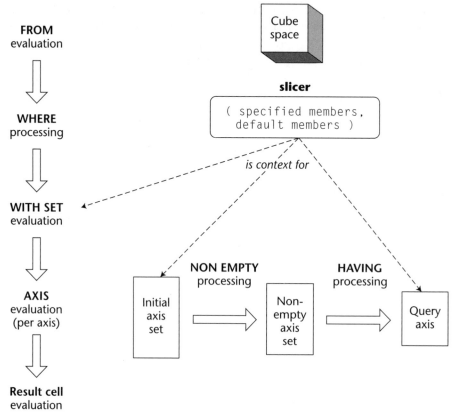

Figure 4-1   Conceptual flowchart of query evaluation.

Along the way, there is always a default cell context and a default iteration context. This starts from outside the query and is always carried from one stage to the next. Each stage can modify this context before passing on to the next stage.

The .DefaultMember Function

Syntax:

```
Dimension.DefaultMember
```

`DefaultMember (Dimension)`	**Hyperion extension**

Every dimension in MDX has associated with it a default member. In Analysis Services, an administrator can set it to be any member, and it can be modified through MDX either by directly modifying it (see Chapter 11) or by altering the effective cube space (*subcube*) you are querying (discussed later in this chapter). The typical default is otherwise the root member of the dimension (or the first level-0 member in Analysis Services). You can explicitly reference the member with the `DefaultMember` function.

Default Context and Slicers

Remember that every cell in the cube is defined by a tuple. Conceptually, before any part of the query is executed, a cell context is set up for a query that is defined by the default member from each dimension. In a cube named `[Sales]` with dimensions of Time, Product, Customer, Promotion, and Measures, it is equivalent to the tuple

```
(
   Time.DefaultMember,
   Product.DefaultMember,
   Customer.DefaultMember,
   Promotion.DefaultMember,
   Measures.DefaultMember
)
```

The Simplest Query: All Context, Nothing Else

The following is a valid query, which selects the cell defined by that default tuple:

```
SELECT
FROM [Sales]
```

This is also an example of a "zero-dimensional" query. The slicer, which is the tuple selected by the `WHERE` clause, is actually another kind of axis, but whose *result* is restricted to a single tuple among other things. This query will return a result consisting of a single cell, shown in Figure 4-2, with slicer information but no axis header information.

Any dimension that is not explicitly part of an axis will implicitly be referenced in the slicer at its default member. If the logged-in user role or the dimension definition itself has a default member defined for this dimension, then that will be the member implicitly referenced. Naming the cube in the `FROM` clause therefore implicitly sets the default member of every dimension in the cube, unless it is otherwise modified by some other part of the query. (In Essbase, the simplest query is just `SELECT`, when the API being used establishes a connection to a default cube.)

23,560,743.90

Figure 4-2 Result of a single-cell query with a default slicer.

The WHERE Clause: Default Context and Slicers

Members that you reference in the slicer override the default context to set that dimension's portion of the default context to that member. For example, the query:

```
SELECT
FROM Cube
WHERE [Time].[2005]
```

selects the cell corresponding to the tuple:

```
( Time.[2005],
  Product.DefaultMember,
  Customer.DefaultMember,
  Promotion.DefaultMember,
  Measures.DefaultMember
)
```

The slicer can hold a tuple, so if you want to modify the context by more than one dimension, then you need to use tuple syntax, for example like this:

```
SELECT
FROM Cube
WHERE ([Time].[2005], [Measures].[Dollar Sales])
```

This selects the tuple, whose value is shown in Figure 4-3:

```
( Time.[2005],
  Product.DefaultMember,
  Customer.DefaultMember,
  Promotion.DefaultMember,
  Measures.[Dollar Sales]
)
```

Both Analysis Services 2005 and Essbase allow sets in the slicer as well. In Analysis Services, if the set contains multiple members for a single dimension, the effect will be to aggregate the measure(s) of the query across all members, which will be discussed later. Essbase allows a set, but only of a single tuple, so the effect is the same, although the syntax and packaging of the tuple may be a bit different.

14,080,419.60

Figure 4-3   Result of a single-cell query with a nondefault slicer.

Adding Axes to a Query

After the slicer is evaluated, the axes are evaluated. Logically speaking, the axes are independent, so it doesn't matter which order they actually are evaluated. (If you use the Axis() function in Analysis Services, you can make them interdependent. We'll focus on the independent case here; look at Chapter 7 for examples of using Axis().) Consider the following query:

```
SELECT
{[Product].[Health], [Product].[Shaving]}
on axis(0)
FROM [Sales]
WHERE ([Time].[2005], [Measures].[Dollar Sales])
```

After the slicer is evaluated, the cell context used in evaluating the product members is still:

```
( Time.[2005],
  Product.DefaultMember,
  Customer.DefaultMember,
  Promotion.DefaultMember,
  Measures.[Dollar Sales]
)
```

Because the axis is defined by enumerating member names, it doesn't matter what the cell context is.

Once the axis is resolved, the cell data can be pulled back. The two tuples effectively pulled back are shown in Figure 4-4.

	Health	Shaving
the values	384,677.84	111,036.00

the tuples	(Time.[2005],
	  Product.[Health],
	  Customer.DefaultMember,
	  Promotion.DefaultMember,
	  Measures.[Dollar Sales]
	)
		(Time.[2005],
		  Product.[Shaving],
		  Customer.DefaultMember,
		  Promotion.DefaultMember,
		  Measures.[Dollar Sales]
		)

Figure 4-4   Query results with two cells, values and tuples.

Cell Context When Resolving Axes

How you resolve the axes may depend on your cell context. The `Filter()` and `Order()` functions are driven by data, therefore they are sensitive to cell context. Let's use `Filter()` for the examples here.

Recall from Chapter 1 that the syntax of `Filter()` is `Filter (set, boolean-expression)`. It effectively loops over each tuple in *set*, and returns a set composed of the tuples for which its related *boolean-expression* is true. The tuples are in the same order as in the *set*, and any duplicate tuples are preserved. Let's consider a modified version of the query above:

```
SELECT
Filter (
  [Product].[Category].Members,
  [Measures].[Dollars Sold] > 900000
)
on axis(0)
FROM Sales
WHERE ([Time].[2005], [Measures].[Dollars Sold])
```

The cell context after the WHERE clause is resolved as before. This means that when the `Filter()` is executing, the values associated with the members are as follows.

The data values that are compared to 900,000 are from the tuples shown in Figure 4-5. *Note that the cell context set up by the slicer is passed along during the evaluation of the axis.* Once the filter has returned a set of members, the axis is resolved and you will see the results, as shown in Figure 4-6.

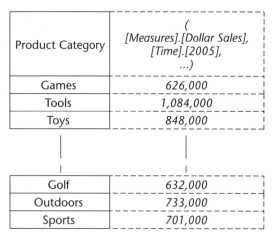

Product Category	([Measures].[Dollar Sales], [Time].[2005], ...)
Games	626,000
Tools	1,084,000
Toys	848,000
Golf	632,000
Outdoors	733,000
Sports	701,000

Figure 4-5   Tuples being evaluated in a simple Filter().

Tools	Computers, Peripherals	Camping, Hiking
1,085,305.02	1,051,540.45	910,998.82

Figure 4-6   Result of the Filter().

Within the `Filter()`, you can take this context tuple and modify it. Consider the following query, which filters the product categories where Dollar Sales increased more than 40 percent from the previous year:

```
SELECT
  Filter (
    [Product].[Category].Members,
    [Measures].[Dollar Sales] >
    1.4 *
      ( [Measures].[Dollar Sales],
        [Time].CurrentMember.PrevMember )
  )
on axis(0)
FROM Sales
WHERE ([Time].[2005], [Measures].[Dollar Sales])
```

The slicer sets up (`[Time].[2005]`, `[Measures].[Dollar Sales]`) again. Within the filter, the Dollar Sales are compared to the Dollar Sales from the previous time member. As the time component of the context is [2005], the previous time member will be 2004. Inside this filter, the comparisons made are shown in Figure 4-7.

Product Category	([Measures].[Dollar Sales], [Time].[2005], ...)	([Measures].[Dollar Sales], [Time].[2004], ...)
Games	626,000	483,000
Tools	1,084,000	894,000
Toys	848,000	768,000
Golf	632,000	380,000
Outdoors	733,000	572,000
Sports	701,000	541,000

Figure 4-7   Comparisons inside the simple filter.

Because the context carries one member from each dimension in it, you can rely even more on it in your expressions. A query that performs the same work as the previous query, but phrased in a different way, is as follows:

```
SELECT
Filter (
  [Product].[Category].Members,
   [Time].CurrentMember >
    1.4 *  [Time].CurrentMember.PrevMember
)
on axis(0)
FROM Sales
WHERE ([Time].[2005], [Measures].[Dollar Sales])
```

The `Filter()`'s comparison expression doesn't refer to any fixed points at all. Because the context of the `Filter()` includes `[Measures].[Dollar Sales]`, that is what is used. You would choose to build a query this way if you only wanted to specify the measure in one place. Looking at this as an example of a `Filter()` expression more than as a complete query, you also might use it against multiple measures without needing to edit it.

Overriding Slicer Context

Just because the slicer provides context doesn't mean you need to use it. Consider the following query with important portions underlined, and whose results are in Figure 4-8:

```
SELECT
{ Filter (
  [Product].[Category].Members,
    ([Measures].[Unit Sales], [Time].[Q4, 2005])
   > 1.4 *  ([Measures].[Unit Sales],
           [Time].[Q4, 2004] )
) }
on axis(0)
FROM Sales
WHERE ([Time].[2005], [Measures].[Dollar Sales])
```

2005					
Dollar Sales					
Auto Electronics	Personal Electronics	Beauty	Bikes, Scooters	Camping, Hiking	Golf
198,813.50	457,966.36	139,280.86	665,878.32	910,998.82	632,340.41

Figure 4-8   Result of Filter() with slicer completely overridden.

REFERENCING THE "CURRENT CELL"

The last example compares the value of the current cell to the value of a related cell. We could have used [Measures].CurrentMember, or [Product].CurrentMember as well to refer to it. MDX has no "this cell" operator**, only a current member operator that requires you to pick the dimension. In the case of the filter expression, we chose Time, since that lets us highlight the logic of the query as comparing values from two related time members.

** The This in MDX Scripts isn't quite a "this cell." It cannot be on the right-hand side of an expression, for one thing.

The slicer sets up ([Time].[2005] and [Measures].[Dollar Sales]), but the Filter() expression compares [Measures].[Unit Sales] at [Time].[Q4, 2005] and [Time].[Q4, 2004]. The expressions used in the Filter(), or in any other part of deciding an axis, can selectively rely on or override any portion of the cell context. So the results are Dollar Sales in 2005, but the filter condition was entirely on Unit Sales from other time periods.

Although we have been highlighting the columns axis, the following is true for all axes:

- Evaluation of each axis takes a cell context from the WHERE clause.

- Each axis evaluates independently from the others (except in Analysis Services when influenced by the Axis() function).

Resolving each axis can involve the computation of an arbitrary number of cells, depending on the expressions involved.

Once the axes are resolved, each cell that is retrieved is identified by the tuple formed by combining each axis' tuple for that cell with the slicer. Any dimension not explicitly mapped to a tuple has its default member in the slicer.

Cell Evaluation (For Any Cell)

If there is a calculation to be performed for any cell, it is logically independent from the calculation to perform to get any other cell value. (Set aliases, discussed in Chapter 5, may have side effects in Analysis Services, and the issues are discussed there.)

THINK ABOUT SOLVE ORDER IN A TOP-DOWN FASHION

When thinking about the order of calculations that solve order creates, many people initially want to think about solve order in terms of "which calculations come first, which ones second and third (and so on)." Although that is a valid way to think about solve order precedence, it is not as easy to get a good grasp of how solve order works as thinking about it top-down from the point of view of the cell being calculated. Solve order specifies how the result is calculated from the input, and working backwards through the inputs is relatively straightforward. Working forward from the inputs to their results is not so easy. It turns out to be much easier to understand it in terms of "A is derived from B is derived from C" than in terms of "C is calculated first, then B, then A."

Regardless of whether a cell is retrieved to determine the tuples for an axis, or to return cell data to the client, the following is true:

- If the cell is not governed by an MDX calculation, it is retrieved from the database. (In an Essbase block-storage application, it could still be dynamically calculated from a non-MDX member formula.)
- If the cell is governed by an MDX calculation, then the formula with the highest solve order is chosen as the formula to calculate the cell. This calculation is performed in terms of its input cells.

In Analysis Services, the expression to calculate a cell value can involve anything that resolves to a number, a string, a Boolean, or NULL. In Essbase, it can be anything that resolves to a number or NULL, and in some cases to a string value as well. All functions are executed dynamically relative to the current cell context brought in from the outside.

Drilling in on Solve Order and Recursive Evaluation

One thing left to walk through is the recursive evaluation of calculated members. Let's examine the evaluation of a cell that is governed by multiple calculated results. You will look at a simple use of solve orders here. However, each of the products that this book treats has different important wrinkles for how solve order affects calculations. Later in this chapter, we will address those wrinkles.

One application design feature encouraged by calculated members is the addition of a time series analysis dimension with a set of calculated members that implement time series calculations, such as period-to-period differences, year-to-date totals, rolling averages, and so on, across all measures and across all other dimensions. This dimension has one member to which all input data is associated. In this example, that member is called [Current]. The Period to Prior difference calculation can be defined as follows, and regardless of the time or measure that you have selected, this member will return the difference between that measure at the chosen time period and that measure at the prior time period:

```
MEMBER [Time Series].[Period to Prior] AS
' ([Time Series].[Current], [Time].CurrentMember)
  - ([Time Series].[Current], [Time].CurrentMember.PrevMember) ',
SOLVE_ORDER = 0
```

Note that you build tuples that include the [Time Series].[Current] member; otherwise, you will get infinite recursion (discussed later in this chapter). A formula for Unit Sales Pct of Parent is:

```
MEMBER [Measures].[Unit Sales Pct of Parent] AS
'[Measures].[Unit Sales] /
  ( [Measures].[Unit Sales], [Product].CurrentMember.Parent )'
, SOLVE_ORDER = 10
```

Given this, to get the difference in Unit Sales Pct of Parent between two time periods, you query for the ([Unit Sales Pct of Parent], [Time Series].[Period to Prior]) tuple. Let's look at this in a single query, the code of which is in Figure 4-9.

```
WITH
MEMBER [Measures] . [Unit Sales Pct of Parent] AS
' [Measures] . [Unit Sales] /
    (    [Measures] . [Unit Sales], [Product].CurrentMember.Parent ) '
, SOLVE_ORDER = 10
MEMBER [Time Series] . [Period to Prior] AS
' ( [Time Series] . [Current], [Time].CurrentMember)
    -  ( [Time Series] . [Current], [Time].CurrentMember.PrevMember) '
, SOLVE_ORDER = 0
SELECT
{    [Measures] . [Unit Sales Pct of Parent]    }
on axis (0),
{    [Time Series] . [Period to Prior]    }
on axis(1)
FROM Sales
WHERE ([Time] . [Q2, 2005], [Product].[Toys])
```

Figure 4-9 Query highlighting solve order rules.

This is a query for one cell, namely the Unit Sales Pct of Parent, Period to Prior, for Q2, 2005 and Toys. Evaluating it requires walking the tree of cells, as shown in Figure 4-10.

Since Unit Sales Pct of Parent has the higher solve order, the two tuples that will be evaluated to make the ratio will be the starting cell modified to the [Unit Sales] for the same product, and the starting cell modified to the [Unit Sales] and Product parent member. Each of those cells, in turn, starts a new context. Because each of those cells is, in turn, calculated by [Period To Prior], they will each in turn retrieve a cell modified to the [Time Series].[Current] and ([Time Series].[Current], [Time].[Q2, 2005].PrevMember).

Notice that, in the end, you are taking the ratio of two differences. This is probably not what you want. Really understanding solve order is the key to understanding where calculations either work correctly or don't. Solve order is a fairly blunt instrument; more precise scoping through cell calculations and MDX Scripts in Analysis Services provides a way to avoid some of these issues, by letting you be more specific about the measures/tuples for which a formula actually is in effect. On the other hand (as we will discuss later in this chapter), AS2005 uses solve order information differently than AS 2000 or Essbase, so generic time-series functionality defined at the server may only work with server-defined calculations, not client-defined calculations.

Resolving NON EMPTY Axes

Once all the axes have been resolved, the process of eliminating the empty tuples on axes can begin. Remember that NON EMPTY can be on any axis, and you can have at least three axes in an ODBO-compliant MDX provider (up to 64 in Essbase and AS2000; up to 128 in AS2005). A tuple on axis(0) would be considered empty if **ALL** cells of the result set that intersect it are empty, which means all rows (and pages, and so on) for that column. Any one cell being not empty across that set of cells would cause the column tuple to be retained. Similarly, a tuple on axis(1) that has only empty result cells across all columns (and pages, and so on) for it would be removed. In practice, it seems that NON EMPTY rows are the most frequent request, and NON EMPTY rows and columns together the secondmost, but the MDX providers can handle whatever combination you want.

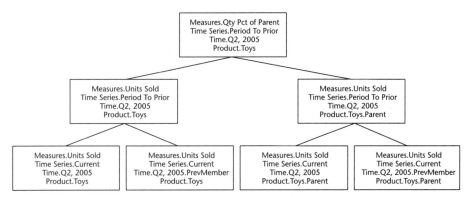

Figure 4-10   Decomposition of cells referenced by solve order rules.

Note that a calculated member may take only a little calculation to determine if the result will be NULL, or it may take a lot of calculation. AS 2000 and AS2005 both have a NON_EMPTY_BEHAVIOR property for calculated members. This property includes the name of a noncalculated measure in Analysis Services 2000. In Analysis Services 2005, it can include noncalculated members of other dimensions for a tuple specification, and it can include a list of non-calculated measure names with the meaning that all of the named measures (or tuples) must be nonempty or else the calculation will be treated as NULL. When a cell is considered for removal by NON EMPTY that has the calculated member as its current member and the calculation is the solve order winner, the emptiness/nonemptiness of the measure/tuple at the overall cell is evaluated, and used instead of actually calculating the cell. This way, execution of the calculation can be deferred until it is known that it will really matter.

Resolving the HAVING Clause in AS2005

The HAVING clause provides you a convenient way to add filtering logic on the tuples of an axis *after* the NON EMPTY logic is performed. It doesn't give you any unique capabilities; it just makes phrasing certain kinds of logic easier. For example, suppose that you want to filter the customer cities in the Northeast to just those that had >=500 dollar sales of a product in 2005, and see only those for which unit sales of that product was not empty over a range of times in the report. One easy way to get the set of customers would be the following query, which returns the cities that had at least one sale in the time period:

```
SELECT
CrossJoin (
  {[Time].[May, 2005] : [Time].[Jul, 2005]},
  { [Measures].[Unit Sales] }
) on axis(0),
NON EMPTY
Descendants ( [Customer].[Northeast], [Customer].[City] )
on axis(1)
FROM Sales
WHERE [Product].[Toys]
```

To add a `Filter()` to this set of customers, you would need to rewrite the query. First, let's look at how you would add HAVING. Syntactically, HAVING is a clause at the axis scope, and operates on the tuples of the axis. In terms of the query execution context that has been discussed so far, it is like a second pass of a `Filter()` function over the axis: The HAVING expression is executed once per tuple on the axis, combining the tuple with the slicer context. So, the modified query would look like this:

```
SELECT
CrossJoin (
  {[Time].[May, 2005] : [Time].[Jul, 2005]},
  { [Measures].[Unit Sales] }
) on axis(0),
NON EMPTY
Descendants ( [Customer].[Northeast], [Customer].[City] )
HAVING ([Measures].[Dollar Sales], [Time].[2005]) >= 500
on axis(1)
FROM Sales
WHERE [Product].[Toys]
```

The use of slicer context and how you modify it are exactly the same as described for evaluating each axis. It's just that the possible tuples for the axis have already been restricted based on the NON EMPTY processing, which is only possible after all result cells of the query have been calculated.

Note that the `axis()` function works also within a HAVING clause. For example, the following filters the rows based on an `axis(0)` offset instead of a particular tuple, which may well be useful for a front-end query generator:

```
SELECT
CrossJoin (
  {[Time].[May, 2005] : [Time].[Jul, 2005]},
  { [Measures].[Unit Sales] }
) on axis(0),
NON EMPTY
Descendants ( [Customer].[Northeast], [Customer].[City] )
HAVING (Axis(0).Item(1) >= 500)
on axis(1)
FROM Sales
WHERE [Product].[Toys]
```

To add a `Filter()` function, by contrast, you need to determine the non-empty range ourselves using set logic. In Analysis Services, the rewrite would use the `NonEmptyCrossJoin()` or `NonEmpty()` function for efficiency, so long as the query doesn't involve calculated members on axis 0. (In fact, this might run faster anyway.)

```
SELECT
CrossJoin (
  {[Time].[May, 2005] : [Time].[Jul, 2005]},
  { [Measures].[Unit Sales] }
) on axis(0),
Filter (
  NonEmptyCrossJoin (
    Descendants ( [Customer].[Northeast], [Customer].[City] ),
    {[Time].[May, 2005] : [Time].[Jul, 2005]},
    { [Measures].[Unit Sales] },
    1  // only return the first dimension
  ),
  ([Measures].[Dollar Sales], [Time].[2005]) >= 500
  // or Axis(0).Item(1) >= 500
)
on axis(1)
FROM Sales
WHERE [Product].[Toys]
```

If the query did have calculated members on axis 0, then you might need to filter on the count of nonempty time/measure tuples being > 0 as well as unit sales >= 500. The expression for that looks like this:

```
Filter (
  Descendants ( [Customer].[Northeast], [Customer].[City] ),
  Count (
    CrossJoin (
      {[Time].[May, 2005] : [Time].[Jul, 2005]},
      { [Measures].[Unit Sales] }
    ),
    EXCLUDEEMPTY
  ) > 0
  AND
  ([Measures].[Dollar Sales], [Time].[2005]) >= 500
)
```

In Essbase, the equivalent would be similar but a little different when using the `NonEmptyCount()` function:

```
Filter (
  Descendants ( [Customer].[Northeast], [Customer].[City] ),
  NonEmptyCount (
    {[Time].[May, 2005] : [Time].[Jul, 2005]},
    [Measures].[Unit Sales]
  ) > 0
  AND
  ([Measures].[Dollar Sales], [Time].[2005]) >= 500
)
```

Named sets (described in the next chapter) provide a way of simplifying the logic of these queries by centralizing the definitions of some of the sets, but if you can use the HAVING clause, that will provide the simplest logic.

Looping Context and .CurrentMember

In addition to the current cell context, there is always a current iteration or looping context. We have already used this to explain the workings of the Filter() function. The Generate() function exists to provide iteration and will be introduced and used extensively starting in Chapter 5. Aggregation functions like Sum(), Max(), and so on also provide a looping context, where the value expression is evaluated once per iteration. You can dynamically create the context as well, which creates very useful possibilities. For example, consider the following query that selects a set of products and for each calculates the percentage of its [Unit Sales] to the maximum [Unit Sales] across its siblings; the results are shown in Figure 4-11:

```
WITH
MEMBER [Measures].[Pct of Max Siblings] AS
'[Measures].[Unit Sales] /
  Max (
    [Product].CurrentMember.Siblings,
    [Measures].[Unit Sales]
  )
'
SELECT
{ [Measures].[Unit Sales],  [Measures].[Pct of Max Siblings] } on
axis(0),
{ [Product].[Doing].Children } on axis(1)
FROM Sales
WHERE [Time].[2005]
```

At each product, within this calculated measure, the current product member's siblings are referenced, and then the formula takes the ratio of the units to the maximum value from the siblings' [Unit Sales]. Within each [Pct of Max Siblings]-related cell, you set up a loop over product's siblings, and implicitly take the [Unit Sales] at each of those products.

	Unit Sales	Pct of Max Siblings
Indoor, Outdoor Games	23,772	56.79%
Tools	41,858	100.00%
Toys	32,373	77.34%

Figure 4-11   Result of calculations with dynamic Max() calculation.

Contexts also nest. Usually, you end up with nested contexts when a number of different formulas are being executed together. To show how you can end up with nested contexts, let us create a query for the following business request that puts all the logic required in a single formula:

"Select quarters whose months include at least one period-to-period increase of at least 13 percent."

We will implement it by selecting quarters whose months have a maximum period-to-period increase that is at least 13 percent. That results in a query like the following, whose results are shown in Figure 4-12:

```
SELECT
Filter (
  [Time].[Quarter].Members,   -- outer loop
  Max (
      [Time].CurrentMember.Children,   -- current in outer loop
      (  [Time].CurrentMember          -- current in Max loop
       / [Time].CurrentMember.PrevMember)
  ) >= 1.13
)
on axis(0)
FROM Sales
WHERE ([Measures].[Unit Sales], [Product].[Tools])
```

This breaks down as follows:

1. `Filter` starts a loop over quarters.

2. The `CurrentMember` that is the first argument to `Max()` is looping over these quarters.

3. The `.Children` tacked onto this starts a loop over `Months`.

4. In the ratio expression that is the second part of `Max()`, the `Time.CurrentMember` is set to each month in turn.

5. `Max() >= 1.13` is true only if `Max()` returns a value `>= 1.13`.

For every nested looping context, cells are evaluated within that context as needed. Solve order rules are in effect for calculating data. Furthermore, if the cells that are required to calculate a value are themselves defined by a calculation, then they are recursively evaluated as necessary. They may themselves set up additional loops and modify the context as necessary as well.

Q2, 2004	Q4, 2004	Q2, 2005	Q4, 2005
5,932	16,555	7,823	18,947

Figure 4-12   Result of query that has multiple nested looping contexts.

Interdependence of Members in AS2005: Strong Hierarchies, Autoexists, and Attribute Relationships

Up to this point, we have described dimensions as being independent of each other, and in our discussion of looping contexts, we have described the "current member" of each dimension as being independent of each other dimension. For AS2005, members of different hierarchy-dimensions may be interdependent with each other as well as dependent on the underlying key dimension. This is a substantial departure from AS2000 behavior, and it carries with it some very interesting consequences. One example is that a CrossJoin() of two hierarchy-dimensions may not return a complete Cartesian product; another is that the current member of hierarchy dimensions may change as the current member of another one changes.

Strong Hierarchies

The term "strong hierarchies" refers to a current-member affinity between attributes used in a hierarchical dimension and members of a related attribute hierarchy. For example, consider the following simple query and the results shown in Figure 4-13:

```
WITH
MEMBER [Measures].[Cust Education] AS
[Customer].[Cust Education].CurrentMember.Name
MEMBER [Measures].[Cust Region] AS
[Customer].[Region attribute].CurrentMember.Name
MEMBER [Measures].[Cust State] AS
[Customer].[State attribute].CurrentMember.Name
SELECT
{ [Measures].[Cust Region], [Measures].[Cust State],
  [Measures].[Cust Education]
} on 0,
{
  Filter (
    [Customer].[Customer].[Cust Identity].Members,
    [Measures].[Units] > 120
  ),
    [Customer].[Customer].[Region].[Midwest],
    [Customer].[Customer].[State].[OH]
} on 1
FROM [Customer Analysis]
```

	Cust Region	Cust State	Cust Education
cust796200	Midwest	IL	All Cust Education
cust1059150	Midwest	OH	All Cust Education
cust1029500	South-Central	MO	All Cust Education
cust797550	Southeast	GA	All Cust Education
cust480650	West	CA	All Cust Education
Midwest	Midwest	All Customer	All Cust Education
OH	Midwest	OH	All Cust Education

Figure 4-13   Query showing CurrentMember impact of hierarchy's current members.

As the current member of the [Customer].[Customer] hierarchy changes, the current members of the related [Region] hierarchy dimension and [State] hierarchy dimension change, too. The current member of the [Customer].[Region] reflects the region the individual customers are in, and the region the states are in. The current member of the [Customer].[Customer] hierarchy reflects the state the individual customers and customer states are in, but becomes the state's All member when the customer level is above the State level. Meanwhile, the [Cust Education] attribute is not part of the hierarchy at all, so its CurrentMember is unchanged.

Note that the slicer may constrain members and aggregate values as well. For example, if you modify the preceding query to include WHERE [Customer].[Region attribute].[South-Central], then the individual customers and their data values considered by the Filter() are constrained to those for the South-Central region. However, consider the result of executing such a query, shown in Figure 4-14. You see only the one customer from the South-Central region, as you might expect. However, the query explicitly requested the Midwest region and the state of Ohio as well. Where did they go? The next section, on the autoexists' behavior, explains why they don't seem to exist when you slice by a different region.

	Cust Region	Cust State	Cust Education	Units
cust1029500	South-Central	MO	All Cust Education	134
All Customer	All Customer	All Customer	All Cust Education	47,374

Figure 4-14   Result of adding a region attribute slicer to the previous query.

Autoexists

Consider the following query, whose results are shown in Figure 4-15. It simply cross-joins region attribute-members with the region name measure across the columns, and picks the same customer members as the last two queries.

```
WITH
MEMBER [Measures].[Cust Region] AS
[Customer].[Region attribute].CurrentMember.Name
SELECT
[Customer].[Region attribute].Members
* {  [Measures].[Units], [Measures].[Cust Region]  }
on 0,
{
  Filter (
    [Customer].[Customer].[Cust Identity].Members,
    [Measures].[Units] > 120
  ),
   [Customer].[Customer].[Region].[Midwest],
   [Customer].[Customer].[State].[OH]
} on 1
FROM [Customer Analysis]
```

Note that you only see values for result cells where the region members visually intersect with customers who are in that region. This is the *autoexists* feature of AS2005 rearing its head. No values will be evaluated for the other cells in the first place. Although it should be intuitive that you would not find any values for Units at those intersections, you cannot interpret the blank Region Name as meaning that the `CurrentMember.Name` reference came up empty—in fact, it was never invoked at all. (You will see this concept of cell existence pop up later when we talk about subcubes.)

	All Customer		Central		Mid-Atlantic		Midwest	
	Units	Cust Region	Units	Cust Region	Units	Cust Region	Units	Cust Region
cust796200	121	Midwest					121	Midwest
cust1059150	136	Midwest					136	Midwest
cust1029500	134	South-Central						
cust797550	127	Southeast						
cust480650	124	West						
Midwest	13235	Midwest					13235	Midwest
OH	4898	Midwest					4898	Midwest

Figure 4-15   Result of crossing hierarchy-attribute members with hierarchy members.

Autoexists prevents tuples of attributes from the same overall dimension (such as customer attributes or time attributes) from existing if the dimension did not have at least one combination of them. This is in contrast to how tuples of attributes from different dimensions (customer or time) can be created even if the fact table never had a record for that combination. At least as of the time this was written, there was no way to get these tuples to exist in a set. For example, the following query ends up having no tuples on axis 0, since the state attribute OR and the region attribute Central never coincide for any customer:

```
SELECT
{ ([Customer].[Region].[Central], [Customer].[State].[OR]) } on 0
FROM [Sales]
```

You can explicitly compose tuples that end up dropping out of any sets. (AS2005 introduces the ability to compose NULL tuples as well, as mentioned in Chapter 1, which will also drop out of sets. This may be useful in some circumstances for composing arguments to .NET stored procedures, which are described in Chapter 10.) A measure evaluated at such a tuple (like the following) will have a NULL result:

```
([Measures].[Unit Sales], [Customer].[Region].[Central],
 [Customer].[State].[OR])
```

One way you might arrive at such a tuple would be by using functions that return members, such as .Item(), .FirstSibling, or others, and composing their results into a tuple with (,).

Autoexists does solve a common application request: "I want to get separate columns back for Regions and States, instead of just one column for both." A cross-join of regions and states returns a two-dimensional set, one dimension being regions and one dimension being states, and you don't need to specify NON EMPTY on its results since AS2005 won't give you any tuples that didn't exist in the dimension table.

Modifying the Cube Context in AS2005

In Analysis Services 2005, the cube space that you are querying from in the first place may be modified, which alters the context against which calculations and selections are made. We will look at two ways this is accomplished. The CREATE SUBCUBE and DROP SUBCUBE statements allow you to sort of restrict the apparent cube space (and unrestrict it) for subsequent operations. Using a SELECT in the FROM clause of a query essentially sets up a query-specific subcube with some similar aspects. These capabilities give you an ability to present different appearances of a cube to different users or applications based on application run-time criteria (as opposed to more design-time criteria, which are the basis for Analysis Services security), or to phrase some kinds of queries in a simpler fashion than if the capability wasn't available. Note that subcubes are not useful for security, because you can reference data outside of the restricted space. The notion of using SELECT in the FROM clause was introduced in the first section of the chapter; we will describe CREATE SUBCUBE first because it will introduce the concepts and some aspects of the syntax. Note that *scopes* in MDX scripts (described more fully in Chapter 13) are a form of nested subcubes.

CREATE SUBCUBE Described

The CREATE SUBCUBE statement performs a restriction of the cube space (or cube perspective's space) that affects a number of aspects of the session context.

NOTE In the following discussion of subcubes, the term "cube" refers to each perspective defined on a cube as well. Subcubes defined on one perspective have no effect on other perspectives.

It does the following:

- Restricts the members that metadata functions such as .Members and .Children will return, according to the scope that you specify in the statement. The members that are returned will be based on the scope you specify but will not be limited to just the ones you specify (as described later).

- Affects the aggregated values returned for base measures, so that measures requested at ancestor members only reflect the aggregation of input values that are within the restricted area.

- Forms a lifespan context for MDX definitions CREATEd while the subcube is in effect. If you execute a CREATE MEMBER, CREATE SET, or another CREATE after executing a CREATE SUBCUBE, then these members, sets, and other things will be automatically dropped when you drop the subcube as well.

- Restricts the members that metadata retrievals from API calls will return to the same that are returned from metadata calls. (You may not see this effect inside the SQL Business Server Management Studio.)

The restriction is in effect until you drop the scope with DROP SUBCUBE. You can still reference and use data outside of the restricted scope using functions like .PrevMember as well as just referencing them directly.

The general syntax is

```
CREATE SUBCUBE cube_or_perspective_name AS (subcube_select)
```

The *cube_or_perspective_name* is the name of the cube or perspective that you are going to restrict. The *subcube_select* is a special form of SELECT, with a few restrictions:

- It cannot contain a WITH clause.
- It cannot contain NON EMPTY or HAVING clauses.
- It cannot request dimension properties or cell properties.

Although it only restricts the logical cube space, the SELECT must be an MDX SELECT with a FROM clause, and axes and/or slicer. The slicer doesn't contribute to the restriction, but if any calculations are involved in evaluating the axes of the SELECT, it will create context for them (as described later).

NOTE The mapping of dimensions to axes and slicer in the subcube has no bearing on how subsequent queries map dimensions onto axes and the slicer. Don't worry about it.

For example, the following subcube definition specifies a restriction of the time dimension to the quarters of 2005. A subcube definition does not restrict the levels available. The subcube will include all members hierarchically related to the ones listed in the restriction, as shown in Figure 4-16:

```
CREATE SUBCUBE [Sales] AS (
   SELECT  [Time].[YQMD].[Year Name].&[2005].Children on 0
   FROM [Sales]
)
```

Note that the name of the subcube is the same as the name of the cube in the FROM clause; this redundancy is required (at least for now).

If the entire time dimension consists of years, quarters, months, and days for 2004 and 2005, then after the foregoing subcube is created, the following will return just the year 2005 and its quarters and months:

```
Descendants (
   [Time].[YQMD].[Year Name].Members,
   [Time].[YQMD].[Month Name],
   SELF_AND_BEFORE
)
```

The .Members function now returns just the one year associated with the quarters, and the only quarters and months apparent are those related to the quarters specified earlier.

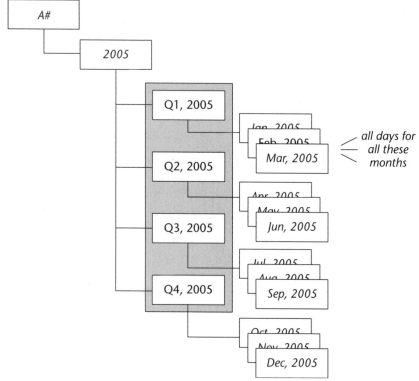

Figure 4-16   Subcube members included on time.

Suppose that the subcube had been defined with the following (the last two quarters of 2004 and the first of 2005):

```
CREATE SUBCUBE [Sales] AS (
   SELECT
   { [Time].[YQMD].[Quarter Name].&[2004Q3]
     : [Time].[YQMD].[Quarter Name].&[2005Q1]
   } on 0 FROM [Sales]
)
```

The foregoing `Descendants()` request would return the year 2004, its two quarters Q3 and Q4, and their months, and also the year 2005, its Q1, and the months of Q1. The time members considered to be part of the subcube are shown in Figure 4-17.

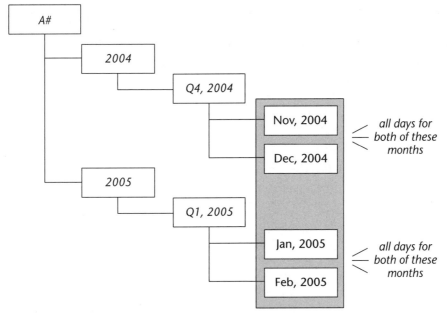

Figure 4-17   Subcube with less regular set of members.

Subcube Restrictions and Attribute Relations

In general, the dimensions that you specify restrictions on are restricted, while the ones you do not specify restrictions on remain unchanged. However, the attribute relationships in a dimension are included in the restrictions, so restrictions on one or more attribute dimensions can imply restrictions on other related attribute dimensions. Consider the following subcube definition, which restricts customers to highly educated unmarried females:

```
CREATE SUBCUBE [Sales] AS (
  SELECT
  {[Customer].[Education].&[Masters],[Customer].[Education].&[PhD] }
  * [Customer].[Married].&[N]
  * [Customer].[Sex].&[F]
  on 0
  FROM [Sales]
)
```

Within this subcube, the only Customer-level descendant under [Mountains] is a single customer. Obviously, this single customer can only have one Num of Children value associated with it, which turns out to be [1]. However, if we

ask for the members of the [Customer].[Num of Children] attribute hierarchy, as shown in Figure 4-18, we will see all of them. This is just the same as
with the autoexists behavior described earlier, since across all of our highly
educated unmarried female customers, we find all number of children. Now
consider the following slightly modified subcube definition:

```
CREATE SUBCUBE [Sales] AS (
  SELECT
    {[Customer].[Education].&[Masters], [Customer].[Education].&[PhD]}
    * [Customer].[Married].&[N]
    * [Customer].[Sex].&[F]
    * [Customer].[State].&[AL]
  on 0
  FROM [Sales]
)
```

Within Alabama, we have two customers that fit this description. When we
request the available customers on rows and the available Num of Children
members on columns, we get the more restricted set of columns as shown in
Figure 4-19. The empty cells, which reflect nonexistent attribute combinations,
cannot have any calculations or retrievals operate on them. However, the filtering of the columns to just the few Num of Children members happens as the
axis is produced; as far as any calculated member is concerned, all members of
the dimension are available.

	All	1	2	3	4+
cust732550	$807.76	$807.76			

Figure 4-18 Across the restricted attributes, all [Num of Children] are found.

	All	3	4+
All	$5,963.92	$3,022.36	$2,941.56
South-Central	$5,963.92	$3,022.36	$2,941.56
AL	$5,963.92	$3,022.36	$2,941.56
Birmingham	$2,941.56		$2,941.56
cust433750	$2,941.56		$2,941.56
Phenix City, AL	$3.022.36	$3,022.36	
cust637200	$3.022.36	$3,022.36	

Figure 4-19 Across sufficiently restricted attributes, only some [Num of Children] are
returned.

> ### RESTRICTING TO MEASURES FROM PARTICULAR MEASURE GROUPS
>
> **One reason to use subcubes, either session-specific or query-specific as described shortly, is to enable the use of functions like** `Leaves()`, **which do not work if measures in scope have different leaf-level granularities for the dimension or cube that you call** `Leaves()` **with. (See Appendix A for syntax details, and Chapter 13 for usage examples in MDX scripts for** `Leaves()`.**)**

You can create restrictions on the measures dimension as well. Since there is no aggregation across the measures dimension, this by itself does not cause any aggregated values to be different. Since you can specifically request members from outside a subcube, it doesn't affect the measures you can reach in a calculation. But it does affect the default measure if the prior default measure was not in the members retained in the subcube. The default member becomes the "first" member in the set of measures that is retained.

Further Details of Specifying a Subcube

Subcube restrictions cannot include calculated members in the members you specify. Session and global calculated members will be retained in the created subcube. They will be calculated as specified in their formulas, although to the degree that their inputs reference aggregate members, the data values they calculate will reflect the subcube.

A valid subcube specification can include any set of members from a dimension, from the same or different levels as desired. Any member included causes all of its descendants to be included, so if a member and its ancestor are both included, all of the descendants of that ancestor end up within the subcube.

Also, the order in which you specify the members has no effect on the dimension's hierarchical order.

Tuple Specifications for Subcubes

In addition to specifying cross-products of members, you can specify subcubes in terms of tuples. For example, consider the following subcube specification:

```
CREATE SUBCUBE [Sales]  AS (
  SELECT {
    ( [Time].[YQMD].[Month].[Jul, 2005],
      [Promotion].[Promotion].[Media].[email] ),
    ( [Time].[YQMD].[Month].[Aug, 2005],
      [Promotion].[Promotion].[Media].[radio] )
  } on axis(0)
  FROM [Sales]
)
```

If this subcube is in effect, the following query will show results like those in Figure 4-20:

```
SELECT
{ [Time].[YQMD].[Month].Members,
    [Time].[YQMD].[Quarter].Members
} on axis(0),
{ [Promotion].[Promotion].Members } on axis(1)
FROM [Sales]
WHERE [Measures].[Dollar Sales]
```

The members all exist as independent members, and metadata requests (either in MDX or through API calls) will show all of the members. However, data cells not part of the subcube will not contribute to aggregates, as Figure 4-20 illustrates.

	Jul, 2005	Aug, 2005	Q3, 2005
All	$4,214.18	$4,622.48	$8,836.66
email	$4,214.18		$4,214.18
E-chain-letter	$648.21		$648.21
E-focused-mail	$2,185.23		$2,185.23
E-Other	$816.91		$816.91
E-spam-attack	$563.83		$563.83
Radio		$4,622.48	$4,622.48
R-Joke		$2,003.58	$2,003.58
R-Other		$1,387.47	$1,387.47
R-Song		$918.94	$918.94
R-Spot		$312.49	$312.49

Figure 4-20   Result of query showing tuple-based subcube restriction.

Subcubes Based on Data Values

Up to now, we have only looked at subcube specifications that use member enumeration or simple metadata functions to specify regions. The specifications have also used SELECT and FROM, but not WHERE. A subcube can contain any set of members from a scope and these members (or tuples whose members conform to the restrictions) can be specified by data-based functions like `Filter()`, `TopCount()`, and others. Functions like `TopCount()`, `Top-Sum()`, and some others perform some sorting of their inputs, but their result sorting is ignored for the subcube definition; only the actual set of members or tuples is used. These functions can use calculated members and named sets already defined in global or session scope, even if they cannot use WITH-defined calculated members. For these functions, the slicer in the subcube's SELECT clause may affect the context for the calculated member(s). For example, the following creates a subcube for the product categories whose average selling price was at least $40 in [Q3, 2004]. However, the subcube that is created does not restrict the [Time] dimension in any way:

```
CREATE SUBCUBE [Sales]  AS (
  SELECT {
    Filter (
      [Product].[ByCategory].[Category].Members,
      [Measures].[ASP] >= 40
    )
  } on axis(0)
  FROM [Sales]
  WHERE [Time].[YQMD].[Quarter].[Q3, 2004]
)
```

Subcubes for Iterative Query Refinement

The capability to base subcubes on data-based or metadata-based selections and to base subcubes on tuple specifications as opposed to just cross-join specifications, along with the fact that subcube definitions nest via CREATE/DROP commands, allows clients to provide a certain kind of precise iterative refinement for query sessions, particularly for those that calculate subtotals and grand totals based on ancestors in the dimensions. For example, one subcube can restrict the subcube to a particular customer territory of interest. Now, another subcube can restrict that subcube to just certain customer attribute values of interest. Another one can restrict that subcube to the customers who increased sales during some time range, and yet another can restrict to just the top 12 products that were bought across all the customers in the latest scope. Each CREATE SUBCUBE corresponds to one more step in a client's interaction, while the exploratory equivalent of a "back" button executes a DROP SUBCUBE. Along the way, requesting a tree of regular dimension members in queries will give you the partial aggregates of all ancestors remaining in scope. Remember that a subcube cannot expand the scope of another subcube currently in effect, only restrict it further.

Points to Consider When Using Subcubes

The way that subcubes restrict metadata but not MDX means that how you compose your MDX will affect whether users obtain the results they want to see. The .Members, .Siblings, Descendants(), and other functions will return their unrestricted sets. For example, when a subcube is defined to restrict the time dimension, you can't readily determine what the first or last period of the subcube space is. Even the Aggregate() function doesn't restrict its values to the subcube. If you create named sets that contain the subcube definition prior to creating the subcube, then you can refer to these named sets for specific members or subsets of interest.

Since the internal aggregation mechanisms are restricted, you can use subcubes in conjunction with calculated members to get grand totals as well as subcube-specific totals (for example, to see total across subcube alongside total in whole cube).

It is entirely possible that you end up with an empty subcube as well, in which case the affected dimensions appear to have no members at any level. This can happen in at least three ways:

- Returning an empty set from a set function like Filter() or .Children

- Specifying an attribute combination for which no leaf dimension members exist

- Accidentally specifying member identifiers for which there are no members, since Analysis Services by default ignores them rather than presenting you with an error

Using SELECT in the FROM Clause in AS2005

Analysis Services 2005 allows the FROM clause to be a slightly limited SELECT statement itself, which is conceptually similar is some ways to the notion in SQL that a FROM clause can contain another SELECT. These nested SELECTs are essentially query-specific subcubes, whose syntax is the same as that for CREATE SUBCUBE. An example of the syntax would be the following query, whose results are shown in Figure 4-21:

```
SELECT
{ [Customer].[Customer].[Region].Members,
  [Customer].[Customer].[State].Members } *
{ [Measures].[Unit Sales], [Measures].[Dollar Sales] } on 0,
[Time].[YQMD].[Quarter].Members on 1
FROM (
  SELECT
  Filter (
    [Time].[YQMD].[Quarter].Members,
    [Measures].[Unit Sales] > 7500
  ) on 0,
  { [Customer].[Customer].[AZ], [Customer].[Customer].[NM],
    [Customer].[Customer].[UT] } on 1
  FROM [Sales]
  WHERE [Product].[ByCategory].[Category].[Tools]
)
```

The nested SELECT is like a subcube definition: It looks like any other one with the following restrictions:

1. It cannot have its own WITH section. No calculated members, named sets, calculated cells, and so on.

2. It cannot use NON EMPTY or HAVING. All nonemptiness and follow-on operations are part of the outer query.

3. It cannot request DIMENSION PROPERTIES on its axes.

These restrictions reflect what the nested SELECT is doing: specifying a restricted portion of the cube's dimensional space that does not depend on the results of any particular outer query. NON EMPTY cannot be assessed until after all axes of a query have been evaluated, and although conceptually this could be done here, it just isn't. Although MDX Scripts aren't discussed until Chapter 13, there is an aspect of scoping a cube to a smaller portion that is similar between this capability and scripts.

The inner SELECT is just creating a restriction on the apparent [Time] dimension and Customer dimension used by the outer SELECT. Note that the outer query requests Time on axis 1, while the inner SELECT requests Time on axis 0. Although you need to specify axis numbers, there is really no result API impact to the layout.

	Central		AZ		NM		UT	
	Unit Sales	Dollar Sales	Unit Sales	Dollar Sales	Unit Sales	Dollar Sales	Unit Sales	Dollar Sales
Q1, 2004	771	$18,552.50	63	$1,604.61	126	$2,566.79	582	$14,351.10
Q4, 2004	2,519	$61,560.91	231	$5,866.57	909	$20,597.08	1,379	$35,097.26
Q2, 2005	748	$19,058.56			338	$7,908.98	410	$11,149.58
Q3, 2005	1,664	$42,620.53	286	$6,862.17	515	$13,688.70	863	$22,069.66
Q4, 2005	3,385	$89,564.24	946	$25,445.65	1,162	$30,106.04	1,277	$34,012.55

Figure 4-21   Results of query using nested SELECT.

The inner SELECT uses context as you might expect from the discussions earlier in this chapter. It selects all the quarters for which the All-customer, Product tools, unit sales were more than 7500, and also a set of three particular customer states. The outer SELECT then retrieves all available customer states and some measures across columns, and all available time quarters down rows. As you can see, the request for [Time].[Quarter].Members in the outer query only returned the few time members obtained from the Filter(), and the result displayed shows only the selected times and customers. Now consider this slight variation to the previous query, whose results are shown in Figure 4-22:

```
SELECT
{ [Customer].[Customer].[State].Members } *
{ [Measures].[Unit Sales], [Measures].[Dollar Sales] } on 0,

[Time].[YQMD].[Quarter].Members on 1
FROM (
   ..// ... Subcube as before
)
```

Note that the inner SELECT returned a set of Customer states, while the outer SELECT didn't refer to Customer at all. What happened? In the outer query, customers is on the slicer and at the default member, in this case the [All] member. In this cube, this implicitly aggregates the set of customers from the inner SELECT, and as a result, the base measures in the query were aggregated across the three Customer members according to their cube-defined aggregation principles.

In terms of execution context, the inner SELECT is evaluated before the outer SELECT, and is isolated from it. The inner SELECT cannot refer to definitions in the WITH section of the outer query. Any formulas or sets that it uses must stand on their own, or be defined previously using CREATE statements. The slicer of the inner SELECT forms context for calculations in the inner SELECT. As with subcubes, it does not form context for any outer queries.

	Unit Sales	Dollar Sales
Q1, 2004	771	$18,552.50
Q4, 2004	2,519	$61,560.91
Q2, 2005	748	$19,058.56
Q3, 2005	1,664	$42,620.53
Q4, 2005	3,385	$89,564.24

Figure 4-22   Results of query aggregating scope from nested SELECT.

The inner SELECT restricts the members visible to the result of the outer SELECT, just as a subcube definition does. If the outer SELECT refers directly to members not returned by the inner SELECT in its axis expressions, those members are not included. However, calculated expressions such as comparison functions for Filter() and calculated members can refer to metadata outside the scope of the inner SELECT, both by absolute reference and by relative reference (using PrevMember, and so on). In short, the subcube really functions as a filter on what members can appear in the final axis sets of the outer query, and forms the set of members for which base measures are intrinsically aggregated in the outer query.

As you see, nested SELECT clauses are essentially query-scoped subcubes.

Infinite Recursion: A "Gotcha" Related to Calculation Context

When you are defining calculated members, you have to take into account the concept of the current context along the dimension in which the calculated member is placed. This includes the measures dimension, which has a current member just like every other dimension. For example, the following calculated measure definition will not quite work, though it is syntactically correct:

```
MEMBER [Measures].[Avg Sale] AS
'Sum (Descendants ([Geography], [Geography].[City]),
     [Measures].[Sales])
/ Count (Descendants ([Geography], [Geography].[City]),
     EXCLUDEEMPTY)'
```

This may look like a perfectly good definition of an average (dividing a sum by a count), but it will not work, because the count cannot be evaluated. When values are being calculated for the count, the current measure is [Measures].[Avg Sale]. When the cells formed by

```
{ Descendants ([Geography], [Geography].[City]) }
```

intersect with the current measure in that context, the server will go into infinite recursion in its attempt to determine whether the set is empty. To evaluate whether any [Measures].[Avg Sale] cell is empty or not, this formula gets uses, which generates infinite recursion. Note that vendor implementations of Count(..., INCLUDEEMPTY) will just count the cells without testing them, so those work fine. The Essbase function NonEmptyCount (set, expression) tests *expression* for emptiness across *set*, making this problem a little harder to run into.

Overall, you need to be cognizant of the cell context. Neither Essbase nor Analysis Services flags a potential infinitely recursive calculated member when it is defined, but you will notice it when you get an error result instead of a value or NULL. Analysis Services will also set an appropriate text message inside the error information retrieved by the client for this cell, indicating the presence of infinite recursion; AS2005 will tell you something about the chain of formulas involved, although it only seems to recognize the involvement of one of the dimensions when formulas on multiple dimensions are involved.

Usually, when you are performing a SUM/COUNT over the same set of non-measure tuples, you are performing the SUM and the COUNT over the same measure. We can remedy this by cross-joining the nonmeasure tuples with the measure of interest to get the right set of cells.

> **TIP** If you want to supply a set to a function (for example, an aggregation like Sum(), Avg(), Max(), Correlation(), and so on), and you want the cells of a specific measure to be used in the function, either cross-join the measure with the set or mention it specifically as the expression to aggregate over. Then, even if the current context includes a different measure, your specific measure's cells will be used.

Product-Specific Solve Order Use

Each of the products here uses solve order specifications in somewhat different ways. The concept is generally compatible, but the details are different. This is especially true between Analysis Services 2005 and Analysis Services 2000; applications that used calculated members defined in the server and calculated members defined in queries will not work without modification. Essbase solve orders are by default the same as Analysis Services 2000, but database settings may make them different.

Use of Solve Order between Global, Session, and Query Calculations in Analysis Services 2005

Analysis Services 2005 follows a different model than its predecessors and other OLAP servers that implement MDX, and while the new behavior is part of a set of semantic changes that make it easier to model complex calculations in server-side definitions than before, the new behavior may break existing applications and force you to think differently about designing new ones. In particular, the functions that you use may affect the apparent solve order.

In AS2005, you define calculated members within an MDX script using the same CREATE MEMBER syntax that we introduced earlier (and is discussed in more detail in Chapter 12) to create globally scoped calculated members. In a client session, you use the same syntax to define a session-scope calculated

member, and in a query you use WITH MEMBER. You can also create cell calculations in each of these scopes as well (also discussed in Chapter 12). Each of
these scopes is its own universe for solve orders, and solve order winners are
only determined by looking at the other definitions in the same scope (where
the query-scope solve orders override session solve orders override global
solve orders). Consider the following sequence:

```
CREATE MEMBER [Sales].[Measures].[Avg Sales Price] AS
[Measures].[Dollar Sales] / [Measures].[Unit Sales]
, SOLVE_ORDER = 10

WITH MEMBER [Product].[My Total] AS
Sum ( { [Product].[A], [Product].[B] } ), SOLVE_ORDER = 0
SELECT
{ [Measures].[Dollar Sales], [Measures].[Unit Sales],
  [Measures].[Avg Sales Price] } on axis(0),
{ [Product].[A], [Product].[B], [Product].[My Total] } on axis(1)
FROM [Sales]
```

The ([Avg Sales Price], [My Total]) cell will contain the sum of the
ratios, even though the solve orders specify the ratio of the sums.

The Aggregate() Function: A Helper with a Twist

There is one exception to this, that you will probably want to take advantage
of, which is sort of a special case. The Aggregate() function does not respect
solve order, and "blasts through" the barriers between different scopes. If you
defined the query aggregation member above as

```
WITH MEMBER [Product].[My Total] AS
Aggregate ( { [Product].[A], [Product].[B] } )
```

then it doesn't matter what solve order you give the member [My Total],
because the aggregate function will always fall to the bottom of the solve
order. *This means that even if you define this member to be solve order 1000, you cannot use the database-defined aggregation function to aggregate the ratios (or whatever
other intersecting formula results you may have).* There is a curious side effect of
this: If your formula has more than one term in it, and one of those terms is an
Aggregate() expression, then different parts of your calculated member
may run at different solve orders. For example, suppose that your query
looked like this (just subtracting an adjustment from an aggregation):

```
WITH MEMBER [Product].[My Total] AS
Aggregate ( { [Product].[A], [Product].[B] } )
- Aggregate ( { [Product].[C], [Product].[D] } )
SELECT
{ [Measures].[Dollar Sales], [Measures].[Unit Sales],
```

```
    [Measures].[Avg Sales Price] } on axis(0),
{ [Product].[A], [Product].[B], [Product].[My Total] } on axis(1)
FROM [Sales]
```

The result for the ([Avg Sales Price], [My Total]) cell will be zero! Furthermore, the following two expressions lead to different result ratio cells:

```
WITH MEMBER [Product].[My Total] AS
Aggregate ( { [Product].[A], [Product].[B] } )
- Aggregate ( { [Product].[C] } ), SOLVE_ORDER = 0

WITH MEMBER [Product].[My Total] AS
Aggregate ( { [Product].[A], [Product].[B] } )
- [Product].[C], SOLVE_ORDER = 0
```

Clearly, the Aggregate() expressions themselves are the parts that go outside the solve order rules, with some surprising results.

> **TIP** One of the great strengths of MDX has been the ability to define calculations at the server, and also in queries, and have them work together. To allow calculated members defined at the server (such as for average sales price, period-to-period ratios, and so on) to operate on aggregates across user-defined groups, use the Aggregate() function in query and session calculated members instead of Sum().

Use of Solve Orders in Essbase

In Essbase, whether the calculated member was defined in the query or in the outline does not matter for determining which calculation to use. At any intersection of two or more calculated members, regardless of their scope, the solve order numbers are compared and a winner chosen. In case of a tie, the winner depends on the type of outline: In an ASO cube built with Essbase 7.1.2 or later, the member in the dimension that appears later in the outline's order wins, whereas in a block-storage cube or a pre-7.1.2 ASO cube, the dimension that appears earlier in the outline order wins. However, solve order number 0 is a special case that may not mean 0.

In an Essbase outline, a default solve order may be set for a dimension as a whole. If you don't set it, the default solve order value is truly 0. If you do set it to number between 1 and 127, then any calculated member for which you specify a solve order of 0 takes on the default solve order for the dimension. If you don't specify a solve order number for a calculated member in the WITH clause of the query, then the solve order takes on that default as well. (Which has the same effect as specifying a value of 0 in this case.) Recall the query of Figure 4-9, in which the [Time Series].[Period to Prior] member is specified as having a solve order of 0. If the [Time Series] dimension has a default solve order of 20, then that member would actually have won the solve order comparison, resulting in the difference of the two ratios. Note that when the default solve order is set to something larger than 0, then the lowest solve order you can specify for a calculated member in that dimension becomes 1.

Use of Solve Orders in Analysis Services 2000

In Analysis Services 2000, whether the calculated member was defined in the query, the session, or the database does not matter for determining which calculation to use. At any intersection of two or more calculated members, regardless of their scope, the solve order numbers are compared and a winner chosen. However, there are a number of other kinds of calculation definitions, with different solve order considerations. Cell calculations and custom member formulas have the same solve order numbering that calculated members have. Custom rollup functions and custom rollup operators inhabit specific documented solve order numbers (between -5120 and -5118 for custom rollup functions, for example, and -4096 for VisualTotals calculations). Analysis Services 2000 allows you to specify solve order ranges from -8181 up to 2^{32}-1.

Within this system, ties occur not just between calculated members, but between various kinds of calculation definitions as well. The winning type of calculation appears earliest in the following list:

1. Cell calculation
2. Custom rollup formulas
3. Calculated member or custom member formula
4. Custom rollup operators

When the winning kind of calculation is a cell calculation, tied cell calculation solve order is won by the cell calculation that was defined earlier. When the winning kind is a calculated member or custom member formula, ties among members are won by the dimension that appears later in the list of dimensions for the cube. Remember, measures are effectively the last dimension in the list. The same dimension list order holds for custom rollup formulas. In testing, custom rollup operator ties are dependent on the actual operators as opposed to the documented dimension order, and in general we would discourage rollup operators on multiple dimensions in Analysis Services 2000.

Nondata: Invalid Numbers, NULLs, and Invalid Members

When performing queries and calculations, you will frequently need to deal with data that isn't valid as well as the empty space in cubes where data could be but isn't. You may encounter three sorts of nondata when evaluating queries: invalid numbers, NULLs (or empty cells), and invalid member specifications (which you have also seen referred to as NULL members). Let us take a look at each of these.

Invalid Calculations: Division by Zero and Numerical Errors

Even though the result of a division by zero is not a valid number, Analysis Services does not treat it as an empty value. In some instances, you can test for the results of a division by zero, or for a floating-point overflow caused by other means, by comparing the cell value with (1/0). For example,

```
iif (1.0e+40 * 1.0e+40 = (1/0), "Overflowed", "Didn't Overflow")
```

multiplies a very large double-float value by itself and will cause an overflow condition. When performing a comparison, Analysis Services will consider the overflow value as being equal to (1/0) (at least on Pentium-class CPUs), so the expression will always return the string "Overflowed." Be aware, however, that this test is dependent upon how the processor of the machine on which Analysis Services is installed handles different types of numeric errors. Different CPUs (different families of Intel CPUs or other processor types to which the product may be ported) may return different values, and different causes of overflowing may cause different values to appear. In short, you may not be able to effectively test for an overflow condition for any given calculation without using an external function. We discussed how to avoid problems like division by zero in Chapter 3.

Note that Analysis Services will never detect an overflow in integer calculations. If you add 2,000,000,000 to 2,000,000,000 in a small-integer calculation, you will not get 4,000,000,000 as a result but rather 1,852,516,354. BigInt calculations are extremely unlikely to overflow; if 2,000,000,000 input cells each contribute a value of 2,000,000,000 to a sum, the result will still not overflow. Numerical errors trapped by external function libraries frequently raise an ActiveX or .NET error rather than return a bogus value. When this happens, the evaluation of the cell will halt, and it will neither be empty nor have a value of any type.

Semantics of Empty Cells

Given the usual sparseness of data in a multidimensional data set, empty cells are the rule rather than the exception. When you are looking at a data set as a set of cells within a big CrossJoin() of all dimensions, you will see a lot more empty cells in the cube than there are NULLs in underlying fact tables. The reason for this, of course, is that not every consumer, supplier, employee, or factory participated in every type of transaction at every possible time period with every possible geographical location. (In Analysis Services 2005, empty values in fact table measure columns can be captured as NULL cell values when the measure's NullProcessing property is set to "Preserve," which is a change from Analysis Services 2000 in which empty values measure columns resulted in zero for cell values.)

Analysis Services has default semantics for handling empty cells in an MDX expression that differs somewhat from the default semantics for handling NULLs in SQL, and also from the standard MDX specification. As you saw in Chapter 3, Analysis Services and Essbase also extend standard MDX with a NULL operator, which can be used to return an empty or NULL value from a formula. (Because MDX has an operator called IsEmpty() and our servers have a NULL operator to make a cell empty, no clear terminology is laid out for us to use. We will, therefore, use both NULL and empty in our discussion here.)

The MDX that Analysis Services provides does not, however, provide any operators for determining whether a cell is empty because the underlying table column values were NULL or because rows were not present for that dimensional combination. Also, there is no standard way in an OLAP model for an application to signify whether an empty cell could possibly have had a value or not (such as the invalidity of a "how many months pregnant" condition for a male patient, or sales values for a store member in the months before the store actually opened).

First, what the standard says: According to the OLE DB for OLAP specification of MDX semantics, empty cells are treated almost identically to zero in a numerical context and as an empty string in a string context. That is, in a numerical context, they should add, subtract, multiply, and divide as though they were zero. In an ascending sort, they will be sorted before zero and after the negative number that has the smallest magnitude. In a string context, concatenating a string with an EMPTY will result in the original string, and empty cells that have a string type will sort immediately before cells that have a real empty string for a value. That is, the following sets of values are sorted according to the MDX specification:

- Numbers: 210, 21, 20.00001, NULL, 0, 0.00001, 1, 10

- Strings: NULL, "", "a," "ab," "z"

When ordering a set, neither Analysis Services nor Essbase adheres to the OLE DB for OLAP specification in treatment of NULLs. In the case of Analysis Services, when ordering a set, NULL values are treated as if they actually were zero or empty strings. Refer to Chapter 3 for information on how to work around this. In the case of Essbase, tuples with related NULL values are eliminated entirely from the results by default, and we also treat this in Chapter 6.

In both Essbase and Analysis Services, NULL values are treated as FALSE in a Boolean expression. In Analysis Services, this is the case whether the value is in a Boolean context like an iif() function or calculating a Boolean cell result.

NULLs in Comparisons and Calculations

Both Analysis Services and Essbase interpret NULL cell semantics differently from the OLE DB for OLAP specification in that the result of a calculation that involves empty cells may be NULL or it may not be NULL.

NULLs in Analysis Services Calculations

In Analysis Services, a NULL value will be treated as zero when it is combined with a non-NULL value in a calculation, but a calculation that involves only NULL values will be regarded as NULL. Let's use as an example the following calculation:

```
([Measures].[Sales] - [Measures].[Costs]) / [Measures].[Costs]
```

If Sales and Costs are both present, you will get a value in return; if Sales are 10 and Costs are 8, then $(10 - 8)/8 = 0.25$. If Sales is present but Costs is not, the expression would be evaluated as $(10 - 0)/0$, and the floating-point overflow value (with a typical string representation of #1.INF) will be returned. If Costs is present but Sales is not, the expression would be evaluated as $(0 - 8)/8 = -1$. However, if neither costs nor sales are present (if both are NULL), the expression will return an empty value.

If you include any constants in a expression, the expression will always return a result because any empty cell value will be combined with a non-empty value (the constant) as a result. For example, a growth projection formula of (1.5 * ([Time].[Q2 2004] + [Time].[Q3 2004])) will return zero if the given measure does not have a value at either [Q2 2004] or [Q3 2004]. It will return 1.5 times the sum of the values that are present, if any are. If we break this down into pieces, the expression ([Time].[Q2 2001] + [Time].[Q3 2001]) will have a NULL result if all of the cells are empty, but (1.5 * (NULL)) will be treated as 1.5 * 0.

Sum(), Min(), Max(), and Avg() over values that are only NULL will result in NULL, regardless of whether the values were aggregates or calculated via MDX.

Member properties can be NULL, and the results of functions on members like .UniqueName can have no result (see the following section on invalid locations). Analysis Services 2005 can perform the IsEmpty() operation on member property values as well as cells and the result of expressions. However, if the value for the property does not exist, IsEmpty() returns false (as though the #Error result was actually a value). You should note that in Analysis Services, if you are testing for an empty member name, you probably are trying to see if the member itself exists, which you can do with the expression member IS NULL as well.

NULLs in Analysis Services Comparisons

In a comparison, a NULL will be equal to zero in all circumstances. That is, the expression iif (NULL = 0, . . . , . . .) will always return the result of the if-true expression. Of course, NULL = NULL is true, and (NULL <> NULL) is always false. Don't fall into the trap of comparing a value with NULL directly, as with iif ([Measures].[Units Sold] = NULL, . . .). The NULL will be silently converted into a zero if the [Units Sold] reference is present. If the [Units Sold] reference is NULL, perhaps a NULL will actually be compared to a NULL (which will result in true). The result will be exactly as if you compared [Units Sold] with zero.

NULLs/MISSINGs in Essbase Calculations and Comparisons

In Essbase documentation, MISSING is used as the term for NULL. In Essbase, whether NULL is treated as a 0 or not depends on the operation it is used in, as shown in Table 4-1.

Table 4-1 Results of Combining MISSING with Values through Operators in Essbase

CALCULATION/OPERATION	RESULT
Value + MISSING	Value
Value – MISSING	Value
MISSING – Value	-Value
Value * MISSING	MISSING
Value / MISSING	MISSING
MISSING / Value	MISSING
Value / 0	MISSING
Value % MISSING	MISSING
MISSING % Value	MISSING
Value % 0	MISSING
Value = MISSING	False, or True if Value is MISSING
Value <> MISSING	True, or False if Value is MISSING
Value <= MISSING	Value <=0

(continued)

Table 8-1   *(continued)*

CALCULATION/OPERATION	RESULT
Value >= MISSING	Value >=0, or true if Value is MISSING
Value > MISSING	Value > 0
Value < MISSING	Value < 0
True AND MISSING	MISSING
False AND MISSING	False
MISSING AND MISSING	MISSING
True OR MISSING	True
False OR MISSING	MISSING
MISSING OR MISSING	MISSING
IIF (MISSING)	IIF (0)

Invalid Locations

Noninformation may need to be dealt with in MDX in another way: when invalid tuples or empty sets are specified. These can arise in a variety of ways. Analysis Services has a very simple logic for dealing with them, which you will need to account for when you are constructing ranges using the colon (:) operator.

An empty set or tuple arises whenever you request a member(s) that just isn't there. For example, take a time dimension whose leaf level is months and whose first month is January 2000. Because there are no children to January 2000, the set expression [Time].[Jan 2000].Children will return an empty set. The MDX parser will treat it as a set, and the set can be combined with other sets, as in {[Time].[Jan 2000], [Time].[Jan 2000].Children}. However, the [Jan 2000].Children term will contribute zero members to the resulting set. Similarly, the member expression [Time].[Jan 2000].PrevMember specifies a nonexistent member. A set that combined this nonexistent member with other members, such as { [Time].[Jan 2000], [Time].[Jan 2000].PrevMember } will only result in the members that were actually present in the dimension metadata ({[[Time].[Jan 2000]}, in this case). If the geography dimension had [City] as its leaf level, then the tuple specification ([Geography].[Atlanta GA].FirstChild, [Time].[Jan 2000].PrevMember) would result in an invalid tuple (as would ([Geography].[Atlanta GA], [Time].[Jan 2000].PrevMember). This is because if only one member in a tuple specification is invalid, the entire tuple is.

> **CHANGE IN LOGIC BETWEEN ANALYSIS SERVICES 2000 AND 2005**
>
> **With the release of Analysis Services 2005, the semantics of providing an invalid location on one or both sides of the colon (`:`) operator have changed.**

References to invalid members, tuples, or sets can occur in queries for a variety of reasons. Only valid locations can return results, however, so you will not get valid values back from invalid locations—only NULL. Invalid locations can spring up in two contexts: when a set is being specified and when a tuple is being specified. We've just talked about the case in which a tuple is being specified; let's take a look at sets next.

When a set is being specified, it will ultimately form the range over which a set of values will be evaluated. This is true whether the set is the axis of a query, is a set created by CREATE SET or WITH SET, or is specified in a calculated member as input to an aggregation function. As the set specification is evaluated, valid tuples are included, and invalid ones will not appear. If the set specifies one valid member and 100 invalid members, only one member will be in the final set, and all values (cell or property) that are evaluated relative to that will be related to the one member. Thus, Analysis Services and Essbase prevent invalid member references (which will lead to invalid tuples) from contributing empty cell values to calculations like Count() and Avg().

It is important to understand the behavior of invalid members when they are used with the colon operator (`:`) provided by Microsoft Analysis Services. (This behavior has changed between releases.) Common usage of MDX functions like .Lag(), .Lead(), Cousin(), and ParallelPeriod() will frequently result in an invalid member. Part of the utility of Cousin() and ParallelPeriod() is that comparable ranges from multiple levels can be specified with one simple operator. The set of time members described by

```
{ ParallelPeriod ([Time].[Year], 1)
  : [Time].CurrentMember }
```

provides you with the last year's worth of members at the level of the current time member, regardless of whether it is month, quarter, or day. The byproduct of constructing ranges like this is that some ranges may not mean what you want them to mean. What does it mean when the current time member is already in the first year, so there is no parallel period a year ago?

In Analysis Services 2005 (as with earlier versions), when you specify a range in MDX in which one member is valid and the other is not, the resulting range extends to the edge of the database's ordering of members on the level of the valid member. For example, consider a time level that has the 12 months January through December in calendar order. The range { [March] : [January].PrevMember } specified a valid member on the left and an invalid member on the right. The set that resulted would be { [March] : [December] }. In Analysis Services 2005, this is the same as { [March] : NULL }, which might be helpful in some cases. For example, an "all time-to-date" specification would be {NULL : [Time].CurrentMember }.

In Analysis Services 2000, when an invalid location is specified on either or both sides of the colon (:), an error occurs when the query is executed. On one hand, this prevents surprising results to a query. On the other hand, it means that you should make sure that an invalid location cannot end up on either side of the colon.

You can use iif() to test indirectly for the existence or nonexistence of members, or you can use other indirect means. A direct test would be asking whether the member itself is NULL (in Analysis Services) or if it IsValid() (in Essbase).

An indirect test would be to test the count of tuples from one member in a dimension back to the edge of the dimension. For example, if you want to calculate a six-month moving average only where at least six months exist over which to calculate it, you can count the number of tuples stretching from the current member backwards and only return the average if there are six of them, as the following expression does:

```
iif (
  LastPeriods (6, [Time].CurrentMember).Count >= 6,
  Avg(LastPeriods (6, [Time].CurrentMember),
      [Measures].[Volume Traded]),
  NULL
)
```

A direct test in Microsoft would involve comparing the member with NULL using the IS operator.

```
iif (
  Not ([Time].CurrentMember.Lag(5) IS NULL),
  Avg({ [Time].CurrentMember.Lag(5) : [Time].CurrentMember },
      [Measures].[Volume Traded]),
  NULL
)
```

A direct test in Essbase would involve checking the validity of the member reference using IsValid().

```
iif (
  IsValid([Time].CurrentMember.Lag(5)),
  Avg({ [Time].CurrentMember.Lag(5) : [Time].CurrentMember },
      [Measures].[Volume Traded]),
  NULL
)
```

Precedence of Cell Properties in Calculations

Another aspect of context that we have not yet talked about is that of a single cell and the calculation chosen as having precedence for that cell. Precedence issues and solve order numbers were introduced in Chapter 2. When a calculated member is used to define the value of a cell, it defines the values for every aspect of that cell. That includes not only the raw numerical quantity for the cell but also all associated properties for that cell. In combination with the data types of the cells that go into calculating the cell, the formula itself will determine the data type of the raw value that is returned to the client or passed to an external function. The other properties of a cell, including textual display formatting and font-rendering information, will be those that are also defined for the calculated member. The following sections explore each of these areas.

Precedence of Display Formatting

Let's revisit the simple query introduced in Chapter 2 that provided the desired results for Figure 2-3, this time with formatting applied. Assuming that the dollar and unit sales are formatted to return zero decimal places, you will see the results shown in Figure 4-23 if you ask for a Q1-Q2 difference to two decimal places and that Avg Sales Price be formatted as a currency value to two decimal places:

```
WITH
MEMBER [Measures].[Avg Sales Price] AS
'[Measures].[Dollar Sales] / [Measures].[Unit Sales]',
SOLVE_ORDER = 0, FORMAT_STRING = '$0.00'
MEMBER [Time].[Q1 to Q2 Growth] AS
'[Time].[Q2, 2005] - [Time].[Q1, 2005]',
SOLVE_ORDER = 1, FORMAT_STRING = '0.00'
SELECT
{ [Measures].[Dollar Sales], [Measures].[Unit Sales],
  [Measures].[Avg Sales Price]
}
on columns,
{ [Time].[Q1, 2005], [Time].[Q2, 2005], [Time].[Q1 to Q2 Growth] }
on rows
FROM [Sales]
WHERE ([Customer].[MA])
CELL PROPERTIES [Formatted_Value]
```

	Dollar Sales	Unit Sales	Avg Sales Price
Q1, 2005	96949	3866	$ 25.06
Q2, 2005	104510	4125	$ 25.34
Q1 to Q2 Growth	7561.10	259.00	$ 0.28

Figure 4-23   Result of requesting formatted values for overlapping calculations in a query.

As you can see from Figure 4-23, the cell formatting defined in the calculated member that calculates the cell is the formatting that is applied to the value of the cell. The server itself takes on the chore of performing the formatting, so your clients will not need to devote any logic to this task. Font choice, size, style, and color information can also be specified by the calculated member; whether this information is used is up to the client application.

Earlier in this chapter, we discussed how in AS2005 the `Aggregate()` function does not follow solve order rules. However, note that the cells calculated by calculated members do follow the solve order rules we discuss here for handling display-related cell properties.

NOTE In MDX scripts (described in Chapter 13), a format may be assigned to a region of cells. When a calculated member defined in a `WITH` or `CREATE` overlaps a script scope, the result cell will be calculated according to the calculated member, but the display formatting will be taken from the script's scope.

Data Types from Calculated Cells

It is a simple matter to describe the rules for the data types that are returned for calculations involving valid data and that return a valid result. The data type for the result of a calculated member depends on the formula as well as the types of cells it uses as inputs. The following rules are used in MDX calculations in Analysis Services 2005 and 2000:

- Two integers added, subtracted, or multiplied result in an integer. If the integers are of different size, the result is of the bigger size.

- An integer added to, subtracted from, or multiplied by a floating-point number in any way results in a floating-point number. The result will be the size of the floating-point number (single-float or double-float).

- Any number divided by any other number results in a double-float result.

- The data type of the value returned by `Count()`, `Rank()`, or `.Ordinal` is a 32-bit integer in 32-bit product versions.

- The data type of the value that is returned by `Max()` and `Min()` is the largest type of any of its inputs (the maximum of an integer and a single-float is a single-float, even if the integer is the larger of the numbers; the maximum of a double-float and any other type is a double-float).

- The `Sum()` or `Avg()` of an empty set or of a set of entirely empty cells is an empty value.

- Any values calculated by an aggregation operator other than those listed in the preceding rules (including `Sum()`, `Max()`, and so on) are returned as a double float. All values that are input to the aggregation operator are converted to a double float prior to aggregation, so if you take the sum of a large number of 32-bit integers, the aggregation operator will not overflow as the sum passes the 2,147,483,647 limit on a 32-bit integer.

- In an external function, a calculation that results in an error will cause a variant containing an Error value (vbError) to be created.

- (AS 2005) When a logical result is used in a numerical context (like `(A > B) * 5`), a true results in an integer value of -1 and a false results in an integer value of 0.

- (AS 2005) When a string value is used in a numerical context (like `5 + "3"`), the string is converted to a number. An error will be raised if the string cannot be converted into a number.

String operations otherwise have no conversion rules. They may be concatenated with other strings within Analysis Services, but otherwise they are simply passed into functions and/or returned from functions. When a calculated member is defined with a formula that just performs a logical operation, as with the following, Analysis Services 2005 will treat the value as a Boolean when conveying the type of the value to external code (through XMLA, for example):

```
CREATE MEMBER [AccountCube].[Measures].[Indebted] AS
'[Measures].[Borrowed] > [Measures].[Assets]'
```

Analysis Services 2000 will convert the Boolean result into a 32-bit integer, with a true result represented by 1 and a false by 0.

Thus, even though a measure may have a defined data type, if the formula of some calculated member has precedence at a cell, the data type returned for the cell is defined by the calculation. For example, suppose that an inventory unit's measure is defined as having an integer type and the following scenario variance member is used:

```
[Scenario].[Budget Pct. Variance] AS
  '([Scenario].[Actual] / [Scenario].[Budget]) - 1'
```

In this case, the result of any ([Scenario].[Budget Pct. Variance], [Measures].[Inventory Units]) tuple is going to be a double float (unless yet another calculation has precedence for that cell).

Cube Context in Actions

Although an action is not executed from an MDX query (instead, it is invoked by manipulating data structures), it executes in a context as though it was a single-cell query, and in fact is basically a single-cell text query. The default context for the action is the default member for the user/role in each dimension. Although actions can be defined over more scopes, if the scope is a member, a tuple, or a set, then the member, tuple, or set provided by the client can affect the query context for the action. In the case of a member or tuple, the context members of the listed dimensions are set to the member(s) provided by the client when the action is invoked. In the case of a set-scoped action, the context is not directly affected by invoking the action, but the set can be referenced by the action itself and use its contents in set functions and tuples. More information on developing actions is presented in Chapter 14, and more information on accessing them in client code is presented in Chapters 14 and 15.

Cube Context in KPIs

A KPI is a set of related calculated members, which are accessed by a client query. These calculated members can be accessed on their own, or through the KPIxxx functions (described in Appendix A). Therefore, all of the techniques described so far apply, including subcubes, and changing the default members for a dimension, which is described in more detail in Chapter 12.

Visibility of Definitions between Global, Session, and Query-Specific Calculations in Analysis Services 2005

In Analysis Services, calculated members, named sets, and cell calculations can be defined both at session scope via CREATE and at query scope via WITH, as well as in an MDX script. It is not an error to define one of these entities in a WITH clause or a session-level CREATE command that has the same name as one defined at the server. That is, if the cube [Sales] has a calculated member [Measures].[Avg Order Size] defined at the server, you can build a query that starts with

```
WITH MEMBER [Measures].[Avg Order Size] AS ...
```

and no error occurs. You could also execute CREATE MEMBER [MyCube].[Measures].[Avg Order Size] AS .... If the entity being redefined is a set, then any reference to that set in the query will use the new definition. If the entity is a calculated member, then querying for the member by name will return your newly defined version, while obtaining it through .AllMembers will return both versions. If you have a calculated member with the same name defined in an MDX script, a session CREATE MEMBER statement, and the WITH clause, .AllMembers will give you all three versions. In addition, each subcube that you create provides a separate scope for CREATE MEMBER definitions. You can CREATE a member with the same name in each of these scopes, and if you use .AllMembers on that dimension, then you will see all of the versions of this member.

While in Analysis Services 2000 you could DROP members (and cell calculations and sets) that were defined by the server, because they were just commands sent to the PivotTable Service, in Analysis Services 2005, a client cannot drop them.

When a CREATE CELL CALCULATION, SET, or MEMBER is executed, if it refers to a specific named set, then the definition of the cell calculation, set, or member is fixed at that moment in time. For example, suppose that you executed the command:

```
CREATE MEMBER [Sales].[Car].[Fast Car Total] AS
' Sum ([Fast Cars] )', SOLVE_ORDER = 1
```

If the set [Fast Cars] consists of the set { [Porsche], [Lotus], [Turbo Yugo] }, then the member [Fast Cars Total] will sum up measure values for these three cars. Now consider the following query:

```
WITH
SET [Fast Cars] AS
'{[Porsche], [Lotus], [Corvette], [Audi]}'
SELECT
{ [Measures].[Units Sold] } on columns,
{ [Fast Cars], [Car].[Fast Car Total] } on rows
FROM [Sales]
```

The [Fast Car Total] member returned in the report will be the sum of { [Porsche], [Lotus], [Turbo Yugo] }, while the car members listed on the rows will be { [Porsche], [Lotus], [Corvette], [Audi] }. This reflects the binding of the [Fast Car Total] to the particular session-level set, which still exists even though it is not visible in the query. Similarly, a set or cell calculation that includes a session-level calculated member will return the results of its calculation, even though a query may redefine the calculated member to have a new definition.

In AS2005, if you define a calculated member in a WITH clause that has the same name as a calculated member created via CREATE MEMBER and you request that member to be returned, you only get the WITH version of the member. This is different from Analysis Services 2000, which returned both versions.

Also, if you create a session-level named set that references a calculated member, but you redefine the calculated member in the WITH clause of the query, the member that is used in the set is the newly defined calculated member, not the session-level calculated member.

NOTE These semantics have changed from version to verson of SQL Server. Because Microsoft does not document these semantics, there is no guarantee that they won't change again.

Summary

In this chapter, you looked at context in a query, the properties that are affected by the cell-by-cell calculation of members within a query, and the way in which Analysis Services handles missing and invalid data in a query. Combined with the base of MDX knowledge you have gained so far, these factors enable you to begin understanding all aspects of a query that are relevant to a client.

CHAPTER 5

Named Sets and Set Aliases

Building and using sets is an important part of MDX. Sometimes, it is most convenient to attach a name to a set that you've defined so that you can reference it later. As introduced in Chapter 2, standard MDX provides *named sets* to do just that. Both Analysis Services and Essbase extend the standard with set aliases to provide names for sets in additional contexts. (Essbase further provides tuple aliases as well.) These are also easy to use and frequently used.

The first half of this chapter builds on Chapter 4's discussion of context and execution flow to add detail to named set evaluation and use. The second half of this chapter introduces some rather involved query requirements that are solved by only a small number of features and functions working together. It both explains how some sophisticated user requests are handled and also continues to work through constructing MDX as assemblies of small simple expressions, so it may bear reading slowly and more than once.

Named Sets: Scopes and Context

Chapter 4 discussed context and query evaluation at some length. To recap briefly here, when a query is evaluated, first the slicer is evaluated, and then named sets are evaluated. This means that the slicer forms the context for all calculations performed in evaluating a named set. So, for named sets defined in the WITH section, you can make named set logic generic by relying on the slicer, or you can make it specific by adding particular members to tuples used them.

However, in the standard CREATE SET, there is no query context available. You need to compose your set expressions to include all relevant context for the members. In Analysis Services, in order to use the same set expressions for CREATE SET as you use for WITH SET, you can alter the default members using the techniques described in the "Altering the Default Member for a Dimension in Your Session" section of Chapter 11 so as to use a more generic set expression. In Analysis Services 2005, you can also a subcube scope (described in Chapter 4) and have the set expression use it for setting members and their related data values. Note that when the subcube is dropped, the created set will be dropped also.

Essbase 9 extends the standard CREATE SET syntax with an optional WHERE clause. For example:

```
CREATE SET [User Selection] AS
'Filter (
  [Product].[Category].Members,
  [Measures].[Dollar Sales] > 5000
)'
WHERE ([Time].[Q1, 2005])
```

This allows you to use the same MDX for named sets in CREATE SET statements as in WITH section definitions.

NOTE Essbase supports up to 16 named sets per session. Note also that when you create a set using CREATE SET, it cannot refer to other named sets. Sets created in the WITH section may do so, however.

Common Uses for Named Sets

Two of the most common uses for named sets are to improve performance of queries, and to tidy up complex set logic and make queries easier to understand. In both the Microsoft and Hyperion MDX implementations, the tuples of a named set are cached when the set expression is evaluated, and every time the set is referenced, the cached set is used. This means that the work of sorting, filtering, ranking, and other expensive actions can be done only once.

For example, look at the following query, whose results are in Figure 5-1:

```
WITH
MEMBER [Measures].[Avg Sales Price] AS
'[Measures].[Dollar Sales] / [Measures].[Unit Sales]',
SOLVE_ORDER = 10
SET [Interesting Cities] AS
'Order (
  Filter (
    [Customer].[City].Members,
    [Measures].[Avg Sales Price]
      > 1.05 * ([Measures].[Avg Sales Price], [Time].[Q2, 2005])
  ),
  [Measures].[Avg Sales Price],
  BDESC
)'
MEMBER [Customer].[Total] AS
'Sum ([Interesting Cities])', SOLVE_ORDER = 0
SELECT
{ [Measures].[Unit Sales], [Measures].[Dollar Sales], [Measures].[Avg
Sales Price] }
on columns,
{
  [Interesting Cities],
  [Customer].[Total]
} on rows
FROM [Sales]
WHERE ([Product].[Category].[Toys], [Time].[Q1, 2005])
```

	Unit Sales	Dollar Sales	Avg Sales Price
Muncie, IN	68	2,280.70	33.5
West Palm Beach, FL	52	1,653.60	31.8
Waltham, MA	54	1,704.20	31.6
Palmyra, PA	47	1,418.90	30.2
Broadalbin, NY	66	1,925.90	29.2
Northbrook, IL	64	1,786.90	27.9
...	...	...	...
Albuquerque, NM	56	1,217.40	21.7
Hopkins, MN	40	782.00	19.6
Total	1,416	37,631.80	26.6

Figure 5-1   Result of query with Order() and Sum().

This query filters cities to find just those where average sales price in Q1 was more than 5 percent higher than in Q2 for the Toys category of product, orders that set by decreasing average sales price, and then adds a calculated total across that set as the bottom line. (Figure 5-1 omits most of the rows that were returned.) If you want to sum over the result set for the total member but don't want to run the filter more than once, assign the result to a named set and then create the calculated member to sum over the result of the named set. It doesn't matter whether you sum over the sorted set or not, so the named set is created with the result of `Order()` instead of `Filter()` for simplicity. You could just as readily express the following to have `Order()` and `Filter()` each operate once:

```
... // skip
SET [Interesting Cities] AS  // just the filtered cities
'Filter (
  [Customer].[City].Members,
  [Measures].[Avg Sales Price]
    > 1.05 * ([Measures].[Av Sales Price], [Time].[Q2, 2005])
),
MEMBER [Customer].[Total] AS
'Sum ([Interesting Cities])', SOLVE_ORDER = 0
SELECT
... // skip
{
  Order (
    [Interesting Cities],  // use the named set here
    [Measures].[Avg Sales Price],
    BDESC
  ),
  [Customer].[Total]
} on rows
FROM [Sales]
WHERE ([Product].[Category].[Toys], [Time].[Q1, 2005])
```

As you can see, named sets are simple to create and use.

Set Aliases

As simple as named sets are to use, they have one drawback. Each named set is defined once in a query or in a session. What if you want to name and reuse a set expression in a smaller context, for example within a calculation? All of the cases we've come across are complex, but as you use MDX for more and more analyses, you will inevitably come across them. We'll address one of the most important reasons—when you absolutely must do this—after we look at the basics.

An Example of a Set Alias

For example, let's say that you want a calculated member to calculate the range of values (max–min) over the leaf-level descendants of the current member. In Analysis Services, you may be able to greatly optimize calculating the value range using measures that aggregate by MAX and MIN, but it's not possible in all cases. Let's say you need to report on a Product Price Range measure across a set of products and months. You want to calculate the range across only cities that sell at least 100 units per month per product. So, each cell that calculates this range will evaluate its own filter on cities. (The example is slightly complicated; there are additional and more natural examples starting in Chapter 6. However, this lets us focus on what the set alias brings to us without opening up new subject areas.)

The naive (and standard) way to calculate this is

```
MEMBER [Measures].[Product Price Range] AS
'Max (
  Filter (
    Decendants (
      [Customer].CurrentMember,
      [Customer].[City]
    ),
    [Measures].[Unit Sales] > 100
  ),
  [Measures].[Avg Sales Price]
) - Min (
  Filter (
    Decendants (
      [Customer].CurrentMember,
      [Customer].[City]
    ),
    [Measures].[Unit Sales] > 100
  ),
  [Measures].[Avg Sales Price]
)'
```

You can see that the Filter() expression is written at least twice. Unless the server is rather smart, it will evaluate it twice as well. You can clean this up and perhaps make it much faster by employing a set alias, as in the following:

```
MEMBER [Measures].[Product Price Range] AS
'Max (
  Filter (
    Decendants (
      [Customer].CurrentMember,
      [Customer].[City]
    ),
```

```
    [Measures].[Unit Sales] > 100
  ) AS [AliasA],
  [Measures].[Avg Sales Price]
) - Min (
  [AliasA],
  [Measures].[Avg Sales Price]
)'
```

AS [AliasA] has been added immediately after the Filter(), before even the comma that separated it from the expression to take the maximum of. Then, it was simply referenced in the Min() expression as the set to take the minimum value over. You can put this into a query such as the following (assuming that Avg Sales Price is available), with results shown in Figure 5-2:

```
WITH
MEMBER [Measures].[Product Price Range] AS
'Max (
  Filter (
    Descendants (
      [Customer].CurrentMember,
      [Customer].[City]
    ),
    [Measures].[Unit Sales] > 100
  ) AS [AliasA],
  [Measures].[Avg Sales Price]
) - Min (
  [AliasA],
  [Measures].[Avg Sales Price]
)'
SELECT
CrossJoin (
  {[Time].[Q3, 2005], [Time].[Q4, 2005]},
  {[Measures].[Avg Sales Price], [Measures].[Product Price Range]}
) on columns,
{ [Product].[Home Audio].Children } on rows
FROM [Sales]
```

There are two cells with no value returned; these were products that did not sell at least 100 units in that quarter in any city! The value of 0 indicates no price variation across cities. Variation was quite high for some subcategories in Q4.

	Q3, 2005		Q4, 2005	
	Avg Sales Price	Product Price Range	Avg Sales Price	Product Price Range
Blank Media	29.2	8.6	27	5.8
CD Recorders & Players	24.2	13.9	25.3	9.0
Headphones	25.9		25.5	
Home Theater & Surround	25.7	0.0	28.1	6.4
Shelf Systems	24.7	0.0	27.1	

Figure 5-2   Result of price range query.

Set Aliases in More Detail

Immediately after the alias is defined, it can be used. Any operation that results in a set can be aliased. For example, the following creates an alias for a set constructed with { }:

```
{ [Time].[2005], [Time].CurrentMember.Children } AS [AliasName]
```

The names you give as aliases must not conflict with other things that you have defined, especially named sets. They must also not conflict with each other; if two different calculations (calculated members, named sets, or other expressions involved in a query) define the same alias name, you will get an error. This is true across all the MDX DDL that you have for a cube; aliases used in all the CREATE SET/CREATE MEMBER (and other DDL) must be distinct. Adopt a practice where aliases have their own naming convention (like [__Alias01], [__Alias02], and so on, which are unlikely to be duplicated as a member name).

You may be surprised to learn that in Analysis Services 2000, an alias defined in one calculation (like the calculated Price Range measure in the preceding example) can be accessed in another calculation! For this product version, this provides a somewhat brittle but quite powerful optimization capability to queries and calculations, because the materialization of the aliased set will be retained until the next time the set is constructed. Other calculations can "reach in" to it and use it.

NOTE Analysis Services 2005 and Essbase allow set aliases defined in one calculation to be referenced in another, but they may not return correct results. You should probably avoid allowing this to happen.

For example, let's say that you want to know the average sales price across the same set of filtered cities as the range. You can alter the query to the following, with the results in Figure 5-3:

```
WITH
MEMBER [Measures].[Product Price Range] AS
'Max (
  Filter (
    Descendants (
      [Customer].CurrentMember,
      [Customer].Levels(1)
    ),
    [Measures].[Unit Sales] >= 100
  ) AS [AliasA],
  [Measures].[Avg Sales Price]
) - Min (
  [AliasA],
  [Measures].[Avg Sales Price]
)'
MEMBER [Measures].[Avg Price In Range] AS
'Sum (
  [AliasA],
  [Measures].[Dollar Sales]
) / Sum (
  [AliasA],
  [Measures].[Unit Sales]
)'
SELECT
CrossJoin (
  {[Time].[Q4, 2005]},
  {[Measures].[Avg Sales Price], [Measures].[Product Price Range],
   [Measures].[Avg Price In Range]}
) on columns,
{ [Product].[Home Audio].Children } on rows
FROM [Sales]
```

In Analysis Services 2000, it is important that the software that retrieves results from the server retrieves results in the right order. If the API retrieves [Avg Price In Range] before [Product Price Range], for example, because the order was changed in the axis and the client retrieves cells in order across each column, you would get a blank value for (Blank Media, [Q4, 2005], Avg Price In Range) since the alias hasn't been evaluated yet. Essbase 7.1.2 and higher will return the correct answer by looking a little harder at the dependencies, but you should still test each use of this capability for correctness and use it with care. However, being able to cut the execution time of slow queries by 90 percent or more (in our experience) is a powerful incentive to give it a try.

When Set Aliases Are Required

Earlier, we said that there is a case when a set alias is required, and we'll discuss that case now. It arises because there is only one "current member" in any dimension. As you saw in Chapter 4, the "current member" context can change, for example inside the iteration over a set in set functions like Sum() and Filter(). What if you need to refer to the current member in some outer layer of looping? You can't do it without a set alias (or a tuple alias or member alias in Essbase).

Imagine that you need to write a report that returns, for any time period, the count of days in that period for which units per transaction were larger than the average units per transaction in that time period. As a generic report, someone may run it at the month level, the quarter level, or the week level. Given a measure [Tx Count] that counts the number of transactions, you know that it is easy to compute the units per transaction with the expression

```
([Measures].[Unit Sales] / [Measures].[Tx Count])
```

and that you can compare this ratio for the days with the ratio at the end of the result time period. You can count the days with a Sum:

```
Sum (
  range,
  iif ( condition, 1, 0)
)
```

You also know that you can find the days to sum over for the time period with:

```
Descendants (
  [Time].CurrentMember,
  [Time].[Day]
)
```

	Q4, 2005		
	Avg Sales Price	Product Price Range	Avg Price In Range
Blank Media	26.36	17.23	26.98
CD Recorders & Players	23.65	11	22.45
Headphones	23.99	4.7	22.99
Home Theater & Surround	24.89	7.23	24.87
Shelf Systems	23.27	2.26	22.7

Figure 5-3   Results of query with reuse of aliases.

Putting it all together, you get this far:

```
WITH
MEMBER [Measures].[Count of Days Gtr Than Avg For This Time] AS
'Sum (
  Descendants (
    [Time].CurrentMember,
    [Time].[Day]
  ),
  iif (
      ([Measures].[Unit Sales] / [Measures].[Tx Count])
    > (  ([Measures].[Unit Sales], [Time]./* what goes here */ )
      / ([Measures].[Tx Count], [Time]./* what goes here */ )
    ),
    1,
    0
  )
)'
```

The problem, which leaves you scratching your head, is how you get your starting point back. Inside the `iif()`, `Time.CurrentMember` is set to each day in turn. Your starting point might have been week or month or quarter or year, and you just can't get at it. That's where the alias comes in. You can use a member alias in Essbase to reference it, as follows:

```
WITH
MEMBER [Measures].[Tx Unit Avg] AS
'[Measures].[Unit Sales] / [Measures].[Tx Count]'
MEMBER [Measures].[Count of Days Gtr Than Avg For This Time] AS
'Sum (
  Descendants (
    [Time].CurrentMember AS [Alias_ReferenceTime],
    [Time].[Day]
  ),
  iif (
      [Measures].[Tx Unit Avg]
    > ( [Measures].[Tx Unit Avg], [Alias_ReferenceTime]),
    1,
    0
  )
)'
SELECT
{  [Measures].[Tx Unit Avg],
   [Measures].[Count of Days Gtr Than Avg For This Time]
} on columns,
{
  [Product].[Home Audio].Children
} on rows
FROM WM2005.Sales
WHERE [Time].[Q4, 2005]
```

In Analysis Services, a set alias requires a little more work, but not much more:

```
'Sum (
  Descendants (
    {[Time].CurrentMember} AS [Alias_ReferenceTime],
    [Time].[Day]
  ),
  iif (
      [Measures].[Tx Unit Avg]
    > ( [Measures].[Tx Unit Avg], [Alias_ReferenceTime].Item(0)),
    1,
    0
  )
)'
```

The member was wrapped with {} to put it into a set and then extract item(0) from the set to reference the tuple. This relies on the fact that Descendants() can take a set of members in Analysis Services. If you need to make a set alias out of a member and you obtain the member in a place that cannot use a set (like, for example, the Ancestor() function), then you would need to put it into a set and take it out again. For example, you would use the following in Analysis Services to return, out of the last 12 time periods, only those time periods whose [Unit Sales] were greater than the original current time period in terms of [Unit Sales]:

```
Filter (
  LastPeriods (
    12,
    {{ [Time].CurrentMember } as [Alias_RefTime]}.Item(0),
  ),
  [Measures].[Unit Sales]
  > ([Measures].[Unit Sales], [Alias_RefTime].Item(0))
)
```

Once you wrap the { [Time].CurrentMember } as an [Alias_Ref-Time] fragment in {}, you have a set that you can take the first tuple/member out of with .Item(0), from which we will get the set of last 12 members.

Summary

Named sets are a simple, powerful, and standard facility for a set to be constructed at the scope of a query or session and used multiple times. Named sets also are used very frequently in queries. Set (and tuple and member) aliases are generally easy to use, very powerful, and not as commonly required as named sets. However, sometimes you must use an alias in order to be able to express the required logic, and sometimes you can achieve dramatic optimization by using their more obscure capabilities. This chapter has covered both these aspects in detail, and you will see them used over and over in the remaining chapters.

Sorting and Ranking in MDX

A very common requirement for analytical applications is providing sorted and ranked views of data. Users are always interested in Top-10 lists, and often in seeing who or what was #1 last month or year. We'll cover the basics of sorting and ranking in this chapter, and also look at some ins and outs for more advanced kinds of sorting and ranking calculations.

Functions used in this chapter are `Order()`, `Hierarchize()`, `TopCount()`, `BottomCount()`, `TopSum()`, `BottomSum()`, `TopPercent()`, `BottomPercent()`, `YTD()`, `CoalesceEmpty()`, `Rank()`, `ParallelPeriod()`, `Generate()`, `Ancestor()`, `Descendants()`, `.Properties()`, `DrillDownLevelTop()`.

The Function Building Blocks

We took a brief look at the `Order()` function in Chapter 1, so we've seen one building block already. The full set of functions provided for sorting and ranking purposes are as follows:

FUNCTION	PURPOSE
`Order()`	Sort a set of tuples
`Hierarchize()`	Sort a set of tuples into hierarchical order.
`TopCount()`	Select the top *N* tuples of a set.
`BottomCount()`	Select the bottom *N* tuples of a set.
`TopSum()`	Select the top tuples of a set whose sum meets a threshold.
`BottomSum()`	Select the bottom *N* tuples of a set whose sum meets a threshold.
`TopPercent()`	Select the tuples of a set corresponding to the top *N*% of all in set.
`BottomPercent()`	Select the tuples of a set corresponding to the bottom *N*% of all in set.
`Rank()`	Find the ordinal position of a tuple in a set.

Note that all of these functions operate on sets of tuples, not just one-dimensional sets of members. The following are additionally provided, and are intended to help support GUI interaction, although any MDX-based application may use them. (They are only mentioned briefly within the chapter.)

`DrillDownLevelTop()`	Drills down on members of a specified level in a set; adds only the top-*N* members.
`DrillDownLevelBottom()`	Drills down on members of a specified level in a set; adds only the bottom-*N* members.
`DrillDownMemberTop()`	Drills down on specified members in a set; adds only the top-*N* children.
`DrillDownMemberBottom()`	Drills down on specified members in a set; adds only the bottom-*N* children.

Classic Top-*N* Selections

The `TopCount()` function is what we would use to create a classic Top-10 list (or Top-*N*). Its syntax is as follows:

```
TopCount (set [ , numeric_expression ] )
```

The optional *numeric_expression* gives the number of tuples to take, and it returns up to that many from the *set*, in order from largest to smallest. Here is a query to return the top 5 product subcategories for the whole quarter in the Northeast, and the results are shown in Figure 6-1:

```
SELECT
{ [Measures].[Dollar Sales] } on columns,
TopCount (
  [Product].[Subcategory].Members,
  5,
  [Measures].[Dollar Sales]
) on rows
FROM [Sales]
WHERE ([Q2, 2005], [Northeast])
```

Note that the members are returned in order from largest Dollar Sales to smallest.

Ranking queries often require a total across the top *N*, and also a total of all others, so you can see how the top 10 performed as a group and compare to all others not in the group. This is a perfect case to use a named set, so we only run the ranking operation once and use its results multiple times. Let's update the last query to incorporate a set total and an all-other total. The fastest way to calculate the all-other total is not to figure out the set of all-other members and total across that, but rather to subtract the top-10 group total from the [All Product] total, which was automatically aggregated. (Remember to leverage precalculated aggregates wherever you can!)

```
WITH
SET [TopSelection] AS
'TopCount (
  [Product].Levels(2).Members,
  5,
  [Measures].[Dollar Sales]
)'
MEMBER [Product].[Total] AS
'Sum ([TopSelection])'
MEMBER [Product].[All Others] AS
'[Product].[All Product] - [Product].[Total]'
SELECT
{ [Measures].[Dollar Sales] } on columns,
{
[TopSelection],
[Product].[Total], [Product].[All Others]
} on rows
FROM WM2005.Sales
WHERE [Q2, 2004]
```

	Dollar Sales
Baseball	29,930.05
Coolers	28,994.72
Foot Massagers, Spas	27,085.48
CD Players	24,589.87
Upgrades	23,941.65

Figure 6-1   Top-5 query result.

The standard behavior for `TopCount()` is to always return as many tuples as you specify, unless the input set had fewer to begin with. Suppose that the set is larger than N, but you have fewer associated data cells that had any data in them. The topmost tuples will be associated with data, while the remaining ones will have no data associated with them but still be in the set. Users often don't want to see the Top-10 list containing 10 items if only 8 had data and the other 2 are arbitrary blank choices. They'd rather see the list trimmed down to just the eight that had data. So, unless you're confident the data is dense enough, you may want to filter the data set. The standard means to do this is to rank on the results of a filter:

```
TopCount ( Filter ( the set, Not IsEmpty (criterion ) ) ), 10, criterion)
TopCount ( Filter ( the set, criterion <> 0 ) ) ), 10, criterion)
```

In Analysis Services 2005 and 2000, you may get much better performance with the following, so long as you don't have real zero values that you also want to remove:

```
TopCount ( NonEmptyCrossJoin(the set, criterion-measure), 10, criterion)
TopCount ( NonEmpty(the set, criterion-measure), 10, criterion)
```

	Dollar Sales
Baseball	29,930.05
Coolers	28,994.72
Foot Massagers, Spas	27,085.48
CD Players	24,589.87
Upgrades	23,941.65
Total	134,541.77
All Others	1,637,019.83

Figure 6-2   Top-5 query result with group total and "All-Others" total.

MISSING VALUES IN ESSBASE SORTING AND RANK SELECTIONS

By default, Essbase strips tuples with associated missing values from a set during sorting and ranking operations. To include these, you would need to use the `CoalesceEmpty()` function to put them in your preferred place. The following would virtually guarantee them to be at the end:

```
TopCount ( the set, CoalesceEmpty( criterion, -1.0e+38))
```

Because this works on tuples, you can use the following to take the top 100 brand-channel combinations in terms of year-to-date units sold:

```
TopCount (
  CrossJoin(
    [Product].[Brand].Members,
    [Channel].[Channel ID].Members
  ),
  100,
  Sum (
    YTD(),
    [Measures].[Unit Sales]
  )
)
```

Adding Ranking Numbers (Using the Rank() function)

Sometimes a report needs to return the actual rank number (1, 2, 3, and so on). Furthermore, rank numbers may be necessary sometimes because the members are being returned in another order. For example, salespeople may be ranked both for this year and last year, or the top-10 suppliers returned in terms of delivery times could have their cost rankings reported as a measure. Note that Analysis Services 2005 has changed the behavior of a Microsoft extension to `Rank()` from its behavior in the 2000 version. The change may be more convenient, with perhaps no major difference in performance, and we will highlight this. (Note also that Essbase 9 does not support the `Rank()` function, although future releases may.)

Let's report on the top 10 suppliers in terms of delivery time (shorter time is better) and their cost rankings. The `[Cost Ranking]` will be a calculated member in the query. MDX offers us the `Rank()` function, which returns the index that a tuple has in a set. We can sort our suppliers by costs and use that as the set within which to rank them. Rank counts start at one, so the first one will be our #1-costing supplier. We don't want to sort the suppliers over and over again, so we'll define a named set to hold the sorted suppliers. Notice that we sort in descending order, so the highest-cost supplier is at position #1, and we break the hierarchy so that the order is meaningful:

```
WITH
SET [Cost-Ordered Suppliers] AS
'Order (
  [Supplier].[Supplier].Members,
  ([Measures].[Total Cost]),
  BDESC
)'
MEMBER [Measures].[Cost Ranking] AS
'Rank (
  [Supplier].CurrentMember,
  [Cost-Ordered Suppliers]
)', FORMAT_STRING = '#;#;-'
SELECT
{ [Measures].[Delivery Time], [Measures].[Cost Ranking] } on columns,
{ BottomCount (
  [Supplier].[Supplier].Members,
  10,
  [Measures].[Delivery Time]
) } on rows
FROM [Purchasing]
WHERE [Time].[Year].[2004]
```

We chose `BottomCount()` instead of `TopCount()` because the business problem wanted the top performers, which is opposite of those that have the top times! BottomCount() is like the reverse of TopCount(). It returns the bottom *N* tuples from the set, ordered from smallest to largest. The supplier with the lowest time appears first in the list.

Note that the cost ranking returned from this query for each supplier is that supplier's rank among all suppliers in the database, not among the set of 10. If we only wanted to take the cost ranking among the 10, then we would rephrase the query like this:

```
WITH
SET [Delivery-Ordered Suppliers] AS
'BottomCount (
  [Supplier].[Supplier].Members,
  10,
  ([Measures].[Delivery Time])
)'
MEMBER [Measures].[Cost Ranking] AS
'Rank (
  [Supplier].CurrentMember,
  [Delivery-Ordered Suppliers]   // our 10 suppliers
)', FORMAT_STRING = '#;#;-'
SELECT
{ [Measures].[Total Cost], [Measures].[Cost Ranking] } on columns,
{ [Delivery-Ordered Suppliers] } on rows
FROM [Purchasing]
WHERE [Time].[Year].[2004]
```

Now, let's tackle a more demanding yet very real-life query. Let's say that you need to generate a report which lists the top-10 salespeople according to the year-to-date units sold, their ranking number according to those units, their previous year's rank, and the difference in units sold between year-to-date and the previous year's YTD.

You need to derive the year-to-date units sold to calculate this. You're also going to take the ranking of the 10 salespeople within an ordered set of all salespeople, so you should name that ordered set. Let's assume that the time dimension is marked as being a time dimension and that the year level in it is tagged as being a year-typed level, so that you can make use of the YTD() function as well:

```
WITH
// define our year-to-date units count
MEMBER [Measures].[YTD Units Count] AS
'Sum(YTD(), [Measures].[Units Sold])'
// define a set of ordered salespeople for repeated references
// break the hierarchy, and put the top-valued ones first in the list
SET [Last Year Ordered SalesPeople] AS
'Order (
  [SalesPerson].[Individual].Members,
  ([Measures].[YTD Units Count], ParallelPeriod ([Time].[Year],1)),
  BDESC
)'
MEMBER [Measures].[Previous Year Rank] AS
'Rank (
  [SalesPerson].CurrentMember,
  [Last Year Ordered SalesPeople]
)', FORMAT_STRING = '#;#;-'
SET [This Year Top 10 SalesPeople] AS
'TopCount (
  [SalesPerson].[Individual].Members,
  10,
  [Measures].[YTD Units Count]
)'
MEMBER [Measures].[This Year Rank] AS
'Rank (
  [SalesPerson].CurrentMember,
  [This Year Top 10 SalesPeople]
)', FORMAT_STRING = '#;#;-'
MEMBER [Measures].[YTD Units Change] as
'[YTD Units Count] -
  ([YTD Units Count], ParallelPeriod ([Time].[Year],1))'
SELECT
{ [Measures].[This Year Rank], [Measures].[YTD Units Count],
  [Measures].[Previous Year Rank], [Measures].[YTD Units Change]
} on columns,
{ [This Year Top 10 SalesPeople] } on rows
FROM Sales
WHERE ([Time].[Aug. 2004])
```

Note that the WHERE clause defines August 2004 to be the date that the year-to-date accumulates all the values to.

TIP Rank() returns 0 when the tuple isn't found in the set. In reports like these, users will probably want to see a blank or a symbol like - to indicate "not found." You can use a format string that replaces zero values with the appropriate indicator in these calculated members. Each of the examples in this section will display a dash (-) instead of 0. See Appendix D for format code details.

Handling Tied Ranks: Analysis Services

What if there's a tie for third place in the top 10? You want to see 3 for each of the tuples in positions 3, 4, and 5, and then you want to see "6" for the tuple in position 6. As an extension to the standard, Analysis Services supports an optional third argument to Rank() that is the sort criteria expression used to sort the set. The semantics for this function have changed between Analysis Services 2000 and 2005. When the expression is provided, it is used to determine if ties exist and what the right rank should be. In Analysis Services 2000, the expression was used when the tuple was found to search neighbors in the set and determine fair ranking numbers. For example, if you had defined the rank calculated members above as the following, you would get fair scoring across the salespeople:

```
MEMBER [Measures].[Previous Year Rank] AS
'Rank (
  [Last Year Ordered SalesPeople],
  [SalesPerson].CurrentMember,
  ([Measures].[YTD Units Count], ParallelPeriod ([Time].[Year],1))
)'
...
MEMBER [Measures].[This Year Rank] AS
'Rank (
  [This Year Top 10 SalesPeople],
  [SalesPerson].CurrentMember,
  [Measures].[YTD Units Count]
)'
```

With these semantics, regardless of whether the set is sorted in ascending or descending order in terms of the expression, the rank numbers reflect tied ordering from the first item. The set was not actually ordered in any way by the Rank() function, so if it wasn't sorted by the expression, then you may or may not get the results you wanted.

In Analysis Services 2005, this extended version of the Rank() function does sort the set, in ascending order. This means two things:

1. You don't actually need to sort the set prior to calling Rank() on it.

2. Whether or not you pass it a sorted set, you need to take the negative of the sort criteria to get the rank number in terms of descending order.

For example, the following rephrases the foregoing example to use the new semantics (note the unary negation operator, -, being used):

```
MEMBER [Measures].[Previous Year Rank] AS
'Rank (
  [Last Year Ordered SalesPeople],
  [SalesPerson].CurrentMember,
  - ([Measures].[YTD Units Count], ParallelPeriod ([Time].[Year],1))
)'
...
MEMBER [Measures].[This Year Rank] AS
'Rank (
  [This Year Top 10 SalesPeople],
  [SalesPerson].CurrentMember,
  - [Measures].[YTD Units Count]
)'
```

Taking the Top-*N* Descendants or Other Related Members across a Set

A single ranked report is as easy as our first example. However, you may need to build a more general report, where you need to drill down on a set of members that is selected by other logic in the query. We have two ways to do this:

■ Employ the DrillDownLevelTop() function or one of its kin: DrillDownLevelBottom(), DrillDownMemberTop(), Drill-DownMemberBottom().

■ Use Generate() to repeat the TopCount() function over the set.

DrillDownLevelTop() is tailor-made if you only need the top/bottom children, and is more convenient if the set has more than one dimension in it. It's really well-suited to a graphical user interface (GUI) that provides a top-*N* drill function, which may not have full knowledge of how the set was constructed in the first place. Otherwise, the for-each capability of Generate() can be used here. (Note that Essbase 9 does not support the DrillDownXXXTop/Bottom functions.) For example, let's say that you want the top three product subcategories for each product family. You can express that with the following:

```
SELECT { [Measures].[Dollar Sales] } on axis(0),
Generate (
  [Product].[Family].Members,
  {[Product].CurrentMember,
   TopCount (
     Descendants (
        [Product].CurrentMember,
        [Product].[Subcategory]
     ),
     3,
     [Measures].[Dollar Sales]
  )}
)
on axis(1)
FROM [Sales]
```

Note that Generate() returns the family-level member followed by the top three results by creating a set using {}.

What if you want to add group totals to the Top-3 lists here? See Chapter 7 for the techniques.

To simply drill from our family members down to the top three children each, the DrillDownLevelTop() function could hardly be easier:

```
SELECT { [Measures].[Dollar Sales] } on axis(0),
DrillDownLevelTop (
  [Product].[Family].Members,
  3,
  ,    // intentionally blank
  [Measures].[Dollar Sales]
)
on axis(1)
FROM [Sales]
```

The empty third argument to the function tells it to drill down on the members at the lowest level in the set (which is all of them because they're all at the same depth in the hierarchy).

You can employ the Generate() function to take the top N of the top N as well, for example, the top five products for each of the top five customers as shown in the following query; the results are shown in Figure 6-3:

```
Generate (
  TopCount (
    [Customer].[Cust ID].Members,
    5,
    [Measures].[Dollar Sales]
```

```
  ),
  CrossJoin (
    { Customer.CurrentMember },
    TopCount (
      [Product].[Subcategory].Members,
      5,
      [Measures].[Dollar Sales]
    )
  ),
  ALL
)
```

		Dollar Sales
667900	Camp Kitchen	36,447.40
	Tents	36,337.90
	Razor Accessories	35,936.50
	Construction	17,705.10
	Action Figures	11,149.10
507450	Games	27,323.50
	Musical	25,131.80
	Baseball	21,104.50
	Blank Media	21,067.50
	CD Players	13,330.70
465300	Cordless Phones With Call	30,601.40
	Headphones	26,872.80
	Garage Door Openers	23,697.80
	Cordless Phones	21,234.30
	Weights	12,791.20
450850	Pools, Pumps	33,520.00
	Rainwear	23,620.90
	Medical Supplies	18,807.80
	Trampolines	18,237.10
	Camp Furniture	16,075.70
479600	Vitamins, Nutrition	38,006.90
	DVD Players	30,529.60
	Electrical Shop	18,907.00
	GamePlace	4,057.40
	Bags	3,751.20

Figure 6-3 Result of Top-5 of Top-5 query.

Getting the Fewest/Most Tuples to Reach a Threshold

Suppose that you want to find the smallest set of products to focus your efforts on in order to reach some target of sales. Or, you want to obtain the largest set of customers for which the total cost to reach them does not exceed some threshold. Another pair of functions, `TopSum()` and `BottomSum()`, rank and select tuples based on a threshold value, and can be used to solve selection problems like the ones described. The syntax of TopSum() and BottomSum() is

```
TopSum (set [, numeric_expression] )
BottomSum  (set [, numeric_expression] )
```

The optional *numeric_expression* provides the target to which values of the set are summed.

Using `TopSum()` is straightforward. For example, the following selects the top products that will meet the expected quota of $5,000,000:

```
TopSum (
  [Product].[Category].members,
  5000000,
  ([Measures].[Dollar Sales], [Scenario].[Quota])
)
```

`BottomSum()` is almost as straightforward. Depending on your application, you may or may not want to exceed the threshold. If you want to include the last tuple that causes you to exceed your threshold, it is just as simple. If you want to get the group of the smallest such that you do *not* exceed your budget, you need to trim the last tuple from the returned set only if the sum was greater than your target. Also, it's almost guaranteed that you want to trim tuples with related values that are missing. You would want to trim the tuples from the input to `BottomSum()`, and you can only remove the extra tuple on the results. So, you would compose MDX like the following for Analysis Services:

```
Head (
  BottomSum (
    NonEmptyCrossJoin (
      [Customer].[City].members,
      {[Measures].[Ad Budget]},
      1
    )
```

```
      5000000,
      [Measures].[Ad Budget]
   ) AS [A],
   Iif (
      Sum ([A], [Measures].[Ad Budget]) > 5000000,
      [A].Count - 1,
      [A].Count
   )
)
```

Note that the set alias [A] is used to refer to the results of BottomSum(), so you don't need to run BottomSum() more than once, and you don't need to create a named set outside of the Head().

NOTE Essbase only supports Count() syntax but does filter out empty values, so the following would be the equivalent:

```
Head (
   BottomSum (
      [Customer].[City].members,
      5000000,
      [Measures].[Ad Budget]
   ) AS [A],
   Iif (
      Sum ([A], [Measures].[Ad Budget]) > 5000000,
      Count ([A], INCLUDEEMPTY) - 1,
      Count ([A], INCLUDEEMPTY)
   )
)
```

BottomSum() (and BottomPercent(), described next) are the ranking functions from which you will most likely want to strip empty and/or zero values.

BOTTOMSUM() AND TOPSUM() USUALLY WANT POSITIVE NUMBERS

While you use BottomSum() to accumulate the set associated with the smallest numbers, note that the function sums values tuples until the sum is greater than the threshold. If your target is positive, summing negative numbers gets you farther away from the goal, not nearer to it. If your target is negative, then you'll either start off above your goal, or you will never get any closer.

Retrieving the Top *N* Percent of Tuples

While many reports are interested in the top *N* tuples, the components of the top *N* percent are also quite useful for understanding true business drivers. (The top 10 customers may account for only 5 percent of the business, which is important but doesn't help you address the 80/20 picture.) The TopPercent() and BottomPercent() functions let you directly request a proportional threshold. The syntax for these functions is

```
TopPercent (set [, numeric_expression] )
BottomPercent  (set [, numeric_expression] )
```

TopPercent() returns the largest values required to hit the percentage, in descending order, while BottomPercent() returns the smallest values required to hit the percentage, in ascending order.

For example, you can determine the top 20 percent of customers in terms of dollar sales with the following:

```
TopPercent (
   [Customer].[Customer ID].Members,
   20,
   [Measures].[Dollar Sales]
)
```

The result set may have one customer, or it may contain many customers.

This is the beginning of Pareto analysis. There are other parts of really providing insight into the 80/20 populations, and we will describe another part of constructing 80/20 reports in Chapter 7.

Retrieving the Top *N* Percent of the Top *N* Percent

When you are attempting to understand business drivers, you may need to see drivers of more than one dimension. For example, once you know the top 20 percent of customers in terms of sales, you may want to understand the top 20 percent of products for each of the customers. This is another case where you see the phrase "for each" in the business statement of the problem and reach for the Generate() function. Say that you want to see the top 20 percent of customers, and for each of them you want to see the total across all products and the top 30 percent of product categories for each customer. The query looks very similar to the one we used for the top *N* of the top *N* earlier:

```
SELECT
{ [Measures].[Dollar Sales] } on axis(0),
Generate (
  TopPercent (
```

```
      [Customer].[Customer ID].members,
      20,
      [Measures].[Dollar Sales]
   ),
   CrossJoin (
      { [Customer].CurrentMember },
      { [Product].[All Product],
        TopPercent (
           [Product].[Category].Members,
           30,
           [Measures].[Dollar Sales]
      ) }
   )
)
on axis(1)
FROM [Sales]
```

One notable difference is that you see `CrossJoin()` used here. Remember from Chapter 1 that you can't make a set of tuples without using it. You want to return (Customer, Product) combinations, where customer is a single member, but product is a list. So, you `CrossJoin()` the current customer, which is one of the top 20 percent, with the set of products, to produce the combinations.

A more sophisticated analysis would look at the products across these customers, and we will continue the example in Chapter 7 to see how you can extract more relevant business information from this selection.

Putting Members/Tuples in Dimension Order (Ancestors First or Last)

There are a number of reasons that you might want to arrange a set of members (or tuples) into the order defined by the dimension(s). They may have been picked via a GUI and sequenced in the order in which they were picked. They may have been selected by one of the ranking functions here. And you may be looking to incorporate parents or ancestors, either to include database aggregates, to include Analysis Services visual totals (discussed in Chapter 7), or to enable more coherent drill-up/drill-down. You may simply be trying to get higher-level aggregates to appear below their children, for example on a financial statement. All of these cases are handled by using the `Hierarchize()` function.

Syntactically, Hierarchize() simply takes a set and returns the set put into hierarchical order. The default and standard behavior is to put parents before children as well. Both Analysis Services and Essbase take an additional option flag (POST) that specifies that parents should follow children, as in a financial statement.

The following simply takes the Terms dimension's members and puts parents after children:

```
Hierarchize (
  [Terms].Members,
  POST
)
```

Let's say that you want to drill up from the top 25 product subcategories, instead of drilling down on product families to the top three subcategories each. Once again, you use Generate(), as shown in the following expression:

```
Hierarchize(
  Generate (
    TopCount (
      [Product].[Subcategory].Members,
      25,
      [Measures].[Dollar Sales]
    ),
    { Ancestor(
        [Product].CurrentMember,
        [Product].[Family]
      ),
      [Product].CurrentMember
    }
  )
)
```

Instead of concatenating a product with its descendants as in the earlier example, you concatenate the ancestor of the product with the product. It doesn't matter whether the ancestor comes first or second, because Hierarchize() is going to sort things afterwards.

However, you may be asking, "Why don't we get duplicates? Can't two subcategories have the same family?" Yes, two subcategories can have the same category, but by default, Generate() strips duplicate values from the set it returns. So, there's no harm in putting the ancestor in twice or more.

Reversing a Set

One technical need that comes up occasionally is reversing a set. There is no direct general way to do this in standard MDX. Depending on the origin of the set, you might be able to just sort them, or else you can use the Rank() function. You can't use the Hierarchize(,POST) function, because that only reverses the order of parents relative to children. Members are still within dimension order overall. In Analysis Services, it's perhaps better done using a stored procedure or external function. You will look at the stored procedure method in Chapter 10. However, maybe you don't have the ability to add a stored procedure, and you need a pure-MDX solution. In Analysis Services, if the set is in the dimension's hierarchical ordering, you can reverse it by sorting on the intrinsic ID property. For example, the following would sort a collection of time members into reverse-hierarchical order (the extra TYPED argument was introduced with AS2005):

```
Order (
  [Time].[2006].Children,
  [Time].CurrentMember.Properties ("ID", TYPED),
  BDESC
)
```

Otherwise, you sort on the rank:

```
Order (
  [Time].[2006].Children,
  Rank( [Time].CurrentMember, [Time].[2006].Children),
  BDESC
)
```

In Analysis Services 2005, you can make use of the .CurrentIndex function to reverse a set without resorting to sorting. The following would accomplish the task (notice that you need to use a named set or alias as the argument for .CurrentIndex):

```
Generate (
  [Time].[2006].Children AS [Alias_Children],
  [Alias_Children].Item (
    [Alias_Children].Count - [Alias_Children].CurrentIndex - 1
  ),
  ALL
)
```

Summary

The sorting and ranking functions directly implement a large number of user requests. Somewhat more advanced requests are readily satisfied by combining these functions with other functions like Generate(), CrossJoin(), and others that are part of the core "moving parts" of MDX. Hopefully, this chapter has both introduced you to the ranking and sorting functions and deepened your capacity for translating user requirements into MDX compositions. The next chapter will start the real focus on patterns of MDX and how to combine component expressions into elegant assemblies of high value to the users.

CHAPTER 7

Advanced MDX Application Topics

In the last four chapters, you have looked at basic calculations and selections in MDX, and expanded the vocabulary of functions and operators with which you can compose expressions. In this chapter, we are going to put together the pieces in many more ways, working through some more advanced concepts and techniques. Many of these come from assistance the author has given to other MDX users over the last seven years, so if some seem esoteric at first, remember that MDX has many different applications!

The same problem may be solved in multiple ways in MDX. The point of this chapter is both to give you a reference to solutions to many common and/or advanced requirements, and to increase your prowess in "thinking in MDX." So, alternatives will be presented when there are interesting differences in approach. Since there are important differences in the capabilities of the three product versions that this book refers to, we will also explore product-specific differences in ways of constructing the expressions that achieve the goal where relevant. As you read through this chapter, you will start to see recurring patterns in the way the various moving parts of MDX are assembled.

The expressions and queries in this chapter are oriented more toward the composition of whole analytical queries, and the principles that go into constructing them are useful for constructing all manner of sophisticated analyses, even if the particular examples presented in this section do not address the applications you are going to build.

The types of expressions and queries explored here are

- Arranging parents/ancestors after children, not before
- Using `Generate()` to turn tuple operations into set operations
- Returning the subtree under a member and the ancestors of that member along with the member
- Calculating dates and date arithmetic
- Defining ratios against the members selected on rows/columns/axes, instead of against a specific dimension
- Report totals-to-parent, totals-to-ancestor, and percentage contribution to report totals
- Hierarchical sorting that skips levels in the hierarchy
- Sorting a single set on multiple criteria
- Multiple layers or dimensions of sorting
- Pareto analysis and cumulative sums
- Returning the top-selling product (or other most significant name) as a measure
- Most recent event for a set of selected members
- Building a set that sums backward in time
- Aggregating by multiplication (Product instead of Sum)
- One formula calculating different things in different places (also called "formula application ranges")
- Including all tuples with tied ranking in sets
- Including generic time-series analysis dimensions in cubes

After working through these expressions and queries, we will apply the same principles for using MDX that we discuss here in a complete series of analytical queries.

The functions and operators that are used or described in this chapter include `Hierarchize()`, `Union()`, `Intersect()`, `CrossJoin()`, `Ancestor()`, `Ascendants()`/`Ancestors()`, `Generate()`, `Rank()`, `.Count`/`Count()`, `.Properties()`, `StrToMember()`, `Axis()`, `.Item()`, `.CurrentMember`, `.Parent`, `.Dimension`, `VisualTotals()`, `Avg()`, `Sum()`, `IsAncestor()`, `IS`, `Order()`, `.Members`, `.FirstSibling`, `.Siblings`, `Head()`, `Tail()`, `TopCount()`, `NonEmpty()`, `NonEmptyCrossJoin()`, `Filter()`, `IsEmpty()`, `iif()`, `CASE`, `.Ordinal`/`Ordinal()`, `.Level`, and `.Generations()`.

Arranging Parents/Ancestors after Children, Not Before

By default, when you get a set of members from metadata, each parent precedes its children. Functions like `Descendants()`, `DrillDownMember()`, and their ilk also place children or descendants after parents. Note that the `Hierarchize()` function takes an optional `POST` flag in both AS and Essbase, so the following puts parents/ancestors after their children:

```
Hierarchize (the_set_to_arrange, POST)
```

Returning the Subtree under a Member and the Ancestors of That Member Along with the Member

This just requires composing two different metadata ranges: the descendants of the member, and the ancestors of the member. The `Union()` function gets rid of any duplicates from the set by default (we leave out the `ALL` flag), and `Hierarchize()` makes sure that it is in appropriate hierarchical order. Between Analysis Services and Essbase, there is a slight difference in the functions that you use. In Analysis Services, you use `Ascendants()`, while in Essbase you use `Ancestors()`. The selection is phrased as follows. In Analysis Services:

```
Hierarchize (
  Union (
    Descendants (target_member),
    Ascendants (target_member)
  )
)
```

In Essbase:

```
Hierarchize(
  Union (
   Descendants (target_member),
   Ancestors (target_member, target_member.Generations(1))
  )
)
```

The `Descendants()` function, with just the single member as an argument, retrieves all descendants of the member. The `Ascendants()` function retrieves all ancestors, whereas the Essbase `Ancestors()` function retrieves members from the given member up to the layer specified in the second argument. Both of these return parents after children, so `Hierarchize()` is necessary to put all the members in the same order. Although the reference member is returned from both, the default behavior of `Union()` strips out duplicates. You can express `Distinct( {Descendants(...), Ascendants(...)} )` as well.

Using Generate() to Turn Tuple Operations into Set Operations

How do I get the descendants, ancestors, children, and so on from a set of members?

Most of the standard MDX functions and operators that return members based on hierarchical references (such as `Descendants()`, `Ancestor()`, and the like) only take a single member for their input. However, you may find that you need to take the descendants or ancestors for a set of members. The way to accomplish this is to use `Generate()` around the function or operator to get it to return the set that you want.

For example, say that you want to take the average of a measure over a set of day-level descendants for a set of quarters or months that the user has chosen. The following query is tempting but will not work:

```
WITH
SET InterestingMonths AS
'LastPeriods ([Time].[Month].[Apr 2000], 3)'
MEMBER [Time].[AverageVal] AS
'Avg (
  Descendants (
    [InterestingMonths],    // problem! (except as in note)
    [Time].[Day]
  )
)', SOLVE_ORDER = 10
SELECT ...
```

Instead, you need to define `[Time].[AverageVal]` as

```
'Avg (
  Generate (
    [InterestingMonths],
    Descendants (
      [Time].CurrentMember,
      [Time].[Day]
    )
  )
)', SOLVE_ORDER = 10
```

which loops over each given time period (be it a month, a quarter, or even a day) and produces the related day members. You'll see another example of this use of Generate() in the "Report-Based Totals-to-Parent" section later in this chapter.

NOTE Beginning with Analysis Services 2000, Service Pack 3, the first argument to Descendants() **can be a set as well as a single member, with behavior equivalent to running** Generate(..., Descendants (), ALL) **on it. So, you can indeed express:**

```
WITH
SET InterestingMonths AS
'LastPeriods ([Time].[Month].[Apr 2000], 3)'
MEMBER [Time].[AverageVal] AS
'Avg (
  Descendants (
    [InterestingMonths],    // Not a problem in AS2000 SP3+)
    [Time].[Day]
  )
)', SOLVE_ORDER = 10
```

Calculating Dates/Date Arithmetic

Sometimes, an application calls for calculating values based on dates. Perhaps you need to calculate the number of days between two dates, or the number of days between a date-valued measure or member property and a day member in a cube. Perhaps you need to calculate the number of weekdays between two day-level members (or in a month, which works out to nearly the same thing). Or, perhaps you need to calculate an expected date for something. SQL has a fairly rigorous definition of dates and a set of date calculation functions built in. Standard MDX provides no special date/time calculation functionality. Analysis Services does not contain a notion of a date/time data type, but numeric measures and member properties can hold or represent date/time values that ActiveX external functions and .NET stored procedures can manipulate. Essbase allows member properties to be declared as having a date type, and provides a function for converting formatted date strings into numbers in the internal format.

As usual, these calculations can be implemented in more than one way. Depending on your database design, your MDX will look different.

NOTE All of the examples here are assuming a U.S. locale for constructing and parsing text representations of date values. If you are implementing in Europe, Canada, or elsewhere, you will need to adjust for our assumptions.

If you are simply trying to calculate the number of days between two day-level members, and every day in the calendar has a corresponding day in the database, then you just need to count the members.

```
{ First_Day : Last_Day }.Count  // Analysis Services
Count({ First_Day : Last_Day })  // Essbase
```

is a brief expression that performs the count of the days (and you could subtract one from it to get the number of days in between the first and last days).

Other types of date-related calculations can rely on VBA (Visual Basic for Applications) or Excel functions. For example, let's say that you are trying to count the weeks between two dates. The VBA DateDiff() function can directly calculate this number, so you only need to pass the two dates into it. Assuming that the date stamp for the day members is stored as the Date-Stamp member property of the time members, you can retrieve it as a date stamp datatype for input to DateDiff() either by using the TYPED flag in AS2005 or by using the VBA CDate() function. You can simply define the member (in the WITH clause of a query) as:

```
MEMBER [Measures].[WeeksBetween] AS
 'VBA!DateDiff (
   "ww",  // this tells it to calculate weeks
   [Time].[Day1].Properties ("DateStamp", TYPED),  // AS2005
   CDate ([Time].[Day2].Properties ("DateStamp"))  // AS2000
 )'
```

(The VBA! prefix makes explicit which library the DateDiff() function is being called from; we discuss this notation in Chapter 10.) This will only produce one number. To count the number of weeks between a particular day and each day returned in a query, define the member as:

```
MEMBER [Measures].[WeeksBetween] AS
 'VBA!DateDiff (
   "ww",
   [Time].[Day1].Properties ("DateStamp", TYPED),
   [Time].CurrentMember.Properties ("DateStamp", TYPED)
 )'
```

Note that if the members are the DateStamp attribute members themselves, or you have assigned the date stamp as a member value for the members, you can also use .MemberValue to retrieve the value, as in the following:

```
[Time].CurrentMember.MemberValue
```

Let's say that the starting date is a member property of the customer dimension that refers to the date the customer enrolled in the organization, named [Date Enrolled]. Then, for each customer you could get the number of weeks the customer has been enrolled. The `[Time].[Day1].Proper-ties("DateStamp")` in these expressions would be replaced by `[Cus-tomer].CurrentMember.Properties ("Date Enrolled")`. If you ever need to reference measures at the date the customer enrolled, then as long as you have unique names across all levels of the time dimension and the format of the string stored in `[Date Enrolled]` matches the format of your time member names (that is, "May 11, 2000"), you could substitute `StrToMember ("[Time].[ " + [Customer].CurrentMember.Properties ("Date Enrolled") + "]")` for `[Time].[Day1]` in the preceding examples. For example, the following provides an expression for Weeks Enrolled and one for Opening Purchase Amount:

```
MEMBER [Measures].[Weeks Enrolled] AS
'iif (
  [Customer].CurrentMember.Properties ("Date Enrolled", TYPED)
  > [Time].CurrentMember.Properties ("DateStamp", TYPED),
  NULL,
  VBA!DateDiff (
    "ww",
    [Customer].CurrentMember.Properties ("Date Enrolled", TYPED)
    [Time].CurrentMember.Properties ("DateStamp", TYPED)
  )
)'
MEMBER [Measures].[Opening Purchase Amount] AS
'( [Measures].[Dollar Sales],
   StrToMember ( "[Time].["
     + [Customer].CurrentMember.Properties ("Date Enrolled")
     + "]"
   )
)'
```

If you were thinking about using the `LinkMember()` function, note that `LinkMember` serves a different purpose: mapping the same member from one dimension to another. (If you weren't thinking about the `LinkMember()` function, go look it up in Appendix A right now.)

Note also that .NET stored procedures can return members, giving you a way to apply any logic you can code into one to the problem of calculating a time member (or member of any other dimension, for that matter).

TIP Using unique names across the members of a time dimension (for example, `[2001]`, `[Q2, 2001]`, `[May, 2001]`, and `[May 11, 2001]`) makes it easier to perform date translations in MDX. Analysis Services 2005 unique names are a bit more complex than Analysis Services 2000 unique names, but when you know the naming scheme for members in your time dimension(s), you can adjust your name construction functions to match it.

Another variation on this occurs when you are forming a query that involves a set of days from the time dimension, perhaps not every day but some days (for example, December 4, 5, 6, 9, and 10, 2004). If you want to find out how many calendar days are between the first and the last day members in the query, then you need to extract those members and plug them into the kinds of expressions that we have been looking at.

Let's assume that you simply need to calculate a time member that returns the span of days represented by the set. This is directly supported both by VBA libraries and by the Essbase built-in functions, so we'll look at it for both products. In Analysis Services, the VBA `DateDiff()` function comes in handy in this example:

```
WITH
SET [Times] AS
'{ [Dec 04, 2004], [Dec 05, 2004], [Dec 06, 2004], [Dec 09, 2004], [Dec
10, 2004] }'
MEMBER [Time].[DaysInQuery] AS
'VBA!DateDiff  (
  "d",
  CDate (
    [Times].Item(0).Item(0).Properties ("DateStamp")
  ),
  CDate (
    [Times].Item ([Times].Count - 1).Item(0).Properties ("DateStamp")
  )
)'
```

In Essbase, once you have an attribute of type Date, it is stored internally as a day number, so calculating the span of days just involves subtracting one from another, as in the following:

```
MEMBER [Time].[DaysInQuery] AS
'[Times].Item(0).Item(0).[DateStamp]
- Tail ([Times]).Item(0).Item(0).[DateStamp]'
```

To calculate a date in the future, you once again might want to look at the VBA functions. For example, given a date value and a calculated measure that yields a number of days, you can use the VBA `DateAdd()` function to add the two together. (The result might be converted to a string and returned to the client as a raw value, or it might be used as an argument to the `Members()` or `StrToMember()` functions to look up a time member for further work.)

Defining Ratios against the Members Selected on Rows/Columns/Axes, Instead of against a Specific Dimension

Sometimes, you want to define calculated members that can take ratios or differences based on whatever the user has selected on rows, columns, or some other axis. Then, users can view these measures in any front-end tool, and depending on the dimension(s) they have selected, they'll get the right ratios. There are a couple of common variations to this:

- Ratio-to-parent for members on rows/columns
- Ratio-to-total across rows/columns

Both of these are handled in Analysis Services by using the Axis() function in the calculation. For each case, you need to decide whether you're going to handle having multiple dimensions nested on the axis of interest; if you are, the MDX is slightly different depending on whether you want the outermost or the innermost dimension to be the one relative to which you are taking the ratio.

Let's start off simply. Let's say you want to have a Dollars pct of Row Parent measure, and you'll assume one dimension only on rows. You want to see results like those shown in Figures 7-1 and 7-2. The member definition would look like the following:

```
MEMBER [Measures].[Dollars % of Row Parent] AS
iif (
  ([Measures].[Dollar Sales],
   Axis(1).Item(0).Item (0).Dimension.Currentmember.Parent) = 0,
  NULL,
  [Measures].[Dollar Sales] /
  ([Measures].[Dollar Sales],
   Axis(1).Item(0).Item (0).Dimension.Currentmember.Parent)
), FORMAT_STRING = '0.00%'
```

	Dollar Sales	Dollars % of Row Parent
Beauty	220,250.48	4.80%
Fragrances	447,511.32	9.76%
Health	697,482.38	15.21%
Massagers, Spas	862,653.50	18.81%
Oral Care	836,282.92	18.24%
Personal Care	958,475.44	20.90%
Shaving	562,687.85	12.27%

Figure 7-1 Result of generic axis calculation with products on rows.

	Dollar Sales	Dollars % of Row Parent
AMEX	527,830.02	2.12%
Check	546,206.69	2.20%
COD	183.48	0.00%
GiftCert		
IH-CHG	11,714,896.32	47.08%
MC-VISA	12,092,552.81	48.60%
Other		

Figure 7-2   Result of generic axis calculation with payment terms on rows.

The meat of the formula is the subexpression

```
Axis(1).Item(0).Item (0).Dimension.Currentmember.Parent
```

which means: "take the dimension of the first member in the first tuple of the Axis 1 set, then take the current member of that dimension, and then take its parent." This is just used in a tuple, to be combined with the measure [Dollar Sales]. Otherwise, this is exactly the same kind of ratio-to-parent formula described in Chapter 3. (This formula does assume that measures are not on axis 1, since that would cause an error!) The usual case is to guard against divide-by-zeros, although generally the parent will have a value even when the child doesn't, so it might not be necessary.

NOTE If you defined this member in a CREATE statement in AS2000, you needed to use a string-based syntax (StrToSet ("Axis(1)") .Item(0) ...) because it couldn't handle the fact that the axis didn't exist when the formula was compiled. AS2005 does not have this problem.

While this formula isn't too complicated, it looks like it breaks down when you nest more than one dimension on the rows. Consider what the results look like if you returned results for product families and payment terms, as shown in Figure 7-3. The sum of the percentages for the payment terms in the Doing family is greater than 100 percent. Is there a problem in the ratio?

		Dollar Sales	Dollars % of Row Parent
Beauty	AMEX	5,676.36	5.68%
	Check	3,120.18	2.81%
	IH-CHG	100,410.34	4.67%
	MC-VISA	111,043.60	4.99%
Fragrances	AMEX	11,279.89	11.29%
	Check	11,210.20	10.08%
	IH-CHG	218,167.04	10.15%
	MC-VISA	206,854.19	9.30%
Health	AMEX	16,011.83	16.02%
	Check	20,315.58	18.27%
	COD	68.48	100.00%
	IH-CHG	343,371.44	15.97%

Figure 7-3   Multiple dimensions on rows, problematic ratios.

No, there is a problem in the dimension selected from the axis. Assuming that conventional browser mapping of dimensions to axes, the `.Item(0)` `.Item(0)` subexpression specifies to use the leftmost dimension as the one you're taking the parent for. So, the 20.29% shown in the top row shows that Doing was 20.29 percent of the All-product value for AMEX, not that AMEX was 20 percent of the All-payment term value for Doing. Fortunately, in Analysis Services, you can count the number of dimensions in a tuple with *tuple*.Count, so you can pick the dimension of the innermost dimension on the axis with the following:

```
Axis(1).Item(0).Item ( Axis(1).Item(0).Count - 1)
```

The whole ratio expression now becomes as follows, and you can see the result in Figure 7-4. This is much more intuitive.

```
MEMBER [Measures].[Dollars % of Row Parent] AS
iif (
  ([Measures].[Dollar Sales],
   Axis(1).Item(0).Item (
     Axis(1).Item(0).Count - 1
   ).Dimension.Currentmember.Parent) = 0,
  NULL,
  [Measures].[Dollar Sales] /
  ([Measures].[Dollar Sales],
   Axis(1).Item(0).Item (
     Axis(1).Item(0).Count - 1
   ).Dimension.Currentmember.Parent)
), FORMAT_STRING = '0.00%'
```

		Dollar Sales	Dollars % of Row Parent
Beauty	AMEX	5,676.36	2.58%
	Check	3,120.18	1.42%
	IH-CHG	100,410.34	45.59%
	MC-VISA	111,043.60	50.42%
Fragrances	AMEX	11,279.89	2.52%
	Check	11,210.20	2.51%
	IH-CHG	218,167.04	48.75%
	MC-VISA	206,854.19	46.22%
Health	AMEX	16,011.83	2.30%
	Check	20,315.58	2.91%
	COD	68.48	0.01%
	IH-CHG	343,371.44	49.23%
	MC-VISA	317,715.05	45.55%
Massagers, S	AMEX	18,873.00	2.19%
	Check	19,553.80	2.27%
	IH-CHG	397,771.34	46.11%

Figure 7-4   A better ratio-to-row-parent calculation for multiple dimensions on rows.

NOTE You can't count the number of dimensions in a set directly. Rather, you count the number of dimensions in some tuple in the set. A set's tuples all have the same dimensionality, so picking the 0th tuple is all you need to do. If the set is empty, without tuples, it has no identifiable dimensionality anyway.

Report-Based Totals-to-Parent, Percentage Contribution to Report Totals

Some reports need to provide a subset of children or a subset of descendants for a member, along with a total of those children or descendants. For example, assume that for a group of interesting customers within a sales region, you want to see summary values for them at the city and state level. In addition to seeing the summary values, you want to see the influence of each of them as a percentage of all the interesting customers in that group. Both Analysis Services and Essbase provide intrinsic aggregation of all children to their parents (and all descendants to their ancestors), but this may include many children and descendants that are not part of the query. (In a query of this sort, in MDX you are really creating a proxy set of levels and ancestor members whose names are the same as the database's but who represent a different and interesting subset of the original dimension.) There is more than one way to perform this common report requirement, depending on which product and version you use. This section will explore three ways, to provide you multiple ways to think about solving the problem. Although the first way explained will help build up your repertoire of MDX "moving parts assemblies," if you are using Analysis Services 2005, you may find the third way the easiest.

NOTE You can set a connection property when the client connects to the server (Default MDX Visual Mode) that can automatically set every query to use a `VisualTotals` aggregation for parent members. We describe this in Appendix B.

Technique 1: Only Standard MDX Techniques

To calculate percentage-of-total contributions for each customer in the [InterestingCustomers] set, we need to create calculated members. The percentage-to-total calculation does not belong in the customer dimension. In this case, it is best suited to the measures dimension. For example, consider the following query in the Essbase style, whose results are shown in Figure 7-5 (note that the percentage calculated measure is given SOLVE_ORDER = 5 so that the ratio is calculated on the sum):

```
WITH
SET [InterestingCustomers] AS
'{[Customer].[385150],
  [Customer].[445100],
  [Customer].[511900]
}'
MEMBER [Customer].[Total of Great Falls, MT] AS
'Sum ( [InterestingCustomers])'
MEMBER [Measures].[Pct to Report Sales Total] AS
'[Measures].[Dollar Sales] /
 ([Measures].[Dollar Sales], [Customer].[Total of Great Falls, MT])',
SOLVE_ORDER = 5
SELECT
{ [Measures].[Unit Sales], [Measures].[Dollar Sales],
  [Measures].[Pct to Report Sales Total] } on columns,
{ [Customer].[Great Falls, MT], [Customer].[Total of Great Falls, MT],
[InterestingCustomers] } on rows
FROM [WM2005.Sales]
```

	Unit Sales	Dollar Sales	Pct to Report Sales Total
Great Falls, MT	529	12992.8	110.1%
Total for Great Falls, MT	479	11805.3	100.0%
385150	19	414.2	3.5%
445100	169	3977.3	33.7%
511900	291	7413.8	62.8%

Figure 7-5   Result for report having "pct of report total" calculation.

You can use this approach of creating a named set, a calculated member on the same dimension, and one or more calculated measures for any set of members that aggregate into one member only.

More difficult, however, is when you wish to see a set of descendants and their contributions to ancestors for more than one ancestor. For example, you may have a set of interesting customers in Colorado and Montana. The last approach runs into a few complications when you try to extend it. The [Percent to Report Sales Total] measure hardwires the Great Falls, Montana, ancestor member within it. One way to handle this is to add a separate percentage measure for each ancestor, which is an ugly solution. It would create a set of two measures here, each of which would only have a valid intersection with one of the two state-level members, something we would prefer to avoid. If there were more states, this would get even uglier. In addition, you would need to do other things like generate multiple sets of interesting customers, one for each Explicit Total pseudo-parent.

You can avoid this ugliness if you create a new calculated report total measure and use some of the set manipulation functions provided in MDX. Let's say that you have a set of interesting customers in two different states:

```
SET [InterestingCustomers] AS
'{ [Customer].[385150],   // from MT
   [Customer].[445100],
   [Customer].[511900],
   [Customer].[567500],   // from CO
   [Customer].[491400]
}'
```

Let's also say you wish to get the sum of unit and dollar sales within each of these customers' states, along with the percentage contribution of each customer to that total. You do need to include the ancestor members within the query. If you are starting only with a set of customers, you can do that with Generate() (because Ancestor() only works on members, not on sets). A hierarchically ordered set to be used as one axis of the query could be obtained from an arbitrary set of customers with the following expression:

```
SET [rowset] AS
'Generate (
  Hierarchize (
    [InterestingCustomers],
    { Ancestor(
        [Customer].CurrentMember,
        [Customer].[State]
      ),
      [Customer].CurrentMember
    }
  )
)'
```

Note that Generate() does not include the ALL flag this time; we want to eliminate duplicates of the parents. As far as creating a hierarchical order, this puts the members in hierarchical order and then builds a set where ancestors come first. To put ancestors last, you could either swap the order of the Customer current member and current member's ancestor references in the second part of Generate(), or you could just use Hierarchize(...,POST) on the result of Generate().

The real heart of the query is in the calculated measures that compute the report total of the sales and cost measures. Each is similar. The one for sales can look like this:

```
MEMBER [Measures].[Report Total Sales] AS
'Sum (
  Intersect (
    [InterestingCustomers],
    Descendants (
      [Customer].CurrentMember,
      [Customer].[Cust ID]
    )
  ),
  [Measures].[Dollar Sales]
)'
```

At each customer member, you take the individual customer(s) that corresponds to that customer member. Intersecting that with the customers of interest gives you only the interesting individual customers that are under our customer member. (Or it will give us the interesting customer back, if one of the customers is the current member.) For each state-level member, the sum over that set gives us the report total sales for the interesting customers within that state.

ADVANCED MDX MECHANICS

If you want to try to calculate Report Total Sales as the sum across members in the set whose ancestor is the current member, it's surprisingly contorted. Let's see how. Remember that within the loop of `Sum()`, the customer currentmember will iterate over the members of the set, and you need to compare those to the current member that the sum is being calculated for. The only way to refer to two different current members is once again to use an alias. But how do we capture that? By using `Generate()` again, in a fashion that is fairly obscure but well-suited to this purpose. Look at the following:

```
MEMBER [Measures].[Report Total Sales] AS
'Sum (
  Generate (
    { [Customer].CurrentMember } AS [AliasCurrCust],
    [InterestingCustomers],
    ALL
  ),
  Iif (
    IsAncestor (
      [AliasCurrCust].Item(0).Item(0),
      [Customer].CurrentMember
    )
    OR [AliasCurrCust].Item(0).Item(0) IS
      [Customer].CurrentMember
    [Measures].[Dollar Sales],
    NULL  // MISSING in Essbase
  )
)'
```

The result of `Generate()` is the result of the second set expression. The first set argument to `Generate()` only exists to wrap up the current member in an alias, because the customer current member at that point in execution is the one for which our result is to be calculated.

Within the loop of `Sum()`, you test each member to see if it has the aliased member as an ancestor, and aggregate either the Dollar Sales for that member or `NULL`, depending on the test's success. Note that you can use `IsAncestor (..., ..., INCLUDEMEMBER)` in Essbase to eliminate the OR condition in the test.

Because you are using real state-level members to organize the report total sales, you can simply take the ratio of individual customer sales to the ancestor's Report Total Sales to obtain the percentage of total, only for members of the [Cust ID] level, as in the following code:

```
MEMBER [Measures].[Sales Pct of Report Total] AS
'iif (
  [Customer].CurrentMember.Level.Ordinal
    = [Customer].[Cust ID].Ordinal,  /* Ordinal(...) = Ordinal(...) in
Essbase */
  [Measures].[Dollar Sales] /
    ([Measures].[Report Total Sales],
      Ancestor ([Customer].CurrentMember, [Customer].[State])
    ),
  NULL  /* MISSING in Essbase */
)'
```

So, the whole query rolled together would be as follows (excluding the details of the individual customers), with the query's result shown in Figure 7-6:

```
WITH
SET [InterestingCustomers] AS '...'
SET [Rowset] AS
'Generate (
  [InterestingCustomers],
  { Ancestor (
      [Customer].CurrentMember, [Customer].[State]
    ),
    [Customer].CurrentMember
  }
)'
MEMBER [Measures].[Report Total Sales] AS
'Sum (
  Intersect ([InterestingCustomers],
    Descendants ([Customer].CurrentMember,
      [Customer].[Cust ID]
  ) ),
  [Measures].[Dollar Sales]
)'
```

```
MEMBER [Measures].[Report Total Units] AS
'Sum (
  Intersect ([InterestingCustomers],
    Descendants ([Customer].CurrentMember,
      [Customer].[Cust ID]
  ) ),
  [Measures].[Unit Sales]
)'
MEMBER [Measures].[Dollars Pct of Report Total] AS
'[Measures].[Dollar Sales] /
([Measures].[Report Total Sales],
  Ancestor ([Customer].CurrentMember, [Customer].[State])
)', SOLVE_ORDER = 5, FORMAT_STRING = '#.00%'
MEMBER [Measures].[Units Pct of Report Total] AS
'[Measures].[Unit Sales] /
 ([Measures].[Report Total Units],
  Ancestor ([Customer].CurrentMember, [Customer].[State])
)', SOLVE_ORDER = 5, FORMAT_STRING = '#.00%'
SELECT
{ [Measures].[Report Total Sales], [Measures].[Report Total Units],
  [Measures].[Dollars Pct of Report Total],
  [Measures].[Units Pct of Report Total]
} on columns,
{ [Rowset] } on rows
FROM [WM2005.Sales]
```

	Report Total Sales	Report Total Units	Dollars Pct of Report Total	Units Pct of Report Total
MT	11,805.30	479		
385150	414.20	19	3.50%	4.00%
445100	3,977.30	169	33.70%	35.30%
511900	7,413.80	291	62.80%	60.80%
CO	53,825.10	2,073		
567500	48,487.20	1,847	90.10%	89.10%
491400	5,337.90	226	9.90%	10.90%

Figure 7-6   Full report totals and percent total results.

Technique 2: Considering Using VisualTotals() in Analysis Services

`VisualTotals()` is a Microsoft Analysis Services–specific function that will give us the report total to a parent member, which makes some of this process easy when only parents and children are involved. The function's semantics changed from AS2000 to AS2005.

Using VisualTotals in Analysis Services 2000

In essence, `VisualTotals()` returns a set that may include new calculated members as a part of it, defined within `VisualTotals()`. For example, the query

```
SELECT
{ [Measures].[Dollar Sales], [Measures].[Unit Sales] } on columns,
{ [Customer].[City].[Great Falls, MT],
  VisualTotals ( {
    [Customer].[Cust ID].[cust385150],
    [Customer].[Cust ID].[cust445100],
    [Customer].[Cust ID].[cust511900]
    }, "Total for *"
  )
} on rows
FROM [Sales]
```

would generate a straightforward report of the three customers in Great Falls, and their total sales and costs, along with the database total for Great Falls for contrast, just as in Figure 7-6 except that you have no ratio-to-report-total here. The result would appear as shown in Figure 7-7. This approach is expedient when you only want the total values for children values, grouped according to their hierarchy. `VisualTotals()` also lets us total up descendants farther away than children and in fact enables us to use descendants at multiple levels without double-counting their results. Using `VisualTotals()` is very convenient because it does not require us to devote any logic to the creation of calculated members to hold the various group totals, as the examples in the prior subsection did. For example, the following gives us subtotals and grand totals for selected customers in Montana and Colorado:

```
SELECT
{ [Measures].[Dollar Sales], [Measures].[Unit Sales] } on columns,
{ VisualTotals ( {
  [Customer].[Mountains],
  [Customer].[State].[MT],
  [Customer].[City].[Great Falls, MT],
  [Customer].[Cust Id].[cust385150],
```

```
      [Customer].[Cust Id].[cust445100],
      [Customer].[Cust Id].[cust511900],
      [Customer].[State].[CO]
      [Customer].[City].[Colorado Springs, CO]
      [Customer].[Cust Id].[cust567500],
      [Customer].[Cust Id].[cust491400]
   },  "Total in *"
   )
} on rows
FROM [Sales]
```

However, when you wish to calculate percentage-of-total contributions for each customer in the [InterestingCustomers] set, you do need to create calculated members as with the standard MDX approach. This is because any subtotal or total member created by VisualTotals() does not have a name that we can reference in the query. When the query is parsed, the name has not yet been generated, and although you could form the expression (sales / [Total in Great Falls, MT]), the MDX parser will not know what member it corresponds to because it will not exist until later.

NOTE VisualTotals() **does not work with DISTINCT COUNT measures in AS2000, but works will all aggregation functions in AS2005.**

Using VisualTotals in AS2005

In AS2005, VisualTotals() is built on a foundation of subcubes. It's a bit more flexible than in AS2000 in that the ancestor members can follow the descendant members, or indeed appear anywhere else. (In AS2000, the ancestor members to total over needed to be immediately followed by the descendant members.)

	Dollar Sales	Unit Sales
Total in Mountains	58,216.59	2,261
Total in MT	4,391.49	188
Total in Great Falls, MT	4,391.49	188
cust385150	414.20	19
cust445100	3,977.29	169
Total in CO	53,825.10	2,073
Total in Colorado Springs	53,825.10	2,073
cust567500	48,487.20	1,847
cust491400	5,337.90	226

Figure 7-7   Result of a VisualTotals() query.

The totals members created by VisualTotals() in AS2005 are effectively renamed versions of the real members, in that they participate in the hierarchy, so you can refer to their parent, their previous member, and so on. They just have a different caption. However, a side effect of this query being based on subcubes is that if you refer to the same member outside of the result of VisualTotals(), you still get the VisualTotals() results. For example, the following set has the same values returned for [Customer].[Customer].[State].[CO] in both places:

```
SELECT
{ VisualTotals (
    { [Customer].[Customer].[State].[CO]
      [Customer].[Customer].[City].[Colorado Springs].&[cust567500]
    },
      "total - *"
    ),
    [Customer].[Customer].[State].[CO]
}
on rows, ...
```

Interestingly, if you include a calculated member in your query that refers to the totals members, the percent-of-total reported is the percent to the database total that includes everything outside the subcube. This mimics the behavior of AS2000 in this regard, so you can't use VisualTotals() to get a percent of report total in AS2005 either.

Technique 3: Using AS2005 Subcubes

Recall from Chapter 4 that when you define an AS2005 subcube as containing a particular set of members, the resulting subcube actually contains all descendants and ancestors of those members as well, and the values for base measures at those ancestor members reflect the aggregation across the members you listed in the subcube definition. So, given a set of interesting members upon which you want to create report totals, you don't need to add in those ancestors using Generate(). One difference between using subcubes and VisualTotals is this: The subtotal/total members for which aggregating is done *are* the real members, not additional calculated members or renamed members.

Using the fact that Descendants() can take a set as its first argument, you can easily make the query for the subtotals and grand totals for the interesting customers from Montana and Colorado generic with respect to the region(s) you want to use as a grand total. A percent-of-parent total calculation, whether defined in the query or defined by a CREATE MEMBER statement, automatically takes the percentage relative to the subcube total. The query would look like the following:

```
SELECT
{ [Measures].[Total], [Measures].[Qty]} on 0,
Descendants (
  [Customer].[Customer].[Region].Members,
  [Customer].[Customer].[Cust Identity],
  SELF_AND_BEFORE
) on 1
FROM (
  SELECT {
    [Customer].[Customer].[City].[Missoula, MT].&[cust064950],
    [Customer].[Customer].[City].[Missoula, MT].&[cust410300],
    [Customer].[Customer].[City].[Colorado Springs, CO].&[cust567500],
    [Customer].[Customer].[City].[Colorado Springs, CO].&[cust491400]
  } on 0
  FROM [Customer Analysis]
)
```

Hierarchical Sorting That Skips Levels in the Hierarchy

The hierarchical sorting provided by the `Order()` function is very convenient when you wish to display data sorted within all hierarchical relationships. Sometimes, however, you may wish to sort by hierarchical relationships but not use all levels in the hierarchy. For example, you may use a customer dimension in a cube that has levels of region, state, city, and individual customer. If you sort the city members hierarchically by average sale price per unit, you will get each city sorted per state and each state sorted per region, whether or not those intermediate levels are in the report. How, in a report, can you sort each city per region, leaving out the states?

The answer is to break apart the sorting so that you are sorting the cities within each region independently. The `Generate()` function provides you with the iterative framework you need to do this. The first set can be the set of regions, and the second set can be an expression that sorts the descendants of the current member of the first set:

```
Generate(
  { [Customer].[Region].Members },    // for each region
  Order(    // sort its cities
    Descendants (
      [Customer].CurrentMember, [Customer].[City],
      SELF),
    [Measures].[ASP],
    BDESC
  )
)
```

It is important, of course, to specify BDESC or BASC rather than ASC or DESC. You will probably want to include the regions along with the cities. In a report where you wish to hierarchically represent the regions with the cities, you can add them into the second set for Generate():

```
Generate(
   { [Customer].[Region].Members },  // for each region
   { [Customer].CurrentMember,         // add the region
     Order(                            // followed by its sorted cities
       Descendants(
         [Customer].CurrentMember, [Customer].[City],
         SELF),
       [Measures].[ASP],
       BDESC
     )
   }
)
```

As an aside, the default hierarchical ordering always places parents before children, whether the sorting is ascending or descending. You can use the same sort of construct to put the regions after their children, in a typical subtotal format:

```
Generate(
   { [Customer].[Region].Members },   // for each region
   { Order(                           // add its sorted cities
       Descendants(
         [Customer].CurrentMember, [Customer].[City],
         SELF),
       [Measures].[ASP],
       BDESC
     )
   },
   [Customer].CurrentMember           //  followed by the region
)
```

> **NOTE** The results described in this section return a single dimension's members. A client will typically render this as a single row or column, with multiple levels of members in a single list. In Analysis Services 2005, if you want different levels of a hierarchy treated as different dimensions, you can use the techniques described later for sorting multiple dimensions to sort multiple attribute hierarchies of the same dimension as different dimensions. A client tool will typically render this with a separate header column or row for each attribute dimension in the set.

Sorting a Single Set on Multiple Criteria

In MDX, sorting a set of tuples based on one criterion is directly supported through the `Order()` function. Somewhat surprisingly, it doesn't support multiple criteria for sorting. However, the MDX specification requires that a provider implement a *stable* sorting algorithm, which means that if two tuples tie in terms of the sorting criterion, their order is preserved from the input set. This means that you can nest one call to `Order()` inside another, and the result will be as if the outermost Order was the primary sorting criterion, and the inner `Order()` expression was the secondary criterion. Both Microsoft and Hyperion implement this.

For example, suppose you want to sort a collection of customers primarily by their gender code, and secondarily by the dollars they spent. If gender code was part of the customer hierarchy, then hierarchical sorting might be relevant, but let's say that it's not. The way you would express this sort (in AS2005 syntax) is

```
Order (
  Order (
    [a customer set],
    [Measures].[Dollar Sales],
    BDESC
  ),
  [Customer].[Customer].CurrentMember.Properties ("Gender"),
    /* or [Customer].[Gender].CurrentMember.MemberValue */
  BDESC
)
```

In Essbase, you would use the Essbase property syntax, for example `[Customer].CurrentMember.[Gender]`. Note that in the foregoing example, in AS2005 we can also use attribute relationships to sort on the MemberValue of the current [Customer].[Gender] member. The current member of the Gender attribute hierarchy is driven by the current member of the [Customer].[Customer] hierarchy in this case.

Multiple Layers or Dimensions of Sorting

There are several different permutations of sorting multiple layers within a dimension or sorting multiple dimensions. This topic explores several of them. Some of them can be approached simply by using `Order()` in the right way, particularly with the ill-understood `ASC`/`DESC` "hierarchical" sorting options. Others require strategic use of the `Generate()` function.

Sort Nested Dimensions with the Same Sorting Criterion for Each Dimension

For example, let's say that you want to sort tuples of (Promotion, Product) by [Unit Sales]. You'd like to sort promotions as a group, and products per promotion. If you use the following, Analysis Services 2000 (and, probably, Service Pack 1 of Analysis Services 2005) sorts Promotions by the all-product Unit Sales, then products per promotion based on [Unit Sales]:

```
Order (
  { (promotion, product) set },
  [Measures].[Unit Sales],
  DESC
)
```

This is the case that is directly handled by Order (..., ASC or DESC), because Order () only takes one expression to sort on. However, note that the outermost dimension is sorted by the all-inner-dimension totals. Suppose that you want to sort promotions by the sum of (or other aggregation across) the products?

In AS2005, this is straightforward if you can use a subcube to limit the set of products, because the totals will be automatically restricted. For example, the following query, whose results are shown in Figure 7-8, shows use of subcube-based totals:

```
SELECT
{ ... } on 0,
Order (
  { [Promotion].[Promotion].[Media].[email].children *
    [Product].[ByCategory].[Family].Members },
  [Measures].[Unit Sales],
  DESC
) on 1
FROM (
  SELECT {
    [Product].[ByCategory].[Family].[Doing],
    [Product].[ByCategory].[Family].[Health & Fitness]
  } on 0
  FROM [Sales]
)
```

(Note that the Order () function in the RTM version does not behave correctly, but a service pack will fix this.)

		Unit Sales	Dollar Sales
E-focused-mail	Health & Fitness	4815	121,938.88
	Doing	4718	120,383.11
E-Other	Health & Fitness	4879	125,460.94
	Doing	4646	116,530.52
E-spam-attack	Doing	4740	119,908.45
	Health & Fitness	4273	106,198.37
E-chain-letter	Doing	4404	111,771.42
	Health & Fitness	4387	111,132.33

Figure 7-8   Result of sorting using subtotals.

NOTE Essbase 9 does not implement the ASC or DESC options. You can get a similar effect for sorting nested dimensions at once by using the techniques described next for sorting by multiple criteria, only using the same criterion for both parts.

Sort Nested Dimensions by Different Criteria

This is a case where you can use nested Order() statements, or use Generate(). You'll look at the nested Order() strategy after you look at using Generate(). The strategy using Generate() is to sort the "outer" dimension by its own criteria, and then sort the inner dimension by its own criteria. Note that you're going to look at two cross-joined dimensions in this case. If you have tuplesets that aren't full cross-products (for example, the top 100 product-promotion tuples), then you may have a harder job defining the criteria.

For a simple case, let's say you want to sort time members in reverse order, and per time period you want to sort product families in descending order of dollar sales. If you phrase this as "for-each time from sorted times, sort families," you can see that Generate() is called for. You will Generate() over the sorted set of times, and sort product families. The following query includes the whole sorted selection, and the results are shown in Figure 7-11:

```
SELECT
Generate (
  Order(
    [Time].[YQMD].[2005].Children,
    [Time].[YQMD].CurrentMember.Name,
            // or .[MEMBER_NAME] in Essbase
    BDESC
```

DYNAMIC SORTING BY NAME IN ANALYSIS SERVICES 2005

One of the reasons to perform multidimensional sorting is to put innermost dimensions into alphabetical ordering, since a dimension hierarchy clumps children within parents, parents within grandparents, and so on. However, in AS2005, when you use `CrossJoin()` to combine attribute dimensions, the inner dimension is dynamically ordered relative to the outer attribute dimension. For example, consider the following set, whose results are shown in Figure 7-9:

```
{ [Customer].[Region].[Midwest]
    * [Customer].[City ID].[City ID].Members }
```

Since the City ID members are ordered by member name in the dimension, they are ordered by that principle per Region here. On the other hand, the following would sort them by name per Education level, as shown in Figure 7-10, even though their cities may appear with multiple education levels:

```
{ [Customer].[Education].[Education].Members
    * [Customer].[City ID].[City ID].Members }
```

Midwest	Akron, OH
Midwest	Bear Lake, MI
Midwest	Belleville, IL
Midwest	Bolingbrook, IL
Midwest	Bridgeview, IL
Midwest	Burnsville, MN
Midwest	Canton, OH

Figure 7-9 Dynamic ordering of hierarchically related attributes.

Grad College	Aberdeen, WA
Grad College	Akron, OH
Grad College	Albany, LA
...	...
Grad High School	Aberdeen, WA
Grad High School	Acton, MA
Grad High School	Akron, OH
Grad High School	Albuquerque, NM
...	...

Figure 7-10 Dynamic ordering of nonhierarchically related attributes.

```
    ),
    CrossJoin (
      { [Time].[YQMD].CurrentMember },
      Order(
        [Product].[ByCategory].[Family].Members,
        [Measures].[Dollar Sales],
        BDESC
      )
    )
  ) on rows,
  { [Measures].[Dollar Sales]} on columns
  FROM [Sales]
```

		Dollar Sales
Q4, 2005	Electronics	2,217,956.40
Q4, 2005	Outdoor & Sporting	2,201,913.23
Q4, 2005	Health & Fitness	1,190,132.04
Q4, 2005	Doing	1,177,974.33
Q3, 2005	Electronics	799,940.47
Q3, 2005	Outdoor & Sporting	780,272.86
Q3, 2005	Health & Fitness	483,750.68
Q3, 2005	Doing	468,279.30
Q2, 2005	Electronics	784,229.72
Q2, 2005	Outdoor & Sporting	706,562.40
Q2, 2005	Health & Fitness	473,656.18
Q2, 2005	Doing	466,185.52
Q1, 2005	Electronics	790,797.05
Q1, 2005	Outdoor & Sporting	650,182.86
Q1, 2005	Doing	446,485.29
Q1, 2005	Health & Fitness	438,187.49

Figure 7-11   Result of nested sort.

Note that you could compose this as a nested `Order()` expression as well, but you need to think about the problem in a different way. The following expresses the same ordering request as the previous query:

```
Order(
  Order (
    CrossJoin (
      [Time].[YQMD].[Quarter].Members,
      [Product].[ByCategory].[Family].Members
    ),
    [Measures].[Dollar Sales],
    BDESC
  ),
  [Time].[YQMD].CurrentMember.Name,
          // or .[MEMBER_NAME] in Essbase
  BDESC
)
```

Whether this is more or less efficient to run is up to your server; whether it is more or less easy to think in terms of is up to you!

Pareto Analysis and Cumulative Sums

When you query for parents and children, you can use `Order()` with `ASC` or `DESC` to preserve the hierarchy while sorting. For example, the following set expression results in the ordering of cities shown in Figure 7-12:

```
Order(
 {[Customer].[Customer].[State].[MI],
  [Customer].[Customer].[State].[MI].Children,
  [Customer].[Customer].[State].[IL],
  [Customer].[Customer].[State].[IL].Children
 },
 [Measures].[Unit Sales],
 DESC  // preserves hierarchy
 )
```

Now, let's say that for each of the children, you want the cumulative sum as you go from the first child in this ordering to the last child. This will essentially give you a Pareto analysis within each state. If you used the following expression, the results would be quite wrong:

```
[Measures].[Cum Unit Sales] AS
'Sum (
  {[Customer].[Customer].FirstSibling
   : [Customer].[Customer].CurrentMember},
  [Measures].[Unit Sales]
 )'
```

MI
Detroit, MI
Romulus, MI
Taylor, MI
Lansing, MI
Bear Lake, MI
Haslett, MI
Dowagiac, MI
Holland, MI
Grand Rapids, MI
Lincoln Park, MI
Wyandotte, MI
IL
Chicago_Inner, IL
Chicago, IL

Figure 7-12   Result of hierarchical sorting on members.

This is so because .FirstSibling is not relative to this ordering, even though .CurrentMember will be.

To get the cumulative sum for each of the children as you go from the first child in this ordering to the last, you must re-create the range of ordered children within our calculated member. We also need to find our current tuple within the range, using Rank(), and you need to create a range from the first tuple in the set to the referent child's tuple, using Head(). The following expression gives us the proper ordering of members:

```
Order (
  [Customer].[Customer].Siblings,
  [Measures].[Unit Sales],
  DESC            // or BDESC here, no hierarchy among sibs
)
```

You obtain the position of any tuple in that set with:

```
Rank ([Customer].[Customer].CurrentMember, Set)
```

The Rank() term gives us the rank of the current store member within that set to use as our cutoff point for aggregating. In this case, you do *not* want to return tied values as having the same rank. In addition, the expression

```
Head( Set, Index)
```

gives you the subset to aggregate. You must use the set once to get the members to aggregate over and another time to get them to rank over. Rolling it all together, you get:

```
MEMBER [Measures].[Cum Unit Sales] AS
Sum (
  Head(
    Order (
      [Customer].[Customer].Siblings,
      [Measures].[Unit Sales],
      BDESC
    ),
    Rank (
      [Customer].[Customer].CurrentMember,
      Order(
        [Customer].[Customer].Siblings,
        [Measures].[Unit Sales],
        BDESC
      )
    )
  ),
  [Measures].[Unit Sales]
)'
```

Note that using set aliases simplifies this:

```
MEMBER [Measures].[Cum Unit Sales] AS
Sum (
  Head(
    Order (
      [Customer].[Customer].Siblings,
      [Measures].[Unit Sales],
      BDESC
    ) AS [AliasSet],
    Rank (
      [Customer].[Customer].CurrentMember,
      [AliasSet]
    )
  ),
  [Measures].[Unit Sales]
)'
```

A sample complete query would look like the following, and its results are shown in Figure 7-13:

```
WITH
MEMBER [Measures].[Cum Unit Sales] AS '...'
MEMBER [Measures].[Cum Pct of Parent] AS
'[Measures].[Cum Unit Sales] /
```

```
([Measures].[Unit Sales],
 [Customer].[Customer].CurrentMember.Parent)
', FORMAT_STRING = "0.00%"
SELECT
{ [Measures].[Unit Sales], [Measures].[Cum Unit Sales],
  [Measures].[Cum Pct of Parent]
} on columns,
{ [Customer].[Customer].[State].[MI],
  Order (
    [Customer].[Customer].[State].[MI].Children,
    [Measures].[Unit Sales],
    BDESC
  ),
  [Customer].[Customer].[State].[IL],
  Order (
    [Customer].[Customer].[State].[IL].Children,
    [Measures].[Unit Sales],
    BDESC
  )
} on rows
FROM [Customer Analysis]
```

	Unit Sales	Cum Unit Sales	Cum Pct of Parent
MI	10,649	239,026	94.62%
Detroit, MI	5,299	5,299	49.76%
Romulus, MI	2,571	7,870	73.90%
Taylor, MI	515	8,385	78.74%
Lansing, MI	455	8,840	83.01%
Bear Lake, MI	419	9,259	86.95%
Haslett, MI	416	9,675	90.85%
Dowagiac, MI	309	9,984	93.76%
Holland, MI	292	10,276	96.50%
Grand Rapids, MI	260	10,536	98.94%
Lincoln Park, MI	102	10,638	99.90%
Wyandotte, MI	11	10,649	100.00%
IL	93,867	192,080	76.04%
Chicago_Inner, IL	41,724	41,724	44.45%
Chicago, IL	39,197	80,921	86.21%

Figure 7-13   Cumulative unit sales.

The exact results for Illinois and Michigan are dependent on the contents of their siblings, of course. If you want to only return results for [Cum Unit Sales] at the city level and omit cumulative counts at higher levels, use the techniques we discuss for "one formula calculating different things in different places" discussed later in this chapter.

If constructing, maintaining, and executing this sort of MDX is less onerous to you than maintaining code in a .NET common language run-time (CLR) language, then you can certainly do it in MDX. If you would rather maintain .NET-based code, then a stored procedure is the way to go (and we provide an example of one way to approach the problem in Chapter 10). For example, within the following query, we call a .NET stored procedure named Partial-Sum() to take an ordered set of customers and the current customer, and return the subset of customers over which to sum [Unit Sales]:

```
WITH
MEMBER [Measures].[Cum Unit Sales] AS
Sum (
  PartialSet (
    Order(
      [Customer].[Customer].CurrentMember.Siblings,
      [Measures].[Unit Sales],
      BDESC),
    [Customer].[Customer].CurrentMember
  ),
  [Measures].[Unit Sales]
)
. . .
```

Notice that you pass a set directly to the stored procedure without using SetToArray(), and you return a set from the function directly into Sum().

Returning the Top-Selling Product (or Top-Selling Month or Other Most-Significant Name) As a Measure

Sometimes you might also phrase this as "the product with the biggest sales" or "the product with the maximum sales across its group." Other requests that fit this pattern include "best month this product sells in" and "top salesperson in office." This is easy to do in Analysis Services. You will accomplish this with the TopCount() function, not the Max() function; Max() gives you the maximum sales, while TopCount() can give you the member associated with those maximum sales. All you do is take the top single member from the appropriate set. The following example returns the top-selling product category per month and per region:

```
WITH
MEMBER [Measures].[Top Product in Children] AS
TopCount (
  [Product].[ByCategory].CurrentMember.Children,
  1,
  [Measures].[Unit Sales]
).Item(0).Item(0).Name
MEMBER [Measures].[Top Product's Units] AS
( [Measures].[Unit Sales],
  TopCount (
    [Product].[ByCategory].CurrentMember.Children,
    1,
    [Measures].[Unit Sales]
  ).Item(0)  // in Essbase, need .Item(0).Item(0)
)
SELECT
CrossJoin (
  { [Time].[YQMD].Children }.
  { [Measures].[Top Product in Children],
    [Measures].[Top Product's Units]
  }
)  on columns,
{ [Customer].[Customer].[Region].Members } on rows
FROM Sales
```

Most Recent Event for a Set of Selected Members

An interesting kind of request that is made in some applications is a request for the most recent event that occurred across a set of selected members. In one instance, it was for the most recent articles given a set of authors (where author and article were separate dimensions). An analogy for this would be "the most recent purchase dates by a customer, along with the products they purchased." In another case, it was the most recent date (before a given date) that the number of requests for a particular item crossed a given threshold, for a given set of items.

The first case is easy to express but a little tricky to explain. It uses `Generate()`, as so many interesting selections do. Let's use the analogy of customers and products again. There is a slightly different way in each product covered to get the last purchase date for each customer. In Analysis Services 2005:

```
Generate (
  { Set_of_customers },
  CrossJoin (
    { [Customer].CurrentMember },
    Tail (
      NonEmpty (
```

```
            [Time].[Day].Members,
            { [Measures].[Unit Sales] }
          )
        )
      ),
   ALL
)
```

In Analysis Services 2000:

```
Generate (
   { Set_of_customers },
   CrossJoin (
     { [Customer].CurrentMember },
     Tail (
       NonEmptyCrossJoin (
         [Time].[Day].Members,
         { [Measures].[Unit Sales] },
         1
       )
     )
   ),
   ALL
)
```

In Essbase:

```
Generate (
   { Set_of_customers },
   CrossJoin (
     { [Customer].CurrentMember },
     Tail (
       Filter (
         [Time].[Day].Members,
         Not IsEmpty ([Measures].[Unit Sales])
       )
     )
   ),
   ALL
)
```

In each of these, the difference is the best way to get the set of days that have some sales values, and then get the last one of those days by using `Tail()`. Using `ALL` with `Generate()` isn't strictly necessary because the set it assembles won't have duplicates anyway, but evaluating the set for duplicates is unnecessary overhead.

What you have so far is just the last purchase date for each customer. Obtaining the products is another exercise, and lo and behold you probably need to use `Generate()` again unless you know how many distinct products were bought. If you know how many distinct products were bought on the last day, you can just use that value as the argument to Tail (instead of the default value of 1). We would like the MDX to look something like the following (in Analysis Services 2005 syntax):

```
Generate (
  { Set_of_customers },
  CrossJoin (
    { [Customer].CurrentMember },
    Tail (
      NonEmpty (
        CrossJoin (
          [Time].[Day].Members,
          [Product].[SKU].Members
        )
        { [Measures].[Unit Sales] }
      ),
      [Measures].[Distinct SKU Count]   // still missing something!
    )
  ),
  ALL
)
```

The problem is that you don't at that point know what day is the last day, do we? Well, once the NonEmpty() has done its work, the *last* tuple in it contains the last day. So, we reach deeper into the same bag of tricks we reached into for the axis-based calculations described earlier. If you name a set alias for the NonEmpty, you can use it here as follows (in AS2005 syntax):

```
Generate (
  { Set_of_customers },
  CrossJoin (
    { [Customer].CurrentMember },
    Tail (
      NonEmpty (
        CrossJoin (
          [Time].[YQMD].[Day].Members,
          [Product].[ByCategory].[SKU].Members
        ),
        { [Measures].[Unit Sales] }
      ) As [AliasSet],
      ([Measures].[Distinct SKU Count],
        Tail ([AliasSet]).Item(0).Item(0)
      )
    )
  ),
  ALL
)
```

You take the Tail of the aliased set, which results in a one-tuple set. The `.Item(0).Item(0)` of that is the time member. In Analysis Services 2000, you'd replace `NonEmpty()` with an equivalent `NonEmptyCrossJoin()` expression. In Essbase 9, if your sets are small, you could just use the following instead:

```
Filter (
 CrossJoin ( ... ),
 Not IsEmpty([Measures].[Unit Sales])
)
```

When the sets are larger, without an optimized equivalent for `NonEmpty()`, you can do the following as well:

```
Generate (
   { Set_of_customers },
   CrossJoin (
     { [Customer].CurrentMember },
     CrossJoin (
       Tail (
         Filter (
           [Time].[Day].Members,
           Not IsEmpty ([Measures].[Unit Sales])
         )
       ) As [AliasSet],
       Filter (
         [Product].[SKU].Members,
         Not IsEmpty (
           ( [Measures].[Unit Sales], [AliasSet].Item(0).Item(0) )
         )
       )
     )
   ),
   ALL
)
```

Suppose that you're uncomfortable about set aliases. If you were to avoid using set aliases altogether, you would need to `Generate()` again, and for each of the customer-days you produced, you would need to get the set of products for that date. Using Essbase syntax this time, you can construct:

```
Generate (
   Generate (
     { Set_of_customers },
     CrossJoin (
       { [Customer].CurrentMember },
       Tail (
         Filter (
```

```
         [Time].[Day].Members,
         Not IsEmpty ([Measures].[Unit Sales])
       )
     )
   ),
   ALL
 ),
 CrossJoin (
   { ([Customer].CurrentMember, [Time].CurrentMember) },
   Filter (
     [Product].[SKU].Members,
     Not IsEmpty ([Measures].[Unit Sales])
   )
 ),
 ALL
)
```

So what about when the recent event is something else, like the last day each customer purchased more than $100 worth of electronics, and what the electronics SKUs were? The mere existence of cells is no longer the condition to use. Instead, you put in the comparison that you need. You'd use variation on one of the last two versions presented for this selection, changing the Not IsEmpty() condition in the day filter to the appropriate condition (for example: ([Measures].[Dollar Sales], [Product].[Electronics]) > 1000) and then either filtering or using NonEmpty() to obtain the products of interest).

How Long Did It Take to Accumulate This Many ? (Building a Set That Sums Backward or Forward in Time)

(How to select a set of times back from some date such that a measure totaled across them reaches some value.)

Suppose that you need to create a set that contains the last time periods required to accumulate 500 new customers from a cube where [New Customer Count] is a measure available per day. This set could then be used to total up advertising and sign-up costs over that time range, or simply counted to provide the number of days. Technically, you want to build a set of time periods such that their sum of a measure is at least greater than a given quantity. You may want to use the ending period as the reference point (from Day X, how far back do you have to go to accumulate these new customers), or you may want to use the starting period as the reference (from Day X, how many days elapsed until the target was reached). Let's look at the ending-period case here—the difference between it and the starting-period case is just in the direction of the range you create.

From a glance at the `TopSum()` function, it seems nearly suited to this need, as it returns a set of tuples based on the overall sum meeting or just exceeding a certain value. However, it sorts all of the tuples first in terms of the value being summed, which scrambles them from the point of view of the goal—you want the set of time periods to be in database order.

There are straightforward solutions to this using either straight MDX or a stored procedure/external function call. The larger the number of time periods being considered, the more efficient an external function call will be compared to straight MDX. We will consider how to do this in Chapter 10.

You can solve this problem with a recursive calculated member that computes the total new customer count backward in time, which lets you build a named set that contains the time members where the accumulated value does not exceed the threshold of 500. You will look for the set of time periods up to October 2005. Since you do not know in advance how far back in time to go, you will take all months prior to the time that you are counting back from.

The heart of this is the calculated measure `[Accum Sum Back]`, which can be expressed either recursively or as a set operation:

```
// Recursively
MEMBER [Measures].[Accum Sum Back] AS
'iif (
  [Time].CurrentMember IS [Time].[Oct, 2005],
  [Measures].[New Customer Count],
  [Measures].[New Customer Count] +
     ([Measures].[Accum Sum Back], [Time].CurrentMember.NextMember)
)'
// As a set operation
MEMBER [Measures].[Accum Sum Back] AS
'Sum (
  { [Time].CurrentMember : [Time].[Oct, 2005] }
  [Measures].[New Customer Count]
)'
```

Then, the set of times is filtered to just the ones that meet the criteria, which keeps all of them below the threshold, and includes the one that meets the threshold by its being next to the last one that didn't:

```
SET [Times Until Sum] AS
'Filter (
  [Time].[Month].Members.Item(0) : [Time].[Month].[Oct 2005],
  [Measures].[Accum Sum Back] < 500
   OR ([Measures].[Accum Sum Back] >= 500
    AND ([Measures].[Accum Sum Back],
        [Time].CurrentMember.NextMember) < 500
  )
)'
```

(There is no way to explicitly walk the time periods backward or forward in MDX, although we'll show a little trick later on.)

The named set [Times Until Sum] contains a set that you can use for a result axis or for further filtering. If you only need to report the number of days, you would just count the members in the set.

The [Times Until Sum] set is defined only for the course of the query. If you wanted to share the set among queries by using CREATE SET to define a named set, you would need to first define the calculated [Accum New Count] member using CREATE MEMBER (or define it at the server). Note that the reference time period needs to be embedded into the calculation in this case.

One step more advanced would be to return, in a grid of multiple dimensions, the number of days it took to accumulate some threshold, such as days it took to sell 100 units of a product. In this case, there is no single day to embed in our calculated member. You need to put all the logic into the Filter() expression which will be evaluated per result cell. The following query includes the straightforward logic in AS2005 syntax and relies upon a set alias because you need to refer to two different Time current members within the Sum():

```
WITH
MEMBER [Measures].[Periods to 100] AS
'Filter (
  NonEmpty (
    { [Time].CurrentMember.Level.Members.Item(0)  :
      [Time].CurrentMember },
    [Measures].[Unit Sales]
  ) AS [AliasSet],
  Sum (
    { [Time].CurrentMember : Tail([AliasSet]).Item(0).Item(0) },
    [Measures].[Unit Sales]
  ) <= 100
).Count'
SELECT
{ [Time].[YQMD].[Month].[Dec, 2004].Children } *
{ [Measures].[Unit Sales], [Measures].[Periods to 100] } on columns,
[Product].[ByCategory].
on rows
FROM [Sales]
```

In Essbase, you can use a member alias to make the expression a little neater, but you need to do things differently to trim out time periods where no units were sold:

```
'Count (
  Filter (
    { [Time].CurrentMember.Level.Members.Item(0)
      : [Time].CurrentMember AS [AliasMbr] },
    Not IsEmpty ([Measures].[Unit Sales])
    AND Sum (
```

```
      { [Time].CurrentMember : [AliasMbr] },
      [Measures].[Unit Sales]
    ) <= 100
  )
)'
```

In both Analysis Services and Essbase, it seems that one could devise a recursive calculated member that returned the unique name or another unique reference to the period upon which the threshold was reached, but it would require two separate time dimensions: one for the reference days used in the query, and the other for the days against which the sum is being recursively calculated. That is beyond the scope of this book.

Aggregating by Multiplication (Product Instead of Sum)

When an application calls for aggregating percentage changes along time, it needs to multiply them all together. MDX does not implement a `Product()` aggregation to go with `Sum()`, but there are a couple of ways to approach it. In Analysis Services, you can use the Excel `Product()` function. In both Analysis Services and Essbase, you can create a recursive calculated member to do the work. Also, if all of the percentages are greater than 0 and are coming from a fact table, you can perform a little algebraic trick: load the logarithms of the values into the cube, and then in your calculation, sum the logarithms and take the exponent. This last method allows you to use the built-in aggregation of base measures for summing as well.

First, let's look at using `Product`. In Analysis Services, to calculate the product of a `[Percent]` measure over the children of the current `[Time]` measure, you can simply write our calculated member formula as:

```
Excel!Product (
  SetToArray (
    [Time].[YQMD].CurrentMember.Children,
    [Measures].[Percent]
  )
)
```

In either Essbase or Analysis Services, you can also create a recursive calculated member to do the same work. Actually, you need to create two calculated members: one to hold the result, and one to recursively perform the calculation, stopping at the right place. The following shows how:

```
MEMBER [Measures].[Compounded Percentage] AS
'( [Measures].[Compounding Percentage],
    [Time].CurrentMember.LastChild
)'
```

```
MEMBER [Measures].[Compounding Percentage] AS
'iif (
  [Time].CurrentMember IS [Time].CurrentMember.FirstSibling,
  [Measures].[Percent],
  [Measures].[Percent] *
  ([Measures].[Compounding Percentage], [Time].CurrentMember.PrevMember)
)'
```

As you see, the compounded result is simply the result of requesting the compounding recursive member at the last child member. For completeness, you should include a test in [Compounded Percentage] that just returns [Measures].[Percent] if you're at a leaf-level member.

One Member Formula Calculating Different Things in Different Places

You have seen that calculated members create slices across all intersections of all other dimensions. Sometimes, however, you need a calculated member to give a different result depending on where in the hypercube it is being evaluated. How can you make one calculated member return two different things at two different places? The answer is to use a conditional function and the various properties of members, levels, hierarchies, tuples, and sets in a calculated member to test for the location where the members are being evaluated, and then choose the correct formula to use for that place in the cube.

> **NOTE** Analysis Services 2005 provides MDX scripts (described in Chapter 13) as a means to provide scoped calculation logic, but these can only be created as server-based, global definitions. Both it and Analysis Services 2000 provide cell calculations (described in Chapter 12) as an additional way to describe scoped calculations that can also be defined at session lifespan scope using CREATE or query scope using WITH. Some aspects of the cube region to which a cell calculation applies are defined using set functions, while other aspects are defined using the functions described here.

For example, if you wish to create a calculated measure that shows a three-month moving average of sales but don't want it to show any values for any level other than month, you can use the Level.Ordinal property to tell you at what level the formula is being evaluated:

```
iif (
  [Time].[CurrentMember].Level.Ordinal = [Time].[Month].Ordinal,
  Avg( LastPeriods (3, [Time].CurrentMember),
    [Measures].[Dollar Sales]
  ),
  NULL
)
```

NOTE In Essbase, you can use the `Ordinal (layer)` **function to achieve the same effect.**

Notice that the test for whether or not this formula is being evaluated at the month level is implemented as a test to determine if the level's ordinal (in Analysis Services, its depth from the root level) is equal to the month level's ordinal. You can test for a hard-wired depth such as 2; some providers support the `.Name` property for a level, which you could compare to "Month." However, this seems to capture the best combination of efficiency (comparing numbers instead of strings) and grace (you know what `[Time].[Month]` refers to, whereas 2 would not be as easily understood). This example has a maintenance issue as well: If the dimension changed and a new level was inserted between the month level and the root, then the 2 would need to be updated to a 3. Using Microsoft's `IS` extension to MDX, you can also use the `IS` statement to test for equivalence of object identity, as with the following:

```
iif (
   [Time].[CurrentMember].Level IS [Time].[Month],
   Avg( LastPeriods (3, [Time].CurrentMember), [Measures].[Dollar
Sales]),
   NULL
)
```

This formulation should not only be efficient, but will also be graceful to changes in the set of levels in the time dimension (so long as the Month level does not disappear).

Sometimes, you may find that you need to use a different formula depending upon what member you are evaluating a calculated member at. For example, a multinational corporation may use a slightly different net profit calculation depending upon the country in which it is performing the calculation. The following example demonstrates three different profit formulas, two of which are specific to a single country as exceptions to the general rule:

```
CASE
WHEN [Geography].CurrentMember IS [Geography].[Japan]
THEN [Sales] - [Deductible Expenses 1]
WHEN [Geography].CurrentMember IS [Geography].[Malaysia]
THEN [Sales] - [Deductible Expenses 2]
ELSE [Sales] - [Deductible Expenses 3]
END
```

Note that Analysis Services 2000 does not support the CASE construct, so you would need to use the following:

```
iif ([Geography].CurrentMember IS [Geography].[Japan],
   [Sales] - [Deductible Expenses 1],
   iif ( [Geography].CurrentMember IS [Geography].[Malaysia],
```

```
    [Sales] - [Deductible Expenses 2],
    [Sales] - [Deductible Expenses 3]
  )
)
```

If you are using IF-THEN logic to specify a constant value based on member name, you might also think about putting that information into a table and using it either as a member property or as a measure. The less conditional the logic in a formula, the easier it is to comprehend and maintain over time. The numbers that you are specifying might be exceptions to a general rule, for example, commission rates to charge based on product. In that case, the logic of the formula would test for the special commission being empty or not and to use the special commission value if it is present or the default value if the special commission is absent. Note that Analysis Services provides the Str-ToValue() function, which introduces quite a large degree of flexibility. In this case, you might compose something like the following to use the right formula per member:

```
StrToValue (
  [Geography].CurrentMember.Properties ("Profit Formula")
)
```

Three types of tests you may wish to perform on the current member are

- Is it at a particular member or members?
- Is it at a particular level or levels? Is it at the leaf level?
- Is it at a descendant of a particular member?

To test whether the current member is at a particular level (or above or below a particular level, including the level of an arbitrary named level), compare its level with the target level using IS. Compare the current member's level ordinal to the ordinal of the level you are interested in using level.Ordinal. To test whether the current member is a descendant of a particular member, you can use the IsAncestor() function.

The only two standard functions you can use against the current member or its related information for this purpose are

- *Member*.Level.Ordinal
- *Member*.Properties ("Property Name") or *Member*.[Property Name]

Microsoft extends the set of tests you can use with the following:

- *Member*.Level.Name
- *Member*.Level.UniqueName
- *Member*.Name
- *Member*.UniqueName
- IsAncestor(*target-member*, *source-member*)
- IsGeneration(*member*, *generation-number*)
- IsLeaf(*member*)
- IsSibling(*member1*, *member 2*)

Hyperion extends the set of tests you can use with the following:

- *Member*.[MEMBER_NAME]
- *Member*.[MEMBER_UNIQUE_NAME]
- Ordinal(*Member*.level-or-generation)
- IsAccType(*target-member*, *account-type*)
- IsAncestor(*target-member*, *source-member*)
- IsGeneration(*member*, *generation-number*)
- IsLeaf(*member*)
- IsLevel(*member*, *level-number*)
- IsSibling(*member1*, *member 2*)
- IsUDA(*member*, "*UDA-name*")

They work as shown in Table 7-1.

Also, Rank([Dimension].CurrentMember, { member1, member2, . . . memberN }) > 0 can be used to test for whether or not the current member is in the given set. Using IsGeneration() in Analysis Services is a bit complicated and requires an understanding of how it assigns generation numbers; please refer to its discussion in Appendix A.

Table 7-1 Functions and Operators for Testing the Member or Level at Which a Cell Is Being Calculated

EXTENSION	EXPRESSION	PURPOSE
	`[dimension].Level.Ordinal = Named_Level.Ordinal`	Tests for being at level
	`[dimension].Level.Ordinal > Named_Level.Ordinal`	Tests for being below level
	`[dimension].Level.Ordinal < Named_Level.Ordinal`	Tests for being above level
MS	`[dimension].Currentmember. Uniquename = [Specific Member] .UniqueName` `[dimension].CurrentMember. UniqueName = "Unique Name"`	Tests for member equivalence
	`[dimension].CurrentMember. Properties("External Property") =Value`	Tests for arbitrary condition on property, can be applied to this purpose
	`[dimension].CurrentMember. [External Property] = Value`	Tests for arbitrary condition on property, can be applied to this purpose
MS,Hyp	`[dimension].CurrentMember IS [member]`	Tests for member equivalence
MS	`[dimension].CurrentMember .Level IS [level]`	Tests for being at level
MS,Hyp	`IsAncestor ([member], [dimension].CurrentMember)`	Tests for current member being descendant of specific member
MS,Hyp	`IsLeaf ([dimension] .CurrentMember)`	Tests for current member being at the leaf level
MS,Hyp	`IsSibling([dimension] . CurrentMember, [Specific Member])`	Tests for current member being sibling of target member
Hyp	`IsUDA([dimension] . CurrentMember, "UDA Name")`	Tests for current member having UDA associated with it
Hyp	`IsAccType([accounts_ dimension]. CurrentMember, Acct_Flag)`	Tests for current accounts member being of a particular account type

DON'T USE *MEMBER = MEMBER* TO TEST MEMBER EQUIVALENCE

It is tempting to use the = sign to test for member equivalence. However, remember that = works only on cell values. What you do when you use `member1 = member2` is to test whether the cell value associated with *member1* in the current context is equal to the cell value associated with *member2*. It might accidentally appear to give you the correct results in some situations, but it isn't doing the right thing.

When you are testing for member equivalence in Analysis Services and Essbase, you should favor the *dimension*.`CurrentMember IS [Specific Member]` construct. This is because unique names can have many different formats, and you are not always in control of the format chosen.

Including All Tuples with Tied Ranking in Sets

Recall, from Chapter 6, the discussion of ranking queries and returning the top *N* products or salespeople, and also reporting on rank numbers for them. If you're truly trying to be fair to your salespeople and it's possible that two or more are tied for 10th place, then you need to apply more MDX than we did in Chapter 6. The trick is simply to add to the set all tuples (products in this case) whose values are equal to the 10th place product, and unite this filtered set with the ranked set. Because MDX preserves the ordering in the sets when they are united, the final set that is created will be in the correct order. Note that you rely on the extension to `Rank ()` that yields tie numbering when there are value ties.

```
WITH
MEMBER [Measures].[YTD Unit Sales] AS
'SUM(YTD(), [Measures].[Unit Sales])'
SET [Last Year Ordered Products] AS
'Order (
  [Product].[ByCategory].[Category].Members,
  ([Measures].[YTD Unit Sales],
   ParallelPeriod ([Time].[YQMD].[Year], 1)
  ),
  BDESC
)'
MEMBER [Measures].[Previous Year Rank] AS
'Rank (
  [Product].[ByCategory].CurrentMember,
  [Last Year Ordered Products],
  ([Measures].[YTD Unit Sales],
```

```
      ParallelPeriod ([Time].[YQMD].[Year], 1)
    )
  )'
SET [This Year Top 10 Products] AS
'TopCount (
    [Product].[ByCategory].[Category].Members,
    10,
    [Measures].[YTD Unit Sales]
  )'
/* We add some new set declarations */

// collect all products whose units are equal to the 10th's
SET [This Year Tied Products] AS
'Filter (
    [Product].[ByCategory].[Category].Members,
    [Measures].[YTD Unit Sales] =
      ([Measures].[YTD Unit Sales],
        Tail ([This Year Top 10 Products]).Item (0)
      )
  )'
// Put the two sets together, and eliminate the duplicated 10th
MEMBER
SET [Top Ranked This Year Products] AS
'Union (
    [This Year Top 10 Products],
    [This Year Tied Products]
  )'

/* Done adding the set declarations */

MEMBER [Measures].[This Year Rank] AS
'Rank (
    [Product].[ByCategory].CurrentMember,
    [This Year Top 10 Products],
    - [Measures].[YTD Unit Sales] /* remember, AS2005 sorts ascending in
Rank() */
  )'
MEMBER [Measures].[YTD Units Change] as
'[YTD Unit Sales] -
    ([YTD Unit Sales], ParallelPeriod ([Time].[YQMD].[Year], 1))'
SELECT
{ [Measures].[This Year Rank], [Measures].[YTD Unit Sales],
    [Measures].[Previous Year Rank], [Measures].[YTD Units Change]
} on columns,
{ [Top Ranked This Year Products] } on rows
FROM [Sales]
WHERE ([Time].[YQMD].[Month].[Aug, 2005])
```

Time Analysis Utility Dimensions

One fairly common design theme is to provide multiple types of time-series analysis for multiple periodicities in time. For example, an application may need to support queries for year-to-date sums, rolling 12-month or rolling 52-week averages, period-to-year-ago differences, and period-to-period differences. For Analysis Services and Essbase, a very clean way to support these is to introduce a time-series analysis or periodicity dimension into a database.

> **NOTE** Analysis Services 2005 has even embedded this capability into the design environment, in the form of the Define Time Intelligence Wizard. It generates calculated member definitions into the cube's MDX script, and also adds a dimension to the cube. The MDX scripting aspects of this are covered in Chapter 13; we cover the main MDX expressions here.

This dimension will have one regular member (let's call it [Current]), to which all measured data is related, and a set of calculated members. One calculated member will have a formula for year-to-date sum at the [Current] member, another will have period-to-year ago percentage at the [Current] member, and so on. In this scenario, if you want the end user to be able to select a set of customers and see the period-to-year-ago percent change in total sales for them, you need to be able to set the solve order of the sum to be less than the solve order of the percent-change member. Meanwhile, another query for the rolling 12-month average of [Units] and [Average Sales Price] will want the 12-month average calculation to either have a higher or lower solve order than the [Average Sales Price] calculation, but in either case to have a higher solve order than the sum of the customers picked in the query.

For example, the Analysis Services 2005 MDX to create the Period-To-Period Pct Diff member and the Year-To-Date Total member would look like the following (assuming that you are creating them as calculated members):

```
CREATE MEMBER CURRENTCUBE.[Time Series].[Series].[Period-To-Period Pct
Diff] AS
'([Time Series].[Series].[Current] /
  ([Time Series].[Series].[Current],
   [Time].[YQMD].CurrentMember.PrevMember)
  ) - 1'
, SOLVE_ORDER = 20, FORMAT_STRING = '0.0%'

CREATE MEMBER CURRENTCUBE. [Time Series].[Series].[Year-To-Date Total]
AS
'Sum (  // or Aggregate(), as necessary
  PeriodsToDate (
    [Time].[YQMD].[Year],
```

```
        [Time].[YQMD].CurrentMember
    ),
    [Time Series].[Series].[Current]
)'
, SOLVE_ORDER = 3, FORMAT_STRING = '0.0%'
```

In Essbase, you would just place the appropriate formulas and solve orders in the outline.

Note that each of these formulas references the one regular member named [Time Series].[Current]. That is the member at which the data to be operated on exists, and without that reference you would end up with infinite recursion in the Periodicity dimension. Given the periodicity dimension that we have just described, to retrieve the year-to-date aggregate for any particular time member, you just retrieve that time member and the year-to-date periodicity. If you want to see year-to-date and period-to-year-ago percent change, you just retrieve both of those periodicity members.

For example, the following query, whose results are shown in Figure 7-14, retrieves the current and period-to-period percentage difference in Units Sold for August and September 2005:

```
SELECT
CrossJoin (
    { [Time].[YQMD].[Aug, 2005], [Time].[YQMD].[Sep, 2005]},
    { [Time Series].[Series].[Current], [Time Series].[Series].[Period-To-
Period Pct Diff] }
) on axis(0),
[Product].[ByCategory].[Category].[Tools].Children
on axis (1)
FROM [Sales]
WHERE ([Measures].[Unit Sales], [Customer].[Customer].[Northeast])
```

	Aug, 2005		Sep, 2005	
	Current	Period-To-Period Pct Diff	Current	Period-To-Period Pct Diff
Bench Power Tools	90	-57.10%	78	-13.30%
Compressors, Air Tools	15	-48.30%	17	13.30%
Electrical Shop	61	-39.60%	57	-6.60%
Garage Door Openers	161	71.30%	148	-8.10%
Hand Tools, Carpentry	42	1.#INF	44	4.80%
Hand Tools, General Purpo	98	55.60%	15	-84.70%
Mechanics Tools		-100.00%	55	1.#INF
Portable Power Tools		-100.00%		-100.00%
Power Tool Accessories	65	712.50%	10	-84.60%

Figure 7-14   Result of query showing time-series analysis members in use.

NOTE In Analysis Services, note that how you create the members affects how they show up in metadata a bit. If you create these members using custom member formulas, the members are real members that will appear in `.Members` calls. If you create these as calculated members, they only show up as results of `.AllMembers`. Furthermore, remember from Chapter 4 that Analysis Services 2005 groups all solve orders by the scopes in which the calculation was defined (global, session, query). This means that the time intelligence calculations will never take as their inputs session-defined or query-defined calculations, except those that use the `Aggregate()` function as their operation.

A Sample Analysis

MDX is rich enough to support advanced analytical queries. Indeed, once you have created a database schema for Microsoft Analysis Services and populated it with data, MDX provides many of the tools you need to support complex analyses within queries. You will spend the next several pages rolling up your sleeves and using MDX to explore a useful set of questions related to the topic. What are the important products to the important customers? Although your applications may not be related to customers and products, a generalization of the analysis we discuss is "What are the important factors to each of a set of interesting members?" This is a form of data mining, even though we are performing it in an OLAP tool. Within the framework of this analysis, we will explore set construction and the use of the `Generate()` and `Extract()` functions, and make extensive use of named sets.

The dimensions of primary interest in this analysis are customer, product, and time. A familiar simple OLAP query to use as a starting point is "Who are our best customers?" If you are interested in the top 10 customers in terms of total profitability in 2005, you may start with the set defined by the following:

```
TopCount ( [Customer].[Individual].Members, 10,
          ([Measures].[Profit], [Time].[2005]) )
```

A query that shows profitability for 2004 and 2005 for these customers is

```
SELECT
{ [Time].[2004], [Time].[2005] } on columns,
{ TopCount ([Customer].[Individual].Members, 10,
([Measures].[Profit], [Time].[2005])) } on rows
FROM Sales
WHERE ( [Measures].[Profit] )
```

Now, this query is useful in its own right, but we want to go a bit deeper and learn about the products that these customers are buying. You can learn about the top three product brands (in terms of profit) that some customers are buying with the following expression:

```
TopCount ( [Product].[Brand].Members, 3,
          ([Measures].[Profit], [Time].[2005]) )
```

Because this is along a separate dimension, you can put it on a different query axis than the customer dimension, or you can put it on the same axis as the customers with CrossJoin(). For example:

```
WITH
SET [Top3Prods] AS
'{ TopCount ([Product].[Brand].Members, 3,
      ([Measures].[Profit], [Time].[2005])) }'
SELECT
{ CrossJoin ([Top3Prods], {[Time].[2004], [Time].[2005]}) } on columns,
{ TopCount ([Customer].[Individual].Members, 10,
      ([Measures].[Profit], [Time].[2005])) } on rows
FROM Sales
WHERE ( [Measures].[Profit] )
```

However, this still doesn't tell us about the products that these top customers are buying. Regardless of the way products are oriented in the query or whether the product set is evaluated as a named set or within the body of the SELECT clause, the context in which the product set is evaluated is going to be at the All-customer member because that is the default member in the query context. What you want is the set of products that these customers are buying. You can explore a couple of different paths for determining this.

One path is to ask about the top three product categories over the entire set of top-10 customers. To do this, you need to calculate profitability across the top-10 customers. Calculating the top-10 customers from the leaf level of a fairly large dimension takes significant CPU time because of the sorting involved, so you should use a named set to hold the result customer set. You can then sum across that directly or use a calculated member to hold the result:

```
WITH
SET [Top10Custs] AS
'{ TopCount ([Customer].[Individual].Members, 10,
      ([Measures].[Profit], [Time].[2005])) }'
MEMBER [Measures].[Top10profit] AS
'Sum (Top10Custs, [Measures].[Profit])'
SET [Top3Prods] AS
'{ TopCount ([Product].[Brand].Members, 3,
      ([Measures].[Top10profit], [Time].[2005])) }'
```

```
SELECT
{ CrossJoin ([Top3Prods], {[Time].[2004], [Time].[2005]}) } on columns,
{ TopCount ([Customer].[Individual].Members, 10,
      ([Measures].[Profit], [Time].[2005])) } on rows
FROM Sales
WHERE ( [Measures].[Profit] )
```

This helps you out. You are now looking at the top three products of the top-10 customers, which gives you a better picture of those products and customers in particular. Although these customers could be a fairly homogeneous group, each of them may be fairly different from the others. (They also may be pretty different from the average customer in terms of product preferences; we will explore that later in this section as well.) In terms of our individual customers' favorite product mixes, we can get even more precise than we have, but the MDX requires a quantum leap in sophistication.

Exploring possibilities that don't give you what you are looking for helps you understand the MDX that gives you what you need. MDX's tuple orientation enables you to take the top-N tuples from a set from multiple dimensions. However, taking the top-N tuples from a customer-product set, by cross-joining customers and products together, won't give you what you are looking for. You are interested in 10 customers and three products for each customer. However, the top 30 customer-product combinations (TopCount (CrossJoin (. . .), 30, . . .) could be dominated by 30 products sold to the most profitable customer. The top-30 customer-products of the top-10 customers aren't any better. Taking the top-3 products of the top-10 customers involves somehow breaking it up among the customers, instead of cross-joining customer and product sets. The MDX function that enables you to do this is Generate().

If you are going to create a set named Top3ProdsOf10Custs, the basic template for this is going to be:

```
WITH
SET [Top10Custs] AS
'{ TopCount ([Customer].[Individual].Members, 10,
      ([Measures].[Profit], [Time].[2005])) }'
. . .
SET [Top3ProdsOf10Custs] AS
'{ Generate ([Top10Custs], . . . )}'
```

Within the Generate() function, for each tuple in the set Top10Custs you want to find the top three products. The following looks tempting:

```
Generate ([Top10Custs], TopCount ([Product].[Brand].Members, 3,
    ([Measures].[Profit], [Customer].CurrentMember, [Time].[2005])))
```

But even that will not get you there. (The `[Customer].CurrentMember` is completely superfluous and is only included to clarify our interest in the operation. The current member of a dimension does not need mentioning in this context unless you are going to modify it or access something related to it.) It will get you partway there, but when you put it into a query, the total result (as shown in Figure 7-15) isn't what you want:

```
WITH
SET [Top10Custs] AS
'{ TopCount ([Customer].[Individual].Members, 10,
       ([Measures].[Profit], [Time].[2005])) }'
SET [Top3ProdsOf10Custs] AS
'{ Generate ([Top10Custs], TopCount ([Product].[Brand].Members, 3,
       ([Measures].[Profit], [Time].[2005]))) }'
SELECT
{ [Time].[2004], [Time].[2005]} on columns,
{ [Top3ProdsOf10Custs] } on rows
FROM Sales
WHERE ( [Measures].[Profit] )
```

Our `Generate()` clause returned the right products but no customers. How do you get the customers in? The `Generate()` function returns a set with the dimensionality of the second set, not the first set. You cannot express

```
Generate( [Top10Custs],
  { [Customer].CurrentMember, TopCount ([Product].[Brand].Members, 3,
       ([Measures].[Profit], [Time].[2005])))
```

because that is syntactically and semantically illegal (you are mixing customer and product members in a single set). Using the following query, you can, however, combine the customer member with the product set using the `CrossJoin()` function, which gives you the customer by product tuples that you want:

```
Generate ( [Top10custs],
  CrossJoin (
    {[Customer].CurrentMember },
    TopCount ([Product].[Brand].Members, 3,
      ([Measures].[Profit], [Time].[2005]))
  )
)
```

	2004	2005
Gobi Crab Cakes	25,000	28,400
Silver Scales	24,500	26,900
Poseidon's Platter	21,100	19,000

Figure 7-15   Results of first try.

At last, you have the tuples that you want (see Figure 7-16). Note that in this last version of the query, you needed to reference the current member of the customer dimension in order to have the result set contain both customers and products.

Analytically, this particular result is useful for the fairly arbitrary cutoffs that we chose to define important products for important customers. Importance is defined for this example as importance to the organization (we are looking at profitability, not units, revenue, value of long-term contracts, and so on). The thresholds are very arbitrary because we are choosing the top-N products and customers. Choosing sets of customers and products based on their percentage contribution to profits, revenues, and the like would be a less arbitrary choice, and these are equally easy. For example, for the set of customers that form the most profitable 10 percent, what are the most profitable 20 percent of the products they each buy? Replacing the TopCount() function in the expression with TopPercent() gives you the following:

```
SET [Top 10% of Custs] AS
'{ TopPercent ([Customer].[Individual].Members, 10,
      ([Measures].[Profit], [Time].[2005])) }'
SET [Top 20% Prods Of Top 10% Custs] AS
'{ Generate ( [Top 10% of Custs],
    CrossJoin ( { [Customer].CurrentMember },
      TopPercent ([Product].[Brand].Members, 20,
        ([Measures].[Profit], [Time].[2005])
      )
    )
  )
}'
```

		2004	2005
Hudson Food Dists.	Gobi Crab Cakes	1,200	1,370
	Silver Scales	1,400	1,250
	Poseidon's Platter	1,100	1,000
Barbara, Levin Inc.	Gobi Crab Cakes	1,120	990
	Silver Scales	1,040	980
	Poseidon's Platter	1,200	1,300

Figure 7-16 Results of desired query.

This can lead to several other useful related queries. For example, this expression gives you the products per customer. If the goal is to then focus on the production, distribution, or pricing of these products, you may be interested in removing the specific customers and looking just at the products. Each customer is likely to have products in common with other customers. In fact, it is not immediately obvious how many different products are in this group. The set of customers is unknown in advance of the query. How can you find out the number of products or the set of products?

The answer can be found by using the MDX Extract() function, which returns a set of selected dimensionality. You can use it to return the unique set of products from our selected customer by product tuples, as with the following expression:

```
SET [Top 10%'s Top 20 Products] AS
'Extract ([Top 20% Prods Of Top 10% Custs], [Product])'
```

Extract() returns only unique tuples, so you don't have to worry about finding duplicates. The products will be in a fairly arbitrary order, and you can sort them further if you want to. You can also take this set and count the tuples to find out how many products make up this group.

If the goal is to understand how these customers are or are not representative of the customers as a whole, you may want to compare the product mix purchased by the top 10 percent of customers with the product mix purchased by the average customer. Which brands that are in the top 20 percent by profitability for our top 10 percent of customers are also in the top 20 percent of profitability for all customers? Which ones are peculiar to the top customers? Which ones, if any, are among the most profitable products for all customers, but not among the most profitable products for our top customers? If you are exploring customers and products by profitability, these are also important questions.

This last set of three questions could be answered in one query, and we will continue our train of thought to create it. We will make one creative leap to put it together. The goal is to create a grouping of products into three different groups: those that correspond to only the top-10 customers, those that correspond to both the top-10 group and across all customers, and those that correspond only across all customers and not within the top 10. These three groups represent customer populations, and you will use three calculated members on the customer dimension to represent these groups. (If no products exist in one of these three groups, you will not have any product-customer group tuples that use that customer group, and that group will not appear in the query result.)

You need to construct two basic sets and then manipulate them to get the third. The first set, of top products for top customers, you have already created as [Top 10%'s Top 20 Products]. The second set, of top products across all customers, is similar:

```
SET [Top 20% Prods Across All Custs] AS
'TopPercent ([Product].[Brand].Members, 20,
     ([Measures].[Profit], [Time].[2005]))'
```

The trick now is to create three divisions between those two sets. You need to pool them before dividing them up, using the following expression:

```
SET [Product Union] AS 'Union ([Top 20% Prods Across All Custs],

[Top 10%'s Top 20 Products])'
```

You could also create the same effect with the following expression:

```
Distinct ({[Top 20% Prods Across All Custs],
     [Top 10%'s Top 20 Products] })
```

Now, you simply create three subsets using set functions in sequence:

```
SET [Top10 Only] AS
'Except ([Product Union], [Top 20% Prods Across All Custs])'
SET [Both Groups] AS
'Intersect ([Top 10%'s Top 20 Products],
     [Top 20% Prods Across All Custs])'
SET [All Customers Only] AS
'Except ([Product Union], [Top 20% Prods Across All Custs])'
```

The last step is to create the calculated members that will group these three subsets. "Calculated members" implies computation; what formula calculates the cells within these sets without altering the contents of the cells?

We know that we want to use some sort of default member for this calculation. These members are on the Customer dimension, so a formula of [Customer].[All Customer] makes sense. That formula causes the values of each of the products to be taken from the [All Customer] member for whatever measure is being calculated. So, the three calculated members can each have a very simple formula:

```
MEMBER [Customer].[Top 10% Only Group] AS '[Customer].[All Customer]'
MEMBER [Customer].[Top 10% And All Group] AS '[Customer].[All Customer]'
MEMBER [Customer].[All Customers Only Group] AS '[Customer].[All
Customer]'
And we can create our final set of tuples for reporting on as follows:
SET [Report Tuples] AS '{
   CrossJoin ( { [Customer].[Top 10% Only Group] }, [Top10 Only] ),
   CrossJoin ( { [Customer].[Top 10% And All Group] }, [Both Groups] ),
   CrossJoin ( { [Customer].[All Customers Only Group] }, [All Customers
Only]) }'
```

When we put it all together, it forms the following (long) query, whose results are shown in Figure 7-17:

```
WITH
SET [Top 10% of Custs] AS
'TopPercent ([Customer].[Individual].Members, 10,
     ([Measures].[Profit], [Time].[2005]))'
SET [Top 20% Prods Of Top 10% Custs] AS
'Generate( [Top 10% of Custs],
  CrossJoin (
    {[Customer].CurrentMember},
    TopPercent ([Product].[Brand].Members, 20,
      ([Measures].[Profit], [Time].[2005])


  )
 )
)'
SET [Top 10%'s Top 20% Products] AS
  'Extract ([Top 20% Prods Of Top 10% Custs], [Product])'
SET [Top 20% Prods Across All Custs] AS
  'TopPercent ([Product].[Brand].Members, 20,
     ([Measures].[Profit], [Time].[2005]))'
SET [Product Union] AS
  'Union ([Top 20% Prods Across All Custs],
    [Top 10%'s Top 20% Products])'
SET [Top10 Only] AS
  'Except ([Product Union], [Top 20% Prods Across All Custs])'
SET [Both Groups] AS
  'Intersect ([Top 10%'s Top 20% Products],
  [Top 20% Prods Across All Custs])'
SET [All Customers Only] AS
  'Except ([Top 20% Prods Across All Custs], [Product Union])'
MEMBER [Customer].[Top 10% Only Group] AS '[Customer].[All Customer]'
MEMBER [Customer].[Top 10% And All Group] AS '[Customer].[All Customer]'
MEMBER [Customer].[All Customers Only Group] AS '[Customer].[All
Customer]'
SET [Report Tuples] AS '{
  CrossJoin ( { [Customer].[Top 10% Only Group] }, [Top10 Only] ),
  CrossJoin ( { [Customer].[Top 10% And All Group] }, [Both Groups] ),
  CrossJoin ( { [Customer].[All Customers Only Group] }, [All Customers
Only])
}'
SELECT
{ [Time].[2004], [Time].[2005] } on columns,
{ [Report Tuples] } on rows
FROM SalesInfo
WHERE ([Measures].[Profit])
```

		2004	2005
Top 10% Only Group	Gobi Crab Cakes	25,000	28,400
	Silver Scales	24,500	26,900
Top 10% and All Group	Poseidon's Platter	21,100	19,000
	Make Steak--o	18,300	21,000
All Customers Only	Atlantic Trench Mo	18,100	16,300

Figure 7-17 Results of full query.

Whew! Although this is an involved query, it is not as complex as it would have been if we had tried to perform the same operation in SQL against the original source tables!

Summary

Although we have discussed a number of topics in this chapter, we have used only a fraction of the MDX functions available. It would not be possible to exhaustively cover all applications and MDX techniques in any one book. Note that we have tended to use the same functions over and over, but we've put them together in slightly different ways to accomplish a range of requirements. If you review the functions and operators available to you in Appendix A, you will begin to see more possibilities than you did before for how to take the "assemblies of moving parts" that we have explained in this chapter, and replace them with other parts to create other selections and calculations that you need. Hopefully, this chapter has given you all of the conceptual tools you need to understand how MDX functions as a language and how your OLAP server and MDX work together so that you can construct as sophisticated an application as your situation requires.

CHAPTER 8

Using the Attribute Data Model of Microsoft Analysis Services

So far you have learned the MDX language and the various ways of creating and applying calculations to solve common business problems. MDX was first introduced by Microsoft along with SQL Server Analysis Services 7.0 in 1998. Since its introduction several OLAP providers such as Hyperion Essbase and SAP have started supporting MDX. Microsoft's Analysis Services 2005 supports the MDX per the OLE DB for OLAP specification, along with its own extensions to enrich the data retrieval from the multidimensional database within Analysis Services 2005.

Analysis Services 2005 combines the power of OLAP with a fair amount of flexibility of relational reporting, providing a unified model to the end users. In this chapter, you will first learn how Analysis Services 2005 is able to provide you the functionality of relational and OLAP databaseswith the help of Unified Dimensional Model (UDM). We will discuss how a multidimensional database is modeled using the dimensions and cubes within Analysis Services. The calculation model of Analysis Services 2005 is primarily based on attributes, which are entities that are part of the dimensions, and the relationships between the attributes. Analysis Services 2005 introduces MDX scripts, an entity that holds all the calculations that are to be applied to a cube. You will be introduced to the attribute-based calculation model, and MDX scripts in this chapter. You will learn properties of UDM and new MDX functions that can affect results of MDX queries in this chapter. Finally, you will learn how to set up security for the dimensions using the attribute hierarchies.

The Unified Dimensional Model (UDM)

Central to the architecture is the concept of the Unified Dimensional Model (UDM), which, by the way, is unique to this release of the product. UDM as the name suggests provides you a way to encapsulate data access to multiple heterogeneous data sources into a single model. In fact, with the UDM, you will be buffered from the difficulties of disparate data sources. The UDM itself is more than multiple data source cube. It actually defines the schema of your cubes and dimensions, including enhancements such as calculations actions, translations, perspectives and key performance indicators. Think of the UDM as providing you the best of the OLAP and relational worlds. UDM provides you the rich metadata needed for analyzing and exploring data along with the functionality such as complex calculation, aggregations of the OLAP world and the complex schemas, capability for supporting ad hoc queries that are needed for reporting needs of the relational world. Creation of cubes with multiple fact tables in Analysis Services 2005 has become significantly easier as compared to Analysis Services 2000 with the help of the UDM. The UDM is your friend and helps you create a single model that can support majority of your business needs. Key elements of the UDM are:

- **Heterogeneous data access support:** UDM helps you to integrate and encapsulate data from heterogeneous data sources. It helps you in combining various schemas into a single unified model that enables end users with the capability of sending queries to a single model.

- **Real-time data access with high performance:** Analysis Services 2005 provides end users with real-time data access. Once you have defined the UDM Analysis Services creates a MOLAP(multi-dimensional OLAP) cache of the underlying data. Whenever there are changes in the underlying relational database a new MOLAP cache is built. When users query the model it provides the results from the MOLAP cache. During the time the cache is being built results are retrieved from the relational database. Analysis Services helps in providing real-time data access with the speed of an OLAP database due to the MOLAP cache. This feature is called Proactive caching. You can learn more about this feature in the book Professional SQL Server Analysis Services 2005 with MDX by Harinath and Quinn (Wiley, 2006).

- **Rich metadata, ease of use for exploration and navigation of data:** UDM provides a consolidated view of the underlying data sources with the richness of metadata provided by the OLAP world. Due to this rich metadata supported by the OLAP end users are able to exploit this metadata for navigation and exploration of data with ease to make business decisions. UDM also provides you with ability to view specific sections of the unified model based on your business analysis needs.

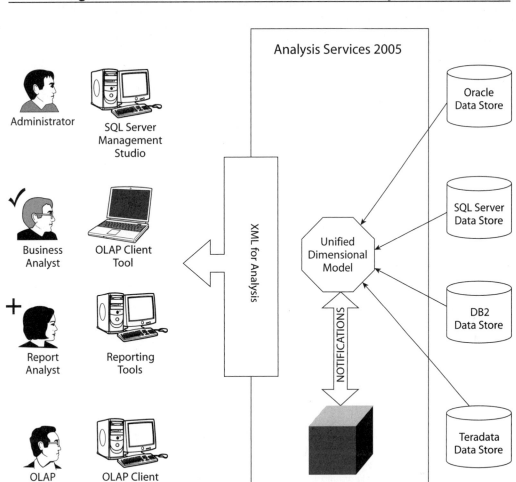

Figure 8-1   The Unified Dimensional Model.

- **Rich analytics support:** In addition to the rich metadata support the UDM provides you with the ability to specify complex calculations to be applied on the underlying data to embed business logic. You can specify the complex calculations by the attribute based calculation model using MDX. All the calculations are contained within the UDM as a single entity called MDX scripts. You learn MDX Scripts in Chapter 13. UDM provides rich analytics such as Key Performance Indicators and Actions that help in understanding your business with ease and take appropriate actions based on change in data.

- **Model for reporting and analysis:** UDM provides the best functionality of both relational and OLAP world. UDM not only provides you with the capability of querying the aggregated data typically used for analysis but also has the ability of providing detailed reporting up to the transaction level across multiple heterogeneous data sources.

     Another handy aspect of using UDM is the storage of foreign language translations for both data and metadata. This is handled seamlessly by the UDM so that a connecting user gets the metadata and data of interest customized to his or her locale. Of course, somebody has to enter those translations into the UDM in the first place; it is not actually a foreign language translation system. The UDM content presented in this chapter has been derived from *Professional SQL Server Analysis Services 2005 with MDX* by Harinath and Quinn (Wiley, 2006).

Dimensions

Dimensions help you to define the structure of your cubes for effective data analysis. They provide you with the ability to slice and dice the cube data. Analysis Services 2005 provides you with the functionality of creating dimensions from star as well snowflake schemas. A star schema dimension is a dimension that is created from a single table, whereas the snowflake schema dimension is one that is created from two or more tables that have relationships established between them. Figures 8-2 and 8-3 show star schema and snowflake schema dimensions that are part of the Adventure Works DW database sample. Figures 8-2 and 8-3 show the dimensions within the Dimension Designer where you can see the tables used to create the dimension within DSV pane.

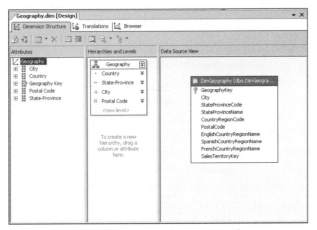

Figure 8-2   Dimension created from star schema.

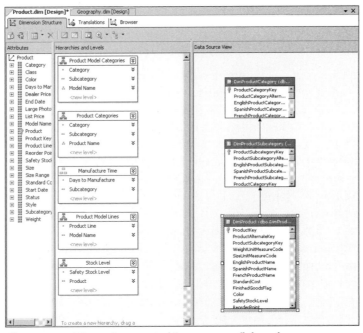

Figure 8-3   Dimension created from a snowflake schema

Dimensions in Analysis Services 2005 are composed of entities called attributes. Typically, there is a one-to-one correspondence between a column in dimension table and the attribute within a dimension. Analysis Services provides you a way to establish relationship between the attributes of a dimension. For example, a customer's address would typically contain city, state, and country. You can certainly establish relationship that there is a many-to-one relationship between city and the state. Attributes along with relationships are fundamental to the calculation model of cubes in Analysis Services 2005. One of the key fundamentals that you learned in Chapter 4 is the fact that cross-joining two attributes within the same dimension does not result in the Cartesian product of the members but only results in the members that exist between themseleves which are referred to as autoexists. For example if you have attributes city and state in a dimension then cross-join of a city member seattle with all the states will only result in (seattle, washington) since seattle only exists with a single state washington.You will see some additional MDX examples of the autoexists behavior later in this chapter.

Attributes, Hierarchies, and Relationships

Analysis Services 2005 has tried to combine the relational and OLAP world using a new model called the attribute-relationship model that helps in defining your cubes, which Microsoft refers to as UDMs. In Analysis Services 2005, dimensions comprise of entities called attributes. Each attribute within a dimension is bound to a column in the dimension table. Each dimension should have at least one attribute that is defined as the key attribute. The key attribute is typically the primary key of the main table that forms the dimension. You have the option to change the key attribute of the dimension based on your business requirements. Analysis Services 2005 provides you the Business Intelligence Development Studio; using this you can design the dimensions for your multidimensional database. We will not be going through the steps of creating dimensions or cube in this chapter. We assume that you have a working knowledge of Analysis Services 2005 tools. If you have not worked with Analysis Services 2005, we recommend reading the book *Professional SQL Server Analysis Services 2005 with MDX* by S. Harinath and S. Quinn (Wiley Publishing, Inc., 2006), which walks you through the entire product including designing dimensions and cubes. Figure 8-4 shows the Dimension Designer for the dimension Geography of the sample Adventure Works DW database that is shipped with SQL Server 2005. You can see in Figure 8-4 that there are three panes called Attributes, Hierarchies and Levels, and Data Source View.

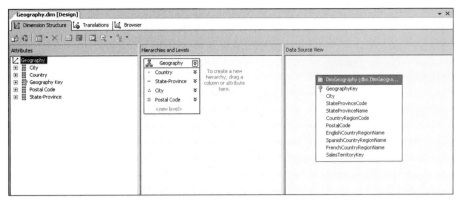

Figure 8-4   Dimension Designer showing Geography dimension.

In order to browse dimensions, Analysis Services provides you a way to navigate the members in the dimension using hierarchies. There are two kinds of hierarchies within a dimension. We define them as attribute hierarchies and multilevel hierarchies. Consider hierarchies as navigational vehicles to explore the space within a dimension or a cube that contains the dimension. Attribute hierarchies are hierarchies that exactly contain two levels. The levels are the default level and the All level. Attribute hierarchies are shown in the Attributes pane within the Dimension editor as shown in Figure 8-4. Attribute hierarchies directly refer to the attributes that form the dimensional space. Attribute hierarchies typically will be used by customers for their relational-style reporting or ad hoc querying.

Multilevel hierarchies are the traditional OLAP-style navigational entities that contain multiple levels. For example, the Geography hierarchy in Geography dimension is a multilevel hierarchy with levels Country, State-Province, City, and Postal Code, as shown in Figure 8-4. When browsing the cube data using the multilevel hierarchy Analysis Services aggregates the right data at each level.

Attributes

Attributes are the building blocks of dimensions in Analysis Services 2005. When you create dimensions using the Dimension Wizard, you are asked to select the attributes for your dimension. You need to select the attributes that are essential for your business analysis. You might only need a subset of the columns from the dimension table to become attributes for business analysis. The number of attributes you add to each dimension affects the space of your cube because the cube space is a product of the attributes of all dimensions. Typically, you would refer to the size of the cube being dependent on the dimensions as dimensionality of the cube. In Analysis Services 2005, we refer to this as hierarchality of the cube space the cube space is affected by the number of hierarchies in the dimensions. Hence you need to make sure that you add the essential attributes to your dimensions.

Figure 8-5:   Dimension Attributes in Dimension Designer.

Figure 8-5 shows the attributes of the Geography dimension in the sample Adventure Works DW project. There are several views to show the attributes of a dimension—tree, list, and grid. In all the views of the attribute pane, the key attribute can be easily distinguished by the key symbol. If you expand each attribute by clicking on the plus sign, you will see the attributes that are related to the current attribute. All the attributes within a dimension are related to the key attribute directly or indirectly. Figure 8-6 shows the attributes pane for the dimensions Customers and Geography in the Adventure Works DW database. You can see that all the attributes in the Customer dimension are directly related to the key attribute Customer because you can see all the related attributes under the Customer attribute. For the Geography dimension, you can see the hierarchical relationship where all the attributes are related to the key attribute Geography Key indirectly. By indirectly related, we mean that an attribute is related to the key attribute through another attribute. For example there is a one-to-many relationship between Postal Code and Geography Key and another one-to-many relationship between Postal Code and City. Therefore, there exists a one-to-many relationship between City and the Geography Key. You might recall from Chapter 4 that an attribute hierarchy and its relationship with other attributes affects the results of the MDX query because of the overriding behavior defined by strong hierarchies. You will see some examples of these later in this section.

Figure 8-6   Dimension Attribute views showing Related Attributes.

Hierarchies and Levels

The term hierarchies in Analysis Services 2005 refers to the traditional OLAP navigation hierarchy that contains multiple levels. These are also referred to as user hierarchies because you as a user define the hierarchy with appropriate levels. There might exist a natural relationship between the various levels at which there is a one-to-many relationship between various levels in the hierarchy. Figure 8-7 shows a multilevel hierarchy called Geography in the Geography dimension. The levels of the hierarchy are basically attributes in the dimension. If there is a relationship between the levels of the hierarchy, then that is indicated in the user interface, as shown in Figure 8-7. For example the existence of one-to-many relationship between Country and State-Province levels is indicated by the fact that there is an attribute relationship between State-Province and Country attribute as shown in Figure 8-7. If your hierarchy has such relationships between attributes at every level, then the hierarchy is called a natural hierarchy. However, if there is at least one level where there is no one-to-many relationship between that level and one of the levels above or beneath it, then such a hierarchy is called unnatural hierarchy. For example if a multilevel hierarchy in dimension contains levels Age, Gender and Name then there is no specific relationship between Age and Gender; i.e. all males or females which are members of the Gender level can be of any age. An example of an un-natural hierarchy is the Employee Department hierarchy in the Employee dimension of the sample Adventure Works DW project.

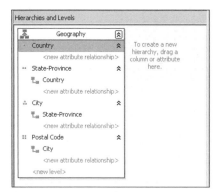

Figure 8-7   Hierarchies and Levels of a dimension with relationships.

You can browse the hierarchies and attributes using the dimension browser in Business Intelligence Development Studio. Figure 8-8 shows the members of the multilevel hierarchy Geography in the Geography dimension. The dimension browser allows you to browse various hierarchies (attribute or multilevel) with appropriate selection using the drop-down list box Hierarchy, as shown in Figure 8-8.

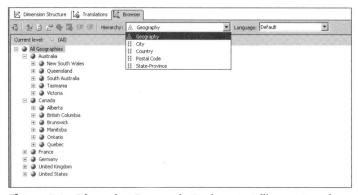

Figure 8-8   Dimension Browser in Business Intelligence Development Studio.

Relationships

Relationships between attributes play a critical role in the calculation model of Analysis Services 2005. The results of an MDX query involving attributes in a dimension depend on whether there exists a relationship between those attributes. Analysis Services 2005 has specific set of overwrite semantics, which is applied to your MDX queries based on the relationships between attributes. The Analysis Services 2005 calculation model is basically derived using the attributes. However, you do have the option of navigating the dimension members using either the attribute hierarchies or multilevel hierarchies. Hence, a user can be browsing the data using a multilevel hierarchy Country→ State-Province→City as well as the attribute hierarchy City. The results of your query can vary, depending on whether the relationships between Country, State-Province, and City are defined or not and the hierarchies involved in the query. This is due to the overwrite semantics (rules that get applied when a member from a user hierarchy cannot reference a cell which results in the member being changed to a valid member in that hierarchy that can access that cell) of Analysis Services 2005.

To establish relationship between two attributes, all you have to do is to drag and drop the attribute under another attribute in the tree view of the attribute pane or in the hierarchies and levels pane. For example, if you need to establish the relationship between Country and State-Province, then you need to expand the attribute or level State-Province and drag and drop the Country attribute below the State-Province attribute where it states "new attribute relationship." Once you have completed this operation a relationship is established between the attributes. You can further refine the type of relationship to be one-to-one or one-to-many, using the property Cardinality in the Properties window.

The attributes along with the relationships form a critical part of the calculation model in Analysis Services 2005. You saw examples of how the results of MDX queries are affected by the relationships between attributes that are part of the query in Chapter 4. In addition, defining relationships between attributes within a dimension greatly helps in improving your processing and query performances.

Querying Dimensions

When you create a dimension in Analysis Services 2005 using Dimension Wizards you have actually created a dimension that is called as the database dimension. Instances of this dimension can then be added to cube(s) within that database. Similarly to querying a cube, you can query the database dimensions. Internally, database dimensions are nothing but a single-dimension cube. Because the MDX query needs to include a cube identifier for queries, Analysis Services provides you with a special way of querying data from database dimension using the syntax $\$<DimensionName>$. One of the simplest queries to issue against the Customer database dimension is to query the various countries of the customers. Figure 8-9 shows the MDX query and the results obtained in querying the database dimension Customer from the sample Adventure Works DW database. Because the cube being queried is the database dimension and there is no default measure, the cell values are NULL in the query.

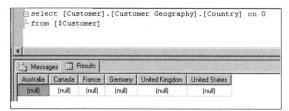

Figure 8-9   Querying a Database Dimension.

You learned about the autoexists feature that is applied when two attributes within the same dimension are queried. Figure 8-10 shows the behavior of autoexists when we query the cross-join of the customers countries and state-province. You can see that Analysis Services 2005 has eliminated all the state-country combinations that do not exist with each other in the result set. You would typically expect the result to be the product of members from both hierarchies. However, the result does not contain "states" of Canada, such as Alberta, cross-joined with Australia. Due to the autoexists behavior in Analysis Services 2005 for hierarchies within a single dimension, states are only shown with their respective country in the results of the MDX query.

```
SELECT
  [Customer].[Country].[Country].MEMBERS *
  [Customer].[State-Province].[State-Province].MEMBERS
ON 0
FROM [$Customer]
```

Australia	Australia	Australia	Australia	Australia	Canada	Canada	Canada	Canada	Canada	Canada
New South Wales	Queensland	South Australia	Tasmania	Victoria	Alberta	British Columbia	Brunswick	Manitoba	Ontario	Quebec
(null)	(null)	(null)	(null)	(null)	(null)	(null)	(null)	(null)	(null)	(null)

Figure 8-10   MDX Query showing AutoExists behavior.

Similarly to having calculations within the query scope, you can have calculations in queries against the database dimension. Figure 8-11 shows an MDX query that retrieves the number of customers in each city. In this query, the function Exists is used to determine if a specific customer exists with the current city used in the context of the query. The Exists function has two flavors. One of the flavors accepts a set and a filter set and returns the tuples from the first set that intersects with members in the filter set. The second flavor takes an additional parameter, MeasureGroupName, in which the Exists is applied across the measure group. You will see an example of the Exists function with a measure group in the "Cubes" section of this chapter. The results of the MDX query are sorted in descending order by the ORDER function used in the query.

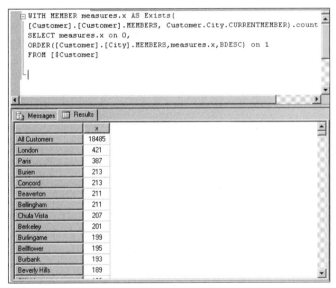

Figure 8-11   Querying Database Dimension with query scope calculation.

The dimension browser you saw Figure 8-8 issues MDX queries against the database dimension to retrieve the members in the database dimension. For example, if you expand the All Geographies member of the user hierarchy Geography in the Customer dimension, the dimension browser needs to retrieve the members in the next level. For that, the dimension browser sends the MDX query shown in Figure 8-12, which retrieves the members and the key value for each member. If you execute this MDX query against the sample database, you will see the results shown in Figure 8-12.

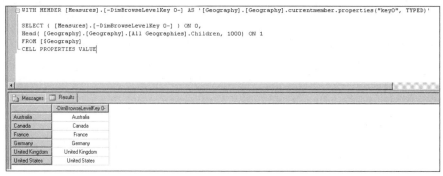

Figure 8-12   MDX Query to database dimension for retrieving members in a dimension.

Member Properties

Analysis Services provides you a way to define properties for members of a hierarchy. Member properties are useful for getting additional information about members in the results of the query. For example, if you perform analysis of sales of products and pick the top-100 customers for your business based on sales information, then you might want to know certain attributes of the customers so that you can target similar ones. Some typical attributes that you might want to look for are salary, age, and number of children.

Analysis Services provides you a way to define member properties in the your model and later query the member properties in your MDX query. By default, there are certain intrinsic member properties that are provided by Analysis Services such as Key, ID, and Name, which are all derived directly from the relational column to which the hierarchy is bound. Additional member properties can be defined within Analysis Services 2005 dimension designer using the related properties or relationship. Whenever you want to define a specific attribute as member property, you drag and drop the corresponding attribute as a relationship to a specific attribute. For example income, marital status, and the like might be attributes that might be of interest when querying customers. Hence, these attributes need to be defined as related attributes to the customer attribute. By default, all attributes are related to the key attribute of a dimension, and the attributes can be retrieved as member properties when you browse the key attributes. However, if you specifically need certain properties to be established as member properties for non-key attributes, then you do need to establish the relationship with appropriate cardinality yourself. Once you have established the relationship, the member properties can be queried in MDX.

Member properties can be retrieved either via the dimension member properties syntax or using the MDX function properties. Figure 8-13 shows an MDX query retrieving the member properties for the customers from Customer dimension using the member properties syntax. Figure 8-13 shows the results of executing the query within SQL Server Management Studios's MDX query editor. There are more members returned by this query. If you double-click on the member Adriana Smith, for example, you will see that the member properties have been retrieved as part of the result. Figure 8-14 shows the member properties dialog for the customer Adriana Smith.

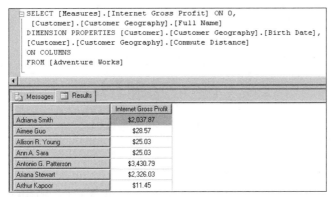

```
SELECT [Measures].[Internet Gross Profit] ON 0,
    [Customer].[Customer Geography].[Full Name]
    DIMENSION PROPERTIES [Customer].[Customer Geography].[Birth Date],
    [Customer].[Customer Geography].[Commute Distance]
    ON COLUMNS
    FROM [Adventure Works]
```

	Internet Gross Profit
Adriana Smith	$2,037.87
Aimee Guo	$28.57
Allison R. Young	$25.03
Ann A. Sara	$25.03
Antonio G. Patterson	$3,430.79
Ariana Stewart	$2,326.03
Arthur Kapoor	$11.45

Figure 8-13   MDX Query retrieving dimension member properties.

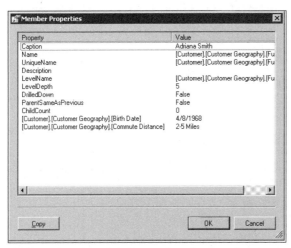

Figure 8-14   Member Properties of a member.

Figure 8-15 shows an MDX query that uses member properties to filter the customers from the result. In this example, the member property for the current customer member is retrieved and compared to the value 0-1 Miles. Because the member property retrieved is a string, an exact matching using the equal to operator is possible. If the member property attribute is an integer data type, then you can perform other logical expressions.

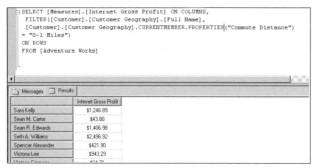

```
SELECT [Measures].[Internet Gross Profit] ON COLUMNS,
  FILTER([Customer].[Customer Geography].[Full Name],
  [Customer].[Customer Geography].CURRENTMEMBER.PROPERTIES("Commute Distance")
  = "0-1 Miles")
ON ROWS
FROM [Adventure Works]
```

	Internet Gross Profit
Sara Kelly	$1,246.89
Sean M. Carter	$43.80
Sean R. Edwards	$1,406.98
Seth A. Williams	$2,496.92
Spencer Alexander	$421.90
Victoria Lee	$943.29

Figure 8-15 Using member properties to filter results.

Some of the attributes that are defined as member properties are typically not used for browsing for the end users. It is highly recommended that you disable such attributes from being browsable by setting the property for the attribute `AttributeHierarchyEnabled` to false. In the Customer dimension, you can see that the attributes Birth Date and Commute Distance Sort are disabled from browsing. By disabling member properties from browsing, you instruct Analysis Services to avoid operations such as building indexes during processing, which are especially very helpful in large dimensions. You will learn more about the intrinsic member properties with examples in Appendix C.

Parent-Child Hierarchies

If you are familiar with Analysis Services 2000, you will know about parent-child dimensions, which are unique and, in modeling, solve various types of business problems. Parent-child dimensions by themselves are not unique across other OLAP providers, but they are special within Analysis Services because they support certain specific properties such as custom rollup and unary operators that help in custom calculations and roll up to the parent in a unique way.

Typically dimensions such as Employee and Accounts are modeled as parent-child dimensions where you have the flexibility of moving members under different parents and the appropriate rollup of data is established through custom calculations. In Analysis Services 2005, parent-child behavior is modeled using attributes, and the results of this process are called parent-child hierarchies. You need to have two columns in the relational table that model the parent-child behavior, where one column indicates the parent key. These two columns are modeled as attributes and are called the key and the parent attribute; within a dimension they form a parent-child hierarchy. You can only have one parent-child hierarchy within a single dimension. Figure 8-16 shows the Account dimension in the Adventure Works DW sample, which contains a parent-child hierarchy Accounts. Analysis Services 2005 only supports a single parent-child hierarchy within a dimension.

The parent attribute is the actual parent-child hierarchy that is used for browsing the members. In Figure 8-17 the attribute Accounts is the parent-child hierarchy and is indicated by the icon that has a relationship pointing to itself. Parent-child hierarchies can also be modeled as multilevel hierarchies with attributes created for each level by appropriately changing the relational data source. However, the main benefit of parent-child hierarchy is the fact that you do not have to know the number of levels and depth of the hierarchy. This is automatically deciphered by Analysis Services during processing based on the data. You do have the option of naming each level of the parent-hierarchy uniquely to distinguish the various levels. By default, while browsing a parent-child hierarchy you will see levels named Level 01, Level 02, and so on. Figure 8-16 shows the members in the Accounts hierarchy as viewed in the dimension browser.

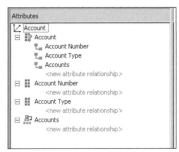

Figure 8-16   Dimension containing Parent-child hierarchy.

Figure 8-17   Browsing a parent-child hierarchy in Business Intelligence Development Studio.

With respect to MDX parent-child hierarchies are treated similar to other hierarchies. However the MDX function DataMember is typically used in conjunction with parent-child hierarchies. Typically leaf level members of a hierarchy have fact data associated with them. Non leaf members of a hierarchy typically get their data aggregated from their children. With Parent-Child hierarchies often non-leaf members also have fact data associated to them. In order to access the value of a non-leaf member in parent-child hierarchy you would typically use the DataMember MDX function.

Time Dimension

The Time dimension is a dimension that is uniquely treated by Analysis Services 2005. the Time dimension is a dimension that would contain hierarchies for various time periods such as Year→Quarter→Month→Date, which can be used for fiscal years or calendar years. Often, business requirements produce a need to analyze data based on calendar and fiscal years for reporting to the stock market and to the IRS for tax purposes. Analyzing your data using the Time dimension provides extremely useful insight into your business data. In the sample project, Adventure Works DW the Date dimension is the Time dimension. The dimension property Type is set to Time to indicate that the dimension is a time dimension. The Dimension Wizard guides you through a sequence of steps that allows you to create multilevel hierarchies that might be needed for analysis, based on the information you provide in the wizard. In Analysis Services, the Time dimension provides you with a unique way of aggregating data in a nonstandard way such as by Sum or Count such as LastChild, FirstChild, LastNonEmpty, and so on. Such aggregation functions are referred to as semi-additive measures because the member's values do not add up to its parent. Semi-additive measures are supported within Analysis Services natively, which provides performance improvements during querying. In addition to semi-additive measures, the Time dimension is also essential for specific rollups across an Account dimension based on the account type, for financial cubes.

In Analysis Services, you can model the attributes within the Time dimension in several ways because of the ability of attribute hierarchies. For example, your Time dimension will typically have attributes Year and Months. Instead of having the years and the standard months 1 through 12, you can now have years numbered 1 through N and months numbered 1 through $12 * N$. You will now be able to browse on the hierarchy Month from 1 though M. Such browsing helps in analyzing how the sales of a company have progressed from the beginning. When you define the granularity attribute above the key attribute Date, which is unique, you need to define the granularity attribute as a combination of multiple attributes such as Month and Year. Such a time dimension can be modeled in versions of Analysis Services prior to the 2005 release. However Analysis Services 2005 make it much easier to model such a dimension Since Time dimension is pretty standard in most cubes Analysis Services 2005 also provides you the option to build a time dimension without a fact table data.

Cubes

Cubes are principal objects in a multidimensional database that help in data analysis. Cubes are multidimensional structures that are composed of dimensions, measures, and the schema that defines the relationships between the measures and the dimensions. Measures are typically numerical data that can be aggregated. For example, the sales of products of various stores is a measure because the sales data is a numerical entity that can be aggregated based on the products or by stores, where products and stores are typically modeled as dimensions in the multidimensional database. Data that can be aggregated across various dimensions is called *fact data*. Fact data is typically stored in a separate relational table along with the IDs of the various dimensions. Such a table is called as a *fact table*. A fact table typically contains one or more fact columns, and each column modeled within the cube is called as a *measure*. Typically, measures from a single fact table are grouped together to form an entity called a *measure group*. Analysis Services 2005 supports the ability to hold fact data from more than one fact table.

The schema of cubes in Analysis Services is referred to as a UDM by Mirosoft because it encapsulates the dimensional model of your business. Figure 8-18 shows the cube designer for the cube Adventure Works in the sample database Adventure Works DW. The cube representation shown within the Data Source View pane is referred to as the UDM because it contains all the dimension and fact tables that are part of the cube.

When you do want to include multiple fact tables within your cube such as the sample Adventure Works cube, you will typically create multiple measure groups, one corresponding to each fact table. Figure 8-18 shows the Adventure Works cube, which contains several measure groups in the Measures pane. The Dimension pane contains all the dimensions that are defined as part of the UDM. When you have multiple measure groups included in a cube, all the measures are located under the measures dimension. Typically, MDX queries query for measures within a single measure group. To query the measures within a single measure group, Analysis Services 2005 provides a new MDX function called `MeasureGroupMeasures`. Figure 8-19 shows an MDX query that retrieves all the measures in the Internet Sales measure group using the `MeasureGroupMeasures` MDX function.

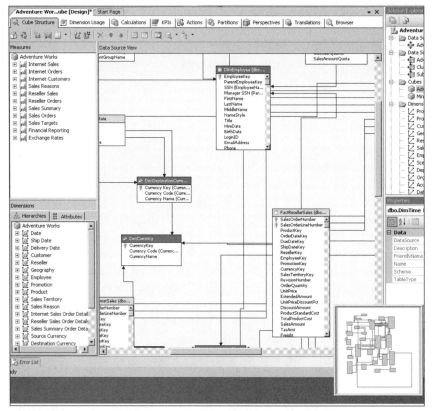

Figure 8-18   Cube designer showing the Adventure Works DW sample project.

```
SELECT MeasureGroupMeasures("Internet Sales") on COLUMNS,
  [Customer].[Customer Geography].[Country].members ON ROWS
FROM [Adventure Works]
```

	Internet Sales Amount	Internet Order Quantity	Internet Extended Amount	Internet Tax Amount	Internet Freight Cost	Internet Total Product Cost	Internet Standard Product Cost
Australia	$9,061,000.58	13,345	$9,061,000.58	$724,880.07	$226,525.61	$5,375,145.51	$5,375,145.51
Canada	$1,977,844.86	7,620	$1,977,844.86	$158,227.59	$49,446.45	$1,147,923.36	$1,147,923.36
France	$2,644,017.71	5,558	$2,644,017.71	$211,521.42	$66,100.70	$1,557,752.99	$1,557,752.99
Germany	$2,894,312.34	5,625	$2,894,312.34	$231,544.99	$72,358.06	$1,706,941.57	$1,706,941.57
United Kingdom	$3,391,712.21	6,906	$3,391,712.21	$271,336.98	$84,793.12	$2,001,221.43	$2,001,221.43
United States	$9,389,789.51	21,344	$9,389,789.51	$751,183.18	$234,745.66	$5,488,808.71	$5,488,808.71

Figure 8-19   MDX query using MeasureGroupMeasures MDX Function.

Analysis Services allows you to specify how the measures values should to be rolled up or aggregated over the hierarchies or dimensions that are being analyzed. Figure 8-20 shows the various aggregation functions that are natively supported in Analysis Services 2005. You might be familiar with some of these from Analysis Services 2000. As mentioned earlier, Analysis Services 2005 natively supports semi-additive measures such as FirstChild, LastChild. Semi-additive support helps you in avoiding writing your own calculations. Semi-additive measure aggregation functions only work when your cube contains a Time dimension. The `ByAccount` aggregation function is used to aggregate the measure value over the hierarchies in the Account dimension based on the type of accounts. If you want the aggregation function to perform a distinct count such as counting the number of distinct customers who provide you the maximum sales for your business, then it is recommended that you have the distinct count measure as a separate measure. Having the distinct count measure as a separate measure allows you to perform aggregations efficiently over the other measures in the same measure group as well as supporting writeback to the measure group.

Figure 8-20 Measure Aggregation Functions supported in Analysis Services 2005.

You must be familiar with the regular aggregation functions such as `Sum`, `Count`, and `Distinct`. Let's look at some MDX examples that include semi-additive measures. Figure 8-21 shows the measure `ExchangeRate`, which has an aggregation function average of children. When you browse the destination currency along with Time, you can see the various exchange rates and how the member's value is aggregated by taking the average of its children. For example, the exchange rate for an Australian dollar for Quarter Q1 CY 2002 is the average of the exchange rates in April 2002, May 2002, and June 2002.

				Australian Dollar Average Rate	Canadian Dollar Average Rate	EURO Average Rate	French Franc Average Rate	United Kingdom Pound Average Rate	US Dollar Average Rate
Calendar Year ▾	**Calendar Semester**	**Calendar Quarter**	**Month**						
⊟ CY 2001	⊟ H2 CY 2001	⊞ Q3 CY 2001		.64	.69	1.01	.15	1.62	1.00
		⊞ Q4 CY 2001		.60	.68	.95	.15	1.58	1.00
		Total		.62	.68	.98	.15	1.60	1.00
	Total			.62	.68	.98	.15	1.60	1.00
⊟ CY 2002	⊟ H1 CY 2002	⊟ Q1 CY 2002	⊞ January 2002	.58	.67	.93		1.50	1.00
			⊞ February 2002	.60	.68	.95		1.51	1.00
			⊞ March 2002	.58	.68	.92		1.50	1.00
			Total	.59	.67	.93		1.50	1.00
		⊟ Q2 CY 2002	⊞ April 2002	.57	.68	.89		1.46	1.00
			⊞ May 2002	.54	.67	.87		1.44	1.00
			⊞ June 2002	.52	.66	.85		1.44	1.00
			Total	.55	.67	.87		1.45	1.00
		Total		.57	.67	.90		1.48	1.00
	⊞ H2 CY 2002			.53	.65	.90		1.45	1.00
	Total			.55	.66	.90		1.46	1.00
⊞ CY 2003				.52	.64	.89		1.43	1.00
⊞ CY 2004				.55	.64	.98		1.54	1.00
Grand Total				.55	.65	.93	.15	1.49	1.00

Figure 8-21 Browsing Exchange Rate for various currencies with Time in Cube Browser.

Figure 8-21 shows the results within the Office Web Components (OWC) embedded within Cube browser of Analysis Services 2005. OWC creates session calculated members and then generates the MDX query to retrieve the cell values. You can also retrieve the above results with the following MDX query.

```
SELECT {[Destination Currency].[Destination Currency].&[Australian
Dollar] ,
[Destination Currency].[Destination Currency].&[Canadian Dollar],
[Destination Currency].[Destination Currency].&[EURO] ,
[Destination Currency].[Destination Currency].&[United Kingdom Pound],
[Destination Currency].[Destination Currency].&[US Dollar] } on COLUMNS,
Descendants([Date].[Fiscal].[All Periods],[Date].[Fiscal].[Fiscal
Quarter], SELF_AND_BEFORE) ON ROWS
from [Adventure Works]
where [Measures].[End of Day Rate]
```

Earlier you saw how the `Exists` function is used to restrict data between hierarchies of the same dimension. You can also use `Exists` function across dimensions and include a measure group to perform the exists operation. For example the following MDX query uses the `Exists` function to restrict the product categories that have been sold in various countries through Internet sales. When you have multiple measure groups and dimensions that have relationships with multiple measure groups, you can use the `Exists` function to perform appropriate filtering operation.

```
WITH SET [productcategoryfilter] as Exists([Product].[Product Model
Categories].[category],
[Customer].[Customer Geography].[Country], "Internet Sales")
select measures.[Internet Sales Amount] on COLUMNS,
[productcategoryfilter] * [Customer].[Customer Geography].[Country]
on ROWS
from [Adventure Works]
```

Dimension Relationships

Dimensions are integral part of cubes for you to slice and dice data for analysis. You need to establish the right relationship between the dimensions and the fact data so that you can analyze the data based on your business need. There are several types of relationships you can establish between the dimensions and the fact data. Figure 8-22 shows some of the relationships that have been established between various dimensions in the Adventure Works DW database and the measure groups. The possible relationship types between a dimension and a measure group are:

1. No relationship
2. Regular

3. Fact

4. Referenced

5. Many-to-many

6. Data mining

Relationship between measure groups and dimensions are through one or more attributes in the dimension. The relationship between dimensions and measure groups is often through the key attribute of the dimensions. However, in certain cases the relationship does not have to be the key attribute. The attribute through which the relationship between dimension and measure group is established is called the granularity attribute. When you have a dimension key in a fact table that is directly joined to an attribute in the dimension table, this is called as the regular relationship. If there is no join between a measure group and a dimension, then there is no relationship. In Figure 8-22, the cells that are grayed out indicate that there is no relationship between the dimension and the measure group. In most cases, the relationship type between the dimension and the measure group is either a regular relationship or no relationship. You are most likely familiar with the regular relationship and querying data for dimensions that have regular relationships with the measure groups in Analysis Services 2000 as well as having seen several examples presented in this book.

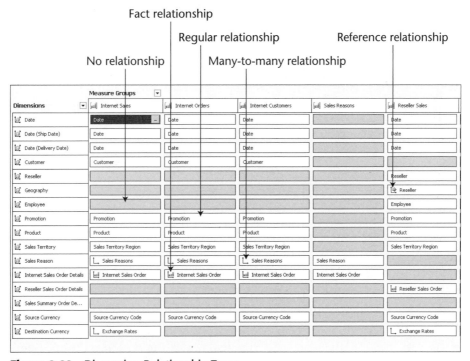

Figure 8-22 Dimension Relationship Types.

When there is no relationship between the measure group and the dimension, you will typically get NULL values when you query the dimension along with measures from the measure group that have no relationship with it. In Analysis Services 2000 you can have a similar scenario with no relationships when you create virtual cubes. In order to avoid having the NULL result returned, the ValidMeasure function was typically used to retrieve the value. In order to retrieve the value the ValidMeasure function used to return the cell value for the All level coordinate for the dimensions that were not common or did not have a relationship. In Analysis Services 2005, you have property for the measure group called IgnoreUnrelatedDimensions. If this is set to true, then this enforces the behavior of ValidMeasure on the query so that you do get results when you query unrelated dimensions. Figure 8-23 shows an MDX query that includes a dimension and measure that are not related. You see the same reseller Sales Amount value for all the members because that is the value for the All level coordinate. If you look at the Reseller Sales measure group, you will see that the property IgnoreUnrelatedDimension is set to true. If you change this property to false and send the MDX query in Figure 8-23, you will see NULL values for all the members. If the IgnoreUnrelatedDimension property is set to false, you can see the results in Figure 8-23 by modifying the MDX query to:

```
with member measures.x as ValidMeasure((([Measures].[Reseller Sales
Amount],
[Customer].[Customer Geography])))
SELECT measures.x on COLUMNS,
[Customer].[Customer Geography].[Country].members on ROWS
from [Adventure Works]
```

Figure 8-23   MDX query with IgnoreUnrelatedDimension set to true.

When the measure group and a dimension are derived from a single table, there is a relationship between the dimension and the measure group. Internally, Analysis Services 2005 treats this fact relationship similarly to a regular relationship. There are, however, optimizations that have been done when you perform a drill-through on a cell. For all practical purposes when using MDX queries, consider fact relationships to be similar to regular relationships.

A reference dimension relationship is a relationship in which you have two dimensions, such as Customer and Geography, where there is a relationship between the Customer and Geography dimensions because a Customer resides in a specific geographical location. Data has a direct relationship to the Customer, typically through the customer key attribute, and has an indirect or reference relationship to the Geography dimension through the customer dimension. Such a relationship allows you to query for information in a form such as "give me sales for all customers in the state of Washington." In the Adventure Works DW sample database, there are a few examples of the reference relationship. One example is the way that the Sales Territory dimension is related to the Sales Targets measure group. Employees belong to a specific territory and they have sales quotas to meet. There is no direct relationship between the sales territories and sales quotas. However, there is an indirect relationship through the Employee dimension. Hence, you can query for the sales quota amount for each territory, as shown in Figure 8-24. Analysis Services aggregates the sales amount quota for all the employees in each territory, and then those values are returned in the results of the query. When you have reference dimensions, you cannot build aggregations unless you mark the dimensions to be materialized at which point Analysis Services will treat the reference dimension similarly to a regular dimension and build indexes. Reference dimension relationship is primarily used for modeling purposes and MDX queries against the reference dimension behave similar to regular dimensions.

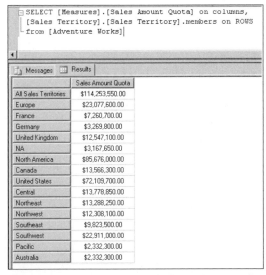

Figure 8-24 MDX query including reference dimension.

A data-mining relationship is a relationship that is established between a measure group and a dimension that was created from a data-mining model. Analysis Services 2005 supports creating data-mining models from cubes that are called OLAP Mining Models. From such a model, you can derive a dimension called a data-mining dimension by querying the information from the model. For example, clustering is a type of algorithm that groups data based on various criteria. If you cluster customers into 10 groups based on their sales, then you can query for the details of these 10 groups and create a data-mining dimension. Such a dimension can then combined with the original cube to form a new cube. The relationship between the measure group used for creating mining model and the dimension that was created from the mining model is referred to as data-mining relationship.

The many-to-many dimension that is introduced in Analysis Services 2005 is an interesting relationship in which a dimension table is joined to an intermediate fact table, which, in turn, is joined to another dimension table, which is finally joined to the measure group. Analysis Services 2005 aggregates the values for distinct regular dimension members related to the many-to-many dimension member by the measure group. This means that data is aggregated to the various levels exactly once. The relationship between the final measure group and the original dimension table is called a many-to-many relationship. In the Adventure Works DW sample project you have two many-to-many relationships defined. One of the relationships is between the Sales Reason Type dimension and the Fact Internet Sales measure group. The intermediate measure group Sales Reasons. When you query Internet Order Quantity with the Sales Reasons Type dimension, you get distinct sum of the values, as shown in Figure 8-25.

Sales Reason Type ▼	Sales Reason	Internet Sales Amount	Internet Order Quantity
⊟ Marketing	Television Advertisement	$27,475.82	730
	Total	$27,475.82	730
⊟ Other	Manufacturer	$5,998,122.10	1,818
	Other	$248,483.34	3,653
	Price	$10,975,842.56	47,733
	Quality	$5,549,896.77	1,551
	Review	$1,694,881.98	1,640
	Total	$18,678,948.02	51,314
⊟ Promotion	On Promotion	$6,361,828.95	7,390
	Total	$6,361,828.95	7,390
Grand Total		$29,358,677.22	60,398

Figure 8-25 Browsing dimension and measure group that have many-to-many relationship.

You can learn more about the various relationship types in the *Professional SQL Server Analysis Services 2005 with MDX* book by Harinath and Quinn (Wiley, 2006).

Role-Playing Dimensions

There are certain dimensions that can act in dual roles within your database. For example, you can have a Time dimension that serves as bill-to-customer date and shipped-to-customer date. In such cases, you can create two Time dimensions to model this scenario. However, modeling scenarios using two different dimensions just increases the cube space. Instead, Analysis Services provides you an efficient way of creating such dimensions so that a single database dimension will be acting as two or more dimensions within one cube. The dimension is said to be role-playing dimension because for each scenario the dimension adopts a particular role and provides the correct results. In the sample Adventure Works DW project, you have the Date dimension, which is role-playing dimension, and plays the role of Date, Shipped Date, and Delivery Date.

When you have a role playing dimension there are instances where your users might want to analyze results on one hierarchy based on a member in another hierarchy. For example you might want to identify all the products delivered on the date product B was shipped. The MDX LinkMember function is typically used in these scenarios in which you specify the member of interest and the hierarchy in which you want to find an equivalent member. Following MDX expression is an example of LinkMember MDX function is used where the the member in Fiscal Year hierarchy is retrieved for a corresponding member in the Calendar hierarchy.

LinkMember([Date].[Calendar].[CY 2004].[Jan], (Fiscal Year])) returns the corresponding member name for Calendar member Jan.

Perspectives

Because Analysis Services 2005 provides UDM to combine the relational and OLAP worlds through the UDM, you might find the UDM to be quite large, and you are typically interested only on a section or slice of the UDM. Analysis Services 2005 provides you with the flexibility to define sections of UDM that can be accessed similarly to a cube. Such entities are called *perspectives*. Consider the perspectives of a cube to be similar to views on top of a relational table. You can choose the dimensions, attributes, and measures that you want to be included within a perspective. Perspectives, for all practical purposes, act very similar to a cube in the sense that you can query the fact and dimension data. However, they are not real cubes. Hence, you will be able to query a dimension that is not part of the perspective through MDX queries. The following MDX query is performed against a perspective Channel Sales that does not contain the Customer dimension:

```
SELECT [Measures].[Reseller Sales Amount] on columns,
[Customer].[Customer Geography].[Country].members on ROWS
from [Channel Sales]
```

When you want to retrieve measures that are not part of the perspective, you need to create them as calculations in the query or session scope. If you do not do that, Analysis Services will elimniate the measure and return empty results. The following MDX query retrieves the Internet Sales Amount measure from the perspective Channel Sales even though Internet Sales measure group was not included in the perspective:

```
with member measures.x as [Measures].[Internet Sales Amount]
SELECT [Measures].x on columns,
[Customer].[Country].members on ROWS
from [Channel Sales]
```

Perspectives also use the attribute model for the calculations because they basically query the data from the real cube. Perspectives are just a way for you to visually restrict some part of your UDM. Perspectives do not provide any level of security because the base cube objects can be queried through the perspectives.

NOTE Perspectives are not a replacement for securing your cubes.

Drill-Through

A drill-through is an operation that is applied on a cell of a cube. As the name suggests *drill-through* means to drill into the details of the cell, exploring the data that make up to the cell value. In Analysis Services 2000, this referred to retrieving the fact data from the relational data source. In Analysis Services 2005, the fact data composing a cell can retrieved from Analysis Services rather than by going to the relational data source. However, if you do specify the storage mode as ROLAP, then the data will be fetched from the relational data source. You will learn about drill-throughs in detail in Chapter 14. It is important to understand drill-throughs with respect to multiple measure groups. Typically, you apply a drill-through on a cell to retrieve data from the same measure group. However, there was a customer scenario where users wanted to apply drill through a different measure group based on the dimensions that represented the cell under consideration. While requesting drill through for a cell you can specify the columns that need to be returned as part of the query. While doing drill through across multiple measure groups it is as simple as just specifying measures from the second measures group. You learn drill through in detail in Chapter 16.

The Calculation Model in UDM

At the core of the Analysis Services engine is the ability to model various complex business problems through calculations. In Analysis Services 2000, calculations were based on dimensions, where each dimension typically contained one or more multilevel hierarchies. The calculation model of Analysis Services 2005 differs from the previous version in that Analysis Services 2005 combines the traditional OLAP and relational world. That combination occurs as a result of leveraging the UDM through attribute hierarchies (which are entities within a dimension). The attribute hierarchies typically have two levels; the optional All level and another level that contains all the members of the attributes. The attributes of dimensions form the basis for the calculation model in Analysis Services 2005. The hierarchies are just used for navigational purposes, and cells in the cube can be referred to through multiple paths. For example, the following MDX queries return the same cells in the Adventure works cube. In these examples, you can navigate through the countries in which there are customers by using either the attribute hierarchy or the user hierarchy.

```
select [Measures].[Internet Sales Amount] on 0,
[Customer].[Customer Geography].[Country].members on 1
from [Adventure Works]

select [Measures].[Internet Sales Amount] on 0,
[Customer].[Country].[Country].members on 1
from [Adventure Works]
```

Most of the calculation definitions for a cube are defined within an object called MDX Script, which is part of a cube. There are some calculations that are specified as properties of dimension attributes such as custom rollups and unary operators. Each MDX script typically contains a `Calculate` statement, which aggregates the cell values across various dimensions. Some of the calculations that are specified in the MDX Script include calculated members, named sets, cell calculations using the `CREATE CELL` Calculation syntax or using the new assignment syntax. You can narrow down your cube space using a new statement in Analysis Services 2005 called `SCOPE`. You will learn more about MDX Scripts and various calculations, and how multiple calculations affecting a single cell are evaluated, in Chapter 13.

Defining Security on UDM

Security in Analysis Services 2005 is performed only through the attribute model. You need to create a role and provide access permissions to the cube and dimensions. Securing your dimension and cell data in Analysis Services 2005 is done through the attributes in various. Analysis Services 2005 provides you with a way to restrict dimension data for the entire database (database dimension) or for a specific cube (cube dimension). If you do restrict the data using database dimensions, then through inheritance the cube dimensions will also have the same security applied. Figure 8-26 shows the Roles editor, where the countries France and Germany are restricted to the member of the current role.

Restrictions on dimension data are specified through MDX expressions in Analysis Services. The Roles editor provides you with a nice user interface to perform the right selections. If you click on the Advanced tab, you can see that you can specify the MDX expression to allow or deny members of an hierarchy. Figure 8-27 shows the MDX expression that is specified in the denied set to allow members France and Germany to be included, as shown in Figure 8-26.

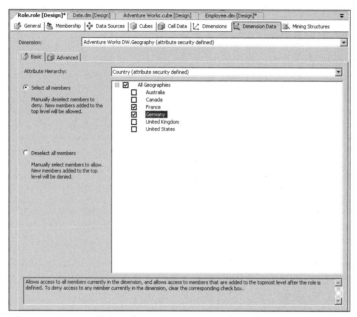

Figure 8-26 Defining dimension security in Roles editor.

You can see, in Figure 8-27, that there are three text boxes to specify an MDX expression for allowing or denying members of an hierarchy and one for specifying a default member when querying the database using the role. The allowed member set is used to specify the members that the users of this role can see. The denied member set disallows the members specified in the set from being seen by the users of the role. The MDX expressions for allowed sets, denied sets, and the default member need to evaluate to a set of members that are part of the hierarchy selected. The default member MDX expression should evaluate to one of the members in the selected hierarchy.

If you have relationships established between attributes and if these attributes form a multilevel hierarchy such as Country→State→County→ City→ZipCode, then disabling a member in the attribute hierarchy using Denied set will disable all its children from being viewed. In the example shown in Figure 8-27, where the countries Australia, Canada, United Kingdom, and United States are disabled, the user will not be able to browse these countries in the attribute hierarchy country or in the user hierarchy Geography. In addition to that, all the children of these countries will not be viewable by a user that belongs to the role. In the cube browser within Business Intelligence Development Studio or in SQL Server Management Studio, you can simulate browsing a specific role using the Change User icon. Figure 8-28 shows the countries seen by a user connected with the role.

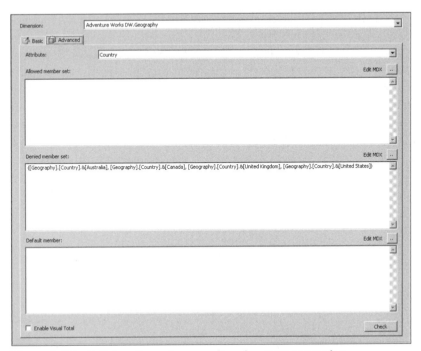

Figure 8-27   Defining dimension security using MDX expression.

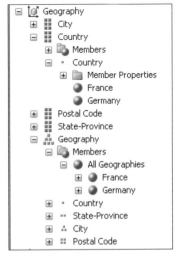

Figure 8-28   Verifying Dimension Security by browsing.

Instead of denying access to countries, you can also deny access to specific states within a country. Having the following MDX expression in the denied set will deny access to all the provinces in Canada.

```
Exists([Geography].[State-Province].members,
[Geography].[Country].&[Canada])
```

When you browse the cube with this specific role, you will see that there are no children for Canada, as shown in Figure 8-29. You will also notice that you do not have access to any of the cities in Canada due to the relationship definition between the state-province and city attributes. It is important to note that if the resulting set does not contain members of the current hierarchy then no security will be applied. For example, if you have the following MDX expression in the denied set, then no security will be applied, because the following MDX expression returns a set whose members have unique name across the multilevel hierarchy rather than the attribute hierarchy.

```
Exists([Geography].[Geography].[State-
Province].members,[Geography].[Country].&[Canada])
```

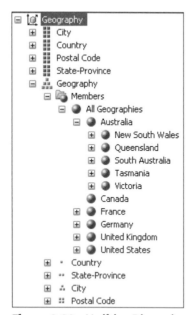

Figure 8-29 Verifying Dimension Security.

If you specify members in the allowed set, then only those members specified in the allowed set will be enabled for users of that role. When a user is part of two roles and a specific member is denied access on one role and allowed access on another one, then when the user browses the cube he or she will have access to the dimension member.

You can use all the MDX functions and operations such as filtering for specifying the MDX expression for allowed and denied set. You can apply dynamic security based on user's profile by using the function `Username`, which returns the current user logged in. You can also write your own custom functions to apply security for dimension data using .NET stored procedures or user-defined COM functions. You will see an example of how a user-defined assembly can be used to apply dimension security in Chapter 10.

Applying security on a parent-child hierarchy is similar to doing so on a multilevel hierarchy, in the sense that if you disable a member access will be denied to all its children. However, for parent-child hierarchy you do see the hierarchical structure of all the members and you can select/deselect members to allow or deny access to them, unlike specifying access to multilevel hierarchies using attributes. Figure 8-30 shows the dimension security being applied to the members of the parent-child hierarchy.

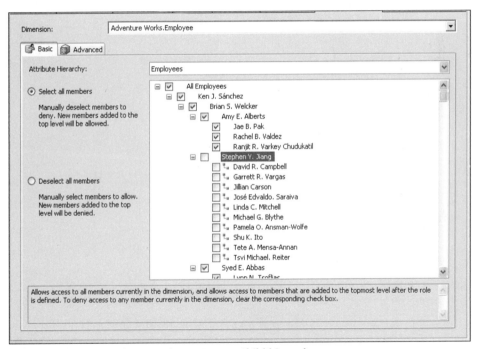

Figure 8-30   Dimension security on Parent-Child hierarchy.

After specifying dimension security the next step would be to apply security on the cells of the cube. You can apply security to the cells using the Cell Security page of the Roles editor, as shown in Figure 8-31. You can specify MDX expressions to allow read access, read contingent access, or read/write access to cells. The MDX expression specified within the Cell Data security page should evaluate to a result true or false. For each cell that is being retrieved this MDX expression will be evaluated. If the expression evaluates to true, then the user is allowed access to the cell, and if the expression evaluates to false, then the user is denied access. You can learn more about dimension and cell security from the book *Professional SQL Server Analysis Services 2005 with MDX* by Harinath and Quinn (Wiley Publishing, Inc., 2006).

Figure 8-31   Cell Security definition pane.

Summary

In this chapter, you have learned the calculation model in Analysis Services 2005 is entirely based on entities called attributes that are part of dimensions. You learned about attributes within dimensions and how the attributes and relationships between attributes play a critical role in the calculation model for a cube. You learned about the hierarchies in dimensions and then briefly about the cube structure in Analysis Services 2005. Calculations are specified through MDX scripts and are applied to each user connecting to the cube. Finally, you learned that the attribute model also plays a critical role in defining security for the UDM. Now that you understand the calculation model in Analysis Services, you will learn about the calculation model in Hyperion Essbase in Chapter 9.

Using Attribute Dimensions and Member Properties in Hyperion Essbase

Essbase *user-defined attributes* (UDAs), attributes, and attribute dimensions surface in MDX as member properties and additional dimensions available to the cube. There are some similarities to and some differences from the Microsoft UDM model of attributes in dimensions. This chapter covers how to reference and use the Essbase attributes and dimensions through MDX.

First, we will recap the difference between UDAs and other attributes, then describe attribute dimensions, and finally look at the ways of using them in MDX.

UDAs and Attributes

Essbase supports two different kinds of attributes, one called UDAs (for historical reasons) and one called simply "attributes." A UDA is just a name, the presence or absence of which is essentially a Boolean flag that can be associated with any member anywhere in the hierarchy from any regular dimension, and many members (even across different dimensions) can share the same UDA. You can associate UDAs with measures/accounts as well as with other members. Several different UDAs can be associated with a member simultaneously. This makes them useful for identifying related groups of members for application purposes.

An attribute is more similar to an attribute in the data warehousing sense. Values for an attribute are collected in an attribute dimension, which may form a single hierarchy with a leaf level, a hierarchy root member, and perhaps other attribute members in between the leaf and the root. Attribute values are typed, and Essbase supports types of number, string, Boolean, and date. An attribute is associated with a regular dimension (we'll call it a *base* dimension in this context). Only the leaf members of the attribute's hierarchy can be associated with regular dimension members. However, either leaf or nonleaf members of the regular dimension can be associated with the attribute values, with the following caveat: When members of a base dimension are associated with the attribute's values, all the members must be from the same height from the leaf level. So, they can all be leaf, or all one step up from the leaf (*level 1* in traditional Essbase terminology), and so on. Note that in a block-storage outline, attribute dimensions can only be associated with sparse dimensions, while in an aggregate storage outline (ASO) database, the attributes can be on any nonaccounts dimension. Any member of the base dimension that does not have a leaf-level attribute member associated with it has an empty attribute value (which will show up as NULL when the value is requested, as described later).

Data is automatically aggregated from base dimension members to an attribute member when the attribute member is part of a cell description, for example when using an attribute dimension as a dimension of the query. There is no automatic aggregation of data to UDA values, although you can set up the calculation yourself in a calculated member.

Neither UDAs nor attribute values can be associated with calculated members. A request for a UDA's association with a calculated member will return false, and a request for an attribute value related to a calculated member will return a NULL.

Retrieving UDAs and Attribute Values on Query Axes

Both UDAs and attributes appear as member properties in MDX, so you can simply query for them using the DIMENSION PROPERTIES clause in an axis specification. For example, the following requests the [Club Level] attribute and the presence or absence of the [Hilltop Promotion Target] UDA for customers:

```
SELECT
{ Descendants (
  [Customer].[Cleveland, OH],
  [Customer].levels(0)    /* in Essbase, easiest way to
                             get leaf members */
) } PROPERTIES [Customer].[Club Level], [Hilltop Promotion Target]
on axis(1),
...
```

For each customer, the related value (if any) of [Club Level] is returned, and the presence or absence of the [Hilltop Promotion Target] is returned as a Boolean value.

Note that you can only retrieve the attribute value directly related to the member as a member property. You cannot request its parent (or other ancestor) in the DIMENSION PROPERTIES clause, but you can request related attribute members as members in their own right as we will discuss shortly.

Predefined Attributes

Essbase provides predefined member properties in MDX as well. They are the following:

PROPERTY NAME	RETURNS
Member_Alias	Member's alias
Member_Name	Member's name
Gen_Number	Generation (depth)
Level_Number	Essbase level (height)
Member_Unique_Name	Member's unique name (if different from name); NULL otherwise
Is_Expense	True if member is an account tagged as Expense
Relational_Descendants	True if the member has descendants in a relational database through Essbase's Hybrid Analysis
Comments	Any associated comments string

Using UDA and Attribute Values in Calculations

While UDAs and attributes are both available as properties on an axis, you incorporate them into calculation expressions a bit differently. Attributes are accessed as values using the MDX standard syntax of member. property_name. For example, the following multiplies the ShipWeight attribute by the [Unit Sales] measure:

```
[Product].CurrentMember.[Shipweight] * [Measures].[Unit Sales]
```

NOTE Essbase uses one of the original standard syntaxes for referencing member property values, while Analysis Services uses a different syntax that is now part of the standard. Until one vendor accepts the syntax that the other uses, this will be an incompatibility allowed by the standard.

Since attribute values are typed, you can use them in appropriate expressions. Boolean attributes need to be used in a Boolean context, for example as a condition for iif(), Case, Filter(), and others. You can also test for their absence at a base member using IsEmpty().

UDA values are tested for with the IsUDA() function. Its syntax is

```
IsUDA (member, "uda-value")
```

where the UDA value is a literal string argument. This function returns true when the member member has the UDA value described in the second argument, and false otherwise. For example, the following expression returns two different values depending on whether the [Hilltop Promotion Target] UDA is present for a customer:

```
iif (
  IsUDA ([Customer].CurrentMember, "[Hilltop Promotion Target]"),
  1.1,
  1.0
)
```

Selecting Base Dimension Members Based on UDA and Attribute Values

One frequent and important use of attribute values and UDAs is to select related base dimension members. For example, let's say that you want to select all customers with a related [Club Level] of "Elite Platinum". While you could filter all customers (at the appropriate level of the Customer dimension) by the condition [Customer].CurrentMember.[Club Level] = "Elite Platinum", there is an easier and faster way. Similarly, although you can select all Customer members that share the "Hilltop Promotion" UDA value by filtering the members using IsUDA(), there is a specialized function for that. Let's look at these functions now.

Using Attribute() to Select Members Based on Shared Attribute Values

The Attribute() function selects members of a base dimension that all share an attribute whose value is a member of an attribute dimension. Its syntax is

```
Attribute (attribute_mbr)
```

If the `attribute_mbr` is at the leaf of the attribute hierarchy, all base dimension members related to that attribute member are returned. If the `attribute_mbr` is at a higher level in the attribute hierarchy, then all base dimension members related to all the leaf descendant attribute members are returned. So, the easier and faster way to obtain all Elite Platinum customers is with the following:

```
Attribute ([Club Level].[Elite Platinum])
```

Note that you do not need to know what the related base dimension is in order to use the function, unless you are going to combine those members with others in some way. For example, the following query takes the top 20 percent of dollar sales of sporting goods across the Elite Platinum customers, and a sum of dollar sales across that group:

```
WITH
SET [Top20PctElite] AS
'TopPercent (
  Attribute ([Club Level].[Elite Platinum]),
  20,
  [Measures].[Dollar Sales]
)'
MEMBER [Customer].[Total Selected] AS
'Sum ([Top20PctElite])'
SELECT
{
  [Top20PctElite],
  [Customer].[Total Selected]
} on rows,
{ [Measures].[Dollar Sales] }
on columns
FROM [WM2005.Sales]
WHERE [Time].[Q3, 2005]
```

If you want to nest attribute dimension members and related base dimension members on the same report, use `Generate()` to make the report most efficient. For example, the following will select the top-3 customers in terms of Dollar Sales for each Club Level, returning the result shown in Figure 9-1:

```
SELECT
Generate (
  [Club Level].Levels(0).Members,  // leaf members
  CrossJoin (
    { [Club Level].CurrentMember },
    TopCount (
      Attribute ([Club Level].CurrentMember),
      3,
```

```
            [Measures].[Dollar Sales]
        )
      )
    ) on axis (1),
    { [Measures].[Dollar Sales] }
    on columns
    FROM [WM2005.Sales]
```

Adding group subtotals for the associated customers requires the techniques covered in Chapter 7. Note that Attribute() returns *all* base members associated with an attribute dimension member. If you want all base members within some more restrained scope, such as all Elite Platinum customers in the Northeast region, then you will need to use Intersect() or Filter() to reduce the returned set.

If what you want is not all base members associated with a single attribute value but all base members associated with a range of attribute values, then you can use a function tuned for this purpose: WithAttr().

Using WithAttr() to Select Members Based on Attribute Values

Hyperion MDX provides the WithAttr() function to select members based on directly associated attribute values (as opposed to their appearance as members in an attribute dimension). The syntax is as follows:

```
WithAttr (Attr_Dim, "comparison", value)
```

		Dollar Sales
Elite Platinum	667900	153,021.10
	507450	148,169.00
	465300	147,760.20
Platinum	508950	125,489.00
	626950	122,318.00
	653150	120,868.80
Gold	684900	102,945.50
	523850	102,291.20
	449650	101,449.90
None	610850	86,907.30
	448450	86,847.60
	434300	85,762.10

Figure 9-1   Attribute and base members nested together.

The first argument is the name of the attribute dimension from which you will select base dimension members. The second argument is a comparison operator, which can be one of the following:

```
>  <  <=  >=  =  <>
```

Since putting one of these operators right in the expression wouldn't mix with the rest of MDX syntax, the operator is wrapped in quotes as a string literal. The third argument is the value to compare with. This value should be of the appropriate type: a string for a string attribute, a numeric value for a numeric attribute, and so on. (More details are found in Appendix A.) But the value does not need to be exactly the same as a value in the dimension.

For example, we can select all Customers whose [Date First Purchase] attribute is less than January 2000 with the following:

```
WithAttr (
  [Date First Purchase],
  "<",
  ToDate("mm-dd-yyyy","01-01-2000")
)
```

To AND and/or OR selections, you can use the Intersect() or Union() functions (for example, to get all of the customers whose Club Level is Elite Platinum and whose first purchase was between January 1, 2000 and January 31, 2000).

Like Attribute(), WithAttr() returns *all* base members that fit the attribute value criterion. If you want all base members within some more restrained scope, such as all customers in the Northeast region who made their first purchase before January 01, 2001, then you will need to use Intersect() or Filter() to reduce the returned set.

Using UDA() to Select Members Sharing a UDA Value

As noted before, a UDA value may be present for many members on any regular dimension. So, selecting a set of members from one dimension that all share a UDA value requires indicating at least the dimension from the members should come. The UDA() function provides this capability. Its syntax is

```
UDA( Member, "UDA_value" )
```

The function returns the set of descendants under the member Member that all share the UDA string value. If you want to combine or restrict the set of members in some way, you can either use Filter(), or a set function, including Intersect(), Except(), or others to refine the set appropriately.

Note that UDA() requires a literal string as its input—it does not take a string expression (for example, a property value). However, since Essbase allows Iif() and CASE to return sets, you can still return different sets based on UDA values if necessary, as shown in the following, which returns a different set of promotions under the [Promotion] dimension root member based on the current customer's club level:

```
Iif (
  [Customer].CurrentMember.[Club Level] = "Elite Platinum",
  UDA ([Promotion], "Soft"),
  UDA ([Promotion], "Normal")
)
```

Connecting Base Members to the Attribute Hierarchy with IN

When you reference an attribute value using the syntax Member.AttributeName, you are referencing the value of the attribute as a value you can calculate with. It's not being referenced as a member. Essbase does not yet provide any function to obtain the attribute member related to a base member. However, you can test whether a base member is related to an attribute member ancestor using the IN operator. The syntax for this is

```
Member IN  [ attribute_member | "string" ]
```

The attribute member cannot be a leaf-level attribute, or the top member of the attribute hierarchy. You can use this test inside Filter() to reduce a set of members to those related to a certain attribute ancestor, or with Iif() or CASE to condition logic. It is analogous to IsAncestor(), but in this case the ancestor member sought is an ancestor in the attribute dimension.

Connecting Base Members to Their Actual Attribute Member

If you want to connect a base member with its leaf-level attribute member, you can't drive it from the base members and obtain their related attribute member. Instead, you need to drive it from the attribute members somehow, for example by using the Attribute() function. Unless you can restrict which attribute values are relevant ahead of time, you need to combine all attribute values with their base dimension values, which will include all of them except those for which no attribute value was associated. The following fragment builds the set of [Club Level], [Customer] tuples:

```
Generate (
  [Club Level].Levels(0).Members,
  CrossJoin (
    Attribute (
      [Club Level].CurrentMember,
    ),
    { [Club Level].CurrentMember }
  ),
  ALL
)
```

This could be wrapped in a named set to be created once in a query. Then, the set can be filtered to just those tuples with customers of interest. Note that while the ALL option to generate is not necessary, since we know that the results won't have any duplicates to remove, we can speed its work by specifying ALL.

Connecting Attribute Members to Their Attribute Values

There may be times when you want to manipulate the members of an attribute dimension in terms of their values. For example, the ShipWeight attribute dimension may have its members helpfully arranged in ascending order, but you may need to sort the members of the ShipWeight attribute dimension into reverse order. Interestingly, Essbase does not provide a direct way to access the attribute value for an attribute member, but you can still get the job done. Since you can access the attribute value from a base member associated with it, you can use the Attribute() function to get the set of base members, and then pick out the first member from that set by using .Item(0).Item(0). To sort the leaf-level members of ShipWeight in reverse order, then, you would use the following expression:

```
Order (
  [ShipWeight].Levels(0).Members,
  Attribute (
    ShipWeight.CurrentMember
  ).Item(0).Item(0).[ShipWeight],   // access the [ShipWeight] value
  BDESC
)
```

Summary

The two attribute models of Essbase, UDAs and attributes, are surfaced in Essbase's MDX without altering MDX concepts. Attributes are values and members at the same time, and different functions let you treat them either way, along with relating attributes with their members. UDAs are available both as member properties and as a way to select groups of members.

CHAPTER 10

Extending MDX through External Functions

In this chapter, we will discuss how to create libraries containing external functions that will work with MDX to perform custom tasks that are not directly supported within MDX. Analysis Services 2005 supports several MDX functions per the MDX specification along with several extensions. In addition to that, Analysis Services supports a subset of VBA (Visual Basic for Applications) and Excel functions, which are useful for most common business scenarios. However, there is always a need to write your function that suits your business application. Analysis Services 2005 provides an extensible architecture by which your external functions can be hosted within Analysis Services so that they can be called via MDX. We refer to the external functions as stored procedures in this chapter and illustrate possible applications for these libraries. Analysis Services 2005 supports two kinds of function libraries, Component Object Model (COM) libraries and .NET common language run-time (CLR) assemblies. COM stored procedures, which are also called user-defined functions (UDFs), are already supported by Analysis Services 2000. Analysis Services 2005 was specifically designed to extend support to .NET stored procedures.

Before we get started, let's clarify some terminology. We will use .NET stored procedure and COM stored procedure to be consistent with the new terminologies introduced by Analysis Services 2005 documentation. The stored procedure and user-defined function (UDF) refer to the same concept. We use stored procedures because Analysis Services 2005 stores function libraries inside server storage and executes the functions on the server side, which helps in custom operations being done on the server. Analysis Services 2005 out of the box supports a subset of functions that are supported within VBA expression services library and Microsoft Excel worksheet libraries. Analysis Services 2000 passed calls to VBA directly to a specific assembly. Since VBA was only supported in 32-bit, users of the 64-bit version did not have the luxury of using UDFs. Analysis Services 2005 supports all the VBA functions supported in Analysis Services 2000; however, most of the VBA functions have been implemented using .NET, allowing the users to utilize the functions in 32-bit as well as 64-bit versions of the product, and some of them have been implemented in native code to achieve best performance.

Libraries of stored procedures are invaluable even though Microsoft Analysis Services 2005 implements a rich subset of the full MDX specification and adds a number of its own functions and operators as extensions. MDX fails to cover all of the analysis functionality that a typical application will need. For example, simple operations, such as rounding a value to a specified number of decimal places, are not present as primitives in the language. Calculations that require iterating over sets of cell values may also be more easily expressed as external functions, because MDX is declarative and has very limited support for iterations. With stored procedures, your custom calculations/operations are just a function call (within certain limits) within your MDX statement or query.

With the support for hosting .NET stored procedures in Analysis Services 2005, your external functions can leverage the powerful .NET libraries and multiple programming language support like other .NET applications. Moreover, stored procedure code can access Analysis Management Objects (AMO) and ADOMD.NET Server objects. The AMO support opens new, exciting opportunities for server management through stored procedures, such as processing cubes or dimensions. The ADOMD.NET Server object model enables functions to accept and return MDX objects such as `Set`, `Tuple`, and `Member`, and access the MDX query running context inside the function.

In this chapter, we will discuss how COM stored procedures and .NET stored procedures are referenced in an MDX expression, what kinds of data they can accept and return, and how to construct them (using Visual Basic for COM stored procedures and C# for .NET stored procedures). We will discuss special MDX functions provided by Analysis Services that are particularly useful in conjunction with COM stored procedures. And we will discuss ADOMD Server objects and their usage in .NET stored procedures. This chapter covers the following:

- Using stored procedures with MDX
  - .NET stored procedures
  - ADOMD Server.NET stored procedures
  - AMO management stored procedures

- COM external functions
  - Argument and return type details
  - MDX functions for use with procedures
- Loading and using libraries
  - Security and library management
  - Name resolution and invoking stored procedures

We refer to stored procedures containing functions using the ADOMD Server object model as ADOMD Server .NET stored procedures. Similarly .NET stored procedures using the AMO object model are referred to as AMO management stored procedures in this chapter. We will illustrate the above mentioned topics with several examples along the way.

Using Stored Procedures with MDX

Stored procedures and MDX operations work together. Stored procedures are called within MDX expressions or queries almost as if they were built-in functions. Let's begin with a simple example to lay the groundwork for an understanding of how MDX and stored procedures interact. Suppose that you are writing MDX expressions that require numerous percentage difference calculations. For example, you need to calculate Profit Percentage as ([Measures].[Sales] – Measures].[Cost])/[Measures].[Cost], and you need to calculate Scenario Percentage Variance as ([Scenario].   [Scenario].[Actual]-[Scenario].[Scenario].[Forecast])/[Scenario].[Scenario].[Forecast]. If you are working on a scenario comparing the relative accuracy of 12 different forecasts to actual results, you may feel like encapsulating this in a single function, which we will call PctDiff(), in a CLR assembly named MyNetAssembly. You would use this function in MDX expressions as shown here:

```
MyNetAssembly.PctDiff([Measures].[Sales], [Measures].[Cost]) and
MyNetAssembly.PctDiff([Scenario].[Scenario].[Actual],[Scenario].
[Scenario].[Forecast]).
```

With MDX expressions or queries, stored procedures are often referenced using the assembly name followed by a period and then the function name with its arguments. For example, the bare name PctDiff would be treated like a member or set name, whereas PctDiff() would be treated like a function.

For example, using the `PctDiff()` function, the complete syntax for creating the Scenario Percentage Variance member in a cube named Scenario Analysis is

```
CREATE MEMBER [Scenario Analysis].[Scenario].[Scenario Pct Variance]
AS MyNetAssembly.PctDiff([Scenario].[Actual], [Scenario].[Forecast])
```

For Analysis Services to use stored procedures, the functions need to be packaged as .NET CLR assemblies or as COM DLLs that are accessible through ActiveX Automation. More than one external function can reside in a library. Since stored procedures are by definition not a part of Analysis Services Server, you need to register .NET assemblies or COM DLLs either in a server's assembly collection or within a database's assembly collection. You can register stored procedures in Analysis Services 2005 via SQL Server Management Studio, Business Intelligence Development Studio (only supports registering .NET assemblies), or with your custom AMO application. Analysis Services 2005 provides fine-grained security control of server-side stored procedures, and we will discuss this in detail in this chapter.

Analysis Services 2005 takes a different approach to user-defined external function support. Analysis Services 2000 only supports COM DLLs. Those DLLs containing UDFs have to be installed on the client side. The client-side component, PivotTable Services, has to load those libraries and executed functions inside a client application process. This is quite cumbersome for multiple-machine deployment, and the server doesn't have control of security for those stored procedures. Analysis Services 2005 supports .NET Assemblies, and manages the user-defined external libraries on server side. The Analysis Services server administrator is the only person authorized to install the assemblies on the server box and register them on a server or database assembly collection. After that is done, all client applications can use those stored procedures without any installation on client machines. All function calls are executed on the server inside a server process. Analysis services provides the administrator with the control to restrict access to resources on the server for the user assemblies and execution accounts for the user assemblies.

.NET Stored Procedures

You can use any language from the set of .NET supported languages (C#, C++, Visual Basic, and so on) to write .NET stored procedures. The easiest approach is to create a new C# project for a class library and define a static public function as in following example:

```
using System;
using System.Collections.Generic;
using System.Text;

namespace MyNetAssembly
{
  public class StoreProcedureExample
  {
    public static double PctDiff(double a, double b)
    {
      return (a - b) / b;
    }
  }
}
```

Compile the project to get an assembly. You are now ready to add the assembly to either the server's assembly collection or the assembly collection of a specific database. The following query will return the percentage difference of Sales from 2003 and 2004:

```
WITH MEMBER [Date].[Fiscal].[PctDiff] AS
    MyNetAssembly.PctDiff([Date].[Fiscal].[Fiscal Year].&[2003],
    [Date].[Fiscal].[Fiscal Year].&[2004])
SELECT [Date].[Fiscal].[PctDiff] ON 0
FROM [Adventure Works]
WHERE [Measures].[Internet Sales Amount]
```

.NET Stored Procedure Parameters and Return Values

.NET stored procedures support more data types than COM stored procedures. Table 10-1 summarizes the supported data types in Analysis Services 2005 for .NET assemblies. Table 10-1 also provides the data types supported via the ADOMD Server object model, which you will see later in this chapter.

Note that Array is not supported for return values. The data type MDX-Value in the ADOMD Server object model is the parent object of Hierarchy, Level, Measure, and so forth, and it can be implicitly converted to its child members. In addition, Dimension, Cube, Property, Measure, and Database objects are not supported for stored procedure parameters.

Table 10-1 Data Types Supported in Analysis Services 2005 for .NET Assemblies

NAMESPACE	DATA TYPE	PARAMETER	RETURN VALUE
System	Object	Y	Y
	Byte	Y	Y
	SByte	Y	Y
	Int16	Y	Y
	UInt16	Y	Y
	Int32	Y	Y
	UInt32	Y	Y
	Int64	Y	Y
	UInt64	Y	Y
	Single	Y	Y
	Double	Y	Y
	Decimal	Y	Y
	String	Y	Y
	Char	Y	Y
	Boolean	Y	Y
	DateTime	Y	Y
	Array	Y	N
System.Data	IDataReader	Y	Y
	DataSet	Y	Y
Microsoft. AnalysisServices. AdomdServer	Hierarchy	Y	Y
	Level	Y	Y
	Member	Y	Y
	Set	Y	Y
	Tuple	Y	Y
	MDXValue	Y	Y

ADOMD Server objects

A key advantage of .NET stored procedures over COM stored procedures is that .NET stored procedures can access ADOMD Server objects within the assembly and perform custom MDX operations. The interface provided by the ADOMD Server object model is just a wrapper for the original server objects. Hence, you do gain performance improvements as compared to doing the operations on the client side because all the operations on the objects are done directly on the server. With ADOMD Server objects, you can pass MDX objects such as `Set`, `Tuple`, and `Member` as parameters to your UDF, and then return such objects as results of your function. If you did not have this support, you would need to perform string operations to convert to MDX objects in your query that typically have a performance impact. The communication between the server and stored procedure extensions is not limited to primitive data types. ADOMD Server objects support the context class, which allows functions to access the query context. Moreover, a static MDX class library is added to allow functions to execute MDX functions such as `crossjoin` and `filter`, within the function code.

Consider the issues examined in Chapter 7 regarding the construction of cumulative sums of members for Pareto analysis. You can use a .NET stored procedure, `PartialSet`, to perform this task. `PartialSet()` takes two arguments: a set with members, and the member at which the return set should stop. The return value will be a set with members from the start to the stop tuple. In C#, you could code the function like this:

```
// <summary>
///  This function returns a partial set from the whole set
///  it only support 1 dimensional set
/// </summary>
/// <param name="wholeSet">the whole member set</param>
/// <param name="stopMember">the member when set should stop</param>
/// <returns>The partial set</returns>
public static AdomdServer.Set PartialSet(AdomdServer.Set wholeSet,
        AdomdServer.Member stopMember)
{
  AdomdServer.SetBuilder returnSet = new AdomdServer.SetBuilder();

  foreach (AdomdServer.Tuple tuple in wholeSet.Tuples)
  {
    //add tuple into the return set
    returnSet.Add(tuple);

    //if the unique name of both tuple is same then go break
    if (string.Compare(tuple.Members[0].UniqueName,
stopMember.UniqueName , true) == 0)
```

```
      break;
   }


   //return the set back to server
   return returnSet.ToSet();
}
```

The code takes an ADOMD Server Set object and an ADOMD Server Member object. The UDF traverses the tuples within the set, and compares the member unique names with the stop member to find a match. The function will end the set construction as soon as it finds a match and returns the set as the result. To keep the example simple, this function only supports a single dimensional set.

A user can invoke the function using an MDX query as shown below. Since the function returns a set, you can directly use the function on Axis.

```
select MyNetAssembly.PartialSet( [Customer].[Customer
Geography].[City].members,
  [Customer].[Customer Geography].[City].&[Wollongong]&[NSW]) on 0
from [Adventure Works]
```

The function can also be used within a calculated member MDX expression to fulfill the partialSum functionality:

```
with Member Measures.PartialSumSales as
sum ( MyNetAssembly.PartialSet( [Customer].[Customer Geography].[City].
members, [Customer].[Customer Geography].currentmember),[Measures].
[Internet Sales Amount])
select  Measures.PartialSumSales on 0,
  [Customer].[Customer Geography].[City].members on 1
 from
[Adventure Works]
```

The ADOMD Server object model supports Hierarchy, Level, Measure, Member, Property, Set, and Tuple as input and output parameters. For ambiguous inputs such as MyFunction(Measures.[Internet Sales Amount]), in which the input can be a value, member, measure, or tuple, Analysis Services will automatically cast the input value to the appropriate object based on the function definition. The return objects are treated the same as any other internal MDX functions, and you can use the stored procedure function anyplace in the MDX query. ADOMD Server also includes many useful classes to facilitate server stored procedure programming.

Expression

The Expression object in the ADOMD Server object model can be used for evaluating an MDX expression, and you get back an MDXValue via the Calculate or CalculateMdxObject function. For example:

```
public AdomdServer.MDXValue ExpressionSample(string expressionText,
AdomdServer.Tuple evaluationTuple)
{
  //create a expression
  AdomdServer.Expression ex = new
AdomdServer.Expression(expressionText);

  //evaluate the value using the evaluation tuple as the current tuple
  AdomdServer.MDXValue value = ex.Calculate(evaluationTuple);
  return value;
}
```

The following MDX query uses the stored procedure illustrated above and uses the ExpressionSample function. In the following example, the Product specified in the slicer axis is used while evaluating the expression within the stored procedure:

```
WITH MEMBER
measures.Test as MyNetAssembly.ExpressionSample(
"[Customer].[Customer Geography].[City].&[Wollongong]&[NSW]",
[Measures].[Internet Sales Amount]
)
SELECT   measures.Test  ON 0
FROM [Adventure Works]
WHERE
([Product].[Product Categories].[Category].&[3])
```

Changing the slice from Product, you will find out that the current evaluation context is taken into account in the value evaluation. A typical usage of the Expression statement is to iterate through a set containing tuples and get the cumulative sum or weighted average for each tuple.

TupleBuilder

The TupleBuilder class can be used for constructing a tuple. It has the Add function to add members to tuple, and its ToTuple function will return a tuple object.

SetBuilder

The SetBuilder class can be used to construct a set. It has the Add function to add tuples to set, and its ToSet function will return a Set object. In the previous example, we used the ToSet function to return a partial set.

MDX

The MDX class contains static methods corresponding to various MDX functions. It allows stored procedures to use MDX functions programmatically. The supported MDX functions in the ADOMD Server object model are shown in Table 10-2.

Table 10-2 MDX Functions Supported in the ADOMD Server Object Model

FUNCTION NAME	RETURN VALUE	PARAMETERS
Aggregate	System.ValueType	Set, Expression
CrossJoin	Set	Set, Set
DrillDownMember	Set	Set, Set
DrillDownMember	Set	Set, Set, DrillDownMemberFlags
DrillDownMember	Set	Set, Set, Hierarchy
DrillDownMember	Set	Set, Set, Hierarchy, DrillDownMemberFlags
Filter	Set	Set, Expression
Generate	MDXValue	Set, Set
Generate	MDXValue	Set, Set, GenerateFlags
Generate	MDXValue	Set, Expression
Generate	MDXValue	Set, Expression, String
ParallelPeriod	Member	
ParallelPeriod	Member	Level

FUNCTION NAME	RETURN VALUE	PARAMETERS
ParallelPeriod	Member	Level, Expression
ParallelPeriod	Member	Level, Expression, Member
StrToSet	Set	String

Following is the code example using MDX functions to implement Par-tialSum, which uses the MDX.Aggregate Function.

```
public static System.ValueType PartialSum(AdomdServer.Set wholeSet,
        AdomdServer.Member stopMember, string expression)
{
  return AdomdServer.MDX.Aggregate(
    PartialSet(wholeSet, stopMember),
      new AdomdServer.Expression[]
      {
        new AdomdServer.Expression(expression)
      }
    );
}
```

Note that this example calls another function, named PartialSet, in the same library that was defined previously. The following MDX query will test the result:

```
with Member Measures.PartialSumSales as

MyNetAssembly.PartialSum( [Customer].[Customer
Geography].[City].members, [Customer].[Customer Geography].currentmember
                                ,"[Measures].[Internet Sales Amount]")
select  Measures.PartialSumSales on 0,
[Customer].[Customer Geography].[City].members on 1
from
[Adventure Works]
```

Context

Context contains a set of static properties that allows a stored procedure to obtain the current execution context. Through the Context object, you can obtain ADOMD Server metadata classes such as CubeDef, Hierarchy, and so on. Context has the following properties related to MDX objects:

NAME	TYPE	DESCRIPTION
ClientCultureInfo	ClientCultureInfo	Culture information on the client that indicates properties such as language
CurrentServerID	String	Server ID (server\instance)
CurrentDatabaseName	String	Name of current database
CurrentCube	CubeDef	Current cube
Cubes	CubeCollection	Collection of cubes in the current database
ExecuteForPrepare	Boolean	This property is used to indicate if the stored procedure has been marked for prepare. When marked for prepare, a client can send a query requesting prepare for execution.
MiningModels	MiningModel Collection	Collection of Mining models within a Mining Structure
MiningServices	MiningStructure Collection	This is the collection of the data mining algorithms
MiningStructures	MiningStructure Collection	Collection of Mining structures within a database
Pass	Integer	Pass number

Server Metadata Objects

Server metadata objects include CubeDef, Dimension, Hierarchy, Level, Member, and more. Through the Context.CurrentCube function, your UDF can access metadata objects such as these. These metadata objects support many useful functions such as Member.GetChildren, Level.Get-Members, which might be useful for your stored procedure, depending on your business needs. Following is an example that goes through all the current cube's hierarchies and KPIs to print out the current member of the hierarchy and KPI names.

```
public static string CurrentContext()
{
  StringBuilder sb = new StringBuilder();
  AdomdServer.CubeDef cube = AdomdServer.Context.CurrentCube;
```

```
    foreach (AdomdServer.Dimension dimension in cube.Dimensions)
    {
      foreach (AdomdServer.Hierarchy hierarchy in dimension.Hierarchies)
      {
        AdomdServer.Member hierMember = hierarchy.CurrentMember;
        sb.Append(hierMember.UniqueName).Append(",");
      }

      //you can even access other objects such as KPIs
      foreach(AdomdServer.Kpi kpi in cube.Kpis)
      {
        sb.Append(kpi.Name).Append(",");
      }
    }

    return sb.ToString();
}
```

You can test the above stored procedure function with the following MDX query, which returns the list of names of KPIs in the cube that is part of the current context:

```
WITH MEMBER measures.Test AS MyNetAssembly.CurrentContext()
SELECT {measures.test} ON 0
FROM [Adventure Works]
WHERE ([Customer].[Customer Geography].[Country].&[Canada])
```

In conclusion, the ADOMD Server object model empowers .NET stored procedure developers with a rich class library with native object support. It is a powerful tool that developers can use to extend the functions available on Analysis Services that can later be used in MDX queries.

AMO .NET Management Stored Procedures

Analysis Management Objects (AMO) is the object model used to perform management operations on an Analysis Services object. .NET stored procedures can access AMO objects and perform system management operations such as processing cubes or dimensions, refining objects within the database, backing up the database, and so on. One advantage of AMO stored procedures is that users can perform server management tasks using MDX and any MDX execution tool.

Although stored procedure functions can be called by any database user, the management tasks can only be performed by administrators. Using AMO, you can make structural changes to Analysis Services objects. Structural changes are changes that would require reprocessing of objects such as adding a hierarchy to a dimension, or adding a measure or measure group to a cube. You can perform nonstructural changes such as changing certain properties for objects. The following is an example of a backup database function, which is an administrative operation on Analysis Services, using a regular server connection that backs up the database to the specified file.

```
public static void BackupDatabase(string databaseName, string
backupFileName, string serverName)
{
  using (AMO.Server asServer = new Microsoft.AnalysisServices.Server())
  {
    // Connect through AMO with connection string *
    asServer.Connect(serverName);
    AMO.Database asDB = asServer.Databases.FindByName(databaseName);
    if (asDB != null)
    {
      asDB.Backup(backupFileName + ".abf");
    }
  }
}
```

MDX has a special syntax `Call` for calling stored procedures without any return parameters. Certain administrative operations where you do not need return values can be executed using the Call statement, which is executed out of context of the MDX query. The following MDX query backs up the database using the above AMO stored procedure:

```
Call MyNetAssembly.BackupDatabase("Adventure Works
DW","C:\AdventureWorksBackUp")
```

You can call most of the functions in the same way as a normal MDX query, and check the function's return value in the `Calculate` member as shown below:

```
with member measures.Test as
MyNetAssembly.BackupDatabase("Adventure Works
DW","C:\AdventureWorksBackUp"localhost")
select {measures.test} on 0
from [Adventure Works]
```

While registering the stored procedures to Analysis Services, you need to specify the `Impersonation` (what account the stored procedure should run as) and `Permission` (what type of permissions or restrictions this stored procedure has, such as having access network to access) under which the stored procedure needs to be executed by Analysis Services. We will discuss the various impersonations and permissions later in this chapter. Note that stored procedures using AMO need to be registered with the "Unrestricted" option in the Permission setting, because AMO is not marked with `Allow-PartialTrustedCallers`.

While using AMO within stored procedures, you can connect to Analysis Services using a special connection string `"*"` which allows you to connect to the current context. Connecting to Analysis Services through this mechanism offers some restrictions on operations that can be executed within the stored procedure for the current context. Operations that deal with multiple versions of objects within the stored procedure, such as backup or processing, fall into this category. Hence, Analysis Services does not allow certain operations while using "*" as a connection string. For example, you can process a dimension within the stored procedure and try to perform a backup at the same time. However, the processing transaction has not committed so far; therefore, the newly processed dimension is not the final version on which to perform the backup. Analysis Services only supports backing up the final version of object. Hence, operations on objects that could have version conflicts are not allowed by Analysis Services. If your operations are on a database that is different than the one in the current context, then you can perform management operations within the stored procedure using this special connection string. For example, you can connect to the default database and perform management operations on all the other databases on Analysis Services.

Performance Considerations of Static Functions and Nonstatic Functions

Analysis Services 2005 supports both static functions and nonstatic functions in a .NET library for stored procedures. We use static functions in all our examples and highly recommend this practice because of its performance benefits.

For static functions, Analysis services needs to load the assembly library only once; it can directly invoke the static functions without any additional cost. No class object is created. For nonstatic functions, the server needs to create a new class object for every function call. The additional cost could be significant for queries that invoke a function multiple times; this is the case, for example, when using a function call in a `Calculate` member like following query:

```
WITH MEMBER measures.InvokeCount AS MyNetAssembly.GetInvokeCount()
SELECT measures.invokeCount ON 0 ,
[Customer].[Customer Geography].[City].members ON 1
FROM [adventure works]
```

The above query calls the nonstatic stored procedure shown below. The query returns values of 1, 2, . . . , 587 for each city member. However, the query causes the server to be called by the function 587 times (the city member count), which is expected. But each time that Analysis Services creates a new `StoreProcedureExample` object, it incurs performance penalties.

```
using System;
using System.Collections.Generic;
using System.Text;
using AdomdServer = Microsoft.AnalysisServices.AdomdServer;
using AMO = Microsoft.AnalysisServices;

namespace MyNetAssembly
{
  public class StoreProcedureExample
  {
    public static int invokeCount = 0;

    public StoreProcedureExample()
    {
      invokeCount++;
    }
    public int GetInvokeCount()
    {
      return invokeCount;
    }

    public static int GetInvokeCountStatic()
    {
      return invokeCount;
    }
  }
}
```

However, the static version shown in the query below will return the same results as for the query shown above that uses `GetInvokeCount`, which means that theserver does not create a `StoreProcedureExample` object even once:

```
WITH MEMBER measures.InvokeCount as MyNetAssembly.GetInvokeCountStatic()
SELECT measures.invokeCount ON  0 ,
[Customer].[Customer Geography].[City].members ON 1
FROM [adventure works]
```

Debugging .NET Stored Procedures

Debugging .NET stored procedures becomes very easy with Visual Studio 2005. In Visual Studio, you can attach to the Analysis Services 2005 (`msmd-srv.exe`) process, and it should automatically load the assemblies that the server loaded for the stored procedures. If you have multiple instances of Analysis Services running on your machine, then you will need to find the right Analysis Services, based on the name or port number, and attach to the right one. Then you can set a breakpoint within your stored procedure functions and invoke the function via any MDX query tool. The debugger will stop at the breakpoint, and you can enjoy all debugging capabilities of Visual Studio.

Figure 10-1 illustrates the debugger window inside Visual Studio. You can run the function step by step and check the variable values. You have all the power of debugging from Visual Studio.

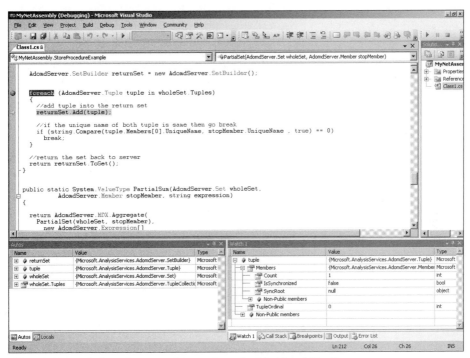

Figure 10-1   Debugging stored procedures inside Visual Studio.

Additional Programming Aspects NULL, ERROR(), and Exception

In general, programmers need to be careful about user input and handle invalid inputs gracefully. Stored procedures can throw exceptions, and Analysis Services will behave differently depending on where the stored procedures are used. Analysis Services 2005 introduced a new function ERROR(), which will raise an error during MDX execution. We will take that into consideration in stored procedure programming.

NULL Value As an Input Parameter

For the input parameter discussion, let's use following example:

```
public static string GetMemberName(AdomdServer.Member member)
{
  return member.Name;
}
public static string GetHierarchyName(AdomdServer.Hierarchy hier)
{
  return hier.Name;
}
```

The following query will return an empty string:

```
WITH MEMBER measures.testMeasure AS
MyNetAssembly.GetMemberName(NULL)
SELECT measures.testMeasure ON 0 FROM
[Adventure Works]
```

If you put a breakpoint inside the function, you will find out that Analysis Services creates a valid empty member object instead of a null pointer. For Set, Member, and Tuple objects, the server always creates an empty object instead of a NULL pointer when you pass NULL as the input parameter. However, the query

```
WITH MEMBER measures.testMeasure AS
MyNetAssembly.GetHierarchyName(NULL)
SELECT {measures.testMeasure} ON 0
FROM [Adventure Works]
```

will return an error such as the following:

```
#Error Internal error: An unexpected error occurred (file
'mdxutils.cpp', line 1176, function 'MDXUtils::VCreateFormula').
```

For `Hierarchy` and `Level` objects, passing a `NULL` value will cause an internal error. The `MDXValue` object can be used as an input parameter, too. You can pass cube objects or values into a stored procedure. The `MDXValue` object supports the `ToHierarchy`, `ToLevel`, `ToTuple`, `ToMember`, and `ToSet` functions to let the user convert an `MDXValue` to a specific object. If the conversion cannot be done, such as calling `ToHierarchy` on a member, it will raise an exception. The conversion from a `NULL` `MDXValue` object is consistent with the previous examples. The server will create an empty object for `ToSet`, `ToMember`, and `ToTuple`, and raise an error for `ToHierarchy` and `ToLevel`.

NULL Value As an Output Parameter

Stored procedures can return a string, or ADOMD Server objects can return `NULL` in stored procedure code, and the compiler won't complain. But be aware that Analysis Services will convert `NULL` to a string (null) no matter what the return type is.

```
public static AdomdServer.Set ReturnNullSet()
{
  return null;
}
```

The query below

```
select MyNetAssembly.ReturnNullSet() on 0 from [Adventure Works]
```

will return the following error:

```
The Axis0 function expects a tuple set expression for the  argument. A
string or numeric expression was used.
```

And the query

```
WITH MEMBER measures.testmeasure AS MyNetAssembly.ReturnNullSet()
SELECT measures.testmeasure ON 0
FROM [Adventure Works]
```

will return a cell with value `"(null)"` !

Exceptions during Execution

If a stored procedure throws an exception during execution, and the stored procedure does not catch and handle the exception, the server will raise an error. Depending on where the stored procedure is called, the query results are different.

If your stored procedure returns a member or set, and you use it on the axis or on the slice, the query will fail with an execution error: Executing the following query in SQL Server Management Studio

```
select {MyNetAssembly.ThrowExceptionTest()} on 0
from [Adventure Works]
```

will result in the error shown below:

```
Executing the query ...

Execution of the managed stored procedure CustomFilter failed with the
following error: Exception has been thrown by the target of an
invocation.the exception message.

Execution complete
```

If the stored procedure is used in a calculated member definition and your query will reference the member, the query will execute successfully, but the individual cell results returned will include the exception message.

```
with member measures.xx as MyNetAssembly.ThrowExceptionTest2()
select {measures.xx} on 0
from [Adventure Works]
```

The query will actually return the cell set with errors inside the cell value.

Error() Function

The `Error()` function is introduced by Analysis Services 2005 to raise an error, and optionally you can present an error message. You can use that in the calculation definition to simply raise an error for some error conditions.

If a stored procedure call has any input parameter that resolves as `error()`, the server will not invoke the stored procedure at all. It will simply return the error and stop the execution. This function is helpful in catching some of the errors returned by Analysis Services while using stored procedures and providing a custom error message to your end users. This function is not limited to catching errors returned by stored procedures.

Using Stored Procedures for Dynamic Security

We mentioned before that stored procedures can be used anywhere in an MDX query or any MDX expression. Stored procedures can be used in user security settings that help you to build custom security for your users. This presents interesting and powerful solutions for dynamic security in systems using Analysis Services.

Dynamic security has become a standard term in the Analysis Services world. It typically means a role in an OLAP system can have a different security context depending on which user is connected to the system. The simplest scenario for dynamic security is that both User A and User B belong to Role X, but User A only can see one product and User B can see another product. The system needs to dynamically adjust the security context according to the logged-in user.

In Analysis Services 2000, this is commonly implemented by setting the role dimension security setting with an MDX expression. The MDX expression will leverage dimension member properties or a user dimension with some lookup function via the MDX username function. The following is a sample MDX expression on the Store dimension's AllowSet:

```
Filter([Store].[Store Name].Members,  Instr(1,[Store].Properties
("AllowAccess"),Username)
```

The above MDX expression filters the stores so the current user logged in can only see the stores for which he or she has access. A user can only see stores whose AllowAccess property includes the particular user's login name. Alternatively, you can create a security cube with User dimension and have all valid User-Store combinations in a fact table. Then an MDX expression like the following will achieve the same results:

```
Filter([Store].[Store Name].Members,
(StrToTuple("[User].["+UserName+"]"),[Measures].[SecureMeasure])>0)
```

The above techniques are also called as data-driven security, because the user's security permissions are stored in data (instead of a cube's metadata). Only one role is defined in Analysis Services, and the MDX expression defined for dimension security dynamically adjusts the security contexts for different users. The previous two techniques will continue to work in Analysis Services 2005. We encourage you to use them when the security context is maintained in Analysis Services objects such as dimension properties and the security cube.

Since .NET stored procedures can return a set that functions like a normal MDX set, you can use stored procedures in users' security settings, too. Stored procedures offer more powerful .NET Libraries for you to use for string manipulations and accessing other data sources such as SQL tables, files, and so on.

Consider the following scenario. The store user's security is managed by another system, and that system will write the username and managed store name into its own SQL table. The change on that SQL table should automatically change the security settings in your cubes. Enclosed below is a function coded in .NET that solves the described scenario. The function GetStoreAllowedSet queries the relational database for the stores that are accessible by a given user passed as an input. The function retrieves the stores corresponding to a username that is passed as an argument by forming an SQL query and querying the information from the database.

```
public static SqlConnection cachedConnection; //cached connection object
public static AdomdServer.Set GetStoreAllowSet(string username)
{
  //Developers need to be careful about multiple user environment
  lock (cachedConnection)
  {
    try
    {
      //Check if the cached connection is still open
      if (null == cachedConnection || cachedConnection.State !=
ConnectionState.Open)
      {
        cachedConnection = new
SqlConnection("Provider=SQLOLEDB.1;Integrated Security=SSPI;Persist
Security Info=False;Initial Catalog=StoreSecurityDB;Data
Source=TestServer");
        cachedConnection.Open();
      }

      StringBuilder setStringBuilder = new StringBuilder();
      setStringBuilder.Append("{");
      int tupleCount = 0;

      // this code is to demonstrate the concept. Please USE storedproc
and pramaterized SQL to avoid sql injection.
      using (SqlCommand command = new SqlCommand("select allowstores
from StoreSecurity where username = '" + username + "'",
cachedConnection))
      {
        // go through the records and build the set
        using (SqlDataReader reader = command.ExecuteReader())
        {
          while (reader.Read())
          {
            if (tupleCount++ > 0)
            {
              setStringBuilder.Append(",");
```

```
            }
            setStringBuilder.Append("[Store].[Store Names].[" +
reader["allowstores"].ToString().Trim() + "]");
            }
            reader.Close();
        }
    }

    setStringBuilder.Append("}");
    return AdomdServer.MDX.StrToSet(setStringBuilder.ToString());


    }
    // Error handling: another important aspect for server store
procedure programing
    catch
    {
    cachedConnection.Close();
    cachedConnection = null;
    //return a empty set
    return AdomdServer.MDX.StrToSet("{}");
    }
  }
 }
}
```

Then in the `[Store].[Store Name]` attribute hierarchy's security setting, you can set the following as `AllowSet`:

```
MyNetAssembly.GetStoreAllowSet(UserName())
```

.NET stored procedures give developers more power and freedom to use all .NET libraries and functions. The previous implementation will pick up the changes in the source security database immediately, and it does not require a dimension update or cube update.

Note that you need to use Unrestricted permission to register the assembly containing the above function since the stored procedure needs to access external resources (relational server over the network) to retrieve data. Set the `Impersonation` to `ImpersonateServiceAccount`. Analysis Services will use the services startup account of Analysis Services to connect to SQL Server. We will discuss security in a later section in this chapter.

COM DLL Stored Procedures

COM stored procedures are both supported by Analysis Services 2000 and Analysis Services 2005 with the exception that Analysis Services 2005 moved the function execution and DLL management to the server side. Note that because of security concerns, the COM stored procedure support is turned off by default. Users need to turn on this feature by setting the server property `Feature\ComUdfEnabled = true`.

The easiest way to create an external function in Visual Basic (version 5.0 and higher) is to simply create, in an ActiveX DLL or other ActiveX library/executable type, a class with `GlobalMultiuse` instancing and then add public functions to it. For example, the `PctDiff()` function would be created with the following:

```
Public Function PctDiff (ByVal A As Double, ByVal B As Double)
As Double
PctDiff = (A - B) / B
End Function
```

This declares the function as taking two double-typed arguments and returning a double result, which is what we want. The key features of the class are that it must be global (not hidden or restricted) and that the functions to be used must all be public. We have included a sample function library and the Visual Basic 6.0 project that generates the library on the CD-ROM accompanying this book.

Stored procedures are useful both for calculating cell values and for defining named sets. Although you can use the results of any stored procedures as a cell value, you can also use a string result to completely specify or partly specify a set by using the `StrToSet()`, `StrToTuple()`, and `Members()` functions. Some of the useful applications of stored procedures involve defining sets and tuples, such as slicers for queries.

Argument and Return-Type Details

You can pass numbers, strings, and arrays of numbers or strings into COM stored procedures, and they can return either numbers or strings. Unlike the .NET stored procedure, there is no native MDX object support for objects such as `Set`, `Tuple`, and `Member`. The arguments for an external function can be declared to be number types, strings, arrays of numbers or strings, or variant types. If the type is specifically declared in the function signature (like double, integer, or string), the value passed from Microsoft Analysis Services for that argument will be coerced into that type when the function is called. For example, if the `PctDiff()` function takes two arguments of type `double`, and it is called with the value of an integer-type measure at some cell, then the integer will be changed into a double. If it is called with a string, such as a property value (which must be a string in Analysis Services), the first digit of the string will be converted into a number when the function is called. (You can use the

Val() function, which is part of the VBA library, to convert the string into a number first. For example, PctDiff(Val("20"), Val("15")) returns 0.333.)

If the argument is a variant type, Analysis Services passes the argument as its own internal type for the value. Depending on the actual type of the cell, the value that is received by the external function may be a 32-bit integer, a 64-bit integer, a single or double float, or a string. An empty cell passed to an external function will be received by the external function as an empty variant.

The return type of an external function is a little more restricted in scope. You can declare the return type to be a number, a string, or a variant. If you declare the type to be a variant, you can only return numbers from it, not strings or arrays. Also, in Analysis Services 2000, if an external function returns an empty variant, the PivotTable Service will return an error condition for the calculation.

Passing Arrays of Values to COM Stored Procedures

You can pass arbitrarily sized arrays of values into COM stored procedures through the MDX extension function SetToArray(). Although the documentation for Microsoft Analysis Services indicates that SetToArray() only creates arrays of numbers, it will in fact create sets of strings as well, which makes it useful for scanning sets of member names and property values as well as for processing a set of numbers. SetToArray() is useful for creating all kinds of custom aggregator functions. For each tuple in the set that is passed to SetToArray(), Analysis Services will place a value in the array at the corresponding location in the array, so there will be one value in the array for each tuple in the set (with one exception case that we will describe later in this section) in the same order.

For example, consider the issues examined in Chapter 7, regarding the construction of cumulative sums of members for Pareto analysis. We proposed an external function, PartialSum(), to perform this task. As envisioned there, PartialSum() takes three arguments: an array of values to sum across, an array of names corresponding to the values, and the name of the tuple at which summing should stop. In VB, we could code the function like this:

```
Public Function PartialSum (ByRef ArgVals() As Double, ByRef ArgNames()
As String, ByVal StopAt As String) As Double
Dim Start As Integer
Dim Finish As Integer
Dim i As Integer

Start = LBound(ArgVals, 1)   ' for safety
```

```
Finish = UBound(ArgVals, 1)

' initialize working sum to zero
PartialSum = 0
For i = Start To Finish
    ' add value for this tuple
    PartialSum = PartialSum + ArgVals(i)
    ' leave if we have encountered the stopping point
    If ArgNames(i) = StopAt Then Return
Next i

' If we get here, there is a problem
' leave the next two commented out in order to simply return the sum we
got
' PartialSum = 0
Err.Raise 9999

End Function
```

The function takes the lower and upper bounds of the array and loops through the argument value array, adding each value to the sum. (Although the documentation for Analysis Services does not discuss the lower-bound number for the array—does the array numbering start at 0, 1, or something else?—the numbering consistently starts at 0.) At each cycle through the loop, the function tests whether the current argument name is equal to the name at which the loop should stop, and when that condition is met, the function returns the value. If the function does not encounter the name to stop at in the array of names, we have three possible choices: return the total across the entire set, return zero, or raise an error.

We have chosen the most conservative approach in the code (to raise an error), but the other two outcomes may make sense for your applications as well. We could then call this function in a query to generate cumulative sums, as with the following simple query, which would yield the result shown in Figure 10-2 as a spreadsheet grid and as a graph:

```
WITH
MEMBER [Measures].[Geog. Name] AS '[Geography].CurrentMember.UniqueName'
SET [Ordered States] AS 'Order ([Geography].[State].Members,
[Measures].[Profit], BDESC)'
MEMBER [Measures].[Cum Profit] AS
'PartialSum (
    SetToArray ([Ordered States], [Geography], [Measures].[Profit]),
    SetToArray ([Ordered States], [Geography], [Measures].[Geog. Name]),
    [Geography].CurrentMember.UniqueName
)'
SELECT
```

```
{ [Ordered States] } on columns,
{ [Measures].[Profit], [Measures].[Cum Profit] } on rows
FROM
[Sales Cube]
```

Microsoft OLAP/Analysis Services makes every value of the array have the same type. That is, arrays passed to functions can be of numbers or of text, but Analysis Services cannot pass arrays of variants to an external function. If Analysis Services could pass variants, then we might be able to pass in a single two-dimensional array containing pairs of "(name, value)" and simplify the MDX a bit more. But the function is still handy enough as it is.

Notice that we passed the string array in by first declaring a measure to simply return the unique name of the current geography member and then using that as the value expression for SetToArray(). Analysis Services generates a parser error if you try to use any value expression that is not the value of a cell here, so we need to make sure to make it a cell value.

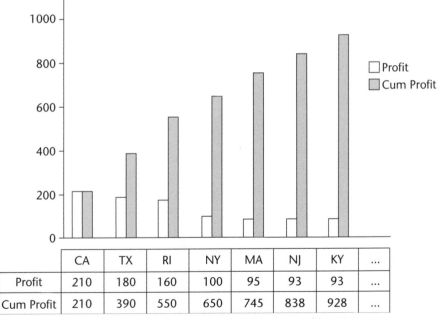

	CA	TX	RI	NY	MA	NJ	KY	...
Profit	210	180	160	100	95	93	93	...
Cum Profit	210	390	550	650	745	838	928	...

Figure 10-2   Result of cumulative sum query using external function.

Because arrays are passed in COM variant types, you can think about accepting arrays through variant arguments. If you declare the array input to be of variant type, then you must understand how Microsoft Analysis Services prepares the array in its native type. Recall from Chapter 4 how the data type for each cell is determined independently of the type of any other cell. When Analysis Services creates the array, it chooses the data type of the first value that it places into the array as the type for the array. If that value is a double, then the variant will contain an array of double-typed values. If that value is an integer, then the variant will contain an array of integer-typed values, and so on. If the first value is an empty cell, then an empty variant is passed, rather than an array whose first element is zero. (Because the variant cannot itself contain an array of variants, no empty argument can be passed in an array.) Any value after the first value that is empty in Analysis Services will have a zero placed in the corresponding array position. Given the issues that handling the array data types entails, you may want to declare your array arguments as being arrays of a specific type.

Raising an error is one of the options that we listed in the code for `PartialSum()` when the stop-at name is not found. If your external function raises an error, then Analysis Services will immediately stop evaluating the formula and return an error condition for the cell instead of a value for it. A well-constructed client will somehow feed this information back to the user to let him or her know that something went wrong when the cell was calculated, in the same way that cell data errors flagged by Analysis Services are processed.

If you are paying attention to run-time performance (and that is a good idea), you may have already seen how the `SetToArray()` function can be made more efficient. Although a member's unique name will uniquely identify the member within the dimension, the member also has an intrinsic integer ID property. Having Analysis Services construct the array of integers is likely to be a little faster, and it will certainly be faster for the external function to test each of them to see if it is the last one to be processed. We can rewrite the function as follows:

```
Public Function PartialSum (ByRef ArgVals() As Double, ByRef ArgIDs() As
Long, ByVal StopAt As Long) As Double
Dim Start As Long
Dim Finish As Long
Dim i As Long

Start = LBound(ArgVals, 1)   ' for safety
Finish = UBound(ArgVals, 1)

' initialize working sum to zero
PartialSum = 0
```

```
For i = Start To Finish
    ' add value for this tuple
    PartialSum = PartialSum + ArgVals(i)
    ' leave if we have encountered the stopping point
    If ArgIDs(i) = StopAt Then Return
Next i


' If we get here, there is a problem
' leave the next two commented out in order to simply return the sum we
got
' PartialSum = 0
Err.Raise 9999


End Function
Our function would be used in our sample query as follows:
WITH
MEMBER [Measures].[Geog. ID] AS
'CLng ([Geography].CurrentMember.Properties("ID"))'
SET [Ordered States] AS 'Order ([Geography].[State].Members,
[Measures].[Profit], BDESC)'
MEMBER [Measures].[Cum Profit] AS
'PartialSum (
    SetToArray ([Ordered States], [Geography], [Measures].[Profit]),
    SetToArray ([Ordered States], [Geography], [Measures].[Geog. ID]),
    CLng([Measures].[Geog. ID])
)'
SELECT
{ [Ordered States] } on columns,
{ [Measures].[Profit], [Measures].[Cum Profit] } on rows
FROM
[Sales Cube]
```

One subtle point to note regarding SetToArray() is how Microsoft Analysis Services constructs the array. Recall from Chapter 4 how an invalid tuple specification in a set specification ends up contributing no tuple to the set. For example, if a Time dimension's month level starts with January 2000, then the set specification { [Time].[Jan 2000], [Time].[Jan 2000].PrevMember, [Time].[Jan 2000].NextMember} will result in a set of only two tuples (for January and February). When this set is used to materialize an array that is passed to an external function via SetToArray(), the set will only contain two values as a result. If you construct your sets using functions like .PrevMember, Cousin(), ParallelPeriod(), SetToArray(), LastPeriods(), and the like, you will need to code your COM store procedures to take this into account.

MDX Functions for Use with COM Stored Procedures

In addition to `SetToArray()`, which can only be used with COM stored procedures, a number of functions specific to Analysis Services's implementation of MDX are most useful in combination with COM stored procedures. We list them in Table 10-3 and describe their utilities in the following paragraphs. All functions are marked by an asterisk (*) because they are Analysis Services extensions to the MDX specification. We will discuss most of these functions in this section. We leave the application of the `Dimensions()` and `Levels()` functions to your imagination and application requirements.

SetToStr(), TupleToStr()

`SetToStr()` converts the given set specification into a string. It does not convert the values associated with the set's tuples into a string. The format of the string is simple and is fully described in Appendix A. We could well have written `PartialSum()` so that it uses `SetToStr()` instead of an array of strings or member IDs. An external function that uses `SetToStr()` might be easier to write and might run faster if it used `SetToArray()` instead of `SetToStr()` because the string will need to be parsed in the external function if the tuples are to be processed there. `TupleToStr()` is similar except that it converts only a single tuple to a string.

Table 10-3   MDX Functions Useful with COM Stored Procedures

EXTENSION	RETURNS	SYNOPSIS
*	string	`SetToStr` **(Set)**
*	string	`TupleToStr` **(Tuple)**
*	set	`StrToSet` **(String Expression)**
*	set	`NameToSet` **(String Expression)**
*	tuple	`StrToTuple` **(String Expression)**
*	string, number	`StrToValue` **(String Expression)**
*	member	`Members` **(String Expression)**
*	member	`StrToMember` **(String Expression)**
*	string	`MemberToStr` **(Member)**
*	dimension	`Dimensions` **(String Expression)**
*	level	`Levels` **(String Expression)**

Members(), StrToSet(), StrToTuple()

Suppose that you want to create an MDX query that always provides requested data for the current day, for example, by using it as a slicer in the query. If you are generating the query dynamically, you can create an MDX expression every time the query is accessed, which puts the current date into the slicer. However, you can get the same effect with a completely static query by using an external function that returns the name of the current day. For example, a query that always returned the year-to-date sales through the current month might be written as follows:

```
WITH
MEMBER [Measures].[Sales YTD] AS
'Sum (PeriodsToDate ([Time].[Year], Members (OurCurDate())),
      [Measures].[Sales])'
SELECT
{ [Products].[Division].Members } on columns,
{ [Geography].[Regions].Members } on rows
FROM
[Sales Tracking]
WHERE ([Measures].[Sales YTD])
```

The logic that makes this query tick can be included in a single VB function that is 17 lines long, including white space. Assuming that the levels of the time dimension are [All], [Year], [Quarter], [Month], and [Day], the following VB code would return the appropriate name (assuming default time member names are used):

```
Public Function OurCurDate() As String
Dim TheDate As Date

TheDate = Date

' e.g. "[Time].[All Time].[1999].[Quarter 1].[February].[Feb 01, 1999]"
OurCurDate = "[Time].[All Time].[" & _
            DatePart("yyyy", TheDate) & _
        "].[" & _
          "Quarter " & Format(DatePart("q", TheDate)) & _
        "].[" & _
          Format(TheDate, "mmmm") & _
        "].[" & _
          Format(TheDate, "mmm dd, yyyy") & _
        "]"

End Function
```

If you are using Microsoft Analysis Services and the names for the day level are unique (which we generally advocate), this function can be much simpler because you don't need to list the parents in order to create the unique name. You can just use the name of the day, as follows:

```
Public Function OurCurDate() As String
Dim TheDate As Date

TheDate = Date

' e.g. "[Time].[Feb 01, 1999]"
OurCurDate = "[Time].[" &
            Format(TheDate, "mmm dd, yyyy") & _
          "]"

End Function
```

You must take care that the name logic is in synch with the name logic of the dimension. For example, if you change the way the quarters are named so that Q1 of 1999 is renamed from [Quarter 1] to [Q1, 1999], then you need to update the function. (If you were generating MDX dynamically to insert the current month, you would need to update its code generator too, so there is no great need to keep the naming principles in synch.)

The major difference between Members() and StrToTuple() is simply that Members() returns a single member, while StrToTuple() returns a tuple of arbitrary dimensionality. You could, of course, construct a tuple using multiple calls to Members(). For example,

```
(Members(MemberF1()), Members(MemberF2()))
```

specifies a tuple that combines the member whose name is returned by MemberF1() with the member whose name is returned by MemberF2().

StrToSet() returns an actual set, so it would be used in contexts where StrToTuple() and Members() cannot be used. You could, of course, express one-tuple sets as { StrToTuple(. . .) } or { Members(. . .) }. For example, the statement

```
CREATE SET [Production].[ProductsToAnalyze] AS
'StrToSet( MyEFThatReturnsAProductSetString( . . . ))'
```

will generate a named set within the context of the production cube that you can use in any number of subsequent queries.

External Function Example: Time Span until Sum

In Chapter 7, you worked through the MDX required to determine the time span required to accumulate a particular quantity (in that case, number of subscribers). The goal was to get the set of times, as opposed to simply counting how many times there were. Let's look at how to implement this operation in an external function.

First, you should understand what the function will return and how it will be called. In the example of Chapter 7, we were interested in a set of members, so let's have this function return a string containing a set specification. In the query, you'll turn this into a set of members using StrToSet(), calling it with something like StrToSet(TimeSpanUntilSum(. . .)). It needs to take an array of cell values to figure out the sums. However, it only needs to take one time member name (the latest time member's name), because it can return a string like [Time].[Feb 2000].lag(5) : [Time].[Feb 2000]. (This string assumes that the members are in database order; we'd construct the function differently if this might not be the case.) So, you can pass it just as an array of cell values and the time member name, and call it like this:

```
SET [Times Until Sum] AS
'StrToSet (
  TimeSpanUntilSum (
    SetToArray (
      {[Time].[Month].Members.Item(0) : [Time].[Month].[Oct 2000]},
      [Measures].[New Customer Count]
    ),
    "[Time].[Month].[Oct 2000]",
    500  // the sum we want to arrive at
  )
)'
```

What would the code for this function look like? It's pretty straightforward in any language; we'll provide a VB implementation here:

```
Public Function TimeSpanUntilSum (ArgVals() As Double, ByVal LastName As
String, ByVal SumTo As Double) As String

Dim i As Integer
Dim RunSum As Double

For i = UBound(ArgVals) to LBound(ArgVals) Step -1
  RunSum = RunSum + ArgVals(i)
  If RunSum >= SumTo Then
    Goto Done
```

```
   End If
Next i


Done:


TimeSpanUntilSum = "{" & LastName & ".Lag(" & UBound(ArgVals) - i _
                   & ") : " & LastName & "}"


End Function
```

Guess what? This tends to run faster than the plain MDX version, and the more time members, the greater the difference. The more members you have in the Time dimension, the more the plain MDX version creates redundant sums. Also, you don't need to create a different calculated measure definition every time you want to run this, whereas you did need to put the ending time member name in the plain MDX's calculated member definition each time you wanted to run it for a new time member. You can also adjust the threshold from 500 to 50,000 without altering any logic.

Loading and Using Stored Procedures

Analysis Services 2005 stored procedure libraries are deployed and executed on the server side. There are two levels of assembly collections to hold the user libraries for .NET assemblies or COM libraries. Libraries in the Server assembly collection will be accessible for all connections to the server. Libraries in database assembly collections will only be accessible by connections to a specific database. Unlike Analysis Services 2000, where the user libraries need to be deployed to every client machine, Analysis Services 2005 only needs to deploy the libraries on the server machine. The USE LIBRARY statement is deprecated for Analysis Services 2005; it is still supported by the parser, but it is a non-op.

The user can load the library into the server through the user interface via SQL Server Management Studio. Using the Business Intelligence Development Studio, you will only be able to add .NET assemblies. You can also add assemblies to your server or database collection using your own AMO application. For COM libraries, Analysis Services will create metadata files including the path of the COM library. For a .NET library, Analysis Services will copy the library over and store it in a folder under the server data folder. If the library has multiple dependent assemblies, Analysis Services will store those dependent assemblies in the same folder as the main assembly, so the CLR can find and load them. The user can choose "Include debug information" to copy debug files (.pdb) into the same folder. Including the symbol information will help you in debugging if any issues arise.

Security of Stored Procedures

Analysis Services 2005 provides fine-grained control for security of stored procedures. There are two security settings for each library: `Permission` and `Impersonation`.

`Permission` indicates which permission set should be applied to the .NET assembly. The permission restricts the access capability of the assembly, such as file system, network, registry, or calling unmanaged code. There are three levels of permission settings:

- **Safe:** This permission only allows the stored procedure to exercise computation, but gives no permissions to access any of the protected resources in the .NET framework.

- **ExternalAccess:** This permission offers access to server external resources, but does not offer general security guarantees (though it is possible to secure this scenario); it does give reliability guarantees.

- **Unrestricted:** This permission is intended for server administrators who are proficient enough to write server code without being given safeguards against programming errors causing server instability. This permission allows the managed library calls unmanaged code.

The unrestricted permission setting is not applied to COM libraries, because the COM library is always unrestricted. The default `Permission` for .NET assemblies is Safe. It is sufficient for functions to only interact with data inside Analysis Services and restrict access to resources outside the system such as files, the network, and so on. ADOMD Server objects are supported for a safe permission set because they are marked as `AllowPartiallyTrusted-Callers`. However, assemblies using AMO objects have to be marked as an unrestricted permission set.

The `Impersonation` property specifies which user the server should impersonate when calling a method in the user's assembly. The assembly can only operate within the capabilities of the specified user.

The following `Impersonations` are supported by Analysis Services:

- **`Default`:** The behavior depends on the setting of the Permission setting and library type. COM libraries treat `Impersonation=Default` as `ImpersonateCurrentUser`; .NET assemblies treat `Imperson-ation=Default` as `ImpersonateServiceAccout` for safe permission sets and `ImpersonateCurrentUser` for `ExternalAccess` and unrestricted permission sets.

- **`ImpersonateServiceAccount`:** Use credentials of the Analysis Services startup account.

- **ImpersonateAnonymous:** The execution context corresponds to the Windows login user account IUSER_servername on the server. This is the Internet guest account, which has limited privileges on the server. An assembly running in this context can only access limited resources on the local server.

- **ImpersonateCurrentUser:** Use credentials of the current user.

- **ImpersonateAccount:** Use credentials of the specified Windows account and password.

Note that ADOMD Server is a wrapper of Analysis Services's server internal objects. When a stored procedure calls an ADOMD Server method, such as MDX.Aggregate, that makes a transition into the server's unmanaged code, the server will revert the impersonation and run under the current user's context.

Stored Procedure Name Resolution

The syntax for calling a stored procedure is

```
COM: [ Assembly {.|!} [ Class {.|!} ] ] Method ( [params] )

.NET: Assembly {.|!} [ Class {.|!} ] Method ( [params] )
```

- Assembly is the name of the COM/CLR assembly object, as specified in the DDL. It is optional for COM assemblies, but mandatory for CLR assemblies.

- In a .NET assembly, Class is the fully/partially qualified name of the class. In a COM assembly, Class is the name of the interface.

- Method is the name of the method being called.

Following are some examples to illustrate the syntax.

1. Using only the method name:

   ```
   StoredProcName()
   ```

2. Using assembly and method names:

   ```
   AssemblyName.StoredProcName()
   ```

3. Using assembly, unqualified class, and method names:

   ```
   AssemblyName.ClassName.StoredProcName()
   ```

4. Using assembly, interface, and method names:

   ```
   COMLibraryName.InterfaceName.StoredProcName()
   ```

Analysis Services uses the type library (for COM assemblies) or reflection (for .NET assemblies) for resolving and executing stored procedures.

When a function call does not contain a separator (Example 1), then the server first tries to find a built-in function with the same name. If none exists, then the server iterates through all COM assemblies (CLR assemblies must be qualified by assembly name) and all classes/interfaces until it finds a method with the same name. Once a matching method is found, the name resolution is considered complete.

When a function call contains one or more separators (Examples 2–4), then Analysis Services assumes that the first part is the assembly name and the last part is the method name. The server limits its search to within the specified assembly. If no assembly with this name exists, an error is raised. If the function call contains exactly one separator (Example 2), then the server iterates through all classes/interfaces in the assembly until it finds a method with the same name. If the function call contains more than one separator (Examples 3–4), then the server uses the part between the first and last separators to resolve the class/interface name within the assembly and raises an error if that fails.

Name resolution failure (inability to find a class/interface with a matching method) results in a parsing error. Once name resolution is complete, the method is executed. If the parameters of the function call do not match the method, an error is raised. Analysis Services does not attempt to find a best match across all classes and assemblies based on the function call parameters. In the interest of resolving ambiguity across classes and assemblies, we suggest that you use fully qualify stored procedure names.

Nothing can prevent you from loading two or more function libraries that each contains a function with the same name. You are encouraged to use fully qualified names to avoid ambiguity.

Invoke Stored Procedures in MDX

Following are some typical usages of stored procedures in MDX. Stored procedures can be invoked in any place of the MDX query.

1. Stored procedure returns a set:

   ```
   SELECT StoredProc(a, b) ON 0 FROM Sales
   ```

2. Stored procedure returns a member, and is used in an MDX function:

   ```
   SELECT DESCENDANTS(StoredProc (a, b), 3) ON 0 FROM Sales
   ```

3. Stored procedure in a calculation:

   ```
   WITH MEMBER Measures.Foo as StoredProc(a, b)
   SELECT {Measures.Foo} on 0, Country.MEMBERS ON 1 FROM Sales
   ```

4. CALL the stored procedure:

   ```
   Call StoredProc(a, b)
   ```

The CALL statement invokes the stored procedure outside the context of an MDX/DMX query. It is useful for calling stored procedures that perform administrative tasks (using AMO) and do not return a result. And for AMO stored procedures that use "*" as a special connection string, you will end up with a server error if the stored procedure tries to change objects in the current context. The CALL statement is also useful for calling stored procedures that return rowsets or datasets that need to be sent directly to the client.

The CALL statement only supports return values of type `IDataReader` and `DataSet`. If the return value is of any other type, it will be ignored and the response will be empty.

Any exception thrown in a stored procedure will be caught by the Analysis Services server, and it will return errors for MDX query cases (Examples 1–3), sometimes the error shows in each cell's return value if you use calculate members to call stored procedures. The exception will directly return to the user for a CALL statement (Example 4).

Additional Considerations for Stored Procedures

The stored procedures' support of Analysis Services 2005 is a powerful tool for application developers, especially for the new .NET stored procedures. Stored procedures may open and read files, read the registry, call a Web service, and so on. The .NET support provides the opportunity for user functions to take advantage of .NET libraries such as regular expressions, Web services support, and so on. These will all be very application-specific, so we will not attempt to go through all of the possibilities here, but you may find that they make a great deal of sense for your own application. Keep in mind that it may not be appropriate for a stored procedure to interact with the production computing environment (for example, popping up a dialog box on a web server). Also, since the functions are global, it is difficult for the function library itself to maintain internal or session state in a stateless web server environment.

One interesting use of an external function is to have an application combine its specific calculations with cube data in MDX queries. Your application may need to perform some amount of data processing that would be inconvenient in MDX queries, and it would then combine the results with data in an Analysis Services cube. One way to perform the combining of the results is to feed them into a fact table and process a cube that provides additional calculations on them. If the scale of the calculations is small enough (in terms of number of cells calculated and their suitability for calculation in a client's session), it may make sense to have your application read its input data through MDX, perform its calculations, and then expose its results to further MDX calculations through an external function that references the results. Candidates for this approach would be any calculations that require iterative methods on the data from Analysis Services and return results that map to cells in the database.

Performance should be another consideration of using stored procedures. .NET stored procedures require transitions between management code and unmanaged code, which could significantly impact the performance. Also stored procedure developers should avoid heavy operations such as accessing files, querying other databases, and the like in stored procedures that need be invoked many times in a query.

Summary

Analysis Services 2005 supports .NET stored procedures and COM stored procedures. The .NET support and new ADOMD Server objects greatly improve the capability and flexibility of server stored procedures, allowing you to perform custom operations. In server library management, it eases the deployment effort and enables administrators to have more security controls on the libraries.

In this chapter, we covered the mechanisms that are used to call into and receive results from a stored procedure as well as how to register them for use with Analysis Services. We also looked at a set of examples to illustrate situations that these mechanisms can be applied to as well as how to implement them, so you can write your own with confidence. Many applications may have no need for them at all, but you may find they are the perfect technique for implementing the functionality that your particular application needs.

CHAPTER 11

Changing the Cube and Dimension Environment through MDX

MDX, like SQL, offers a Data Manipulation Language (DML) as well as a Data Description Language (DDL). Using DDL statements, it is possible to significantly alter the given cube environment through a client application. Some of the things that you can do for a user's session regardless of the source of the cubes are

- Alter the default member for a dimension
- Refresh the cell data and dimension members

If the dimension has writeback-enabled, you can

- Create a new member
- Drop a member
- Move a member within the hierarchy
- Update the custom member formula or member properties associated with the member

If a cube has writeback enabled, you can also update data cells within it, either programmatically or with the UPDATE CUBE statement.

These commands enable you to build applications, such as budgeting and forecasting applications, in which end users can alter the database without being granted administrative access to the cubes, using the old Decision

Support Objects (DSO) or the new Analysis Management Objects (AMO) code to update the databases.

The result of each command in this last set of four is that the database and all sessions connected to it immediately see the changes to the dimension structure, and the table that underlies the dimension is immediately updated. Thus, a certain amount of collaborative construction and analysis is supported.

Note that creating a new member in a writeback dimension is not the same as creating a new calculated member, and updating a member is not the same as altering the definition of a calculated member. These operations actually affect the underlying dimension table and cause the results to be visible to all users connected to their cubes, while calculated members do not exist in dimension tables and only really live in the context of a user's own session. For the collaborative application, differences in solve order and execution order for calculated members and custom member formulas can be significant. We discuss these issues in Chapter 12.

Altering the Default Member for a Dimension in Your Session

Every dimension in each cube has a default member, which is the member chosen when the dimension is not referenced in a query or by the `Dimension .DefaultMember` function. This default is chosen by the DBA or database designer and can be for the dimension as a whole, within the cube, or for the user's login role. However, this default can also be changed by MDX during the course of a session.

The general syntax to do this is

```
ALTER CUBE Cube
    UPDATE DIMENSION Dimension, DEFAULT_MEMBER = 'MDX Rule'
```

The MDX rule can be any valid MDX expression that results in a single member of that dimension. It could be the name of a member, but it could also be the results of selecting an item from a named set, or the result of an external function. Whatever it is, it is evaluated immediately; if it is an expression that relies on changing data, it will need to be reevaluated to pick up the changes in the data.

For example, suppose that the rule was `'Tail([Time].[Day].Members, 1).Item(0).Item(0)'`, which will pick up the last day defined in the time dimension (`.Item(0).Item(0)`, which picks the member from the tuple picked from the set, can be omitted in AS 2005). An incremental update of the time dimension during the session might introduce a new last day that would be available in metadata, but the default member would not be changed until the ALTER CUBE statement was run again. Suppose that you had an external function that returned the name of the time member to use. If the rule was 'StringToSet (ExternalDayNameFunction()).Item(0) .Item(0)', then this rule would be evaluated at the moment the ALTER CUBE statement was run, and once again, the default will not be changed until the ALTER CUBE statement is run again.

In AS2005 a dimension can have many hierarchies: attribute hierarchies, user hierarchies and natural hierarchies. Each of them has its own separate default, which can be set independently from the others. That means that we can set separate default members for [Customer] .[Martial Status] and [Customer].[Gender], for example.

Moreover, a default member created in a subcube (i.e. a default member created after the issue of a CREATE SUBCUBE command) lives within the context of the subcube; dropping the subcube restores the original default member.

Dimension Writeback Operations

If your cube contains write-enabled dimensions, then you can use the following Microsoft-specific MDX commands to manipulate these dimensions. These commands each take effect immediately, regardless of the transaction isolation mode in effect for the session. They are also committed immediately, unlike the UPDATE CUBE and cell writeback operations that require an OLE DB or ADO commit in order to take effect on the server. Although they can be phrased as ALTER CUBE statements, they affect the dimension in every cube that the dimension appears in, so they can affect many cubes at once.

Some of these commands are only supported, in AS 2005, with parent-child dimensions, or are more constrained, with respect to AS 2000, in case of regular dimensions.

Moreover, there are restrictions on write enabling dimensions: for instance, hierarchies cannot have discretization set, you should have write permissions to source tables, the table cannot have auto-increment, and a few similar conditions. This information is retrieved from data source and saved in data source view.

Creating a New Member

To create a new member in a parent-child dimension, you can use the ALTER CUBE CREATE DIMENSION MEMBER statement. The general syntax for this is

```
ALTER CUBE Cube
    CREATE DIMENSION MEMBER [ParentUniqueName.]MemberName
    , KEY='KeyValue'
    [ PropertyName = 'PropertyValue' [, PropertyName = 'PropertyValue'
 . . . ]]
```

The result of this command is that a new row is actually entered into the underlying dimension table.

The property names are database-defined member properties such as [Manager Name] or [Reporting Units], not OLE DB member properties such as FORMAT_STRING.

For example, given a parent-child dimension that is write-enabled, the following will add a new [Family Assistance] member under the [Human Resources] member:

```
ALTER CUBE IntegratedReporting
CREATE DIMENSION MEMBER [Accounts].[Net Cash].[Expenses].[Human
Resources].[Family Assistance]
, KEY='175'
, [RollupColumn] = '+'
```

Moving a Member within Its Dimension

If a member already exists, but it needs to be moved, you can move it with the ALTER CUBE MOVE DIMENSION MEMBER command. The general syntax of this command is

```
ALTER CUBE Cube
   MOVE DIMENSION MEMBER MemberUniqueName
[, SKIPPED_LEVELS = '<value>'] [WITH DESCENDANTS]
   UNDER ParentUniqueName
```

If you specify the WITH DESCENDANTS clause, then the entire subtree of members starting with the member and extending to the leaves is moved under the new parent. Otherwise, the member alone is moved, and the member's children immediately prior to the command's execution become the children of the member's original parent (or root members if it was a top-level member). The effect of the operation on the underlying dimension table is simply to alter the values of the parent key column for the row that defined the member, and possibly for the rows that defined its immediate children. The new parent key is that of the member listed in MemberUniqueName. If the SKIPPED_LEVELS clause is used, then the member is effectively placed that many hierarchical steps below the parent member, so that it will appear in metadata requests for members at that deeper level from the parent or root.

Note that this does not always provide a good means to make the member a root member. If the dimension does not have a database-defined all level, there is no way that this member can become a child member of anything and be a root member. You can, of course, work around this by moving the member under a dummy member and then deleting the dummy.

AS2005 introduces some constraints on the possible movements of members within a dimension: If the dimension is a parent/child dimension, a member can be moved to any level other than the All level, whereas in "regular dimensions," members can be moved only within the same level, so a City, for instance, cannot become a State.

Dropping a Member

You can delete a member from the dimension by using the ALTER CUBE DROP MEMBER command. The general syntax for the command is

```
ALTER CUBE Cube
    DROP DIMENSION MEMBER MemberUniqueName
    [WITH DESCENDANTS]
```

This simply deletes the member and the corresponding row in the dimension table. If the WITH DESCENDANTS clause is included, then all descendants (and their dimension table rows) are also deleted. If the WITH DESCENDANTS clause is omitted, then the children of the member become the children of the member's parent. If the member being dropped is a root member and WITH DESCENDANTS is omitted, then the member's children become root members.

To drop a calculated member, the command is

```
ALTER CUBE Cube
    DROP CALCULATED MEMBER MemberUniqueName
```

Updating a Member's Definition

You can also update some aspects of a member's definition by using the ALTER CUBE UPDATE DIMENSION MEMBER command. This command enables you to alter the custom member formula associated with the member and one or more property values as well. The general syntax for the command is

```
ALTER CUBE Cube
    UPDATE DIMENSION MEMBER MemberUniqueName
[ AS 'MDXExpression' ] [ , Property = 'Value' [, Property = '<value>'  .
  . . ]]
```

or simply (no `MDXExpression`):

```
ALTER CUBE Cube
    UPDATE DIMENSION MEMBER MemberUniqueName
    Property = 'Value' [ , Property = 'Value'  . . . ]
```

The definition of the custom member formula and/or member property values are updated in the OLAP database and also in the underlying dimension table.

For example, the following will alter the rollup operator associated with our member to subtraction (-):

```
ALTER CUBE IntegratedReporting
UPDATE DIMENSION MEMBER [Accounts].[Net Cash].[Expenses].[Human
Resources].[Family Assistance]
   , [RollupColumn] = '-'
```

NOTE This command does not alter the formula for a calculated member. In order to do that, you will need to drop the calculated member and then re-create it.

Refresh Cell Data and Dimension Members

During the course of a client session, it is possible for data to be updated at the server. These updates can include new members appearing, cell data changing, member property values changing, and in some cases, members being deleted or renamed as well. Ordinarily, after some time, the client will detect these changes and begin to provide the new or altered members and data to new queries. However, depending on the connection settings, it may take too long for these to appear. It will always be possible for a client to refresh its cached data with the REFRESH CUBE command. The general syntax for refreshing a cube is

```
REFRESH CUBE CubeName
```

For example, the following command will refresh the Sales cube:

```
REFRESH CUBE [Sales]
```

Note that only one cube at a time can be updated with this command. Also, although the members of dimensions may have changed, any named sets defined on the Sales cube will not be updated.

When a client is connected to a local cube file as opposed to a server-based cube, the REFRESH CUBE command will cause the cube contents to be rebuilt from its definition and tables. (Local cube files are discussed in Chapter 17.)

Writing Data Back to the Cube

Writing data back to the cube (assuming that the cube has been write-enabled) can be done in two ways. One way (supported by standard OLE DB for OLAP) is through data structures, while the other way uses Microsoft's UPDATE CUBE statement. We'll talk about both of these here, although we will discuss UPDATE CUBE in much greater detail. UPDATE CUBE can be used in place of the standard writeback facility as well.

Standard Cell Writeback

The standard cell writeback capability involves programmatically changing the data value for a cell that has already been retrieved from the database. This requires that a query already has been formulated to produce the cell. In OLE DB for OLAP, when the results of the query are requested for insertion into a range rowset (via IMDRangeRowset:GetRangeRowset), it is possible for the cells to be updated by obtaining an IRowsetChange interface on the range rowset and altering the cell values as though they were updatable fields in a relational database. The details for this are covered pretty well in the OLE DB for OLAP documentation. Through ADOMD, after retrieving the results of a query into a Cellset object, you can update a cell value by simply assigning a new data value to the cell. You must remember two important details about Microsoft Analysis Services:

- Only leaf-level cells of a cube can be updated by writing back to the data structures. This means that no cell for a calculated member can be updated. If the cells are not leaf cells in a regular cube, they cannot be written back to.

- Only the Value column (or the ADOMD .Value property of the Cellset object) can be written to. Formatted_Value and the other cell properties cannot be written to.

In ADOMD, the following snippet of VB code updates the cell:

```
Dim ResultCS As ADOMD.CellSet
Dim cmd AS ADODB.Command

Set ResultCS = cmd.Execute ("SELECT  . . . ")

ResultCS (1, 1) = 45    ' update cell 1,1 with the value 45
```

Commit and Rollback

Note that updating cell data in the actual database will always involve programming in addition to using MDX. Cell updates are controlled via OLE DB transactions. When you update cell data through the techniques described in this section, you initially update data held in the session cache. This enables you to perform a variety of what-if? calculations. (You cannot drop the results of a particular update; if you want to roll back a particular what-if?, you need to remember what the change was and apply its opposite. You can roll back all uncommitted changes issued, however.) If you want to update the shared database so that your database will persist the results and all users can see your changes, then you need to programmatically commit the work. With OLE DB, you will use `IRowsetUpdate:Update()`, and in ADOMD, you will use the ADODB's `Connection.CommitTrans` method to commit all updates for the connection. Similarly, you can also use `IRowsetUpdate:Undo()` and `Connection.RollbackTrans` to undo changes.

When a transaction is committed in Microsoft Analysis Services, all accumulated deltas for changed cells are written to the writeback table. If a cell has been changed more than once, only one row is entered into the writeback table that contains the sum of all deltas.

Using UPDATE CUBE

Microsoft's UPDATE CUBE extension to MDX provides a couple of enhancements over the standard cell update mechanism. Functionally, it enables aggregate cells to be updated and provides a set of options for allocating data to leaf-level cells. It also provides a language-based interface which makes the description of the task to perform easier than lower-level programming, which requires opening a query and programmatically placing new data into the cell data structures returned by the query. As with standard writeback, cells associated with calculated members cannot be updated. Also, the measure associated with the cell must be aggregated by SUM.

> **NOTE** Updating a cell associated with a member from a level-based dimension actually causes the associated leaf cells to be updated via one of four allocation functions. This is true even for parents in parent-child dimensions where nonleaf data may be entered from underlying fact tables. However, writing to the parent only, allowed in AS2000 via the `.DataMember` function, is not possible anymore in AS2005.

When Analysis Services executes an UPDATE CUBE statement, it first determines the set of leaf-level cells that will be affected by the update, and then it calculates new values or deltas for them. The outcome will be that the updated cell will have the value specified by the UPDATE CUBE command, but when multiple cells contribute to the aggregated cell, the values in those cells may change in different ways. We will describe the allocation methods in the course of describing the syntax.

The general syntax for the UPDATE CUBE command is

```
UPDATE [CUBE] CubeName
SET tuple [.VALUE] = New_aggregate_value
[ USE_EQUAL_ALLOCATION |
  USE_EQUAL_INCREMENT |
  USE_WEIGHTED_ALLOCATION [BY Weight_value_expression ] |
  USE_WEIGHTED_INCREMENT [BY Weight_value_expression ]
]
```

The cell specified by tuple expression can be any cell in the multidimensional space (that is, it does not have to be a leaf cell). However, the cell must be aggregated with the Sum aggregate function and must not include a calculated member in the tuple used to identify the cell.

If a dimension in the cube does not have a member listed in the tuple, the default member for that dimension is used. Notice that no quotes are around either the New_aggregate_value or the weight_value_expression.

Four different allocation methods are available:

1. USE_EQUAL_ALLOCATION. Every leaf-level cell contributing to the updated cell will be assigned the same value. *New leaf cell value = New_aggregate_value/*Count *(leaf cells related to aggregate cell).*

2. USE_EQUAL_INCREMENT. Every leaf-level cell contributing to the updated cell will be changed by the same increment: *New leaf cell value = Original leaf cell value + (New_aggregate_value – Original aggregate value)/*Count *(leaf cells related to aggregate cell).*

3. USE_WEIGHTED_ALLOCATION. Every leaf-level cell contributing to the updated cell will be assigned a value that is a fraction (weight value) of the updated cell. *New leaf cell value = New_aggregate_value * Weight_value_ expression.*

4. USE_WEIGHTED_INCREMENT. Every atomic cell contributing to the updated cell will be changed by a value that is a fraction (weight) of the increment (positive or negative) of the updated cell. *New leaf cell value = Original leaf cell value + (New_aggregate_value - Original aggregate value) * Weight_value_expression.*

If the `Weight_value_expression` is not provided, the following expression is assigned to it by default (fractional contribution of the original leaf to the original aggregate):

```
Original leaf cell value/Original aggregate cell value
```

Regardless, you should ensure that the `weight_value_expression` evaluates to a number between 0 and 1 per cell. If the sum of all the leaf-level cell evaluations for weight_value_expression is 1, then the sum of the leaf cells after the UPDATE CUBE instruction has been executed will be the `New_aggregate_value`. However, if the sum of all the leaf-level cell evaluations for weight_value_expression is not 1, then the result of the UPDATE CUBE instruction will be that the cell specified will have a value proportionately greater than or less than `New_aggregate_value`. Generally speaking, you will use a `weight_value_expression` that generates a ratio of some measures across multiple levels in one or more dimensions, which will guarantee that the sum of the weights is 1. If the dimensions taken into account are more than one, attention must be paid! Suppose, for instance, that you want to allocate a sales target between different shops. You can use, as the `weight_value_expression`, the previous year sales contribution of each shop to the total (see Chapter 3):

```
([Measures].[Sales], Parallelperiod([Time].[Year],1)) /
([Measures].[Sales], Parallelperiod([Time].[Year],1), [All Geography])
```

This fraction is the "marginal contribution" of each `[Geography].currentmember` to the total.

Suppose that you want, instead, to allocate your target according to Products. You'd use:

```
([Measures].[Sales], Parallelperiod([Time].[Year],1)) /
([Measures].[Sales], Parallelperiod([Time].[Year],1), [All Products])
```

But if you want to allocate your target according to Shops AND Products, you have to use the "joint contribution" of Shops and Products, in this way:

```
([Measures].[Sales], Parallelperiod([Time].[Year],1)) /
([Measures].[Sales], Parallelperiod([Time].[Year],1), [All Geography],
[All Products])
```

You *cannot*, for instance, define the `weight_value_expression` by multiplying the two ratios:

```
([Measures].[Sales], Parallelperiod([Time].[Year],1)) /
([Measures].[Sales], Parallelperiod([Time].[Year],1),  [All Products]))
*
([Measures].[Sales], Parallelperiod([Time].[Year],1))/
([Measures].[Sales], Parallelperiod([Time].[Year],1),  [All Geography]))
```

Such an approach will indeed provide you with a `weight_value_ expression` whose sum over all leaf-cells is usually not 1, as it should be. This is due to the statistical fact that Products and Shops are usually correlated (certain Products are sold more in certain Shops/Cities/Countries than in others), which means that the "joint distribution" is not the product of the "marginals." (Do you remember? The "joint probability" of two events can be computed as the product of the individual probabilities only when the two events are independent, which is usually not the case . . . if the OLAP dimensions were independent, multidimensional analysis would be useless!)

Remember also, that the calculations in `weight_value_expression` can be influenced by cell calculations, custom member formulas, and all other techniques of calculating available when executing an expression. The `USE_EQUAL_ALLOCATION` and `USE_EQUAL_INCREMENT` methods guarantee that each of the associated leaf cells ends up with a value. If some of the cells were empty prior to the `UPDATE CUBE` command, they will have appropriate data values afterwards. Cells that contained data values prior to the execution of the command will be adjusted.

NOTE Because `USE_EQUAL_ALLOCATION` and `USE_EQUAL_INCREMENT` ultimately assign a data value to every leaf-level cell associated with the aggregate cell, assigning a cell with many associated leaf cells can consume a great deal of memory and take substantial time.

The `USE_WEIGHTED_ALLOCATION` and `USE_WEIGHTED_INCREMENT` methods increment data values for cells that already have data. They do not create new cells for related leaf-level cells that are empty, unless all of the cells related to the aggregate cell are empty. If that is the case, the first cell (the cell related to the first leaf descendant in database ordering along each of the dimensions) related to the aggregate cell is assigned the entire `New_aggregate_value`.

Each of these allocation options can be useful for different purposes in budgeting and forecasting applications. For example, when leaf-level cells already contribute different quantities to an aggregate cell, `USE_EQUAL_INCREMENT` preserves the absolute differences between the cells (albeit changing empties into nonempty cells), whereas `USE_WEIGHTED_INCREMENT` can be used to maintain their proportional differences while not assigning values to empty cells.

For example, the following statement updates the month-level, store-level, and Provision-VAT account cells related to Q2-2002 and Austria, incrementing the current values by the ratio of the related store-month estimated sales:

```
UPDATE CUBE [Transfer Budget]
SET (
    [Time].[Q2-2002]
  , [Operating Unit].[Austria]
  , [Account].[Provision-VAT]
) = 65000
USE_WEIGHTED_INCREMENT BY
    [Account].[Est Sales]
    / ([Operating Unit].[Austria], [Time].[Q2-2002], [Account]. [Est
Sales])
```

If the [Account].[Provision-VAT] member is itself a parent member, the previous expression would write back to each of its leaf-level descendants as well.

Summary

The commands covered in this chapter are useful for a number of applications. In particular, the virtual cube version of CREATE CUBE and the ALTER CUBE UPDATE DIMENSION can be used by any application to adjust the cubes and dimensions provided by the DBA. The other commands that were discussed are important pieces of interactive budgeting and collaborative analysis applications. These commands complement the queries and calculations covered in the first chapters. In the next chapter, we will look at the different types of calculations available in AS2005 (as well as in AS2000).

CHAPTER 12

The Many Ways to Calculate in Microsoft Analysis Services

Microsoft Analysis Services 2000 provided many different ways of calculating a cell, and not much guidance on which one to choose for your application. Microsoft Analysis Services 2005 has added a new way of MDX programming, via MDX scripting. In this chapter, we describe the mechanics and interactions of the "traditional ways of calculating," while the description of MDX scripting is left to another chapter. An important difference between the two approaches is that, while Scripts can only be defined at the server, some of the techniques described here can be defined and/or modified within user sessions or even per query. We will provide a few simple tips to keep in mind when applying them.

The ways to calculate a cell are

1. Intrinsic aggregation for a measure
2. Rollup by custom unary rollup operator
3. Custom member formula
4. Calculated member
5. Cell calculation

We have described calculated members in some detail already because they are part of standard MDX and useful in almost every application. We haven't discussed the intrinsic aggregation for a measure very much, but then again it's simple enough almost to take for granted. (It's also something that you don't have any control over in MDX, except when creating a local cube using Microsoft's CREATE CUBE statement.) We'll discuss the custom rollups in some depth in this chapter. The custom member or custom rollup formulas are MDX expressions, whereas the unary rollup operators are a simplified (and non-MDX) way of specifying calculations within a hierarchy. The application designer and DBA ordinarily set up the various custom rollups (they live on the server). However, if they are in a write-enabled parent-child dimension, they can be modified using the ALTER CUBE UPDATE DIMENSION command (described in Chapter 11). Cell calculations are a way of layering calculation specifications over cell regions of a cube, and provide another way to perform calculations without adding new members.

Overview of Calculation Mechanisms

Before looking at how all of the ways to calculate interact with each other, let's set the stage by looking at each calculation method individually. We will briefly describe how each technique works on its own and how it is created and edited. For calculated members and cell calculations, we will also look at the syntax used to create them.

Intrinsic Aggregation for a Measure

If a cell has no other calculations applied to it, it is calculated by intrinsic aggregation. This is achieved by the default CALCULATE command, the first expression in an MDX script. It specifies that the measures should be aggregated according to their AggregateFunction properties. In Microsoft's Analysis Services, every measure has indeed an aggregation function associated with it. While in AS2000 the aggregation functions were simply SUM, COUNT, MIN, MAX, and DISTINCT COUNT, in AS2005 many more have been included, that make the handling of semi-additive measures easier (see Table 12-1)

Remember that an additive measure is a measure that can be aggregated along any dimension (for example, sales), a nonadditive measure is a measure that cannot be aggregated at all (for example, a percentage profit margin, an interest rate, and the like), and a semi-additive measure can be aggregated along some dimensions and not along others (usually the time dimension, as with a bank balance, an inventory level, and the like).

If you look at the following table, you can see that, if you have a bank balance, you can't SUM it over the days of one month, but you can take the AVERAGEOFCHILDREN (daily average over one month), the FIRSTCHILD (value at the first day), the LASTCHILD, and so on.

If two or more fact records are associated with a particular cell, then the column associated with that measure is aggregated by that aggregation function and the results appear in that cell. In a parent-child hierarchy, it is possible for a parent member to aggregate records for itself, and also to incorporate the aggregates for its descendants in the hierarchy, but the data is still aggregated by the built-in function. Thus, even leaf-level cells are essentially aggregated (and without drilling through to the fact records, you cannot tell whether a leaf cell was in fact atomic or if it was an aggregation of two or more records).

AGGREGATE FUNCTION	RETURNED VALUE
Sum	Calculates the sum of values for all members/rows. This is the default aggregate function.
AverageOfChildren	Calculates the average of values for all nonempty child members.
ByAccount	Calculates the aggregation according to aggregate functions assigned by an account dimension. If no account dimension exists in the measure group, treat as the None aggregate function.
Count	Retrieves the count of all members/rows.
FirstChild	Retrieves the value of the first child member along the time dimension.
FirstNonEmpty	Retrieves the value of the first nonempty child member along the time dimension.
LastChild	Retrieves the value of the last child member along the time dimension.
LastNonEmpty	Retrieves the value of the last nonempty child member along the time dimension.
Max	Retrieves the highest value for all child members/rows.
Min	Retrieves the lowest value for all child members/rows.
DistinctCount	Retrieves the count of all unique members/rows.
None	No aggregation is performed, and all values for leaf and nonleaf members in a dimension are supplied directly from the fact table for the measure group containing the measure. If no value can be read from the fact table for a member, the value for that member is set to NULL.

Rollup by Unary Operator

In a parent-child dimension, it is possible to use a column of the underlying dimension table (or a related table) to specify rollup operators, which provide a simple technique for specifying calculations within the hierarchy. The syntax is borrowed from Hyperion Software's Essbase server and will be familiar to everyone who has built a system from that product. Every child member under a parent can have a single-character operator associated with it. The cell associated with the parent member forms an accumulator for the results; based on the symbol associated with each child member, the value associated with the child is combined with the accumulated value to that point using the operator. The operators are shown in the following table.

OPERATOR	FUNCTION
+	Adds the child's data value to the accumulated value.
–	Subtracts the child's data value from the accumulated value.
*	Multiplies the accumulated value by the child's value.
/	Divides the accumulated value by the child's value.
%	Divides the accumulated value by the child's value and then multiplies by 100.
~	The child's value is ignored (contributes NULL to the accumulated value).
Weight	Adds/subtracts the value weight * child's data value to/from the accumulated vale.

The last operator in the table (Weight) has been introduced in AS2005, where it is possible to aggregate or subtract a percentage (weight) of the child's data value to the accumulated value, instead of the entire value.
So, instead of the + operator, you can specify, for instance, 0.5, meaning that you want to add only 50 percent of the child value to the parent, or -0.25, to subtract 25 percent of the value.

The operators + and – become, therefore, special cases, representing a weight of +1 and -1 respectively. ~ is then equivalent to the weight 0.

Unary operators are stored in a column of the dimension table (or a related table) defined by the UnaryOperatorColumn property of the parent attribute.

The child members and their operators are applied in database order (according to the member ordering per level specified at the server). The first operator applied must be +, -, or ~; no value is in the accumulator before the first operator is applied, and no default value of 1 or 0 is assumed if the *, /, or % operator is used first. If all child operators used are ~, the parent's value will be NULL or empty. Typically, the ~ operator is used for members that function as placeholders in the hierarchy, serving to organize other members. For example, in a dimension of financial accounts, the hierarchy of accounts that make up the proper P&L may all connect to each other using + and –, whereas a separate subtree of the dimension that holds important ratios would have each of its members using the ~ operator to prevent spurious calculations further up. If the parent member has associated fact data from a fact table that has been aggregated to it, that data is overridden by the results of the rollup operators. Figure 12-1 shows a sample outline of members, operators, and calculated results.

Rollup operators cannot be specified for the measures dimension because you cannot specify hierarchy or member properties for measures. However, a cube that uses rollup operators usually has just one measure named something like Amount or Value, whereas another dimension named Accounts or Indicators functions as the measures dimension.

In the absence of any other specified calculations, rollup operators cut across all measures in cubes that use the dimension. Whereas rollup operators are used on two or more dimensions, dimension ordering in the cube determines how the rollups are applied to calculate a cell. (We'll talk about that in the "How Types of Calculations Interact" section further along in this chapter.)

NOTE The `RollupChildren()` function in Analysis Services provides a way to explicitly roll up children using particular unary operators through MDX as well. Because that is an MDX function, it executes as part of one of the other calculation forms (custom member formula, custom rollup, calculated member, and cell calculation). However, the rules for combining the child members using unary operators in this function follow the rules described here. We discuss `RollupChildren()` in Appendix A.

Custom Member Formula

A custom member formula is an MDX formula that is associated with a regular member of a dimension. Member formulas are typically used with parent-child dimensions but may also be used in any dimension. They are similar in some ways to a calculated member and different in others. The formula is ultimately stored in a column of a dimension table and may be altered in a write-enabled dimension by the `ALTER CUBE UPDATE DIMENSION` command.

A custom member formula is like a calculated member in that it is an MDX expression (for example, `[Accounts].[Profit]/[Accounts].[Head-Count]`), and intersects all members of all other dimensions. Unlike a calculated member, it intersects all members of all other dimensions in every cube that the dimension appears. If the custom member formula is intended for use in calculating values for some measures but not others, you need to craft its formula or other calculations accordingly using `Iif()` or `Case` to distinguish between the measures.

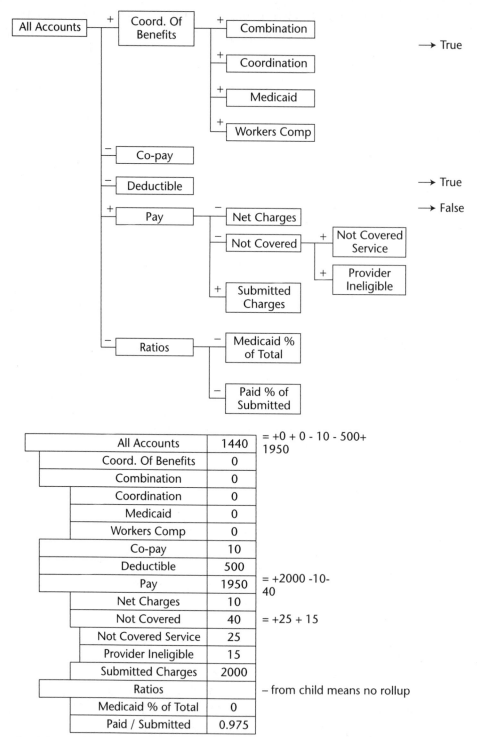

Figure 12-1   Effect of rolling up by unary operators.

Unlike a calculated member, the member that holds a custom member formula can have children as well as a parent, and is considered a regular member by OLE DB for OLAP. Actually, the member itself is a regular member; it just happens to have this formula associated with it. Data can be entered for it and aggregated from fact tables, but at the member itself, the calculation overrides the intrinsic aggregation. The calculated custom member may be overridden as well, by an MDX Script that touches its cells.

A custom formula can even be specified for the All member of a dimension through the `All Member Formula` property. The formula for the custom member is stored in a column of the dimension table, and is enabled by setting the `CustomRollupColumn` property of an attribute to that column. When the formula column is empty, the cell value for the corresponding member is returned normally; otherwise, it is defined by the formula, which overrides the aggregation function.

The properties of the custom members, such as the `SOLVE_ORDER`, the `FORMAT_STRING`, and the like, are stored in another column of the dimension, separated by commas, and enabled by setting `CustomRollupPropertiesColumn`.

> **NOTE** AS2000 Custom rollup formulas, that is, MDX formulas that were not associated with a member-such as a custom member formula-but with an entire level of a dimension, are now implemented (in AS2005) via an MDX Script "scoped" to that level.

Calculated Member

A calculated member is a member defined by a command and associated with an MDX formula. As such, it is treated differently from regular members by certain metadata functions. Although a calculated member can be defined to appear as a child of a nonleaf regular member, a calculated member cannot itself have children.

Calculated members can be created with the `CREATE MEMBER` statement and dropped by the `DROP MEMBER` command. They can be defined either by the database designer/DBA at the server or during the course of a session. The formula associated with a calculated member cannot be modified without dropping and re-creating the member (and, in the process, invalidating every calculation that references it). Query-specific calculated members can be defined using the `WITH MEMBER` construct.

Unlike the custom calculations, a calculated member is only defined in a single cube. Two different cubes that have a calculated member with the same name can have the same definition for the calculated member or two different definitions. Calculated members can, of course, be defined in the measures dimension as well as in other dimensions.

Like custom calculations and cell calculations, a calculated member also can influence the formatting of cell values. A calculated member can hold a format string, and font and color information for use in representing cells that were directly calculated by the member. Calculated members can be assigned a specific solve order number, which gives their creator fine-grained control over their precedence when intersecting other calculated members, custom members, and cell calculations.

Defining a Calculated Member

The general syntax for defining a calculated member at a session or global level is

```
CREATE MEMBER cube-member-name AS 'expression' [, optional-property . .
. ]
like in AS2000, or
CREATE MEMBER cube-member-name AS expression [, optional-property . . .
].
```

The use of the quotation marks around the expression was required in AS2000, despite the fact that the OLE DB for OLAP spec (the formal MDX spec) did not include them. Now, AS2005 allows the quotation marks for compatibility with the previous version, but prefers the "no-quotes" version (the parser behaves slightly differently).

The general syntax for defining a calculated member within the context of a query is

```
WITH MEMBER member-name AS [']expression['] [, optional-property . . . ]

(with or without quotes)
```

The OLE DB for OLAP specification also specifies an ALTER MEMBER construct, but this is not implemented in Microsoft Analysis Services.

The CREATE MEMBER statement is a DDL statement that defines a new calculated member. It can be used both on the client side and, by scripting, on server side. The calculated member is defined within the context of a particular cube or subcube, so the name of the member must also be qualified with the name of the cube/subcube; in a script or local cube DDL, the token CURRENTCUBE can also be used to indicate the cube that the CREATE MEMBER statement is associated with. Like any other calculated member, the expression may reference any MDX function, including user-defined functions (UDFs). It may also reference any other members, whether created with the CREATE MEMBER statement or not. Members created through the CREATE MEMBER statement are accessible in member-related metadata through OLE DB for OLAP, despite the specification saying they must not be.

Following the expression, one or more optional properties may be defined. The most important properties that you may define are the following:

```
SOLVE_ORDER = integer-number (from -8181 to 65535)
FORMAT_STRING = 'Microsoft-Office-cell-format' (literal or expression)
LANGUAGE = 'LCID', or Language Code Id (for instance, 1033 for US)
VISIBLE = 'number'
NON_EMPTY_BEHAVIOR = {measure list}  (in AS200 just a single measure
could be specified)
```

The LANGUAGE property, combined with the FORMAT_STRING property, allows AS2005 to properly format currencies (for instance, $ for USD and € for Euros).

You could also set, literally or via an expression (see the "Conditional Formatting" section later in this chapter), some formatting properties:

```
FORE_COLOR = 'color-code'
BACK_COLOR = 'color-code'
FONT_NAME = 'font-name'
FONT_SIZE = 'font-size'
FONT_FLAGS = 'font-flags'
```

For example, the statement

```
CREATE MEMBER [Production].[Measures].[Avg Failure Cost] as
[Measures].[Failure Cost Sum Per Incident] / [Measures].[Failure
Incident Count], SOLVE_ORDER = 10, FORMAT_STRING = '#.##'
```

creates the calculated measure [Avg Failure Cost] as the ratio of total failure incident cost to count of incidents, specifies its SOLVE_ORDER number as 10, and indicates that wherever this formula is used to calculate cells, the result should be formatted with two decimal places.

The SOLVE_ORDER property is used when a value is calculated for a cell that is related to a number of different calculations (custom members, calculated members, or calculated cells); the calculation with the highest solve order wins. The FORMAT_STRING property, if provided, is used to format the data values into character strings. The VISIBLE flag controls whether the calculated member is visible to the query through .AllMembers and AddCalculatedMembers(); a zero value means the member is hidden, and a nonzero value means that the member is visible.

The NON_EMPTY_BEHAVIOR property contains a list of base measures to use to determine whether or not to attempt calculation of the calculated member. If all named measures are empty at the same nonmeasures intersection, then the calculated member will not be evaluated and taken as NULL. This can dramatically speed up complex calculations and NON EMPTY queries against sparse data. Note that only measure names are listed, not their unique names. For example, you would use { [Unit Sales] } instead of { [Measures].[Unit Sales] }.

The default is for the member to be visible. The other properties are specified and stored as character strings and are provided to the client in response to queries that explicitly reference cell properties. The OLE DB data types of these properties as they are delivered back to the client are shown in the following table.

PROPERTY	TYPE
FORMAT_STRING	DBTYPE_WSTR
FORE_COLOR	DBTYPE_UI4
BACK_COLOR	DBTYPE_UI4
FONT_NAME	DBTYPE_WSTR
FONT_SIZE	DBTYPE_UI2
FONT_FLAGS	DBTYPE_I4

For more information on creating programs that use cell properties, refer to the developer's documentation for OLE DB for OLAP.

Within a CREATE MEMBER statement, the SESSION keyword is supported to make explicit the fact that the created member is valid for the OLE DB session in which the statement was issued. In Microsoft Analysis Services, there is no difference between using SESSION and leaving it out. For example, the expression

```
CREATE SESSION MEMBER [Production].[Measures].[Failure rate] AS...
```

explicitly creates the member within the scope of that single session, whereas

```
CREATE MEMBER [Production].[Measures].[Failure rate] AS...
```

implicitly creates the member within the session.

The only difference between WITH MEMBER and CREATE MEMBER is that the scope of a member created with WITH MEMBER is limited to the query that contains the WITH MEMBER statement. A member created by WITH MEMBER is invisible to any other query in any other session, and it is not accessible as part of the OLE DB for OLAP metadata.

Multiple members may be defined in one CREATE MEMBER or WITH MEMBER statement. After the CREATE (or WITH) and optional session scope identifier, each member's definition is listed in order. For example, the following expression creates two members in the Production cube:

```
CREATE
MEMBER [Production].[Measures].[Failure rate] AS ' . . . ', SOLVE_ORDER
= 10, FORMATSTRING = '#.##'
MEMBER [Production].[Scenarios].[VarianceOverTrials] AS '. . . ',
SOLVE_ORDER = 20, FORMATSTRING = '#.##%', FONT_NAME = 'Times New Roman'
```

Note that you do not separate the different MEMBER definitions with commas.

You cannot define a calculated member so that it has the same unique name as another member in the same cube or subcube, either base or calculated (but a new subcube creates a new scope). If you want to redefine a calculated member, use DROP MEMBER to discard it first and then execute CREATE MEMBER. Also, note that you can use WITH MEMBER to create a member whose name is identical to a member created with CREATE MEMBER. If you request all calculated members in their scope with AddCalculatedMembers(), you will get both of them; if you request a member by that specific name, you will only get the results of the WITH MEMBER definition.

Dropping a Calculated Member

The general syntax for dropping a calculated member is

```
DROP MEMBER cube-member-name [,cube-member-name . . . ]
```

The DROP MEMBER statement removes one or more calculated members and all associated definitions from the current subcube. When more than one calculated member is to be dropped, each name is separated by a comma. When a calculated member is dropped, it disappears from the member-related metadata accessible through OLE DB for OLAP. For example, the following statement drops the two named members:

```
DROP MEMBER
   [Production].[Measures].[Failure Rate],
   [Production].[Scenarios].[Variance Over Trials]
```

You can even drop members whose CREATE MEMBER statements were part of the database (stored at the server), but not from the client side. You may also drop members that have other calculated members defined on them, and no warning is issued. The definitions of the dependent calculated members remain, but they are internally invalid and return a #ERR cell value when they are included in a query. In Microsoft Analysis Services, it is not ever possible to return the dependent members to a valid state, even by re-creating the dropped input member.

Cell Calculation

A cell calculation is a definition of a pass or set of passes of calculations for the cells in a region of a cube, often conceived in terms of calculation layers. When you have multiple cell calculations defined for a cube, they can be arranged in different sets of passes, which helps you organize which ones are ultimately executed for each cell of a query. Cell calculations interact with all other types of calculations in a cube, including calculated members, custom rollups, and custom member formulas. All of these types of calculations are performed in cell calculation passes as well. Cell calculations can calculate values for cells that would otherwise be calculated by one of these other techniques in the cell calculation's absence. For example, the value for a cell related to a calculated member or custom member formula may actually be calculated by a cell calculation if you desire to override the member's formula. In order to understand how cell calculations function, you need to spend a little time working through calculation passes.

Cell calculations can be created with the CREATE CELL CALCULATION statement and dropped by DROP CELL CALCULATION. They can be defined either by the database designer/DBA at the server or during the course of a session. The formula associated with a cell calculation cannot be modified without dropping and recreating the cell calculation, but because cell calculations are not referred to by name, this does not invalidate any dependents. Query-specific cell calculations can be created using the WITH CELL CALCULATION construct.

Like custom and calculated members, a cell calculation also can influence the formatting of cell values. A cell calculation can hold a format string, font, and color information for use in representing cells that were directly calculated by the cell calculation. Cell calculations can be defined to be in effect over a certain range of calculation passes; different cell calculations that overlap in cell space can be organized to contribute to each other. In addition, each cell calculation can be assigned a specific solve order number, which gives their creator fine-grained control over their precedence with intersecting calculated members and cell calculations within each calculation pass.

Calculation passes are a significant source of flexibility and complexity; we will discuss calculation passes in detail further along.

Defining a Cell Calculation

The general syntax for defining a cell calculation is

```
CREATE CELL CALCULATION Cube.CellCalcName
FOR '( dimset [, dimset ...] )' AS 'formula'
[ CONDITION = 'MDX_Condition_Formula' ]
[ , DISABLED = {TRUE | FALSE} ]
[ , DESCRIPTION = 'description string' ]
[ , CALCULATION_PASS_NUMBER = number ]
[ , CALCULATION_PASS_DEPTH = number ]
```

or (the ALTER CUBE variation):

```
ALTER CUBE Cube
CREATE CELL CALCULATION Name
FOR '( dimset [, dimset ...] )' AS 'formula'
[ CONDITION = 'MDX_Condition_Formula' ]
[ , DISABLED = {TRUE | FALSE} ]
[ , DESCRIPTION = 'description string' ]
[ , CALCULATION_PASS_NUMBER = number ]
[ , CALCULATION_PASS_DEPTH = number ]
```

A cell calculation can also be defined for a query in the WITH section of the query in a manner analogous to creating a calculated member or named set for the query.

The CREATE CELL CALCULATION statement is a client-side DDL statement that defines a new cell calculation. The cell calculation is defined within the context of a particular cube, so the name of the calculation must also be qualified with the name of the cube, but if cube name has been specified in the connection string (Cube=*Cubename*), we can leave out the [Cube].prefix on the names. Microsoft extends the standard OLE DB for OLAP schema rowsets with a CELL FORMULAS schema rowset, so a client can obtain limited metadata about the cell calculations defined.

For each cell calculation, the following properties available for calculated members can also be used (separated by commas as the other cell calculation properties are):

```
SOLVE_ORDER = integer-number (from -8181 to 65535)
FORMAT_STRING = 'Microsoft-Office-cell-format'
LANGUAGE = 'LCID', or Language Code Id
FORE_COLOR = 'color-code'
BACK_COLOR = 'color-code'
FONT_NAME = 'font-name'
FONT_SIZE = 'font-size'
FONT_FLAGS = 'font-flags'

where the formatting options can be  "literals" or the result of an
expression.
```

Note that cell calculations have a SOLVE_ORDER property; this is very important to include when using cell calculations along with calculated members.

Each DimSet can be resolved into a set of members from one dimension, with the following restriction. Each dimension's expression must have one and only one of the following:

- No members
- One member

- A set consisting of one entire level
- A set of all descendants of a particular member at a particular level
- A set of all descendants of a particular member
- All members in a dimension

The region of the cube over which the cell calculation is in effect is the cross-join of the individual DimSets. It can be thought of as a "cone" in the multidimensional space of the cube. If a dimension is not specified (which could happen if a dimension's expression has no members), then the cell calculation ranges over all members of the dimension. In the "outer space," out of the "cone," the results of the cell calculation are aggregated as usual, from the highest levels of the calculated cell region to the higher-level cells. If the members have associated rollup operators, then the rollup operators are applied to the results of the cell calculations.

To specify a set consisting of one member, you can simply name the member (enclosed by braces { }). The member can be a calculated member or a regular member. In addition to naming the member, you can reference a single member-set constructed from a wide variety of means. For example, the following four expressions are all perfectly fine:

```
{ [Accounts].[Interest Rate] }
{ [Named Set 1].Item (0) }
{ Tail ([Named Set 1]).Item (0) }
StrToSet ("{[Accounts].[Interest Rate]}")
```

One of the few restrictions that we have noted in building these expressions is that if you are using a named set, it must have been created by CREATE SET at the session level and not by WITH SET within a query.

To specify a set consisting of one level in a level-based dimension, you must use the `level.Members` construct. This won't ordinarily include the calculated members assigned to that level; to do that, you need to use `level.AllMembers`. In a parent-child or ragged hierarchy, if you want to specify all leaf-level members, you can use the Descendants (`member`, , LEAVES) construct using the All member or the root member of the hierarchy for the starting member. For example, in a parent-child dimension, if you want to specify a cell calculation for all of the leaf-level members only, you would use:

```
WITH
CELL CALCULATION LeafCalcs FOR
'( Descendants ( [Accounts].[All Accounts],, LEAVES) )'
...
SELECT ...
```

To obtain a set of all descendants of a particular member at a level, use the `Descendants ( member, level)` construct. For example, the following sets up a cell calculation at the Assembly-level descendants of facility [South Bend 45]:

```
WITH
CELL CALCULATION Assumptions_01 FOR
'( Descendants ( [Facility].[South Bend 45], [Facility].[Assembly]) )'
...
SELECT ...
```

To include all members of a dimension, you can either not reference the dimension in the DimSet section of the cell calculation definition, or you can reference `Dimension.Members`. One reason to reference the dimension's members is to include calculated members, which by default are not included. In this case, you would reference `Dimension.AllMembers`.

The condition specified in the `CONDITION` clause can be used for both dimension and cell data conditions. For example, if a cell calculation is to apply to every member in a level where some member property is "true," then the condition could state 'Project.CurrentMember.Properties ("Requires Travel") = "1"'. If a cell calculation is to apply to every cell in a region where the associated `[Measure].[Reserve]` value is negative, then the condition could state '[Measures].[Reserve] < 0'.

Given the constraints on calculation regions and the flexibility of the conditions, more than one way to compose equivalent cell calculations is available. For example, if a calculation applies to more than one member of a level, you could compose one cell calculation per member and give them the same pass number and depth, or you could create one cell calculation for the level and use the condition to filter only the members that the calculation is for. In terms of efficiency, the use of conditional filters can be worse than defining more cells. Maintenance issues are different (for example, how many cell calculations are you managing?, might the target member set change?, and so on).

Let's put all these together into a complete definition. For example, let's say that you have a Production Cost member that combines production labor cost, production overhead cost, and material costs. You also have a Service Cost member that combines service labor and service overhead. However, for the "service" products, you really want the material costs to be assigned away from the Production Cost and into the Service Cost member.

The cell calculations shown in Figure 12-2 exclude material costs from the [Production Cost] member (assuming they were already added in) and add them to the [Service Cost] member where the product category is [Service].

```
CREATE CELL CALCULATION CPI.ServiceMaterialAdjustment_Production
FOR '( {[Accounts].[Production Cost]},
  Descendants ( [Products].[Service Products] ) )'
AS
'CalculationPassValue (
 [Accounts].[Production Cost],
  -1,        // take the value from the previous pass
  RELATIVE
)
- CalculationPassValue (
  [Accounts].[Material Cost],
  -1,        // take the value from the previous pass
  RELATIVE
)'
, CALCULATION_PASS_NUMBER = 10

CREATE CELL CALCULATION CPI.ServiceMaterialAdjustment_Service
FOR '( {[Accounts]. [Service Cost]},
  Descendants ([Products].[Service Products] ) )'
AS
'CalculationPassValue (
  [Accounts].[Service Cost],
  -1,        // take the value from the previous pass
  RELATIVE
)
+ CalculationPassValue (
  [Accounts].[Material Cost],
  -1,        // take the value from the previous pass
  RELATIVE
)'
, CALCULATION_PASS_NUMBER = 10
```

Figure 12-2   Cell calculation example.

Dropping a Cell Calculation

A cell calculation can be dropped with one of two statements:

```
DROP CELL CALCULATION CubeName.CellCalcName

ALTER CUBE CubeName DROP CELL CALCULATION CellCalcName
```

Although not documented by Microsoft, multiple cell calculations can be dropped by separating their names with commas.

For example, the following statement drops the cell calculations that we just created:

```
DROP CELL CALCULATION
  CPI.ServiceMaterialAdjustment_Production,
  CPI.ServiceMaterialAdjustment_Service
```

Conditional Formatting

You have seen that by defining calculated members, as well as custom members and calculated cells, you can set some formatting properties. Two are of special interest: FORE_COLOR and BACK_COLOR. Both properties can contain any MDX expression that returns a numeric value, and you can then use the VBA RGB function to easily work out which numeric value equates to which color (RGB(255,0,0)=red, RGB(0,255,0)=green, RGB(0,0,255)=blue, and RGB(x,y,x) is a mixture of the three colors). For instance, if you want to see the sales in green if they are greater than 10,000, and otherwise in red, you use:

```
WITH MEMBER Measures.Demo AS
[Measures].[Reseller Sales Amount],
FORE_COLOR=
'iif( [Measures].[Reseller Sales Amount]>10000, RGB(0,255,0),
RGB(255,0,0))'

SELECT {Measures.DEMO} ON 0,
[Product].[Product Categories].MEMBERS ON 1
FROM [Adventure Works]
CELL PROPERTIES VALUE, FORMATTED_VALUE, FORE_COLOR
```

To apply the formatting properties, the query expressed by SELECT must retrieve not only the value of the cells (the default), but also the formatting properties, by specifying CELL PROPERTIES VALUE, FORMATTED_VALUE, and FORE_COLOR.

How Types of Calculations Interact

Essentially, three different orderings of calculations are available in a cube, of which you have fine-grained control over two. Calculated members, custom members, and cell calculations have a specified solve order, and a wide range of solve order numbers can be used. Pass number can also be used with cell calculations, and referred to by other calculations. The third kind of ordering is the order of dimensions in a cube, which determines the order in which calculations take place in case of a "tie."

Interaction without Any Cell Calculations

The simplest case to consider is custom calculations and calculated members in the absence of any cell calculations. The rules for combining data types are the same when custom calculations are considered, but custom calculations introduce wrinkles in picking what calculation to perform.

Precedence of Custom Member Formulas on Multiple Dimensions

For any given cell, if it is not associated with a calculated member, and a custom calculation is on it from any dimension, the cell is calculated according to the formula of the custom calculation. If custom formulas are used on two or more dimensions, the calculation from the dimension with the highest solve order is used to calculate the cell.

Precedence of Unary Operators on Multiple Dimensions

When a cell is defined by two intersecting regular members that each have rollup operators defined for their children, the actual cell calculation that takes place depends on what the rollup operators are. If the rollup operators involved are only + and -, or only *, /, and %, then it does not really matter. However, if the two members have child rollups between them that involve a mixture of + or - with *, /, or %, then the operators are chosen by an assumed precedence (which may or may not be what you want). The following rules are followed:

- If the children from each dimension contain only + and -, then precedence does not matter.

- If the children after the first child contain only * and /, then precedence does not matter. (The first child that does not have ~, must have either + or -; subsequent children can have any valid operator.)

- A member that has child operators of *, /, or % takes precedence over a member whose children contain purely + and - operators.

- Dimension precedence is used when child operators contain a mixture of + or - with * and / on each of the dimensions (each dimension's children contain a mixture).

For many applications, it would be preferable if a + or - took precedence over *, so that sums of products (like a summation of units * price) would be taken. We do not know whether a service pack will alter the functionality to include that capability.

Cell Calculation Passes

Every cell calculation has an associated pass number, which is part of arranging the cell calculations into different passes. Like solve orders, pass numbers help to order calculations when more than one calculation (of any kind) could provide the value for a cell. Like solve orders, higher numbers are essentially calculated after lower numbers (potentially overruling a result provided by a calculation with a lower number). The pass numbers for a cube and query start at zero, although the lowest pass number that a defined cell calculation can use is 1. If you don't specify a pass number, then 1 is the default. (Calculation pass 0 is reserved for calculations that take place prior to any cell calculation.) Unlike solve order, which is used to choose a formula as the "winner" to calculate a cell once, passes may end up calculating the value for a cell multiple times.

Every cell calculation also has an associated pass depth, which determines the number of passes (starting from the pass number and working toward lower numbers) in which its formula is in effect. A pass depth of 1 (the default) means that the calculation is only in effect during its stated pass. A pass depth greater than 1 means that it is in effect from the stated pass back by one less than the given number of steps. For example, a pass number of 9 and a pass depth of 3 means that the calculation will be in effect in passes 7, 8, and 9.

There is no way to declare that a cell calculation is to occupy a set of passes after or before another cell calculation, except by keeping control over the pass numbers.

When a query is executed, the passes required for each cell are determined. One pass will be performed for the highest pass number defined across all cell calculations. For example, if there are three cell calculations defined on a cube with pass numbers 5, 10, and 15, then a pass 15 is performed on every cell in a query (regardless of whether the cells accessed by the query fall into the subcubes for the cell calcs or not). This does not mean that 3 or even 15 passes will be performed for any cell, but that even if only one pass is performed for a cell (for example, to simply retrieve a preaggregated value from MOLAP storage), it will occur at pass 15. Depending on the mix of defined calculations that overlap at that cell, other passes may take place. The solve order values for these calculations partly determines the order, and if two separate cell calcs share the same, highest solve order number, then the calc that was defined last wins.

Although calculation passes are only assigned to cell calculations, all other calculations will take place at any calculation pass deemed necessary to compute a cell. Thus, a calculated member, custom member, or custom rollup may be calculated in any (or every) pass for each cell. So, in each pass you define for a cell calculation, all other calculations may be executed as well. These calculations may have a solve order higher than the cell calc, which will let them compute the cell's value.

Any MDX calculation (custom or otherwise) may refer to data values calculated in earlier passes through the use of the `CalculationPassValue()` function. (This function is described in Appendix A, and we will use it here without further description.) This allows each to have a definition that refers to earlier passes, and even to be recursive through the passes. In the case of a calculation for a cell that otherwise is not the target of a cell calculation, the cell is evaluated for the highest-numbered pass number among all cell calculations defined in the cube. (For example, if a cube has three cell calculations defined and the highest pass number among them is 5, then any cell being calculated for the cube starts off at pass number 5.) As a cell is calculated (by any means), if it references a value at a lower pass number, then that value and pass are calculated (so passes are calculated from highest to lowest). In other words, a calculated member `[Forecast Factor]` whose definition reads:

```
iif (
  CalculationCurrentPass() > 1,
  1.1 * CalculationPassValue (
    [Measures].[Forecast Factor],
    -1,
    RELATIVE
  ),
  1
)
```

and that is executed starting at pass 5 will cause pass 4 to be executed, which will cause pass 3 to be executed, and so on down to pass 1 (at which pass it results in 1, and the value returned from pass 5 is 1.4641). Figure 12-3 illustrates this recursive process.

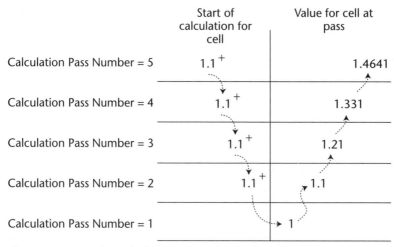

	Start of calculation for cell	Value for cell at pass
Calculation Pass Number = 5	1.1 +	1.4641
Calculation Pass Number = 4	1.1 +	1.331
Calculation Pass Number = 3	1.1 +	1.21
Calculation Pass Number = 2	1.1 +	1.1
Calculation Pass Number = 1	1	

Figure 12-3   Earlier calculation passes invoked from later passes.

In the case of a cell in a cell calc that references earlier passes of cell calculations, the earlier passes are calculated first and then the later passes. A pair of cell calculations that were defined as

```
CREATE CELL CALCULATION [Fcst].[A1]
FOR '({[Measures].[Forecast Factor]})'
AS
'1.1 * CalculationPassValue (
  [Measures].[Forecast Factor],
  -1,
  RELATIVE
)'
, CALCULATION_PASS_NUMBER = 5
, CALCULATION_PASS_DEPTH = 2
```

```
CREATE CELL CALCULATION [Fcst].[A2]
FOR '({[Measures].[Forecast Factor]})'
AS
'1'
, CALCULATION_PASS_NUMBER = 3
, CALCULATION_PASS_DEPTH = 1
```

would first generate a 1 for `[Measures].[Forecast Factor]` at pass 3, then create a 1.1 for `[Measures].[Forecast Factor]` at pass 4, and finally create 1.21 as the value for `[Measures].[Forecast Factor]` at pass 5. This is diagrammed in Figure 12-4.

Note that in the case of a calculated member referencing calculation passes, the execution of the calculated member at pass 5 is what caused earlier passes to be executed, and passes were executed in the order that they were requested by the recursive definition. In the case of the cell calculation referencing earlier passes, the calculation passes are produced from earlier to later in order.

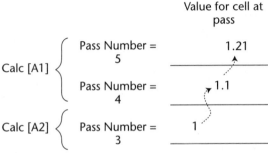

Figure 12-4   Calculation passes invoked in order.

Only the passes actually required are calculated for each cell. For example, consider the following skeletal cell calc definition:

```
CREATE CELL CALCULATION Budgeting.Layer5
FOR '( { [Measures].[Adjustment] } )'
AS
'Measures.[Amount]
+ CalculationPassValue (
   Measures.[Amount],
    1,
    ABSOLUTE
 )'
, CALCULATION_PASS_NUMBER = 10
, CALCULATION_PASS_DEPTH = 8
```

in which a cell calculation for the measure [Adjustment] is defined to start at pass 10 and run back to pass 3, and this results in the value of the measure [Amount] at the current pass plus the value of [Amount] from pass 1. In the absence of other computations actually referencing the values of [Adjust- ment] between passes 9 and 3, Analysis Services only calculates the value of [Adjustment] from [Amount] at pass 10 and [Amount] at pass 1 and adds those two values together. If some other computation references the value of [Adjustment] at, say, pass 5, then [Adjustment] for pass 5 would be cal- culated from [Amount] at pass 5 and the value of [Amount] at pass 1. (The value for [Amount] at pass 1 would be cached from the first time it was refer- enced, so it would only be calculated once.)

While we are on the topic, consider again the definition for the preceding Budgeting.Layer5 cell calculation. If another cell calculation is in the cube whose calculation pass is, say, 20 and does not calculate a value for the [Adjustment] measure, then Budgeting.Layer5 is calculated at passes 20 and 1 instead of 10 and 1. If another calculation references the value at pass 10, then this makes no material difference; the value of the cell at pass 20 is the same as at pass 10 because no other calculations get in the way, so no other cal- culation pass is executed. However, let's consider the case that some other cal- culations may intersect this cell. If a calculation references the value of [Adjustment] at a pass above 10, then the results depend on any other inter- secting calculations. For example, if a calculated member intersects [Adjust- ment], the value for [Adjustment] at pass 15 will be determined by the calculated member. (As we said, constructing and maintaining calculations in the face of calculation passes can get complicated!)

Equation Solving and Financial Modeling

Calculated cells can be used to implement more complex modeling, involving simultaneous equations. Consider, for instance, this system of equations:

Profit = Revenues - Costs - Tax

Tax = TaxRate * Profit

or even econometric modeling, like the Keynes macroeconomic model, where:

Aggregate Demand = Investments + Consumption

Consumption = Coefficient * Aggregate Demand

These equations, usually solved by the Excel Solver, can be implemented with calculated cells and solved with an iterative calculation using the `Calcu-lationPassValue` function.

Try this query:

```
WITH
—set initial value of consumption  to 0. This is just to have a member
on which we can define later a calculated cell
MEMBER [Measures].[Consumption]
as 'iif(calculationcurrentpass()=1, 0,
calculationpassvalue([Measures].[Consumption],-1,relative)) '

—set constant Investment to 100
MEMBER [Measures].[Investment]
as '100'

—set Coefficient of Propensity to Consumption to 0.6
MEMBER [Measures].[Coefficient]
as '0.6'
—Calculate Aggregate Demand
MEMBER [Measures].[Aggregate Demand]
as '[Measures].[Consumption] + [Measures].[Investment]'

— Recalculate consumption
CELL CALCULATION [Consumption Calculation]
FOR '({[Measures].[Consumption]})'
as 'iif(calculationcurrentpass()=1, 0,
Coefficient*calculationpassvalue([Measures].[Aggregate Demand],
-1,relative))',
CALCULATION_PASS_NUMBER=100, CALCULATION_PASS_DEPTH=99

select
{[Measures].[Consumption], [Measures].[Investment],
[Measures].[Aggregate Demand]}
ON COLUMNS
FROM  [Adventure Works]
```

To understand how this works, consider that, at the beginning, there are only Investments (= 100) and Consumption is zero. Aggregate Demand is therefore 100. But Consumption is proportional to Aggregate Demend, by a factor given by Coefficient, which takes Consumption to 0.6 * 100 = 60. You can see this by setting CALCULATION_PASS_DEPTH=1, to stop at the first iteration. Aggregate demand becomes, therefore, 100 + 60 = 160. But then consumption becomes 0.6 * 160 = 96, which results in an Aggregate Demand of 196 (try this with CALCULATION_PASS_DEPTH=2).

But we know the solution of the equation: with Coefficient = 0.6 and Investments = 100, the Aggregate Demand is 100 / (1 - 0.6) = 250, which means that the iteration schema above converges; try this with CALCULATION_PASS_DEPTH=50, the solution shown is 249.9999999.

With CALCULATION_PASS_DEPTH=99, you get a nice 250.

You have to take into account that not every iteration schema converges. For instance, if the Coefficient in the model above was greater than 1, the model would "explode" (mathematically, not just computationally!).

In Analysis Services 2000, when the number of iterations increased above the stack capability, you got an error. In AS2005, the problem seems to be solved.

> **TIP** One thing to be aware of and guard against when using cell calculations and calculated members is that infinite recursion can occur. If a cell calculation refers to a calculated member in its formula (directly or indirectly) and the calculated member itself draws data from the cell being calculated at the same calculation pass, then an infinite recursion error will occur. The key to breaking out of this recursion is for the calculated member to draw its data from some other calculation pass. This could be accomplished by having the calculated member itself refer to data at a particular pass, or by having the cell calculation formula refer to the calculated member at a different pass. Try, for instance, to modify the calculated cell above by removing the calculationpassvalue, and you'll get the infinite recursion error:

```
CELL CALCULATION [Consumption Calculation]
FOR '({[Measures].[Consumption]})'
as 'iif(calculationcurrentpass()=1, 0,
Coefficient* ([Measures].[Aggregate Demand])',
```

Using Solve Order to Determine the Formula in a Pass

For any cell referenced by a query, at least one calculation pass (pass 0) and perhaps more will be executed. Within each pass, solve orders for the potentially applicable formulas are resolved to determine which formula actually calculates the cell. Cell calculations, calculated members, and all custom rollups each have their own solve order. (In fact, data retrieval from intrinsic aggregations has its own solve order as well.) The type of calculation does not matter; ultimately, it's the solve order number that makes the difference. In the case of a tied solve order, the order of definition decides which calculation is applied.

When defining a set of calculations on a cube, it is very important to understand global solve orders. Consider the definition of a calculated member and a cell calculation in Figure 12-5. The intent is to round the total time per call to the nearest two units (using the Excel Round() function).

Because no solve order is specified for the cell calculation, the default solve order of 0 is assumed. Now, consider what happens when a [Time Per Call] member is calculated at pass 1. Consider these two formulas: the cell calculation and the calculated member. The calculated member has the higher solve order, so the calculated member wins and the cell calculation is ignored.

Suppose, however, that we redefine the [Calls].[Rounding] cell calculation to have SOLVE_ORDER=15. Now, at pass 1, the cell calculation will perform the rounding against the [Time Per Call] value from pass 0. At pass 0, the only formula to consider is the [Measures].[Time Per Call], so that will be calculated as the ratio.

```
CREATE MEMBER [Calls].[Measures].[Time Per Call] AS
'[Measures].[Total Call Time] / [Measures].[Count of Calls]'
, SOLVE_ORDER = 10

CREATE CELL CALCULATION [Calls].[Rounding]
FOR '({[Measures].[Time Per Call]})' AS
'CalculationPassValue (
  Excel!Round(
    [Measures].[Time Per Call],
    2
  )
  , 0
  , ABSOLUTE
)'
, CALCULATION_PASS_NUMBER = 1
```

Figure 12-5   System of calculated member and cell calculation.

Why did we define the ratio as being at solve order 10? Perhaps the application allows a user to select a set of call center operators to calculate the total call time, count of calls, and time per call as a group. The sum of total call time and sum of count of calls needs to occur at a lower solve order than the ratio. Defining key ratios at a higher solve order such as 10 allows us space in the global solve order list to insert other, possibly unforeseen calculations earlier in the list. For example, we could use this in the following query:

```
WITH
SET [Interesting Operators] AS
'{ [John], [Suzie], [Harold] }'
MEMBER [Operators].[Total] AS 'Aggregate ( [Interesting Operators] )'
, SOLVE_ORDER = 0
SELECT
{ [Measures].AllMembers } on columns,
{ [Interesting Operators], [Operators].[Total] } on rows
FROM [Calls]
```

Note the use of `Aggregate` in AS2005, which will automatically compute the sum at a lower solve order (and we could even avoid `SOLVE_ORDER=0`), whereas in AS2000 we had to use `Sum` (`Aggregate` doesn't work on calculated members in AS2000) with a low SOLVE_ORDER, in order to take the ratio of sums.

By the same token, custom rollups are themselves calculated at each pass. According to their solve order, they will, at any pass, provide data to cell calc or calculated members, or use data calculated by them.

Calculated Members Not Themselves Aggregated

A cell calculated by a calculated member is not aggregated by the intrinsic aggregation machinery, which makes sense because calculated members aren't considered part of any hierarchy. A calculated measure has no intrinsic aggregation function specified, either. (A calculated member can, of course, contain its own aggregation logic to perform aggregation along one or more dimensions if desired.)

Intrinsic Aggregation of Custom Rollups, Custom Members, and Calculated Cell Results

If the parent of a member with a custom formula does not itself have any formulas applied, then the result of the custom formula is aggregated to the parent as if it was drawn from the underlying fact table(s). This is handy when the

custom member formula involves only addition or subtraction. It is also frequently useful when the custom member calculation involves multiplication
of a rate and some unit (such as units and price), because the results are automatically summed up the hierarchy instead of requiring additional MDX. This
can be a source of problems if the custom member formula is a ratio, however,
and you do not want to sum the ratio with other values.

Similarly, if a cell calculation region does not include the topmost level in
one or more dimensions, the calculated cells in the region that have parent
members outside the region will have their results aggregated to the parent
member. The result of the query below is simply that months whose measure
values are less than 100 are not included in the total. If the raw cell values for
[Jan. 2001], [Feb. 2001], and [Mar. 2001] are 50, 200, and 300, then the
raw value for [Q1, 2001] is 550. However, the results of the cell calculations
from the months are aggregated to the quarter, so the result of the query for
[Q1, 2001] is 500. The process is diagrammed in Figure 12-6.

```
WITH
CELL CALCULATION Calc1
FOR '( {[Time].[Month].Members} )'
AS 'NULL',
CONDITION = 'Measures.CurrentMember.Value < 100'
SELECT
{ [Time].[Jan, 2001], [Time].[Feb. 2001], [Time].[Mar. 2001],
  [Time].[Q1, 2001]
} on columns
FROM [Cube]
```

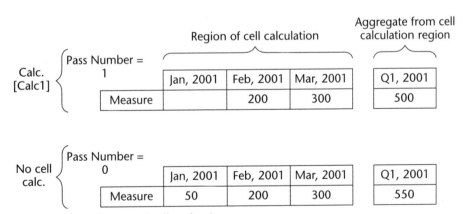

Figure 12-6   Diagram of cell evaluation.

Tips on Using the Different Calculation Techniques

In accounting dimensions, custom rollup operators typically are used to combine accounts. A parent-child dimension is the ordinary way to implement an accounting dimension. Most accounting lines are combined with +, and a few with – or ~. Key ratios may be implemented either by the / rollup operator or by custom member formulas. These usually do not present a difficulty when combined with other dimensions such as time, product, branch office, and so on. Lines that roll up to their parent using the * operator or that have custom formulas which perform multiplication need to be looked at carefully in conjunction with the entire set of dimensions and calculations that they will be used in. At aggregate levels of the other dimensions, the results may be the product of sums rather than the sum of products.

Custom member formulas and calculated members need to be considered carefully. Custom member formulas can be more easily managed because they are stored once for all cubes and are stored in the dimension table. Moreover, custom member formulas can be organized, for instance in a parent/child dimension, allowing to create indicator trees or similar structures.

The results of a calculated member are not aggregated up the hierarchies of any dimensions, but the results of all other calculations are. This makes the other ways of calculating suitable for specifying complex calculations for a low level that must be aggregated up the hierarchies, and restricts the use of calculated members mainly to "linear operators," that is, operators that give the same result if applied to the aggregated value or to the addends (for instance, the multiplication by a constant, or simple addition or subtraction).

Only intrinsic aggregations may be precalculated and stored. This means that a complex calculation at the leaf levels, which is aggregated up to a high level in several dimensions, may be slow to calculate.

Summary

In this chapter, we have worked through the different kinds of calculations that are available through Microsoft Analysis Services, both in AS2000 and (with some small differences) in AS2005. Given the number of different types of calculation techniques and the subtle differences between them, we have worked through their individual operation and their combined operations so as to demonstrate the impact of choosing one technique over another. These methods allow you to get the values that you want. Choosing among them requires an understanding of an application's usage and maintenance requirements as well as calculation needs.

The description of the intricacies of the calculation passes should have made clear that writing complex logic with calculated cells, while possible, is not an easy task. The use of MDX Scripting, available in AS2005 and described in the next chapter, should make MDX programming easier.

CHAPTER 13

MDX Scripting in Analysis Services 2005

MDX Scripting represents an evolution of the calculated cells functionality available in Analysis Services 2000. It would be wrong to say that it is a complete replacement for Calculated Cells though: Calculated Cells are still supported in Analysis Services 2005, and they are still necessary for some tasks (such as creating goal-seeking calculations). Instead, think of MDX Scripting and Calculated Cells as two different interfaces on top of the same calculation engine, with MDX Scripting offering a more sophisticated and intuitive abstraction of the functionality available.

Nonetheless, mastering MDX Scripting represents a challenge even for those who are comfortable with multidimensional concepts. Whereas in Analysis Services 2000, Calculated Cells could be safely ignored by most developers because their performance was suspect, in Analysis Services 2005, the development team has made it clear that proper use of MDX Scripting is the key to getting the best possible performance for calculations. This, then, is a challenge that must be met by everyone who is designing cubes and writing MDX professionally.

The approach taken with this chapter is to introduce the core functionality with the use of a very simple cube, then to illustrate how this functionality behaves when new features are added to that cube. You can download the cubes we use from the web site accompanying this book so that you can follow the examples and see for yourself how things work.

MDX Scripting Basics

What Is an MDX Script?

An MDX Script is simply a list of commands that affect the data in an Analysis Services 2005 cube. These commands can create calculated members, named sets, and calculated cells, all subjects dealt with elsewhere in this book; the focus of this chapter will be on the commands that allow you to assign new values to areas within the cube, either explicitly or through the use of MDX expressions. Each command in an MDX Script must be followed by a semicolon (;).

Here is an example of a very simple MDX Script showing a CALCULATE statement (see below for what this does), a CREATE MEMBER statement that creates a calculated member, and a CREATE SET statement, which creates a named set:

```
CALCULATE;

CREATE MEMBER
CURRENTCUBE.[MEASURES].[Demo]
AS [Measures].[Sales]*2,
FORMAT_STRING = "#,#",
NON_EMPTY_BEHAVIOR = { [Sales] },
VISIBLE = 1  ;

CREATE SET
CURRENTCUBE.[Important Regions]
AS {[Geography].[Geography].&[1],
[Geography].[Geography].&[4]} ;
```

A cube can have zero, one, or many MDX Scripts associated with it. If a cube doesn't have an MDX Script, then the server assumes the presence of an empty one with a single CALCULATE() statement. When there are multiple MDX Scripts attached to a cube, only one can be active at any one time; the active script is the first one in the cube definition with the <DefaultScript> tag either omitted or set to true. When you create a cube using Visual Studio, it will automatically have an MDX Script added to it, and you do not have the ability to delete it or create others. This MDX Script can be viewed and edited in Visual Studio by selecting the Calculations tab when the Cube editor is open.

In Analysis Services Scripting Language (nothing to do with MDX Scripts, but rather the Data Definition Language for building objects like databases, dimensions, and cubes), an MDX Script can be subdivided by using command tags as follows: <Command><Text>/*insert MDX here*/</Text></Command>. Each <Command> tag can contain any number of MDX calculations. If there is an error in an MDX Script, this will be detected during processing, and by default, the processing will fail. You can, however, change this behavior by changing

`ScriptErrorHandlingMode` from `IgnoreNone` to `IgnoreAll`, which then means that only the command tag that contains the error will be ignored rather than the whole script (depending on the type of error Analysis Services may also be able to ignore individual statements within the script, but we found that it was unable to do so consistently). Unfortunately, Visual Studio puts all of the contents of an MDX Script inside a single command tag, so if you want to make use of this feature, you will have to edit the ASSL definition of your cube manually. Furthermore, if you have an MDX Script with multiple command tags and you edit it in Visual Studio, the contents of all the command tags will be merged into a single command tag.

This should not be confused with the way that Visual Studio allows you to switch between a form view and a script view of an MDX Script, which is purely to make editing code easier. In the form view, each statement in the script appears as a numbered line in the Script Organizer pane; the currently selected statement is then displayed in the central pane either as MDX or, in the case of calculated members or named sets, in special forms that break out each of their properties into separate textboxes. When in script view, the entire MDX Script is displayed all at once in the central pane in code form.

The Calculate Statement

As you've already seen, when you create a cube in Visual Studio, it automatically includes an MDX Script containing a `CALCULATE` statement. But what does this do? Put simply, `CALCULATE` instructs the cube to aggregate all of the data in each of the measure groups from the lowest level of granularity—the "leaves" of all of the dimensions in the cube—up to the higher levels. Almost all cubes are going to want this to happen, and this is why the command is there by default, but there may be some scenarios where you might not want any aggregation to take place automatically, or where you might want some operations to take place before the `CALCULATE` statement is executed.

Let's take a look at the first of our example databases, DB1, and its sole cube CUBE1. You'll see that this cube has only got one measure, [Sales], and two dimensions [Geography] and [Period], which each have only one attribute hierarchy, [Region] and [Month], respectively; if you look at the MDX Script, you'll see it consists of a single `CALCULATE`. Deploy and process this cube and then run the following query in either SQL Server Management Studio or MDX Sample Application:

```
SELECT
[Geography].[Region].MEMBERS ON 0,
{[Period].[Month].[All],[Period].[Month].[January 2005],
[Period].[Month].[February 2005], [Period].[Month].[March
2005],[Period].[Month].[April 2005]} ON 1
FROM CUBE1
```

The results are shown in Table 13-1.

Table 13-1

	ALL	NORTH	SOUTH	EAST	WEST
ALL	324	36	66	96	126
JANUARY 2005	104	11	21	31	41
FEBRUARY 2005	108	12	22	32	42
MARCH 2005	112	13	23	33	43
APRIL 2005	(null)	(null)	(null)	(null)	(null)

You can see that data has been aggregated up from the leaf levels of [Month] and [Region] to the All levels of both dimensions, as you would expect. Now go back to the MDX Script, and comment out the CALCULATE statement, so that it looks like this:

```
//CALCULATE;
```

Now if you redeploy the cube and run the same query, you'll see that the results are now as shown in Table 13-2.

No aggregation has taken place—data only appears at the intersections of the lowest levels of both attribute hierarchies. The important thing to note at this point is that CALCULATE acts like a switch, turning on the aggregation mechanism from the point in the script at which it appears: Aggregation does not happen just when the CALCULATE statement executes, but potentially many times after that. You will see this in action in the next section.

Subcubes

The real usefulness of MDX Scripting comes from the ability to overwrite values inside the cube space. This is a two-step process: First you have to define the area within the cube whose values you wish to overwrite, then you either supply the new value or an MDX expression (which may in part rely on the value you're overwriting), which returns a new value.

Using the same cube as in the previous section, imagine that you have decided that the value for the Sales measure in the North region for January 2005 should be 50 instead of 11. The easiest way of doing this is simply to assign a new value to the tuple by adding a statement to the existing MDX Script so that it looks like this (notice that CALCULATE remains commented out):

```
//CALCULATE;

([Measures].[Sales], [Geography].[Region].[North],
[Period].[Month].[January 2005])=50;
```

Table 13-2

	ALL	NORTH	SOUTH	EAST	WEST
ALL	(null)	(null)	(null)	(null)	(null)
JANUARY 2005	(null)	11	21	31	41
FEBRUARY 2005	(null)	12	22	32	42
MARCH 2005	(null)	13	23	33	43
APRIL 2005	(null)	(null)	(null)	(null)	(null)

MDX SCRIPT SUBCUBE DEFINITION RULES

A subcube in an MDX Script assignment can be thought of as being the result of the cross-join of either the All Member from, or a set of one or more members from the lower level of, all the attribute hierarchies in the cube. Thus, it must form a regular *N*-dimensional shape in the same way that the cube does; a subcube cannot be defined as just any arbitrary collection of cells from within the cube.

Knowing this, we can derive some rules that we must follow in order to define a valid subcube. Each set within a subcube definition must be

◆ A set of any members, except the All Member, from an attribute hierarchy

◆ A single member from an attribute hierarchy or a user-defined hierarchy, or an MDX expression that resolves to one

◆ A set of any members taken from a single level in a natural user-defined hierarchy

◆ Descendants of any single member at one or more levels of a natural user-defined hierarchy

◆ Children of any single member in an unnatural user-defined hierarchy

◆ All members of either an attribute hierarchy or a user-defined hierarchy

◆ The leaf members of either an attribute hierarchy or a user-defined hierarchy

A "natural" user-defined hierarchy is one where the attributes that make up each level are member properties of the attributes that make up the level below. For example, using the sample data used in this section, it would be possible to build a user-defined hierarchy on the Period dimension with, in descending order, Year, Quarter, and Month levels. This is a natural hierarchy because Year is a member property of Quarter, and Quarter is a member property of Month. It would also be possible to build a user-defined hierarchy consisting of the levels Quarter, Year, and Month in that order. This would be an unnatural hierarchy because Quarter is not a member property of Year.

If you run the same query as before, you see the results shown in Table 13-3.

In actual fact, when we defined the part of the cube we wished to overwrite, we were not defining a tuple (although it looked very much like one), we were defining a subcube. Whereas a tuple is a list of individual members from dimensions that define an area in a cube, as you learned in Chapter 4, a subcube is a list of individual members or sets of members from dimensions that can define more easily a large subset of the cube space. However, in contrast to the subcubes you encountered in Chapter 4, the subcubes used in MDX Scripts do not need a SELECT statement or axes in their definitions.

To see a bit more of what is possible with a subcube, change the MDX Script so that there is no reference to the Period dimension:

```
//CALCULATE;

([Measures].[Sales], [Geography].[Region].[North])=50;
```

Rerun the query, and you can see in Table 13-4 that the values for January 2005, February 2005, March 2005, April 2005, and the All Member on the [Period].[Month] attribute hierarchy have been overwritten with the value 50.

Notice that (April 2005, North), which was previously NULL, now contains 50: when you make this kind of assignment, you are not simply overwriting all not-NULL cells, but rather all the cells that exist with ([Measures].[Sales], [Geography].[Region].[North]) in the cube space whether they originally had values or not. This is easy to forget and is a common source of confusion when trying to debug MDX Scripts.

You can overwrite all the values for both North and South by including a set in the subcube definition containing these members:

```
//CALCULATE;

([Measures].[Sales],
{[Geography].[Region].[North],[Geography].[Region].[South] })=50;
```

Table 13-3

	ALL	**NORTH**	**SOUTH**	**EAST**	**WEST**
ALL	(null)	(null)	(null)	(null)	(null)
JANUARY 2005	(null)	50	21	31	41
FEBRUARY 2005	(null)	12	22	32	42
MARCH 2005	(null)	13	23	33	43
APRIL 2005	(null)	(null)	(null)	(null)	(null)

Table 13-4

	ALL	NORTH	SOUTH	EAST	WEST
ALL	(null)	50	(null)	(null)	(null)
JANUARY 2005	(null)	50	21	31	41
FEBRUARY 2005	(null)	50	22	32	42
MARCH 2005	(null)	50	23	33	43
APRIL 2005	(null)	50	(null)	(null)	(null)

The query would then return the results shown in Table 13-5.

You could even overwrite the values of every cell in the cube using the * operator, which equates to every member on every hierarchy on every dimension:

```
//CALCULATE;

(*)=50;
```

This would mean that the query would return the results shown in Table 13-6.

Assignments and Aggregation

So far, all of the examples of assigning values to subcubes have deliberately had the CALCULATE statement commented out. But what happens if CALCULATE is uncommented? The simple answer is, of course, that aggregation once more takes place. If you go back once more to the original example and do this, the MDX Script will be as follows:

```
CALCULATE;

([Measures].[Sales], [Geography].[Region].[North],
[Period].[Month].[January 2005])=50;
```

Table 13-5

	ALL	NORTH	SOUTH	EAST	WEST
ALL	(null)	50	50	(null)	(null)
JANUARY 2005	(null)	50	50	31	41
FEBRUARY 2005	(null)	50	50	32	42
MARCH 2005	(null)	50	50	33	43
APRIL 2005	(null)	50	50	(null)	(null)

Table 13-6

	ALL	NORTH	SOUTH	EAST	WEST
ALL	50	50	50	50	50
JANUARY 2005	50	50	50	50	50
FEBRUARY 2005	50	50	50	50	50
MARCH 2005	50	50	50	50	50
APRIL 2005	50	50	50	50	50

The results will then be as shown in Table 13-7.

You can see that even though the assignment happened after the CALCULATE statement in the script, aggregation has taken place taking into account this newly inserted value. So, the value for (North, All Month) is 50 + 12 + 13 = 75, and the value for (January 2005, All Region) is 50 + 21 + 31 + 41 = 143. It is very important to remember the fact that aggregation can be thought of as taking place after every single assignment because in many cases it can result in values you've just inserted being overwritten in turn.

Going back to the second example where we overwrote all the values for the North region, including the All Month member, if you uncomment CALCULATE like this:

```
CALCULATE;

([Measures].[Sales], [Geography].[Region].[North])=50;
```

you get the results shown in Table 13-8.

Notice how the value for (All, All) is calculated. Without the assignment you've just made, its value could have been found by either adding up all of the months at the All Region level or adding up all of the Regions at the All Month level—the results were the same. Now, though, because you have over-written (All, North) with the value 50 so that it is no longer the sum of (January 2005, North), (February 2005, North), (March 2005, North), and so on, the original symmetry has been broken. Adding up all the Regions at the All Month level gives the value 50 + 66 + 96 + 126 = 338, but adding up all the Months at the All Region level gives 143 + 146 + 149 + 50 + 50 + 50 + 50 = 638. So, which value is correct? You can see from the results above that it's the first value, 338; the reason is that whenever there is a question about which set of values Analysis Services should choose to aggregate when calculating the value of a given cell, it will always choose one that has been affected by an assignment in the MDX Script over one that hasn't.

Table 13-7

	ALL	NORTH	SOUTH	EAST	WEST
ALL	363	75	66	96	126
JANUARY 2005	143	50	21	31	41
FEBRUARY 2005	108	12	22	32	42
MARCH 2005	112	13	23	33	43
APRIL 2005	(null)	(null)	(null)	(null)	(null)

> **NOTE** If, when calculating the value of a cell, Analysis Services has more than one aggregation path that has been affected by assignments to choose from, then it will choose the one that has been affected by the assignment that appears closer to the end of the script. This behavior is called the "last pass wins" rule.

Let's look at a few more examples of how the "last pass wins" rule gets enforced in order to properly understand how it works. If you make two assignments that each affect one cell on the two possible aggregation paths for (All, All), as follows:

```
CALCULATE;

([Measures].[Sales],
[Geography].[Region].[North], [Period].[Month].[All])=50;
([Measures].[Sales],
[Geography].[Region].[All], [Period].[Month].[January 2005]) =50;
```

you can see from the results in Table 13-9 that, when you rerun the query, the (All, All) value is calculated based on the second assignment.

Table 13-8

	ALL	NORTH	SOUTH	EAST	WEST
ALL	338	50	66	96	126
JANUARY 2005	143	50	21	31	41
FEBRUARY 2005	146	50	22	32	42
MARCH 2005	149	50	23	33	43
APRIL 2005	50	50	(null)	(null)	(null)

Table 13-9

	ALL	**NORTH**	**SOUTH**	**EAST**	**WEST**
ALL	270	50	66	96	126
JANUARY 2005	50	11	21	31	41
FEBRUARY 2005	108	12	22	32	42
MARCH 2005	112	13	23	33	43
APRIL 2005	(null)	(null)	(null)	(null)	(null)

Analysis Services is adding up the sum of the members on the Month level at the All level on Region to get the (All, All) value, and so it is 50 + 108 + 112 = 270. If you swap the order of the assignments, for example:

```
CALCULATE;
([Measures].[Sales],
[Geography].[Region].[All], [Period].[Month].[January 2005]) =50;
([Measures].[Sales],
[Geography].[Region].[North] , [Period].[Month].[All])=50;
```

then, as shown in Table 13-10, (All, All) will return 338 again because the aggregation path last affected by an assignment is the sum of all the Regions at the All level of Month.

If you make a third assignment, so that the script is as follows:

```
CALCULATE;
([Measures].[Sales],
[Geography].[Region].[All], [Period].[Month].[January 2005]) =50;
([Measures].[Sales],
[Geography].[Region].[North] , [Period].[Month].[All])=50;
([Measures].[Sales],
[Geography].[Region].[All], [Period].[Month].[February 2005]) =50;
```

then (All, All) will revert to being the sum of the Months at All Region once again, as shown in Table 13-11.

Table 13-10

	ALL	**NORTH**	**SOUTH**	**EAST**	**WEST**
ALL	338	50	66	96	126
JANUARY 2005	50	11	21	31	41
FEBRUARY 2005	108	12	22	32	42
MARCH 2005	112	13	23	33	43
APRIL 2005	(null)	(null)	(null)	(null)	(null)

Table 13-11

	ALL	NORTH	SOUTH	EAST	WEST
ALL	212	50	66	96	126
JANUARY 2005	50	11	21	31	41
FEBRUARY 2005	50	12	22	32	42
MARCH 2005	112	13	23	33	43
APRIL 2005	(null)	(null)	(null)	(null)	(null)

You also need to be careful when making assignments "underneath" each other in the cube space. Bearing in mind some of the scenarios you've just been looking at, you might well think that the following MDX Scripts would produce the same results:

```
CALCULATE;

([Measures].[Sales], [Geography].[Region].[North])=50;
```

and

```
CALCULATE;

([Measures].[Sales], [Geography].[Region].[North],
[Period].[Month].[All])=50;

([Measures].[Sales],[Geography].[Region].[North],
{[Period].[Month].[January 2005],[Period].[Month].[February 2005],
[Period].[Month].[March 2005], [Period].[Month].[April 2005]})=50;
```

We have, after all, overwritten exactly the same cells with exactly the same values, just in two assignments rather than one. However, running the test query with the second of these two scripts produces the results shown in Table 13-12.

Table 13-12

	ALL	NORTH	SOUTH	EAST	WEST
ALL	488	200	66	96	126
JANUARY 2005	143	50	21	31	41
FEBRUARY 2005	146	50	22	32	42
MARCH 2005	149	50	23	33	43
APRIL 2005	50	50	(null)	(null)	(null)

PASS ORDER IN ANALYSIS SERVICES 2005

Pass order as a concept was present in Analysis Services 2000, but in Analysis Services 2005 it has undergone a few subtle changes. At Pass 0, a cube now only contains *unaggregated* data. Every subsequent `Calculate()` statement or assignment then creates a new Pass, and you can see this in action by using the `CalculationCurrentPass` function inside your script to return the current Pass number; this does not apply to Calculated Cells, however, for which you can still give specific Pass numbers. Unary Operators and Custom Members are given the same Pass as the CALCULATE statement.

The value for (North, All Month) is no longer 50 but 50 + 50 + 50 + 50 = 200. What has happened is that the Analysis Services calculation engine has realized that if aggregation was carried out after our second assignment, it would result in a conflict with the first assignment. This demonstrates another aspect of the last pass wins rule, which dictates that assignments can be aggregated up to replace values that have been specifically assigned at higher levels in assignments earlier in the MDX Script. This behavior can be confusing, so the ability to step through the script using the MDX Debugger built into Visual Studio is very useful when it comes to trying to understand these sorts of conflicts.

Assignments and Calculated Members

Very often you will find yourself assigning values to subcubes that include calculated measures or members, and in this scenario you need to remember that calculated measures and members take no part in the aggregation process but are evaluated after it has taken place. Take the following MDX Script, for example:

```
CALCULATE;

CREATE MEMBER CURRENTCUBE.[MEASURES].Test
  AS NULL,
VISIBLE = 1  ;

(
{[Measures].[Sales], [MEASURES].Test},
[Period].[Month].[January 2005]
)=50;
```

It creates a calculated measure called Test, which has a value of NULL, and then uses an assignment to set its value and the value of Sales to 50 for January 2005. If you run the following query:

```
SELECT
{[Measures].[Sales], [MEASURES].Test}
ON 0,
{[Period].[Month].[All], [Period].[Month].&[1],
[Period].[Month].&[2],[Period].[Month].&[3],[Period].[Month].&[4]}
ON 1
FROM CUBE1
```

you can see from the results in Table 13-13 that, as you would expect, no aggregation has taken place on the measure Test.

> **NOTE** In the RTM version of Analysis Services 2005, there is a bug, which means that if you do not specify a measure or measures in your assignment subcube, and there are calculated members present in the cube, you may see unexpected behavior. For this reason, as well as for the sake of clarity in your code, it is best practice to always include the measures dimension in your assignment subcube definitions.

Assignments and Named Sets

When there are assignments present in your MDX Script, where you put the definition of your named sets with regard to these assignments becomes an important issue because it can affect the contents of these sets. Named sets are resolved at the point in the script that they are defined, so, for example, if you are ordering or filtering a set by a particular measure and then you subsequently make an assignment to that measure, you could get unexpected results.

Table 13-13

	SALES	TEST
ALL	270	(null)
JANUARY 2005	50	50
FEBRUARY 2005	108	(null)
MARCH 2005	112	(null)
APRIL 2005	(null)	(null)

This behavior is very easy to see in action. Consider the following MDX Script, which contains two identical named sets that order the members of the Region hierarchy by the Sales measure:

```
CALCULATE;

CREATE SET CURRENTCUBE.[BEFORE]
  AS ORDER([Geography].[Region].[Region].MEMBERS, MEASURES.SALES,
BDESC) ;

([Measures].[Sales], [Geography].[Region].[North]) = 100;

CREATE SET CURRENTCUBE.[AFTER]
  AS ORDER([Geography].[Region].[Region].MEMBERS, MEASURES.SALES,
BDESC) ;
```

The only difference between the two sets is that the first is defined before the assignment on [North], while the second comes after. If you run a query to retrieve the contents of the first named set, for example:

```
SELECT [Measures].[Sales] ON 0,
[BEFORE] ON 1
FROM CUBE3
```

you can see from the results in Table 13-14 that it has been ordered based on the value of the measure before the assignment took place, even though, of course, the value displayed for Sales reflects the assignment: North comes last in the set, even though its value after the assignment is greater than that of East and West.

Running the same query but for the second of the two sets ([AFTER]) returns more sensible results, as shown in Table 13-15.

TIP For the reasons outlined in this section, in general, it is a good idea to declare all your named sets at the end of your MDX Script after all assignments have taken place. The only time you might want to break this rule would be if you intended to use the set in some complex scopings for an assignment.

Table 13-14

	SALES
WEST	126
EAST	96
SOUTH	66
NORTH	100

Table 13-15

	SALES
WEST	126
NORTH	100
EAST	96
SOUTH	66

MDX Scripting and More Complex Cubes

So far we have seen how very simple MDX Scripts behave with a very simple cube. In this section, we will introduce more complex cubes, which are more likely to reflect real-world designs, and try to understand the impact of specific cube design features.

Multiple Attribute Hierarchies

If we take a look at the second example database, DB2, and the cube, CUBE2, you'll see that on the Period dimension there are now four attribute hierarchies: Year, Season, Quarter, and Month. You'll also see that the relationships between these four attribute hierarchies are defined so that Quarter and Season are member properties of Month, and Year is a member property of Quarter. Similarly, on the Geography dimension there is now a Country attribute hierarchy and Region is linked to it by making Country a member property of Region. Understanding the relationships between attribute hierarchies is crucial to understanding how MDX Scripts behave when multiple attribute hierarchies are present, so at this point it might be helpful to run a slightly modified version of our test query to illustrate them:

```
WITH MEMBER MEASURES.DEMO AS
PERIOD.YEAR.CURRENTMEMBER.NAME
+ "," +
PERIOD.SEASON.CURRENTMEMBER.NAME
+ "," +
PERIOD.QUARTER.CURRENTMEMBER.NAME
+ "," +
PERIOD.MONTH.CURRENTMEMBER.NAME
+ "," +
GEOGRAPHY.COUNTRY.CURRENTMEMBER.NAME
+ "," +
GEOGRAPHY.REGION.CURRENTMEMBER.NAME

SELECT
```

```
{[Geography].[Region].[All],[Geography].[Region].[North],[Geography]
.[Region].[South]} ON 0,
{[Period].[Month].[All],[Period].[Month].[January 2005],
[Period].[Month].[February 2005], [Period].[Month].[March 2005]} ON 1
FROM CUBE2
WHERE MEASURES.DEMO
```

The results of this query are as shown in Table 13-16.

As you learned in Chapters 4 and 8, the relationships between the attribute hierarchies dictate that even though we have only included the Month and Region attributes in the query, the CurrentMembers on the Quarter, Year, Season, and Country attributes vary too, depending on the CurrentMember on Month and Region. One point of interest is that [Period].[Month].[All] exists only with the default member on [Period].[Year] which, because there is no All Member on that hierarchy, is [Period].[Year].[2005]. It does not exist with [Period].[Year].[2006] despite the fact that it has children that exist with [Period].[Year].[2006].

Table 13-16

	ALL	NORTH	SOUTH
ALL	2005, All, All, All, All, All	2005, All, All, All, Cubovia, North	2005, All, All, All, Cubovia, South
JANUARY 2005	2005, Winter, Quarter 1 2005, January 2005, All, All	2005, Winter, Quarter 1 2005, January 2005, Cubovia, North	2005, Winter, Quarter 1 2005, January 2005, Cubovia, South
FEBRUARY 2005	2005, Spring, Quarter 1 2005, February 2005, All, All	2005, Spring, Quarter 1 2005, February 2005, Cubovia, North	2005, Spring, Quarter 1 2005, February 2005, Cubovia, South
MARCH 2005	2005, Spring, Quarter 1 2005, March 2005, All, All	2005, Spring, Quarter 1 2005, March 2005, Cubovia, NorthSouth	2005, Spring, Quarter 1 2005, March 2005, Cubovia,

Bearing all this in mind, let's see how assignments referring to one attribute affect the others. If you modify the cube's script so that it reads as follows:

```
CALCULATE;

([Measures].[Sales], [Period].[Year].[2005])=99;
```

and run the following query:

```
SELECT
[Geography].[Region].MEMBERS ON 0,
{[Period].[Month].[All],[Period].[Month].[January 2005],
[Period].[Month].[February 2005], [Period].[Month].[March 2005]}
ON 1
FROM CUBE2
```

the results are as shown in Table 13-17.

The assignment only mentioned the Year attribute hierarchy, and so the implicit scope on the [Period].[Month] hierarchy is [Period].[Month].[All]; if the assignment had been on [Period].[Year].[2006] instead, the results of the above query would be the same as if there had been no assignment in the MDX Script at all.

So, what would happen if you made an assignment to a particular Month and then ran a query on the [Period].[Year] hierarchy? You can probably guess, but since this raises the whole question of how data aggregates up through a dimension, we should discuss some theory before we look at an example. In Analysis Services 2000, this was a fairly straightforward process: Data simply aggregated up from level to level on every hierarchy of every dimension. In Analysis Services 2005, data aggregates up through the attribute hierarchies in a similar way, from the lowest level of each attribute up to the All level (if one exists); contrary to what you might think, data does not aggregate from attribute to attribute according to the relationships defined in the member properties though.

Table 13-17

	ALL	NORTH	SOUTH	EAST	WEST
ALL	99	99	99	99	99
JANUARY 2005	104	11	21	31	41
FEBRUARY 2005	108	12	22	32	42
MARCH 2005	112	13	23	33	43

ROOTS AND LEAVES

The set of "leaves" of an Analysis Services 2005 dimension is defined as the set of tuples containing the members from the lowest level of every attribute hierarchy from the granularity attribute upwards that exist with each other. Because the granularity attribute of a dimension can vary from measure group to measure group, the leaves of a dimension can vary from measure group to measure group.

The MDX function `Leaves(Dimension_Expression)` returns the set of leaves of a dimension. It represents the lowest level of granularity within the dimension for a given measure group, the level that all data is aggregated up from. The set of leaves of a dimension should not be confused with the set of members from the lowest level of the granularity attribute of a dimension: the first is a set of tuples, and the second is a set of members, although querying by either of them will return exactly the same data.

Note that if the `Leaves` function is used on a dimension that has different granularity attributes in different measure groups, and if you have not specified any measures within the current scope, or if you have specified measures from measure groups where the dimension has different granularities, it will raise an error. For example, in the DB3 database, the Period dimension has different granularites in the Fact and Demographics measure groups, so the two following assignments will raise errors:

```
(LEAVES(PERIOD))=10;
```

and

```
({MEASURES.POPULATION, MEASURES.SALES},LEAVES(PERIOD))=10;
```

But the following assignment is legal because it only refers to a subcube where the Period dimension has consistent granularity:

```
({MEASURES.POPULATION},LEAVES(PERIOD))=10;
```

The "root" of a dimension is defined as the tuple consisting of either the All Member from every attribute hierarchy (or if an attribute hierarchy is not aggregatable, the Default Member) and every user hierarchy on the dimension. The MDX function `Root(Dimension_Expression)` returns this tuple. It represents the highest level of granularity within a dimension, the highest level that data can be aggregated up to.

In the example cube, the following query returns just the leaves of the Period dimension:

```
SELECT {} ON 0,
LEAVES(PERIOD) ON 1
FROM CUBE2
```

The results are shown in Table 13-18.

Table 13-18

Spring	February 2005	Quarter 1 2005	2005
Spring	March 2005	Quarter 1 2005	2005
Spring	April 2005	Quarter 2 2005	2005
Spring	May 2005	Quarter 2 2005	2005
Summer	June 2005	Quarter 2 2005	2005
Winter	January 2005	Quarter 1 2005	2005
Winter	January 2006	Quarter 1 2006	2006

Looking at the first tuple in the set of leaves, (Spring, February 2005, Quarter 1 2005, 2005) and remembering the member properties defined on each attribute hierarchy, we can, therefore, say that there are six possible paths to take to aggregate up to the root of the dimension at (All, All, All, 2005): for example (Spring, February 2005, Quarter 1 2005, 2005) to (Spring, All, Quarter 1 2005, 2005) to (Spring, All, All, 2005) to (All, All, All, 2005). Since we have no assignments in the cube, all paths will produce exactly the same value for the root; if there are assignments that overlap one route, the last pass wins rule comes into effect again so that the path affected by the assignment closest to the end of the MDX Script is the one that is taken.

Now that you know how aggregation works, you can then be confident about knowing the effect of any assignments you make, and we can answer the original question of what effect an assignment on the Month attribute will have on the Year attribute.

If you delete everything apart from the CALCULATE statement and run the following query:

```
SELECT {[Measures].[Sales]} ON 0,
{
([Period].[Month].[All], [Period].[Quarter].[All],
[Period].[Year].&[2005]),
([Period].[Month].[All], [Period].[Quarter].[Quarter 1 2005],
[Period].[Year].&[2005]),
([Period].[Month].[January 2005], [Period].[Quarter].[Quarter 1 2005],
[Period].[Year].&[2005]),
([Period].[Month].[February 2005], [Period].[Quarter].[Quarter 1 2005],
[Period].[Year].&[2005]),
([Period].[Month].[March 2005], [Period].[Quarter].[Quarter 1 2005],
[Period].[Year].&[2005])
}
ON 1
FROM CUBE2
```

the results are shown in Table 13-19.

Table 13-19

			SALES
ALL	**ALL**	**2005**	324
ALL	**QUARTER 1 2005**	**2005**	324
JANUARY 2005	**QUARTER 1 2005**	**2005**	104
FEBRUARY 2005	**QUARTER 1 2005**	**2005**	108
MARCH 2005	**QUARTER 1 2005**	**2005**	112

Now, if you make the following assignment on January 2005 in the Month attribute in the MDX Script:

```
CALCULATE;

(MEASURES.SALES, [Period].[Month].[January 2005])=0;
```

and rerun the same query, you can see in Table 13-20 that the new value for January 2005 looks like it has been aggregated upwards just as you would expect.

Similarly, a query that just referred to the [Period].[Year] attribute hierarchy would show the same effects, so that

```
SELECT [Measures].[Sales] ON 0,
{[Period].[Year].&[2005]} ON 1
FROM CUBE2
```

returns the results shown in Table 13-21.

Table 13-20

			SALES
ALL	**ALL**	**2005**	220
ALL	**QUARTER 1 2005**	**2005**	220
JANUARY 2005	**QUARTER 1 2005**	**2005**	0
FEBRUARY 2005	**QUARTER 1 2005**	**2005**	108
MARCH 2005	**QUARTER 1 2005**	**2005**	112

Table 13-21

	SALES
2005	220

This all seems very straightforward so far, but when making mutliple assignments, you need to properly understand the aggregation process in order to understand how the last pass wins rule is going to be applied. For example, if you modify the MDX Script so that it reads:

```
CALCULATE;
  (MEASURES.SALES, [Period].[Quarter].[Quarter 1 2005])=0;
  (MEASURES.SALES, [Period].[Month].[January 2005])=0;
```

and rerun the query before last, you get the results shown in Table 13-22.

Even though (All, Quarter 1 2005, 2005) was explicitly assigned the value 0, the subsequent assignment of 0 to (January 2005, Quarter 1 2005, 2005) at the lower level of granularity means that aggregation took place again from that lower level and overwrote the earlier assignment.

Although the relationships between attributes do not affect aggregation, they do of course affect the implicit selections made in subcube definitions. For instance an asssignment on ([Measures].[Sales], [Period].[Quarter] .[Quarter 1 2005]) is implicitly also assigning to [Period].[Month] .[All], [Period].[Year].&[2005] and every member on the Season attribute that exists with [Period].[Quarter].[Quarter 1 2005]. This behavior can be extremely useful when defining subcubes that need to cover large areas of a dimension. For example, a common requirement is to make an assignment to all areas of a dimension apart from its leaves, and this can be achieved by making an assignment to the All Member of the granularity attribute since it exists with every member on every other attribute; in the example cube, you could use a subcube such as ([Measures].[Sales], [Period].[Month].[All]).

Table 13-22

			SALES
ALL	**ALL**	**2005**	220
ALL	**QUARTER 1 2005**	**2005**	220
JANUARY 2005	**QUARTER 1 2005**	**2005**	0
FEBRUARY 2005	**QUARTER 1 2005**	**2005**	108
MARCH 2005	**QUARTER 1 2005**	**2005**	112

The final point to make in this section is that although you can assign a value to a tuple that doesn't exist together in an MDX Script, and no errors will be raised during deployment or processing, it will have no effect on the cube (see Chapter 4 for more discussion of this topic). For example, the members `[Period].[Year].&[2006]` and `[Period].[Month].[January 2005]` obviously do not exist together, but you can still make an assignment such as the following one without realizing this fact:

```
CALCULATE;
([Measures].[Sales],[Period].[Year].&[2006],[Period].[Month].[January
2005] )=0;
```

User Hierarchies

User hierarchies, as you already know, simply organize attribute hierarchies into user-friendly multilevel structures. Bear in mind that it is the attribute hierarchies alone that describe the space of the cube and that user hierarchies are something like views on top of them, so that any assignments you make on a user hierarchy will behave in exactly the same way as if you had made them to the equivalent coordinates on one or more attribute hierarchies.

For example, on the user hierarchy on the Period dimension in the sample cube, the member `[Period].[Year-Month].[Month].[January 2005]` represents exactly the same coordinate as the member `[Period].[Month].[January 2005]` on the `[Period].[Month]` attribute hierarchy. You can see this by modifying the MDX Script on the sample cube as follows:

```
CALCULATE;
(MEASURES.SALES, [Period].[Year-Month].[Month].[January 2005])=0;
```

If you then rerun the same query as at the end of the last section, you will get exactly the same result again as shown in Table 13-23.

Table 13-23

			SALES
ALL	ALL	2005	220
ALL	QUARTER 1 2005	2005	220
JANUARY 2005	QUARTER 1 2005	2005	0
FEBRUARY 2005	QUARTER 1 2005	2005	108
MARCH 2005	QUARTER 1 2005	2005	112

The [Period].[Year-Month] user hierarchy is an example of a natural hierarchy, where each level is a member property of the level beneath it. The [Period].[Season-Quarter] user hierarchy is, on the other hand, an unnatural hierarchy: Season is not a member property of Quarter, and a Quarter can appear in many Seasons. Assignments to unnatural hierarchies behave in exactly the same way as assignments to natural hierarchies.

Parent/Child Attribute Hierarchies

Parent/child attribute hierarchies behave in a very similar way to user hierarchies in terms of aggregation. Moving onto the third of the sample databases and cubes, take a look at the structure of the [Employee].[Employee Reports] attribute hierarchy, then run the following query:

```
WITH MEMBER MEASURES.SHOWANCESTORS AS
GENERATE(
ASCENDANTS([Employee].[Employee Reports].CURRENTMEMBER)
,[Employee].[Employee Reports].CURRENTMEMBER.NAME, ",")
SELECT {MEASURES.SHOWANCESTORS, MEASURES.SALES} ON 0,
[Employee].[Employee Reports].MEMBERS ON 1
FROM CUBE3
```

The results give the ancestors of each member on the dimension and the Sales measure, as shown in Table 13-24.

As you might expect, an assignment to one member affects all of its ancestors in the same way as an assignment to a member on a user hierarchy affects all of its ancestors. So, for example, changing the MDX Script on the cube as follows:

```
CALCULATE;
(Measures.Sales, [Employee].[Employee Reports].[Chris])=99;
```

gives the results shown in Table 13-25 if you rerun the query above.

Table 13-24

	SHOWANCESTORS	SALES
ALL	All	324
HELEN	Helen, All	324
CHRIS	Chris, Helen, All	324
JON	Jon, Chris, Helen, All	(null)
NATASHA	Natasha, Chris, Helen, All	324
COLIN	Colin, Helen, All	(null)

Table 13-25

	SHOWANCESTORS	SALES
ALL	All	99
HELEN	Helen, All	99
CHRIS	Chris, Helen, All	99
JON	Jon, Chris, Helen, All	(null)
NATASHA	Natasha, Chris, Helen, All	324
COLIN	Colin, Helen, All	(null)

Remember that if you have nonleaf members on your parent/child attribute hierarchy that have data in the fact table, and if you have the `MembersWithData` property set to `NonLeafDataHidden`, there will be extra members called `DataMembers` on your hierarchy that are not visible (unless you specifically include them in a query) but that will have values that are aggregated and to which you can assign new values.

NOTE In the RTM version of Analysis Services 2005, there is a bug, which means that the behavior described in the section "Multiple Attribute Hierarchies", above, whereby selecting a member or one attribute implicitly changes the current member on other attribute hierarchies, and is not applied to parent and key attributes involved in a parent-child hierarchy.

Many-to-Many Dimensions

If a dimension has a many-to-many relationship with a measure group, then assignments that involve that dimension behave slightly differently from what you have seen so far. Running the following query on the sample cube (making sure that all previous assignments in the MDX Script have been deleted and it only contains a `CALCULATE()` statement) shows how aggregation works with many-to-many dimensions and a measure with aggregation type `Sum`:

```
SELECT
[Geography].[Region].MEMBERS
ON 0,
[Geography Description].[Geography Description].MEMBERS
ON 1
FROM CUBE3
WHERE([Measures].[Sales])
```

The Geography dimension has a direct relationship with the measure group we are querying; the Geography Description dimension has a many-to-many relationship; and the effect is one of "distinct sum" so that the value for each Region is repeated for each of the Geography Descriptions that that Region has a relationship with, as shown in Table 13-26.

Table 13-26

	ALL	NORTH	SOUTH	EAST	WEST
ALL	324	36	66	96	126
MOUNTAINOUS	102	36	66	(null)	(null)
RAINY	192	(null)	66	(null)	126
TROPICAL	(null)	(null)	(null)	(null)	(null)
URBAN	(null)	(null)	(null)	(null)	(null)
WILD	102	36	66	(null)	(null)
WINDY	222	(null)	(null)	96	126

If you make an assignment to the many-to-many dimension, such as:

```
CALCULATE;

([Measures].[Sales], [Geography Description].[Geography
Description].[Mountainous])=0;
```

and rerun the same query, the results are as shown in Table 13-27.

The top row shows no change, illustrating that the aggregation process has been unaffected by the assignment. However, if you make an assignment to the dimension that forms the link between the many-to-many dimension and the fact table whose measure you are querying, for example like this:

```
CALCULATE;

([Measures].[Sales], {[Geography].[Region].[North],[Geography]
.[Region].[South]})=0;
```

Table 13-27

	ALL	NORTH	SOUTH	EAST	WEST
ALL	324	36	66	96	126
MOUNTAINOUS	0	0	0	0	0
RAINY	192	(null)	66	(null)	126

(continued)

Table 13-27 *(continued)*

	ALL	NORTH	SOUTH	EAST	WEST
TROPICAL	(null)	(null)	(null)	(null)	(null)
URBAN	(null)	(null)	(null)	(null)	(null)
WILD	102	36	66	(null)	(null)
WINDY	222	(null)	(null)	96	126

then rerun the query, you can see from the results in Table 13-28 that there is an impact.

You can see that, for example, the cell containing the value for (Mountainous, All) is now zero and that the cell (All, All) contains the value 222 rather than 324. As a general rule, then, we can say that assignments that only reference a many-to-many dimension will affect the area of the cube below the Root of that dimension but nowhere else; conversely, assignments involving dimensions that have a regular relationship with the cube may affect the area below the Root of a many-to-many dimension.

Many-to-many dimensions connect to a measure group via an intermediate measure group that models the many-to-many relationship; so for example, in the sample cube, Geography Description is linked to the Geography dimension by the [Geo Geo Desc Link] measure group. As a result, it would be fair to wonder if assignments to the intermediate measure group have an effect on how the many-to-many relationship is resolved—the answer is, unfortunately, that they do not.

Fact Dimensions and Reference Dimensions

Fact dimensions and Reference dimensions behave like regular dimensions as far as MDX Scripts and assignments are concerned.

Semi-additive and Nonadditive Measures

So far in this chapter, you have only looked at additive measures—those that have the aggregation function Sum. Semi-additive measures (those with aggregation functions Count, Min, Max, AverageOfChildren, FirstChild, LastChild, FirstNonEmpty, and LastNonEmpty) and nonadditive measures (those with aggregation functions DistinctCount and None) do not behave in the same way as additive measures when it comes to assignments. In both cases, you can still assign values to subcubes, but the difference is the effect that these assignments have on cells outside the subcube.

Table 13-28

	ALL	NORTH	SOUTH	EAST	WEST
ALL	222	0	0	96	126
MOUNTAINOUS	0	0	0	(null)	(null)
RAINY	126	0	0	(null)	126
TROPICAL	0	0	0	(null)	(null)
URBAN	0	0	0	(null)	(null)
WILD	0	0	0	(null)	(null)
WINDY	222	0	0	96	126

Assignments to nonadditive measures never affect values outside the sub-cube of the original assignment, and the same goes for semi-additive measures where the assignment is above the granularity attribute of the Time dimension. For example, in the sample cube, the measure [Opening Period Sales] has the aggregation function FirstChild. Running the following query on the test cube (making sure that the MDX Script only consists of a Calculate() statement) shows how this semi-additive aggregation works (see Table 13-29):

```
SELECT
{[Measures].[Sales], [Measures].[Opening Period Sales]} ON 0,
{[Period].[Year-Month].[Year].[2005], [Period].[Year-
Month].[Quarter].[Quarter 1 2005],
  [Period].[Year-Month].[Month].[January 2005], [Period].[Year-
Month].[Month].[February 2005], [Period].[Year-Month].[Month].[March
2005]}
ON 1
FROM CUBE3
```

You can see that the value for 2005 is the same as for Quarter 1 2005, which is the same as for January 2005. If you make an assignment on Quarter 1 2005, as follows:

```
CALCULATE;
  ([Period].[Year-Month].[Quarter].[Quarter 1 2005])=0;
```

and then rerun the query, you can see from Table 13-30 that although the 2005 value for Sales has changed as a result of the assignment, the 2005 value for Opening Period Sales has not.

Table 13-29

	SALES	OPENING PERIOD SALES
2005	324	104
QUARTER 1 2005	324	104
JANUARY 2005	104	104
FEBRUARY 2005	108	108
MARCH 2005	112	112

Table 13-30

	SALES	OPENING PERIOD SALES
2005	0	104
QUARTER 1 2005	0	0
JANUARY 2005	104	104
FEBRUARY 2005	108	108
MARCH 2005	112	112

However if you were to make an assignment on January 2005, because Month is the granularity attribute for the Period dimension here, you would see an impact on the 2005 and Quarter 1 2005 values. So, for example, if you changed the script to read as follows:

```
CALCULATE;
  ([Period].[Year-Month].[Month].[January 2005])=0;
```

and then reran the query again, you'd get the results shown in Table 13-31.

Table 13-31

	SALES	OPENING PERIOD SALES
2005	220	0
QUARTER 1 2005	220	0
JANUARY 2005	0	0
FEBRUARY 2005	108	108
MARCH 2005	112	112

Unary Operators and Custom Member Formulas

Attribute hierarchies with unary operators or custom member formulas are special cases in that the last pass wins rule for aggregation does not apply to them. For instance, take a look at the following query on the sample cube:

```
SELECT
{[Period].[Month].[All], [Period].[Month].[January 2005],
[Period].[Month].[February 2005],[Period].[Month].[March
2005],[Period].[Month].[April 2005]}
ON 0,
[Account].[Account Structure].MEMBERS
ON 1
FROM CUBE3
WHERE([Measures].[Fact Value])
```

It returns the results shown in Table 13-32.

Table 13-32

	ALL	JANUARY 2005	FEBRUARY 2005	MARCH 2005	APRIL 2005
All	4089	119	439	959	(null)
Profit (+)	4089	119	439	959	(null)
Book					
Sales (+)	63	11	21	31	(null)
Consulting Revenue (*)	66	12	22	32	(null)
Expenses (-)	69	13	23	33	(null)
Goodwill (~)	72	14	24	34	(null)

You can see that Profit for the All Member on Month is calculated as ((All, Book Sales) * (All, Consulting Revenue)) - (All, Expenses) or (63 * 66) - 69 = 4089, and not (Profit, January 2005) + (Profit, February 2005) + (Profit, March 2005) or 119 + 439 + 959 = 1517. This is so because unary operators are always applied last of all in the aggregation process, to make sure that they actually aggregate up in the way that the unary operators imply, and this behavior continues to be enforced even after assignments have been made to the cube using MDX Scripts.

If you make a simple assignment to the cube, such as

```
CALCULATE;

([Measures].[Fact Value], [Account].[Account Structure].[Book Sales
(+)], [Period].[Year-Month].[Month].[January 2005])=99;
```

and then rerun the same query, you get the results shown in Table 13-33.

Table 13-33

	ALL	JANUARY 2005	FEBRUARY 2005	MARCH 2005	APRIL 2005
All	9897	1175	439	959	(null)
Profit (+)	9897	1175	439	959	(null)
Book					
Sales (+)	151	99	21	31	(null)
Consulting Revenue (*)	66	12	22	32	(null)
Expenses (-)	69	13	23	33	(null)
Goodwill (~)	72	14	24	34	(null)

Profit is once again calculated in the same way, so that (All, Profit) is ((All, Book Sales) * (All, Consulting Revenue)) – (All, Expenses), and this will be true in all cases except when there is a direct assignment on Profit. So, for example, if you alter the script like this:

```
CALCULATE;
  ([Measures].[Fact Value], [Account].[Account Structure].[Profit
(+)])=99;
```

and rerun the same query again, you'll see from Table 13-34 that Profit is now 99 as per the assignment, rather than being calculated according to the unary operators.

Table 13-34

	ALL	JANUARY 2005	FEBRUARY 2005	MARCH 2005	APRIL 2005
All	99	99	99	99	99
Profit (+)	99	99	99	99	99
Book					
Sales (+)	63	11	21	31	(null)
Consulting Revenue (*)	66	12	22	32	(null)
Expenses (-)	69	13	23	33	(null)
Goodwill (~)	72	14	24	34	(null)

The rule, then, for dimensions with unary operators and custom member formulas (which behave in the same way), is that any given cell will always be calculated according to the unary operators or custom member formulas, unless the cell itself is overwritten by an assignment. This rule is called "closest pass wins."

Advanced MDX Scripting

Now that you understand how simple MDX Scripting statements behave in a complex cube, it is time to look at what is possible with more complex MDX Scripting statements.

Defining Subcubes with SCOPE

So far in this chapter you have explicitly defined a subcube for every assignment you've made, but for a complex series of assignments, this will lead to dense and unreadable MDX. A better alternative is to build up subcube definitions incrementally, using one or more SCOPE statements. Taking a very simple subcube example of overwriting the cell for Sales, North, and January 2005, the assignment

```
([Measures].[Sales], [Geography].[Region].[North],
[Period].[Month].[January 2005])=50;
```

can be rewritten using the SCOPE statement as follows:

```
SCOPE([Measures].[Sales], [Geography].[Region].[North],
[Period].[Month].[January 2005]);
    THIS=50;
END SCOPE;
```

The SCOPE statement takes one argument, which is a subcube definition, and all subsequent MDX expressions until the closing END SCOPE statement can then refer to this subcube using the THIS function. So, in the example above, the assignment THIS=50 sets all values within the subcube defined in the preceding SCOPE statement to 50.

SCOPE statements can be nested. This means we can rewrite our assignment once again and get the same result:

```
SCOPE([Measures].[Sales]);
    SCOPE([Geography].[Region].[North]);
        SCOPE([Period].[Month].[January 2005]);
            THIS=50;
        END SCOPE;
    END SCOPE;
END SCOPE;
```

Each nested SCOPE statement narrows down the definition of the subcube even further. Of course, you do not need to put all of your assignments within the innermost SCOPE statement. For example, if you use the following script on the cube:

```
//CALCULATE;

SCOPE([Measures].[Sales]);
    SCOPE([Geography].[Region].[North]);
        THIS=100;
        SCOPE([Period].[Month].[January 2005]);
            THIS=50;
        END SCOPE;
    END SCOPE;
END SCOPE;
```

and then run the following query:

```
SELECT
[Geography].[Region].MEMBERS ON 0,
[Period].[Month].MEMBERS ON 1
FROM CUBE3
```

you get the results shown in Table 13-35.

Table 13-35

	ALL	NORTH	SOUTH	EAST	WEST
All	(null)	100	(null)	(null)	(null)
January 2005	(null)	50	(null)	(null)	(null)
February 2005	(null)	100	(null)	(null)	(null)
March 2005	(null)	100	(null)	(null)	(null)
April 2005	(null)	100	(null)	(null)	(null)
May 2005	(null)	100	(null)	(null)	(null)
June 2005	(null)	100	(null)	(null)	(null)
January 2006	(null)	100	(null)	(null)	(null)

Each assignment using THIS within a SCOPE block acts just like the individual explicit assignments you have looked at so far, and this means that the last pass wins rule will still be enforced if you uncomment the CALCULATE statement from the previous MDX Script example and rerun the query. Table 13-36 shows the results.

Table 13-36

	ALL	NORTH	SOUTH	EAST	WEST
All	838	550	66	96	126
January 2005	143	50	21	31	41
February 2005	196	100	22	32	42
March 2005	199	100	23	33	43
April 2005	100	100	(null)	(null)	(null)
May 2005	100	100	(null)	(null)	(null)
June 2005	100	100	(null)	(null)	(null)
January 2006	100	100	(null)	(null)	(null)

Finally, you can override inheritance within a nested SCOPE block simply by making another SCOPE declaration, which references a hierarchy you've already referenced in an outer block. So, in the following example:

```
CALCULATE;

SCOPE([Measures].[Sales], [Period].[Month].[January 2005]);
    SCOPE([Period].[Month].[February 2005]);
        THIS=100;
    END SCOPE;
    THIS=50;
END SCOPE;
```

you can see from the results in Table 13-37 that (January) is set to 50 and (February) gets set to 100, because the inner block declaration has overridden the outer one.

Table 13-37

	ALL	NORTH	SOUTH	EAST	WEST
All	262	163	173	183	193
January 2005	50	50	50	50	50
February 2005	100	100	100	100	100
March 2005	112	13	23	33	43

Assignments That Are MDX Expressions

Assigning static values to subcubes has only limited use in real-world cubes: Most of the time you will want to manipulate values already in the cube by applying formulas to them. Here's an example that adds 50 to every cell within the subcube ([Measures].[Sales],[Period].[Month].[January 2005]):

```
SCOPE([Measures].[Sales], [Period].[Month].[January 2005]);
    THIS = [Measures].[Sales] + 50;
END SCOPE;
```

Unfortunately, the THIS keyword can't be used on the right-hand side of an assignment. You can't use an expression like THIS = THIS + 50 or THIS += 50; you have to always state what it is you're modifying. Hard-coding the measure you're modifying works if you are scoping only on one measure, though. You can remove the hard-coded measure name and, therefore, create an assignment that will work for multiple measures by rewriting the assignment as follows:

```
SCOPE(MEASUREGROUPMEASURES("FACT"), [Period].[Month].[January 2005]);
    THIS = [Measures].CURRENTMEMBER + 50;
END SCOPE;
```

You can also easily create assignments that allow the subcube to mirror values found elsewhere in the cube. For example, the following MDX Script sets the value of January 2005 to be the same as February 2005:

```
CALCULATE;

SCOPE([Measures].[Sales], [Period].[Month].[January 2005]);
    THIS = [Period].[Month].[February 2005];
END SCOPE;
```

If you run the following query:

```
SELECT
[Geography].[Region].members
ON 0,
{[Period].[Month].[All], [Period].[Month].[January 2005],
[Period].[Month].[February 2005],[Period].[Month].[March
2005],[Period].[Month].[April 2005]}
ON 1
FROM CUBE3
```

you can see from the results in Table 13-38 that the values for January 2005 are indeed the same as those for February 2005.

Table 13-38

	ALL	NORTH	SOUTH	EAST	WEST
All	328	37	67	97	127
January 2005	108	12	22	32	42
February 2005	108	12	22	32	42
March 2005	112	13	23	33	43
April 2005	(null)	(null)	(null)	(null)	(null)

By doing this kind of assignment, it is important to understand that you are assigning a formula that points to the values of February 2005 rather than overwriting January 2005 with those values. That's to say that if you subsequently make an assignment in the MDX Script that alters the values of February 2005, then the values of January 2005 will change too. You can see this if you alter the existing MDX Script as follows:

```
CALCULATE;

SCOPE([Measures].[Sales], [Period].[Month].[January 2005]);
    THIS = [Period].[Month].[February 2005];
END SCOPE;

SCOPE([Measures].[Sales], [Period].[Month].[February 2005]);
    THIS=0;
END SCOPE;
```

Rerunning the last query now gives the results shown in Table 13-39.

Table 13-39

	ALL	NORTH	SOUTH	EAST	WEST
All	112	13	23	33	43
January 2005	0	0	0	0	0
February 2005	0	0	0	0	0
March 2005	112	13	23	33	43
April 2005	(null)	(null)	(null)	(null)	(null)

If you don't want this to happen, you can use the FREEZE() statement. When a FREEZE() statement is executed on a subcube, it makes sure that subsequent assignments to cells outside that subcube will have no effect on the values within the subcube. If you alter the MDX Script to use it on January 2005, as follows:

```
CALCULATE;

SCOPE([Measures].[Sales], [Period].[Month].[January 2005]);
    THIS = [Period].[Month].[February 2005];
    FREEZE(THIS);
END SCOPE;

SCOPE([Measures].[Sales], [Period].[Month].[February 2005]);
    THIS=0;
END SCOPE;
```

and rerun the query again, you can see from the results in Table 13-40 that January 2005 is now unaffected by the later assignment to February 2005.

Table 13-40

	ALL	NORTH	SOUTH	EAST	WEST
All	220	25	45	65	85
January 2005	108	12	22	32	42
February 2005	0	0	0	0	0
March 2005	112	13	23	33	43
April 2005	(null)	(null)	(null)	(null)	(null)

FREEZE() also allows us to stop the aggregation process overwriting cell values. For example, a FREEZE() statement placed before the CALCULATE statement in the MDX Script will prevent nonleaf cells from ever being populated by values through aggregation. Take the following script, which freezes (All, North):

```
FREEZE([Measures].[Sales], [Geography].[Region].[North],
[Period].[Month].[All]);

CALCULATE;
```

Rerunning the query once more returns the results shown in Table 13-41, and sure enough, (All, North) is now NULL.

Table 13-41

	ALL	NORTH	SOUTH	EAST	WEST
All	288	(null)	66	96	126
January 2005	104	11	21	31	41
February 2005	108	12	22	32	42
March 2005	112	13	23	33	43
April 2005	(null)	(null)	(null)	(null)	(null)

Here's another example, this time showing how FREEZE() can prevent a value explicitly written to a cell from being overwritten by values aggregated up from a subsequent assignment at a lower granularity:

```
CALCULATE;

SCOPE([Measures].[Sales], [Geography].[Region].[North],
[Period].[Month].[All]);
    THIS=50;
    FREEZE(THIS);
END SCOPE;

SCOPE([Measures].[Sales], [Geography].[Region].[North],
[Period].[Month].[Month].MEMBERS);
    THIS=100;
END SCOPE;
```

The results of the query we've been using (see Table 13-42) show how (All, North) is not overwritten by the sum of all the months below it.

Table 13-42

	ALL	NORTH	SOUTH	EAST	WEST
All	338	50	66	96	126
January 2005	193	100	21	31	41
February 2005	196	100	22	32	42
March 2005	199	100	23	33	43
April 2005	100	100	(null)	(null)	(null)

In this scenario, the aggregation process will continue aggregating up to higher levels of granularity above the frozen subcube using the values within that subcube. Using the same MDX Script as previously, the following query (and its results in Table 13-43) shows this in action:

```
SELECT MEASURES.SALES ON 0,
{
[Period].[Year-Month].[Year].&[2005],
[Period].[Year-Month].[Quarter].[Quarter 1 2005],
[Period].[Year-Month].[Month].[January 2005]
}
ON 1
FROM CUBE3
WHERE([Geography].[Region].[North])
```

Table 13-43

	SALES
2005	50
Quarter 1 2005	50
January 2005	100

Assigning Error Values to Subcubes

As well as assigning static values and formulas to subcubes, you can also display an error within all the cells within a subcube using the ERROR() function. This function takes a single string argument, which is the error message to be displayed to the user; the following example script shows how it can be used:

```
CALCULATE;

SCOPE([Measures].[Sales], [Period].[Year-Month].[Month].[January 2005]);
    THIS=ERROR("Hello World");
END SCOPE;
```

Querying the affected area of the cube would show that the cells for January 2005 would all show the value #Error, and inspecting the Value and Formatted_Value cell properties (for example by double-clicking on the cell in SQL Server Management Studio) would show the value #Error MdxScript(Cube3) (9, 10) Hello World.

Assigning Cell Property Values to Subcubes

It isn't just the values of cells that can be modified using MDX Scripts: Certain other cell properties can also be changed. The FORMAT_STRING(), NON_EMPTY_BEHAVIOR, LANGUAGE(), FORE_COLOR(), BACK_COLOR(), FONT_SIZE(), FONT_FLAGS(), and FONT_NAME() statements can all be used to assign values to the properties of the same name for a subcube.

For example, the following script shows how the format string used can be altered only for January 2005:

```
CALCULATE;

SCOPE([Measures].[Sales], [Period].[Year-Month].[Month].[January 2005]);
    FORMAT_STRING(THIS)='#.00';
END SCOPE;
```

The results can be seen clearly in Table 13-44, which shows the results of a query on that part of the cube.

Table 13-44

	ALL	NORTH	SOUTH	EAST	WEST
All	324	36	66	96	126
January 2005	104.00	11.00	21.00	31.00	41.00
February 2005	108	12	22	32	42
March 2005	112	13	23	33	43

One very useful application for the LANGUAGE() statement is to make a measure that has its format string defined as Currency, display different currency symbols for different members on a dimension. The following script shows how this can be achieved:

```
CALCULATE;

CREATE MEMBER CURRENTCUBE.[MEASURES].[Currency Test]
 AS [Measures].[Fact Value],
FORMAT_STRING = "Currency",
VISIBLE = 1  ;

SCOPE([MEASURES].[Currency Test]);
    SCOPE([Account].[Account Structure].&[2]);
        LANGUAGE(THIS)=1033;
    END SCOPE;
    SCOPE([Account].[Account Structure].&[4]);
        LANGUAGE(THIS)=2055;
    END SCOPE;
END SCOPE;
```

Table 13-45 shows the results of the following query when run on a server whose default locale is 2057 (UK English):

```
SELECT [Measures].[Currency Test] ON 0,
[Account].[Account Structure].MEMBERS ON 1
FROM CUBE3
```

Table 13-45

	CURRENCY TEST
All	£4,089.00
Profit (+)	£4,089.00
Book Sales (+)	$63.00
Consulting Revenue (*)	£66.00
Expenses (-)	SFr. 69.00
Goodwill (~)	£72.00

Conditional Assignments

The IF statement in an MDX Script allows you to make an assignment only if a condition is fulfilled; it should not be confused with the IIF function or the CASE statement, both of which can only return values or objects and cannot be used for control flow. The following example shows how it can be used:

```
CALCULATE;

SCOPE([Measures].[Sales], [Period].[Year-Month].[Month].[January 2005]);
    IF
        MEASURES.SALES>21
    THEN
        THIS=0
    END IF;
END SCOPE;
```

If you run the following query, you can see in Table 13-46 what the effect is:

```
SELECT
[Geography].[Region].MEMBERS ON 0,
{[Period].[Month].[All],[Period].[Month].[January 2005],
[Period].[Month].[February 2005], [Period].[Month].[March 2005]}
ON 1
FROM CUBE3
```

Table 13-46

	ALL	NORTH	SOUTH	EAST	WEST
All	220	36	66	65	85
January 2005	0	11	21	0	0
February 2005	108	12	22	32	42
March 2005	112	13	23	33	43

It is very important to realize that even when the condition evaluates to false and no change to a cell's value is made, Analysis Services still acts as though an assignment has been made and the last pass wins rule comes into play. As a result, using the following MDX Script will not alter the results of the previous query at all:

```
CALCULATE;

SCOPE([Measures].[Sales],[Period].[Month].[All]);
    THIS=0;
END SCOPE;

SCOPE([Measures].[Sales], [Period].[Year-Month].[Month].[January 2005]);
    IF
        MEASURES.SALES>21
    THEN
        THIS=0
    END IF;
END SCOPE;
```

Even though the value of (January 2005, South) is less than 21 and the condition evaluates to false, the value of 0 in the cell (All, South) is still overwritten by aggregation.

NOTE Assignments that use the IF statement are no better in terms of query performance than equivalent assignments that use the IIF() function.

Real-World MDX Scripts

Theory is all very well, but how do you actually use MDX Scripts in practice? This final section of the chapter will consider some common calculations, several of which are dealt with elsewhere in this book, and consider how they can be implemented using MDX Scripts as opposed to simple calculated members.

The Time Intelligence Wizard

The best set of examples of calculations implemented with MDX Scripts is built into Visual Studio: The scripts created using the Add Business Intelligence wizard for "Time Intelligence" calculations not only demonstrate several best practices, but they need to be understood because it's very likely that at some point you will need to alter them to meet the requirements of your project. Before you read this section, it might be worth going back to Chapter 3 to review the section "Time-Based References and Time Series Calculations" so that you can compare the more generally applicable MDX statements there with the MDX Script-specific implementations you'll encounter below.

In the DB3 database, you can see that the MDX Script contains two calculations created with the wizard: Twelve Months to Date, which returns the sum of
the 12 months up to and including the current month, and Month Over Month
Growth, which returns the difference between the current month and the previous month. The approach taken is that of creating a Time Utility Dimension, as
described in Chapter 7, and if you haven't already read that section, we recommend that you do so now to familiarize yourself with the concept.

The first section of script generated by the wizard creates the two calculated
members on the [Period].[Year-Month Period Calculations]
attribute hierarchy, which will return the calculated values when the user
selects them in a query:

```
Create Member CurrentCube.[Period].[Year-Month Period Calculations].
[Twelve Months to Date] AS "NA" ;

Create Member CurrentCube.[Period].[Year-Month Period Calculations].
[Month Over Month Growth] AS "NA" ;
```

In contrast to the method described in Chapter 7, you'll see that these calculated members do not contain formulas; they simply return the value NA for
Not Applicable. This value will be overwritten later on in the script but only
for areas of the cube where the calculation is relevant: For example, a Twelve
Months to Date calculation makes no sense when looking at Years, so in that
scenario the original NA value will be returned.

Next comes the section containing all the assignments. It is surrounded by a
SCOPE block, which contains the measures selected in the wizard:

```
Scope(
        {
            [Measures].[Sales]
        }
) ;
```

Although it is recommended that you run the wizard only after the rest of
your cube design has been finalized, it's almost inevitable that at some point
you will want to add more measures (calculated or otherwise) to your cube. If
you want the time intelligence calculations to apply to these new measures,
you will need to add them to this set, which is simply a case of editing the
SCOPE() statement.

If you take a look at the first of the time intelligence calculations, Twelve
Months to Date, it is very straightforward:

```
/* On the left hand side, the subcube to be assigned to*/
( [Period].[Year-Month Period Calculations].[Twelve Months to Date],
    [Period].[Month].[Month].Members ) =
```

```
/* On the right hand side, the formula assigned to the subcube */
Aggregate(
        { [Period].[Year-Month Period Calculations].DefaultMember }

*

        {
        ParallelPeriod(
                        [Period].[Year-Month].[Month],
                        11,
                        [Period].[Year-Month].CurrentMember
        ) : [Period].[Year-Month].CurrentMember
        }
) ;
```

The calculation is scoped on the [Period].[Year-Month Period Calculations].[Twelve Months to Date] calculated member and [Period].[Month].[Month]. The fact that the wizard has chosen to scope on the attribute hierarchy [Period].[Month].[Month] rather than the equivalent user hierarchy level [Period].[Year-Month].[Year] is significant: It is always preferable to scope on an attribute hierarchy rather than a user hierarchy, because user hierarchies are much more likely to change over the lifetime of a cube. For instance, users might want to drill directly from Year to Month, so the Quarter level of [Period].[Year-Month] would be deleted, and any calculations that relied on this level would fail. The same goes for the right-hand side of an assignment, but, as this example shows, the ability to use functions such as ParallelPeriod on user hierarchies can provide a strong argument to break this rule.

The second calculation created by the wizard, Month Over Month Growth, is similar but displays another best practice: It is deliberately not scoped for the first month of data because we know that the first month has no previous month to calculate a growth from, so the calculation will never return a useful value:

```
( [Period].[Year-Month Period Calculations].[Month Over Month Growth],
  [Period].[Month].[Month].Members ( 1 ) : Null ) =

( [Period].[Year-Month Period Calculations].DefaultMember ) -
( [Period].[Year-Month Period Calculations].DefaultMember,
  ParallelPeriod(
                [Period].[Year-Month].[Month],
                1,
                [Period].[Year-Month].CurrentMember
  )
) ;
```

The special case of the first month is handled in a second assignment:

```
( [Period].[Year-Month Period Calculations].[Month Over Month Growth],
  [Period].[Month].[Month].Members ( 0 )
) = Null ;
```

If we didn't do this we would have to include a check within the formula for this condition and handle it appropriately (for example returning NULL) if it was true, a test that would have to be run every time a cell was evaluated and that would result in worse performance. Of course, it isn't possible to avoid all run-time checks of this nature, but in general you should try to scope to avoid them.

NOTE In the RTM version of Analysis Services 2005, we have noticed several instances where the Time Intelligence Wizard generates MDX, which does not work properly, for example year-to-date calculations are only scoped on year attributes. Hopefully, this will be fixed in a subsequent service pack.

Basic Allocations Revisited

Referring back to Chapter 3 again, another common application for MDX Script assignments is to perform various types of allocations. Once again, it should be pointed out that this section does not attempt to supersede the information given in Chapter 3 but instead show how an MDX Script–specific approach would work; using calculated measures alone to solve these problems may be easier for you to understand and is certainly more concise in terms of the amount of code needed, so in some respects, using MDX Scripts is not necessarily the best choice.

Out of the two types of allocation mentioned in Chapter 3, the first, proportional allocation of one quantity based on another, should always involve the use of calculated measures, although as you have seen already, their values can be populated using assignments. The following script shows how an advertising budget (specified in the calculated measure [Advertising]) could be allocated in proportion to the Sales of any member on any hierarchy of the Geography dimension:

```
CALCULATE;

CREATE MEMBER CURRENTCUBE.[MEASURES].[Advertising]
  AS 1000,
VISIBLE = 1;

CREATE MEMBER CURRENTCUBE.[MEASURES].[Advertising Budget Allocated]
  AS NULL,
VISIBLE = 1  ;

SCOPE([MEASURES].[Advertising Budget Allocated]);
    THIS =
```

```
        [MEASURES].[Advertising]
        *
        (
            [Measures].[Sales]
            /
            ([Measures].[Sales], ROOT([Geography]))
        );
    FORMAT_STRING(THIS) = "#,#.00";
END SCOPE;
```

The use of the `Root()` function is the most important thing to notice here, because it allows you to avoid having to hard-code the name of every All Member on every hierarchy in the Geography dimension.

The second type of allocation mentioned, unweighted allocations down a hierarchy, presents more of a challenge. Imagine that you now want the advertising budget allocated evenly across all the months in the Period dimension, and to see the correct result for every attribute hierarchy and user hierarchy in that dimension. You could use a calculated measure to do this but it would involve some very complex MDX; it is much easier to create a real measure in your cube, use a script to allocate the values you want only to the leaves of the Period dimension, and then let the Analysis Services aggregation engine do the work for you. In the sample cube, there is already a measure in the Fact measure group called `[Advertising Allocated By Month]` which only contains NULL values (it is created as a named calculation on the measure group's fact table in the data source view); the following MDX Script shows how you can use it to solve the problem:

```
CALCULATE;

CREATE MEMBER CURRENTCUBE.[MEASURES].[Advertising]
  AS 1000,
VISIBLE = 1;


SCOPE([Measures].[Advertising Allocated by Month]);
    SCOPE(LEAVES(PERIOD));
        THIS =
            [MEASURES].[Advertising]
            /
            COUNT([Period].[Month].[Month].MEMBERS)
            ;
    END SCOPE;
    FORMAT_STRING(THIS) = "#,#.00";
END SCOPE;
```

In this example, you can see that we have used the `Leaves()` function for the scope of the calculation, but did not use it when calculating the ratio for allocating `[Advertising]`. This is so because, as we found earlier, Period has mixed granularity across different measure groups in the cube, and although the `Leaves()` function can understand the current context when it is used within a `SCOPE()` statement, if you try to use it within the `COUNT()` function, it will raise an error because there is no way to tell it that we want it to return the leaves for a certain measure group.

Summary

In this chapter, we have introduced the topic of how to perform calculations using MDX Scripts. You have seen how to describe an area within the cube, a subcube, which can have a value assigned to it. You have also seen how the process of aggregation and overlapping assignments can alter values outside the subcube that was defined. A thorough understanding of all of this should put you in a position where, at the very least, you can maintain MDX Scripts created by the various wizards built into Visual Studio; if you are feeling confident, you should be able to go on to model quite complex sets of calculations. What we have not discussed, however, is how to ensure that the calculations created perform as well as possible, and that is what you will learn about in Chapter 16, "Optimizing MDX."

CHAPTER 14

Enriching the Client Interaction

In addition to normal MDX queries, OLAP-based systems usually support some advanced user interactions with OLAP objects such as cubes, dimension members, and cells. This chapter will discuss drill-through, action, and KPI support of Analysis Services 2005.

OLAP-based systems are usually intermediaries—they draw on detailed data that was collected from various operations, and supply results that are used in making decisions. Frequently, we would like them to extend their reach a little bit in both directions, so that we may see the raw data that they derived their results from and to help us implement the actions that their results suggest. Enabling these two possibilities is the subject of this chapter, and for Microsoft these are provided by drill-through and actions. Drill-through is an industry-standard term for reaching into the underlying fact table records for a cell or cells in an OLAP system.

An action is a term created by Microsoft and used in the OLE DB for OLAP specification. It refers to a textual command that can be generated by the OLAP database for use in an arbitrary application, for example to implement a decision.

KPIs (key performance indicators) are frequently used in business performance management systems. Analysis Services 2005 provides a framework for categorizing the KPI MDX expressions into a set of predefined data roles (actual, goal, trend, status, and the like). Quantitive KPIs are managed via

MDX expressions. Analysis Services 2005 maintains the metadata for user KPI definition and introduced a new set of MDX functions for applications to easily retrieve those KPI values from cubes.

Using Drill-Through

Drill-through enables a client application to access data from the tables that underlie a cube. For example, suppose that a cell for quarterly sales for a particular region shows a number for which an analyst wishes to look at the supporting transaction detail. Figure 14-1 shows the relationship of the underlying table to the cell, and represents the result that the analyst would like to see.

To perform a drill-through, the client issues a drill-through query in MDX, which is very similar to an ordinary query. The result of the drill-through query is an OLE DB rowset that appears the same as one that results from an SQL query. A client that uses ADO.NET or ADOMD.NET can access this result as a regular `System.Data.DataReader`.

	Q1-2005		Q2-2005		Q3-2005	
	Hours	Revenue	Hours	Revenue	Hours	Revenue
Detroit	450	450	400	450	425	8500
Lansing	305	6010	350	7000	380	7400
Columbus	275	5500	280	5600	325	6500
Toledo	405	8100	400	8000	350	7000
Bowling Green	550	11000	510	1020	470	9400
Lexington	120	2400	115	2300	175	3500

Location	Date	Customer	Hours	Billing
Columbus	April 06, 2005	Acme Mfg	50	1000
Columbus	April 23, 2005	Bower's Flowers	20	400
Columbus	May 14, 2005	Acme Mfg	35	700
Columbus	May 30, 2005	Specialty Inc.	75	1500
Columbus	June 12, 2005	eXen Design	100	2005

Figure 14-1   Representation of a drill-through.

Improvements and Changes in Microsoft Analysis Services 2005 for Drill-Through

Analysis Services 2000 generates one or many SQL queries to get drill-through results from the backend SQL data source. However, Analysis Service 2005 fetches the results directly from its MOLAP data storage; no SQL query is issued unless there are ROLAP partitions or ROLAP dimensions in the measure group. This provides a great performance advantage for drill-through queries. Note that the analysis server will combine fact table rows with the same dimension keys because they store in the OLAP system as one cell. You can achieve the same behavior as Analysis Service 2000 by adding a ROLAP dimension—especially a fact table dimension with a unique RowID column as the dimension key.

The `AllowDrillthrough` flag on a cube in Analysis Services 2000 is deprecated in Analysis Services 2005. User security settings will control drill-through. The administrator of Analysis Services 2005 can set allow/deny drill-through for each role on each cube. The administrator of Analysis Services 2005 can perform a drill-through (run a drill-through query) against any cube without any special settings on cubes. A drill-through query will return a security error if the user does not have drill-through rights on a specific cube.

In addition, the properties `DrillThroughFilter`, `DrillThroughForm`, and `DrillThroughJoin` in Analysis Services 2000 are no longer valid in Analysis Services 2005. The same functionality can be achieved by using the data source view.

A new action type—`DrillThrough` action—is introduced in Analysis Services 2005. The cube designer can set the drill-through return column set in Action designer.

MDX for Drill-Through I

A Drill-Through MDX query is simply a single-cell query that starts with `DrillThrough`. For example, for the Adventure Works cube, Internet sales Measures group, the following query will retrieve rows from Internet Sales in March 2004, from United States, and the product is Mountain Bikes:

```
DrillThrough
select
FROM
    [Adventure Works]
WHERE
(
    [Measures].[Internet Sales Amount],
    [Date].[Calendar].[Month].&[2004]&[3],
```

```
        [Geography].[Geography].[Country].&[United States]
        ,[Product].[Product Categories].[Subcategory].[Mountain Bikes]
)
```

Because the major syntactic requirement for a drill-through query is that no more than one member be specified for each axis, the following would result in the same rowset:

```
DRILLTHROUGH
select
{[Measures].[Internet Sales Amount]} on Axis(0),
{[Date].[Calendar].[Month].&[2004]&[3]} on Axis(1),
{[Geography].[Geography].[Country].&[United States]} on Axis(2),
{[Product].[Product Categories].[Subcategory].[Mountain Bikes]} on
Axis(3)
FROM
    [Adventure Works]
```

A drill-through can query a leaf-level cell or an aggregate cell for a base measure. You can only drill through a single cell. And you cannot start a drill-through from a cell related to a calculated member. If a default member in any of the dimensions is a calculated member, you must override it with a specific uncalculated member for that dimension as a result. For example, if you are using a calculated measure as the default measure, you must pick an arbitrary uncalculated measure (perhaps with `[Measures].Members.Item(0)`) for the drill-through query.

The type of dimension you drill through on does not make a difference. If you drill through a cell for a parent member in a parent-child hierarchy, all rows that contribute to that cell, including the cells of the children members, will be included in the result.

In Analysis Services 2005, if the drill measure belongs to a measure group, drill-through commands, by default, will return records for the querying measure group. Columns include all granularity attributes for all measure group dimensions, including referenced dimension and fact dimension. Columns also include all fact measures of that measure group. Only many-to-many dimension attributes are excluded from the default return column, because a single fact record can resolve to 0, 1, or many members in many-to-many dimension cases. A user can explicitly request dimension attributes not limited to granularity attributes in the return clause.

A new `Return` clause is introduced in Analysis Services 2005 to control the columns returned by a drill-through query. In the `Return` clause, the user can list the dimension attributes and measures. The following query will only return Date and Product style attributes and Internet Sales Amount and Tax Amount; in the query, `Product.Style` is not the granularity attribute and won't be returned by default.

```
DrillThrough
select (
    [Measures].[Internet Sales Amount],
    [Date].[Calendar].[Month].&[2004]&[3],
    [Geography].[Geography].[Country].&[United States]       ,
    [Product].[Product Categories].[Subcategory].[Mountain Bikes]
    ) on 0
from
    [Adventure Works]
Return
    [$Date].[Date],
    KEY([$Product].[Style]),
    [Internet Sales].[Internet Sales Amount],
    [Internet Sales].[Internet Tax Amount]
```

You may notice that we put $ before the dimension to reference the cube dimension, and the measures need to be specified with the measure group name in the Return clause. The KEY() function is supported to return the attribute key instead of name (default). Eight functions are supported in the Return clause:

Key(attr[, N]): Returns the Nth part of the composite key of the member. N by default is equal to 1.

Name(attr): Returns the name of the member. By default, the server will return the name.

MemberValue(attr): Returns the value of the member. This is the default.

Caption(attr): Returns the caption of the member.

UniqueName(attr): Returns the unique name of the member.

CustomRollup(attr): Returns the custom rollup expression of the member.

CustomRollupProperties(attr): Returns the custom rollup properties of the member.

UnaryOperator(attr): Returns the unary operator of the member.

Programmatic Aspects of Drill-Through

In Analysis Services 2005, a drill-through query always returns one rowset, no matter how many partitions are involved in the query. All rows from different partitions are combined. (An Analysis Services 2000 drill-through query can return one rowset, or it can return one rowset per partition involved.)

For a developer using managed code, ADOMD.NET has the functionality to execute both a multidimensional results query (ExecuteCellset) and a tabular results query (ExecuteReader). Although developers can use ADO.NET's OledbConnection and OledbCommand to execute the drill-through query just like any SQL query, using ADOMD.NET is more convenient and you are using one set of object models to perform all cube-related queries.

The OLEDB interface is unchanged from Analysis Services 2000 to Analysis Services 2005. Using OLE DB, when multiple partitions contribute to the result, they can be accessed as rowsets by retrieving an IMultipleResults object from the drill-through query instead of an IRowset object. A single IRowset object is retrieved from the query, and the resulting rowset contains the union of all columns with the union of all rows from the individual partitions accessed.

NOTE The OLE DB rowset(s) and records from ADOMDDataReader are read-only.

C# Code that executes a drill-through and loops through the resulting ADOMDDataReader.

```
string connectionString = "Provider = MSOLAP.3;Data
Source=localhost;Initial Catalog=Adventure Works DW";
AdomdConnection acCon = new AdomdConnection(connectionString);
try
{
  acCon.Open();
  using (AdomdCommand command = new AdomdCommand(
      @"DrillThrough
            select (
                [Measures].[Internet Sales Amount],
                [Date].[Calendar].[All],
                [Geography].[Geography].[Country].&[United States]
                ,[Product].[Product
Categories].[Subcategory].[Mountain Bikes]) on 0
            from
                [Adventure Works]
            Return [$Date].[Date],KEY([$Product].[Style]),[Internet
Sales].[Internet Sales Amount],
                    [Internet Sales].[Internet Tax Amount]
                ", acCon))
  {
    using (AdomdDataReader reader = command.ExecuteReader())
    {
      //output the column information
      DataTable schema = reader.GetSchemaTable();
      foreach (DataRow row in schema.Rows)
      {
```

```
          Console.Write(row[0]); //0 is ColumnName
          Console.Write(",");
        }
      Console.WriteLine();

      //output data columns
      while (reader.Read())
      {
        for (int i = 0; i < reader.FieldCount; i++)
        {
          Console.Write(reader[i]);
          Console.Write(",");
        }
        Console.WriteLine();
      }

    }
  }
}
finally
{
  acCon.Close();
}
```

If you replace ADOMDConnection, ADOMDCommand, and ADOMD-
DataReader with OledbConnection, OledbCommand, and Oledb-
DataReader, the sample code will still work, only this time the query will go
through the OLE DB layer instead of ADOMD.NET, which uses XML/A
directly.

MDX for Drill-Through II

As described earlier, a drill-through query in MDX is any query that returns a
single cell, does not use any calculated members, and begins with
DRILLTHROUGH. The general form is

```
DRILLTHROUGH
  [MAXROWS N]
SELECT
...
FROM Cube
[WHERE ...]
[RETURN Attributes, Functions of attributes and Measures]
```

It does not matter at all how dimensions map to query axes or to the slicer.
The MAXROWS option is followed by a positive integer and specifies the maximum number of records to retrieve. Note that you do not get the opportunity
to specify an ordering for the records, so the set returned will essentially be

arbitrary. Analysis Services 2005 honors the MAXROWS specification because the drill-through query is resolved inside the server and against its own data storage. In Analysis Services 2000, since the drill-through query is translated into an SQL query and executed against a relational database, if the underlying OLE DB provider does not support the DBPROP_MAXROWS property, then this value is ignored.

To avoid having a user inadvertently retrieve millions of records from the server, Analysis Services 2005 has a server property, OLAP \ Query \ DefaultDrillthroughMaxRows, which has a value of 10,000 by default. If a user does not specify the MAXROWS option in a query, this value will be used to retrieve a maximum of 10,000 fact rows for the query. The administrator can change the property.

In a drill-through query, although you cannot reference calculated members, you can reference items from named sets. For example, if a client application had created a set [Customer Set] as { [Customer].[Cust 007], [Customer].[Cust M] }, then the following would be perfectly valid:

```
DRILLTHROUGH
SELECT
FROM [Purchases]
WHERE ([Customer Set].Item (0))
```

Note that no WITH clause is available in a drill-through query, so you cannot define sets in the context of the query.

The Return option allows a user to specify the desired dimension attributes and measures (inside the same measure group) to be returned. Note that you need to put a $ before the dimension to specify a cube dimension, and a measure group name before measures. Eight functions (KEY, NAME, CAPTION UNIQUENAME, and the like) are supported to get different values from the attribute.

The FIRSTROWSET option in Analysis Services 2000 is deprecated because Analysis Services 2005 always returns one rowset with rows from all partitions.

Drill-Through Security

Drill-through security is controlled by roles' drill-through settings on cubes. Cell security is also honored for drill-through queries. If a user cannot read some data using an MDX query, a drill-through query will restrict the user access to the cells in the same manner. Dimension security will be honored, too. A drill-through query will succeed and filter out all secured records if the user drills through a higher-level cell, while the lower-level dimension members are secured.

Using Actions

Actions are a feature that allows a string to be generated by the analysis system along with a suggestion as to how it should be used by a client application. This allows the developer of the analysis system to include application functionality that a relatively generic client can invoke. An application developer can also include functionality that is very specific to the application. An action is sort of like a stored procedure that is limited to returning a string. Like a calculated member, every action is defined against a particular cube. The string that the action returns can be the result of any MDX string expression that can be invoked against the cube. The action can also be directed against some context in the cube: the entire cube, a dimension, a level, a member of a dimension, a cell within the cube, or a set defined for the cube.

The main part of an action is simply a string expression, expressed in MDX. Any MDX expression that results in a string can be used, which includes simple operators and functions that return strings and any combinations that result in strings as well. The result is a single string, as if it was the result of calculating a single cell in a query.

Somewhat surprisingly, only a little language aspect is used to invoke an action; they are not invoked like MDX commands and queries are. Mostly, invoking an action requires a client application to prepare a data structure and use it as a means of restricting the rows. In OLE DB, you prepare a set of restrictions on the schema rowset for actions (a table interface used to retrieve metadata). In ADOMD.NET, you prepare an array of restriction values for the Actions schema recordset. One of the restrictions is the context for the action, which can be a string identifying a dimension, a level, a member, a tuple, or a set name. (When you define an action to use on a set, note that the set name must be passed in when obtaining the action string. You cannot pass in a set expression instead of a set name.) We'll look at C# code for invoking actions using ADOMD.NET later in this section. (We won't elaborate on OLE DB for OLAP programming. If you are familiar with OLE DB and a suitable language like C++, the techniques for invoking actions using OLE DB for OLAP are quite similar.)

What Can You Do with an Action?

The strings returned by the execution of an action can be interpreted in a variety of ways. The point, however, is to try to use some result from the analysis system to influence the world outside of itself, beyond just contributing a number to a graph or spreadsheet. An action type associated with each action indicates to a client application how to treat the result string. Table 14-1 lists the types of action types supported by Analysis Services 2005.

Two of the predefined action types are connected with Web usage. The first, URL, results in a string that should be suitable for use as a browser's URL. For example, it could be the name of a Web page, or the URL of an Active Server Pages (ASP) or Common Gateway Interface (CGI) script adorned with one or more arguments to the script. For example, the expression

```
"http://www.dsslab.com/search.dll?" +
Product.Product.CurrentMember.Properties ("SKU ID")
```

will concatenate the URL of the search DLL with the SKU ID property associated with the product context's member, perhaps producing the following as a result:

```
http://www.dsslab.com/search.dll?WUY3391
```

The second type, HTML, provides interesting possibilities. For example, an action directed against a set can build a HyperText Markup Language (HTML) table of member names and default cell values (identified through the default members of all other dimensions) with the following:

```
"<HTML><TABLE>" +
"<TR><TD>Name</TD><TD>Value</TD></TR>" +
"<TR><TD>" +
Generate (
  ActionParameterSet,
  ActionParameterSet.Current.Item(0).Properties ("Caption") +
    "</TD><TD>" +
    iif (Not IsEmpty ([Measures].CurrentMember),
      CStr ([Measures].CurrentMember),
      ""
    )
  , "</TD></TR><TR><TD>"
) +
"</TD></TR></TABLE></HTML>"
```

This uses the string version of `Generate()` to emit rows of the table; for each row, a column of member captions (appropriately localized, if set up in the database!) and the associated values is produced. We use the `[Measures]`
`.CurrentMember.Value` as a proxy for "current cell"; current cell has no syntax, so we simply reference the current member of one of the cube's dimensions, and every cube always has a dimension called Measures. Because `CStr()` will return an error if the underlying value is NULL, we test for the cell value being empty first and substitute an empty string if the cell is NULL. Note the use of the special set name `ActionParameterSet`. For an action that is targeted at sets, the name of the set to run it on may not be known when the action is created. `ActionParameterSet` is set to the contents of the set that the action is actually invoked on.

Table 14-1   Action Types Supported by Analysis Services 2005

CODE	MEANING
URL	The resulting string is a URL, preferably launched using an Internet browser.
HTML	The resulting string is HTML. The string should be rendered using an Internet browser, usually by saving it to a file first. A whole script may be executed as part of the generated HTML.
STATEMENT	The resulting string is a statement that needs to be executed in OLE DB or OLE DB for OLAP. In OLE DB, set the `ICommand:SetText` method of a command object to the string and call the `ICommand:Execute` method. In ADOMD.NET, set the `CommandText` of a command or connection object and call `Execute` on it. If the command does not succeed, an error should be returned to the client application.
DATASET	The resulting string is an MDX query to execute. In OLE DB, set the `ICommand:SetText` method of a command object to the string and call the `ICommand:Execute` method with a requested interface ID (`IID`) of `IDataset`. The client application should allow the user to browse or manipulate the returned dataset.
ROWSET	Similar to `DATASET`. In OLE DB, instead of requesting an `IID` of `IDataset`, the client application should request an `IID` of `IRowset`. In ADO.NET, the result string should be used to set the `CommandText` of a `Recordset` object, and that `Recordset` should be opened against a connection. The client application should allow the user to browse or manipulate the returned rowset.
COMMANDLINE	The resulting string is a command line. The client application should execute it.
PROPRIETARY	The resulting string is meaningful to some other application. A client application should not display or execute the action unless it has specific knowledge of the specific action. A proprietary action is not returned to the client application unless the client application explicitly asks for it by setting the appropriate restriction on the application name.
REPORT	The resulting string is a URL connecting to a Microsoft Reporting Service server. A client application can display the results using an Internet browser. This action has customized properties such as `ReportServer`, `Path`, `ReportParameter`, and `ReportFormatParameter`. (This action type is new in Analysis Services 2005.)

(continued)

Table 14-1 *(continued)*

CODE	MEANING
DRILLTHROUGH	The resulting string is a drill-through statement that needs to be executed against the server to return a predefined drill-through rowset. User can define proper drill-through return columnsets and MaximumRows in the DrillThrough action, and the server will return the proper DrillThrough query for that action. (This action type is new in Analysis Services 2005.)

An example of code (in C#) that would invoke a Cells-scoped action and retrieve the resulting content is shown below. It assumes that a cube is named [Adventure Works] and it queries for the DrillThrough action type for Cell ([Measures].[Internet Sales Amount]), and it retrieves the action without regard to the invocation type. Note that none of the names (CATALOG NAME, CUBE NAME) in the restriction are enclosed by brackets, []; if any of them were, the name would not be recognized and the action content would not be retrieved!

Three of the other types—STATEMENT, DATASET, and ROWSET—are geared for use with the client's OLE DB and OLE DB for OLAP connections. The result of an action of these types should be capable of being executed as a database query or command would be (for example, CREATE MEMBER, UPDATE CUBE, DRILLTHROUGH SELECT, and so on). The OLE DB for OLAP specification does not specify whether the command is to be presented as an OLAP command or an SQL command; in general, you should be cautious in your assumptions and know what your client applications are going to do. A DATASET action is only useful against an OLE DB for OLAP or ADOMD.NET connection, but ROWSET or STATEMENT might be useful against a relational OLE DB or ADO.NET connection as well.

Here is C# code to retrieve a cell drill-through action's results:

```
string connectionString = "Provider = MSOLAP.3;Data
Source=localhost;Initial Catalog=Adventure Works DW";
AdomdConnection acCon = new AdomdConnection(connectionString);
try
{
  acCon.Open();
  DataSet ds = acCon.GetSchemaDataSet(AdomdSchemaGuid.Actions,
      new object[]{
        "Adventure Works DW",    //CATALOG_NAME
        null,                    //  SCHEMA_NAME
        "Adventure Works",       // CUBE_NAME
        null,                    // ACTION_NAME
        256,                     //ACTION_TYPE 256 DrillThrough
        "([Measures].[Internet Sales Amount])",   //COORDINATE  Cell
        6                                  //COORDINATE_TYPE  Cell
      });
```

```
    DataTable dtDrillthroughActions = ds.Tables[0];
    StringBuilder sbSchemaRow = new StringBuilder();
    foreach (DataRow dr in dtDrillthroughActions.Rows)
    {
       sbSchemaRow.Length = 0;   //clean the stringbuilder
       sbSchemaRow.Append("CATALOG_NAME").Append(":
").Append(dr[0]).Append("\n");
       sbSchemaRow.Append("SCHEMA_NAME").Append(":
").Append(dr[1]).Append("\n");
       sbSchemaRow.Append("CUBE_NAME").Append(":
").Append(dr[2]).Append("\n");
       sbSchemaRow.Append("ACTION_NAME").Append(":
").Append(dr[3]).Append("\n");
       sbSchemaRow.Append("ACTION_TYPE").Append(":
").Append(dr[4]).Append("\n");
       sbSchemaRow.Append("COORDINATE").Append(":
").Append(dr[5]).Append("\n");
       sbSchemaRow.Append("COORDINATE_TYPE").Append(":
").Append(dr[6]).Append("\n");
       sbSchemaRow.Append("INVOCATION").Append(":
").Append(dr[7]).Append("\n");
       Console.WriteLine(sbSchemaRow.ToString());
       Console.WriteLine("-----------------------------------------------");
    }

}
finally
{
   acCon.Close();
}
```

The COMMANDLINE action type indicates that the client should execute the returned string as an operating system command. Use of this type may require you to be aware of which operating system your clients are running and applications that they have installed.

Actions whose type is PROPRIETARY are meant to be executed by a particular client program. In order to execute a proprietary action, a client must fill in the name of the application in the APPLICATION_NAME restriction that is passed to the OLE DB schema rowset. Third-party browser tools may publish specifications for actions that they will accept, and in addition you can define your own. If you are developing a client that may use proprietary actions, take care to create an application name that is unlikely to collide with anyone else's. Incorporating your company's name ("DSS Lab.Special Browser") increases the odds of uniqueness, and using the string form of a GUID virtually ensures uniqueness along with the potential for factoring action functionality by the GUIDs of objects that know how to interpret the action.

One class of very useful actions requires that the statements be presented to an RDBMS connection. An MDX query could result in a set of rows; let's take a look at following statement:

```
INSERT INTO MyTable
SELECT * FROM OpenQuery (
  OurOLAPServer,
  'SELECT
  { [Measures].[Calculated Potential] } on columns,
  { [Current Customer Set] } on rows
  FROM PredictionCube'
)
```

The statement could transfer data calculated or filtered by the OLAP system into a table for use in preparing a mailing list in the RDBMS. However, the overall statement would need to be presented to an RDBMS connection. This could be addressed by using the Proprietary action type instead, although for more than one commercial client to support the related application, the name would need to indicate that RDBMS statements are the purpose of this action.

Targets for Actions

Each action can be targeted against a different region or element of a cube, as described in Table 14-2.

Table 14-2   Action Types

SCOPE OF ACTION	APPLICATION
Cube	Actions that are global to a cube (not to be parameterized).
Dimension	Actions that apply across a dimension, but are not defined specifically for any member(s) or level(s) within it. The dimension is supplied when the action is invoked.
Level	Actions that apply to an entire level of a dimension, but are not defined specifically for any member in that dimension. The dimension and level are supplied when the action is invoked.
Member	Actions that apply to a specific member of a dimension or a level of a dimension. The dimension and member are supplied when the action is invoked.
Cell	Actions that apply to a specific cell. One or more members that define the cell are supplied when the action is invoked (the remaining dimensions are set to their default members for the user role invoking the action).
Set	Actions that apply to a named set. The name of the set is supplied when the action is invoked. In order to allow the action to be generic with respect to the actual set, the name ActionParameterSet is used in the action expression to refer to the set that is the argument.

> **WEB SERVER SECURITY NOTE FOR COMMANDLINE ACTIONS**
>
> If you are providing a Web interface to OLAP and are running the PivotTable Service on the web server, you should very carefully evaluate how you run actions of the COMMANDLINE type, if you do this at all. Actions are useful in the context of a web server, because the logic for the action remains on the server. However, executing a command on the server raises significant security concerns. If a client of the web server (for example, a browser) can pass MDX to be executed, it can pass a CREATE ACTION statement to the server that creates a COMMANDLINE action and then request execution of the action.

When an action is invoked, the context for the action starts with all dimensions at their default members. If the scope of the action is Member or Cell, then the member(s) provided as the argument to the action will alter this default context. For example, in a typical cube, the default member for every nonmeasures dimension is the all member, and the default measure is the first one listed in the cube definition. A cube-scoped action that returned a constant string would be independent of any members, whereas a cube-scoped action defined by

```
[Time].[Calendar].CurrentMember.UniqueName + ": " + CStr
(Measures.CurrentMember.Value)
```

would return a string like [Time]. [Calendar]. [All]: 948235350. If the same expression was used for a cell-scoped action and it was invoked with a coordinate of ([Time].[Calendar].[Quarter].[Q3, 2000], [Measures].[Profit], [Department].[Department].[Clothing]), the string returned might be [Time].[Calendar].[Quarter].[Q3, 2000]: 22123.95.

Defining an Action

Normally, in addition to BI Workbench, developers for Analysis Services 2005 are encouraged to use AMO to create action objects and update those objects on the Analysis Services server. The AMO object model has two specific Action classes, ReportAction and DrillThroughAction, with new properties that are only valid for each action type.

Following is an example of the C# code using AMO to add ReportAction and a URL action to the Adventure Works cube:

```
Server serverObject = new Server();
    try
    {
```

```
        serverObject.Connect("Localhost");
        Database dbObject = serverObject.Databases.GetByName("Adventure
Works DW");
        Cube cubeObject = dbObject.Cubes.GetByName("Adventure Works");

        //Add report Action Object
        if (cubeObject.Actions.ContainsName("NewReportAction") )
        {    //if the object is already exists, remove it

cubeObject.Actions.RemoveAt(cubeObject.Actions.IndexOfName("NewReportAct
ion"),true);
        }

        ReportAction reportActionObject = new
ReportAction("NewReportAction","NewReportAction");
        reportActionObject.TargetType =
ActionTargetType.AttributeMembers;
        reportActionObject.Target = "[Product].[Category]";
        reportActionObject.Description = " This action will launch a
report comparing sales reasons for a given product category.";
        reportActionObject.Caption = "\"Sales Reason Comparisons for \"
+ [Product].[Category].CurrentMember.Member_Caption + \"...\"";
        reportActionObject.CaptionIsMdx = true;

        //Report Action spefic properties
        reportActionObject.ReportServer = "localhost";
        reportActionObject.Path = "ReportServer?/AdventureWorks Sample
Reports/Sales Reason Comparisons";

reportActionObject.ReportFormatParameters.Add("rs:Command","Render");

reportActionObject.ReportFormatParameters.Add("rs:Renderer","HTML5");

reportActionObject.ReportParameters.Add("ProductCategory","UrlEscapeFrag
ment( [Product].[Category].CurrentMember.UniqueName)");
        //have to set type even it should be automatically set
        reportActionObject.Type = ActionType.Report;
        cubeObject.Actions.Add(reportActionObject);

        //Add report Action Object
        if (cubeObject.Actions.ContainsName("NewURLAction"))
        {    //if the object is already exists, remove it

cubeObject.Actions.RemoveAt(cubeObject.Actions.IndexOfName("NewURLAction
"), true);
        }

//Add URL Action Object
        StandardAction stdActionObject = new
StandardAction("NewURLAction", "NewURLAction");
        stdActionObject.Description = "This action will display the map
for a given city.";
```

```
        stdActionObject.Caption = "\"View Map for \" +
[Geography].[City].CurrentMember.Member_Caption + \"...\"";
        stdActionObject.CaptionIsMdx = true;

        //Add translation
        stdActionObject.Translations.Add(1036, "Carte de la Ville");
        stdActionObject.TargetType = ActionTargetType.AttributeMembers;
        stdActionObject.Target = "[Geography].[City]";
        stdActionObject.Type = ActionType.Url;
        stdActionObject.Expression =
"\"http://maps.msn.com/home.aspx?plce1=\" +
[Geography].[City].CurrentMember.Name";
        cubeObject.Actions.Add(stdActionObject);

        cubeObject.Update();

    }
    finally
    {
        serverObject.Disconnect();
    }
```

Although users can define actions using MDX CREATE ACTION statements,
the MDX CREATE ACTION statement is only for backward compatibility, and it
will keep working in Analysis Services 2005.

The general form of a CREATE ACTION statement is

```
CREATE ACTION CubeName.ActionName FOR Target
AS 'MDXExpression'
[, TYPE = 'ActionType']
[, INVOCATION = 'ActionInvocation']
[, APPLICATION = 'ApplicationName']
[, DESCRIPTION = 'Description']
[, CAPTION = '<MDX expression>']
```

Using the ALTER CUBE syntax, it is

```
ALTER CUBE CubeName
  CREATE ACTION ActionName FOR Target
  AS 'MDXExpression'
  [, TYPE = 'ActionType']
  [, INVOCATION = 'ActionInvocation']
  [, APPLICATION = 'ApplicationName']
  [, DESCRIPTION = 'Description']
  [, CAPTION = '<MDX expression>']
```

If the CREATE ACTION statement is held in the Commands collection of a
server-side cube or cube role, or if it is in the COMMANDS section of a local cube
definition, you can use CURRENTCUBE in place of the cube name because the
target is obvious.

```
CREATE ACTION [Budgeting].[An Action]
FOR CELLS
AS
' "\\CentralServer\Processes\MarkCurrent.EXE " +
  Customers.CurrentMember.Properties ("KEY") + " " +
  Time.CurrentMember.Properties ("KEY") + " " +
  CStr (Measures.CurrentMember.Value)
'
, TYPE = 'COMMANDLINE'
, INVOCATION = 'BATCH'
, DESCRIPTION = 'Mark projections as current for this customer/time'
, CAPTION =
'"Mark projection current for " + Customers.CurrentMember.Properties
("CAPTION") + ", " Time.CurrentMember.Properties ("CAPTION")
'
/* possible result:

\\CentralServer\Processes\MarkCurrent.EXE TX_005 200143 65000.75

*/
```

Programmatic Aspects of Actions

You have seen the C# code sample that retrieves the schema rowset for the drill-through action in the previous section. We'll talk a little more about that now. In order to invoke an action (as well as to find out what actions are available to invoke in the first place), you need to restrict the Actions schema rowset. The lengthy `Array()` construct in the previous example contained a set of restrictions. Table 14-3 shows the set of restriction columns (also contained in the OLE DB for OLAP and Analysis Services documentation).

The codes for coordinate types are listed in Table 14-4. The codes for action types are listed in Table 14-5. They can be OR'd together or added together (except for the zero no-restriction value) to obtain multiple types of actions in the resulting rowset.

Table 14-3   Restriction Columns

COLUMN	REQUIRED/OPTIONAL	TYPE
CATALOG_NAME	Optional	String
SCHEMA_NAME	Optional	String
CUBE_NAME	Required	String
ACTION_NAME	Optional	String
ACTION_TYPE	Optional	Integer
COORDINATE	Required	String

Table 14-3 *(continued)*

COLUMN	REQUIRED/OPTIONAL	TYPE
COORDINATE_TYPE	Required	Integer
INVOCATION	Optional	Integer

Table 14-4   Target Scopes and Numerical Codes

COORDINATE TYPE	NUMERICAL CODE
CUBE	1
CELLS	2
HIERARCHY	3
LEVEL	4
DIMENSIONMEMBERS	5
HIERARCHYMEMBERS	6
LEVELMEMBERS	7
ATTRIBUTEMEMBERS	8

Note that in Analysis Services 2005, the target type numbers are different than in Analysis Services 2000.

Table 14-5   Action Types and Numerical Codes

ACTION TYPE	NUMERICAL CODE
(no restriction)	0
URL	1
HTML	2
STATEMENT	4
DATASET	8
ROWSET	16
COMMANDLINE	32
PROPRIETARY	64
REPORT	128
DRILLTHROUGH	256

The codes for invocation types are listed in Table 14-6. We haven't discussed invocation types yet, but we will later.

Table 14-6   Invocation Types and Numerical Codes

INVOCATION TYPE	NUMERICAL CODE
(no restriction)	0
INTERACTIVE	1
ON_OPEN	2
BATCH	3

Table 14-7 Actions Schema Rowset Return Columns

CATALOG_NAME
SCHEMA_NAME
CUBE_NAME
ACTION_NAME
ACTION_TYPE
COORDINATE
COORDINATE_TYPE
ACTION_CAPTION
DESCRIPTION
CONTENT
APPLICATION
INVOCATION

For standard actions, the content returns the string of the command (depends on action type) after the MDX resolution. For the report and drill-through actions, the content string is defined by the properties in the following two tables, since they have custom properties.

Report Action Custom Properties

ReportServer	The name of the report server
Path	The path exposed by the report server
ReportParameters	Extra parameters for the report
ReportFormatParameters	Extra parameters for the report format

The content generated by Analysis Services is

```
http://ReportServer/Path&ReportParameter1Name=
ReportParameter1Value& ReportParameter2Name=
ReportParameter2Value.......&
ReportFormatParameter1Name=ReportFormatParameter1Value&
ReportFormatParameter2Name=ReportFormatParameter2Value ...
```

Drill-Through Custom Properties

`Default`	A Boolean value to specify if this action is the default drill-through action
`Columns`	A column collection to specify columns returned by the drill-through query
`MaximumRows`	Maximum return rows

The content generated by Analysis Services is

```
DRILLTHROUGH
SELECT
     (COORDINATE Inputted in Schema rowset query) on 0
FROM CUBE
RETURN (COLUMNS)
```

Following is an example of the C# code to invoke a URL Action:

```
string connectionString = "Provider = MSOLAP.3;Data
Source=localhost;Initial Catalog=Adventure Works DW";
AdomdConnection acCon = new AdomdConnection(connectionString);
try
{
  acCon.Open();
  DataSet ds = acCon.GetSchemaDataSet(AdomdSchemaGuid.Actions,
     new object[]{
  "Adventure Works DW",    //CATALOG_NAME
  null,                 //  SCHEMA_NAME
  "Adventure Works",       // CUBE_NAME
  null,                 // ACTION_NAME
  1,                //ACTION_TYPE URL
  "[Geography].[City].[Seattle]",     //COORDINATE  attribute member
  8                         //COORDINATE_TYPE  attribute
member
}
     );

  DataTable dtDrillthroughActions = ds.Tables[0];
```

```
   foreach (DataRow dr in dtDrillthroughActions.Rows)
   {
     ProcessStartInfo psi = new ProcessStartInfo();
     psi.FileName = "IEXPLORE.exe";
     psi.Arguments = dr["Content"].ToString();
     Process.Start(psi);
   }

}
finally
{
  acCon.Close();
}
```

Dropping an Action

You can use AMO to drop actions using the following code:

```
//Add report Action Object
if (cubeObject.Actions.ContainsName("NewReportAction") )
{   //if the object already exists, remove it

cubeObject.Actions.RemoveAt(cubeObject.Actions.IndexOfName("NewReportAct
ion"),true);
        }
```

As with other created objects, the client can drop actions at any time. Two variations on the syntax for this are

```
ALTER CUBE CubeName
   DROP ACTION ActionName

DROP ACTION CubeName.ActionName
```

Using KPIs

KPIs (key performance indicators) track the performance of significant business metrics. Analysis Services 2005 introduces the support for cube KPIs. Many client tools such as Microsoft Scorecard Manager understand and display the KPIs in intuitive graphical reports.

Analysis Services 2005 provides a framework to store the metadata of a set of standard KPI data metrics, (Value, Goal, Status, Trend, and Weight). Users can specify each data metric's MDX expression, and the recommended graphical representation for KPI status and trend. Users can also define the display folders and relationship between KPIs to inform the UI components how to display those KPIs in folders and the parent-child relationship. Analysis Services 2005 also supports a set of convenient KPI MDX functions to help application developers to access the KPI metrics. Applications can query KPI metadata via SchemaRowset and get KPI values through MDX queries.

Creating KPI

A cube can contain a set of KPIs. A KPI definition includes the following attributes. Developers can use AMO to programmatically create, modify, and delete KPIs in cubes. Table 14-8 lists the properties for a KPI.

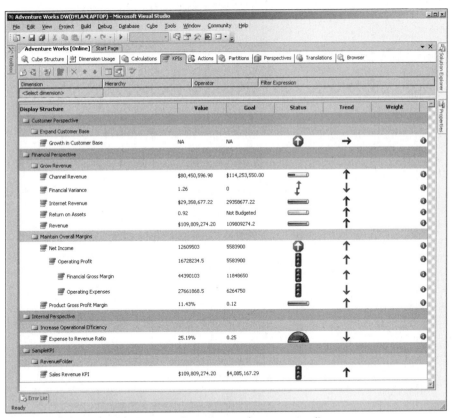

Figure 14-2 Sample KPI report from BI Development Studio.

Table 14-8 KPI Properties

PROPERTY	DESCRIPTION
Name	The name of the KPI.
ID	The ID of the KPI.
Description	The description of the KPI.
Translation	A set of translations for the caption of the KPI.
DisplayFolder	A display folder. This can be used by client applications to determine presentations of KPIs.
KPI-Specific Properties	
Value	An MDX expression that returns the actual value of the KPI. It is mandatory for a KPI.
Goal	An MDX expression that returns the goal of the KPI.
Status	An MDX expression that returns the status of the KPI. To best represent the value graphically, we suggest that it be a normalized expression returning values between -1 and 1.
Trend	An MDX expression that returns the trend of the KPI over time. We suggest that it be a normalized expression returning values between -1 and 1.
Weight	An MDX expression that returns the weight of the KPI. If a KPI has a parent KPI, you can define the weight to control the contribution of this KPI to its parent.
StatusGraphic	A string showing the recommended graphical representation for the status. Such as "Status Arrow – Ascending" or "Road Signs."
TrendGraphic	A string of the recommended graphical representation for the trend.
CurrentTimeMember	An MDX expression that defines the current time member that is relevant for the KPI. This allows different KPIs to have different time members.
AssociatedMeasureGroupID	The associated measure group for the KPI. This is used to specify the dimensionality of the KPI. If not specified, the KPI will be dimensioned by all measure groups. The referenced measure group must exist in the cube.
ParentKPIID	The parent of the KPI, allowing KPIs to be organized in a hierarchical manner. The referenced KPI must exist in the cube.

Here is C# sample code for adding new KPI using AMO:

```
Server serverObject = new Server();
try
{
  serverObject.Connect("Localhost");
  Database dbObject = serverObject.Databases.GetByName("Adventure Works
DW");
  Cube cubeObject = dbObject.Cubes.GetByName("Adventure Works");

  if(cubeObject.Kpis.ContainsName("NewKPI"))
  {
    cubeObject.Kpis.RemoveAt(cubeObject.Kpis.IndexOfName("NewKPI"),
true);
  }

  Microsoft.AnalysisServices.Kpi newKpi = new
Microsoft.AnalysisServices.Kpi("NewKPI","NewKPI");
  newKpi.Value = "( [Account].[Accounts].&[47],
[Scenario].[Scenario].&[1], [Measures].[Amount] )";
  newKpi.Goal = "( [Account].[Accounts].&[47],
[Scenario].[Scenario].&[2], [Measures].[Amount] )";
  newKpi.Status = "KpiValue ( \"Net Income\" )/KpiGoal ( \"Net Income\"
)";
  newKpi.Trend = "KpiValue( \"Net Income\" ) - (KpiValue ( \"Net
Income\" ),ParallelPeriod([Date].[Fiscal].[Fiscal
Year],1,[Date].[Fiscal].CurrentMember))";

  newKpi.DisplayFolder = "Financial Perspective\\Maintain Overall
Margins";
  newKpi.StatusGraphic = "Standard Arrow";
  newKpi.TrendGraphic = "Standard Arrow";

  cubeObject.Kpis.Add(newKpi);
  cubeObject.Update();
}
finally
{
  serverObject.Disconnect();
}
```

Under the hood, Analysis Services 2005 creates calculated members on the measure dimension, for each KPI metric (Value, Goal, Status, Trend, and Weight). The only exception is that if the expression of a metric directly references a measure, the server directly uses the measure instead of creating a new calculated measure.

The calculated measure's name is <Kpi Name> + ' ' + <Component: Value, goal etc>. The userss need to be careful with KPI names to avoid potential name collisions with regular measures. The KPI related calculated measures are treated exactly the same as any other hidden calculated member.

Users can access them in MDX directly by using the calculated measure's name or by using the new KPI functions discussed in next section. The KPI metric's MDX expression definition can reference other KPIs' metrics or even others of its own metrics by using the calculated measure name or KPI*xxx* functions. We have included KPI function samples in the previous code example.

The NewKPI KPI, which we created using the previous program, will create a calculated measure like the following for its Value metric:

```
Create Member CurrentCube.[Measures].[NewKPI Value]
AS([Account].[Accounts].&[47],[Scenario].[Scenario].&[1],
[Measures].[Amount] )
```

The ParentKpiID property for a KPI is used purely for the purpose of organizing the KPIs. For example, Figure 14-2 demonstrates the KPI organization with Net Income as the parent of Operating Profit, and Operating Profit as the parent of Financial Gross Margin and Operating Expenses. Unlike the parent-child hierarchy, this parent-child relationship does not impose any aggregation rules, and the parent KPI does not get the value from child KPIs by default. However, it is common for the parent KPI metric MDX expression to reference the child KPI's value or weight to get its own number.

Following is an example of a parent KPI status definition for Revenue. Suppose the Revenue KPI has two children (Revenue Per HeadCount) and (Revenue Growth).

```
((KPIStatus([Revenue per Headcount]) * KPIWeight([Revenue per
Headcount])) + (KPIStatus([Revenue growth]) * KPIWeight([Revenue
growth])))) / (KPIWeight([Revenue per Headcount]) + KPIWeight([Revenue
growth]))
```

MDX KPI Function

Analysis Services 2005 introduces several new KPI member functions. All functions take a KPI name string as the input parameter and return the calculated measure member (or the measure member) corresponding to the KPI metric. KPICurrentTimeMember will return the member on time dimension for the KPI.

KPIValue (<KPI Name>)	Return value member for the KPI
KPIGoal (<KPI Name>)	Return Goal member for the KPI
KPIStatus (<KPI Name>)	Return Status member for the KPI
KPITrend (<KPI Name>)	Return Trend member for the KPI
KPIWeight (<KPI Name>)	Return Weight member for the KPI
KPICurrentTimeMember (<KPI Name>)	Return the time member for the KPI

NOTE For security reasons, especially the risk of MDX injection, applications supporting KPIs or in general Analysis Services 2005 should not directly construct MDX queries from user input. The input in the following example should be replaced with a parameterized query (there is a full sample in the next section.)

Suppose that the `KPIname` is a user input string:

```
//Code with MDX injection problem.
string commandText = @"SELECT { KPIValue("+KPIname+") } ON COLUMNS FROM
[Adventure works]";
```

This should be replaced with:

```
string commandText = @"SELECT { StrToMember(@KPIParameter)} ON COLUMNS
FROM [Adventure works]";
```

Then you can include the user input in `@KPIParameter`.

Using KPI

A user can query a KPI schema rowset to get the metadata of a cube's KPIs. Table 14-9 lists the schema rowset for KPI metadata. For the `KPI_Metrics` columns, such as `KPI_VALUE`, `KPI_GOAL`, and so on, the server returns the unique name of the created calculated measures.

Table 14-9

COLUMN	DESCRIPTION
CATALOG_NAME	Source database.
SCHEMA_NAME	Not supported for KPIs.
CUBE_NAME	Parent cube for KPI.
MEASUREGROUP_NAME	The associated measure group for the KPI. This is used to specify the dimensionality of the KPI. The default value is <NULL>. If <NULL>, the KPI will be dimensioned by all measure groups.
KPI_NAME	Name of KPI.
KPI_CAPTION	
KPI_VALUE	The unique name of the member in the measures dimension for the KPI value.

(continued)

Table 4-9 *(continued)*

COLUMN	DESCRIPTION
KPI_GOAL	The unique name of the member in the measures dimension for the KPI goal. NULL if there is no goal defined.
KPI_STATUS	The unique name of the member in the measures dimension for the KPI status. NULL if there is no status defined.
KPI_STATUS_GRAPHIC	This is the default graphical representation.
KPI_TREND	The unique name of the member in the measures dimension for the KPI trend. NULL if there is no trend defined.
KPI_TREND_GRAPHIC	Default graphical representation.
KPI_WEIGHT	The unique name of the member in the measures dimension for the KPI weight. NULL if there is no weight defined.
KPI_CURRENT_TIME_MEMBER	The unique name of the member in the time dimension that defines the temporal context of the KPI. NULL if there is no time member defined.
KPI_DESCRIPTION	Textual description of the metric.
KPI_DISPLAY_FOLDER	Slash-delimited categorization structure such as "Category\Goal\Metric." This can be used by client applications to determine the presentation of the catalog of KPIs to users. This can also be completely arbitrary.

Alternatively, ADOMD.NET has native support for KPIs. It has a Kpi class, and you can access the KPI via the CubeObject's Kpi collection. The properties of a KPI can be retrieved by Kpi.Properties("KPI_xxx"). The following is the code example of accessing KPI via ADOMD.NET and send KPI MDX queries using a parameterized MDX query. Since KPI metrics are nothing but calculated measures, the query execution part is exactly the same as in regular MDX queries.

```
connectionString = "Provider = MSOLAP.3;Data Source=localhost;Initial
Catalog=Adventure Works DW";
AdomdConnection acCon = new AdomdConnection(connectionString);
try
{
```

```
   acCon.Open();
   CubeDef cubeObject = acCon.Cubes["Adventure Works"];
   foreach (Microsoft.AnalysisServices.AdomdClient.Kpi cubeApi in
cubeObject.Kpis)
   {
      string commandText = @"SELECT { strtomember(@Value),
strtomember(@Goal), strtomember(@Status), strtomember(@Trend) }
      ON COLUMNS FROM [" + cubeObject.Name + "]";
      AdomdCommand command = new AdomdCommand(commandText, acCon);
      command.Parameters.Clear();
      command.Parameters.Add(new AdomdParameter("Value",
kpi.Properties["KPI_VALUE"].Value));
      command.Parameters.Add(new AdomdParameter("Goal",
kpi.Properties["KPI_GOAL"].Value));
      command.Parameters.Add(new AdomdParameter("Status",
kpi.Properties["KPI_STATUS"].Value));
      command.Parameters.Add(new AdomdParameter("Trend",
kpi.Properties["KPI_TREND"].Value));
      CellSet cellset = command.ExecuteCellSet();

      Debug.WriteLine("KPI Name:" + kpi.Name);
      Debug.WriteLine("Value:" + cellset.Cells[0].FormattedValue);
      Debug.WriteLine("Goal:" + cellset.Cells[1].FormattedValue);
      Debug.WriteLine("Status:" + cellset.Cells[2].FormattedValue);
      Debug.WriteLine("Trend:" + cellset.Cells[3].FormattedValue);
    //Code with MDX injection problem.
    //string commandText = @"SELECT { KPIValue("+KPIname+") } ON COLUMNS
FROM [Adventure works]";
   }
}
finally
{
  acCon.Close();
}
```

Summary

This chapter has been devoted to three topics: drill-through queries, actions, and KPIs. Drill-through queries are very simple MDX expressions with great utility for exploring underlying data. Actions can provide an end user with additional application functionality. Actions make use of MDX string expressions to provide their results, so understanding the MDX string functions available can be important. KPIs present a metadata framework for applications to easily define, query, and retrieve key metrics from an OLAP database. In the next chapter, we will chage gears and look at client programming basics.

CHAPTER 15

Client Programming Basics

We've spent the majority of this book describing the use of MDX without very much discussion on how a client program issues MDX and retrieves results from a query. As with SQL, we can consider data structures and analyses in the abstract, but to bring a system to a user, we do need some code. This chapter will briefly introduce programming issues related to the use of MDX. Our point is not to construct a full-fledged client browser, but rather to expose you to bread-and-butter issues that every type of client application may need to deal with.

Since the first edition of this book, support for MDX has broadened significantly beyond Microsoft's OLE DB for OLAP and ADOMD. Most naturally, it has extended into XML for Analysis, the successor to OLE DB for OLAP based on the Web services model. Note OLE DB for OLAP and XML for Analysis are distinct standards with differing overseers. As well, because MDX was first proposed as part of OLE DB for OLAP, the MDX specification resides within the OLE DB for OLAP documentation. You will not find any documentation on MDX within the XMLA for Analysis documentation.

With the advent of Microsoft's .NET, ADOMD has spawned ADOMD.NET, a Microsoft .NET class library for working with XML for Analysis within the .NET environment.

More exciting is that a handful of vendors have added MDX support to their own proprietary and open APIs and integrated the language into the core of their own multidimensional database engines: Hyperion Solutions via their C

API, MIS AG via XMLA, and SAP AG via RFC/BAPI. This is an important shift because, as an MDX developer, you need to be aware of the challenges up front if you wish to write MDX that functions across the spectrum of API and/ or backends.

In this chapter, we will focus on the ADOMD.NET API because it is simple to use and easy to follow. For people familiar with ADOMD or ADO, ADOMD.NET will be extremely approachable because it is very similar. Best of all, since it is a .NET class library, you can use ADOMD.NET from any managed language. We will use C# for its clarity. Also, we assume that you are using the Microsoft Visual Studio development environment.

> **NOTE** Both OLE DB for OLAP and XML for Analysis have grown beyond OLAP and into data mining. Data mining adds new capabilities and a new language (Data Mining Extensions, or DMX). ADOMD.NET also includes facilities for data mining. However, these are all outside the scope of this chapter and book, and we will not cover them here.

ADOMD.NET Basics

ADOMD.NET's object model is similar to ADOMD and ADO but differs in a few important details. First, unlike ADOMD's dependence on ADO, ADOMD.NET has no dependence upon ADO.NET. All objects within the ADOMD.NET library are accessed through the single ADOMD.NET assembly: `Microsoft.AnalysisServices.AdomdClient.dll`. (Despite the name of the DLL, this same DLL is used irrespective of the actual server that you are connecting to.) Other notable differences between ADOMD.NET and ADOMD are

1. There is no correspondence to ADOMD's `Catalog` object in ADOMD.NET. Instead, use ADOMD.NET's `AdomdConnection` object's `Cubes` property to access the available cubes.

2. ADOMD.NET uses an explicit `AdomdCommand` object in place of ADOMD's `CellSet` to execute MDX commands. ADOMD.NET has a `CellSet` object but it is used solely for navigating the results of a query.

A general-purpose client may need to perform various tasks, including but certainly not limited to the following:

- Connecting to a data source
- Getting metadata
- Listing databases and cubes

- Listing dimensions, hierarchies, and levels
- Listing KPIs
- Listing members
- Listing sets
- Listing external functions
- Listing actions
- Listing cell calculation functions

ADOMD.NET 9.0 (distributed with Analysis Services 2005) supports all of these activities. Listing sets, actions, and external functions are relevant to the MDX a client may attempt to execute, but little programming is required to handle the results of these metadata inquiries. (Listing cell calculation functions is more awkward than listing the other types of metadata.) Executing MDX statements may affect which sets and external functions and actions are defined (as well as the members). The programming side of executing these DDL statements is simple, and we will cover it in this chapter.

Prerequisites

Using ADOMD.NET requires adding a reference to the ADOMD.NET assembly `Microsoft.AnalysisServices.AdomdClient.dll`. To do this with the C# project in Visual Studio .NET:

- Go to the Solution Explorer and right-click on the References node under your project.
- Select Add Reference.
- Under the .NET tab, select the component named Microsoft.Analysis-Services.AdomdClient. Click OK.
- You should now have an entry Microsoft.AnalysisServices.Adomd-Client under the References node of your Solution Explorer.
- In your C# code, you need to insert a using clause in any source file where you need to work with ADOMD.NET objects:

```
using Microsoft.AnalysisServices.AdomdClient;
```

Making a Connection

Establishing a connection in ADOMD.NET is similar to doing so in ADOMD in that you use a connection string. The connection string can specify one of three types of connections:

- A binary wire-protocol connection to Microsoft Analysis Services
- An XMLA connection to Microsoft Analysis Services or any other XMLA 1.1 provider
- A connection to a Microsoft cube file

If you specify a hostname in the connection string, ADOMD.NET will attempt to connect via Microsoft Analysis Services' binary wire-protocol over TCP/IP.

Alternately, you can specify the URL to Microsoft Analysis Services configured as a Web service in the connection string. Note that because it is using a Web service, you can connect to an XMLA provider other than Microsoft Analysis Services. ADOMD.NET makes use of many Microsoft Analysis Services assumptions and extensions to the XMLA standard. If you are connecting to a non-Microsoft XMLA provider, you need to be aware of the differences between your XMLA provider and Microsoft Analysis Services to reduce programming difficulties. We will provide some guidance on this matter in this chapter. The last option is to specify the pathname of a Microsoft cube file. If you know the database that you want to connect to, you can provide that in the Catalog field of the connection string.

For example, the following code will create a connection to the local machine, open it, and immediately close it:

```
AdomdConnection conn = new AdomdConnection("Data
Source=localhost;Catalog=Adventure Works DW");
conn.Open();
conn.Close();
```

To connect via XMLA to Analysis Services 9, you only need to change the connection string above to this:

```
AdomdConnection conn = new AdomdConnection("Data
Source=http://localhost/msxmla/msmdpump.dll;Catalog=Adventure Works
DW");
```

Any given XMLA provider may support additional connection properties that affect client behavior, including how metadata is represented and how MDX is executed. We provide a full list of connection properties for Microsoft Analysis Services 9 in Appendix B.

Working with Metadata

Client programs often need to work with multidimensional metadata such as cubes, hierarchies, levels, and their members. In ADOMD.NET, there are two methods to access multidimensional metadata. The first and most direct method is to read the raw data from the schema rowsets. Accessing schema rowsets directly provides more flexibility at the expense of more work on your part. An alternate method you may prefer is to work with the ADOMD.NET metadata object model, which is built from the information in the schema rowsets. The metadata object model is easier to use and will be sufficient for most client applications.

Retrieving Schema Rowsets

Schema rowsets are retrieved using the `AdomdConnection` method `GetSchemaDataSet`. This method is overridden to take as input either the name of the schema rowset that you would like to retrieve or the schema GUID of the rowset.

When retrieving schema rowsets by name, you specify the discovery method you are invoking (for example, `DISCOVER_DATASOURCES`) or the name of the schema rowset (for example, `MDSCHEMA_CUBES`). The restrictions are passed in using an `AdomdRestrictionCollection`, so you also need to specify the restrictions by name. No validation of the schema name or restriction names is done; they are passed directly through to the server as they are passed in. The following code snippet illustrates how you would retrieve the dimensions belonging to the Adventure Works cube using this technique:

```
AdomdConnection conn = new AdomdConnection("Data
Source=localhost;Catalog=Adventure Works DW");
conn.Open();

DataSet ds;
String s;

AdomdRestrictionCollection restrictions = new
AdomdRestrictionCollection();
restrictions.Add("CUBE_NAME", "Adventure Works");
ds = conn.GetSchemaDataSet("MDSCHEMA_DIMENSIONS", restrictions);

foreach (DataRow r in ds.Tables[0].Rows)
{
  s = r["CUBE_NAME"].ToString();
  s = r["DIMENSION_NAME"].ToString();
  s = r["DIMENSION_UNIQUE_NAME"].ToString();

int i = Int32.Parse(r["DIMENSION_CARDINALITY"].ToString());
}
```

The alternative to using the data source names is to use the schema GUIDs. These are the same GUIDs that were assigned to each rowset in the OLE DB for OLAP specification. When using this method, ADOMD.NET cross-references the guid that was passed in with the results of a `DISCOVER_SCHEMA_ROWSETS` call. It finds the matching schema rowset and submits the request. Restrictions are passed in as an array of strings, and are assigned to the restrictions in the order that they appear in the array. ADOMD.NET provides the `AdomdSchemaGuid` class, which defines the GUID constants for each of the rowsets available in Microsoft's Analysis Services.

With this method, the GUID is validated before being sent to the server. If the GUID cannot be found in the `DISCOVER_SCHEMA_ROWSETS` rowset, then ADOMD.NET will throw an exception. However, any restrictions passed in are not checked. Analysis Services 2005 will return an exception if an invalid restriction is passed in, and ADOMD.NET will pass this through accordingly. There are some XMLA providers that merely ignore invalid restrictions. Continuing from the code above, the following uses the `AdomdSchemaGuid` class:

```
restrictions.Clear();
ds = conn.GetSchemaDataSet(AdomdSchemaGuid.SchemaRowsets, restrictions);
foreach (DataRow r in ds.Tables[0].Rows)
{
  s = r["SchemaName"].ToString();
  s = r["Restrictions"].ToString();
  s = r["SchemaGuid"].ToString();
  s = r["Description"].ToString();
  s = r["RestrictionsMask"].ToString();
}
```

Interoperability Considerations When Using Schema Rowsets

When programming an ADOMD.NET client for non-Microsoft XMLA providers, you need to be aware of the Microsoft Analysis Services extension that ADOMD.NET uses. Schema GUIDs are a Microsoft extension and are not part of the XMLA 1.1 standard. In order to use GUIDs to retrieve the schema rowsets, the XMLA provider needs to provide them in the `DISCOVER_SCHEMA_ROWSETS`, and the GUIDs need to be of the same type and value as those defined within Microsoft Analysis Services. If your client application is meant to connect to non-Microsoft XMLA providers, it may make sense to use only the names of the rowsets and avoid using schema GUIDs altogether.

You also need to pay attention to schema rowsets that are specified in the XMLA provider as optional, that have optional columns, or that are vendor-specific extensions. Since not all XMLA providers will provide support for these, you may sacrifice your client's interoperability when you use them.

Working with the Metadata Object Model

The metadata object model makes working with metadata relatively easy. The model structure intuitively mirrors the familiar multidimensional structure, as depicted in Figure 15-1. The subobjects of a given object are accessed through properties. When you query a property from one of these objects, the corresponding schema rowset request is made automatically with the appropriate restrictions so that the contained objects can be built. Note that catalogs are not represented in this object model. The only way to retrieve catalog information is to retrieve the schema rowset manually using `GetSchemaDataset`.

NOTE Note that in Analysis Services 2005, all of the dimensions within a database will appear as cubes within the Cubes collection retrieved from an `AdomdConnection`. Your application may want to filter out the dimension cubes by examining the `Type` property on each `CubeDef` object.

Interoperability Considerations When Working with the Metadata Object Model

Some parts of the metadata object model rely on Microsoft-specific extensions to XMLA. To remain interoperable with other XMLA providers, these parts should be avoided.

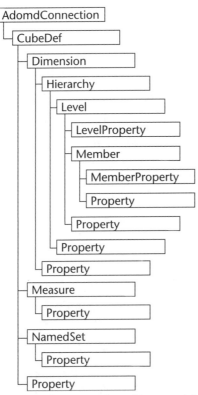

Figure 15-1   Metadata object model.

For instance, when working with the `Hierarchy` object, avoid retrieving the `HierarchyOrigin` property. The getter for this property will internally query the optional `STRUCTURE` column from the `MDSCHEMA_HIERARCHIES` rowset. If your XMLA provider does not include a `STRUCTURE` column, then an exception will be thrown when you attempt to retrieve this property.

Dimension Particularities

Under Microsoft Analysis Services 2005, aside from each dimension being enumerable via the `MDSCHEMA_DIMENSIONS` schema rowset, each dimension is also presented as a distinct cube. These cubes are named by prefixing a $ to the dimension name. These special cubes are restricted to users with database administrator rights. And to obfuscate matters, these cubes are also not visible from the various schema rowsets unless you provide the appropriate restrictions requesting them specifically. For the `MDSCHEMA_CUBES` schema rowset, you need to add the `CUBE_SOURCE` restriction:

```
AdomdRestrictionCollection restrictions = new
AdomdRestrictionCollection();
restrictions.Add("CUBE_SOURCE", 2); // 2 indicates DIMENSION cubes
ds = conn.GetSchemaDataSet("MDSCHEMA_CUBES", restrictions);

foreach (DataRow r in ds.Tables[0].Rows)
{
    // . . .
}
```

For the `MDSCHEMA_DIMENSIONS` and `MDSCHEMA_HIERARCHIES` schema rowsets, you need to add at least the `CUBE_NAME` restriction:

```
restrictions.Clear();
restrictions.Add("CUBE_NAME", "$Product");
ds = conn.GetSchemaDataSet("MDSCHEMA_DIMENSIONS", restrictions);

foreach (DataRow r in ds.Tables[0].Rows)
{
    // . . .

}
```

Concretely speaking, this addition allows you to reformulate the MDX statement

```
SELECT [Product].[Manufacture Time].MEMBERS ON 0, {} ON 1 FROM
[Adventure Works]
```

to this slightly more succinct form:

```
SELECT [Product].[Manufacture Time].MEMBERS ON 0 FROM [$Product]
```

However, these two statements are, in general, not equivalent. First, as stated earlier, only database administrators can execute the second query. Furthermore, the dimension's members may be renamed within the cube, or security roles could be set up to restrict the members that a user can see within a dimension. In short, the administrator's view will not necessarily match that of any given end user's.

Handling ADOMD.NET Metadata Caching

Any part of the metadata object model is populated on the fly the first time that part of the object model is requested. This information is cached so that subsequent accesses of these objects need not result in repeated XMLA DISCOVER requests to the server. It is possible that, after this metadata has been retrieved, changes may be made to the metadata. Such changes may result in a disagreement between the metadata displayed by your client and the actual metadata of the cube.

For example, a client may traverse the Dimensions, Hierarchies, and Levels collections to reach member metadata. (Member metadata is actually handled separately from the Member objects that are returned from a query.) If your client creates new calculated members or alters the members through the UPDATE CUBE commands, they will not be reflected in the metadata objects, although they can be used by queries and commands and will be fully available through their corresponding schema rowset. With Microsoft's Analysis Services, the same is true for changes made to a dimension via incremental processing.

In order to account for changes, you need to execute the Refresh Metadata method of the AdomdConnection object. This will invalidate all metadata already retrieved so that subsequent requests to the metadata properties result in new DISCOVER requests.

```
AdomdConnection conn = new AdomdConnection("Data
Source=localhost;Catalog=Adventure Works DW");
conn.Open();

// do something to invalidate ADOMD.NET's metadata cache
...

conn.RefreshMetadata();
```

Executing a Query

A central programming activity in MDX is executing a query or statement and retrieving the query results. ADOMD.NET uses a distinct object for each of these two steps. You execute an MDX statement using the `AdomdCommand` object and retrieve the results using a `CellSet` or one of two new alternative result set representations: the `AdomdDataReader` or the `XmlReader`. Each representation provides its own blend of ease of use, efficiency, scalability, and flexibility.

A `CellSet` provides a fully multidimensional view of the data and is the easiest to work with. An `AdomdDataReader` presents a forward-only flattened view of the data, which can be very efficient, since the data can be streamed row by row. We will defer discussion on flattening to the latter portion of this chapter. An `XmlReader` provides a straight passthrough of the XML that is returned from the provider, which allows you to implement your own XML processing if desired.

We focus on the `CellSet` representation in this section because it will be appropriate for the majority of client applications.

Executing Commands

The `AdomdCommand` object is a straightforward representation of a multidimensional command. Before executing a command, you first need to set up the `AdomdCommand` object, as in the following code sample:

```
AdomdConnection conn = new AdomdConnection("Data
Source=localhost;Catalog=Adventure Works DW");
conn.Open();

// create the command
AdomdCommand cmd = new AdomdCommand();

// set the connection
cmd.Connection = conn;

// set the command text
cmd.CommandText = "SELECT [Customers].[Northeast].Children FROM
[Budgeting]";
```

You can alternately create a command using `AdomdConnection`'s `CreateCommand` method:

```
AdomdConnection conn = new AdomdConnection("Data
Source=localhost;Catalog=Adventure Works DW");

// create the command
AdomdCommand cmd = AdomdConnection.CreateCommand();
```

```
// set the command text
cmd.CommandText = "SELECT [Customers].[Northeast].Children FROM
[Budgeting]";
```

In either case, you may defer the opening of the connection up to the point when you execute the command.

To execute the command, you call either the general `Execute` method, or one of four specific execute methods: `ExecuteCellSet`, `ExecuteReader`, `ExecuteXMLReader`, or `ExecuteNonQuery`. The general `Execute` method will return a generic object, the type of which will depend on the data received from the server. For a typical `SELECT` statement, this will usually be a `CellSet`. For DDL commands (for example, `CREATE ACTION` or `DROP SET`), the object will be `NULL`. The other four execute methods return the data representation implied by their name, or nothing at all in the case of `Execute NonQuery`. Note that you cannot execute a DDL command using `Execute CellSet` or `ExecuteReader`, as these variants expect data to be returned and ADOMD.NET will throw an exception when no results are returned. The reverse case of executing a DML command using `ExecuteNonQuery` is allowed though probably not very useful.

Parameterized Commands

A very handy feature of Microsoft Analysis Services 2005 supported by ADOMD.NET is the parameterized command. It is a feature of convenience that, as the name suggests, allows you to parameterize your MDX command and execute the command with various parameter values. This is the same idea as the SQL parameter, but in MDX's case, there is no equivalence to `SQL- Prepare()`. To use it, you would typically replace a literal with a placeholder. The following code will make this clear:

```
// create the command
AdomdCommand cmd = new AdomdCommand();

// set the connection
cmd.Connection = conn;

// Parameterize to filter Products based on Color
cmd.CommandText = "select filter([Product].members, " +
"[Product].properties("Color") = @Color ) . . . from [Cube]";

// Select only Yellow Products
cmd.Parameters.Clear();
cmd.Parameters.Add(new AdomdParameter("Color", "Yellow"));

// Execute query
CellSet cellset = cmd.ExecuteCellSet();
```

Note that this feature will only work with Analysis Services 2005. Using parameters against a different data source will result in an exception being thrown when the command is executed.

Working with the CellSet Object

A CellSet consolidates all the metadata, axis data, and result data for a query into one object. It makes this information readily available through its Cell, Axes, FilterAxis, and OlapInfo properties. This convenience comes at a cost both in terms of memory-usage—since this information is stored in-memory—and query retrieval times—since more information needs to be retrieved and processed.

A CellSet object is created like so:

```
CellSet cs = cmd.ExecuteCellSet();
```

Once you have your CellSet object, you can begin to work with the meta-data, and axis and cell information.

OlapInfo Holds Metadata

ADOMD.NET separates the metadata objects from the data objects by introducing a hierarchy of new OlapInfo classes to encapsulate all the CellSet metadata, as depicted in Figure 15-2.

This model provides richer metadata than was previously available in ADOMD; however, since the metadata and data are contained in separate objects, processing a CellSet now usually requires a few more steps compared to doing this in ADOMD.

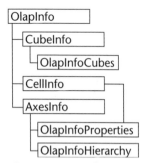

Figure 15-2   OlapInfo class hierarchy.

For example, the `Type` property of the `CellProperty` object is no longer contained in the `CellProperty` object itself. To determine the type of a `CellProperty`, you need to retrieve the `OlapInfoProperties` object corresponding to the cell property of interest and check its `Type` property. Contrast the two approaches via the following two code fragments:

```
'*** ADOMD Example in VB ***
Dim conn As New ADODB.Connection
conn.Open "Provider=MSOLAP; Data Source=localhost"
Dim cs As New ADOMD.Cellset
cs.ActiveConnection = conn
cs.Source = "Select { [Measures].[Unit Sales]} on columns ,
{[Time].members} on rows from [Sales]"
cs.Open

If cs.Item(0).Properties("CELL_ORDINAL").Type != adUnsignedInt Then
...
End If
```

```
// ADOMD.NET Example in C#
AdomdConnection conn = new AdomdConnection("Data
Source=localhost;Catalog=Adventure Works DW");
conn.Open();

AdomdCommand command = conn.CreateCommand();
command.CommandText =
 "Select { [Measures].[Internet Sales Amount], [Measures].[Internet Order
Quantity] } on columns,"
+ "{ [Date].[Calendar].[Date].&[1097], [Date].[Calendar].[Date].&[1200]}
on rows "
+ "from [Adventure Works]";

// we're making use of the multi-dimensional CellSet
CellSet cs = command.ExecuteCellSet();

OlapInfo oi = cs.OlapInfo;
CellInfo ci = oi.CellInfo;
OlapInfoPropertyCollection oips = ci.CellProperties;

// we're going to check the default CellOrdinal property
OlapInfoProperty  oip = oips["CellOrdinal"];

int  ti = 0;
if ( oip.Type != ti.GetType() )
{
...
}
```

Axes Hold Axis Information

The `Axes` collection of the `CellSet` contains an axis object for each of the query's named axes. The contents of the `Axes` collection are ordered so that the first item (`Cellset.Axes[0]`) holds the set of tuples for axis 0 (the columns), the second item holds the results for axis 1 (the rows), and so on. The slicer axis (defined by the `WHERE` clause) is held in a separate `FilterAxis` property of the `CellSet`. If the query has no axes defined (a zero-dimensional query, as described in Chapter 2), then the `Axes` collection is empty.

All dimensions not referenced in the named axes of the query will end up in the `FilterAxis`. Remember from Chapter 5 that if the members of a dimension are not placed in one of the named axes, the default member of that dimension forms part of the context for the query. That context is reflected in the `FilterAxis`; all dimensions of the cube will end up being reflected in either the named axes or the slicer if the MDX that was executed was a query.

The axis data itself can be accessed through either the `Positions` or the `Set` property. The `Positions` property parallels the ADOMD property of the same name while the `Set` property is new with ADOMD.NET. Both properties contain the result tuples for an axis. Through the `Positions` property, the `Position` class represents the tuples. Through the `Set` property, the `Tuple` class represents the tuples. The difference between the two is that the `Set` object contains additional hierarchy information that is not contained in the `Positions` collection. The `Hierarchies` property of the `Set` class contains information about each hierarchy referred to in the set, in the order in which they appear in each tuple. The number of hierarchies in the `Hierarchies` collection tells you the dimensionality of the axis (which is also the dimensionality of the set and the dimensionality of each tuple contained within). This is the most convenient way to determine the dimensionality of an axis. (ADOMD.NET's `AxesInfo` object does not contain a `DimensionCount` property as it did in ADOMD.) If a query returns an empty set for an axis, the `Tuples` collection in the `Set` and the `Positions` collection will both be empty (as will the set of result cells).

Each `Tuple` contains a list of members, one member for each dimension in the tuple. The first dimension represented in the `Tuple` will be the one listed first in the MDX query for the axis and should correspond to the first hierarchy in the hierarchy collection contained in the set. If the query started off with

```
SELECT
CrossJoin (
  [Time].[2001].Children,
  [Salesperson].[Eastern].Children
) on columns
...
```

then, in each `Tuple` in the `Axes[0].Set.Tuples` collection, the first member will be a Time member and the second will be a Salesperson member. In the `Axes[0].Set.Hierarchy` collection, the first hierarchy will be the Time hierarchy, and the second will be the Salesperson hierarchy.

Each member in the `Members` collection of a `Tuple` will contain information about the member, including its name, unique name, display caption, and some provider-defined properties that will assist in displaying the member. Additionally, if the query requested any member properties for members of that dimension, their names and values will be held in the `Properties` collection of the member.

Working with tuples and members can be highly streamlined when you are working in C#. For example, the following fragment illustrates the key elements of iterating over the results:

```
// Loop over Tuples
foreach ( Tuple  t in cs.Axes[0].Set.Tuples )
{
    foreach (Member m in t.Members)
    {
        // do what we need with m.Caption
    }
}
```

Cells Hold Cell Information

A `CellSet` also holds a collection of `Cell` objects in its `Cells` collection. Each `Cell` object holds various properties for each retrieved cell. The `Value` property contains the raw, unformatted number or string value for the cell and is the default, so simply requesting a value from the `CellSet`'s collection of `Cells` will retrieve the unformatted value. The `FormattedValue` property is also available by name. Other cell properties can be retrieved through the cell's `CellProperties` property (such as through `cellset.Cells[0].CellProperties["FORE_COLOR"]`).

In MDX, the names of the cell properties that you can retrieve are listed here and are repeated in Appendix C:

`ACTION_TYPE`	Microsoft extension
`BACK_COLOR`	
`CELL_EVALUATION_LIST`	Microsoft extension
`CELL_ORDINAL`	
`FONT_FLAGS`	

```
FONT_NAME
FONT_SIZE
FORE_COLOR
FORMAT_STRING
FORMATTED_VALUE
LANGUAGE                    Microsoft extension
NON_EMPTY_BEHAVIOR          Microsoft extension
SOLVE_ORDER                 Microsoft extension (deprecated)
UPDATEABLE                  Microsoft extension
VALUE
```

Except for CELL_ORDINAL, you would use the name as above to retrieve the cell properties from the CellProperties collection. For CELL_ORDINAL, you need to use the name "CellOrdinal". CELL_ORDINAL is also the only property that is always returned irrespective of whether it was requested or not. The indexer ([]) for the CellProperties collection is overloaded to allow use of either a string or an integer parameter. It is preferable to use the string overload for legibility, but if you want to use the integer overload, the properties are sequenced in the collection in the order in which they were listed in the CELL PROPERTIES section of the query beginning with CELL_ORDINAL ("CellOrdinal") at index 0.

NOTE Remember that if you ask for any specific cell properties, you need to request every cell property that you are interested in. By default, you get back VALUE, FORMATTED_VALUE, **and** CELL_ORDINAL.

If you are aiming to present information in Microsoft Excel or through another interface that enables the user to perform further calculations against the retrieved data, it may be helpful to retrieve the raw value and the format string in each query. If you retrieve the formatted value only, then the number of decimal places may be limited and the numbers represented may not be correct for further calculations. If you retrieve the raw value only, you lose the formatting information provided by the database designer.

For example, the code that follows retrieves formatted value and color information from a query that requests these cell properties.

```
AdomdConnection conn = new AdomdConnection("Data
Source=localhost;Catalog=Adventure Works DW");
conn.Open();
```

```
AdomdCommand command = conn.CreateCommand();
command.CommandText = "Select { [Measures].[Internet Sales Amount],
[Measures].[Internet Order Quantity] } on columns,"

 + "{ [Date].[Calendar].[Date].&[1097], [Date].[Calendar].[Date].&[1200]}
on rows "

 + "from [Adventure Works] CELL PROPERTIES ACTION_TYPE, BACK_COLOR,
UPDATEABLE , FORMATTED_VALUE, FORMAT_STRING, FORE_COLOR";

CellSet cs = command.ExecuteCellSet();

foreach (Cell c in cs.Cells )
{
    string  s = c.CellProperties["FORMATTED_VALUE"].ToString();
    . . .
}
```

Further Details on Retrieving Information from a Query

A couple more common details are worth bringing up here: how to retrieve member properties from a result set, and how to retrieve and use additional member information provided by XMLA and ADOMD.NET.

Retrieving Member Property Information

The following are always going to be returned in specific named properties of the Member object:

- Caption
- Name
- UniqueName
- Description
- LevelName
- LevelDepth

For example, the caption for the member can always be retrieved by referencing Member.Caption.

These properties can also be retrieved by specifically listing them in the DIMENSION PROPERTIES clause of the query's specification for that axis. In that case, their values will also appear in the Properties collection of the Member object in the order in which they were specified in the query. Database-defined member properties will also be listed in that clause and retrieved in the member's Properties collection.

Member properties retrieved through the `Properties` collection are named using unique names, which can cause some complication to your code if you need to search them by name or translate the name to a user-readable format. The unique name style for member properties is discussed in Chapter 1. With some XMLA providers, a human-accessible caption can usually be inferred by isolating the text enclosed by the rightmost [and "] characters in the string.

One important use for member unique names returned from queries, apart from holding them for insertion into subsequent queries, is to augment the members retrieved from the database with ancestor information, which may not have been retrieved in the query. For example, a geography dimension may have two Portland members at the city level, one in Oregon and another in Maine. If a query retrieves only city-level members, a user has no way of clearly knowing which state the city belongs to.

Deriving this ancestor information was frequently needed in Analysis Services 2000 for the time dimension because member names were frequently vague. For example, there are 12 members in each year with a name of [1]. Analysis Services 2005 changes this. The default name in Analysis Services 2005 for a time member contains the chronological details starting from the year and down to the member's level. For instance, the name for the first day of the first month of 2006 is now [January 1, 2006]. Previously, the name was [1]. Similarly, the name for the first month of 2006 is now [January 2006].

There are two ways that you can add ancestor information to the display. The simpler way is to lean on the metadata model and use the `Parent` property of the member to traverse the hierarchy from the member in question to the top of the hierarchy. For example, the following fragment will prepend all ancestor's captions to a given member's caption, separating the captions with "/":

```
// retrieve an arbitrary member
Member member = cs.Axes[0].Set.Tuples[i].Member[0];

String caption = member.Caption;
Member parent = member.Parent;
// Stop when member has no more parents
while (parent != null)
    {
caption = parent.Caption + "/" +  caption;
  parent = parent.Parent;
    }

// Now caption holds full hierarchy of captions
// e.g. "USA/Oregon/Portland"
```

However, this method will only work with XMLA providers that return cube information within a `Cellset` and support using the tree operator to retrieve member information. When this is not the case, you need to work somewhat harder and derive the information from the schema rowset directly. In this situation, you can use the `UniqueName` property of the member along with the `AdomdConnection`'s `GetSchemaDataSet` method to retrieve ancestor information. You can use the member's `LevelDepth` to detect when you've reached the top of the hierarchy. For example, the code below has the same functionality as the previous example but is slightly more complex:

```
// retrieve an arbitrary member
Member member = cs.Axes[0].Set.Tuples[i].Member(0);

String caption;

if (member.LevelDepth > 0)
{
    int levelDepth = member.LevelDepth;
    string uniqueName = member.UniqueName;

    while (levelDepth!= 0)
        {
        AdomdRestrictionCollection restrictions =
                new AdomdRestrictionCollection();
        restrictions.Add("CUBE_NAME", "Adventure Works");
        restrictions.Add("MEMBER_UNIQUE_NAME", uniqueName);

        DataSet ds = connection.GetSchemaDataSet("MDSCHEMA_MEMBERS",
                                          restrictions);
        DataRow row = ds.Tables(0).Rows(0);
        caption = row["MEMBER_CAPTION"] + "/" + caption;

        if (row["PARENT_UNIQUE_NAME"] == DBNull.Value)
        {
            break;
        }

        uniqueName = Convert.ToString(row["PARENT_UNIQUE_NAME"]);
        levelDepth = Convert.ToInt32(row["LEVEL_NUMBER"]);
    }
}

// Now caption holds full hierarchy of captions
// e.g. " USA/Oregon/Portland "
```

Rather than try to traverse the object hierarchy of the cube to figure out the dimension and level of the member and then walk up the ADOMD.NET object trees, you can make use of the underlying schema rowsets to first access the member's parent unique name. Then you would use the rowsets to access for each parent its caption and its own parent's unique name, repeating as necessary to move up the hierarchy until all ancestors have been accounted for. If you used the ParentSameAsPrev property described in the next section, you could probably economize the searching. (We're assuming only one parent per member here, which won't be a valid assumption for providers like TM1.) In order to understand the specifics of the XML for Analysis schema rowsets, you should refer to the XML for Analysis documentation.

Retrieving Additional Member Information

In addition to standard and database member properties, the following properties will also be returned for each member in a Tuple:

- DrilledDown
- ParentSameAsPrev
- ChildCount

The DrilledDown flag basically indicates if a parent member is immediately followed by one of its children. This can be useful for indicating to an end user whether an action on the parent member will initiate a drill-down or -up. If the client is attempting to render children together under a parent, perhaps by using indenting or HTML table rows, ParentSameAsPrev provides a low-cost way for the client to determine, as it loops through result tuples, whether it should break out of a child group to start a new parent or not. ChildCount is an approximate count of the number of children that a member has. It is not reliable (the MDX specification requires that the number returned here need only be an approximation but doesn't say how good the approximation needs to be), but in general, if the ChildCount is zero, then a member cannot be drilled down on, and if it is greater than zero, then it can be.

Further Details about Retrieving Cell Data

ADOMD.NET provides three ways to retrieve data from a CellSet. At the lowest "level," it allows retrieval using the cell ordinal. The cell ordinal for a cell is a scalar representation of the multiaxis coordinate of the cell. It is efficient, powerful, and usually inconvenient. ADOMD.NET has a second, optimized, way for retrieving data from a two-axis CellSet. This is the recommended way to use, especially since most of you will be using two-axis CellSet in your work. Finally, ADOMD.NET also has a generalized mechanism to allow for the use of a multiaxis coordinate.

To calculate the cell ordinal for a cell, the position number in each axis will be multiplied by the product of the number of positions at each lower-numbered axis. The column position number will be multiplied by 1, because no lower-numbered axes exist.

Let's say that you have a three-dimensional result set with four columns, five rows, and six pages. If you want to access the cell at zero-based positions (2, 3, 1), then you will calculate the cell index as $(2 * 1) + (3 * 4) + (1 * 20) = 34$. The cell at positions (2, 3, 2) would be at index $(2 * 1) + (3 * 4) + (2 * 20) = 54$. When the query is executed, an array can be filled with the multipliers of 1, 4, and 20, and a short function can use this to convert any array of coordinate values from the user interface into a cell index. (If performance on queries with more than two dimensions is an issue, you may seriously want to implement your client code in C++ or Delphi, with OLE DB for OLAP or XML for Analysis instead of ADOMD.NET.)

In the case of a zero-dimensional result set, there are no axes for the result set, but there is a slicer. You can reference cell 0 to obtain the sole cell returned by the query.

The following code sample demonstrates all three methods of retrieving data from a CellSet:

```
AdomdConnection connection = new AdomdConnection
  ("Data Source=localhost");
connection.Open();
AdomdCommand command = connection.CreateCommand();
command.CommandText = "select Crossjoin(
{[Measures].[Internet Gross Profit Margin]}, "
+ "{[Sales Reason].[Sales Reason].members } ) on columns,"
+ "{[Product].[Category].[Category].members} on rows "
+ "from [Adventure Works] CELL PROPERTIES VALUE,
FORMAT_STRING, FORMATTED_VALUE";

CellSet cs = command.ExecuteCellSet(); // this CellSet
contains 11 columns and 4 rows

// this method two is highly optimized
//  and convenient for a 2@@hyaxis CellSet
for (int irow = 0; irow < cs.Axes[1].Set.Tuples.Count; irow++)
// this count will be 4
{
  for (int icol = 0; icol < cs.Axes[0].Set.Tuples.Count; icol++)
  // this count will be 11
  {
    if (cs.Cells[icol,irow].CellProperties ["FORMATTED_VALUE"].Value
        != null)
    {
      string s = cs.Cells[icol,irow]
        .CellProperties["FORMATTED_VALUE"].Value.ToString();
    }
```

```
        }
    }

    // Or we can use cell ordinals to go through the cells as follows
    // these are some hints that we pre-calculate to help us
    // compute the cell ordinal
    int[] AxisHints;
    AxisHints = new int[cs.Axes.Count];
    AxisHints[0] = 1;
    for (int i = 1; i < cs.Axes.Count; i++)
      AxisHints[i] = AxisHints[i - 1] *
          cs.Axes[i-1].Set.Tuples.Count;

    // here's a random coordinate into the cellset
    int[] cellsetCoordinate;
    cellsetCoordinate = new int[2];
    cellsetCoordinate[0] = 6;  // axis 0
    cellsetCoordinate[1] = 2;  // axis 1

    // we calculate the cell ordinal using AxisHints
    int cellOrdinal = 0;
    for (int iAx = 0; iAx < cellsetCoordinate.Length; iAx++)
        cellOrdinal += cellsetCoordinate[iAx] * AxisHints[iAx];

    // this is method one using the cell ordinal
    if (cs.Cells[cellOrdinal].CellProperties["FORMATTED_VALUE"].Value
        != null)
    {
        string s = s.Cells[cellOrdinal].CellProperties["FORMATTED_VALUE"]
          .Value.ToString();
    }

    // this third method is a general mechanism that handles
    // an arbitrary number of axes as well. Note how similar it is
    // to our optimized 2-D case
    if (cs.Cells[cellsetCoordinate].
          CellProperties["FORMATTED_VALUE"].Value != null)
    {
      string s = cs.Cells[cellsetCoordinate].
          CellProperties["FORMATTED_VALUE"].Value.ToString();
    }
```

Retrieving Drill-Through Data As a Recordset

Drilling through to the source data is possible via the MDX DRILLTHROUGH statement. More detail about DRILLTHROUGH is available in Chapter 14. The only way to retrieve drill-through results in ADOMD.NET is to call the ExecuteReader method on a command object. In addition, there is an important limitation in Analysis Services 2000 when performing a drill-through. When using XMLA (and correspondingly ADOMD.NET), results are only returned for the first partition from a cube with multiple partitions. It is not possible to retrieve the drill-through results for other partitions. In Analysis Services 2005, this limitation has been removed so drill-through results will be returned for all partitions. The following example shows how to retrieve drill-through results:

```
command.CommandText = "Drillthrough MAXROWS 100
select {[Geography].[State-Province].&[CT]&[US] } on columns,
 {[Product].[Product].&[328]} on rows from [Channel Sales]";

AdomdDataReader reader = command.ExecuteReader();
// move to next row
while (reader->Read())
{
           // ... do actions with the reader such as print out values
Console.WriteLine("{0}", reader->GetValue(0));
}
reader.Close();
```

Key Performance Indicators

Key performance indicators (KPIs) are a new feature of Analysis Services 2005. It's easiest to think of a KPI as a multivalued measure. Each KPI consists of a value, a goal, a status, and a trend. To use a KPI, you reference the particular component of it as you would a measure.

Using KPIs is a three-part process. Applications must first discover the KPIs available in each cube, execute an MDX query with the KPIs, and then format the results for display appropriately.

Information about the KPIs within a cube is available via schema rowsets or the metadata model. Within the metadata model, each CubeDef object contains the cube's KPIs. Of course, you need to first determine if KPIs exist in a given environment. Currently, only Microsoft Analysis Services 2005 support KPIs. An exception will be thrown if attempts are made to access KPI information from an earlier version of Microsoft Analysis Services or any other XMLA provider. One way to determine if your data source supports KPIs is to use GetSchemaDataset on an open connection to retrieve the DISCOVER_ SCHEMA_ROWSETS rowset and to check if the MDSCHEMA_KPI schema is present.

After the appropriate KPIs have been selected, they can be used in MDX queries via the various KPI MDX functions. Finally, after an MDX query is executed, the StatusGraphic and TrendGraphic properties can help determine what graphical representation should be used when displaying the status and trend values for a KPI. The example below illustrates how this process occurs.

```
AdomdConnection connection = new AdomdConnection("Data
Source=localhost;Catalog=Adventure Works DW");
connection.Open();
CubeDef cube = connection.Cubes["Adventure Works"];
Kpi kpi = cube.Kpis["Revenue"];
AdomdCommand command = connection.CreateCommand();

// Use KPI in an MDX statement
command.CommandText = "SELECT NON EMPTY { " +
        "KPIValue(\"" + kpi.Name + "\"), " +
        "KPIGoal(\"" + kpi.Name + "\"), " +
        "KPIStatus(\"" + kpi.Name + "\"), " +
        "KPITrend(\"" + kpi.Name + "\"), " +
        "[Measures].[Internet Order Count]} ON COLUMNS " +
        "FROM [Adventure Works] " +
        "CELL PROPERTIES VALUE, BACK_COLOR, FORE_COLOR, " +
        "FORMATTED_VALUE, FORMAT_STRING, FONT_NAME, FONT_SIZE,
FONT_FLAGS";

CellSet cs = command.ExecuteCellSet();
// Use Status Graphic for displaying results

// we're picking off the Revenue KPI's status at ordinal value 2
// and rendering it appropriately
CellProperty cp = cs.Cells[2].CellProperties["VALUE"];
switch (kpi.StatusGraphic)
{
    case "Cylinder":
        // handle value
        break;
    case "RoadSigns":
        // etc. . .
        break;
}
```

Executing Actions

As described in Chapter 9, actions are not executed by issuing MDX. Instead, an action is executed by retrieving a text value from a schema dataset. The action text is retrieved from the CONTENT field of the actions table returned by calling AdomdConnection's GetSchemaDataSet method with the appropriate restrictions. With AdomdConnections, there are two ways to specify restrictions when opening a schema rowset. The first way is similar to the ADO and OLE DB technique of providing column restrictions through an array of column values. The second way is similar to the XMLA technique of providing column restrictions by specifying key/value pairs. Some of the restrictions are typical, such as the name of the action, the name of the cube in which it is found, and the type of the action.

However, the COORDINATE restriction (at the fifth position in the array) provides whatever argument the action may require, such as the tuple for a cell action, the set name for a set action, the member name for a member action, and so on. This restriction needs to be coordinated with the restriction value provided for the COORDINATE_TYPE restriction (in the sixth position), which indicates how to interpret the coordinate. The actual numerical codes to provide are detailed in Chapter 9.

The following code snippet executes a cell action named Retrieve Details and retrieves the value into the string actionToDo:

```
AdomdRestrictionCollection restrictions = new
AdomdRestrictionCollection();

restrictions.Add("CUBE_NAME", "Budgeting");
restrictions.Add("ACTION_NAME", "Retrieve Details");
restrictions.Add("COORDINATE", " ([Time].[Q1, 2002], [Customers].[NJ],
[Products].[Clothing]) ");
restrictions.Add("COORDINATE_TYPE", 6);

System.Data.DataSet dataset =
connection.GetSchemaDataSet("MDSCHEMA_ACTIONS", restrictions);
System.String actionToDo;

actionToDo = dataset.Tables(0).Rows(0).Item("CONTENT");  // e.g.
"DRILLTHROUGH SELECT  . . . "
```

Note that the names provided are not unique names, nor are they delimited by brackets or another character. By way of another example, the following code snippet executes a statement-type set action named Update Selected with a set named Picked Customers and retrieves the statement text into the string actionTodo:

```
AdomdRestrictionCollection restrictions = new
AdomdRestrictionCollection();

restrictions.Add("CUBE_NAME", "Budgeting");
restrictions.Add("ACTION_NAME", "Update Selected");
restrictions.Add("ACTION_TYPE", 4);
restrictions.Add("COORDINATE", "Picked Customers");
restrictions.Add("COORDINATE_TYPE", 5);

System.Data.DataSet dataset =
connection.GetSchemaDataSet("MDSCHEMA_ACTIONS", restrictions);
System.String actionToDo;

actionToDo = dataset.Tables(0).Rows(0).Item("CONTENT");  // e.g. "
UPDATE INVENTORY_REQ  . . . "
```

As you can see, integrating actions with the rest of your client code involves different programming techniques.

Handling "Flattened" MDX Results

In some programming situations, you may need to use the results of an MDX query as though they came from an SQL query. For example, this may occur because you are using the MDX query in an application that expects tables and that you cannot adequately modify to use cellsets. Or more commonly, you may need to use a reporting tool such as Microsoft SQL Server Reporting Services, which outputs to the screen and/or the page and needs a "flat" presentation of a query. ADOMD.NET provides a mechanism for retrieving an MDX query in a tabular format so that a program sees them as if they were the results of SQL.

DataReader and Tabular Results for MDX Queries

The ADOMD.NET `DataReader` class implements ADO.NET's `IDataReader` and `IDataRecord` interfaces to provide a means for reading a forward-only stream of result sets. Conceptually, the result sets returned are similar to tables with rows and columns. Each result set has a set of columns that contains information such as the column name. Rows can only be read in a forward-only fashion, so implementations are only required to store one row of data in memory. ADO.NET comes with implementations of `IDataReader` that can be used to read tables from SQL Server, Oracle, ODBC, and OLE DB data providers. Within ADOMD.NET, the `AdomdDataReader` class implements the `IDataReader` and `IDataRecord` interfaces for reading results from an MDX query in a tabular format. Although the `IDataReader` interface supports multiple result sets, the `AdomdDataReader` only contains the result set for a single MDX query, as multiple result sets are not supported.

Although an MDX query specifies an N-dimensional result space, an XMLA client can specify two different formats in which to return the data when it submits the query. One format is as a multidimensional dataset and the other is as a normal tabular rowset. An OLAP client normally requests the multidimensional dataset because it retains the full dimensional layout of the query. However, the client can request that the results be returned in tabular form, even though the query is in MDX. In this case, the client will receive a result data rowset that is almost indistinguishable from the result data rowset coming from any SQL query. There are some restrictions on what data comes back from an MDX query when it is requested as a rowset, which we will discuss in this section. In addition, the column names will not be like those from an SQL database. However, neither of these poses an obstacle.

The format for a tabular result set retrieved via XMLA is documented in the XMLA and OLE DB for OLAP specifications. The process of laying out the tabular format is called "flattening" the result set. We will explain in this section the aspects of the flattening you need to understand in order to use the results. (If you are programming an application that will directly use XMLA to retrieve the rows, you will want to refer to the programming documentation for XMLA and OLE DB for OLAP to get additional programming details.) Let's look at how a query is mapped into tabular form.

An MDX query specifies results that are organized along a set of axes. Flattening orients the axes of the result set into rows and columns. There is a special division between axis 0 (the "columns" axis) and the other axes of the query. To prevent confusion between MDX "columns" and table columns, we will refer to the axes of an MDX result set as "axis 0" and "non-axis 0."

Axis 0

Each tuple from axis 0 will appear as its own column of the result rowset. For each of these columns, the column name will be formed from the unique names of the tuple's members, joined together by periods. (This naming system can be quite awkward to use.) For example, the following tuple on axis 0

```
([Time].[All Time].[1965], [Geography].[USA].[IL].[Chicago])
```

would correspond to a column named

```
[Time].[All Time].[1965].[Geography].[USA].[IL].[Chicago]
```

On each row of the resulting table, the columns for the axis 0 tuples will contain cell-related values. Member properties cannot be returned for the dimensions of axis 0. An MDX query can request member properties for axis 0 without generating an error, but the request will be ignored (note that Analysis Services 2005 is an exception, as documented below). Only the cell values will be returned. If the query requests specific cell properties (as listed in Appendix C), the request will be ignored. The actual cell values can be of any type, and the type may change from row to row. As a result, the `AdomdDataReader` class has numerous methods for accessing column values in their native data types or as a generic `System.Object` type.

Analysis Services 2005 Cell Property Behavior

By default, Analysis Services 2005 behaves in the same way as Analysis Services 2000 with respect to handling cell properties when flattening is used. That is, it ignores the CELL PROPERTIES qualifier. For example, the CELL PROPERIES clause in the following MDX code is ignored:

```
Select { [Measures].[Internet Sales Amount], [Measures].[Internet Order
Quantity] } on columns,
{ [Product].[Category].[Category].members} on rows
from [Adventure Works] CELL PROPERTIES VALUE, FORMATTED_VALUE,
FORMAT_STRING
```

However, in Analysis Services 2005, you can now set a property on the command before executing an MDX query to retrieve any specified cell properties. Adding the `ReturnCellProperties` property with a value of `true` to the command before executing an MDX statement will result in a column being returned for each cell property requested. For example, if axis 0 contains two tuples, and three cell properties are requested, then axis 0 contributes a total of six columns to the resulting rowset. Each tuple corresponds to three columns for each cell property request. The example that follows shows how to request that all cell properties be returned:

```
command.CommandText = "Select { [Measures].[Internet Sales Amount],
[Measures].[Internet Order Quantity] } on columns,
{ [Product].[Category].[Category].members} on rows
from [Adventure Works] CELL PROPERTIES VALUE, FORMATTED_VALUE,
FORMAT_STRING";
// Set the property asking for all cell properties
command.Properties.Add(new AdomdProperty("ReturnCellProperties", true));
AdomdDataReader reader = command.ExecuteReader();
// The FieldCount property on the reader will now contain 1 field
// for the Product captions and 6 fields for the cell values.

// do stuff with reader.
reader.Close();
```

Other Axes

The tuples for the non-axis 0 axes are essentially cross-joined and placed in the result rows. The information that is returned for each dimension can be divided into two different cases, depending on whether or not any properties have been specified in the query for the axis that contains the dimension (through the PROPERTIES . . . on axis clause).

When no properties have been specified on the axis, then for each hierarchy of each of the non-axis 0 axes there will be one result column for each level of that hierarchy from its root down to the lowest level of that hierarchy for which there will be a result member. (The All level, if it exists in a hierarchy, will not have a corresponding column.) Each column will have a name that consists of the level's unique name and [CAPTION], joined by a dot (.). For example, consider the use of a geography dimension with only one hierarchy that has country, region, state/province, and city levels. If a query only requests region members, there will be one column for that hierarchy's region level and another for its country level. If a query results in a mix of country members, region members, and city members, there will be a column for each of the country, region, state/province, and city levels (even though no state/province was specifically requested). In the event that the members returned for any dimension are not all from the same level, some rows will have

NULL member values. For example, using the geography dimension as just described, a query for

```
{[Geography].[France], [Geography].[France].[Bordeaux],
 [Geography].[France].[Bordeaux].[Cadillac]}
```

will produce the names for the following members in the rows:

[Geography]. [Country]. [CAPTION]	[Geography]. [Region]. [CAPTION]	[Geography]. [State/Province]. [CAPTION]	[Geography]. [City]. [CAPTION]
France	,null.	,null.	,null.
France	West	Bordeaux	,null.
France	West	Bordeaux	Cadillac

Note that by the same token, the [Geography].[All Geography] member would be represented by a NULL in each column.

When any level's member properties are specified for an axis, there will be one column for each member property that is listed in the properties clause. Intrinsic properties such as ID, KEY, and NAME can be requested, along with any member properties defined by the database. It is important to note that only the properties you list will have corresponding columns. For example, the following axis specification will only return a column for the Manufacturer property values in the rowset:

```
CrossJoin ([Product].[Brand].Members, [Time].[Quarter].Members)
PROPERTIES [Product].[Brand].[Manufacturer] on rows
```

If you also wanted a single column for each dimension's member names, you would need to specify the following:

```
CrossJoin ([Product].[Brand].Members, [Time].[Quarter].Members)
PROPERTIES [Product].[Brand].[Manufacturer], [Product].Name, [Time].Name
on rows
```

Note that all slicer information is lost when an MDX query is flattened into a rowset. No member information will be returned for any dimensions that you fail to place on an axis. If it is important to retain the slice context for the cell data, place all relevant dimensions into an explicit axis of the query (for example, axis 2).

From ADOMD.NET, obtaining and using MDX results in tabular format from an AdomdDataReader is trivial. The steps are identical to retrieving a cellset except that the ExecuteReader method is called on a command object instead of ExecuteCellSet. The following code sample demonstrates this:

```
// create reader
AdomdDataReader reader = command.ExecuteReader();

// move to next row
while (reader->Read())
{
// ... do things like with any other IDataRecord
                                    // such as print out row values
Console.WriteLine("{0}", reader->GetValue(0));
}

// always call Close when done reading
reader.Close()
```

The only major difference between how we used this data reader and how we used any other is that we executed an MDX query, and we used it on a connection to an OLAP database instead of a relational database.

Summary

We have touched on the very basics of client programming in ADOMD.NET using C# for the purposes of executing MDX. Any given client that you are going to create will need to use the techniques that we have outlined here. Your clients will doubtlessly involve a great deal more; we could have devoted several chapters to building a client using ADOMD.NET and XML for Analysis. However, if this topic is new to you, we hopefully have demonstrated that it can be quite straightforward to interact with an OLAP database and put your MDX to use.

Optimizing MDX

Just as with any other language, there is more than one way to say the same thing in MDX. Some alternatives, however, may be more efficient than others in their execution. In this chapter, we look at some of the factors that control efficiency (in terms of CPU and memory used) when executing MDX in Microsoft Analysis Services. If you are interested in efficiency but use a different OLE DB for OLAP provider, some of the techniques described may still apply.

We are not going to discuss optimal database design in this chapter. In our experience building analysis systems using OLAP and Analysis Services, we have found many other issues and factors in total system efficiency, some of which affect MDX execution. However, in keeping with the thrust of this as an MDX book, we will restrict our discussion to the issues most directly connected to composing and using MDX, and only look at one design issue that trades MDX work for cube construction work.

Although we will present different areas of optimization, it is also important to remember that faster is not necessarily "better." If your applications respond too slowly, then something may need to be made faster. If it's fast enough and it works, it doesn't need to be fixed. Composing queries that are optimal from a resource point of view may require more cumbersome database designs or front-end query builders as well. But when you need to tune it up, this chapter may help.

Architecture Change from Analysis Services 2000 to 2005

Analysis Services 2000 has a rich client component—PivotTable Services (PTS). PivotTable Services cache data on a client machine's memory, perform MDX statement parsing, and even resolve calculations on the client side. The communication protocol between server and client is proprietary. A user query could invoke zero round trips (all data is cached on the client side) or multiple round trips (PTS sends multiple subdata queries to get slices of data). Users can choose Execution Location and Default Isolation mode connection parameters to have partial control over the query execution location on either the server or the client.

Analysis Services 2005 has a totally different thin client architecture. The OLE DB client component (PTS) becomes a thin wrapper of XMLA. The managed client component ADOMD.NET is also an object wrapper for XMLA with no dependence on PTS, unlike its predecessor ADOMD. The client components simply wrap query requests with XMLA SOAP requests, send the over to the server, and deserialize the server's XMLA responses (mostly cellset) into client-side objects (`CellSet` or `ADOMDNET.Cellset`). Analysis Services 2005 client components do not have a data cache and do not perform any tasks such as parsing and client-side calculations. All client query requests have to be executed on the server side, and there is no control of execution location. Any client MDX query will invoke exactly one server round trip: The client sends an MDX query to the server and the server sends results back to the client.

The new Analysis Services 2005 architecture supports the standard communication protocol (XMLA). Any client tool that sends XMLA and consumes XMLA will be able to communicate with the Analysis Services 2005 server. The client tool is not limited to any particular OS or programming language. It is a more secure model because no data is cached on the client side and all security checks happen on the server side. The Analysis Services 2005 PTS consumes much less memory (no cache), and requires much fewer client CPU cycles (no complex calculations). It is optimal for typical three-tier applications (web browser, middle tier, and backend server), where the middle-tier server usually maintains many connections to the backend Analysis Services server. The middle tier can support more PTS connections or more concurrent users, due to the thin client design. For slow network applications or cross-continent client/server applications, the thin client design guarantees that there is only one round trip between server and client for each query, contrary to sometimes having many round trips for a single query using Analysis Services 2000. To further improve the performance, Analysis Services 2005 PTS supports Binary XML and XML compression by default. It cuts the network traffic significantly between the server and client.

The new architecture improves performance in most cases. However, there are some cases in which a thin client could have a worse user query response compared to Analysis Services 2000. This could be the case with two-tier applications, such as multiple users using Excel pivot table and that directly connect to an Analysis Services server. If many MDX queries require heavy calculations such as session calculations, cell calculations, and calculated members, or if the target cube has many calculations (MDX Scripts), the server could become CPU- and memory-bound by user query requests. While PTS in Analysis Services 2000 can help resolve most user queries from the client cache, and can utilize client machine resources to do calculations, Analysis Service 2005 can only resolve all the user queries on the server side. A more powerful server machine with more CPUs and more memory will help the query performance in this case. Creating local cubes for clients can be another solution for heavy analytic applications. A user can precache the data slices in local cubes, which are stored on his/her own client machine. When the user does slice and dice data or performs online analysis, all communications go to his/ her own local cube, and there is no server hit. Because client applications will load the local cube DLL (MSMDLocal.dll) into its own memory space, user queries are resolved inside the application process, which means no network traffic and no cross-process communications.

Optimizing Set Operations

When a server executes queries, it behaves as though every set was fully materialized in memory prior to use. This introduces significant resource issues for the server.

```
Topcount ([Customer].[Customer].[Individual Customer].Members, 50,
       [Measures].Sales)
```

will be evaluated at the server for the whole set of [Customer].[Customer] .[Individual Customer].Members. Suppose that you have 500 customers and 100 product categories. Suppose also that you request the following:

```
Topcount (
  CrossJoin(
    [Customer].[Customer].[Individual Customer].Members,
    [Product].[Product].[Category].Members
  ),
  50,
  [Measures].[Sales]
)
```

You will get the top-50 customer-product tuples in terms of sales. In this case, the 50,000 combinations will be generated and examined on the server.

To obtain good performance, you may need to rephrase very resource-intensive calculations. The key to rephrasing is breaking up an operation on a large set into a set of operations on smaller sets. We'll work through some common types of set-related optimizations now. A common thread that runs through them is replacing an expensive `CrossJoin()` with a less expensive series of operations.

Sums along Cross-Joined Sets

For example, producing sums across multiple dimensions that are phrased as the sums of the sums of individual dimensions will be less resource-intensive than producing a single sum of a cross-join. That is, instead of this expression:

```
Sum (
   CrossJoin (
      Descendants (
         [Customer].[Customer].CurrentMember,
         [Customer].[Customer].[Individual Customer]
      ),
      Crossjoin (
         Descendants (
            [Time].[Time].CurrentMember,
            [Time].[Time].[Day]
         ),
         Descendants (
            [Product].[Product].CurrentMember,
            [Product].[Product].[Category]
         )
      )
   ),
   [Measures].[Sales in Euros] *
   ([Measures].[Currency Conversion],
      Ancestor ([Geography].[Geography],
[Geography].[Geography].[Country]))
)
```

you would want to express it as follows:

```
Sum (
   Descendants (
      [Customer].[Customer].CurrentMember,
      [Customer].[Customer].[Individual Customer]
   ),
   Sum (
      Descendants (
         [Time].[Time].CurrentMember,
         [Time].[Time].[Day]
      ),
```

```
    Sum (
       Descendants (
          [Product].[Product].CurrentMember,
          [Product].[Product].[Category]
       ),
       [Measures].[Sales in Euros] *
       ([Measures].[Currency Conversion],
          Ancestor ([Geography].[Geography],
 [Geography].[Geography].[Country])
 ) ) )
```

This avoids the `CrossJoin()` and provides exactly the same results. When you are calculating the results, the order of dimensions is not likely to make any semantic difference. However, if you nest the larger sets within the smaller sets, the `Sum()` will execute noticeably more quickly. For example, if the number of customer descendants in the previous `Sum()` is likely to be larger than the number of product descendants, you should move the customers to be inside of the products. The performance boost will vary as a function of the number of dimensions and members involved, but it can easily make a difference of 5 to 20 percent in the time it takes to calculate. (See the "Optimizing Summation" section later in this chapter for more notes.)

Filtering across Cross-Joined Sets

Frequently, you will need to filter the results of one or more cross-joined sets. Depending on what your filter criterion is, you may or may not be able to create a high-performing expression.

Let's take the simplest case: filtering out tuples with associated empty cells. In straightforward, standard MDX, you might express this as:

```
Filter (
  CrossJoin (
    [Geography].[Geography].[Region].Members,
    CrossJoin (
      [Product].[Product].[Category].Members,
      [Payment Terms].[Terms].Members
    ),
  ),
  Not IsEmpty ([Measures].[Sales])
)
```

In Analysis Services, cross-joining is pretty expensive, because the entire cross-joined set appears to be instantiated in memory prior to any filtering taking place. However, if the [Sales] measure is directly fed into the cube from a fact table, you can make this much more efficient by using Microsoft's own `NonEmptyCrossJoin()`, as in the following:

```
NonEmptyCrossJoin (
   [Geography].[Geography].[Region].Members,
   [Product].[Product].[Category].Members,
   [Payment Terms].[Terms].Members,
   { [Measures].[Sales] },
   3
)
```

We'll leave the detailed definition of this function to Appendix A. You can see that it accepts more than two sets for its input. Analysis Services uses internal information gleaned from reading fact table information to provide the most rapid response it can. The NonEmptyCrossJoin(. . .) works much better than Filter (CrossJoin (. . .), Not IsEmpty(. . .)). However, NonEmptyCrossJoin() doesn't deal with calculated members on any dimension.

Analysis Services 2005 introduced a new function NonEmpty(). The NonEmpty function will take calculated members into account and automatically use a fast algorithm if there is no calculation involved (same as NonEmptyCrossJoin). The NonEmptyCrossJoin function will be depreciated and replaced by NonEmpty, and we will discuss the NonEmpty() function in a later section. For now, we can rewrite the previous statement as the following:

```
NonEmpty (
   [Geography].[Geography].[Region].Members*
[Product].[Product].[Category].Members*
   [Payment Terms].[Terms].Members,
   { [Measures].[Sales] }
)
```

Alternatively, using generate() we can factor calculations in (for example, members calculated by custom member formulas or calculated members):

```
Generate (
   [Geography].[Geography].[Region].Members,
   CrossJoin (
     [Geography].[Geography].CurrentMember,
     Generate (
       [Product].[Product].[Category].Members,
       CrossJoin (
         [Product].[Product].CurrentMember,
         Filter (
           [Payment Terms].[Terms].Members,
           Not IsEmpty ([Measures].[Calculated Member])
) ) ) )
```

The previous example is much faster than the equivalent filter of a large number of CrossJoin() operators. In our own lab, testing on sample data sets, when the difference is noticeable, CrossJoin() takes about twice as long as `NonEmpty()`, but only about a third as much time as the straightforward filter of a `CrossJoin()`.

Optimizing TopCount() and BottomCount()

`TopCount()` and `BottomCount()` are valuable and somewhat resource-intensive operations. If you are simply taking the top or bottom count against members of a single dimension, you can't really optimize the MDX used. However, if you are taking the top or bottom count of a set of tuples formed from a `CrossJoin()`, then you can significantly optimize the processing through MDX. Consider the following extreme example, which potentially generates a huge set in memory:

```
TopCount (
    { [Customer].[Customer].[Individual Customer].Members
    * [Time].[Time].[Day].Members
    * [Product].[Product].[Category].Members },
    50,
    [Measures].[Qty Returned]
)
```

Creating the set and then accessing the top members is very time- and memory-consuming. However, it can be broken up into the following to get the same result:

```
TopCount (
  Generate (
     [Customer].[Customer].[Individual Customer].Members,
     TopCount (
        { [Customer].[Customer].CurrentMember } *
        [Time].[Time].[Day].Members *
[Product].[Product].[Category].Members,
        50,
        [Measures].[Qty Returned]
     )
  ),
  50,
  [Measures].[Qty Returned]
)
```

This last expression means "for each customer, generate a top-50 set, combine all of these top-50 sets, and take the top 50 from them." The overhead of creating the larger number of smaller sets is less than the overhead of extracting the top 50 from the single larger set, and the results will be the same.

Note that `TopPct()` and `BottomPct()` cannot be optimized in this way, because the inner `TopPct()` will remove tuples and cell values that need to be considered by the outer `TopPct()`.

NonEmpty function In Analysis Services 2005

Cube space is very sparse, and users can easily construct a query that requires a large set of cells. The interesting cells most of time are limited to the non-empty cells—the cells that have data. Think of the cube space as a pyramid with the leaf-level cells located at the bottom. Because leaf-level cells get their measure values from fact data (with very limited rows), the Analysis Services server stores the fact data and dimension data in such a way that it can leverage the fact table dimension key information to quickly locate nonempty cells in the huge sparse cube space—both the leaf-level cells and the aggregated upper-level cells.

The NonEmpty() function takes in a set as one of the parameters, filters all the tuples that contain a null cell value, and returns a set of nonempty tuples. Analysis Services is optimized to identify nonempty data and return results to a user query. The Optimized method leverages a much smaller searching space (fact table rows) and has advanced algorithms to quickly locate non-empty cells. The performance difference is significant for queries with large cross-joined member sets.

In addition to the techniques for set optimization described in previous sections, MDX developers should use NonEmpty() as much as possible in their calculations whenever it applies. Here is a sample query:

```
TopCount (
    { [Customer].[Customer].[Individual Customer].Members
    * [Time].[Time].[Day].Members
    * [Product].[Product].[Category].Members },
    50,
    [Measures].[Qty Returned]
)
```

The first step to optimize this query is

```
TopCount (
    NONEMPTY ([Customer].[Customer].[Individual Customer].Members *
[Time].[Time].[Day].Members * [Product].[Product].[Category].Members,
{[Measures].[Qty Returned]}),50,[Measures].[Qty Returned]
)
```

Note that the previous query specified the filter set as { [Measures].[Qty Returned]} in a nonempty function to avoid having the server choose the default query evaluation context (which could be done for other measures).

The old function NonEmptyCrossjoin in Analysis Services 2000 will be deprecated and will be replaced by the new function NonEmpty. While NonEmptyCrossjoin stills works in Analysis Services 2005, the user must be aware that NonEmptyCrossjoin does not take calculated members into account. This problem has been fixed in the NonEmpty function.

If a cube has calculated cells, MDX Scripts, or calculated members, the fact table rows are not a valid indication of the cell emptiness. In the worst case, to return correct results, Analysis Services has to iterate over the entire region of the user query and evaluate cell values individually to see if the cell value is null. This is usually a slow operation for large and sparse data queries, especially for calculated members or cells.

Analysis Services provides you the choice to provide hints so that the server can use the optimized algorithm to determine cells' emptiness with the NON_EMPTY_BEHAVIOR keyword. The following query returns the Forecast sales by applying different rates:

```
with member [Measures].[ForecastSales] as
iif([Measures].[Internet Sales Amount] >500 , [Measures].[Internet Sales
Amount]*1.2, [Measures].[Internet Sales Amount]*1.5)
Select
NonEmpty(
[Customer].[Customer Geography].[Full Name].members* Descendants(
[Product].[Product Categories].[Category].&[3],[Product].[Product
Categories].[Product Name]), {[Measures].[ForecastSales]}) on 1 ,
{[Measures].[ForecastSales]} on 0
from [Adventure Works]
```

Even though the above query uses the NonEmpty function, you will find that the server still takes a long time to execute the query (14 seconds on the author's machine). This is so because the optimized code path cannot be applied to complex calculated members.

Take a second look at the calculated member [Measures].[ForecastSales]; it should have the exact same nonempty behavior as the fact measure ([Measures].[Internet Sales Amount]). You can specify NON_EMPTY_BEHAVIOR for this member, and tie the calculated measure to a real fact measure. Then the server will use the optimized code path for the nonempty determination. The following modified query that contains NON_EMPTY_BEHAVIOR will have better performance.

```
with member [Measures].[ForecastSales] as
iif([Measures].[Internet Sales Amount] >500 , [Measures].[Internet Sales
Amount]*1.2, [Measures].[Internet Sales Amount]*1.5),
NON_EMPTY_BEHAVIOR = [Measures].[Internet Sales Amount]
Select
NonEmpty(
[Customer].[Customer Geography].[Full Name].members* Descendants(
[Product].[Product Categories].[Category].&[3],[Product].[Product
Categories].[Product Name]), {[Measures].[ForecastSales]}) on 1 ,
{[Measures].[ForecastSales]} on 0
from [Adventure Works]
```

Optimizing Sorting: Order()

Fortunately, the Order() function doesn't need a lot of optimizing. When a set of tuples is to be ordered, the ordering expression is evaluated once over the set, the results are placed into a work area, and the tuples are sorted from that. This means that complex expressions are only evaluated once per tuple, and any converting of data types (for example, text versions of member properties into dates or numbers) will also only happen once.

There isn't any straightforward way of optimizing the sorting of cross-joined sets; you cross-join the sets and then you order them. If you are both ordering and filtering a set, it is usually most efficient to filter the set first and then order it, unless the filter condition is somehow dependent on the ordering.

UnOrder Function for a Query with a Large Dataset

Analysis Services 2005 has a new UnOrder function. This function will provide better performance for large datasets if the order of the members in a set is not important. For example, OLAP local cube generation uses MDX queries with UnOrder to get flat rowset fact data. Following is an MDX example of the UnOrder function:

```
Select
unorder ([Customer].[Customer Geography].[City].members)  on 0 ,
[Date].[Calendar].[Calendar Year].members on 1
from [Adventure Works]
where ([Measures].[Internet Sales Amount])
```

Optimizing Summation

When discussing dimensional calculations and time analysis calculations in previous chapters, we looked very briefly at expressing a calculation across measures as a calculation on another dimension that would intersect existing measures. In various examples, we created calculated measures that would aggregate another measure. One technique creates a calculated member that, when combined with a measure, produces the right calculation for the measure, whereas another technique puts all of the calculation logic into its own calculated measure. Although computationally equivalent, there is a surprising performance difference between the two ways of expresssing a calculation. Summation is the most common calculation that this will be seen in.

To recap, consider the two possible ways of phrasing the summation of two measures for a given set of customers, products, and channels:

```
WITH
MEMBER [Customer].[Customer].[Total] AS
'Sum ( { Set of Customers } )'
MEMBER [Product].[Product].[Total] AS
'Sum ( { Set of Products } )'
MEMBER [Channel].[Channel].[Total] AS
'Sum ( { Set of Channels } )'
SELECT
{ [Measures].[Units], [Measures].[Revenue] } on columns,
{ [Time].[Time].[Quarter].Members } on rows
FROM Sales
WHERE ([Customer].[Customer].[Total], [Product].[Product].[Total],
[Channel].[Channel].[Total])
```

and

```
WITH
MEMBER [Measures].[Total Units] AS
'Sum (
  { Set of Channels },
  Sum (
    { Set of Products },
    Sum (
      { Set of Customers },
      [Measures].[Units]
) ) )'
MEMBER [Measures].[Total Sales] AS
'Sum (
  { Set of Channels },
  Sum (
    { Set of Products },
    Sum (
      { Set of Customers },
      [Measures].[Sales]
) ) )'
SELECT
{ [Measures].[Total Units], [Measures].[Total Revenue] } on columns,
{ [Time].[Time].[Quarter].Members } on rows
FROM Sales
```

Both of these methods will result in exactly the same set of cell values, although they will have slightly different measure names. However, there is a notable performance difference between them. Although your mileage will vary depending on the query, we have seen the second phrasing take only 60 percent of the time of the first phrasing. In short, the more dimensionally compact phrasing can easily be 40 percent slower. Both take time in proportion to the number of measures being aggregated, so querying for fewer measures or more measures in the first phrasing of the query will not affect the time required, despite the fact that the number of formulas hasn't changed.

Although the more dimensional phrasing is slower, remember that in many cases the difference will be negligible. Also consider that the phrasing lends itself to a simple way of constructing ratios and performing further calculations on those sums at the server.

Designing Calculations into Your Database (Putting Member Properties into Measures and the New MDX function MemberValue)

You have seen over and over that there are certain useful calculations that junior designers will initially compose against member properties, but that are more efficient and manageable when put directly into OLAP cubes. This is an area that is straightforward to explain, so even though it delves into cube design as well, we will describe it here.

A number of simple numerical data types are often expressed as member properties. Typical examples include the square footage of stores or the number of days in a month (or a higher-level time period). As a member property, these are relatively straightforward to use in calculations at the level they are defined for:

```
CREATE MEMBER [Sales].[Sales Per Square Foot] AS
'[Measures].[Sales] / Val ([Store].[Store].CurrentMember.Properties
("Store Sq Ft"))'
```

However, these calculations are desirable at any level, so there is an impetus to define a calculated member that works at any level:

```
CREATE MEMBER [Sales].[Sales Per Square Foot] AS
'[Measures].[Sales] / Sum (
  Descendants (
    [Store].[Store].CurrentMember,
    [Store].[Store].[Individual Store]
  ),
  Val ([Store].[Store].CurrentMember.Properties ("Store Sq Ft"))
)'
```

If you have more than one calculation that involves square footage (costs per square foot, employees per square foot, and shrinkage per square foot), you may also define a calculated member that is just the square footage aggregated appropriately:

```
CREATE MEMBER [Sales].[Store Square Feet] AS
'Sum (
  Descendants (
    [Store].[Store].CurrentMember,
    [Store].[Store].[Individual Store]
```

```
    ),
    Val ([Store].[Store].CurrentMember.Properties ("Store Sq Ft"))
    )'
CREATE MEMBER [Sales].[Sales Per Square Foot] AS
'[Measures].[Sales] / [Measures].[Store Square Feet]'
```

However, this makes for unnecessary work in every query that executes against the cube. It also forces you to deal with any client-side and logistical issues that arise because [Store Square Feet] is not a "real" member, but a calculated one.

The simplest (and most efficient) way to provide this calculation is to create a one-dimensional measure group with a measure of [Store Square Feet], using the Store dimension. Then combine this one-dimensional measure group with your original measure group into a cube. Now your sales per square foot calculated member will only need to be defined as:

```
CREATE MEMBER [Sales].[Sales Per Square Foot] AS
'[Measures].[Sales] / [Measures].[Store Square Feet]'
```

Similarly, the number of days per time period can be placed into a one-dimensional cube by simply counting the number of day-level time dimension records (or by summing the number 1). If your time dimension starts above the day level, you can use an appropriate column function or a stored column value in the time dimension table to bring in the right number.

In Analysis Services 2005, the new MemberValue function is introduced to allow a Typed ValueColumn property for an attribute. The MemberValue function allows you to get this property value of a member in MDX. Since the MemberValue function is a native MDX function, it is a much better choice performance wise than VBA function VAL(). If you set the Store square feet as a member value of the store key, you can easily write more readable and better-performing queries like the following. Note that this MemberValue is not aggregatable, so to calculate the higher-level store square footage, you still need to use the method in the previous section.

```
CREATE MEMBER [Sales].[Sales Per Square Foot] AS
'[Measures].[Sales] / [Store].[Store].CurrentMember.MemberValue)'
```

MDX Script Optimization

MDX Script is a big step forward, allowing Analysis Services 2005 to support complex cube calculations. It is particularly useful for financial applications, because most of them involve complex business rules to perform calculations such as budget allocation, cash flow calculations, and currency conversion.

The functionality of MDX Script is much richer and more user-friendly than calculated cells in Analysis Services 2000. While the performance of MDX script is highly tuned, all MDX Script calculations are evaluated when user queries are resolved. MDX developers should be aware that any calculation involves extra steps on top of the normal aggregation and data scan operations (storage engine query). Because MDX Script is a calculation definition language (not a procedure), and Analysis Services does not persist any calculation results, MDX Script calculations are performed in server memory space and are calculated on the fly for every user query. Calculations in MDX Script will consume more server memory and CPU resources for each user query, and excessive calculations will cause not only performance problems but also scalability problems in multiple-user analytic systems. In a nutshell, writing an efficient MDX Script is necessary to minimize the server calculations while giving users the correct results.

(The `Cache` statement, which was available in Analysis Services 2000, becomes an undocumented and unsupported function in Analysis Services 2005. While the `Cache` statement could improve the query performance in some cases, we discourage you from using it in SQL 2005 because it is not fully tested and is not guaranteed to work in all cases.)

Scope the Calculation in Detail

For user queries that do not touch the cube space that contains a calculation, Analysis Services will simply fetch the data (often in cache) with simple aggregation and return the results without invoking the calculation module. Cutting down the region of calculation area will reduce the chance of user queries hitting calculations, which consumes more server resources.

Often MDX developers design an MDX Script right from the business rule requirements. However, business requirements are not always accurate, and developers need to take further steps to understand the actual business logic.

For example, suppose that a business rule requires that current year's forecast value equal to prior year's actual * 1.2:

```
Scope ([Measures].[Dollars Sold], [Scenario].[Scenario].[Forecast]);
    this = ([Scenario].[Scenario].[Actual],
ParallelPeriod([Time].[ByMonth].[Year],1,[Time].[ByMonth].currentmember)
)*1.2 ;
end scope;
```

However, forecast values only make sense for future years, and the real business need is to forecast a 2005 value based on 2004's actual results. It is better to put the constraint in the query. All queries querying Forecast before 2004 will directly return NULL from the storage engine query. It also makes more sense to return NULL for the year 2004 and before that for the future scenario:

```
Scope ([Measures].[Dollars Sold], [Scenario].[Scenario].[Forecast],
        Descendants([Time].[ByMonth].[Year].[2005]));
    this = ([Scenario].[Scenario].[Actual],
ParallelPeriod([Time].[ByMonth].[Year],1,[Time].[ByMonth].currentmember)
)*1.2 ;
end scope;
```

Because the MDX Script is evaluated whenever a user query touches those calculation slices, it is good practice for MDX developers to fully understand the business requirements and data distribution to specify the exact Scope, which is only calculated when necessary.

Avoid Leaf-Level Calculations

Leaf-level calculations are calculations that are performed on very low-level members in the cube space. They typically involve tuples with low-level members in multiple dimensions (or hierarchies in dimensions).

Think of the cube space as a pyramid—the lower the level, the bigger the space. The bottom of the pyramid (the true leaf tuples) consists of tuples with members from the leaf level of every dimension. Those cells are aggregated up to a much smaller number of cells in the upper level. For example, in the Adventure Works database, using three dimensions as an example, the number of leaf-level tuples for the Date, Product, and Customer dimensions is 1461 * 395 * 18,484 = 1.67 * 10^10 cells. Suppose that most system users are only interested in Year, Product Category, and State-Province Level—there are only 4 * 4 * 71 members for that combination:

```
with member Measures.LeafCount as
            [Product].[Product Categories].[Product Name].Members.Count*
            [Customer].[Customer Geography].[Full Name].Members.Count*
                                [Date].[Calendar].[Date].Count
Select {Measures.LeafCount} on 0
from [Adventure Works]
```

The cell values from the higher level are aggregated from the leaf-level cells. So, theoretically, a simple MDX like the following

```
select measures.members on 0 from [Adventure Works]
```

would require server aggregate values from a huge number of leaf-level cells (10^{20} and more), because all dimension default members are the top-level member All.

The optimization lays to sparsity of the cube space. The lower the level is, the sparser it is. The actual number of not-null leaf-level tuples is equal to the size of your fact table (if every row has distinct dimension keys) or less than the size of the fact table rows. Analysis Services has many optimizations to accelerate user queries by getting the aggregate value only from those cells that have values. In addition to that, Analysis Services can build aggregation data during processing time for higher-level cells for better query performance.

If there is any calculation on any region of your cube, the sparsity heuristics from the fact table are no longer valid for the server to optimize the aggregations. Calculations can set the value to any cell anywhere in the cube space. A simple assignment like `"this =1;"` will set the whole cube's space to 1.

If the MDX script defines a calculation on the leaf level or lower level with large cells involved, whenever a query queries the tuples on the calculated region, the cell calculation will be evoked. Since users will issue queries on higher-level cells, in most cases, the server has to go to the leaf level to evaluate every single leaf cell where the calculation is defined. Then the server will aggregate the values up to higher-level cells. Using the previous example, if your query is `(year.members, category.members, country.members)`, the query only asks for 4 * 4 * 6 = 96 cells. But if you have leaf-level calculations, which prevent the server from using the fact table heuristic to get the nonempty cells for aggregation, the server will calculate all leaf-level cells (1.2 * 10^10) and then aggregate them to give you the answer. It could take minutes if not hours for the server to return results.

Table 16-1   Adventure Works Dimension and Level Members

[DATE] [CALENDAR]		[PRODUCT]. [PRODUCT CATEGORIES]		[CUSTOMER]. [CUSTOMERGEOGRAPHY]	
Year	(4)	Category	(4)	Country	(6)
Semester	(8)	SubCategory	(37)	State-Province	(71)
Quarter	(16)	Product Name	(395)	City	(587)
Month	(48)			Postal Code	(646)
Date	(1461)			Full Name	(18484)

One typical leaf-level calculation is `calculation Amount = Price* Volume`. If a cube has Price and Volume measures, to get the correct Amount across every level of the cube space, the calculation has to be applied on the lowest level. Another typical leaf-level calculation is currency conversion. Currency conversion has to happen on the leaf level of the time dimension and currency dimension because the currency exchange rate is different for every time period.

Cube Design to Avoid Leaf-Level Calculation

Similarly to design calculations in the OLAP database, the OLAP developer can create measures instead of using an MDX Script to perform leaf-level calculations. Then the leaf-level calculation is precalculated during cube processing time via an SQL query, and the expensive on-the-fly calculation is avoided.

For the Amount = Price * Volume type of calculation, a simple calculated column in DSV and a simple measure Amount added to the cube will ease the calculation burden of the MDX Script. For currency conversion, it is also very easy to build an SQL query to get converted values, and then you can create measures such as Amount and `ConvertedAmount`. A simple cube structure change will give you great performance because Analysis Services is very efficient and highly optimized for fact data scan and aggregation.

The only drawback to this approach is in the writeback scenario. Because the calculated data is precalculated and is stored directly in cube storage, the changes on one member won't affect the calculated results. Using currency conversion as example, if a user issues an update cube query to change the currency rate, the converted amount cannot be automatically calculated.

If applications don't have requirements for writeback or what-if (user changes a cell value and then rolls back the transaction) scenarios, most of the leaf-level calculations can be transferred to an SQL statement, precalculated in the SQL relational database, and cached in the OLAP database.

Measure Expression to Optimize Leaf-Level Calculation

If your application does support writeback or what-if scenarios, Analysis Services 2005 has a specific feature called measure expression that you can use to accelerate the price * unit or currency conversion type of calculation (see Figure 16-1). Analysis Services 2005 cube measures have an optional property `MeasureExpression`, which is the measure expression for that measure. The expression can be defined as Measure1 * | / Measure2 where `Measure1` is a measure from its own measure group (`Main Measuregroup`) and `Measure2` is a measure from a different measure group (`Lookup Measuregroup`) with at least one dimension shared with the main `Measuregroup`. Let's discuss it using a price * unit example.

From the schema, you can identify two measure groups, SalesInUnit, with the Customer, Product, Time dimension, and Unit measures; and Price, with the Product, Time dimension, and Price measures. You can define a measure `Sales` on `SalesInUnit Measuregroup` with `MeasureExpression` as `[UNIT]*[Price]`.

When a user query asks for Sales value, the Analysis Services server will first get all leaf-level fact rows from `Main Measuregroup` that correspond to the query. Then Analysis Services will build an index on shared dimension leaf members (Product and Time). Then Analysis Services will get all related fact rows from the `Lookup MeasureGroup` and build an index on those members too. Then it will merge these two recordsets, calculate the sales value on the leaf level, and then return the aggregation value if necessary.

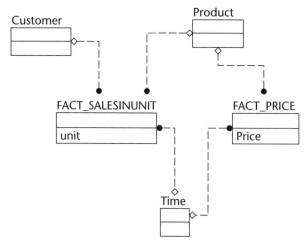

Figure 16-1   Price * Unit measure expression example.

Measure expression has better performance then a normal MDX Script for this type of calculation because the server only scans the data once and does it in batch mode with specific indices. A normal MDX Script might invoke multiple scans of the same data, and the calculation is done for each leaf cell individually.

Measure expression is a powerful tool for solving many business problems such as currency conversion and percentage ownership problems. It usually involves a many-to-many dimension, and you can refer to SQL book online for detailed designs of those scenarios.

Measure expression has some limitations. The granularity of a measure's measure expression must be the same as the granularity of measures used in the measure expression. Using the previous example, Unit and Price have to link to the same level of product and time dimensions. Also, measure expression does not support the distinct count aggregation function.

Since the target measure with measure expression is calculated on the fly, any writeback to one related measure will cause the target measure to change. That is the advantage of using a measure expression over the previous cube design method. However, since the calculation still happens during query time, the performance is worse than the direct measure solution.

MDX Script Optimization for Leaf-Level Calculation

When an MDX script has leaf-level calculations, normally the performance is not bad for queries asking for the exact leaf-level members. It is because user query space is usually limited, and the overall performance is still acceptable although every cell needs to be calculated. The worse case for leaf-level calculations is when a user queries higher-level cells; the server needs evaluate large numbers of lower-level leaf cells, which aggregate up to the higher-level cells. This is called a "calc and aggregate" type of calculation.

Avoid Unnecessary Leaf-Level Calculation

Sometimes, business requirements are too detailed, which results in the MDX Scripts having unnecessary lower-level calculations.

Using the forecast system as example, if the customer requirement is for every product, and every customer, the optimistic value is equal to the actual value of last year * 1.2. The most straightforward translation from the customer requirement would be the following:

```
Scope ([Measures].[Dollars Sold], [Scenario].[Scenario].[Forecast],
Product.Product.ProductName.Members,
Customer.Customer.Customer.Members);
    this = ([Scenario].[Scenario].[Actual],
ParallelPeriod([Time].[ByMonth].[Year],1,[Time].[ByMonth].currentmember)
)*1.2 ;
end scope;
```

For a query asking for higher-level cells:

```
Select {Product.Product.Category.members} on 0,
{Customer.Customer.Country.Members} on 1
From Sales
Where ([Scenario].[Scenario].[Forecast], ([Measures].[Dollars Sold],
[Time].[TimeByMonth].[2005])
```

As described earlier, the server needs to evaluate leaf cells on the product name and customer name levels and aggregate them.

Are the two sets (customer and product leaf-level members) in the scope really needed? Thinking about it a little bit further, the calculation is not really a leaf-level calculation. The cell values don't have to be calculated on leaf level; the higher-level cells can use the exact same calculation formula. Simply remove the two set constraints, as in the following:

```
Scope ([Measures].[Dollars Sold], [Scenario].[Scenario].[Forecast]);
    this = ([Scenario].[Scenario].[Actual],
ParallelPeriod([Time].[ByMonth].[Year],1,[Time].[ByMonth].currentmember)
)*1.2 ;
end scope;
```

When the user queries `Product.Product.Category.members` for (`[Scenario].[Scenario].[Forecast]`, (`[Measures].[Dollars Sold]`), server optimization will use (`[Scenario].[Scenario].[Actual]`,

ParallelPeriod([Time].[ByMonth].[Year],1,[Time].[ByMonth]
.currentmember), Product.product.category.members) value *
1.2 to get the forecast value. The actual value is a natural aggregation.

This section seems to contradict the first section on MDX optimization, "Scope the Calculation in Detail," but the ultimate goal is the same—to minimize the calculation required and to use natural aggregation as much as possible.

Using NONEMPTY for Higher-Level Calculations

There is another solution for the calc and aggregate problem: For nonleaf or up-level calculations, you can use NonEmpty() and use a normal measure (with no calculation) to obtain much fewer leaf-level cells and calculate them to get the aggregate number. This technique is typically effective in Analysis Services 2000 and should be considered as a performance improvement method for Analysis Services 2005.

Using currency conversion as an example, in the following script for measures.ConvertedAmount, the script applies to the leaf level of time (month), currency. If you just have a calculated script, for upper-level cells, the query will return the correct answer, but the query performance will be slower.

```
SCOPE ([Source Currency].[Source Currency].[Source Currency].members,
        [Date].[Calendar].[Date].members,
        [Measures].[ConvertedAmount]);
   This = [Measures].[Internet Sales Amount]* [Measures].[End of Day
Rate];
End Scope;
```

To improve the performance, you can add the following MDX Script to define the calculation of higher-level cells along the Time dimension. The script gives Analysis Services a hint by first using NonEmpty to get those cells that have data for [Internet sales amount]. Because there is no calculation associated with the measure, the server can use the fact data to quickly locate the nonempty cells. Then the server will calculate each of them using the first calculation. The calculated cell count is greatly reduced (especially in the multiple-dimension leaf-level case). We have seen many cases in which such a change will improve the performance from minutes to seconds, especially for Analysis Services 2000.

```
SCOPE ([Source Currency].[Source Currency].[Source Currency].members,
        Descendants([Date].[Calendar].[All
Periods],[Date].[Calendar].[Month],SELF_AND_BEFORE),
        [Measures].[ConvertedAmount]);
   This =
SUM(NONEMPTY(Descendants([Date].[Calendar].Currentmember,[Date].[Calendar].
[Date],SELF), ;
```

```
[Measures].[Internet Sales Amount]), ([Measures].[ConvertedAmount]));
End Scope;
```

Note that in Analysis Services 2005, the calculation engine, especially the query optimizer, will automatically detect whether or not it is safe to automatically apply the NonEmptyCrossJoin algorithm to reduce the number of cells to iterate over. We suggest that you use the first expression because it is intuitive and usually the server optimizer will provide good query performance.

Using NonemptyBehavior to Provide a Hint for Server Calculations

Like calculate member in an MDX query, MDX Script supports NON_EMPTY_BEHAVIOR, which can help the server to determine the cell's emptiness. We can rewrite the example in the previous section:

```
SCOPE ([Source Currency].[Source Currency].[Source Currency].members,
       [Date].[Calendar].[Date].members,
       [Measures].[ConvertedAmount]);
   This = [Measures].[Internet Sales Amount]* [Measures].[End of Day
Rate];
   NON_EMPTY_BEHAVIOR(this) = { [Measures].[Internet Sales Amount]};
End Scope;
```

Analysis Services 2005 does have optimizations that try to analyze the expression and automatically choose the Non_Empty_Behavior for some simple expressions. However, it is good practice to always specify Non_Empty_Behavior for MDX scripts, because Analysis Services does not deduce complex calculations, and the user can provide precise hints using business requirements.

Analysis Service 2005: Use Attribute Hierarchy Instead of Member Property

In Analysis Services 2000, MDX developers frequently use properties to control the calculation logic in IIF statements. Following is an MDX Script that uses the Account Type property to control the aggregation behavior of the account dimension:

```
SCOPE ([Account].[Accounts].MEMBERS,
       DESCENDANTS([Date].[Fiscal].[All
Periods],[Date].[Fiscal].[Month], SELF_AND_BEFORE),
       [Measures].[Amount] );
this = IIF ([Account].[Accounts].CURRENTMEMBER.PROPERTIES("Account
Type") = "Balances",
```

```
                            ([Date].[Fiscal].CURRENTMEMBER.LASTCHILD),
                IIF ( [Account].[Accounts].CURRENTMEMBER.PROPERTIES("Account
        Type") = "Rate",
                        Avg([Date].[Fiscal].CURRENTMEMBER.CHILDREN),
                        Sum([Date].[Fiscal].CURRENTMEMBER.CHILDREN)));
        End SCOPE;
```

In Analysis Services 20005, most of the properties are created as attributes, and they have their own attribute hierarchy associated with them. Analysis Services 2005 builds indices for attributes and has optimized the code path to quickly locate values via attributes. You should leverage attributes and the attribute hierarchy to avoid slower member property fetching and string comparison. The scripts are more readable in addition to performing better.

```
SCOPE ([Account].[Accounts].MEMBERS,
        DESCENDANTS([Date].[Fiscal].[All
Periods],[Date].[Fiscal].[Month], SELF_AND_BEFORE),
        [Measures].[Amount] );
([Account].[Account Type].[Balances]) =
([Date].[Fiscal].CURRENTMEMBER.LASTCHILD);
([Account].[Accounts].[Rate] =
Avg([Date].[Fiscal].CURRENTMEMBER.CHILDREN);
-- default sum, we don't need to specify
End SCOPE;
```

Analysis Services 2005 supports the following Account types, and each has different aggregation rules by default. Users can easily extend Account types and aggregation rules using Database editor and Account Intelligence Wizard in BI workbench. If you use the member property to control calculation, and the member property is discrete, we highly recommend building it as an attribute hierarchy and using it in your queries and MDX scripts.

Analysis Service 2005: Use Scope Instead of IIF

In many cases, some members need to get special calculations. In some other cases, members of some levels must have special treatment. MDX developers are likely to choose IIF because in Analysis Services 2000 it is a common practice. Take a look at the following MDX script. All departments' forecast values equal 1.5 times actual, except Sales and Marketing and Quality Assurance, which have different rates.

```
SCOPE ([Department].[Departments].[Department Level 01].members,
        [Scenario].[Scenario].[Forecast],
        [Measures].[Amount]) ;
```

```
this = IIF ([Department].[Departments].CURRENTMEMBER is
[Department].[Departments].[Sales and Marketing],
               1.2 * ([Scenario].[Scenario].[Actual]),
            IIF ([Department].[Departments].CURRENTMEMBER is
[Department].[Departments].[Quality Assurance],
               1.1 * ([Scenario].[Scenario].[Actual]),
               1.5 * ([Scenario].[Scenario].[Actual])));
END SCOPE;
```

You should write the MDX Script in the following fashion in Analysis Services 2005. It has better performance and is more readable.

```
SCOPE ([Department].[Departments].[Department Level 01].members,
       [Scenario].[Scenario].[Forecast],
       [Measures].[Amount]) ;

this = 1.5 * ([Scenario].[Scenario].[Actual]);
([Department].[Departments].[Sales and Marketing]) = 1.2 *
([Scenario].[Scenario].[Actual]);
([Department].[Departments].[Quality Assurance]) = 1.1 *
([Scenario].[Scenario].[Actual]);

END SCOPE;
```

Another common practice among Analysis Services 2000 users is to perform a level check using `IIF`:

```
SCOPE ([Department].[Departments].members,
       [Account].[Accounts].[Square Footage],
       [Measures].[Amount],
       [Scenario].[Scenario].[Forecast]
) ;
-- Corporate (level 1) doesn't have square footage
-- Department level the forecast square footage = actual * 1.2

this = IIF([Department].[Departments].CURRENTMEMBER.LEVEL is
[Department].[Departments].[Department Level 01],
           NULL,
           [Scenario].[Scenario].[Actual]*1.2);
END SCOPE;
```

The different level members should belong to different `Scope` statements:

```
SCOPE ([Department].[Departments].[Department Level 01].members,
       [Account].[Accounts].[Square Footage],
       [Measures].[Amount],
       [Scenario].[Scenario].[Forecast]
) ;
```

```
this = NULL;
END SCOPE;


SCOPE ([Department].[Departments].[Department Level 02].members,
       [Account].[Accounts].[Square Footage],
       [Measures].[Amount],
       [Scenario].[Scenario].[Forecast]
) ;
this = 1.2 * ([Scenario].[Scenario].[Actual]);
END SCOPE;
```

The previous two sections on avoiding IIF also apply to calculated members and even to session calculated members. In MDX query session calculations, users can use a combination of calculated members and calculated cells to achieve the same behavior as an MDX Script:

```
With Member Measures.OptimisticAmount as
     IIF ([Department].[Departments].CURRENTMEMBER is
[Department].[Departments].[Sales and Marketing],
              1.2 * ([Scenario].[Scenario].[Actual]),
           IIF ([Department].[Departments].CURRENTMEMBER is
[Department].[Departments].[Quality Assurance],
             1.1 * ([Scenario].[Scenario].[Actual]),
             1.5 * ([Scenario].[Scenario].[Actual]))))


Select [Department].[Departments].members on 0 ,
Descendants([Account].[Accounts].[Net Income]) on 1
from [Adventure Works]
where Measures.OptimisticAmount
```

The query can be rewritten to following with better performance:

```
With Member Measures.OptimisticAmount as 1.5 *
([Scenario].[Scenario].[Actual])
Cell calculation DepartmentA FOR '({[Department].[Departments].[Sales
and Marketing]},


{Measures.OptimisticAmount})' AS 1.2 * ([Scenario].[Scenario].[Actual])
Cell calculation DepartmentB FOR '({[Department].[Departments].[Quality
Assurance]},


{Measures.OptimisticAmount})' AS 1.1 * ([Scenario].[Scenario].[Actual])

Select [Department].[Departments].members on 0 ,
Descendants([Account].[Accounts].[Net Income]) on 1
from [Adventure Works]
where Measures.OptimisticAmount
```

Avoid Slow Functions in MDX Scripts

Certain functions in Analysis Services are powerful, but they are less efficient or involve lengthy operations. You should avoid them in intensive calculation definitions, such as inner loops and lower-level calculations.

Functions such as STRTOMEMBER, STRTOTUPLE, and the like will ask the server to parse the string, and locate the member at run time. It is fine to use it in user queries, but it could cause a performance problem if you use the function inside an MDX script and the function is called too many times during query execution.

The LOOKUPCUBE function will look up a cell value in a different cube, and it is much slower than referencing a cell inside the cube. Linking the cube to the current cube using linkmeasuregroup, or directly creating a measure group for the lookup cube, would give the calculation much better performance.

VBA functions such as VAL() should be avoided in MDX scripts. The VBA function requires a native-to-managed transition to call the VBA library, and it is much slower than the regular data fetch and native MDX functions.

Managed Store procedures require the server to perform interops for native and managed code transitions. This should also be limited to only user queries. Store procedures are useful for some calculations that are not easy to implement using MDX functions (for example, random sampling a set). Those functions are valuable for MDX queries where the query scopes are small and the number of calls to those functions is limited. MDX script developers need to be very careful when using them in MDX scripts. For inner loops and lower-level calculations, it is best not to use those functions and to find alternatives.

Change the Calculation Logic for Better Performance: Flow Calculation

Financial applications need to deal with balance sheet calculations. Flow-type calculations are frequently encountered.

Given a flow dimension with four members—opening, addition, deletion, and closing—the calculation rules are simple:

```
Current Period's opening equals to last Period's closing.
Current period's Closing = opening + addition - deletion.
Opening aggregation along time dimension (Firstchild)
Closing aggregation along time dimension (LastChild)
Addition and Deletion aggregation along time dimension (Sum)
```

If we directly translate the business rule into an MDX Script, the script is:

```
SCOPE (DESCENDANTS([Account].[Accounts].[Balance Sheet],, LEAVES),
      [Flow].[Flow].Members,
      [Date].[Fiscal].[Month].members,   -- Lowest level for time
      {Measures.[Amount]} );

([Flow].[Flow].[Opening]) =
([Flow].[Flow].[Closing],[Date].[Fiscal].Currentmember.PrevMember);
([Flow].[Flow].[Opening],[Date].[Fiscal].[Month].&[2001]&[7]) = this;
([Flow].[Flow].[Closing]) = ([Flow].[Flow].[Opening]) +
                            ([Flow].[Flow].[Addition]) -
                            ([Flow].[Flow].[Deletion]);
END SCOPE;

-- Time Aggregation
SCOPE (DESCENDANTS([Account].[Accounts].[Balance Sheet],, LEAVES),
      [Flow].[Flow].Members,
      Decendants([Date].[Fiscal].[All Periods],[Date].[Fiscal].[Fiscal
Quarter], SELF_AND_BEFORE),
      {Measures.[Amount]} );
 ([Flow].[Flow].[Opening]) = ([Date].[Fiscal].currentmember.firstChild);
 ([Flow].[Flow].[Closing]) = ([Date].[Fiscal].currentmember.LastChild);
END SCOPE;
```

In Analysis Services 2005, MDX developers no longer need to fight with "infinite recursion" and struggle with calculation passes, calculation pass depth, and solve order; the server now takes care of those issues by automatically creating a calculation pass for every statement. However, although the script is mathematically correct and it returns correct results, it creates unnecessary recursive calculations, which results in poor performance.

Suppose that a user query asks for the closing of the year 2005. From the calculation dependency, the server will need to first get the number for the first child of Year 2005, which is Quarter 1, 2005. Then further down, the server needs to calculate the number of Month July, 2004, which is the first month of Quarter 1, 2005. To get (July 2004, Opening), the server needs to trace back to (June 2004, closing). Go further: (June 2004, closing) = (June 2004, Opening) + (June 2004, Addition) - (June 2004, deletion). For (June 2004, Opening), the server needs (May 2004, Closing), then the same calculation rules are applied to get (May 2004, Closing). The recursive calculation goes on until it hits the first month of the system, where the opening value is obtained. It is quite amazing for Analysis Services to track the calculation dependencies and return the correct results, but does the server need to go through the recursion to calculate the correct answer?

Let's change the business rule of opening to the following:

```
Current Period's opening = first period opening + addition - deletion
for all periods in between.
```

We can change the first scope statement to the following. This statement cuts the calculation interdependency between the flow's opening and closing. Any query for the opening or closing becomes a straightforward sum of a set of members. It provides much better performance in our lab tests.

```
SCOPE (DESCENDANTS([Account].[Accounts].[Balance Sheet],, LEAVES),
       [Flow].[Flow].Members,
       [Date].[Fiscal].[Month].members,   -- Lowest level for time
       {Measures.[Amount]} );
([Flow].[Flow].[Opening]) =
    ([Flow].[Flow].[Opening],[Date].[Fiscal].[Month].&[2001]&[7])
        +
Sum([Date].[Fiscal].[Month].&[2001]&[7]:[Date].[Fiscal].CurrentMember,
[Flow].[Flow].[Addition]))
        - Sum
([Date].[Fiscal].[Month].&[2001]&[7]:[Date].[Fiscal].CurrentMember,
[Flow].[Flow].[Deletion]))
      );
([Flow].[Flow].[Closing]) = ([Flow].[Flow].[Opening]) +
                              ([Flow].[Flow].[Addition]) -
                              ([Flow].[Flow].[Deletion]);
END SCOPE;
```

Use Server Native Features Rather Than Scripts for Aggregation-Related Calculations

Analysis Services 2005 supports more aggregation operations than Analysis Services 2000 to handle semi-additive measures. Measures can have a choice of Sum, Max, Min, Count, Distinct Count, and Average in Analysis Services 2000. New aggregation choices, First Child, Last Child, Last Nonempty Child, First Nonempty Child, and None, are supported in Analysis Services 2005.

It is recommended to use server native aggregation methods, which are optimized and have better performance then general MDX script. In addition to that, Analysis Services can leverage the aggregation settings to return meaningful results in aggregation functions, and in cases such as set in slicer.

```
Select {Measures.[Balance]} on 0
from [Adventure Works]
where([Date].[Fiscal].[Fiscal Year].&[2002],[Date].[Fiscal].[Fiscal
Year].&[2005])
```

If you set the aggregation function `measures.balance lastnonempty`, Analysis Services will return the balance of year 2005 instead of the sum of 2002 and 2005.

Analysis Services 2005 supports not only measures with different aggregation functions but also the same measure with different aggregation behaviors controlled by account type. It is very useful in financial applications because different accounts usually have different aggregation behaviors along the Time dimension.

Analysis Services 2005 supports the following Account types, and each has different aggregation rules.

Table 16-2   Account Types and Aggregation Behavior

ACCOUNT TYPE	AGGREGATION BEHAVIOR
Statistical	None
Liability	LastNonEmpty
Asset	LastNonEmpty
Balance	LastNonEmpty
Flows	Sum
Expense	Sum
Income	Sum

Summary

Some general rules that you should take away from this chapter include

- You need to determine what level of server resources you are willing to use to support client queries because this will impact your choice of default large levels. This will involve looking at the query mix and client machine resources. You can adjust the server-side large-level setting and the client-side large-level and execution location settings in order to push more queries to the server or to the clients.

- CrossJoin() can be expensive. The relationship between CrossJoin() and Generate() can be leveraged when operations that involve sorting and selection are involved to make the operation more efficient. The relationship is: CrossJoin(A, B) is equivalent to Generate(A, CrossJoin({A.Current}, B)). Any sort of filtering done on the results of a cross-join can be transformed into this, and if the difference in time is noticeable, then using Generate() will be faster.

- Consider using NonEmpty() instead of CrossJoin() when appropriate; it is much faster.
- The commutative nature of SUM (and MIN and MAX) can be leveraged when operations that involve aggregating over multiple dimensions are involved—that is, Sum({A} * {B} * {C}, d) is equivalent to Sum({A}, Sum ({B}, Sum ({C}, d))). Operations involving Count() must be treated a little differently: Count({A} * {B} * {C}) is equivalent to Sum ({A}, Sum ({B}, Count ({C}))).

For MDX Scripts:

- Avoid excessive calculations, especially leaf-level calculations. You can perform the same calculation by changing the database design or writing more efficient MDX Scripts.
- Use scopes and attribute hierarchies to replace IIF statements.
- Avoid slow functions in MDX Scripts, especially in inner loop or lower-level calculations.
- Use server native aggregation settings instead of writing MDX Scripts.

CHAPTER 17

Working with Local Cubes

Local cube files provide a way for users to work with data in a disconnected client setting. In fact, local cubes are required if your users are to access data without being connected to a server. As far as client software is concerned, a local cube can be very similar to a server cube that is created in a limited database. Only a few areas of MDX do not work with a local cube, so it is possible (accepting a variety of requirements and constraints) to construct applications where a user can work with either server cubes or local cubes and not see any difference between them.

Unfortunately, this area of functionality has been subject to some indecision on the part of the designers of Analysis Services: With the release of Analysis Services 2005, there are now three distinct syntaxes for the creation of local cubes. OLAP Services introduced the CREATE CUBE statement, which allowed a great deal of flexibility when creating cubes but was extremely complicated and difficult to use. As a result, in Analysis Services 2000 Service Pack 1, the CREATE GLOBAL CUBE statement was added to make building local cubes from server-based cubes much easier, at the expense of losing some of the flexibility of the CREATE CUBE statement. Finally, in Analysis Services 2005, with the introduction of Analysis Services Scripting Language, it is now possible to create local cubes using the same syntax as you would use to create server-based cubes.

This chapter details the syntax and semantics of all three of these sets of MDX statements, along with some subtle wrinkles in their use, and talks about some of the logistics of creating and managing local cubes. We'll discuss some of the capabilities and limitations of local cubes along the way, although that is not our primary focus in this chapter.

Choosing Which Syntax to Use

The first question that must be answered when choosing which of the three syntaxes for creating local cubes you are going to use is: Does your application need to be able to create local cubes from Analysis Services 2000 server cubes? If not, then the recommendation is to use Analysis Services Scripting Language (ASSL). It is the native method of creating local cubes in Analysis Services 2005 and offers full access to all the new functionality available in them, such as many-to-many dimensions. Furthermore, in addition to Analysis Services 2005 server cubes, you can use it to create local cubes from relational databases. Note that for a user to query any local cube created using ASSL, they will need to have the MSOLAP.3 (OLE DB for OLAP 9.0) provider installed on their machine.

If, however, you do need to create local cubes from Analysis Services 2000 server cubes as well as Analysis Services 2005 server cubes, then you will have to use the CREATE GLOBAL CUBE syntax. The CREATE CUBE syntax is not able to create local cubes from Analysis Services 2005 server cubes (although it still works against Analysis Services 2000 cubes), so we recommend that you only use it if you are going to create local cubes from relational databases and have users who do not have the MSOLAP.3 provider installed on their machine.

The following table shows which syntax you can use against which type of data source.

	AS2000 CUBES	AS2005 CUBES	RELATIONAL DATABASES
ASSL	No	Yes	Yes
Create Global Cube	Yes	Yes	No
Create Cube	Yes	No	Yes

Using the CREATE CUBE Statement

Overview of the Process

Creating a local cube involves specifying the outline structure of a local cube through the CREATE CUBE statement and then populating the local cube by use of an MDX INSERT INTO statement, which will contain an SQL SELECT clause. Both components (CREATE CUBE and INSERT INTO . . . SELECT) are character strings, which are placed into OLE DB/ADO connection properties. At the ADO/OLE DB layer, opening a connection to the cube file when these connection properties are set will cause the cube to be created. Depending on the details of the INSERT INTO statement, the cube can be populated with data right then, and the cube is available for use.

Once a cube has been created, it can be updated by using the REFRESH CUBE statement (described in Chapter 11) as well as by re-creating it from scratch.

Anatomy of the CREATE CUBE Statement

At its heart, the CREATE CUBE statement consists of the following framework:

```
CREATE CUBE CubeName (
Dimension definitions
Measure definitions
Command definitions
)
```

Dimensions are defined first, followed by measures, followed by any commands. The following is a very simple CREATE CUBE statement:

```
CREATE CUBE Sales
(
  DIMENSION [Time] TYPE TIME
,    LEVEL [All Time] TYPE ALL
,    LEVEL [Year]
,    LEVEL [Month]

, DIMENSION [Customer]
,    LEVEL [All Customer] TYPE ALL
,    LEVEL [State]
,    LEVEL [City]
,    LEVEL [Customer]

, DIMENSION [Product]
,    LEVEL [All Product] TYPE  ALL
,    LEVEL [Type]
,    LEVEL [Product]

,  MEASURE [Units]
     FUNCTION SUM

,  MEASURE [Dollars]
     FUNCTION SUM
     FORMAT 'Currency'

, COMMAND ( CREATE MEMBER CURRENTCUBE.[Measures].[Avg Price] AS
     '[Measures]].[Dollars] / [Measures].[Units]' )
)
```

Within each dimension definition, hierarchy, level, and member property, information is spelled out. Within each measure definition, data type, measure aggregation function, and default format, information is specified. Following measures, one or more commands can optionally be specified as well.

Note that a comma is placed between the DIMENSION information and the LEVEL information, but no comma is placed between each MEASURE and its FUNCTION or FORMAT.

Defining Dimensions

The definition of each dimension begins with the DIMENSION keyword and the name of the dimension. You can define regular level-based dimensions, parent-child dimensions, and ragged variations on level-based and parent-child dimensions. You can also define data-mining dimensions. Dimensions can contain multiple named hierarchies as well. As with a server-based dimension, you can define member properties at each level, and you can declare dimensions and hierarchies as hidden.

You can also define custom rollup expressions for each level; in conjunction with Microsoft's RollupChildren() extension to MDX, you can provide the functionality found in server-based rollup operators because they are not directly supported in the CREATE CUBE syntax. Although you can't directly define custom member formulas, you can define a custom rollup expression for the level that executes an MDX formula stored in a member property, which accomplishes the same thing.

Overall Dimension

The overall dimension is defined with the following general expression:

```
DIMENSION DimName [ TYPE TIME ] [ DIMENSION_STRUCTURE PARENT_CHILD ]
[ HIDDEN ] [ OPTIONS Options ] [MEMBERS_WITH_DATA_IF
NonLeafDataOptions],
```

The allowable options to use for Options are shown in the following table.

ALLOWSIBLINGSWITHSAMENAME	Let sibling members (having different member keys) have the same name.
UNIQUE_NAME	Declare that every member in the dimension has a unique name.
UNIQUE_KEY	Declare that every member in the dimension has a unique key.
NOTRELATEDTOFACTTABLE	Specify a mining dimension.

If `ALLOWSIBLINGSWITHSAMENAME` is set to true (the default is false), then a query for a particular member by name or unique name (following the OLAP Services 7.0 unique name style), or for a set of members, may turn up two or more members that have the same name, and two members with the same name (but different member keys) may be children of the same parent.

If the dimension is `PARENT_CHILD`, then only one level (and perhaps also an `ALL` level) may be defined for it. Depending on whether the dimension is `PARENT_CHILD` or not, different options are available. If the dimension is to appear as a time dimension to MDX functions, then the `TIME` keyword must be specified.

Additionally, if the dimension is `PARENT_CHILD`, then `MEMBERS_WITH_DATA_IF` allows nonleaf members to have data in the fact table. The allowable options for `NonLeafDataOptions` are described in the following table.

`NON_LEAF_MEMBERS_HIDDEN`	Data members are hidden.
`NON_LEAF_MEMBERS_VISIBLE`	Data members are visible.

Named Hierarchies

If named hierarchies are provided in the dimension, the very next thing after the dimension expression is the hierarchy name expression, which has the general form of:

```
HIERARCHY HierName [ HIDDEN ] ,
```

As you may guess, the hierarchy may be hidden. Following the `HIERARCHY` expression, or following the `DIMENSION` expression, if no named hierarchies are present, come the level expressions.

Levels

Levels are listed for the dimension or hierarchy in order from the root level down. If the top level is to be an intrinsic `ALL` level, then its form is

```
LEVEL LevelName TYPE ALL ,
```

Otherwise, its form is (for the levels of non-parent-child dimensions):

```
LEVEL LevelName [ TYPE LevelType ]
[ FORMAT_NAME name_format [ FORMAT_KEY key_format ]]
[ OPTIONS ( level_options ) ] [ HIDDEN ]
[ HIDE_MEMBER_IF hide_options ]
[ CUSTOM_ROLLUP_EXPRESSION rollup_expression ]
'
```

For a parent-child dimension, the level you define has the following form, which adds one option:

```
LEVEL LevelName [ TYPE LevelType ]
[ FORMAT_NAME name_format [ FORMAT_KEY key_format ]]
[ OPTIONS ( level_options ) ] [ HIDDEN ]
[ HIDE_MEMBER_IF hide_options ]
[ ROOT_MEMBER_IF root_member_options ]
[ CUSTOM_ROLLUP_EXPRESSION rollup_expression ]
,
```

If you want to create a level-naming template for a parent-child dimension, then LevelName must take the form of a semicolon-delimited list of level names inside square brackets, for example [firstlevelname; secondlevelname; thirdlevelname;]. Also for parent-child dimensions, if you want to define a ragged dimension where children can be more than one level below their parent, you set that option in the INSERT INTO statement.

For either parent-child or regular dimensions, if the level holds member properties, then they are defined immediately after. The allowed options are as shown in the following table.

LEVEL TYPES
YEAR
QUARTER
MONTH
WEEK
DAY
DAYOFWEEK
DATE
HOUR
MINUTE
SECOND

LEVEL OPTION	MEANING
SORTBYNAME	Sort sibling by name.
SORTBYKEY	Sort siblings by key value.
SORTBYPROPERTY member_property	Sort siblings by value of member_property. (Must define the property.)
UNIQUE	Members are fully unique in level.

LEVEL OPTION	MEANING
UNIQUE_NAME	Member names are unique in level.
UNIQUE_KEY	Member keys are unique in level.
NOTRELATEDTOFACTTABLE	Level is a mining level.

HIDE OPTION	MEANING
ONLY_CHILD_AND_BLANK_NAME	Member hidden if no other siblings and name is blank.
ONLY_CHILD_AND_PARENT_NAME	Member hidden if no other siblings and name is same as its parent's.
BLANK_NAME	Member hidden if its name is blank.
PARENT_NAME	Member hidden if its name is the same as its parent's.

ROOT MEMBER OPTION	MEANING
ROOT_IF_PARENT_IS_BLANK	Member is considered a root if its parent name is empty.
ROOT_IF_PARENT_IS_MISSING	Member is considered a root if its parent key is NULL.
ROOT_IF_PARENT_IS_SELF	Member is considered a root if it is listed as its own parent.
ROOT_IF_PARENT_IS_BLANK_ OR_SELF_OR_MISSING	Member is considered a root if any of the other conditions is met.

For example, a Time dimension with levels of All, Year, Quarter, and Month that sorted its members by key value (derived from an appropriate column) would be minimally defined by the following snippet:

```
DIMENSION [Time] TYPE TIME,
   LEVEL [All Time] TYPE ALL,
   LEVEL [Year] TYPE YEAR OPTIONS (SORTBYKEY),
   LEVEL [Quarter] TYPE QUARTER OPTIONS (SORTBYKEY),
   LEVEL [Month] TYPE MONTH OPTIONS (SORTBYKEY),
```

A ragged geography dimension with levels of Country, Region, City, and Store (ragged in cities and stores) would be minimally defined by the following snippet:

```
DIMENSION [Geography],
   LEVEL [All Geography] TYPE ALL,
   LEVEL [Country],
   LEVEL [Region],
   LEVEL [City] HIDE_MEMBER_IF BLANK_NAME,
   LEVEL [Store] HIDE_MEMBER_IF BLANK_NAME,
```

Member Properties

Each member property in a level of a dimension is defined with the following:

```
PROPERTY PropertyName [ TYPE PropType ] [ HIDDEN ]
[ CAPTION Caption ] ,
```

A comma must separate each property definition from the next thing being defined (dimension, hierarchy, level, property, or measure). The Caption can be any string (in double quotation marks). The property types accepted are listed in the following table.

PROPERTY TYPE NAMES
REGULAR
ID
RELATION_TO_PARENT
ORG_TITLE
CAPTION
CAPTION_SHORT
CAPTION_DESCRIPTION
CAPTION_ABBREVIATION
WEB_URL
WEB_HTML
WEB_XML_OR_XSL
WEB_MAIL_ALIAS
ADDRESS
ADDRESS_STREET
ADDRESS_HOUSE
ADDRESS_CITY
ADDRESS_STATE_OR_PROVINCE
ADDRESS_ZIP

PROPERTY TYPE NAMES

ADDRESS_QUARTER

ADDRESS_COUNTRY

ADDRESS_BUILDING

ADDRESS_ROOM

ADDRESS_FLOOR

ADDRESS_FAX

ADDRESS_PHONE

GEO_CENTROID_X

GEO_CENTROID_Y

GEO_CENTROID_Z

GEO_BOUNDARY_TOP

GEO_BOUNDARY_LEFT

GEO_BOUNDARY_BOTTOM

GEO_BOUNDARY_RIGHT

GEO_BOUNDARY_FRONT

GEO_BOUNDARY_REAR

GEO_BOUNDARY_POLYGON

PHYSICAL_SIZE

PHYSICAL_COLOR

PHYSICAL_WEIGHT

PHYSICAL_HEIGHT

PHYSICAL_WIDTH

PHYSICAL_DEPTH

PHYSICAL_VOLUME

PHYSICAL_DENSITY

PERSON_FULL_NAME

PERSON_FIRST_NAME

PERSON_LAST_NAME

PERSON_MIDDLE_NAME

PERSON_DEMOGRAPHIC

(continued)

(continued)

PROPERTY TYPE NAMES
PERSON_CONTACT
QTY_RANGE_LOW
QTY_RANGE_HIGH
FORMATTING_COLOR
FORMATTING_ORDER
FORMATTING_FONT
FORMATTING_FONT_EFFECTS
FORMATTING_FONT_SIZE
FORMATTING_SUB_TOTAL
DATE
DATE_START
DATE_ENDED
DATE_CANCELED
DATE_MODIFIED
DATE_DURATION
VERSION

None of these property type codes conveys the meaning of "function," which would be useful if you were using a member property to hold either MDX functions that simulate Analysis Server custom member formulas or unary rollup operators for use by RollupChildren().

For example, the following snippet defines a customer dimension with an All level and a single customer level, ordered by a [Zip Code] property, and the [Zip Code] property itself:

```
DIMENSION [Customer],
  LEVEL [All Customer] TYPE ALL,
  LEVEL [Customer] OPTIONS SORTBYPROPERTY [Zip Code],
    PROPERTY [Zip Code],
```

FORMAT_NAME and FORMAT_KEY

If FORMAT_KEY and/or FORMAT_NAME are specified, they each take a format string like that used for a calculated member (surrounded by double quotation marks) and generate a textual name (or textual member key) that corresponds to that format. For example, consider the following:

```
DIMENSION [Time] TIME,
   LEVEL [Year]  FORMAT_NAME "yyyy" FORMAT_KEY "yyyy",
   LEVEL [Day]   FORMAT_NAME "mmm dd, yyyy"
```

When these two levels are created from columns having a `datestamp` data type, the names for the year members will be the year portion of that date stamp and the internal member keys for the years will also be the four-digit text form of the year (for example, "2001"). The day names will be of the form "Aug 27, 2001." The day key is left unspecified by this, which is probably a good idea because, generally, we want compact numbers (such as integers and possibly date stamps) and not text strings for the member keys. If you specified `FORMAT_NAME "mmm dd, yyyy"` for the member keys as well, then the days would be ordered alphabetically within the years (for example, [Apr 01, 2001], . . . [Dec 31, 2001] . . . [Jan 01, 2001] . . .) unless you also specified an appropriate member property and `OPTIONS (SORTBYPROPERTY)`.

`FORMAT_NAME` and `FORMAT_KEY` can be used to format strings from data types other than `datestamp`, such as adding currency formatting, thousands separators, or percentages to numbers.

Note that the use of `FORMAT_NAME` and `FORMAT_KEY` is a convenience; the formatting facilities may well be available in the SQL `SELECT` clause of `INSERT INTO` (described below), but by using `FORMAT_NAME` and `FORMAT_KEY`, you won't have to adjust your SQL to any particular dialect.

Defining Measures

After all of the dimension information for the cube is defined, you list the measures for the cube. The cube must have at least one measure. The general form for a measure is much simpler than that for a dimension. It consists of the following:

```
MEASURE MeasureName AggregationFunction [ FORMAT format_string ]
[ TYPE OLEDB_type_def ] [ HIDDEN ]
```

A comma must separate a measure from its following measure or command definition, if one follows.

`AggregationFunction` can be one of the functions in the following table (`DISTINCT COUNT` is not supported).

AGGREGATION FUNCTIONS
SUM
COUNT
MAX
MIN

The `format_string` can be any measure format string. See Appendix D for the format strings accepted (in general, these follow VBA and Excel format strings).

The `OLEDB_type_def` can be one of those in the following table (refer to the OLE DB documentation, if necessary, for their meaning).

OLE DB MEASURE TYPE DEFINITION
DBTYPE_I1
DBTYPE_I2
DBTYPE_I4
DBTYPE_I8
DBTYPE_UI1
DBTYPE_UI2
DBTYPE_UI4
DBTYPE_UI8
DBTYPE_R4
DBTYPE_R8
DBTYPE_CY
DBTYPE_DECIMAL
DBTYPE_NUMERIC
DBTYPE_DATE

Adding Commands

After all of the measures are defined for the cube, you can list a set of commands that will be executed when the cube is opened. These commands include USE LIBRARY, CREATE MEMBER, CREATE SET, and ALTER CUBE UPDATE DIMENSION.

Each command is listed individually, using command syntax virtually identical to that you would use if you were executing it at a client session or defining it at the server using DSO. You must get used to one important syntactic quirk, due to the general form of the command definition in a local cube. This general form (which looks innocuous enough at high level) is

```
COMMAND command
```

The quirk is that if the command contains any spaces, then the executable MDX command must be wrapped in matched delimiters. Interestingly, what these delimiters are is somewhat up to you: Both square braces, [ ], and parentheses ( ) can be used. Parentheses are easy to use. If you wrap the expression in square braces and some part of the command (for example, a unique name) uses square braces as well, then you need to remember how MDX nests braces. A nested right brace is represented by two adjacent right braces,]]. So, a command may look like this:

```
COMMAND [ CREATE MEMBER CURRENTCUBE.[Measures]].[Price]] AS
'[Measures]].[Dollars]] / [Measures]].[Units]]' ]
```

although it would be rendered most easily as

```
COMMAND ( CREATE MEMBER CURRENTCUBE.[Measures].[Price] AS
'[Measures].[Dollars] / [Measures].[Units]' )
```

If you are writing code to automatically place command expressions into local cubes, you should use parentheses, or make sure that your code transforms the right braces appropriately.

ROLAP versus MOLAP

It is possible to create local cubes that are either ROLAP or MOLAP using CREATE CUBE. In a MOLAP local cube, the data is read from the relational data source at the time the cube is connected, and is stored in the local cube file. Only the leaf-level data is stored; no precalculated aggregates are stored in the file. In a ROLAP cube, in constrast, data is only read from the relational data store when cells are needed by queries (assisted, of course, by caching in Pivot Table Services).

By default, if no options are specified, a MOLAP cube will be created. In the INSERT INTO statement, the OPTIONS keyword controls how the cube data will be treated. The "Options for INSERT INTO" section later in the chapter discusses the conditions under which one kind or the other is built.

Note that if you create a ROLAP local cube, you need to make sure that the relational database login is set up appropriately. The Source_DSN property provided, when the cube is created, is retained in the cube file, whereas any information provided in the Source_DSN_Suffix property must be supplied at every subsequent connection to the cube. This means that if a user ID and/or password is required, embedding it in Source_DSN will place it in the cube definition, whereas placing it in Source_DSN_Suffix will require the application to provide it in subsequent uses (which you may want for security purposes).

ROLAP cubes mean smaller cube files, although cube file size frequently isn't much of a problem. If the size of a cube file is a problem for transmission over a slow network (or modem) link, remember that they compress very well using Zip compression.

Note that the options used when constructing a cube affect what members appear in each dimension. If a ROLAP cube is built, then the dimensions for the cube will include all members listed in the dimension tables regardless of whether they join to facts or not. This appears to be enabled because PTS can parse the SQL and can internally create SQL SELECT statements against the underlying database that obtains dimension information. In Analysis Services 2000 (but not 2005), though, if a MOLAP cube is built without any member properties, then the only members created for each dimension are those that actually have corresponding facts in the fact table. The difference between these two modes is important. However, if a dimension has member properties defined for it, for a MOLAP cube that is created without the SELECT query being passed through, that dimension will always have all members listed. This difference between how dimensions are constructed may be accidental, but if you're using Analysis Services 2000 and you want a MOLAP cube to be created using all members from a dimension table regardless of whether they have facts in the fact table, you can harmlessly add a member property to the leaf level of that dimension (for example, one that holds the member name or a constant string value).

PTS will return an error if PASSTHROUGH and DEFER_DATA are specified together.

Anatomy of the INSERT INTO Statement

Whereas the CREATE CUBE statement lays out the outline of the cube, the INSERT INTO statement describes the connection of that cube structure to relational columns and contains an SQL SELECT statement that fills the cube with data. The INSERT INTO statement lists all of the levels, member properties, and measures of the cube, which are matched to columns in the SELECT clause. It is somewhat analogous to the INSERT INTO . . . SELECT statement in SQL.

The framework of the INSERT INTO statement is as follows:

```
INSERT INTO CubeName (
Target1,
Target2,   . . .
)
[ OPTIONS options ]
SELECT ...
```

The order of cube entities (levels, member properties, and measures) in the list of targets should not make any difference, although for consistency, we tend to follow the same order in which they are listed in the CREATE CUBE statement. To repeat ourselves a little, the order of columns in the SELECT clause must match the order of targets. The following is a very simple INSERT INTO statement:

```
INSERT INTO Sales (
   [Time].[Year]
, [Time].[Month]
, [Time].[Day]
, [Customer].[State]
, [Customer].[City]
, [Customer].[Customer]
, [Product].[Product]
, [Measures].[Units]
, [Measures].[Dollars]
)
SELECT
 t.year_name
,t.month_name
,t.day_name
,c.cust_state
,c.cust_city
,c.cust_name
,p.prod_name
,s.units
,s.dollars
FROM sales s, timetable t, customer c, product p
WHERE s.time_id = t.time_id AND s.cust_id = c.cust_id AND s.prod_id =
p.prod_id
```

Cube Targets

A few options are available for the targets. For any level, you can specify the key and name columns separately, and you can specify some options for the construction of a Time dimension.

The All type level of a dimension is never a target for a column (as in a server-defined dimension).

Regular Dimension Levels

A regular dimension level can be specified by one or two columns. If it is specified by one column, then the name and key of the members in the level are the same. In this case, you would just name the level with its name or unique name. We'll use unique names in the examples:

```
[Dimension].[Level] or [Dimension].[Hierarchy].[Level]
```

If it is specified by two columns, then you append .Name to the reference for the name column and .Key to the reference for the key column, like this:

```
[Time].[Month].Name,
[Time].[Month].Key
```

Any member properties for the level would be defined as described later in the chapter.

Parent-Child Dimensions

A parent-child dimension has only one internal level, and this level requires at least member and parent columns. To define the members, you don't actually list the name of the level, but instead list the name of the dimension. As with a regular level, if the key and name are provided by separate columns, you use `.Name` and `.Key` to identify them; otherwise, you list the dimension name only once. You also use `.Parent` to identify the parent column. For a parent-child dimension named account, the following snippet identifies three columns as corresponding to member key, member parent (key), and member name:

```
[Account].Key,
[Account].Parent,
[Account].Name
```

Parent-child dimensions can also be created as ragged, which in their case, requires a column that identifies the number of levels to insert between a member and its parent. The `.SkipLevelColumn` term is used to indicate that column, as in:

```
[Account].SkipLevelColumn
```

Any member properties for the parent-child dimension would be defined as described later in the chapter.

Member Properties

For each level that has member properties, each member property is identified just by naming it. For example, if a member property `[Address]` has been defined for the `Customer.Customer` level, then the following reference would indicate it in the selected columns:

```
[Customer].[Customer].[Address]
```

If the member property is defined on a parent-child dimension, then you just use the name of the dimension as the name of the level:

```
[Account].[Ledger Code]
```

If you use the name for the internal level that you provided in the CREATE CUBE statement, you will get an error message stating that it cannot find the column expression for level PropertyName.

> **NOTE** An INSERT INTO **statement with** OPTIONS PASSTHROUGH **will raise an error if a member property is specified for any level of a level-based dimension or if a parent-child dimension is present in the cube.**

Custom Rollups

A custom rollup operator would be specified by listing the name of the level (or dimension name if it is a parent-child dimension) and .Custom_Rollup. An example of this is

```
[Account].Custom_Rollup
```

Measures

Each measure is identified just by naming it, as in:

```
[Measures].[Units Sold]
```

Column Placeholders in the Targets

If for some reason the SELECT clause returns columns that are not going to be used by the INSERT INTO targets, you can use the SKIPCOLUMN keyword in the target list at the position or positions in which the column to ignore appears. For example:

```
SKIPONECOLUMN
```

Options for the INSERT INTO

The OPTIONS clause that can appear between the INSERT INTO (. . .) and the SELECT clauses governs how Pivot Table Services will populate the cube and how it will attempt to interpret the SELECT statement.

The options available can be divided into analysis and defer options, as shown in the following table. You can specify zero or one of each in the OPTIONS section of the INSERT INTO statement.

DEFER OPTION	MEANING
DEFER_DATA	Do not populate the cube with data (build a ROLAP cube).
ATTEMPT_DEFER	Try not to populate the cube with data (depends).
ANALYSIS OPTION	**MEANING**
PASSTHROUGH	Do not try to interpret the SELECT statement.
ATTEMPT_ANALYSIS	Try to interpret the SELECT statement.

The following table indicates what the results are for the different combinations of options.

DEFER OPTION	ANALYSIS OPTION	CUBE FORM SUCCESSFUL	CUBE FORM FAILED PARSE
(none)	(none)	MOLAP	(Error)
(none)	PASSTHROUGH	MOLAP	(can't fail)
(none)	ATTEMPT_ANALYSIS	MOLAP	MOLAP
DEFER_DATA	(none)	ROLAP	(Error)
DEFER_DATA	PASSTHROUGH	(Error)	(can't fail)
DEFER_DATA	ATTEMPT_ANALYSIS	ROLAP	(Error)
ATTEMPT_DEFER	(none)	ROLAP	MOLAP
ATTEMPT_DEFER	PASSTHROUGH	MOLAP	(can't fail)
ATTEMPT_DEFER	ATTEMPT_ANALYSIS	ROLAP	MOLAP

The SELECT Clause

The SELECT statement is an ordinary SQL-compatible SELECT statement, although if you do not specify the PASSTHROUGH option, then it can only use a subset of available SQL-89 syntax. The reason for this is that Pivot Table Services will attempt to parse the SQL to some degree, and this is not a simple task with either a large subset of SQL or any RDBMS's particular extensions. If for some reason your SELECT statement is not being parsed correctly or you get a mysterious "column expression cannot involve multiple tables" error message, you may need to either hide table joins under a view (if you need a ROLAP cube) or use OPTIONS PASSTHROUGH.

The order of columns selected by the SELECT statement must match the order of levels, properties, and measures identified in the INSERT INTO

statement. This is similar to the requirements on an SQL `INSERT INTO ( . . . )`
`SELECT . . .` statement.

The following discussion is most relevant if you are using `OPTION`
`ATTEMPT_ANALYSIS` or leaving out `OPTION PASSTHROUGH`, as it is most concerned with the SQL that PTS can parse. If you use `OPTION PASSTHROUGH`,
then the syntax limitations of PTS won't come into play.

The `SELECT` statement can use the following syntax if PTS is to
attempt/succeed at parsing it, and use it against a relational database:

```
SELECT
  ColumnRef [ AS ColumnAlias1]
  [, ColumnRef [AS ColumnAlias2] ...]
FROM
  Table1 [ [AS] TableAlias1]
  [, Table2  [[AS] TableAlias2] ...]
WHERE
  Where-clause
```

Each `ColumnRef` can consist of a column name or a `table.column` pair,
an expression enclosed by parentheses, or an ODBC scalar function of
columns. For example, the following are acceptable:

```
CustomerCity,
A.CustomerState,
(B.Price * B.Qty) AS Total,
MONTH(TimeTable.Day_Date) AS Month
```

However, because there is no provision for a `GROUP BY` clause, aggregate
functions such as `Sum()` or `Count(*)` are of limited use.

The `FROM` clause cannot contain SQL-92 join clauses (`INNER JOIN`, `OUTER`
`JOIN`, and so on). It can only contain a list of table names, each one optionally
with a corresponding table alias.

The `WHERE` clause can contain zero or more equi-join clauses and zero or
more constraint clauses. Individual join and constraint clauses can be combined with AND. The equi-join clauses can only be of the form `ColumnA =`
`ColumnB` or (`ColumnA = ColumnB`), as in the following:

```
WHERE
  T.Day_ID = Tx.Day_ID AND (P.SKU = Tx.SKU)
```

The constraint clauses can be combined with OR as well as AND, and NOT
can be used to negate them.

If you are going to include constraints, such as (`T.Day_ID , 366`), then
you need to enclose all of your constraints in parentheses. Otherwise, it will
complain of too many tables being involved in the query. Although Microsoft
does not document any join constraint besides = as being usable, we find that
comparisons such as < and > can be used as well as constructs (such as

`p.prod_id` in (`select prod_id from Johnson_products`)), so we really can't say what the true limits are.

Select Statements That Are Not SQL

If you provide `OPTION PASSTHROUGH` or `ATTEMPT_ANALYSIS` in the `INSERT INTO` statement, then the contents of the `SELECT` clause do not need to necessarily be SQL at all. It needs to be understood by the underlying data ODBC source or OLE DB provider as something that will result in rows, but the only key is that it returns suitable rowsets for constructing a cube.

We need to provide the caveat that we have attempted to make this work, but as of the time of this writing, have not found a working case. You might, therefore, think it should be possible to issue an MDX `SELECT` statement and get the result as a flattened rowset that can be read as a cube, but we have only seen data type errors or "parameter type incorrect" errors after the query has run for some time.

More Advanced Programming: Using Rowsets in Memory

Instead of a `FROM` clause, the `SELECT` statement can select columns from an OLE DB rowset already initialized in memory by using a rowset option. This allows an application to build a local cube from anything that represents its information as an OLE DB rowset, without resorting to a full SQL interface. In this case, there will be no `FROM`, no tables listed, and no `WHERE` clause. The options and meanings are listed in the following table.

ROWSET OPTION	MEANING
`DIRECTLYFROMCACHEDROWSET  hex-number`	Populate from rowset found at address *hex-number*
`DIRECTLYFROMMARSHALLEDROWSET hex-number`	Populate from marshalled rowset found at address *hex-number*

PTS is an in-process OLE DB provider, which means that it operates in the same address space as the process that is creating the connection to the cube file. If that process holds a pointer to an OLE DB rowset, the text form of the pointer value converted into hexadecimal is passed as the hex-number value following the rowset option. The following would be an example of this (assuming that the rowset has columns named Col1, Col2, and Col3):

```
SELECT
Col1, Col2, Col3
DIRECTLYFROMCACHEDROWSET 87e011c0
```

Tips for Construction

Overall, the following connection properties are relevant when you are creating a local cube:

CreateCube

DataSource

InsertInto

Source_DSN

Source_DSN_Suffix

UseExistingFile

We encourage you to review their descriptions in Appendix B.

If you are creating multiple local cubes for a user, you can package them into a single cube file. All you need to do is specify the name of an existing cube file when you create the cube, and the cube will be added to the file or updated if it already exists. By using the UseExistingFile connection parameter, you can also direct PTS to preserve the cube, or to fail to create the cube if the file does not already exist.

When you do create multiple cubes in a single cube file, keep in mind that each cube appears in its own catalog or database, which has the same name. This means that the cubes are separate and cannot be combined in a session virtual cube.

As far as maintaining the cube files goes, keep in mind that the REFRESH CUBE statement will refresh the MOLAP data when executed. It is roughly the same as a full process of a cube on a Microsoft OLAP/Analysis Services server—all data is reread from the source databases and the MOLAP storage is rebuilt. Along the way, the dimensions are fully refreshed, too. This means that you don't have to go through the process of respecifying and executing the full CREATE CUBE/INSERT INTO process. Of course, if any of the dimension levels change, any measure definitions change, or commands change, you will need to re-create the cube from scratch.

Local Cubes from Server Cubes

As already mentioned, it is possible to use the CREATE CUBE syntax to create local cubes from Analysis Services 2000 server cubes. For reasons of simplicity, you will usually want to use the CREATE GLOBAL CUBE syntax (see below) rather than CREATE CUBE for this task, but using CREATE CUBE is also fairly straightforward so long as you bear a few things in mind.

You can create local cubes from an SQL query against a server cube. We will not discuss the SQL syntax supported by Analysis Services 2000 (this is, after all, a book on MDX). It is a reasonably restricted and easy-to-understand subset of SQL that treats the entire cube as a table; Books Online has more details.

In Analysis Services 2000, if the server cube is a virtual cube that combines measures with differing leaf levels in their regular cubes or with different base dimensionality, you will need to pay attention to which measures you are querying for and from where. All measures in the local cube will have the same dimensionality and enter at the leaf level of its dimensions, so you may need to provide placeholder members at the leaf level for one or more measures for one or more dimensions to make all measures enter at the leaf level. In addition, although you can create a UNION ALL query in standard SQL to combine multiple separate table queries, you cannot create a UNION ALL query against multiple regions of an Analysis Services cube to query separate regions of the virtual cube and combine them into one rowset. However, you can readily compose a UNION ALL query that combines each fact table that feeds the virtual cube and inserts placeholder members if necessary to ensure that all data actually feeds into the leaf level. The CREATE GLOBAL CUBE syntax handles this problem automatically.

Creating local cubes from server cubes via connections that have cell and dimension security enforced can lead to sporadic errors in Analysis Services 2000, even when the user has access to the part of the server cube that the local cube is to be based on. As a result, if you need to use local cubes but must also have security on your server cubes, it is best to set up a centralized production process that runs under an account with no security restrictions and then distribute the resulting local cubes to your users, for example by email or FTP.

Finally, one last barrier to using the CREATE CUBE syntax in Analysis Services 2000 is the fact that you cannot use it against server cubes that contain custom rollup formulas: You get the error "Unable to run SQL queries against cubes that have custom rollup formulas" when you do. One way of working around this is to create a linked server in SQL Server that points to your cube, create a view from that cube, and then build your local cube from the view, but given that the CREATE GLOBAL CUBE syntax does not suffer from this limitation and successfully re-creates the custom rollups, you are probably better off using the newer syntax in this case.

Rollups and Custom Member Formulas

In order to use unary rollup operators, you need to be able to define a custom rollup formula. The following ought to work for a dimension named [Account] that holds its rollup operators in a property named [RollupOp]:

```
CUSTOM_ROLLUP_EXPRESSION
'iif (
  IsLeaf ([Account].CurrentMember),
  [Account].Ignore,
  RollupChildren (
    [Account].CurrentMember,
    [Account].CurrentMember.Properties ("RollupOp")
  )
)'
```

In order to simulate custom member formulas, you can use a custom rollup formula that references a member property that contains the member formula. The formula would look like this:

```
CUSTOM_ROLLUP_EXPRESSION
'iif (
  [Account].CurrentMember.Properties ("CustomFunc") = ""
  [Account].Ignore,
  StrToValue (
    [Account].CurrentMember.Properties ("CustomFunc")
  )
)'
```

The whole definition of the dimension looks like this:

```
DIMENSION [Account] DIMENSION_STRUCTURE PARENT_CHILD
, LEVEL [Account1]
ROOT_MEMBER_IF ROOT_IF_PARENT_IS_BLANK_OR_SELF_OR_MISSING
CUSTOM_ROLLUP_EXPRESSION
'iif (
  [Account].CurrentMember.Properties ("CustomFunc") = ""
  [Account].Ignore,
  StrToValue (
    [Account].CurrentMember.Properties ("CustomFunc")
  )
)'
, PROPERTY CustomFunc
```

And, where a dimension has both custom member formulas and custom rollup operators, the formula overrides the operators for a member, so simulating that requires the following:

```
CUSTOM_ROLLUP_EXPRESSION
'iif (
  [Account].CurrentMember.Properties ("CustomFunc") = "",
  /* no function, check for operators */
  iif (
```

```
      IsLeaf ([Account].CurrentMember),
      [Account].Ignore,
      RollupChildren (
        [Account].CurrentMember,
        [Account].CurrentMember.Properties ("RollupOp")
      )
    ),
    /* got a function, execute it */
    StrToValue (
      [Account].CurrentMember.Properties ("CustomFunc")
    )
  )'
```

Using the CREATE GLOBAL CUBE Statement

Overview of the Process

The CREATE GLOBAL CUBE statement defines the structure of a local cube in terms of the server-based cube that is to act as the data source, and bears more than a few similarities to the CREATE CUBE statement. It is, however, much simpler because rather than having to specify the various properties of the measures, dimensions, and levels included, as in the CREATE CUBE statement, these are automatically read from the source cube. Calculated members don't need to be specified either: These are also automatically copied from the source cube, although if the local cube does not include all dimensions or measures from the source cube, any calculated members that rely on the missing entities will not appear in the local cube. For example, if you had a calculated measure in your server cube that multiplied the real measures [Units] and [Dollars], but you didn't include [Dollars] in your local cube, then the calculated measure wouldn't appear in the local cube either.

Another improvement in terms of ease of use is that the CREATE GLOBAL CUBE statement is not placed in the connection string—it can be run like any other MDX statement through the Source property of an ADOMD cellset. This means you can run a CREATE GLOBAL CUBE statement by pasting it into the query pane of the MDX sample application, for example. In Analysis Services 2000, when the statement is executed, Pivot Table Services translates it into the equivalent CREATE CUBE and INSERT INTO statements and opens a second connection in the background to create the local cube; in Analysis Services 2005, the statement is translated into Analysis Services Scripting Language and then executed.

Anatomy of the CREATE GLOBAL CUBE Statement

The CREATE GLOBAL CUBE statement is structured as follows:

```
CREATE GLOBAL CUBE CubeName
STORAGE CubeLocation
FROM SourceCubeName (
Measure definition
Dimension definition
)
```

After the cube name, the location of the .cub file where the cube is to be created, and the source server cube have been specified, all that is needed is a list of one or more measures and one or more dimensions from the server cube. Within the dimension definition, you have the option to specify which levels you wish to include and which members on those dimensions to slice by. The following is a simple CREATE GLOBAL CUBE statement:

```
CREATE GLOBAL CUBE Sales
STORAGE 'C:\Sales.CUB'
FROM Sales (
MEASURE Sales.[Qty],
DIMENSION Sales.[Customer] (
LEVEL [State],
LEVEL [City],
MEMBER [Customer].[State].[AZ]
))
```

Defining Measures

Defining measures is straightforward, consisting of the following:

```
MEASURE ServerCubeName.ServerMeasureName
[HIDDEN] [AS NewMeasureName]
```

The HIDDEN flag has the same effect as setting the Visible property to false on a server-based measure: It means that the measure is no longer visible in metadata and isn't returned by set expressions such as Measures.Members but can be referenced directly in an MDX expression. The only other option is to rename the measure.

Defining Dimensions

The definition for a dimension is marginally more complex, taking the form:

```
DIMENSION ServerCubeName.ServerDimensionName
[HIDDEN] [AS NewDimensionName]
[(LevelList, [MemberSliceList], [DefaultMemberDefinition])]
```

Note that when specifying the name of a dimension on the server, when the target is an Analysis Services 2000 cube where multiple hierarchies are present on a dimension, each hierarchy is treated as a separate dimension. For example, to re-create a server Time dimension with two hierarchies, you would need to use something similar to the following:

```
CREATE GLOBAL CUBE Sales
STORAGE 'C:\Sales.CUB'
FROM Sales (
MEASURE Sales.[Qty],
DIMENSION Sales.Time.ByMonth,
DIMENSION Sales.Time.ByWeek
)
```

However, in Analysis Services 2005, simply specifying the name of the dimension results in all of the hierarchies on that dimension being transferred to the local cube, so the following statement would be sufficient:

```
 CREATE GLOBAL CUBE Sales
STORAGE 'C:\Sales.CUB'
FROM Sales (
MEASURE Sales.[Qty],
DIMENSION Sales.Time
)
```

There is no way of choosing which hierarchies you want to include in your local cube when using Analysis Services 2005 as your source—you always get all of them—but by specifying individual hierarchies in the CREATE GLOBAL CUBE statement, you can still choose to include only certain levels from those hierarchies or filter levels by certain members.

Defining Levels

Within a dimension, level definitions take the form:

```
LEVEL LevelName
[HIDDEN] [AS NewLevelName]
[PropertyList]
```

The first two options are as shown above; PropertyList takes the form of a list of member properties to be included on the level, or the NO_PROPERTIES flag, which indicates that none of the properties present are to be included. The following example illustrates this:

```
CREATE GLOBAL CUBE Sales
STORAGE 'C:\Sales.CUB'
FROM Sales (
```

```
MEASURE Sales.[Qty],
DIMENSION Sales.Time.ByMonth
(
LEVEL [Year],
LEVEL [Day] (PROPERTY [Ordering])
),
DIMENSION Sales.Customer
(
LEVEL [Region],
LEVEL [Cust Identity] NO_PROPERTIES
))
```

Defining Members for Slicing

Within a dimension, after the list of level definitions, you can specify a list of members from the topmost specified level to slice the cube by. For example, the following statement creates a local cube containing only two months of data:

```
CREATE GLOBAL CUBE Sales
STORAGE 'C:\Sales.CUB'
FROM Sales (
MEASURE Sales.[Qty],
DIMENSION Sales.Time.ByMonth
(
LEVEL [Month],
LEVEL [Day],
MEMBER [Time].[ByMonth].[All Time].[1998].[Q1, 1998].[Jan,1998],
MEMBER [Time].[ByMonth].[All Time].[1998].[Q1, 1998].[Mar,1998]
))
```

Note that trying to slice by a member from any level that is not the first in the list of specified levels will result in an error.

Things to Look Out For

For all its convenience, the CREATE GLOBAL CUBE statement suffers from more than its fair share of bugs and quirks. This sections lists, in no particular order, all of the problems we are aware of that are still valid for Analysis Services 2000 Service Pack 4. Only the first is applicable to Analysis Services 2005.

- If you are creating calculated members using the CREATE MEMBER statement, or you are using DSO to add calculated members to your server cube, you should always use the CURRENTCUBE token instead of the cube name in the calculated member definition. This will ensure that the calculated members still work when they are copied to the local cube. Calculated members created using Analysis Manager are automatically declared using CURRENTCUBE.

- When the CREATE GLOBAL CUBE statement opens its own connection in the background, not all the connection string properties from the original connection are copied across. No list of which properties are copied and which aren't exists, but one significant property that isn't copied is the Roles property—as a result, it isn't possible to use this property along with server-based security to control the contents of your local cubes.

- The background connection that the CREATE GLOBAL CUBE statement opens is always TCP/IP-based. Therefore, it is not possible to use this method to create local cubes when you only have HTTP access to a server.

- When creating local cubes from virtual cubes, one extra member with an empty caption appears on every level of every dimension. The purpose of these members is to make sure that measures show the correct values for dimensions they are not related to.

- The LookUpCube() function is not supported in local cubes, so any server calculated member (and, in turn, any calculated members that depend on it) that uses it will not appear in a local cube.

- Although Analysis Manager will prevent this, it is possible to create dimensions on the server that have names longer than 24 characters using DSO. However, CREATE GLOBAL CUBE will fail if you try to use it against a cube that contains such a dimension.

Using Analysis Services Scripting Language

Overview of the Process

Analysis Services Scripting Language (ASSL) is the new XML dialect used to create server objects and perform tasks such as processing, as well as creating local cubes. In fact, to create a local cube using ASSL, you follow exactly the same steps as you would to create a server cube: You open a connection to your target (in this case a .cub file), then execute your ASSL statement in the same way as you would any other MDX query.

Anatomy of an ASSL Statement

The easiest way to see an example of an ASSL statement used to create a local cube is to run a CREATE GLOBAL CUBE statement against your cube, and at the same time run a Profiler trace on the server. In Analysis Services 2005, CREATE GLOBAL CUBE statements are translated to ASSL when they are run, so you will see the ASSL statement created in the trace and you can then copy and paste it out for closer examination.

At the highest level, the ASSL statement consists of a `Batch` containing two commands: one to create the local cube structure and one to process it. Here's an example of one with only the cube definition removed to save space:

```
<Batch
xmlns="http://schemas.microsoft.com/analysisservices/2003/engine"
xmlns:xsd="http://www.w3.org/2001/XMLSchema"
xmlns:xsi="http://www.w3.org/2001/XMLSchema-instance">
    <Create AllowOverwrite="true">
            <ObjectDefinition>
                    <!--insert cube definition here -->
            </ObjectDefinition>
    </Create>
    <Process>
            <Type>ProcessFull</Type>
            <Object>
                    <DatabaseID>MyDatabase</DatabaseID>
            </Object>
    </Process>
</Batch>
```

Generating the contents of the `<ObjectDefinition>` tag yourself is not recommended as it is an extremely complicated structure. If you need to create local cubes from an Analysis Services 2005 server cube, then you can automatically generate this information by right-clicking on a cube in the Object Explorer pane of SQL Server Management Studio and selecting the "Script Cube as" menu item. Even if you want to create local cubes directly from a relational database, it may be worth creating a server cube first so that you can use this method to generate the object definition more easily.

Remember that although many more features of server cubes are supported in Analysis Services 2005 local cubes than was the case with Analysis Services 2000, there are still some (such as distinct count measures, partitioning, COM user-defined functions, and stored procedures) that are not, so you cannot simply always copy a server cube definition.

Security

In Analysis Services 2005, you must now explicitly give an end user the permission to create local cubes from server cubes. This is achieved by selecting the Cubes page in the Role dialog box, and then selecting Drillthrough and Local Cube in the drop-down list in the Local Cube/Drillthrough Access column next to your cube. If your application is going to read the definition of a server cube to generate the contents of the `<ObjectDefinition>` tag dynamically for an ASSL statement, you will also need to check the Read Definition box on the General page.

It is also now possible to secure access to a local cube with a password, by specifying the Encryption Password connection string property when you connect to a new local cube file. So, the connection string property `Encryption Password=Test` will set the password of the new local cube file to `Test`. After creating the local cube, you will need to specify the same connection string property value in order to open it again to query it. The password is case-sensitive.

Summary

In this chapter, we have focused on the mechanics of building and maintaining local cube files, and we have explored the different Microsoft MDX syntaxes available to build and populate these cubes. When this is combined with at least a basic understanding of good dimension and cube design principles, you should be able to use local cube files for delivering data and analyzing it in a variety of ways.

MDX Function and Operator Reference

This appendix is a detailed reference to the functions and operators of standard MDX, and extensions as implemented in Microsoft's Analysis Services 2000 and 2005 and Hyperion's Essbase 9. The main body of the appendix lists the functions and operators in alphabetical order, along with any arguments and the result's data type. We have included a pair of indexes at the beginning to help you navigate.

Index to Functions

We have found that two different types of indexes are useful for looking up a function or operator: by name and by return type.

Alphabetical Index

Return Type Index

The functions are all listed here by return type:

Number

String

Logical

Dimension, Hierarchy, and Level

The following functions return references to dimensions, hierarchies, or levels:

Miscellaneous

Call: 549

Error(): 572

Scope: 615

SetToArray(): 615

Basic Operators

This section lists the basic operators for manipulating strings, numbers, and logical conditions.

Value Operators

Table A-1 lists the basic operators. A *ValueExpr* can be either numeric or string, but it must be the same type on both sides of the operator. An *ObjectExpr* can refer to any metadata object or to NULL.

Expressions can be grouped with parentheses () to make the ordering of operations clear.

Table A.1   List of Operators

OPERATOR	RESULTS IN
NumericExpr + NumericExpr	Addition
NumericExpr - NumericExpr	Subtraction
*NumericExpr * NumericExpr*	Multiplication
NumericExpr / NumericExpr	Division
NumericExpr1 % NumericExpr2	"Percentage of": equivalent to *(NumericExpr1/ NumericExpr2) * 100.* (Hyperion extension)
- NumericExpr	Unary negation
StringExpr + StringExpr	String concatenation (Microsoft extension)
StringExpr || StringExpr	String concatenation (standard MDX)
ValueExpr < ValueExpr	Less than
ValueExpr > ValueExpr	Greater than
ValueExpr <= ValueExpr	Less than or equal to
ValueExpr >= ValueExpr	Greater than or equal to
ValueExpr <> ValueExpr	Not equal to

Table A-1   *(continued)*

OPERATOR	RESULTS IN
ValueExpr = ValueExpr	Equal to
BooleanExpr **AND** *BooleanExpr*	True if both expressions are true, false otherwise.
BooleanExpr **OR** *BooleanExpr*	True if either expression is true.
NOT *BooleanExpr*	True if expression is not true, false otherwise.
BooleanExpr **XOR** *BooleanExpr*	True if either of the expressions is true but not both of them, and false otherwise.
PropertyValue **IN** *MemberExpr*	True if the property value's corresponding attribute dimension member is a descendant of the member described in *MemberExpr*. (Hyperion extension).
PropertyValue **IN** *StringLiteral*	True if the property value's corresponding attribute dimension member is a descendant of the attribute member named in the string literal. (Hyperion extension).
MemberExpr **IS** *MemberExpr*	True if the two member expressions evaluate to the same member. This is an extension to OLE DB for OLAP that both Microsoft and Hyperion implement. Note that *NULL* may be used in AS2000 and AS2005 to test if the other member reference is not valid.
ObjectExpr **IS** *ObjectExpr*	True if the two object expressions refer to the same object, and false otherwise. Any reference to a nonexistent object will return true when combined with NULL, as in Time.[All Time].Parent.Level IS Null. (Microsoft extension to OLE DB for OLAP).
SetExpr1 + SetExpr2	Set union, preserving duplicates as sequence (like { *SetExpr1, SetExpr2* }; see below; Microsoft extension).
SetExpr1 - SetExpr2	Set difference (Microsoft extension).
-SetExpr	Complement of *SetExpr* (Microsoft extension). The *SetExpr* must consist only of members from one level of one hierarchy-dimension. Returns all members of that level except those appearing in *SetExpr*.
*SetExpr1 * SetExpr1*	Cartesian product of sets; see *CrossJoin()* (Microsoft extension).
Existing *set_expression*	Evaluates *set_expression* within the current member context. If the existence of the set's members or tuples depends on the current member context (in all dimensions other than those of the *set_expression*), the returned set will reflect the context

Constructing Tuples

```
( member [, member . . .] )
```

Tuples can be explicitly constructed by listing members from one or more dimensions, enclosed within parentheses and separated by commas. If only one dimension is present in the tuple, the parentheses can be omitted as well. Any member specification will work, not just explicitly named members. For example, the following examples are all tuple specifications:

```
[Time].[1997]
([Time].[1997])
([Time].[1997], [Customer].[All Customers])
([Time].[1997], {[Customer].Members}.Item (0))
```

Note that when a function requires that a tuple be one of its arguments within parentheses, the parentheses must be placed around the tuple as well as used to enclose the argument list for the function. For example, the following would be a correct tuple specification to be passed to TupleToStr():

```
TupleToStr( ([Time].[1997], [Customer].[All Customers]) )
```

Trying to create an empty tuple with () will result in a syntax error. In Analysis Services 2005, you can create an essentially empty tuple with null member references. For example (null, null) specifies an empty tuple.

Constructing Sets

```
{ tuple or set   [, tuple or set   . . . ] }
```

Sets can be explicitly constructed by enclosing one or more tuples or sets with the same dimensionality within curly braces, "{" and "}". Each tuple or set specification must be separated from the next by a comma. For example, the following are all sets:

```
{ [Time].[1997] }
{ ([Time].[1997], [Customer].[All Customers]) }
{ [Time].[All Time], [Time].[Year].Members,
  { [Time].[Quarter].Members } }
```

The first two are sets of one tuple each, and the last one is a set composed of one member and two sets, in order. Note that in the last example, one set is syntactically inside the other, and the inner one is also enclosed in curly braces. This is not required, and it does not affect the interpretation in any way. Although an empty set is not usually of much practical use, it may be created with an empty pair of curly braces: {}

```
member : member
```

This operator constructs a set from two members and uses the two members as endpoints. The two members must be on the same level; if they are not, a parse error will occur. If you use the database ordering of the members in the dimension, all members between the endpoints will be included. It is not an error for the two members to be the same (that is, {[Time].[2006] : [Time].[2006]}).

In Microsoft Analysis Services 2005, and 2000, if the member on the right-hand side of the colon is earlier in the database ordering than the member on the left, a range is constructed from the member on the right to the member on the left (as though the members were flipped around the colon; the set will be in dimension order). In AS2005, if only one member is invalid and the other is valid, a range is constructed from the valid member to the end of the level. An invalid left-hand member creates a range from the first member in the level, and an invalid right-hand member creates a range to the last member in the level. In AS2000, if either of the members is invalid, a parse error occurs.

In Essbase, if a member in the right-hand side of the colon is earlier than the member on the left-hand side, the range is constructed in the reverse of the dimension's order. For example, [July] : [May] returns the set {[July], [June], [May]}. If either member reference is invalid, then the set returned is empty.

See also: MemberRange()

Standard MDX Operators Not Supported by Microsoft Analysis Services

The | | operator is not used for string concatenation. Instead, the + operator is supported for string concatenation.

Function and Operator Reference

A

Abs(_numeric_expr_**)**   Returns: number
Extension: Essbase

Returns the absolute value of *expr*, and NULL if *expr* is NULL.

AddCalculatedMembers(_set_**)**   Returns: set
Extension: AS2000, AS2005

By default, when a set of members is specified using a function that retrieves a set based on metadata (such as .Members, .Children, Descendants(), and so on), only base members are returned, even though calculated members may be within that range. The AddCalculatedMembers() function adds in all of the calculated members that are siblings of the members specified within the *set*. Each calculated member that was not already in the set is added in database order after its last sibling member in the *set*. The *set* is limited to only one dimension. Note that this function adds all calculated members defined, whether they were defined by CREATE MEMBER at the server or at the client, or in the query through WITH MEMBER.

See also: .AllMembers, StripCalculatedMembers()

Aggregate(_set_ **[,** _numeric value expression_**])**   Returns: number
Standard (not in Essbase 9)

This function aggregates the cells formed by the set according to the default aggregation operator for any measures in context. If a numeric value expression is provided, then this function sums the expression's set of values over the cells. In the event that the cells are of a base measure, the aggregation function specified for the measure is used. In AS2000, if the aggregation functions of the measure is COUNT, MIN, or MAX, then COUNT, MIN, or MAX, respectively, is the aggregation operation used; otherwise, the aggregation operation used is summation. In AS2005, the list of intrinsic measure aggregation functions with which the Aggregate() function will work is much longer, including:

Sum

AverageOfChildren

ByAccount

Count

FirstChild

FirstNonEmpty

LastChild

LastNonEmpty

Max

Min

DistinctCount

Aggregate() will not aggregate measures whose aggregation function is None, however.

NOTE Although you may specify an expression to be evaluated by this function, this function does not work if you use calculated members as its inputs. (If a calculated member "M" has a higher SOLVE_ORDER than a calculated member on a different dimension that is performing the Aggregate(), then "M" will use the results of the aggregating member.)

This comes in handy when you have a set of different measures with different aggregation rules that are all being queried for. Calculated members performing period-to-date aggregations as well as aggregations on other dimensions will often be best constructed out of this operator. (Essentially, this is the implicit operation carried out within Analysis Services's hierarchies.) Consider the following calculated member:

```
CREATE MEMBER [Time].[MonthsOf2006ToDate] AS
'Aggregate ( {[Time].[Jan 2006] : [Time].[May 2006]} )'
```

When combined with a summing measure, this member will yield the sum of its values over the range of January through May 2006. When combined with a measure aggregating by MAX, this member will yield the MAX of its values over that same time period.

NOTE In Analysis Services 2000, measures aggregated by DISTINCT COUNT cannot be aggregated by this function. This is fixed in Analysis Services 2005.

See also: Sum(), Count(), Min(), Max(), Avg(), DistinctCount()

dimension.**AllMembers**

hierarchy.**AllMembers**   Returns: set   E,M2000,M2005

level.**AllMembers**

All return: set

All are extensions: AS2000, AS2005

> Generally, the .AllMembers functions are semantically equivalent to Add-CalculatedMembers(Scope.Members), but they provide a more intuitive syntax. Although the Microsoft documentation only refers to .AllMembers for dimensions and levels, we note that in the case of multiple hierarchies on a dimension, you can only use this against one hierarchy.

> The only case where .AllMembers and AddCalculatedMembers() differ is when no members are visible in the scope of [Dimension].Members, [Hierarchy].Members, or [Level].Members. This can occur on the measures dimension if all measures are hidden in a cube.

> The following two statements will generally return the same set:

```
[Measures].AllMembers
AddCalculatedMembers([Measures].Members)
```

> *See also: AddCalculatedMembers(), StripCalculatedMembers()*

Ancestor(*member, level*)   Returns: member
Standard

Ancestor(*member, distance*)   Returns: member
Extension: Essbase, AS2005, AS2000

> This function finds the source *member*'s ancestor at the target *level* or *distance*. If the target level is the level of the source member, then the source member is returned. If a distance number is specified, it is the number of hierarchical steps above the member. A distance of 0 will return the source member. The behavior of Ancestor() is shown in Figure A-1.
> *See also: Descendants(), .Children*

Ancestors(*member, level*)   Returns: set
Standard. (Essbase has same syntax, but different behavior)

Ancestors(*member, distance*)   Returns: set
Standard. (Essbase has same syntax, but different behavior)

> **NOTE** Essbase implements a different semantics for the function named Ancestors, although the function signature is exactly the same as the standard.

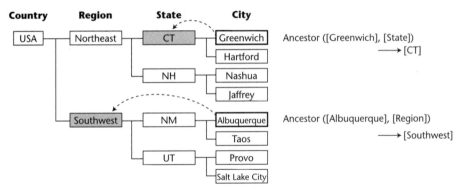

Figure A-1   Behavior of Ancestor().

The standard and Microsoft implementations of this function find the set of ancestors for the source *member* at the target *level*. If the database supports multiple parents for a single member in a hierarchy (as Applix TM1 does), then this function may return multiple members. Other databases (like Microsoft Analysis Services) will return a set of one member. If the target *level* is the level of the source *member*, then the source member is returned as a set.

The target level can be expressed either by name as a string expression or by distance as a numeric expression where 1 represents a parent, 2 represents a grandparent, and so on. Using 0 as a distance will return the member itself.

Note that although this function in theory may return multiple ancestors, the ancestors must be from the same hierarchy and the same level.

In Essbase, this function returns the tree of ancestor members from the given member up to a higher level or generation, as indicated by the argument. If *distance* is specified, then the member and that number of ancestors will be returned. If *layer* is specified, then it returns all ancestors having a height from the leaves that is no greater than the *layer*.

See also: Ancestor(), Ascendants(), Descendants(), .Children

expr1 **AND** *expr2*   Returns: Boolean
Standard

The AND operator returns true if both *expr1* and *expr2* are true, and false otherwise. In Microsoft Analysis Services, if *expr1* is false, then *expr2* is not evaluated (there is no need to; the result is guaranteed to be false); this may be relevant when *expr2* could have side effects or is costly to evaluate.

Ascendants(*member***)**   Returns: set
Extension: AS2005, AS2000

This function returns the full set of ancestors for the given member all the way up to the root of the hierarchy or dimension. The ancestors are ordered from the bottom up, so that parents follow children. The given member is included in the set. It is very useful in queries when you want to include all higher level totals for a given member or set of members. The behavior of Ascendants() is shown in Figure A-2.

Note that the order of the resulting set must be changed by using Hierarchize() to get a top-down ordered set before being used in conjunction with any of the drill-related or VisualTotals() functions.

See also: Ancestor(), Ancestors(), Descendants(), .Children

Attribute(*member_of_attribute_dim***)**   Returns: set
Extension: Essbase

This function takes a member of an attribute dimension and returns the base dimension members that it maps to. (Similar to the AS2005 Exists() function.)

See also: WithAttr(), Exists()

Avg(*set* [, *numeric expression*]**)**   Returns: number
Standard

This function takes the average of the nonempty values found across cells related to the *set*. If a numeric expression is supplied, then its values are averaged across the cells in the set. Note that the average is formed out of the sum of the cells divided by the count of the nonempty cells. If you want to take the average over all cells, treating empty as zero, then you can either create a numeric value expression that converts missing to zero, or you can take the Sum() over the set divided by the Count() of the set, including empty cells.

See also: Aggregate(), Sum(), Count(), Min(), Max()

Axis(*Axis number***)**   Returns: set
Extension: AS2005, AS2000

This function returns the set of members or tuples that are included on a specified axis. Axis(0) returns the column tuples, Axis(1) returns the row members, and so on. This function is likely to be used most often in client applications when building queries. The following example uses Axis() in conjunction with Generate() and TopCount() to select the top two stores for each of the four quarters of 2006. Note that this statement will return results for all selected stores for each of the four quarters:

```
SELECT
Generate(
  Axis (1),
  TopCount(
    [Store].[Store Name].Members,
    2,
    ([Measures].[Amount],
     Axis(1).Current)
  ),
  ALL
) on 0,
{[Time].[2006].Children} on 1
FROM Sales
```

You can use this set as the source for various set-related functions, such
as .Count, Extract(), Distinct(), Except(), and so on. The .Item() function
can be used as well. To use this function to select the top two stores
based on the first member in the set down the rows, you would write
the following:

```
SELECT
TopCount(
  [Store].[Store Name].Members,
  2,
  ([Measures].[Amount],
   Axis(1).Item(0))
) on 0,
{[Time].[2006].Children} on 1
FROM Sales
```

Regardless of which dimensions were involved in the rows, the query
would work fine (so long as [Store] is not in the rows!).

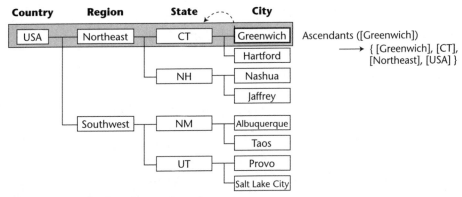

Figure A-2   Behavior of Ascendants().

However, the execution of a query (building the axes and calculating cell values) does not provide a context on its own for iterating over the tuples in the set. For example, the following results in an error with the message stating that .Current cannot be used in this context:

```
WITH
MEMBER [Measures].[Disp] AS
'[Measures].[Unit Sales]',
FORE_COLOR = 'iif (Axis(1).Current.Item(0).Level.Ordinal > 1, 0, 5)'
SELECT
{ [Time].[Quarter].members } on 0,
{ Ascendants ([Customers].[Name].&[2659]) } on 1
FROM Sales
WHERE  [Measures].[Disp]
CELL PROPERTIES FORMATTED_VALUE, FORE_COLOR
```

This can be explained by the fact that the filter is always evaluated first. However, the following will also fail with the same error:

```
WITH
MEMBER [Measures].[Disp] AS
'[Measures].[Unit Sales]',
FORE_COLOR = 'iif (Axis(1).Current.Item(0).Level.Ordinal .> 1, 0, 5)'
SELECT
{ CrossJoin (
    [Time].[Quarter].members,
    { [Measures].[Disp] }
) } on 0,
{ Ascendants ([Customers].[Name].&[2659]) } on 1
FROM Sales
CELL PROPERTIES FORMATTED_VALUE, FORE_COLOR
```

B

BottomCount(*set, index* [, *numeric expression*])   Returns: set
Standard

See the description for TopCount()

BottomPercent(*set, percentage, numeric expression*)   Returns: set
Standard

See the description for TopPercent()

BottomSum(*set, value, numeric expression*)   Returns: set
Standard

See the description for TopSum()

C

CalculationCurrentPass()   Returns: number (integer)
Extension: AS2005, AS2000

This returns the current pass number for which the expression is being calculated. Typically, this will be used with iif() to pick out a particular expression based on the pass number. The lowest pass number is 0. Calculated cells begin calculations with pass 1.

See also: CalculationPassValue(), iif()

CalculationPassValue (*numeric expression, pass number* [, *flag*])   Returns: number
Extension: AS2005, AS2000

CalculationPassValue (*string expression, pass number* [, *flag*])   Returns: string
Extension: AS2005, AS2000

This function evaluates the given expression at the calculation pass identified by pass number and returns the value to the current calculation pass. If the flag is specified, it may be one of the following:

FLAG	DESCRIPTION
ABSOLUTE	The pass number is the absolute number of a pass (starting from zero). If you refer to a pass number that is higher than the currently executing pass, you will begin invoking the higher numbered pass for the cells that are referenced in the expression if they have not already executed that pass.
RELATIVE	This indicates to take the value from the pass that was pass number passes later. A negative pass number will refer to an earlier pass, and a positive pass number will invoke a later pass. A pass number that would refer to a pass earlier than pass 0 will silently cause a reference to pass 0.

Note that in AS2005, passes for session-scoped cell calculations (created by CREATE CELL CALCULATION) and those for query-scoped cell calculations (created by WITH CELL CALCULATION) are separated, so that query, session and global passes (from MDX scripts) cannot refer to calculations in each other.

See also: CalculationCurrentPass(), iif()

Call UDF-Name ([*arguments*])   Returns: Void or rowset
Extension: AS2005, AS2000

This function executes a registered external function that does not return anything (that is, a procedure in Visual Basic). Data can be passed to the function as if it were any other external function. In AS2005, Call can return either nothing or a rowset. In AS2000, the Call itself will return an empty cell value. Unlike other MDX functions and operators, this one cannot be combined with any other operators or functions; when used in an expression, the sole contents of the expression will be the Call invocation. Here's an example:

```
Call MailMsgToUser (
   [Employee].CurrentMember.Properties ("Email Address"),
   "Look at department" + [Department].CurrentMember.Name
   )
```

CASE

```
CASE reference-expression WHEN test1 THEN result1
    [ ... WHEN testN THEN resultN ]
    [ ELSE DefaultResult ]
    END
```

Returns number, string (except Essbase), member, tuple, set, level, hierarchy, array (all AS2005 only)

Standard (except AS2000)

```
CASE WHEN textExpr1 THEN result1
    [ ... WHEN testExprN THEN resultN ]
    [ ELSE DefaultResult ]
    END
```

Returns number, string (except Essbase), member, tuple, set, level, hierarchy, array (all AS2005 only)

Standard (except AS2000)

This operator provides a multiway conditional test for values to return. It is similar to the iif() function, but can handle more conditions. The different implementations provide different capabilities.

The *expression* in the first form can be either a numeric expression or a string expression, and each *test* must the same type (numeric or string). Each *test* from *test1* through *testN* is evaluated in sequence until the result of a test is equal to the *reference-expression*. When that happens, the corresponding *result* following the THEN clause is returned. If no *test* expression is equal to *reference-expression*, then the *DefaultResult*, if any, is returned. If none is specified, then the result of the function is NULL.

In the second form of CASE, each *testExpr* is evaluated as a Boolean expression in sequence until one evaluates as true. The *result* expression of the corresponding THEN clause is returned. If no *testExpr* evaluates to true, then the *DefaultResult*, if any, is returned. If none is specified, then the result of the function is NULL.

In AS2005, the type of result from any THEN clause can be different from that of any other THEN clause. A single CASE operator could return strings, numbers, and/or any of the other types listed depending on the *reference-expression*

and/or *test* expressions. When no test evaluates to true and there is no default
clause, a NULL is returned.

In Essbase, the results can either be all numeric or all set expressions. When
the results are numeric, a MISSING value is returned if no other result or
default expression is returned. When the results are sets, an empty set is
returned if no other result or default expression is returned.

For both AS2005 and Essbase, this allows the CASE expression to serve as an
axis expression or as the input to other functions that use sets, such as Avg() or
Generate(). For AS2005, since CASE can return most MDX objects, you can
write expressions such as the following, which uses the CASE construct to pick
an attribute dimension whose members end up in a named set [ASet]:

```
WITH SET [ASet] AS
CASE
WHEN condition1 THEN [Customer].[Region]
WHEN condition2 THEN [Customer].[State]
ELSE [Customer].[City]
END.Members
. . .
```

See also: CoalesceEmpty(), iif()

member.**Children**   Returns: set
Standard

> This function returns the children of the given member. *member*.Children is
> equivalent to {*member*.FirstChild : *member*.LastChild}. As you might expect,
> if you apply *member*.Children to a leaf member, the result is no members
> (an empty set). Figure A-3 illustrates the behavior of the .Children function.
>
> *See also: Ancestor(), Descendants(),.Parent, .Siblings*

ClosingPeriod (*[level [, member]]*)   Returns: member
Standard

> *See description of OpeningPeriod()*

CoalesceEmpty (*value expression [, value expression* . . .])   Returns: number
or string
Standard

> This function evaluates the first *value expression* listed. If it is not NULL,
> then the value of that expression is returned. If it is NULL, then the second
> *value expression* is evaluated and it is returned if it is not NULL. Each
> subsequent expression, if present, is evaluated in turn; if the last one is
> NULL, the entire operator returns NULL.
>
> CoalesceEmpty() can either take all number-valued expressions and return
> a number or it can take all string-valued expressions and return a string.
>
> *See also: iif(), IsEmpty(), CASE*

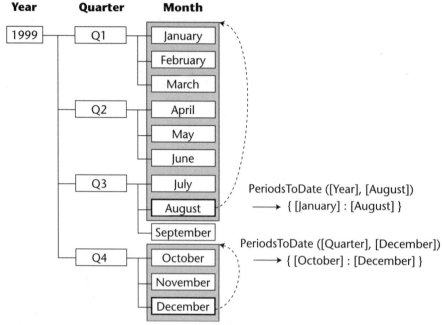

PERIODS TO DATE

PeriodsToDate ([Year], [August])
⟶ { [January] : [August] }

PeriodsToDate ([Quarter], [December])
⟶ { [October] : [December] }

Figure A-3 member.Children.

Correlation (*set, y numeric value expression* [*, x numeric value expression*])
Standard (not in Essbase 9)

> This function calculates a correlation coefficient between x-y pairs of values. The *y numeric expression* is evaluated over the set to get the y values for each pair. If the *x numeric expression* is present, then it is evaluated over the set. Otherwise, the cells formed by the set are evaluated within the current context, and their values are used as the x values. The formula for the correlation coefficient is as follows:

$$\frac{n\sum_{i=1}^{n} x_i y_i - \sum_{i=1}^{n} x_i \sum_{i=1}^{n} y_i}{\sqrt{n\sum_{i=1}^{n} x_i^2 - \left(\sum_{i=1}^{n} x_i\right)^2}\sqrt{n\sum_{i=1}^{n} y_i^2 - \left(\sum_{i=1}^{n} y_i\right)^2}}$$

> If either the *y* or the *x numeric expression* is a logical or text value, or if the value is NULL, then that tuple and its related values are not included in the correlation. Zero values for y and x are included.

Count(*set* [, **INCLUDEEMPTY | EXCLUDEEMPTY**])   Returns: number (integer)
Extension: AS2005, AS2000

Count(*set* [, **INCLUDEEMPTY**])   Returns: number (integer)
Standard (except by AS2005 and AS2000)

This function counts the cells in the range formed by the *set* (as opposed to counting the tuples in the set). In Analysis Services, without the INCLUDEEMPTY flag, only nonempty cells are counted; with the flag, all cells are counted. INCLUDEEMPTY is the default. In Essbase, the function returns the count of cells regardless of whether the INCLUDEEMPTY is specified or not. (You must use Hyperion's NonEmptyCount() to count nonempty tuples.) In the standard, only nonempty cells are counted, unless the INCLUDEEMPTY flag is specified.

See also: .Count, Sum(), Avg(), DistinctCount(), NonEmptyCount()

Set.**Count**   Returns: number (integer)
Extension: AS2005, AS2000

This function counts the tuples present in *Set*. It is equivalent to `Count (Set, INCLUDEEMPTY)` but is syntactically simpler.

See also: Rank(), Count(), Avg(), Set.Item()

Tuple.**Count**   Returns: number (integer)
Extension: AS2005, AS2000

This function counts the dimensions present in *Tuple*.

See also: Tuple.Item()

Cousin(*member, ancestor_member*)   Returns: member
Standard

This function returns the member that has the same relative position under a specified ancestor member as the initial member specified. The Cousin() function is best understood by walking through its algorithm. Figure A-4 shows the behavior of the Cousin() function. From the *member*'s level to the *ancestor_member*'s level, Cousin() tracks which sibling it is related to under its ancestor at that level. [March 2001] is the third child of the first child of [2001]. The same path is then followed from the ancestor member down to the level of *member*. [March 2002] is the third child of the first child of [2002]. Because of the straightforwardness of this algorithm, it works best when you can guarantee the same number of descendants under each ancestor. For example, it is likely that years, quarters, and months or days, hours, and minutes can be used with Cousin(), because each of these levels has a fixed relationship within itself. However, a cousin of January 31 in February will not exist because February will not have a thirty-first day.

See also: ParallelPeriod(), PeriodsToDate()

Covariance(*set, y numeric expression* [*, x numeric expression*])   Returns: number
Standard (not in Essbase 9)

CovarianceN(*set, y numeric expression* [*, x numeric expression*])   Returns: number
Standard (not in Essbase 9)

Covariance() calculates the population covariance and uses the biased population formula (dividing by the number of x-y pairs). CovarianceN() calculates the sample covariance and uses the unbiased population formula (dividing by the number of x-y pairs minus 1). If either the *y* or the *x numeric value expression* is a logical or text value, or if the value is NULL, then that tuple and its related values are not included in the correlation. Zero values for y and x are included.

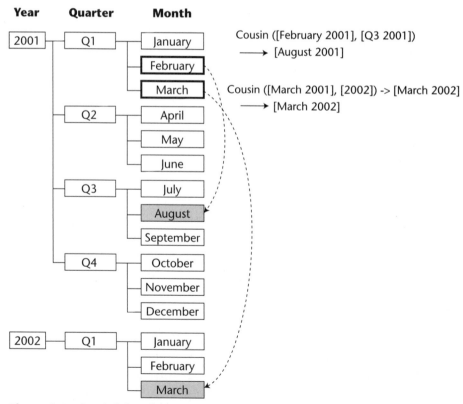

Figure A-4   Cousin() function.

These functions calculate the statistical covariance across x-y pairs of values. The *y numeric expression* is evaluated over the set to get the y values for each pair. If the *x numeric expression is present*, then it is evaluated over the set. Otherwise, the cells formed by the *set* are evaluated within the current context, and their values are used as the x values. The biased population formula for covariance is as follows:

$$\frac{\sum_{i=1}^{n}(\bar{x}-xi)(\bar{y}-yi)}{n}$$

CrossJoin(*set1*, *set2***)**   Returns: set
Standard (additional behavior in AS2005)

set1 * set2   Returns: set
Extension: AS2005, AS2000

These functions return a set forming the Cartesian product of the two sets (except for a Microsoft extension to the semantics noted below). The two sets must represent different dimensions; you will get an error if the same dimension appears in both of them. CrossJoin() only takes two sets as arguments. However, because it takes two sets as input and returns a set as its output, you may nest multiple calls to CrossJoin() to take the Cartesian product of three or more dimensions. Following the same rules used for composing tuples by hand, the order of the dimensions in the resulting tuples is the same as the order of dimensions in the set arguments. Using an asterisk between two sets, as with {set1 * set2}, is a Microsoft-specific synonym for CrossJoin(). The expression set1 * set2 * set3 is the same as CrossJoin(set1, CrossJoin(set2, set3)).

In Analysis Services 2005, if the two sets are composed of tuples from the same base dimension but different attribute hierarchy-dimensions, then only the combinations of tuples that actually exist in the underlying dimension are returned. There is no way to produce tuples that do not have corresponding entries in underlying tables.

See also: Extract(), Generate(), Distinct(), NonEmptyCrossJoin()

Set.**Current**   Returns: tuple
Standard

This function returns the current tuple from a set within an iteration over the set. *set*.Current is only valid while there actually is an iteration occurring over the set. It returns a full tuple from the set. The set needs to be named, and can be either a set alias or a named set.

See also: .CurrentMember, .CurrentTuple, Generate()

dimension[**.CurrentMember**]   Returns: member
Standard

> This function returns the current member in that dimension. "Current" is relative to the context that the calculation is taking place in. That context may be the axis of a query being executed or a Generate() function within that query. We indicate that .CurrentMember is optional. The default operator applied to a dimension is .CurrentMember.

> Note that the MDX specification states that .CurrentMember may be applied to any set to return the current tuple. Both Analysis Services and Essbase restrict the application of this operator to a set that has a single dimension, which will then return a single member. The .Current operator is applied to an arbitrary set to retrieve a tuple.

> In Analysis Service 2005, keep in mind that the current member of an attribute dimension is influenced by the "current" members of other related attribute dimensions and the underlying base dimension.

NOTE In Essbase, the name of the dimension is the same as the name of the top member of that dimension, so .CurrentMember is not optional. Using *dimension* alone is treated as a reference to the root member of the dimension

See also: .Current, .CurrentOrdinal

set.**CurrentOrdinal**   Returns: number
Extension: AS2005

This function returns the current iteration number within a context that iterates over *set*. The Filter() and Generate() functions provide an appropriate iteration context. Functions like Sum() and Order() do not. The *set* must be an alias name — it cannot be a named set.

> *See also:. Current, .Current Tuple, .CurrentMember*

set.**CurrentTuple**   Returns: tuple

CurrentTuple (*set*)   Returns: tuple
Extension: Essbase

> This function returns the current tuple of *set* being iterated over. Useful from a context that provides a notion of iteration, such as Generate() or Filter(). The *set* should be a named set or a set alias. Note that Microsoft Analysis Services supports .Current instead of .CurrentTuple.

> *See also: .Current, .CurrentMember*

CustomData   Returns: string
Extension: AS2005

This function returns the current value of the CustomData connection property. If this property was not set, then the function returns NULL. This can be used to pass in one arbitrary configuration setting to be used by MDX functions.

See also: UserName, Call()

D

*Member.***DataMember**   Returns: member
Extension: AS2005, AS2000

This function returns the system-generated data input member associated with a member (as opposed to the input data). In AS2000 this function generally applies to parent-child dimensions where data is input at the parent level and also calculated by aggregating the parent's children. In AS2005, you can use this on any hierarchy. The following example produces both the input individual salary and the aggregated organizational salary for each employee:

```
WITH MEMBER [Measures].[Individual Salary] AS
'([Employees].CurrentMember.DataMember, [Measures].[Salary])'
SELECT
{ [Employees].Members } on columns,
{ [Measures].[Salary], [Measures].[Individual Salary] } on rows
FROM HRCube
```

Note that when using the UPDATE CUBE command, the .DataMember function enables you to write data to the actual member, as opposed to the member's leaf descendants.

*dimension.***DefaultMember**
Standard

*hierarchy.***DefaultMember**
Standard

Each of these returns the default member for the *dimension* or *hierarchy*. If the dimension has an All level and member, then the default member is the All member. If the dimension does not have an All member, then an arbitrary member from its top level will be the default member. Microsoft Analysis Services also allows you to override these defaults at the server or through their ALTER CUBE UPDATE DIMENSION command; see the section "Altering the Default Member for a Dimension in Your Session" in Chapter 12.

See also: .CurrentMember

Descendants (*member*, [*level* [, *desc_flag*]])
Standard

Descendants (*member*, *distance* [, *desc_flag*])
Standard

This function returns a set of descendants of the given member using the indicated level, or numeric distance from the specified member's level, as a reference point. The desc_flag parameter is used to pick from the many possible sets of descendants. If no level or desc_flag is provided, then the member and all of its descendants are returned. Figures A-5 through A-12 illustrate the behavior of the Descendants() operator. The flags are:

SELF	SELF_AND_AFTER
AFTER	SELF_AND_BEFORE
BEFORE	SELF_BEFORE_AFTER
BEFORE_AND_AFTER	LEAVES

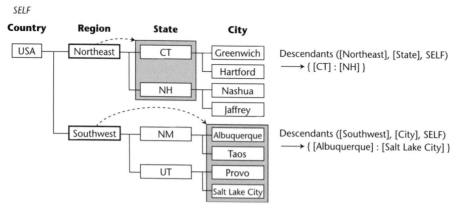

Figure A-5   Behavior of descendants() with SELF FLAG.

AFTER

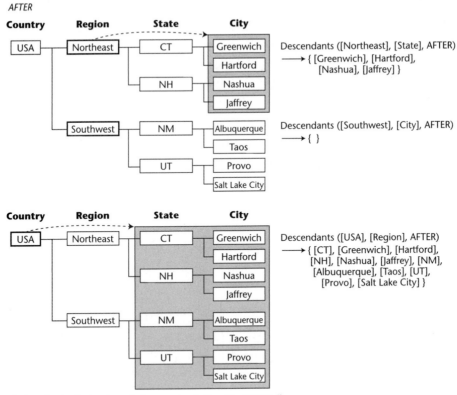

Descendants ([Northeast], [State], AFTER)
⟶ { [Greenwich], [Hartford],
      [Nashua], [Jaffrey] }

Descendants ([Southwest], [City], AFTER)
⟶ { }

Descendants ([USA], [Region], AFTER)
⟶ { [CT], [Greenwich], [Hartford],
      [NH], [Nashua], [Jaffrey], [NM],
      [Albuquerque], [Taos], [UT],
      [Provo], [Salt Lake City] }

Figure A-6   Behavior of descendants() with AFTER flag.

BEFORE

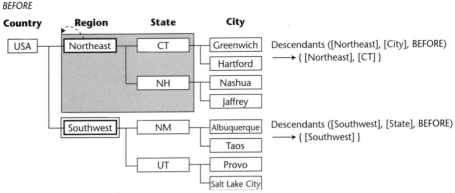

Descendants ([Northeast], [City], BEFORE)
⟶ { [Northeast], [CT] }

Descendants ([Southwest], [State], BEFORE)
⟶ { [Southwest] }

Figure A-7   Behavior of descendants() with BEFORE flag.

SELF_AND_AFTER

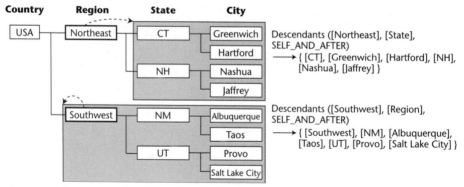

Figure A-8 Behavior of descendants() with SELF_AND_AFTER flag.

SELF_AND_BEFORE

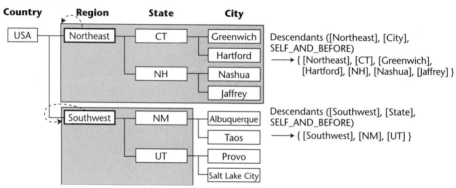

Figure A-9 Behavior of descendants()with SELF_AND_BEFORE flag.

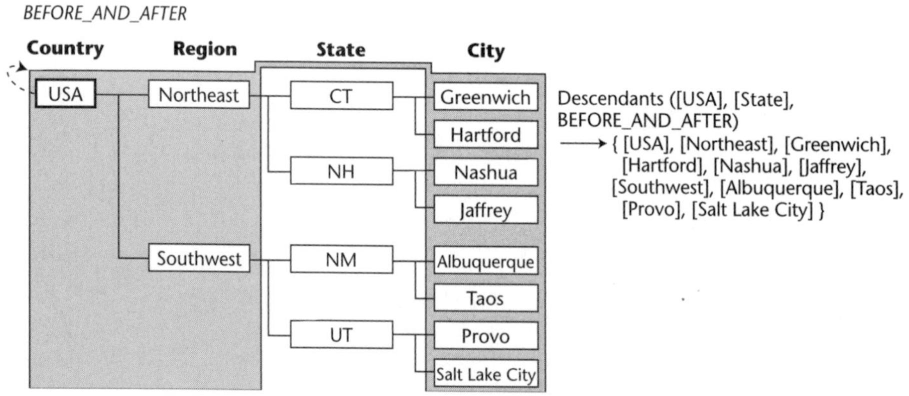

BEFORE_AND_AFTER

Figure A-10 Behavior of descendants() with BEFORE_AND_AFTER flags.

SELF_BEFORE_AFTER

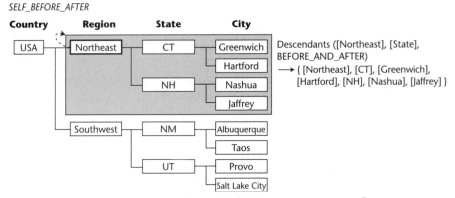

Figure A-11   Behavior of descendants() with SELF_BEFORE_AFTER flags.

SELF refers to the level listed as the second argument and means to take the members at that level. AFTER refers to the level or levels that appear below the level listed as the second argument. BEFORE refers to the level or levels that appear above the level listed and below the member given as the first argument. The BEFORE_AND_AFTER, SELF_AND_AFTER, SELF_AND_BEFORE, and SELF_BEFORE_AFTER flags combine these basic options, as shown in Figures A-5 through A-12.

The LEAVES flag is used in conjunction with a depth number and is intended for use with ragged and parent-child hierarchies. If a depth number is specified without LEAVES, then only members that are at that depth are returned. If a depth number is specified with LEAVES, then any leaf members encountered up to that depth are retained. In Analysis Services, you can request leaf-level members regardless of their depth by leaving the depth argument empty. The following would perform that:

```
Descendants (
  [Accounts].CurrentMember,
  , /* empty */
  LEAVES
)
```

In Essbase, you don't need to use LEAVES, since you can request leaf-level members by referring to the dimension's level 0 (remember that in Essbase, levels refer to heights while generations refer to depths). The following would retrieve leaf-level members in Essbase:

```
Descendants (
  [Accounts].CurrentMember,
  [Accounts].Levels (0)
  /* LEAVES is optional at this point */
)
```

If no flag is specified, the default behavior is SELF.

See also: Ancestor(), Ancestors(), Ascendants(), .Children

Hierarchy.**Dimension**   Returns: dimension
Extension: AS2005, AS2000

This function returns the dimension that the hierarchy is in. Because Microsoft Analysis Services 2000 and, to some degree, 2005 semantically treat different hierarchies as different dimensions, this function is essentially a "no-op" in those products.

Level.**Dimension**   Returns: dimension
Extension: AS2005, AS2000, Essbase

The function returns the dimension that contains Level.

Member.**Dimension**   Returns: dimension
Extension: AS2005, AS2000, Essbase

This function returns the dimension that contains Member.

Dimensions(*numeric expression***)**   Returns: dimension
Extension: AS2005, AS2000

This function returns the dimension whose zero-based position within the cube is *numeric expression*. Note that the Measures dimension is always Dimensions(0), while the order of the other dimensions depends on the order in which they were added to the cube when it was being constructed (and/or modified).

Dimensions(*string expression***)**   Returns: dimension
Extension: AS2005, AS2000

This function returns the dimension whose name is given by string expression.

See also: Dimension.Name

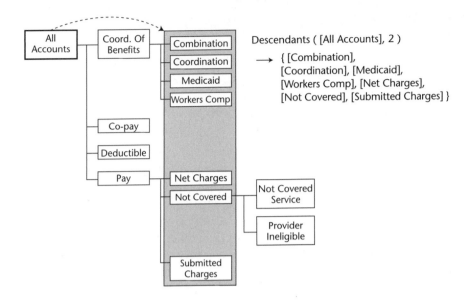

Descendants ([All Accounts], 2)

→ { [Combination],
[Coordination], [Medicaid],
[Workers Comp], [Net Charges],
[Not Covered], [Submitted Charges] }

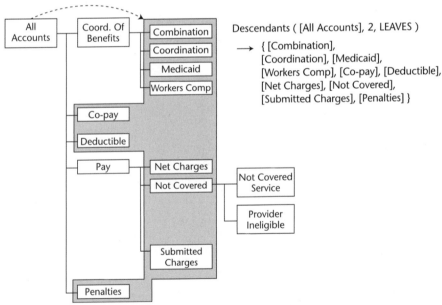

Descendants ([All Accounts], 2, LEAVES)

→ { [Combination],
[Coordination], [Medicaid],
[Workers Comp], [Co-pay], [Deductible],
[Net Charges], [Not Covered],
[Submitted Charges], [Penalties] }

Figure A-12 Behavior of Descendants() with LEAVES flag.

Distinct(*set***)**   Returns: set
Standard

This function removes any duplicates from the *set*. The first instance of each tuple is retained in the order in which it appears.

See also: DistinctCount(), Except(), Extract()

DistinctCount(*set*)   Returns: number (integer)
Extension: AS2005, AS2000

This function counts the distinct, nonempty tuples in a set. It is equivalent to Count (`Distinct (set)`, `EXCLUDEEMPTY`). Only a measure can use this function. If you define a calculation on another dimension that uses DistinctCount(), you will get a syntax error. (If you want this functionality on another dimension, you can use the equivalent Count(. . .) expression.)

When this function is used to calculate a cell, the distinct tuples in *set* are determined, and the nonempty cells formed by intersecting those tuples with the current member in every other dimension are counted. This function can be used to simulate the DistinctCount measure aggregation type in Analysis Services, but its strength is when you want the distinct count along only a subset of cube dimensions (one or two), when you are limiting the scope within the dimensions, when you are taking the distinct count at aggregate members in one or more of the dimensions, or when one or more dimensions involve a calculated member. Remember that the DistinctCount aggregation is handled to some degree by the server during cube aggregation, while this function is calculated at client query time.

See also: Distinct(), Count(), .Count

DrillDownByLayer(*set* [, { *layer* | *index* }])   Returns: set
Extension: Essbase

See definition of DrillDownLevel. DrillDownLevel() can be used as a synonym for DrillDownByLayer() in Essbase. When a numeric *index* is provided, a *set* containing multiple dimensions has the dimension in the *index* tuple position drilled down on. *Index* value 0 is the first dimension. If the *set* contains only one dimension, then only an *index* value of 0 is valid.

See also: DrillUpByLayer(), DrillUpLevel()

DrillDownLevel(*set* [, *level*])   Returns: set
Standard

This function returns a set resulting from a particular drill-down operation performed by the function. *Set* can be of arbitrary dimensionality. When the *level* argument is specified, all members or tuples in *set* that are in *level* are drilled down into the next lowest level (if there is one). When the *level* argument is not specified, only those members or tuples that are at the lowest level in the first dimension of the *set* are drilled down into, and they are drilled down into the next lower level. The behavior of DrillDownLevel() is shown in Figure A-13. All children are inserted immediately after their parents; otherwise, the order is preserved. If *level* is specified, but there is no member at *level* in the *set*, then the given set is returned without modification.

In Essbase, the *layer* can be a generation or level specification.

NOTE If one or more children of a member to be drilled down into immediately follow a parent in set, then that parent will not be drilled down into.

DrillDownLevel(*set,* , *index*)   Returns: set
Extension: AS2005, AS2000

This variation is a Microsoft – specific extension to DrillDownLevel(). It enables the dimension to be drilled down into by leaving the level field empty and providing a zero-based dimension index to specify which dimension should be drilled down into. This is really only useful when *set* has tuples with more than one dimension. The first dimension to drill down into is at index 0, the second dimension is at index 1, and so on. As with the rules for the standard version of DrillDownLevel(), tuples containing the lowest level members of that dimension are drilled down into.

NOTE If one or more children of a member to be drilled down into immediately follows a parent in set, then that parent will not be drilled down into.

DrillDownLevelBottom(*set, index* [,[*level*] [, *numeric expression*]])   Returns: set
Standard (not in Essbase 9)

Similarly to DrillDownLevel() and DrillDownLevelTop(), this function drills down through all members in the *set* that are at the specified *level*, if the *level* is provided (or the lowest *level* of members that are present in the *set* if *level* is not provided). However, instead of returning all children, this function returns only the bottom *index* members or tuples. The *set* can be of arbitrary dimensionality. The ranking is determined through the *numeric expression*, if one is provided, or through the values of cells found in the default context when the set is evaluated, if the *numeric expression* is left out. Figure A-14 illustrates the behavior of DrillDownLevelBottom().

NOTE If one or more children of a member to be drilled down on immediately follow a parent in the set, then that parent will not be drilled down into.

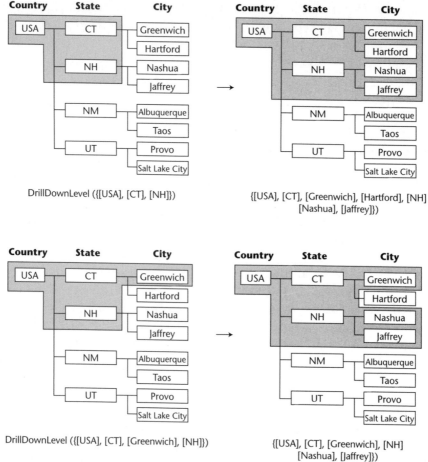

DrillDownLevel ({[USA], [CT], [NH]})

{[USA], [CT], [Greenwich], [Hartford], [NH]
[Nashua], [Jaffrey]})

DrillDownLevel ({[USA], [CT], [Greenwich], [NH]})

{[USA], [CT], [Greenwich], [NH]
[Nashua], [Jaffrey]})

Figure A-13   DrillDownLevel().

DrillDownLevelTop(*set*, *index* [, [*level*] [, *numeric expression*]])   Returns: set
Standard (not in Essbase 9)

Similarly to DrillDownLevel() and DrillDownLevelBottom(), this function drills down all members in *set* that are at the specified *level*, if the *level* is provided (or the lowest level of members that are present in the *set* if *level* is not provided). However, instead of returning all children, this function returns only the top *index* members or tuples. The set can be of arbitrary dimensionality. The ranking is determined through the *numeric expression*, if one is provided, or through the values of cells found in the default context when the set is evaluated, if the numeric value expression is left out. Figure A-15 illustrates the behavior of DrillDownLevelTop(). As with DrillDownLevel(), if a member at *level* is immediately followed by one of its children, it will not be drilled down on.

NOTE If one or more children of a member to be drilled down into immediately follows a parent in set, then that parent will not be drilled down into.

DrillDownMember(*set1*, *set2* **[, RECURSIVE])**   Returns: set
Standard

This function returns a set that is formed by drilling down one level on
each member in *set1* that is present in *set2*. *Set1* can be of arbitrary
dimensionality; *set2* must be of only one dimension. The ability of *set1* to
consist of more than one dimension is an extension to the OLE DB for
OLAP specification.

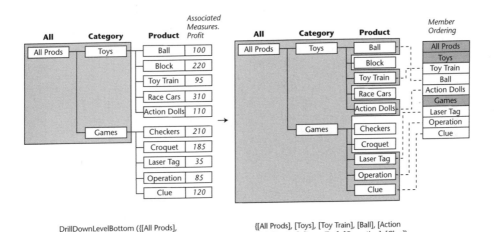

DrillDownLevelBottom ([[All Prods],
[Toys], [Games]], 3, [Category],
[Measure].[Profit])

{[All Prods], [Toys], [Toy Train], [Ball], [Action
Dolls], [Games], [Laser Tag], [Operation], [Clue]}

Figure A-14   DrillDownLevelBottom().

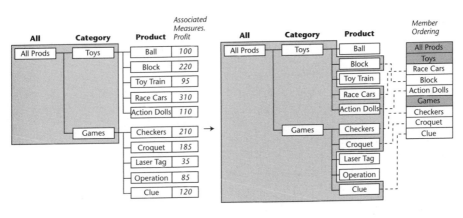

DrillDownLevelTop ([[All Prods],
[Toys], [Games]], 3, [Category],
[Measure].[Profit])

{[All Prods], [Toys], [Race Cars], [Block], [Action
Dolls], [Games], [Checkers], [Croquet], [Clue]}

Figure A-15   DrillDownLevelTop().

If *set1* contains tuples, this function will return a set that is formed by drilling down each tuple in *set1* that has a matching member from *set2* in it. If RECURSIVE is not specified, then only one pass through *set1* is performed, matching each member or tuple with each member in *set2*. If RECURSIVE is specified, then the set resulting from the first pass is again matched with each member in *set2*, and so on until no more members in the set being constructed are found in *set2*. Figure A-16 illustrates the behavior of DrillDownMember().

> **NOTE** If one or more children of a member to be drilled down into immediately follows a parent in set, then that parent will not be drilled down into.

See also: DrillUpMember()

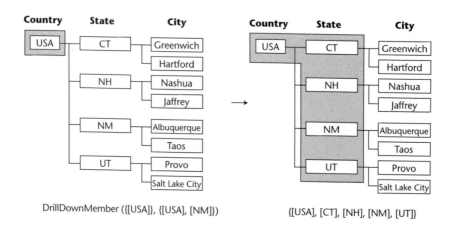

DrillDownMember ({[USA]}, {[USA], [NM]})

{[USA], [CT], [NH], [NM], [UT]}

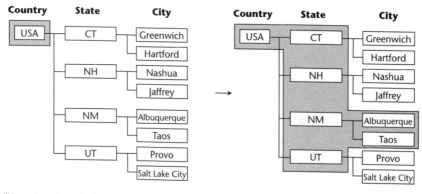

DrillDownMember ({[USA]}, {[USA], [NM]}, RECURSIVE)

{[USA], [CT], [NH], [NM], [Albuquerque], [Taos], [UT]}

Figure A-16   DrillDownMember().

DrillDownMemberBottom(_set1_, _set2_, _index_ [, _numeric expression_][,
RECURSIVE])   Returns: set
Standard (not in Essbase 9)

Much like DrillDownMember(), this function returns a set that is formed
by drilling down one level on each member in _set1_ that is present in _set2_.
However, it returns the bottom _index_ children for a parent rather than all
children. _Set1_ can be of arbitrary dimensionality; _set2_ must be of only
one dimension.

If _set1_ contains tuples, this will return a set that is formed by drilling
down each tuple in _set1_ that has a matching member from _set2_ in it. If
RECURSIVE is not specified, then only one pass through _set1_ is performed, matching each member or tuple with each member in _set2_. If
RECURSIVE is specified, then the set that results from the first pass is
again matched with each member in _set2_, and so on until no more members in the set being constructed are found in _set2_. At each step of
drilling, the bottom _index_ child members or tuples are returned instead
of all children. The ranking is based on the _numeric expression_, if specified; otherwise, values from the set of children are evaluated in the current context, and those results are used. Figure A-17 illustrates the
behavior of DrillDownMemberBottom().

DrillDownMemberTop(_set1_, _set2_, _index_ [, _numeric expression_][,
RECURSIVE]])   Returns: set
Standard (not in Essbase 9)

Like DrillDownMember(), this function returns a set that is formed by
drilling down one level on each member in _set1_ that is present in _set2_.
However, it returns the top _index_ children for a parent rather than all
children. _Set1_ can be of arbitrary dimensionality; _set2_ must be of only
one dimension.

If _set1_ contains tuples, this will return a set formed by drilling down
each tuple in _set1_ that has a matching member from _set2_ in it. If RECUR-
SIVE is not specified, then only one pass through _set1_ is performed,
matching each member or tuple with each member in _set2_. If RECUR-
SIVE is specified, then the set that results from the first pass is again
matched with each member in _set2_, and so on until no more members in
the set being constructed are found in _set2_. At each step of drilling, the
top _index_ child members or tuples are returned instead of all children.
The ranking is based on the _numeric expression_, if specified; otherwise,
values from the set of children are evaluated in the current context, and
those results are used. Figure A-18 illustrates the behavior of DrillDown-
MemberTop().

DrillUpByLayer(*set* [, *layer*])   Returns: set
Extension: Essbase

> See definition of DrillUpLevel(). DrillUpLevel() can be used as a synonym for DrillUpByLayer() in Essbase.
>
> *See also: DrillDownByLayer(), DrillDownLevel()*

DrillUpLevel (*set* [, *level*])   Returns: set
Standard

> This function strips away all members in the set that are below the given *level*. (In Essbase, either a generation or level may be used.) If the *level* is not provided, then it is assumed to be one level higher in the hierarchy than the level of the lowest level member(s) in the set (the lowest-level members in the set are removed). Figure A-19 illustrates the behavior of DrillUpLevel(). A set returned by DrillDownMember() or DrillDownLevel() will be suitable for cleanly drilling up with this function.
>
> *See also: DrillDownLevel(),DrillDownByLayer(),DrillUpByLayer(),*

DrillUpMember (*set1, set2*)   Returns: set
Standard

> This step strips away members in *set1* that are descendants of members in *set2*. Figure A-20 illustrates the behavior of DrillUpMember(). *Set1* can contain tuples of arbitrary dimensionality; *set2* must contain only members of one dimension.
>
> Note that only descendants that are immediately after the ancestor member in *set2* are stripped away. If an ancestor member specified in *set2* is not present in *set1*, any descendants will remain. Descendants that precede the ancestor or that appear after another member that is not a descendant has intervened will not be stripped away. A set returned by DrillDownMember() or DrillDownLevel() will be suitable for drilling up cleanly with this function. Figure A-20 illustrates the behavior of DrillUpMember().
>
> *See also: DrillDownMember()*

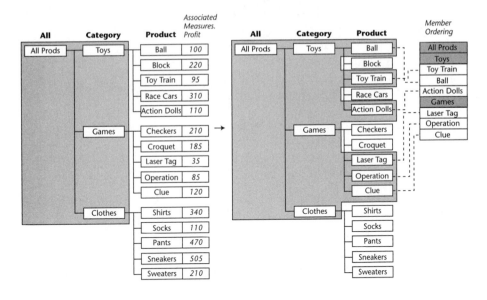

DrillDownMemberBottom ({[All Prods],
[Toys], [Games], [Clothes]} , { [Toys], [Games] },3,
[Measures].[Profit])

{ [All Prods], [Toys], [Toy Train], [Ball], [Action
Dolls], [Games], [Laser Tag], [Operation], [Clue] }

Figure A-17   DrillDownMemberBottom().

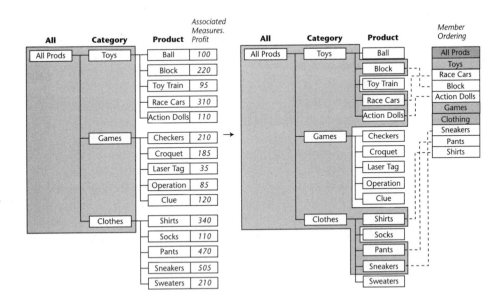

DrillDownMemberTop ({ [All Prods],
[Toys], [Games], [Clothes]} , { [Toys], [Games] }, 3,
[Measures].[Profit])

{ [All Prods], [Toys], [Race Cars], [Block], [Action
Dolls], [Clothing], [Sneakers], [Pants], [Shirts] }

Figure A-18   DrillDownMemberTop().

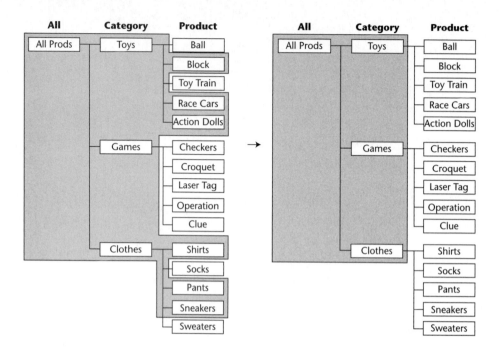

DrillUpLevel ({ [All Prods],
[Toys], [Race Cars], [Block], [Action Dolls],
[Clothing], [Sneakers], [Pants], [Shirts] }, [Category])

{ [All Prods], [Toys], [Games], [Clothes] }

Figure A-19   DrillUpLevel().

E

Error([*string_expr*] **)**   Returns: (no return)
Extension: AS2005

The Error() function raises an error. This will propagate to callers; if an error occurs for evaluating a cell that is an input to a function like Filter() or Order() in an axis or slicer, the query will not successfully execute. If the error occurs while calculating a result cell, then the client will receive an error result when retrieving that cell's value. It may be possible to detect and work around the error with the IsError() function that is part of VBA and .Net, although this may not work correctly until service pack 1 of AS 2005.

Except(*set1*, *set2* **[, ALL]**)   Returns: set
Standard

set1 – set2   Returns: set
Extension: AS2005, AS2000

> The Except() function removes all elements from *set1* that also exist in *set2*. The ALL flag controls whether duplicates are retained or eliminated. When ALL is specified, duplicates in *set1* are retained, though any tuples matching them in *set2* are discarded. When ALL is not specified, no duplicates are returned. The members returned are determined by the order in which they appear in *set1*.
>
> *See also: Union(), Intersect(),and the unary – (complement) operator for sets*
>
> Microsoft Analysis Services also provides "-" as an alternate way of specifying Except(). Duplicates are removed from the resulting set. The expression `Set1- Set2` is equivalent to `Except (Set1, Set2)`.
>
> *See also: Union(), Intersect(), and the unary– (complement) operator for sets*

Existing *set*   Returns: set
Extension: AS2005

> This function applies the attribute relationships in effect in the current context to restrict the tuples in *set*. For example, if the [Product].[Ship Weight] current context consists of the member [12], then Existing [Product].[SKU].Members will return only those [SKU] members associated with the ship weight [12]. The current context may contain multiple members for each related attribute (for example, due to a set in the slicer or in a defined subcube), in which case the set will be restricted to tuples which are associated with at least one of the members in context.
>
> *See also: Exists*

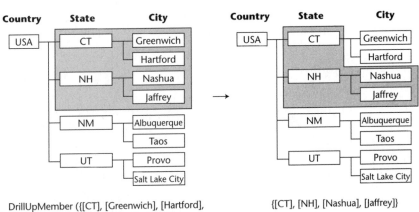

DrillUpMember ({[CT], [Greenwich], [Hartford],
    [NH], [Jaffrey], [Nashua]} , {[CT]})

{[CT], [NH], [Nashua], [Jaffrey]}

Figure A-20   DrillUpMember().

Exists (*set1, set2* [*, measure_group_name*])   Returns: set
Extension: AS2005

> Returns all tuples in *set1* which exist with respect to the tuples in *set2*. *Set1* and *set2* may or may not include related attribute hierarchy-dimensions. When the optional *measure_group_name* is provided, it uses existence of fact records for the measure group as the basis for relating members. members when *set1* and *set2* contain tuples from different dimensions (not just different hierarchy-dimensions). In this case, it is similar to NonEmpty(). If all measures in the measure group are NULL in a fact table row, Exists() will consider the relationship to exist, whereas if a fact table row doesn't exist at all, it will consider the relationship to not exist. This is different from NonEmpty(), which requires at least one non-NULL measure value to exist for non-emptiness to be established.
>
> *See also: CrossJoin(), Extract(), NonEmpty()*

Exp (*expr*)   Returns: number
Extension: Essbase

> Returns the value of *e* raised to the power of *expr*. Returns NULL if *expr* is NULL.

Extract (*set, dimension*[*, dimension* ...])   Returns: set
Standard

> This function behaves as an opposite to the CrossJoin() function. The resulting set consists of tuples from the extracted dimension elements. For each tuple in the given *set*, the members of the dimensions listed in the arguments are extracted into new tuples. Since this could result in a great deal of redundancy, this function always removes duplicates from its results.
>
> *See also: CrossJoin(), Generate()*

F

Factorial (*expr*)   Returns: number
Extension: Essbase

> Factorial() returns the factorial of *expr*. If *expr* is fractional, the fractional portion is truncated and the integer portion is used. If *expr* is fractional, the result is MISSING.

Filter (*set, search condition*)   Returns: set
Standard

Filter returns those tuples of set for which the search condition (a logical expression) is true. If none are true, an empty set is returned. The tuples in the resulting set follow the same order in which they appeared in the original set. Note that the search condition must be phrased as a Boolean expression; you cannot use the assumption that a nonzero numerical result means "true" and a zero numerical result means "false."

See also: iif(), CoalesceEmpty()

member.**FirstChild**   Returns: member
Standard

member.**LastChild**   Returns: member
Standard

These functions return the first child or last child of the *member* according to the database ordering of the child members. Their behavior is illustrated in Figure A-21.

See also: .FirstSibling, .LastSibling, .Children, .Siblings

member.**FirstSibling**   Returns: member
Standard

member.**LastSibling**   Returns: member
Standard

Figure A-22 shows the behavior of the .FirstSibling and .LastSibling operators. The first child of a parent is its own first sibling, and the last child is its own last sibling. If no parent exists, then the first member in that level is the first sibling and the last member in the level is the last sibling. For example, the All or root member of a dimension is its own first and last sibling. In a dimension without an All level, the first member of the top level is the first sibling of all members at that level, and the last member of the top level is the last sibling of all members at that level.

See also: .Siblings, .FirstChild, .LastChild

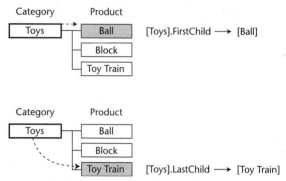

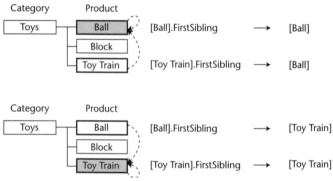

Figure A-21 .FirstChild and .LastChild.

Figure A-22 .FirstSibling and .LastSibling.

G

Generate(*set1*, *set2* [, **ALL**])   Returns: set
Standard

Generate(*set*, *string expression*, [*delimiter*])   Returns: string
Extension: AS2005, AS2000

The set version of Generate() iterates over each tuple in *set1*, and for each element in *set1*, it puts every element specified by *set2* into the result set. The dimensionality of the result set is the dimensionality of *set2*. If ALL is specified, then duplicate result tuples are retained. If ALL is not specified, duplicates after the first are removed. *Set1* and *set2* may be composed of completely different dimensionality, or they may be composed of exactly the same dimensionality. When *set2* is a relatively static set of members, this function behaves much like CrossJoin(). Generate() gains its iterative power when *set2* is an expression that depends on the current member or tuple in *set1*.

The string version of this function iterates over each tuple in the set specified as the first argument, evaluates the string expression for the current member of the set, and returns the concatenated result, optionally with a delimiter. For example, the following generates an HTML table of member names:

```
"<table><tr><td>"
+ Generate (
   [Product].[ByCategory].CurrentMember.Children,
   [Product].[ByCategory].CurrentMember.Name,
   "</tr></td><tr><td>"
) + "</tr></td></table>"
```

See also: CrossJoin(), Extract()

*Member.***Generation**   Returns: generation
Extension: Essbase

Returns a reference to the entire generation in the hierarchy that *member* is in. (This is equivalent to a level of members in Analysis Services, being all members at the same depth from the root in the hierarchy.) Used primarily as an input to metadata functions like .Members.

See also: Generations(), .Level

*Dimension.***Generations** (*index*)   Returns: generation
Extension: Essbase

Returns a reference to the entire generation of members in the hierarchy of *Dimension* at *index* depth. *Index* 1 is the tip member of the generation. This is similar to a level of members in Analysis Services, being all members at the same depth from the root in the hierarchy, except that depth numbers start at 1 in this function and 0 in OLE DB for OLAP. Used primarily as an input to metadata functions like .Members.

See also: .Generation, Levels()

H

Head (*Set* [, *Count*])   Returns: set
Extension: AS2005, AS2000, Essbase

This function returns a set of the first *Count* elements from the given *set*. The order of elements in the given set is preserved. If *Count* is omitted, the number of elements returned is 1. If *Count* is less than 1, an empty set is returned. If the value of the *Count* is greater than the number of tuples in the set, the original set is returned.

See also: Tail(), Subset(), Rank(), .Item()

Hierarchize (*set***)**   Returns: set
Standard

Hierarchize (*set***, POST)**   Returns: set
Extension: AS2005, AS2000, Essbase

Hierarchize() returns the set that it is given after it puts all the members in each dimension of *set* into hierarchical order. By default, within each level, members are put into their database ordering, top down. Children are sorted to immediately follow after their parents. The optional POST keyword returns the members in bottom-up rather than top-down order; that is, the children precede their parents. When the tuples are composed of more than one dimension, they are sorted primarily on the first dimension, then on the second dimension, and so on. Any duplicate tuples are retained.

In Analysis Services, Hierarchize() is similar to sorting on the members' internal ID property.

See also: Order(), Ascendants(), Ancestor(), .Parent

level.**Hierarchy**   Returns: hierarchy
Standard (not by Essbase 9)

This function returns the hierarchy that contains the level. Because Analysis Services semantically treats different hierarchies as different dimensions, this function is essentially equivalent to *Level*.Dimension.

member.**Hierarchy**   Returns: hierarchy
Standard (not by Essbase 9)

This function returns the hierarchy that contains the member. Because Analysis Services semantically treats different hierarchies as different dimensions, this function is essentially equivalent to *Member*.Dimension.

I

dimension.**Ignore**   Returns: member
Extension: AS2000

When used in an expression, .Ignore fixes the member of *dimension* at the current one in the context and prevents any further recursion along that dimension. In recursive calculations, sometimes a cell reference will end up being circular. For example, the level-wide custom rollup expression

```
IIf (IsLeaf ([Accounts].CurrentMember),
  [Accounts].CurrentMember,
  RollupChildren ( [Accounts].CurrentMember,
    Accounts.CurrentMember.Properties ("UNARY_OPERATOR") )
)
```

becomes recursive at leaf levels, because the evaluation of the [Accounts].CurrentMember at the leaf level will still result in another cycle through the whole iif() clause. Modifying the expression to

```
IIf (IsLeaf ([Accounts].CurrentMember),
  [Accounts].Ignore,
  RollupChildren ( [Accounts].CurrentMember,
    Accounts.CurrentMember.Properties ("UNARY_OPERATOR") )
)
```

fixes the problem; no more recursion will take place on the Account dimension.

Iif (*search_condition, true_part, false_part*)   Returns: number, string (except in Essbase), set (EssbaseAS 2000), member, tuple, level, hierarchy, array (all only in AS2005)

The standard version of the `iif()` function can either take numerical expressions for the true part and the false part and return a number, or it can take string expressions for the true part and the false part and return a string. Analysis Services 2005 extends this to allow the parts to have separate types, and for the results to be almost any MDX object (numeric and string values, members, sets, tuples, levels, hierarchies, dimensions and arrays). be numeric or string separately from each other. Hyperion Essbase extends the standard to allow the parts to return sets in addition to numbers, so for example an axis or a set to average over can be specified with an `Iif()` function.

Since both AS2005 and Essbase allow you to return sets, you can write expressions like the following:

```
SELECT IIF( condition, set1, set2) on axis(0) ...

Avg (
  iif ( condition, LastPeriods (3), LastPeriods(4)),
  [Measures].[Units]
)
```

AS2005 allows iif() to return other kinds of things as well. For example, you can select the members from a level determined dynamically with the following:

```
SELECT
IIF (condition,
  [Customer].[Customer].[Region],
  [Customer].[Customer].[State]
).Members on axis(1) ...
```

This function evaluates *search_condition*, which needs to be a logical value in Essbase but can be any value expression in AS 2005 and any logical or numeric expression in AS 2000. If the result is true, or at least nonzero in Analysis Services, then the *true_part* expression is evaluated and returned. If the result is not true, then the *false_part* expression is evaluated and returned. The standard version of the iif() function can either take numerical expressions for the true part and the false part and return a number, or it can take string expressions for the true part and the false part and return a string. Microsoft extends this to allow the parts to be numeric or string separately from each other. Hyperion extends this to allow the parts to return sets in addition to numbers, so for example an axis or a set to average over can be specified with an Iif() function.

Note that when the search condition contains a logical expression that involves comparison operations, since NULL cells compare as equal to zero with any comparison operator, the result of the search condition cannot be NULL. However, either the *true_part* or the *false_part* may evaluate to NULL, in which case NULL will be the result when that condition is met.

See also: CoalesceEmpty(), Filter(), CASE

Int (*expr***)** Returns: number
Extension: Essbase

The Int() function truncates the result of *expr* to the next-lower integer value.

See also: Round()

Intersect(set1, set2 [,ALL]) Returns:
Standard

The ALL flag controls whether duplicates are retained or eliminated. When ALL is not specified, only the unique tuples appearing in *set1* that also appear in *set2* are returned. When ALL is specified, then duplicated tuples in *set1* that appear anywhere in *set2* are returned. If duplicates of a tuple occur in *set2*, only the duplicates that exist in *set1* will end up in the resulting set. The members are returned in the order in which they appear in *set1*. For example, the expression

```
Intersect (
    {[Customer].[AZ].[Phoenix], [Customer].[AZ].[Scottsdale],
     [Customer].[KS].[Pittsburg], [Customer].[AZ].[Phoenix]},
    {[Customer].[NM].[Albuquerque], [Customer].[AZ].[Phoenix],
     [Customer].[AZ].[Scottsdale], [Customer].[AZ].[Phoenix]},
)
```

yields the following set:

```
{ [Customer].[AZ].[Phoenix], [Customer].[AZ].[Scottsdale] }
```

The expression

```
Intersect (
   {[Customer].[AZ].[Phoenix], [Customer].[AZ].[Scottsdale],
     [Customer].[KS].[Pittsburg], [Customer].[AZ].[Phoenix]},
   {[Customer].[NM].[Albuquerque], [Customer].[AZ].[Phoenix],
     [Customer].[AZ].[Scottsdale], [Customer].[AZ].[Phoenix]},
     , ALL
)
```

yields the following set:

```
 { [Customer].[AZ].[Phoenix], [Customer].[AZ].[Scottsdale],
   [Customer].[AZ].[Phoenix]}
```

object1 **IS** *object2*   Returns: boolean
Extension AS2005, AS2000, Essbase (for objects that are members)

The Is operator is used to determine if two objects are equivalent. For example, the expression

```
[Customers].CurrentMember
   IS [All Customers].[Canada].[BC].[Vancouver]
```

will only return TRUE when the current customer member in the context is Vancouver, BC. In Analysis Services, you can compare objects of any kind, and you can compare objects with NULL as well to see if they exist. For example, if the first month in the Time dimension is [Jan 2000], then the following two expressions will return TRUE:

```
[Jan 2000].PrevMember IS NULL
[Jan 2000].Level IS [Time].[Month]
```

See also: IsEmpty(), IsValid()

IsAccType (*member_spec* , *acct_tag*)   Returns: Boolean
Extension: Essbase

IsAcctType() returns true if the member has the associated accounts tag. Account tags apply only to members in the dimension marked as Accounts. Returns false if the *member_spec* specifies a member in another dimension. The tags can be one of the following:

- First
- Last
- Average
- Expense
- TwoPass

This makes it easy to filter a set of members to those having just a particular account type.

IsAncestor (*AncestorMember*, *StartingMember*)   Returns: boolean
Extension: AS2005, AS2000

IsAncestor (*AncestorMember*, *StartingMember* [, **INCLUDEMEMBER**])
Returns: boolean
Extension: Essbase

> This function returns true if the *AncestorMember* is indeed a proper ancestor of *StartingMember*, and false otherwise. No error is returned if the two members are from different dimensions (just false). Essbase will broaden the test to consider a member as its own ancestor if you include its optional INCLUDEMEMBER flag.
>
> *See also: IsChild(), IsGeneration, IsSibling(), IsLeaf(), iif(), Is, .Ordinal*

IsChild(*ChildMember*, *ParentMember* [, **INCLUDEMEMBER**])   Returns:
Boolean
Extension: Essbase

> This function returns true if the *ChildMember* is a child of *ParentMember*, and false otherwise. No error is returned if the two members are from different dimensions (just false). Essbase will broaden the test to consider a member as its own child if you include its optional INCLUDE-MEMBER flag.
>
> *See also: IsAncestor(), IsGeneration, IsSibling(), IsLeaf(), iif(), Is, .Ordinal*

IsEmpty(*ValueExpression*)   Returns: boolean
Standard

> This function returns true if the *ValueExpression* is NULL, and false otherwise. Note that in Analysis Services, if the *ValueExpression* is a tuple instead of a simple member reference, then it must be enclosed by parentheses to distinguish the use of parentheses for tuple construction from parentheses for delimiting the argument to IsEmpty(), as in:

```
IsEmpty ( ([Measures].[Units], [Time].PrevMember) )
```

Also, in Analysis Services, note that `IsEmpty()` will return false if a property reference is not valid for the member (like `IsEmpty ([Time].CurrentMember.Properties("Mailing Address"))`). More generally, in AS 2005, it will return false if evaluation of *ValueExpression* raises an error.

See also: iif(), IS, IsValid(), Error()

IsGeneration(*member, generation_number***)**   Returns: boolean
Extension: AS2005, AS2000, Essbase

(Analysis Services and Essbase implement different semantics for this function, although the syntax is the same.)

In Analysis Services, this function returns true if the *member* is *generation_ number* steps from the leaf level, and false otherwise. The definition of a generation is as follows: The leaf level is considered to be generation 0. For every non-leaf member, the generation number is 1 plus the range of generation numbers from all of the children of its parent. In an irregular hierarchy, this means that a member may belong to more than one generation. For example, the generation numbers for a simple hierarchy are shown in Figure A-23

In the case of a ragged level-based dimension, the generations are counted from the visible members. If a leaf member has a hidden parent and a visible grandparent, for example, the visible grandparent will be considered to be generation 1.

The expression `IsGeneration ([Account].CurrentMember, 0)` is equivalent to `IsLeaf ([Account].CurrentMember)`.

In Essbase, a generation is the depth from the root, where the top member of a dimension is at generation 1. The function returns true if the *member* is at *generation_number* within the hierarchy, so `IsGeneration ([Time].CurrentMember, 3)` returns true if the current time member is a grandchild of the top member (or two steps *below* the top member).

See also: IsAncestor, IsSibling(), IsLeaf(), IsLevel() iif(), IS, .Ordinal

IsLeaf (*Member***)**   Returns: Boolean
Extension: AS2005, AS2000, Essbase

This function returns true if the *Member* is a leaf member in its dimension, whether the dimension is a parent-child dimension or a regular dimension.

In the case of a ragged level-based dimension, a member is considered to be a leaf member if it has no visible children.

Essbase accomplishes the same thing with IsLevel().

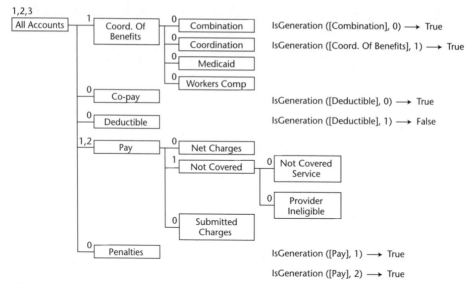

Figure A-23   Microsoft Implementation of IsGeneration().

IsLevel (*member, level_number***)**   Returns: boolean
Extension: Essbase

In Essbase, a level is the height from the leaf level of a dimension. The leaf level of a dimension is level 0. The function returns true if *member* is at the level indicated by *level_number,* and false otherwise. `IsLevel (Customer.CurrentMember, 0)` returns true if the current customer member is a leaf member. When different children are at different heights from the leaf level in a dimension, the member is considered to only be at the level corresponding to the maximum level of its children, plus one. So, a member that has one level-one child and one level-two child will be considered only to be at level 3 and `IsLevel( ..., 2)` will return false for it.

Note that Analysis Services has a special test for leaf members with the IsLeaf() function.

See also: IsAncestor(), IsSibling(), IsGeneration(), IsLeaf(), iif(), IS, .Ordinal, CASE

IsSibling(*Member1, Member2***)**   Returns: boolean
Extension: AS2005, AS2000, Essbase

IsSibling(*Member1, Member2***, INCLUDEMEMBER)**   Returns: Boolean
Extension: Essbase

This function returns true if the *Member1* is a sibling of *Member2*. In Analysis Services, IsSibling() considers a member to be a sibling of itself. In Essbase, a member is not by default a sibling to itself; the

INCLUDEMEMBER option must be used in the function to return true when *member1* and *member2* are the same member.

In Analysis Services, in a ragged, level-based dimension, the sibling relationship is determined by the visibility of members. If a parent has one hidden child and one visible child, and the hidden child has a visible child, the two visible children will be considered as siblings.

See also: IsAncestor, IsLeaf(), IsGeneration(), iif(), IS, .Ordinal

IsUDA(*member_spec*, **"UDA Name"**)   Returns: boolean
Extension: Essbase

This function returns true if the UDA is defined at the member specified by *member_spec*.

See also: UDA()

IsValid (*member* | *tuple* | *set* | *layer* | *property*)   Returns: boolean
Extension: Essbase

This function returns true if the member, tuple, set, layer, or property reference is valid. Examples of invalid references would be: an ancestor of the top member, a reference using *set*.Item() with an index out-of-range, a request for the children of a leaf member, the level below the bottom level, or a property value at an invalid level.

See also: IsEmpty()

tuple[**.Item**](*index*)   Returns: member
Standard: AS2005, AS2000, Essbase

Item (*tuple*, *index*)   Returns: member
Extension: Essbase

This function returns the member at the index position within the tuple. The index is based at 0. For example, (`[Product].[Jackets]`, `[Time].[2006]`).Item (0) is [Product].[Jackets], and (`[Product]`
`.[Jackets]`, `[Time].[2006]`).Item (1) is `[Time].[2006]`.
We indicate that Item() is optional because it is the default operator. The following are equivalent:

```
Tuple(index)
Tuple.Item(index)
```

set[**.Item**](*index*)   Returns: tuple
Standard

Item (*set*, *index*)   Returns: tuple
Extension: Essbase

set[**.Item**](*string expression*[,*string expression* ...])   Returns: tuple
Standard (except by Essbase 9)

The first variation of the .Item() operator returns the tuple at the index position within the set. The index is based at 0. For example, consider:

```
{ [Time].[1996], [Time].[1997] }.Item (0) is [Time].[1996]
{ [Time].[1996], [Time].[1997] }.Item (1) is [Time].[1997]
```

The second variation returns the first tuple in the set whose name is matched by the string expressions. When using the string form, you can use either one string or more than one string. If you use one string, it must contain a complete tuple specification. If you use more than one string, then the number of strings must match the number of dimensions, but each string will identify only one member from one dimension. In either case, the order of dimensions listed in the string(s) must match the order of dimensions in the set. If some member from the strings is not found in the metadata when the expression is parsed, then a parse error results. If the member is found in the metadata, but not in any tuple in the set, then an empty tuple is returned. For example, the following two item specifications are identical:

```
Crossjoin ([Time].[Year].members, _[Customer].[State].Members).Item(
"[1997]", "[FL]")
Crossjoin ([Time].[Year].members, _[Customer].[State].Members).Item(
"([1997], [FL])")
```

Note that in the tuple specifications, member expressions can be used as well as named members. For example, the following are also equivalent to the two-item specifications just given:

```
Crossjoin (
   [Time].[Year].members,
   [Customer].[State].Members
).Item( "[1998].lag(1)", "[FL]")
Crossjoin (
   [Time].[Year].members,
   [Customer].[State].Members).Item( "([1997].[Q1].Parent, [FL])")
```

We indicate that .Item() is optional because it is the default operator. The following are equivalent:

```
Set(index)
Set.Item(index)
```

Remember: If you are trying to use Rank() to pick out an index for Item(), that Rank returns a 1-based index, and you will need to subtract 1 from it to use it with Item().

K

KPICurrentTimeMember (*KPI_name*)   Returns: member
Extension: AS2005

This function returns the time member associated with the KPI named *KPI_name*. The *KPI_Name* is a string expression. See Chapters 10 and 15 for more information on developing and using KPIs.

KPIGoal (*KPI_name*)   Returns: member
Extension: AS2005

This function returns the member that calculates the value of the goal for the KPI named *KPI_name*. The *KPI_Name* is a string expression. See Chapters 10 and 15 for more information on developing and using KPIs.

KPIStatus (*KPI_name*)   Returns: member
Extension: AS2005

This function returns the member that calculates status value associated with the KPI named *KPI_name*. To conform to the conventions used in constructing the KPI graphic images, you should try to have this function return a value that is the KPIStatusValue() result somehow normalized between -1 and 1, although there is no technical requirement that you do so. The *KPI_Name* is a string expression. See Chapters 10 and 15 for more information on developing and using KPIs.

KPITrend (*KPI_name*)   Returns: member
Extension: AS2005

This function returns the member that calculates a trend value associated with the KPI named *KPI_name*. To conform to the conventions used in constructing the KPI graphic images, you should try to have this function return a value normalized between -1 and 1, although there is no technical requirement that you do so. The *KPI_Name* is a string expression. See Chapters 10 and 15 for more information on developing and using KPIs.

KPIValue (*KPI_name*)   Returns: member
Extension: AS2005

This function returns the member that calculates the value of the KPI named *KPI_name*. The *KPI_Name* is a string expression. See Chapters 10 and 15 for more information on developing and using KPIs.

KPIWeight (*KPI_name*)   Returns: member
Extension: AS2005

> This function returns the number that calculates weighting of the contribution of the KPI named *KPI_name* to its parent KPI. To conform to the conventions used in constructing the KPI graphic images, you should try to have this function return a value normalized between -1 and 1, although there is no other technical requirement that you do so. The *KPI_Name* is a string expression. See Chapters 10 and 15 for more information on developing and using KPIs.

L

member.**Lag**(*index*)   Returns: member
Standard

> .Lead() returns the member that is *index* number of members after the source member along the same level, and .Lag() returns the member that is *index* number of members before the source member on the same level. .Lead(0) and .Lag(0) each result in the source member itself. Lagging by a negative amount is the same as leading by the positive quantity and vice versa. Figure A-24 shows examples of .Lead() and .Lag().

member.**LastChild**   Returns: member
Standard

> *See definition for .FirstChild*

LastPeriods(*index* [, *member*])   Returns: set
Standard

> This function returns the set of *index* periods from member back to the member lagging by *index*-1 from member. This is almost equivalent to

```
{ member.LAG(index - 1) : member }.
```

> If member is not specified, then it defaults to the current member of the Time-typed dimension in the cube. If the index is a negative number, then the range goes forward from the member to *index* –1 members instead of backward. If *index* is 0, then an empty set is returned (which makes it slightly different from using .Lag()). If member is omitted, and no dimension in the cube is marked as being Time-typed, the statement will be parsed and execute without error. However, when a client attempts to retrieve a cell calculated in part by the LastPeriods() function, a cell error will occur.

> The behavior of LastPeriods() is shown in Figure A-25.

> *See also: OpeningPeriod(), ClosingPeriod(), .Lag(), .Lead()*

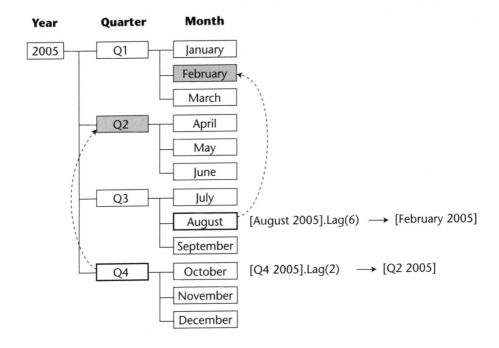

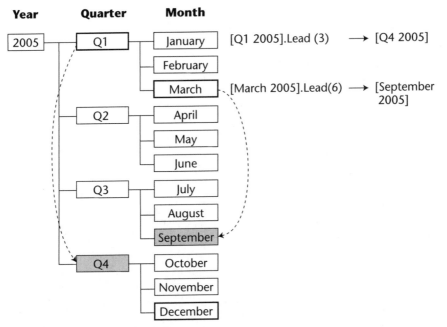

Figure A-24   .Lag() and .Lead().

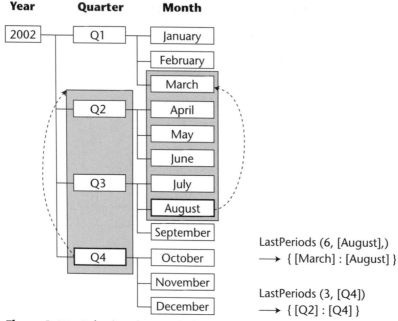

Figure A-25   Behavior of LastPeriods().

*member.***LastSibling**   Returns: member
Standard

> *See definition for .FirstSibling*

*member.***Lead**(index)   Returns: member
Standard

> *See definition for .Lag()*

Leaves ()   Returns: set

Leaves (*dimension***)**   Returns: set

> This function returns a set of the cross-join of the lowest level of all attribute hierarchies in the dimension. This includes the dimension's key attribute and all leaf-level attributes. If the *dimension* is omitted, the leaf level space is a set for the entire leaf level of the cube (!).

> Note that the Leaves() function cannot be used if different measure groups in scope in the cube use the dimension at different levels of granularity (including if some are dimensioned by it and some do not). You can select from a subcube that only includes measures from a suitable measure group or groups; see chapter 4 for details on specifying subcubes and Chapter 13 for details on specifying subcube scopes in MDX scripts.

While you can use this function in any MDX expression, it is most likely to be useful as part of specifying subcubes either in an MDX script or in a query or session subcube.

See also: MeasureGroupMeasures(), Root()

member.**Level**   Returns: level
Standard

This function returns a member's level.

Levels (*string expression***)**   Returns: level
Extension: AS2005, AS2000

This function returns the level whose name is given by string expression. It is typically used with user-defined functions (UDFs) that return a name. The string expression can be any expression that results in a level reference. For example, the string "[Time].[Year]" will result in the year level of the Time dimension. However, the string "[Time].Levels(1)" in a Time dimension where the year level is the first one down from the root level will also result in the year level. (See the following description for the Dimension.Levels() function as well.)

Dimension.**Levels (***numeric expression***)**   Returns: level
Standard

This function returns the dimension level specified by numeric expression. Note that in Analysis Services, the number is zero-based, starting at the root level, while in Essbase the number is one-based starting at the leaf level.

For example, in Analysis Services, if the levels of the [Time] dimension are [All], [Year], and [Month], then [Time].Levels(0) returns the [Time].[All] level, and [Time].Levels(2) returns the [Time].[Month] level. In Analysis Services, you can obtain the number of levels in the dimension with *Dimension*.Levels.Count, which lets you refer to the leaf level by the expression *Dimension*.Levels (*Dimension*.Levels.Count).

LinkMember(*member, dimension***)**   Returns: member
Extension: AS2005, AS2000

The LinkMember() function is used to reference a member in one hierarchy based on a member from another related hierarchy. The hierarchies may either be from the same dimension (where a dimension has multiple hierarchies) or from different dimensions. (Remember that different hierarchies are different dimensions in Microsoft OLAP/Analysis Services.) The members are matched by key rather than by name, so members with the same key but with different names will be linked. For example, the expression

```
Hierarchize(
    Ascendants(
        Linkmember([Time].[Calendar].[Jan 1 1999],[Time].[Fiscal])
))
```

will return the ascendants in the fiscal hierarchy for the calendar hierarchy member [Jan 1 1999].

LinRegIntercept(*set*, *y numeric expression* [, *x numeric expression*])   Returns: number
Standard (not in Essbase 9)

This function returns the intercept of the linear regression line calculated from the given data points (where the regression line intersects 0). For the linear equation $y = ax + b$, which will be determined over some set of y and x, the values of the *y numeric expression* are evaluated over the set to get the y values. If the *x numeric expression* is present, then it is evaluated over the set to get the values of the x axis. Otherwise, the cells formed by the set are evaluated within the current context and their values are used as the x values. Empty cells and cells containing text or logical values are not included in the calculation, but cells with zero values are included.

Once the linear regression line has been calculated, this function returns the x-intercept of the line (represented by b in the equation $y = ax + b$).

See also the other LinRegXXX functions.

LinRegPoint(*x slice numeric expression*, *set*, *y numeric expression* [, *x numeric expression*])   Returns: number
Standard (not in Essbase 9)

This function returns the value of the calculated linear regression line $y = ax + b$ for a particular value of x. For the linear equation $y = ax + b$, which will be determined from a set of y and x values, the values of the *y numeric expression* are evaluated to get the y values. If the *x numeric expression* is present, then it is evaluated over the *set* to get the values of the x axis. Otherwise, the cells formed by the *set* are evaluated within the current context and their values are used as the x values. Empty cells and cells containing text or logical values are not included in the calculation, but cells with zero values are included.

Once the linear regression line has been calculated, the value of $y = ax + b$ is calculated for the value given in the *x slice numeric expression* and is returned.

LinRegR2(*set*, *y numeric expression* [, *x numeric expression*])   Returns: number
Standard (not in Essbase 9)

This function returns the statistical R^2 variance of the given data points to the linear regression line calculated from them. For the linear equation

$y = ax + b$, which will be determined over some set of y and x, the values of the *y numeric expression* are evaluated to get the y values. If the *x numeric expression* is present, then it is evaluated over the *set* to get the values of the x axis. Otherwise, the cells formed by the *set* are evaluated within the current context and their values are used as the x values. Empty cells and cells containing text or logical values are not included in the calculation, but cells with zero values are included.

Once the linear regression line has been calculated, this function returns the statistical R^2 variance between the points on it and the given points.

See also the other LinRegXXX functions.

LinRegSlope(*set* [, *y numeric expression* [, *x numeric expression*]])   Returns: number
Standard (not in Essbase 9)

This function returns the slope of the linear regression line calculated from the given data points. For the linear equation $y = ax + b$, which will be determined over some set of y and x, the values of the *y numeric expression* are evaluated to get the y values. If the *x numeric expression* is present, then it is evaluated over the *set* to get the values of the x axis. Otherwise, the cells formed by the *set* are evaluated within the current context and their values are used as the x values. Empty cells and cells containing text or logical values are not included in the calculation, but cells with zero values are included.

Once the linear regression line has been calculated, this function returns the slope of the line (represented by a in the equation $y = ax + b$).

See also the other LinRegXXX functions.

LinRegVariance(*set*, *y numeric expression* [, *x numeric expression*])   Returns: number
Standard (not in Essbase 9)

This function returns the variance of fit of the calculated linear regression line to the actual points given for it. For the linear equation $y = ax + b$, which will be determined over some set of y and x, the values of the *y numeric expression* are evaluated to get the y values. If the *x numeric expression* is present, then it is evaluated over the *set* to get the values of the x axis. Otherwise, the cells formed by the *set* are evaluated within the current context and their values are used as the x values. Empty cells and cells containing text or logical values are not included in the calculation, but cells with zero values are included.

Once the linear regression line has been calculated, this function returns the statistical variance between its points and the given points.

See also the other LinRegXXX functions.

Ln (*numeric expression***)**   Returns: *number*
Extension: Essbase

Ln() returns the natural logarithm of the value calculated by *numeric expression*. If that value is zero, negative, or NULL, returns NULL.

See also: Exp(), Log(), Log10(), Power()

Log (*numeric expression* [*,base*]**)**   Returns: *number*
Extension: Essbase

Log() returns the base-*base* logarithm of the value calculated by *numeric expression*. If that value is zero, negative, or NULL, returns NULL. If *base* is omitted, base 10 is assumed.

See also: Exp(), Ln(), Log10(), Power()

Log10(*numeric expression***)**   Returns: *number*
Extension: Essbase

Log10() returns the base-10 logarithm of the value calculated by *numeric expression*. If that value is zero, negative, or NULL, returns NULL.

See also: Exp(), Ln(), Log(), Power()

LookupCube(*cube_string***,** *numeric_expression***)**   Returns: number
Extension: AS2005, AS2000

LookupCube(*cube_string***,** *string_expression***)**   Returns: string
Extension: AS2005, AS2000

LookupCube() can be used to retrieve a single value from another cube. This function can look up values from a regular cube or a virtual cube. The expression can also reference calculated members within the designated cube. The function is most likely to be used as part of a calculated member or custom rollup expression, although care must be taken to ensure that the result is as expected, because LookupCube() returns only a single value and does not respect the context of the current query. This means that any necessary current members need to be placed in the numeric expression or string expression. For example, the following calculated member only makes sense if we are looking at the All level on the other dimensions:

```
WITH MEMBER [Measures].[Store Net Sales] AS
 '[Measures].[Store Sales] - LookupCube("Budget","[Account].[Total
Expense]")'
```

The following will include time and product dimensions from the sales cube:

```
WITH MEMBER [Measures].[Store Net Sales] AS
'[Measures].[Store Sales] - LookupCube("Budget",
  "([Account].[Total Expense]," + [Time].CurrentMember.UniqueName +
","
  + [Product].CurrentMember.UniqueName + ")"
)'
```

See also: StrToVal()

M

Max(*set* [, *numeric expression*])   Returns: number
Standard

This function returns the maximum value found across the cells of the set. If a numeric expression is supplied, then the function finds the maximum of its nonempty values across the set. Note that in Analysis Services, a positive number divided by zero will cause an erroneous value that will be reported as the maximum.

See also: Min(), Median()

MeasureGroupMeasures (*string_expression*)   Returns: set
Extension: AS2005

This function returns the set of measures contained in the measure group named by *string_expression*. Note that the name should be exactly as specified when designing the cube, e.g. "Sales" or "Currency Rates", not "[Sales]" or "[Currency Rates]".

See also: .Members, .AllMembers

Median(set [, numeric expression])   Returns: number
Standard (not in Essbase 9)

This function returns the median value found across the cells of the set. If a numeric expression is supplied, then the function finds the median of its values across the set.

See also: Min(), Max()

MemberRange (*member1, member2* [, { **LEVEL | GENERATION** }])
Returns: set
Extension: Essbase

MemberRange() is a more flexible version of the colon operator { *member1 : member2* }. It returns a range extending from *member1* through *member2,* but allows you to specify whether that range is of all members

at the same generation/depth in the hierarchy or all members at the
same level/height in the hierarchy. If the third argument is omitted,
members are from the same depth in the hierarchy, just like the colon
operator (equivalent to specifying GENERATION).

See also: Colon (:)

dimension.**Members**   Returns: set
Standard

hierarchy.**Members**   Returns: set
Standard (not in Essbase 9)

level.**Members**   Returns: set
Standard

generation.**Members**   Returns: set
Extension: Essbase

Each of the variations of the .Members function returns the set of all
members within the scope of the given metadata object in the database's
default order. Figure A-26 shows the scope of the members operator.
Dimension.Members, shown in Figure A-26a, returns the members of the
entire dimension and includes the All member of the hierarchy if present.
Because in OLAP/Analysis Services a hierarchy is implemented as a
dimension, the Hierarchy.Members function is also shown. Level.Mem-
bers, shown in Figure A-26b, selects all members in the specified level.

*See also: .AllMembers, MeasureGroupMeasures(), AddCalculatedMembers(),
StripCalculatedMembers()*

Members(*string expression***)**   Returns: member
Extension: AS2005, AS2000

This function returns the member whose name is given by *string expression*. (Yes, it only returns a single member, even though its name is
plural.) The most common use for this function is to take a string from a
user-defined function (UDF) that identifies a member and convert it to a
member. For example, consider a UDF named UDF_GetMySalesTerri-
tory on the client that returned the member name for the user's sales territory. Given this UDF, the following expression,

```
([Measures].[Sales], Members ( UDF_GetMySalesTerritory() ) )
```

would refer to the sales value for that user's sales territory.

See also: StrToMember(), StrToTuple(), StrToSet(), .Name, .UniqueName

Members(*dimension* | *level* | *generation***)**   Returns: set
Extension: Essbase

This function returns the set of members in the specified dimension, level or generation. It is a variation of *dimension*.Members, *level*.Members, and *generation*.Members.

See also: .Members

MemberToStr (*member***)**   Returns: string
Standard (not in Essbase 9)

This function returns the unique name of a member. In Analysis Services, the MDX Compatibility and MDX Unique Name Style connection parameters will determine the format of the name generated. This is identical in function to .UniqueName.

See also: Member.UniqueName

Min (*set* [, numeric *expression*])   Returns: number
Standard

This function returns the minimum value found across the cells of the set. If a numeric expression is supplied, then the function finds the minimum of its values across the set. Note that in Analysis Services, a negative number divided by zero will cause an erroneous value that will be reported as the minimum.

See also: Max(), Median()

DIMENSION.Members
HIERARCHY.Members

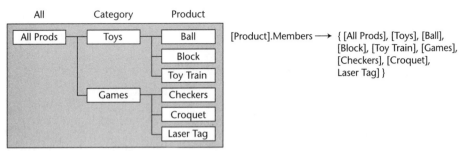

Figure A-26a   Members selected by .Members operator.

LEVEL.Members

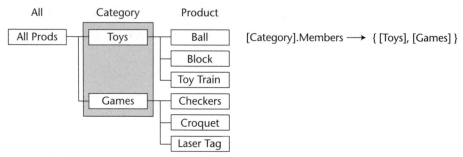

Figure A-26b Members selected by Level.Members

MTD ([*member***])**   Returns: set
Standard

MTD() is the equivalent of PeriodsToDate() with the level set to Month. If member is not specified, it defaults to the current member of the Time-typed dimension. If no Time-typed dimension is in the cube, or if it does not have a level tagged as Month, then an error results.

See also: PeriodsToDate(), YTD(), QTD(), WTD()

N

dimension.**Name**   Returns: string
Extension: AS2005, AS2000

This function returns the name of the dimension.

See also: .UniqueName, Dimensions()

hierarchy.**Name**   Returns: string
Extension: AS2005, AS2000

This function returns the name of the hierarchy.

See also: .UniqueName

level.**Name**   Returns: string
Extension: AS2005, AS2000

This function returns the name of the level.

See also: .UniqueName, .Ordinal, Levels()

member.**Name**   Returns: string
Extension: AS2005, AS2000

This function returns the name of the member. (Essbase uses the predefined member property *member*.[MEMBER_NAME] to achieve the same
effect.)

See also: StrToMember(), StrToTuple(), StrToSet(), TupleToStr(), .UniqueName

NameToSet (*membername***)**   Returns: set (of one member)
Extension: AS2005, AS2000

This function returns a set containing one member specified by the
member name. If no member can be found with this name, then the set
is returned empty (and it cannot be identified with .Dimension). The
contents of *membername* must be only a member name or unique name.
It cannot be a member expression, as StrToSet() would allow.

See also: Member.UniqueName, StrToSet(), StrToMember()

member.**NextMember**   Returns: member
Standard

See description of .PrevMember

NonEmpty (*set1* [, *context_set*]**)**   Returns: set
Extension: AS2005

This function returns the tuples of *set1* that are non-empty across the
tuples of *context_set*. Non-emptiness is a characteristic of cells, not
tuples. The measure(s) to use in determining whether or not a tuple is
"empty" are found in one of the sets. If the *context_set* is omitted, the
current context of all current members from all dimensions not part of
set1 is used. Even if context_set is provided, the current context of all
attributes is present, whether or not they explicitly participate in either
of the sets.

*See also: NonEmptyCrossJoin(), Filter(), Count(), NonEmptyCount(),
IsEmpty()*

NonEmptyCrossJoin (*set1*, *set2* [,*set3* . . .] [, *set-count*]**)**   Returns: set
Extension: AS2005, AS2000

This function returns the nonempty cross-join of two or more sets. It is
based on data actually present in fact tables. This means that it filters out
all tuples involving calculated members.

*Note that while this function is supported in Analysis Services 2005, Microsoft
is recommending that you use NonEmpty instead.*

Nonemptiness is a characteristic of cells as opposed to tuples. Non-EmptyCrossJoin() takes a different approach to specifying the cells than the other functions that deal with empty/nonempty cells associated with tuples. If the set-count is present, then the number specified for it will be used as the number of sets (starting at *set1*) to actually cross-join. The remaining sets listed will be used to form the slices used to find the cells that are nonempty. (Any dimensions not listed will have their current member used to determine cells.)

If the *set-count* parameter is provided, then only that number of sets (in the order that they appear) will contribute tuples to the resulting set. The remaining sets will provide the context or add members for consideration in the nonemptiness. The other sets may have only one member, or they may have multiple members. If they have multiple members, it is possible that more than one contributes to result tuples. Only the distinct tuples from the dimensions listed in the first *set-count* sets will be returned, though.

Note that if a measure field is NULL in the underlying fact table, Analysis Services 2000 will treat the measure as zero, so the associated tuple will show up in the nonempty set (unless all measures in the row are NULL). Analysis Services 2005 allows measures to be NULLable, however, so the tuple won't show up unless there actually was a value for it in the underlying table.

Note that NonEmptyCrossJoin() always eliminates duplicate tuples, and ignores all calculations by calculated members, cell calculations, MDX scripts, and so on. This makes it less useful than NonEmpty() for determining true non-emptiness of a set of tuples, so in general NonEmpty() seems preferable.

See also: CrossJoin(), Extract(), Except(), Union(), Intersect()

NonEmptyCount (*set* **[,***numeric_expression***])** Returns: number
Extension: Essbase

Returns the number of tuples in *set* for which the *numeric_expression* was not NULL. If *set* is empty, the function returns 0.

See also: Count()

NOT *expr* Returns: Boolean
Standard

The NOT operator returns false if *expr* is true, and false otherwise.

O

OpeningPeriod ([*level* [, *member*]]**)**   Returns: member
Standard

ClosingPeriod ([*level* [, *member*]]**)**   Returns: member
Standard

The OpeningPeriod() and ClosingPeriod() functions are essentially first-descendant and last-descendant operators that are intended primarily to be used with the Time dimension, though they may be used with any dimension. The OpeningPeriod function returns the first member among the descendants of member at level. For example, `Opening-Period(Month, [1991])` returns [January, 1991]. If no member is specified, then the default is the current member of the Time-type dimension in that cube. If no level is specified, then it is the level immediately below that of member. `OpeningPeriod (level, member)` is equivalent to `Descendants(member, level).Item(0)`. Closing-Period() is very similar, only it returns the last descendant instead of the first descendant. Opening-Period() and ClosingPeriod() are illustrated in Figure A-27.

If member is omitted, and no dimension in the cube is marked as being Time-typed, the statement will parse and execute without error. However, when a client attempts to retrieve a cell calculated in part by the OpeningPeriod() or ClosingPeriod() function, a NULL member reference will occur in Analysis Services.

See also: PeriodsToDate(), ParallelPeriod(), Is

expr1 **OR** *expr2*   Returns: Boolean
Standard

The OR operator returns true if either *expr1* is true or *expr2* is true. In Analysis Services, if *expr1* evaluates to true, then *expr2* is not evaluated (because the result is already guaranteed to be true).

See also: AND, NOT, XOR, iif(), Filter()

Order (*set*, {*string_expression* | *numeric_expression*} [,**ASC** | **DESC** | **BASC** | **BDESC**]**)**   Returns: set

Standard (of which Essbase supports a subset)

Order() returns the set that it is given after it sorts it based on the given expression. If a numeric or string value expression is provided, then that is used to sort the tuples; otherwise, the values of the cells in context are used. This function also takes an optional flag to indicate how to sort. The default ordering is ASC (ascending without breaking the hierarchy).

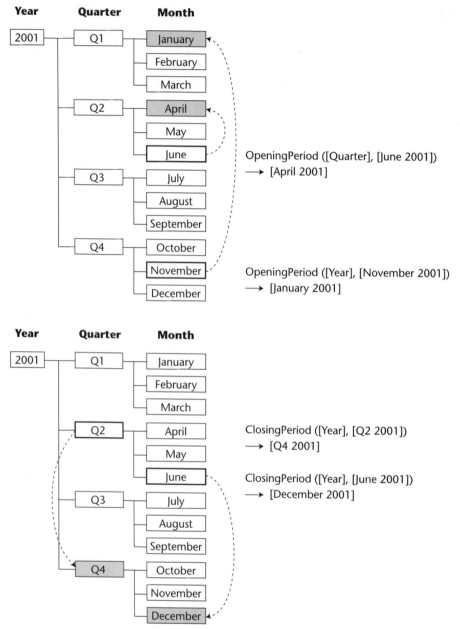

Figure A-27   OpeningPeriod() and ClosingPeriod().

Order() has two modes for sorting: breaking hierarchy and preserving hierarchy. The BASC and BDESC options break the hierarchy, while ASC and DESC do not. When the hierarchy is broken, the values associated with each tuple in the set are treated as peers, and the set is ordered only by the values. When the hierarchy is preserved, a more complex ordering algorithm is used, which can lead to very useful results.

ESSBASE SUPPORT Note that Essbase only supports the BASC and BDESC sort options, and its default sort is BASC.

Note that there is no explicit way to sort a set based on more than one criterion. For example, if you want to sort a set based primarily on a string member property and secondarily on a numerical value, no good way is available for specifying this. We do describe techniques for performing this in Chapter 4.

Preserving Hierarchy: Set Containing One Dimension

When the set consists only of one dimension's worth of members, sorting and preserving the hierarchy orders each parent before its children. At each level of members from the top down, the children of each parent are sorted relative to each other. For example, the product hierarchy for a fictional fishcake manufacturer is shown in Figure A-28 and the units shipped per product are shown in Figure A-29. Ordering these members while preserving the hierarchy would give us the orderings shown in Figure A-30.

Also, an extra sophistication in the sorting process is not immediately evident. Let us imagine that the category-level members [Standard], [Premium], and [Diet] were not part of the set being queried, while the ProductName members still were. Therefore, the category-level [Units] value does not come directly into play when the set is ordered. However, when sorting without breaking hierarchy, the [Units] value is still calculated at each parent member when Microsoft OLAP Services is trying to figure out how to order the groups of children relative to their cousins.

For example, suppose that the following set of product names was ordered by Units: {[Product].[Briny Deep], [Product].[Anglers Choice], [Product].[Ancient Mariner], [Product].[Gobi Crab Cakes], [Product].[Thin Fins]}. The ordering shown in Figure A-31 would be returned.

Category	Product Name
Premium	Ancient Mariner
Premium	Gobi Crab Cakes
Premium	Moby Dick
Premium	Neptunes Glory
Diet	Silver Scales
Diet	Thin Fins
Standard	Anglers Choice
Standard	Briny Deep
Standard	Gill Thrill
Standard	Mako Steak-o

Figure A-28 Sample product hierarchy.

Product	Units
Ancient Mariner	221,871
Gobi Crab Cakes	223,351
Moby Dick	200,745
Neptunes Glory	210,745
Premium	856,274
Silver Scales	425,604
Thin Fins	434,482
Diet	860,086
Anglers Choice	207,662
Briny Deep	201,443
Gill Thrill	209,962
Mako Steak-o	215,521
Standard	834,588

Figure A-29   Units shipped in hierarchy.

ASC

Product	Units
Standard	834,588
Briny Deep	201,443
Anglers Choice	207,662
Gill Thrill	209,962
Mako Steak-o	215,521
Premium	856,274
Moby Dick	200,745
Neptunes Glory	210,745
Ancient Mariner	221,871
Gobi Crab Cakes	223,351
Diet	860,086
Silver Scales	425,604
Thin Fins	434,482

DESC

Product	Units
Diet	860,086
Thin Fins	434,482
Silver Scales	425,604
Premium	856,274
Gobi Crab Cakes	223,351
Ancient Mariner	221,871
Neptunes Glory	210,745
Moby Dick	200,745
Standard	834,588
Mako Steak-o	215,521
Gill Thrill	209,962
Anglers Choice	207,662
Briny Deep	201,443

Figure A-30   Hierarchy preserved in ordering.

ASC

Product	Units	Parent's Units
Briny Deep	201,443	834,588
Anglers Choice	207,662	
Ancient Mariner	221,871	856,274
Gobi Crab Cakes	223,351	
Thin Fins	434,482	860,086

DESC

Product	Units	Parent's Units
Thin Fins	434,482	860,086
Gobi Crab Cakes	223,351	
Ancient Mariner	221,871	856,274
Anglers Choice	207,662	
Briny Deep	201,443	834,588

Figure A-31   Hierarchy preserved when ordering a set without parents.

Preserving Hierarchy: Set Containing Multiple Dimensions

When the set consists of multiple dimensions, the tuples are sorted so that the hierarchical ordering of the first dimension in the tuples is the primary ordering. According to this ordering, within each member of the first dimension, the members of the second dimension are sorted. Within each ([member from dim 1], [member from dim 2]) tuple, the members of the third dimension are sorted, and so on. For example, let's expand the example to include some customers and time periods and order the cross-join of

```
{ [Product].[Briny Deep], [Product].[Anglers Choice],  [Product].[Mako
Steak-o] }
```

with

```
{ [Time].[Quarter 2], [Time].[Quarter 3] }
```

with

```
{ [Customer].[Supernaturalizes Food Service], [Customer].[Hanover
Distributors], [Customer].[Subcommittees Anticipates Farms] }.
```

The ordering and values shown in Figure A-32 will appear. The products are arranged in order of decreasing quantity over year and customer parent. For each product, the quarters are arranged in order of decreasing quantity based on that product and customer parent. For each (Product, Time) tuple, the customers are arranged in order of decreasing quantity. Where tuples are tied (at the blank cells), the original ordering of the tuples is retained rather than the dimension's ordering (which was alphabetical).

See also: Hierarchize()

*Level.***Ordinal**   Returns: number (integer)
Standard (not in Essbase 9)

This function returns the index of the level in the cube. The root level of a cube is number 0, the next level down (if there is one) is number 1, and so on. This is typically used in conjunction with IIF() to test whether a cell being calculated is at, above, or below a certain level in the cube (for example, below the All level or below the Quarter level). In Analysis Services, you can obtain the number of levels in the dimension with `Dimension.Levels.Count`.

See also: Is, .Name, Dimension.Levels(), Levels()

			Qty.
	Quarter 2	Subcommittee Anticipation Farms	199.00
		Supernatural Food Service	87.00
Mako		Hanover Distributions	64.00
Steak-o	Quarter 3	Hanover Distributions	185.00
		Supernatural Food Service	151.00
		Subcommittee Anticipation Farms	105.00
	Quarter 3	Hanover Distributions	181.00
		Supernatural Food Service	179.00
Anglers		Subcommittee Anticipation Farms	
Choice	Quarter 2	Supernatural Food Service	127.00
		Hanover Distributions	73.00
		Subcommittee Anticipation Farms	
	Quarter 3	Subcommittee Anticipation Farms	213.00
		Supernatural Food Service	
Briny		Hanover Distributions	
Deep	Quarter 2	Subcommittee Anticipation Farms	204.00
		Supernatural Food Service	
		Hanover Distributions	

Figure A-32   Hierarchy preserved when ordering a set with multiple dimensions.

Ordinal (*level* | *generation*)   Returns: number (integer)
Extension: Essbase

Returns the level number for *level* or the generation number for *generation* in the hierarchy. The top member of the dimension is generation 1. The leaf level of the dimension is level 0.

See also: .Ordinal, .Levels(), .Generations(), Level(), Generation()

P

ParallelPeriod ([*level* [, *index* [, *member*]]])   Returns: set
Standard

This function is similar to the Cousin() function. It takes the ancestor of member at level (call it "ancestor"), then it takes the sibling of ancestor that lags by index (call it "in-law"), and it returns the cousin of member among the descendants of in-law. Figure A-33 illustrates the process of finding the parallel period. `ParallelPeriod (level, index, member)` is equivalent to `Cousin (member, Ancestor (Member, Level).Lag(index)`.

See also: Cousin(), OpeningPeriod(), ClosingPeriod(), Is

member.**Parent**
Standard

This function returns the source member's parent member, if it has one. The behavior of Parent() is shown in Figure A-34.

See also: Ancestor(), Ascendants(), IsAncestor(), IsGeneration()

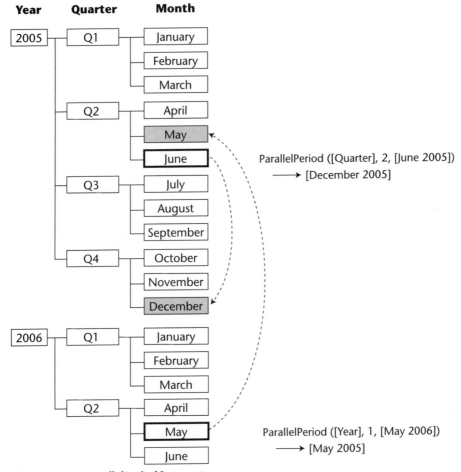

Figure A-33   ParallelPeriod() operator.

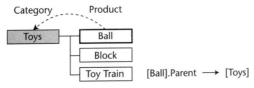

Figure A-34   Behavior of .Parent.

PeriodsToDate ([*level* [, *member*]])   Returns: set
Standard

This function returns a set of members at the same level as *member*, starting at the first descendant under *member*'s ancestor at *level* and ending at *member*. If neither *level* nor *member* is specified, then the default member is the current member of the cube's Time-typed dimension, and *level* is the parent level of that member. If the *level* is specified but the *member* is not, then the dimension is inferred from the level, and the current member on that dimension is used. The function is identical to the following:

```
{ Descendants (Ancestor(member, level), member.Level).Item (0)
  : member }
```

If member is omitted, and no dimension in the cube is marked as being Time-typed, the statement will be parsed and execute without error. However, when a client attempts to retrieve a cell calculated in part by the PeriodsToDate() function, a cell error will occur.

The behavior of PeriodsToDate() is shown in Figure A-35.

See also: .Siblings, OpeningPeriod()

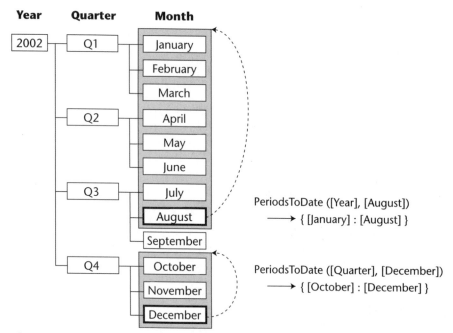

Figure A-35   Behavior of PeriodsToDate().

Predict (*mining_model_name, numeric_mining_expression***)**   Returns: Number
Extension: AS2005, AS2000

Predict() evaluates the given numeric_mining_expression against the
data-mining model identified by mining_model_name. The actual syntax of the numeric_mining_expression is not part of MDX, but part of
Microsoft's OLE DB for Data Mining specification.

*member.***PrevMember**
Standard

*member.***NextMember**
Standard

.PrevMember gives the previous member along the level implied by the
member, while .NextMember gives the next member along the level
implied by the member. Figure A-36 shows examples of .PrevMember
and .NextMember. Note that these functions return the next or the previous member within the same level regardless of whether the new member shares the same parent or not.

See also: OpeningPeriod(), ClosingPeriod(), Is

Power (*numeric_expression, exponent***)** Returns: number
Extension: Essbase

Returns the value of *numeric_expression* raised to the power of *exponent*.
If either argument is NULL, returns NULL. For example, Power(2, 0.5)
returns 1.41421356237.

See also: Ln(), Log(), Log10()

member.**Properties(**property name**)** Returns: string
Standard (except Essbase 9)

*member.***Properties(***property name***, TYPED)** Returns: various
Extension: AS2005

Returns the value of the named property at the member. The property
name can be a string expression. If it is, the name expression is evaluated
cell by cell every time the property reference is.

Even though Analysis Services 2000 and 2005 support member properties in a variety of data types, the return value of the .Properties() function is coerced to be a string unless you include the TYPED flag. Then,
the property value is returned in its internal data type.

In Analysis Services, every member has associated properties named
CAPTION, NAME, ID, and KEY.

*See also: .PropertyName, .MemberValue, StrToMember(), StrToSet(),
StrToTuple(), StrToValue(), Members(), Dimensions(), Levels()*

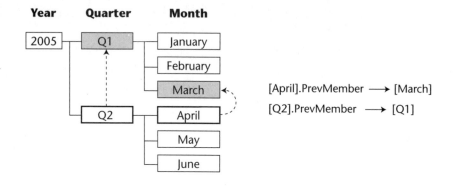

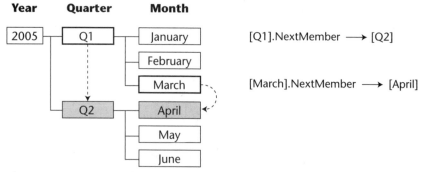

Figure A-36   NextMember and .PrevMember.

*member.**PropertyName*** Returns: string, number, boolean
Standard (except AS2000, AS2005)

In Essbase, a property value associated with a member is referenced by
member.PropertyName, where the name of the property is literally placed
in the MDX. For example, the following retrieves the ClubStatus property value for the current Customer member:

```
[Customer].CurrentMember.[ClubStatus]
```

Since the syntax for this kind of property reference is similar to the syntax for a number of functions, you should always use delimited names
(in []) for property names.

*See also: .Properties(), .MemberValue, StrToMember(), StrToSet(), StrToTu-
ple(), StrToValue(), Members(), Dimensions(), Levels()*

Q

QTD ([*member*])   Returns: set
Standard

QTD() is the equivalent of PeriodsToDate() with the level set to Quarter. If member is not specified, it defaults to the current member of the Time-typed dimension. If no Time-typed dimension is in the cube, or if one is in the cube without a level tagged as Quarter, then an error results.

See also: PeriodsToDate(), YTD(), MTD(), WTD()

R

Rank(*tuple, set*)   Returns: number (integer)
Standard (not by Essbase 9)

Rank(*tuple, set, numeric_expression*)   Returns: number (integer)
Extension: AS2005, AS2000

This function returns the (one-based) index of the *tuple* in the *set*. If the *tuple* is not found in the set, Rank() returns 0.

If the optional numeric expression is provided, then it is evaluated for tuple. In AS2005, when this expression is found, the given ordering of the set is ignored. Instead, AS2005 puts the tuples of the set in ascending order according to *numeric_expression*, and returns the tied rank number according to that numbering. In AS2000, the numeric expression is evaluated for the neighbors of *tuple* in the ordering of the set as it is passed to Rank(). If two or more tuples share the same value in the set, then the rank number returned is the tied rank. Note that if the set is not sorted by the same numeric expression, then the rank numbers will reflect the (possibly tied) rank according to the set as it is actually sorted.

MEMBER	SALES	UNITS
Leather Jackets	100	5
Leather Pants	120	4
Leather Gloves	150	200
Leather Bags	150	16
Leather Skirts	200	4

Consider the following examples against a simple set of numbers:

Against this set of tuples (which we will call Set1) and associated values, the following is true:

Rank ([Product].[Leather Pants], Set1) is 2.

Rank ([Product].[Leather Bags], Set1, [Measures] .[Sales]) is 3 (tied with leather gloves).

Rank ([Product].[Leather Skirts], Set1, [Measures] .[Units]) is 5 in AS2000 (the tie with leather pants is not noticed). In AS2005, it is 1 (tied for first place when sorted in ascending order).

Note that the .Item() and Subset() functions use a zero-based index; the rank of Set.Item(0) is 1.

See also: .Item(), Subset(), Head(), Tail()

RelMemberRange (*member, lead_count, lag_count,* [, *layer_type*])   Returns: set
Extension: Essbase

This function is a generalization of LastPeriods() that makes it easier to express ranges that extend on both sides of a single member, for example to express ranges for seasonally adjusted averages. It returns a range that extends from *lead_count* members before *member* to *lag_count* members following *member*. By default, the members are drawn from the same depth in the hierarchy. If you specify a *layer_type* of LEVELS, the lead and lag range will be taken from members at the same height from the leaf level in the hierarchy. If you specify a *layer_type* of GENERATIONS, the behavior is the default. For example, the following returns the range { [Mar, 2005], [Apr, 2005], [May, 2005], [Jun, 2005], [Jul, 2005], [Aug, 2005] }:

```
RelMemberRange ([May, 2005], 2, 3)
```

If the range extends beyond the edge of the dimension, the set returned will go to the edge of the dimension. In order to only use ranges that are of the full size requested, test both the lead and the lag members for existing with IsValid (*member*.Lead(*lead_count*)) and IsValid ((*member*.Lag(*lag_count*)).

See also: LastPeriods(), Lead(), Lag()

Remainder (*numeric_expression*)   Returns number
Extension: Essbase

The Remainder() function returns the fractional component of a number. For example, Remainder (12.34) returns 0.34, and Remainder (-12.78) returns -0.78

See also: Truncate()

RollupChildren(*member, string expression*)   Returns: number
Extension: AS2005, AS2000

This function is used to return the value generated by rolling up the children of a specified parent member using the specified unary operator. The string expression is evaluated once per child of member. You can use a constant string value for the expression, as well as a string value that changes with each member. The first (or only) unary operator may be one of +, -, ~, or a number, while subsequent operators may be one of +, -, *, /, ~ or a number. When a number is used, it is a weighting value; the effect is to multiply the cell value related to the child member by the number, and add it to the accumulating rollup value. Frequently, a reference to a member property ([Dimension].CurrentMember.Properties ("Some Property")) will be the string expression. You may also use a string expression based on a property. For example, the following expression will create the positive sum of all children that would ordinarily be subtracted from the sum:

```
iif ([Accounts].CurrentMember.Properties ("UNARY_OPERATOR") <> "-",
  "~",
  "-"
)
```

This function could be used, for example, in a budgeting application where there may be more than one way to roll up the Accounts dimension, and perhaps some costs are ignored in the alternate rollup. You could create a member property "alternate operators" to hold the operators of this alternate rollup. The following expression would return the results of this alternate rollup (note that the current member is evaluated once per child of [Account].[Net Profit]):

```
RollupChildren([Account].[Net Profit],
        [Account].CurrentMember.Properties("ALTERNATE_OPERATORS") )
```

Note that if you use this function as a custom rollup operator (for example, in a local cube), you may need to use it in conjunction with an iif() test and the .Ignore function to avoid infinite recursion at leaf-level members.

See also: Sum()

Root ()   Returns tuple
Extension: AS2005

Root (*dimension*)   Returns tuple
Extension: AS2005

Root (*tuple***)**   Returns tuple
Extension: AS2005

The Root() function returns a tuple of the root attribute-dimension members for each attribute hierarchy in the scope. If an attribute dimension does not have an All member, then the default member is included instead. It may return an empty or null tuple, as described below.

If the argument is a dimension, then all the related attribute dimensions/ hierarchies for that dimension are included. In this case, it does not matter whether you pick the overall dimension (for example, [Product]) or a hierarchy within the dimension (for example, [Product].[ByCategory] or [Product].[Ship Weight]).

If the argument is a tuple, then the result tuple contains the original members and all of the root members for the other attribute hierarchies in the respective dimensions. Note that the result tuple puts the members in a server-defined order, not the dimension order of members in the tuple. For example, you may have a tuple such as

```
( [Product].[Shipweight].[12],
  [Time].[YQMD].[Oct, 2005] )
```

but if Time appears before Product in the order of dimensions in the cube designer, the time components of the result tuple will appear first. However, the Shipweight member will be [12] and the YQMD hierarchy member will be [Oct, 2005]. The tuple can contain a member from different attribute hierarchies of a single logical dimension, like [Time] or [Product], but if the members do not have a corresponding tuple in the dimension, the result tuple is null. If they do, each of the members is retained in the tuple.

If this function is called with no argument, a tuple composed of the root members for each hierarchy is returned.

Note that this function can be used anywhere, not just in MDX scripts

See also: Leaves()

Round (*numeric_expression*, *digits_expression***)**   Returns number
Extension: Essbase

The Round() function returns the value of *numeric_expression* rounded to the number of decimal places in *digits_expression*. For example, Round (5.1357, 2) returns 5.14, and Round (-5.1357, 2) returns -5.14.

See also: Truncate()

S

Scope
Extension: AS2005

Scope is an MDX Scripting statement that defines a subcube, within which the actions of other statements is limited. The general syntax is:

```
Scope subcube ;
  statement1 ; [ ... statementN ; ]
End Scope ;
```

Chapter 13 discusses in depth the syntax and impact of Scope in scripts. Please refer to it for details.

SetToArray(*set* [, *set* ...][, *numeric or string expression*])
Standard (not in Essbase 9)

The SetToArray() function creates an array as a COM Variant type that holds an array of values. The only use for this function in OLAP and Analysis Services is to pass the constructed array to an external function that is defined as taking an array.

The constructed array will hold values of only one type (which might be, for example, long integer, single float, double float, or string). That type is determined by the type of the first value that is actually placed into the array. The dimensionality of the array that is created is determined by the number of sets that appear as arguments to SetToArray(). If the optional numeric or string expression is provided, it is evaluated over the cross-join of the sets, and the values are placed in the array. If the numeric or string expression is not provided, then the cross-join of the sets is evaluated in the current context, and the results obtained are placed in the array.

SetToStr(*set*)   Returns: string
Standard (not in Essbase 9)

This function constructs a string from a set. It will frequently be used to transfer a set to an external function that knows how to parse the string, even though the string is syntactically suitable for OLAP Services to parse into a set. OLAP Services constructs the string as follows: The first character is { and the last character is }. Between the braces, each tuple is listed in order. A comma and a space separate each tuple from the next name. If the set contains only one dimension, then each member is listed using its unique name. If the set contains more than one dimension, then each tuple begins with an open parenthesis ["("] and ends with a closing parenthesis, ")". The unique name of the member from each dimension is listed in the order of the dimensions in the set, separated by a comma and a space. For example, in a Time dimension that has three years, the expression

```
SetToStr ([Time].[Year].Members)
```

would yield the following string:

```
"{[Time].[All Times].[1998], [Time].[All Times].[1999], [Time].[All
Times].[2000]}"
```

Moreover, the expression

```
SetToStr ( {([Time].[1998], [Customer].[Northeast]), ([Time].[1999],
[Customer].[Southwest])} )
```

yields the following string:

```
"{([Time].[All Times].[1998], [Customer].[All Customers].[Northeast]),
([Time].[All Times].[1999], [Customer].[All Customers].[Southwest])}".
```

Fairly large strings (greater than 16K) will take significant time to create, and the first release of OLAP Services was released with problems that led to the truncation of strings. The further down the hierarchy the members are, the longer and more numerous their unique names are likely to be. So, you may need to perform your own performance evaluations when using this function.

The style of the unique names generated into the string by this function will be affected by the MDX Unique Name Style and MDX Compatibility settings (see Appendix B for more information).

See also: Generate(), StrToValue(), StrToSet(), StrToMember(), LookupCube()

*Member.***Siblings**   Returns: set
Extension: AS2005, AS2000, Essbase

This function returns the set of metadata siblings of a specified member in the database's default order. The resulting set includes the specified member itself. It does not include calculated members. Figure A-37 diagrams the selection of .Siblings.

See also: .Children, .FirstSibling, .LastSibling

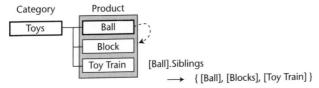

Figure A-37   Diagram of .Siblings.

StdDev(*set* [, *numeric value expression*])   Returns: number
Standard

StdDevP(*set* [, *numeric value expression*])   Returns: number
Extension: AS2005, AS2000, Essbase

StDev(*set* [, *numeric value expression*])   Returns: number
Extension: AS2005, AS2000

StDevP(*set* [, *numeric value expression*])   Returns: number
Extension: AS2005, AS2000

These functions return the standard deviation of a numeric expression evaluated over a set. If the numeric value expression is not supplied, these functions evaluate the set within the current context to determine the values to use. The formula for obtaining the standard deviation is as follows:

$$\sqrt{\frac{\sum_{i=1}^{n}(\bar{x} - x_i)^2}{n}}$$

StDev() calculates the sample standard deviation and uses the unbiased formula for population (dividing by n - 1 instead of n). On the other hand, StDevP() calculates the population standard deviation and uses the biased formula (dividing by n). StdDev() and StdDevP() are aliases of StDev() and StDevP(), respectively.

StripCalculatedMembers(*set*)   Returns: set
Extension: AS2005, AS2000

The StripCalculatedMembers() function returns the members of *set* after removing all the calculated members. The set is limited to only one dimension. Note that this function removes all calculated members defined, whether they were defined by CREATE MEMBER at the server or at the client, or in the query through WITH MEMBER.

See also: AddCalculatedMembers(), .AllMembers

StrToMember (*string_expression*)   Returns: member
Standard (not in Essbase 9)

StrToMember (*string_expression*, **CONSTRAINED**)   Returns: member
Extension: AS2005

This function refers to a member identified by the *string_expression*. This
will frequently be used along with external functions to convert a string
returned by the external function to a member reference within the
query. The string expression can be dynamic as well as a fixed string.
When the CONSTRAINED flag is omitted, the expression can resolve to
an MDX expression that evaluates to a member as well as just the name
of a member When the CONSTRAINED flag is present, the *string_
expression* can still be a string expression instead of a literal string, but
when the string is evaluated, it must be a qualified or unqualified member name, or else the evaluation results in an error. If the error occurs in
evaluating a slicer or axis, the query execution will stop. If the error
occurs in evaluating a result cell, the cell will have an error result.

See also: Members(), StrToTuple(), StrToSet(), .Properties(), IsError()

StrToSet(*string_expression*)   Returns: set
Standard (not in Essbase 9)

StrToSet (*string_expression*, **CONSTRAINED**)   Returns: set
Extension: AS2005

This function constructs a set from a *string expression*. This will frequently
be used to transfer a set specification returned by a UDF back to the MDX
statement. When the CONSTRAINED flag is omitted, the string must be
a syntactically valid MDX set specification relative to the cube in whose
context it is executed. For example, the set of all years in a Time dimension that has three year-level members could be created by passing either
of the following strings into StrToSet:

```
"{[Time].[All Times].[2004], [Time].[All Times].[2005],
  [Time].[All Times].[2006]}"
"[Time].[Year].Members"
```

When the CONSTRAINED flag is provided, the string expression must
contain either a valid MDX tuple composed of named members, or a set
of tuples composed of named members and enclosed by {}. Of the two
examples above, the first would be allowed with the CONSTRAINED
flag while the second one would not. If the error occurs in evaluating a
slicer or axis, the query execution will stop. If the error occurs in evaluating a result cell, the cell will have an error result.

*See also: StrToTuple, SetToStr(), TupleToStr(), Members(), .Properties(), .Name,
.UniqueName, IsError()*

StrToTuple (*string_expression*)   Returns: tuple
Standard (not in Essbase 9)

StrToTuple (*string_expression*, **CONSTRAINED**)   Returns: tuple
Extension: AS2005

This function constructs a tuple from a string expression. This will frequently be used to transfer a tuple specification that is returned by an external function back to the MDX statement. The string must be a syntactically valid MDX tuple specification relative to the cube in whose context it is executed. When the CONSTRAINED flag is omitted, the *string_expression* can contain any MDX expression that results in a tuple. For example, the following two strings would give identical results in the customer dimension, where [AZ] is a child of [Southwest], in that both would result in the Southwest region member:

```
"([Customer].[Southwest],[Time].[2006])"
"([Customer].[AZ].Parent,[Time].[2006])"
```

When the CONSTRAINED flag is provided, the string expression must contain valid MDX tuple composed of named members, or else an error will result. Of the two examples above, the first would be allowed with the CONSTRAINED flag while the second one would not. If the error occurs in evaluating a slicer or axis, the query execution will stop. If the error occurs in evaluating a result cell, the cell will have an error result.

See also: StrToSet(), SetToStr(), TupleToStr(), Members(), .Properties(), .Name, .UniqueName, IsError()

StrToValue (*string expression*)   Returns: number or string
Extension: AS2005, AS2000

StrToValue (*string_expression*, **CONSTRAINED**)   Returns: number or string
Extension: AS2005

This function takes the results of an arbitrary string expression and evaluates it as an MDX expression in the current context of the cube or query. The string expression can be dynamic as well as a fixed string. When the CONSTRAINED flag is omitted, the MDX expression can be arbitrarily complicated so long as it returns a single cell value. When the CONSTRAINED flag is provided, the string expression must contain only a constant value, or else an error will result. If the error occurs in evaluating a slicer or axis, the query execution will stop. If the error occurs in evaluating a result cell, the cell will have an error result.

See also: StrToSet, SetToStr(), TupleToStr(), Members(), .Properties(), .Name, .UniqueName

Subset (*set*, *start* [, *count*])   Returns: set
Extension: AS2005, AS2000, Essbase

This function returns up to *count* elements from *set*, starting at *start*. The start index is zero-based: the first element in the set is at index 0, and the last is at one less than the number of tuples in the set. If *count* is not specified or is greater than the number of elements in the set following *Start*, all elements from *Start* to the end of the set are returned. If *count* is less than 1, then an empty set is returned.

See also: Head(), Tail(), Index(), .Count, Count(), Rank()

Sum (*set* [, *numeric value expression*])   Returns: number
Standard

This function returns the sum of values found across all tuples in the *set*. If *numeric value expression* is supplied, then it is evaluated across *set* and its results are summed; otherwise, *set* is evaluated in the current context and the results are summed.

See also: Aggregate(), Avg(), Count(), .Count, Min(), Max()

T

Tail(*set* [, *count*])   Returns: set
Extension: AS2005, AS2000, Essbase

This function returns a set of the last *count* elements from the given *set*. The order of elements in the given *set* is preserved. If *count* is omitted, the number of elements returned is 1. If count is less than 1, an empty set is returned. If the value of the count is greater than the number of tuples in the set, the original set is returned.

See also: Subset(), Head(),Index(), .Count, Count(), Rank()

This   Returns: subcube

This function returns the currently specified scope in an MDX script. May be assigned to or have properties set for it. See chapter 13 for details on writing and using MDX scripts.

See also: .CurrentMember

ToDate (*date_fmt_string*, *date_value_string*)   Returns: number
Extension: Essbase

This function converts the date named in *date_value_string* using the format given in *date_fmt_string* to a number that Essbase uses as a date reference. Member properties of "Date" type use the same date reference, so this is especially helpful in expression a filter criterion for date-related properties. The allowable *date_fmt_string* values and corresponding example *date_value_string* values are shown in the following table.

Date_fmt_string value	Date_value string example
"dd-mm-yyyy"	"31-03-2005" meaning March 31, 2005
"mm-dd-yyyy"	"03-31-2005" meaning March 31, 2005

See also: Attribute(), WithAttr()

ToggleDrillState (*set1*, *set2* **[, RECURSIVE]**)   Returns: set
Standard (not in Essbase 9)

This function returns a set in which those members or tuples in *set1* that are drilled up are drilled down and those members or tuples in *set1* that are drilled down are drilled up. This function combines the operations of DrillUpMember() and DrillDownMember(). *Set1* can contain tuples of arbitrary dimensionality; *set2* must contain only members of one dimension. A member or tuple in *set1* is considered drilled down if it has any descendant immediately following it and is considered drilled up otherwise. When a member is found without a descendant immediately after it, DrillDownMember() will be applied to it, with the RECURSIVE flag if the RECURSIVE is present.

See also: DrillDownMember(), DrillUpMember()

TopCount (*set*, *index* **[,** *numeric expression***]**)   Returns: set
Standard

BottomCount (*set*, *index* **[,** *numeric expression***]**)   Returns: set
Standard

TopCount() returns the top *index* items found after sorting the *set*. The *set* is sorted on the *numeric expression* (if one is supplied). If there is no *numeric expression*, the cells found in the evaluation context are used. The Bottom-Count() function is similar to TopCount(), except that it returns the bottom index items. TopCount() returns elements ordered from largest to smallest in terms of the cells or expression used; BottomCount() returns them ordered from smallest to largest. Any duplicate tuples are retained during sorting, and those that make the cutoff are retained.

These functions always break the hierarchy. If members from multiple levels are combined in the set, then they are all treated as peers. If duplicate values exist for some of the cells in set, these functions may pick an arbitrary set. For example, suppose the set of values (when sorted) is as follows.

FRUIT	VALUE
Strawberries	12
Cantaloupes	10
Peaches	8
Apples	8
Kiwis	8
Bananas	4

In this case, selecting the top three or bottom two fruits based on values will cause an arbitrary choice to be made at the value of 8. The results are functionally equivalent to Head(Order(*set, numeric value expression,* BDESC), *index*) and Head(Order(*set, numeric value expression,* BASC), *index*).

Note that Essbase always removes tuples from the set whose numeric expression is NULL. If you want them included at some position, use CoalesceEmpty() in the numeric expression to convert the NULL to some value.

See also: TopSum(), BottomSum(), TopPercent(), BottomPercent()

TopPercent(*set, percentage, numeric expression***)**   Returns: set
Standard

BottomPercent(*set, percentage, numeric expression***)**   Returns: set
Standard

TopPercent() returns the top percentage tuples of set, based on numeric expression if specified. The cells or expression are summed over the set, and the top set of elements whose cumulative total of the numeric expression is at least percentage is returned. Percentage is a numeric expression. For example, using the sorted set of fruits and values, TopPercent(fruit, 50, Value) will result in {Strawberries, Cantaloupes}. Strawberries is 24 percent of the total, Cantaloupes 1 Strawberries is 44 percent of the total, and Peaches would push the set over the 50 percent limit to 56 percent.

BottomPercent() behaves similarly, except that it returns the bottom set of elements whose cumulative total from the bottom is less than the specified percentage. TopPercent() returns elements ordered from largest to smallest in terms of the cells or expression used; BottomPercent() returns them ordered from smallest to largest.

The percentage is specified from 0 to 100 (not 0 to 1.0). These functions always break the hierarchy. Like TopCount() and BottomCount(), they may pick an arbitrary cutoff when some cells have the same values. Any duplicate tuples are retained during sorting, and those that make the cutoff are retained. Note that these functions do not have anything to do with taking tuples in the top or bottom percentile ranges according to the statistical definition of percentiles.

Note that Essbase always removes tuples from the set whose numeric expression is NULL. If you want them included at some position, use CoalesceEmpty() in the numeric expression to convert the NULL to some value.

See also: TopCount(), BottomCount(), TopSum(), BottomSum()

TopSum(*set, value, numeric expression***)**   Returns: set
Standard

BottomSum (*set, value, numeric expression***)**   Returns: set
Standard

TopSum() returns the subset of set, after sorting it, such that the sum of the cells (or numeric value expression, if supplied) is at least value. This function always breaks the hierarchy. For example, given the sorted set of fruits and values, TopSum(fruit, 24, value) would return {Strawberries, Cantaloupes}. Strawberries' 12 is less than 24, and Strawberries 1 Cantaloupes is 22, while adding Peach's 8 to the 22 would push it over the limit of 24 to 30. The BottomSum() function behaves similarly, except that it returns the bottom set of elements whose cumulative total from the bottom is less than the specified value. TopSum() returns elements ordered from largest to smallest in terms of the cells or expression used; BottomSum() returns them ordered from smallest to largest.

These functions always break the hierarchy. Like TopCount() and BottomCount(), they may pick an arbitrary cutoff when some cells have the same values. Any duplicate tuples are retained during sorting, and those that make the cutoff are retained.

Note that Essbase always removes tuples from the set whose numeric expression is NULL. If you want them included at some position, use CoalesceEmpty() in the numeric expression to convert the NULL to some value.

See also: TopCount(), BottomCount(), TopPercent(), BottomPercent()

TupleRange (*start_tuple, end_tuple***)**   Returns: set
Extension: Essbase

This function returns a raveled set of tuples from the *start_tuple* through the *end_tuple*. Both *start_tuple* and *end_tuple* must have the same dimensionality. For example, in the conventional use, both *start_tuple* and *end_tuple* will be a tuples with dimensionality (year, period_within_year). The expression

```
TupleRange (
  ([Year].[2004], [Period].[November]),
  ([Year].[2005], [Period].[February])
)
```

returns the set

```
{ ([Year].[2004], [Period].[November])
  ([Year].[2004], [Period].[December])
  ([Year].[2005], [Period].[January])
  ([Year].[2005], [Period].[February]) }
```

Cubes in which the year is in one dimension and subyear periods are in another dimension will have an easier time expressing some ranges using this function. In general, starting from the *start_tuple*, the second dimension of the tuple is advanced to the next member in the same generation until the end of that dimension, at which point the first dimension of the tuple is set to the next member in the same generation as the corresponding member in *start_tuple*, and the second dimension is set to the first member at the same generation as the original member in *start_tuple*. The tuples are enumerated in this fashion until the *end_tuple* is reached. If there are more than two dimensions in the tuples, all members of the more nested dimensions at the same generation as their specified members are simply cross-joined in.

See also: CrossJoin(), Generate().

Truncate (*numeric_value_expression***)**   Returns: number
Extension: Essbase

Returns the integral portion of the expression provided, keeping the sign of the number the same. `Truncate (3.57)` yields 3, and `Truncate (-12.87)` yields -12.

See also: Round(), Remainder()

TupleToStr(*tuple***)**   Returns: string
Standard (not in Essbase 9)

This function constructs a string from a tuple. This will frequently be used to transfer a tuple specification to an external function. If the tuple contains only one dimension, the unique name for its member is placed in the string. (In this use, it is identical to Member.UniqueName.) If the tuple contains more than one dimension, Analysis Services constructs the string as follows. The string begins with an open parenthesis ["("] and ends with a closed parenthesis ["("]. In between the parentheses, the member's unique name is placed in the string for each dimension in the order they follow in the tuple. Each member is separated by a comma and a space. For example, the expression

```
TupleToStr ( (Time.[1997], Customer.[AZ]) )
```

which uses names that are not quite the members' unique names, might return the following string:

```
"([Time].[All Times].[1997], [Customer].[All
Customers].[Southwest].[AZ])"
```

If the tuple is a result of an invalid member reference, then the resulting string is empty (instead of an error result).

The style of name generated depends on the MDX Unique Name Style and MDX Compatibility settings (see Appendix B for more details).

See also: SetToStr(), StrToTuple(), .Name, .UniqueName, StrToMember(), Members(), StrToValue(), LookupCube()

U

UDA({ *member* | *dimension* **},** *string_literal***)**   Returns: set
Extension: Essbase

This function returns all descendants of *member* or all members of *dimension* that have the associated UDA value given in *string_literal*. It is equivalent to filtering all members within that scope (at all layers in the hierarchy) using the IsUDA() function, but will operate much more quickly and is more direct in expression the intent.

See also: IsUDA()

Union(*set1*, *set2* **[, ALL])**   Returns: set
Standard

set1 + set2   Returns: set
Extension: AS2005, AS2000

This function returns the union of the two sets. The ALL flag controls whether duplicates are retained or eliminated; by default, they are eliminated. When duplicates of each tuple are eliminated, the first instance of each tuple is retained according to the order in which it appears. The effect of this function is that *set2* is appended to *set1*, and then all copies of each tuple are removed after the first instance of that tuple in the appended version. When duplicates are retained, any duplicates in the *set1* are retained, and any additional copies in *set2* are also retained. The effect of the union is that *set2* is appended to *set1*. For example, the expression

```
Union (
    { [Customer].[AZ].[Phoenix], [Customer].[AZ].[Scottsdale],
      [Customer].[KS].[Pittsburg], [Customer].[AZ].[Phoenix] },
    { [Customer].[NM].[Albuquerque], [Customer].[AZ].[Phoenix],
      [Customer].[AZ].[Scottsdale], [Customer].[AZ].[Phoenix]
)
```

yields the following set:

```
{ [Customer].[AZ].[Phoenix], [Customer].[AZ].[Scottsdale],
  [Customer].[KS].[Pittsburg], [Customer].[NM].[Albuquerque] }
```

The expression

```
Union (
    { [Customer].[AZ].[Phoenix], [Customer].[AZ].[Scottsdale],
      [Customer].[KS].[Pittsburg], [Customer].[AZ].[Phoenix] },
    { [Customer].[NM].[Albuquerque], [Customer].[AZ].[Phoenix],
    [Customer].[AZ].[Scottsdale], [Customer].[AZ].[Phoenix] }
    , ALL
)
```

yields the following set:

```
{ [Customer].[AZ].[Phoenix], [Customer].[AZ].[Scottsdale],
[Customer].[KS].[Pittsburg], [Customer].[AZ].[Phoenix],
[Customer].[NM].[Albuquerque], [Customer].[AZ].[Phoenix],
[Customer].[AZ].[Scottsdale], [Customer].[AZ].[Phoenix] }
```

Microsoft OLAP Services and Analysis Services also provide + as an alternate way of specifying Union(). Duplicates are removed from the resulting set. The expression Set1 + Set2 + Set3 is equivalent to Union (Set1, Union (Set2, Set3)).

See also: Intersect(), Except(), {}

Dimension.**UniqueName**   Returns: string
Extension: AS2005, AS2000

This function returns the unique name of a dimension. In Microsoft's OLAP products, this does not include the name of the cube.

See also: .Name

Level.**UniqueName**   Returns: string
Extension: AS2005, AS2000

This function returns the unique name of a level. In Microsoft's OLAP products, this does not include the name of the cube. It will be either

[Dimension].[Level] or [Dimension].[Hierarchy].[Level], depending on the structure of the dimension.

See also: .Name, Levels()

Member.**UniqueName**   Returns: string
Extension: AS2005, AS2000

This function returns the unique name of a member. In Microsoft's OLAP products, this does not include the name of the cube, and the results are dependent on the MDX Unique Name Style connection property or the equivalent server-side setting (see Appendix B for more details).

See also: StrToMember(), StrToTuple(), StrToSet(),TupleToStr(), .Name

member.**UnknownMember**   Returns: member
Extension: AS2005

This function returns the member created by AS2005 for handling "unknown hierarchy" conditions in fact data. Unknown members can be created at one of the following levels:

- The top level, in attribute hierarchies that cannot be aggregated
- The level beneath the (All) level for natural hierarchies
- Any level (for other hierarchies)

If the unknown member is requested for a member, then the child of the given *member* that is an "unknown member" is returned. If the unknown member does not exist under the given *member*, a NULL member reference is returned.

See also: .CurrentMember, .DefaultMember

Unorder()   Returns: set
Extension: AS2005

This function relaxes MDX-specified ordering from the tuples or members of a set. Generally speaking, this function is a hint for optimization of a set operation. For example, a set that is input to NonEmpty(), Top-Count() or Order() may not have any need to have the sequence of input tuples preserved. (For functions that sort the input sets, like TopCount() and Order(), this is because the stable sorting requirement becomes relaxed.) Therefore, `NonEmpty (Unorder(set))` may run more quickly than `NonEmpty (set)`. Note that AS2005 automatically attempts to perform this optimization for functions like Sum(), Aggregate(), so you may not notice any performance gain attempting to aggregated Unorder()'d sets.

UserName   Returns: string
Extension: AS2005, AS2000

This function returns the username of the user executing the function. The name is returned in Domain\Name format. For example, if user Lisa in the domain ITCMAIN invokes a calculation that uses this function, it will return "ITCMAIN\Lisa".

See also: CustomData

V

ValidMeasure (*tuple***)**   Returns: tuple
Extension: AS2005, AS2000

This function returns the value of the measure specified by the tuple where the measure has been projected to a meaningful intersection in a virtual cube. When a virtual cube joins two or more regular cubes that have different dimensionality, all base data values in the virtual cube are found at the ALL levels of each dimension that is not shared by all cubes. You can always reference these base data cells by explicitly qualifying the measure reference to the ALL level of each dimension (for example, ([Measures].[Employee Count], [Product].[All Products], [Customer].[All Customers])). This function is a convenience because you do not need to explicitly reference all of the dimensions that are not relevant to the measure.

The tuple may contain members from any dimensions of the virtual cube (and it does not need to have a measure in it). Any members for noncommon dimensions for the measure are projected to the ALL member. Any members for dimensions that are in common are used to locate the value returned. The function can be used with regular cubes, but in that case it does nothing to change the location of reference for the measure.

Note that you need an extra set of parentheses to define the tuple if it contains more than one member

```
ValidMeasure ( ([Measures].[Qty Purchased], [Time].PrevMember) )
```

instead of

```
ValidMeasure ( [Measures].[Qty Purchased], [Time].PrevMember )
```

In AS2005, keep in mind that setting the IgnoreUnrelatedDimensions option on a measure group will turn on an automatic ValidMeasure behavior, which obviates the need for this function

measure[.Value]   Returns: number or string
Standard (except AS2000)

The .Value operator returns the value of the specified measure at the location formed by the current members of all other dimensions in context. We show this operator as optional because it is the default operator on a measure in a calculation or query context. If you leave it off, you get the value of the measure anyway because the default interpretation of a measure is to take its value. This operator exists simply as a specific counterpart to the other functions that return aspects of a member, such as .Name (which would return the name of the measure).

Var(*set [, numeric value expression]*)   Returns: number
Standard (except by Essbase 9)

Variance(*set [, numeric value expression]*)   Returns: number
Extension: AS2005, AS2000

VarianceP(*set [, numeric value expression]*)   Returns: number
Extension: AS2005, AS2000

VarP(*set [, numeric value expression]*)   Returns: number
Extension: AS2005, AS2000

These functions return the variance of a numeric expression evaluated over a set. If the numeric expression is not supplied, these functions evaluate the set within the current context to determine the values to use. The formula for obtaining the variance is

$$\frac{\sum_{i=1}^{n}(\bar{x} - x_i)^2}{n}$$

Var() calculates the sample variance and uses the unbiased population formula (dividing by n − 1), while VarP() calculates the population variance and uses the biased formula (dividing by n). Variance() and VarianceP() are aliases of Var() and VarP(), respectively.

See also: Stdev(), StdevP()

VisualTotals (*set, pattern*) **Returns set**
Extension: AS2005, AS2000

The function accepts a *set* that can contain members at any level from within one dimension. (The set can only include members from one dimension.) Typically, the *set* contains members with some ancestor/descendant relationship. For the set that is returned, aggregate data values for the ancestor data values are calculated as aggregates of the children or descendants provided in the *set* instead of using all children from the dimension. (When the *set* corresponds to children visible in the GUI, the parents are totaled according to the visible members, which is the origin of the "visual totals" name). The *pattern* is a string that is used to identify visual-total members- "visually" totaled members are identified in the results using this pattern string. . Wherever an asterisk appears in the string, the name (the simple name, not the unique name) of that parent member is inserted. A double asterisk (**) causes an asterisk character to appear in the name.

NOTE While this function exists in both AS 2005 and AS 2000, its behavior has changed substantially between the releases. In AS2005, the function works with all measure aggregation types, in contrast with AS2000 in which it did not work with DISTINCT COUNT measures. We will describe the AS 2005 behavior first and then the AS 2000 behavior.

In Analysis Services 2005, VisualTotals() effectively redefines the parent members listed in the set to have only children/descendants as they appear in the set, changing the display caption of the parent members to match the naming pattern as well. This affects all uses of the members in the entire query, not just within the set. In terms of calculations, it is similar to, but not the same as defining a subcube consisting of the just the lowest-level members in the *set*.

Consider the following query, whose results are shown in Figure A-38:

```
WITH
SET [VT1] AS
VisualTotals (
   { [Product].[ByCategory].[Category].&[2],
     {[Product].[ByCategory].[Subcategory].&[12],
      [Product].[ByCategory].[Subcategory].&[15]}
   },
   "(total *)"
)
SELECT
{ [Measures].[Unit Sales], [Measures].[Dollar Sales]} on 0,
{ [VT1],
   [Product].[ByCategory].[Category].&[2],
   [Product].[ByCategory].[Family].&[1] }
} on 1
FROM [Sales]
```

	Unit Sales	Dollar Sales
(total Outdoor Gear)	13,505	$346,008.44
Inflatable Boats	4,625	$199,377.93
Multi-Tools, Knives	8,880	$226,631.05
(total Outdoor Gear)	13,505	$346,008.44
Outdoor & Sporting	256,691	$6,493,322.31

Figure A-38   Results of VisualTotals() in AS 2005.

You can see that the first three rows represent the VT1 set, which includes two product subcategories and their Outdoor Gear parent. The fourth row was a request for the Outdoor Gear member outside of the VisualTotals(), but it returns the same value as the VisualTotals() result since the member has been redefined for the whole query. The last row is a request for the Outdoor & Sporting member which is the parent of Outdoor Gear. Its aggregates include only the visible Outdoor Gear values, but also all the values from the siblings of Outdoor Gear. Unlike a subcube, VisualTotals() does not effectively make members invisible, but it does change the set of children/descendants that contribute to an ancestor.

This global impact has a slightly surprising effect. Consider the following query, whose results are shown in Figure A-39:

```
WITH
SET [VT1] AS
VisualTotals (
   { [Product].[ByCategory].[Category].&[2],
      { [Product].[ByCategory].[Subcategory].&[12],
         [Product].[ByCategory].[Subcategory].&[15] }
   },
   "(total *)"
)
SET [VT2] AS
VisualTotals (
   { [Product].[ByCategory].[Category].&[2],
      { [Product].[ByCategory].[Subcategory].&[9],
         [Product].[ByCategory].[Subcategory].&[12] }
   },
   "(total *)"
)
SELECT
{ [Measures].[Unit Sales], [Measures].[Dollar Sales]} on 0,
{  [VT1], [VT2] } on 1
FROM [Sales]
```

	Unit Sales	Dollar Sales
(total Outdoor Gear)	14,536	$385,402.15
Inflatable Boats	4,625	$199,377.93
Multi-Tools, Knives	8,880	$226,631.05
(total Outdoor Gear)	14,536	$385,402.15
Coolers	9,911	$266,024.76
Inflatable Boats	4,625	$119,377.93

Figure A-39 Results of two VisualTotals() using same parent member.

You can see two different VisualTotals() calls, with the same parent member in each. This results in that member appearing twice in the query result. The aggregated values are calculated by the second call's set.

Note that placement of members is more flexible in AS2005 than in AS2000. In particular, you can have visual totals parents following their children instead of only preceding them, which enables more display requirements to be fulfilled.

In Analysis Services 2000, VisualTotals() returns a set that includes dynamically created calculated members that total up the given descendants for an ancestor. When a parent member is followed by one or more of its children in the given set, or an ancestor by one or more of its descendants, the function replaces that parent or ancestor member with a synthesized member that totals the values taken only from the children or descendants that follow it in the set. The name of the synthesized member is formed from the pattern given in the pattern argument. The order of the appearance of members is important; a parent that is to be replaced by a synthetic visual total must appear immediately before its children. The sets created by the DrillDownXXX functions are likely to fit VisualTotal()'s member ordering requirements.

The synthesized members are named using the text from the pattern string, per the rules described earlier. Consider the following Visual-Totals() expression, which contains numerous parents and ancestors (its results are shown in Figure A-40).

```
WITH
MEMBER [Measures].[AvgPrice] AS '[Measures].[Total] /
[Measures].[Qty]', FORMAT_STRING = '#.00000'
SET [Rowset] AS 'VisualTotals (
{
[Time].[All Time].[2001].[Q1, 2001],
[Time].[All Time].[2001],
[Time].[All Time].[2001].[Q1, 2001].[January],
[Time].[All Time].[2001].[Q1, 2001].[February],
```

```
[Time].[All Time].[2001].[Q2, 2001],
[Time].[All Time].[2001].[Q2, 2001].[May],
[Time].[All Time].[2001].[Q2, 2001].[June],
[Time].[All Time].[2001].[Q1, 2001],
[Time].[All Time].[2001].[Q2, 2001],
[Time].[All Time],
[Time].[All Time].[2001].[Q1, 2001].[January].[Jan 01, 1998],
[Time].[All Time].[2001].[Q1, 2001].[January].[Jan 02, 1998]
}
, "vt *")'
SELECT
{ {[Measures].[Qty],  [Measures].[Total],  [Measures].[AvgPrice} } on
axis(0),
{ [Time].[All Time].[2001].[Quarter 1], [Rowset]
} on axis(1)
FROM cakes03
```

This highlights some of the useful aspects of VisualTotals() and also some of its quirks, which you will need to be aware of. Looking at the [vt All Time] member toward the bottom of the report, the All Time total is simply the sum of the two day-level members following it, and a similar look at [vt Q2, 2001] shows that it is the sum of the two Q2 months following it. Looking at the Qty measure for [vt 2001], the value 1,186,056 is the sum of values found for January, February, [vt Quarter 2], [Quarter 1], and [Quarter 2]. In other words, [vt Quarter 2] was not double-counted with [May] and [June]. You do need to be careful in how you place descendants, however. [Quarter 1] and [Quarter 2] are included in the total without regard to the fact that their descendants have already been incorporated into the total.

	Qty	Total	Average Price
Quarter 1	1,811,965.00	44,166,000.00	24.37464
vt 2001	5,965,904.00	133,988,515.00	22.45905
January	620,829.00	16,343,870.00	26.32588
February	572,194.00	13,863,990.00	24.26447
vt Quarter 2	1,186,056.00	23,660,064.00	19.94852
May	614,945.00	12,267,870.00	19.94954
June	571,111.00	11,392,190.00	19.94743
Quarter 1	1,811,965.00	44,166,000.00	24.37464
Quarter 2	1,774,860.00	35,934,600.00	20.24644
vt All Time	39,239.00	1,220,641.20	31.10786
Jan 01, 2001	16,127.00	492,969.90	30.56799
Jan 01, 2001	23,112.00	727,671.30	31.48457

Figure A-40 Sample results from VisualTotals().

The bottom three rows of the VisualTotals() expression just presented show that VisualTotals() can work against ancestors and descendants of arbitrary depth. The [All Time] member is the higher level member in the dimension, while each day is at the leaf level. If you observe the values for the [AvgPrice] measure in the query, you can see that it is calculated after the visual totals, despite the fact that it is at solve order precedence 0. The VisualTotals() aggregation is documented to be at solve order –4096, so calculated member definitions will ordinarily override VisualTotals() synthetic aggregates. Meanwhile, VisualTotals() synthetic aggregates should be calculated from the results of custom rollups, because they are at solve order -5119.

Note that the synthetic members in the set returned by VisualTotals() are almost fully equivalent to calculated members created by other means. They cannot exist outside of a set as a calculated member, so they will not appear as metadata items through OLE DB for OLAP. They can be part of a set held in a CREATE SET statement and are treated as another calculated member by StripCalculatedMembers(). They can be filtered by name and unique name. They cannot, however, be referenced by a tuple reference in a formula because they are not entered into Microsoft Analysis Services's internal list of metadata objects.

W

WithAttr (*attribute_dim, comp_string, numeric_expression | string_literal*)
Returns: set
Extension: Essbase

WithAttr() returns all base members of the attribute dimension whose associated attribute values in the *attribute_dim* meet the criteria expressed by the *comp_string* and the string_literal or numeric_expression. The *comp_string* must be a string literal from the set of possibilities in the following table.

STRING	ATTRIBUTE VALUE RELATION TO LITERAL
"=="	Equal to literal
"!=" or "<>"	Not equal to literal
">"	Greater than literal
"<"	Less than literal
">="	Greater than or equal to literal
"<="	Less than or equal to literal
"IN"	At or under the attribute member identified by the literal in the attribute dimension's hierarchy

It is equivalent to filtering all of the base dimension's members and comparing their values using the expression in *comp_string*, but will operate more quickly. While strings must be literals, you can use numeric expressions to compute the comparison numbers, for example arithmetic functions or the ToDate() function for date-valued attributes.

See also: Attribute(), IN, ToDate(), Filter()

WTD([*member*])   Returns: set
Standard

WTD() is the equivalent of PeriodsToDate() with the level set to Week. If *member* is not specified, it defaults to the current member of the Time-typed dimension. If no Time-typed dimension exists in the cube, or if it does not have a level tagged as Week, then a parser error results.

See also: PeriodsToDate(), QTD(), MTD(), YTD()

X

expr1 **XOR** *expr2*   Returns: Boolean
Standard

The result of this operator is true if only either *expr1* or *expr2* is true, and false if they both are true or both false. Both expressions must be evaluated in order to determine this.

Y

YTD([*member*])   Returns: set
Standard

YTD() is the equivalent of PeriodsToDate() with the level set to Year. If member is not specified, it defaults to the current member of the Time-typed dimension. If no Time-typed dimension exists in the cube, or if it does not have a level tagged as Year, then a parser error results.

See also: PeriodsToDate(), QTD(), MTD(), WTD()

Connection Parameters That Affect MDX

This appendix collects all of the connection parameters that affect MDX usage and results in Microsoft Analysis Services 2000 and Analysis Services 2005. The OLE DB for OLAP and ADO MD identifiers for them are both provided. This includes most of the implemented connection parameters for Analysis Services.

A list of the connection parameters and the Microsoft product versions that implement them are shown in Table B-1. The fact that no client-side processing of queries takes place in Analysis Services 2005 means that several connection string parameters that controlled the behavior of this functionality in Analysis Services 2000 are now deprecated.

Table B-1 Connection Properties Affecting MDX and Query Results*

ADO MD NAME	OLE DB FOR OLAP PROPERTY ID	ANALYSIS SERVICES 2000	ANALYSIS SERVICES 2005
Auto Synch Period	DBPROP_MSMD_ AUTOSYNCHPERIOD	Y	D
Cache Policy	DBPROP_MSMD_ CACHEPOLICY	Y	D

(continued)

Table B-1 *(continued)*

ADO MD NAME	OLE DB FOR OLAP PROPERTY ID	ANALYSIS SERVICES 2000	ANALYSIS SERVICES 2005
Cache Ratio	DBPROP_MSMD_ CACHERATIO	Y	D
Cache Ratio2	DBPROP_MSMD_ CACHERATIO2	Y	D
CompareCaseNot SensitiveStringFlags	DBPROP_MSMD_ COMPARECASENOT SENSITIVESTRING FLAGS	Y	Y
CompareCase SensitiveStringFlags	DBPROP_MSMD_ COMPARECASE SENSITIVESTRING FLAGS	Y	Y
CreateCube	DBPROP_MSMD_ CREATECUBE	Y	Y
Cube	DBPROP_MSMD_CUBE	N	Y
CustomData CUSTOMDATA	DBPROP_MSMD_	N	Y
Data Source	DBPROP_INIT_ DATASOURCE	Y	Y
Default MDX Visual Mode	DBPROP_MSMD_ DEFAULT_MDX_ VISUAL_MODE	Y	Y
Execution Location	DBPROP_MSMD_ EXECLOCATION	Y	D
Initial Catalog	DBPROP_INIT_ CATALOG	Y	Y
InsertInto	DBPROP_MSMD_ INSERTINTO	Y	Y
Large Level Threshold	DBPROP_MSMD_ LARGE_LEVEL_ THRESHOLD	Y	D
Locale Identifier	DBPROP_INIT_ LCID	Y	Y
Log File	DBPROP_MSMD_LOG_ FILE	Y	D

Table B-1 *(continued)*

ADO MD NAME	OLE DB FOR OLAP PROPERTY ID	ANALYSIS SERVICES 2000	ANALYSIS SERVICES 2005
MDX Compatibility	DBPROP_MSMD_MDXCOMPATIBILITY	Y	Y
MDX Missing Member Mode	DBPROP_MSMD_MDXMISSINGMEMBERMODE	N	Y
MDX Unique Name Style	DBPROP_MSMD_MDXUNIQUENAMES	Y	Y
Non Empty Threshold	DBPROP_MSMD_NONEMPTYTHRESHOLD	Y	D
Real Time Olap	DBPROP_MSMD_REALTIMEOLAP	N	Y
Restricted Client	DBPROP_MSMD_RESTRICTED_CLIENT	Y	Y
Roles	DBPROP_MSMD_ROLES	Y	Y
Safety Options	DBPROP_MSMD_SAFETY_OPTIONS	Y	Y
Secured Cell Value	DBPROP_MSMD_SECURED_CELL_VALUE	Y	Y
Source_DSN	DBPROP_MSMD_SOURCE_DSN	Y	Y
Source_DSN_Suffix	DBPROP_MSMD_SOURCE_DSN_SUFFIX	Y	Y
UseExistingFile	DBPROP_MSMD_USEEXISTINGFILE	Y	Y

*Where a property is deprecated for Analysis Services 2005 (marked D in the final column), including it in the connection string will not raise an error but it may not have any effect.

Auto Synch Period

This property controls the intervals (in milliseconds) for client/server synchronization.

Default setting: 10,000 (10 seconds).

Set: May be set when connecting, and you can change it during the session.

If you set this value to 0 or NULL, no automatic synchronization will occur. Instead, synchronization will only take place whenever a query goes to the server for resolution. Because data to resolve queries may be cached in Pivot Table Services, you may not get updates.

The smallest value is 250 milliseconds (1/4 second). If you specify a number between one and 249, then 250 is used.

Connection string example: `Auto Synch Period=20,000;`

Cache Policy

This property controls what data Pivot Table Services requests from the server to answer a query.

Default: 0

Set: When connecting, and can be changed during the session.

In Analysis Services 2000, a single MDX query can result in zero, one, or many requests for data from the client to the server. If a query can be satisfied entirely from the client cache, no request will be made to the server; otherwise Pivot Table Services will make one or more requests (which can be monitored using the Last Query\Query Number counter in Performance Monitor on the server) not only to retrieve data for the current query, but also in some cases to try to ensure that any future queries are answered from the client cache. In the latter case, Pivot Table Services will request data for the descendants of cells needed by the query rather than the cells themselves and then aggregate the values it needs on the client. The Cache Policy connection string property determines which algorithm should be used to decide what data to request in this case.

The performance of any given algorithm is highly dependent on the nature of the query and the design of the cube, so it is hard to provide any specific advice on which setting should be used when. That said, Value 7 is generally useful when queries request data from many different places in a dimension: It allows Pivot Table Services to OR these requests together and can result in far fewer requests being issued. If Value 7 is used, it has the side effect of the query results not being registered in the server cache, but most of the time this is outweighed by the performance benefit of fewer requests.

Table B-2 describes the meaning of this property's values.

Connection string example: `Cache Policy=7`

Table B-2 Cache Policy Settings and Meanings

VALUE	DESCRIPTION
0	Default, which is the same as Value 2 unless the Default Isolation Mode property is set to 1, in which case it is the same as Value 1
1	Windowing
2	AllScan
3	Isolated
4	Ignore Virtual Pyramid
5	Infinite Virtual Pyramid
6	Largest Area First
7	OR Queries

Cache Ratio

This property controls what data Pivot Table Services requests from the server to answer queries that don't contain either the NonEmptyCrossjoin() function or a NON EMPTY clause that results in the use of the NonEmptyCrossjoin algorithm.

Default: 0.5

As part of the process of Pivot Table Services retrieving data from the server to answer a query (described in more detail under the Cache Policy property above), it will consider the ratio of members needed to answer the current query, "useful" members, to the total number of members in a potential request, members that might help answer future queries. The Cache Ratio property specifies a threshold for this ratio so that the lower its value is the more likely it is that only "useful" members are retrieved when answering a query.

In practice, setting this property to a very low value, such as 0.01, can improve query performance on cubes that have large parent-child dimensions or regular dimensions that are relatively flat, that is, they have few levels and many members, and as a result most members have many children. It is usually used in conjunction with the Cache Ratio2 property and is set to the same value.

Connection string example: Cache Ratio=0.1

Cache Ratio2

This property controls what data Pivot Table Services requests from the server to answer queries that contain either the NonEmptyCrossjoin() function or a NON EMPTY clause that results in the use of the NonEmptyCrossjoin algorithm.

Default: 0.5

This property performs exactly the same role as the Cache Ratio property, but for queries that contain either the NonEmptyCrossjoin() function or a NON EMPTY clause that results in the use of the NonEmptyCrossjoin algorithm. It is usually used in conjunction with that property and is set to the same value.

Connection string example: Cache Ratio2=0.1

CompareCaseNotSensitiveStringFlags

This property adjusts how case-insensitive string comparisons are performed for a specified locale.

Default: None (taken from CompareCaseNotSensitiveStringFlags registry entry on the client computer).

Set: Only when connecting; cannot be changed during session.

The value for this property is made up of discrete flags that can be combined via the bitwise OR. The flags specified in this property are used in case-insensitive string comparisons and control string comparisons and sort order. This property also controls how comparisons are made in character sets that do not support uppercase and lowercase characters, such as Katakana (for Japanese) and Hindi.

If not specified, the default value is taken from the value of the Compare CaseNotSensitiveStringFlags registry entry on the client computer. The client application can override this registry entry for case-insensitive string comparisons by setting this property in the connection string.

Pivot Table Services can have only one value for this property for each process. The value of this property, as set in the first connection of the process thread, affects all subsequent connections in that process thread. If the first connection specifies a value for this property and other connections are opened in the same process, each connection after the first connection must specify the same value as that of the first connection.

Table B-3 describes the meaning of each flag.

Table B-3 Case-Insensitive Comparison Settings and Meanings

VALUE	DESCRIPTION
1	Case is ignored.
2	Binary comparison. Characters are compared based on their underlying value in the character set, not on their order in their particular alphabet.
4	Nonspacing characters are ignored.
8	Symbols are ignored.
16	No differentiation is made between Hiragana and Katakana characters. Corresponding Hiragana and Katakana characters, when compared, are considered to be equal.
32	No differentiation is made between single-byte and double-byte versions of the same character.
64	Punctuation is treated the same as symbols.

This setting overrides the setting found in following registry value:

```
HKEY_CLASSES_ROOT\CLSID\{a07ccd0c-8148-11d0-87bb-00c04fc33942}\
CompareCaseNotSensitiveStringFlags
```

Connection string example: `CompareCaseNotSensitiveStringFlags =52`

CompareCaseSensitiveStringFlags

This property adjusts how case-sensitive string comparisons are performed for a specified locale.

Default: None (taken from `CompareCaseSensitiveStringFlags` registry entry on the client computer).

Set: Only when connecting; cannot be changed during session.

The value for this property is made up of discrete flags that can be combined via bitwise OR. The flags specified in this property are used in case-insensitive string comparisons, and control string comparisons and sort order. This property also controls how case-sensitive comparisons are made in character sets that do not support uppercase and lowercase characters, such as Katakana (for Japanese) and Hindi.

If not specified, the default value is taken from the value of the Compare CaseSensitiveStringFlags registry entry on the client computer. The client application can override this registry entry for case-insensitive string comparisons by setting this property in the connection string.

Pivot Table Services can have only one value for this property for each process. The value of this property, as set in the first connection of the process thread, affects all subsequent connections in that process thread. If the first connection specifies a value for this property and other connections are opened in the same process, each connection after the first connection must specify the same value as that of the first connection.

Table B-4 describes the meaning of each flag.

> **NOTE** The flag value 2 is not valid for use in this context.

This setting overrides the setting found in the following registry value:

```
HKEY_CLASSES_ROOT\CLSID\{a07ccd0c-8148-11d0-87bb-00c04fc33942}\
CompareCaseSensitiveStringFlags
```

Connection string example: CompareCaseSensitiveStringFlags =52;

Table B-4   Case-Sensitive Comparison Settings and Meanings

VALUE	DESCRIPTION
1	Case is ignored.
4	Nonspacing characters are ignored.
8	Symbols are ignored.
16	No differentiation is made between Hiragana and Katakana characters. Corresponding Hiragana and Katakana characters, when compared, are considered to be equal.
32	No differentiation is made between single-byte and double-byte versions of the same character.
64	Punctuation is treated the same as symbols.

CreateCube

This property contains the CREATE CUBE statement that is used during creation of a local cube.

Default: None.

Set: Only when connecting; cannot be changed during session.

You can only use this property together with the InsertInto and Source_ DSN properties.

Connection string example: CreateCube=CREATE CUBE MyCube (...)

Cube

This property indicates that DDL statements (such as CREATE MEMBER and CREATE SET) should default to a particular cube or perspective.

Default: None

Set: Only when connecting; cannot be changed during session.

Connection string example: Cube=Adventure Works;

CustomData

This property specifies the value that the CustomData() MDX returns.

Default: NULL

Set: When connecting, can be changed during a session.

This property is intended for use in middle-tier scenarios. For example, you could have an architecture where you authenticate the connection from the middle tier to the server in any way you want, pass in a value to the CustomData property, and then reference it using the CustomData() function in an MDX expression for dimension or cell security.
Connection string example: CustomData=MyUserID

NOTE The CustomData **connection string property is not supported in the RTM version of Analysis Services 2005, but should be available in Analysis Services 2005 Service Pack 1.**

Data Source

This property specifies the name of the server computer or a local cube file.

Default: None.

Set: Only when connecting; cannot be changed during session.

This is a standard OLE DB property. For Microsoft OLAP/Analysis Server, the value given for this property will set the mode of operation.

Specifying a server name, LOCALHOST, LOCAL, an HTTP or HTTPS URL, or an IP address will attempt a connection with an Analysis Services server.

Specifying the path and name of a cube file (ending in .CUB) will attempt the creation or opening of a local cube file.

A NULL value will attempt the creation of a temporary cube file that will be deleted when the session ends. This file will be located in the directory named in the TMP environment variable.

Connection string example: `Data Source=C:\Work Files\` `Michael.cub`

Default MDX Visual Mode

This property determines the behavior for automatic visual totals.

Default: DBPROPVAL_VISUAL_MODE_DEFAULT

Set: Only when connecting; cannot be changed during session.

Depending on the value set for this property, aggregate members may show either the true total for measures, or they may show the total only for their descendants that the user has queried for. (This property does not affect the ability of a client program to use the `VisualTotals()` function.) Table B-5 describes the meaning of the property's values.

Connection string example: `Default MDX Visual Mode=2`

Table B-5   Visual Mode Values and Meanings

PROPERTY VALUE	DESCRIPTION
0	Provider-dependent. In Analysis Services 2000, this is equivalent to 2.
1	Automatic visual totals are enabled.
2	Automatic visual totals are not enabled.

Execution Location

This property influences where queries will be resolved.

Default: 0 (meaning of default subject to change in future versions).

Set: When connection is established, and at any time during session.

The two possible execution locations for a query are client and server. When left to its own devices, Analysis Services will make a decision about where to execute a query depending on a number of factors, among which the Large Level Threshold and Client Cache Size values in effect are important. In general, it will try to distribute query processing between the client and the server, and as a result in most cases more data will be downloaded from the server to the client when a query is run than just the results. This architecture works well in most scenarios and is intended to make the most effective use of resources across both the client and the server.

However, there may be circumstances in which you want to ensure that as much processing is done on the server as possible; for example, when you have a low-bandwidth and/or high-latency network between the client and the server and you want to minimize network traffic, or when you have complex calculations that would execute faster on superior server hardware. In these cases, you can influence the decision that Analysis Services makes in favor of execution on the server by using the following combination of connection string properties: Execution Location=3; Default Isolation Mode=1. Note that this does not guarantee that query execution will take place on the server—execution must take place on the client when:

- The version of the server is much older than the version of the client.
- ROLAP dimensions are present in the cube that is to be queried.
- The Default MDX Visual Mode connection string property is set to 1.
- The cube that is being queried is a session cube, that is, one that has been created with a CREATE SESSION CUBE statement.
- The CompareCaseSensitiveStringFlags and CompareCaseNot SensitiveStringFlags are different on the client and the server.
- The locale of the client or the locale specified in the Locale Identifier connection string property does not match the locale of the server.
- The query uses the following MDX functions: LookUpCube, Predict, CreatePropertySet, CreateVirtualDimension, or any user-defined function registered using a USE LIBRARY statement earlier in the session.

Table B-6 lists this property's values and their meanings.

Connection string example: Execution Location=3

Table B-6   Execution Location Values and Meanings

VALUE	MEANING
0	Default. For compatibility with OLAP 7, this means the same as 1.
1	Pivot Table Services selects the query execution location (client or server) based on internal heuristics.
2	Queries are executed on the client.
3	Queries that can be executed on the server are executed on the server.

Initial Catalog

This property is used to set the name of the database (or catalog) on the server when connecting.

Default: None.

Set: Only when connecting.

Connection string example: `Initial Catalog=FoodMart`

InsertInto

This property contains the `INSERT INTO` statement used during creation of a local cube.

Default: None.

Set: Only when connecting.

This property must be used in conjunction with the `CreateCube` and `Source_DSN` properties. See Chapter 17 for a description of the `INSERT INTO` command syntax.

Connection string example: `InsertInto=INSERT INTO MyCube (...)`

Large Level Threshold

This property determines the point at which a level is too large to be sent to the client application in a single piece, and at which point the number of members used from a level force Pivot Table Services to try to execute it at the server.

Default: Set at server, server default is 1,000.

Set: Only when connection is established.

Using this property can help manage both memory and CPU usage for the client application. In metadata requests, a request for a level larger than this is broken up into a transmission of groups no larger than this size. If the level is smaller than this threshold, then the entire level is downloaded. Additionally, if a query involves more than this number of members from a single level, OLAP/Analysis Services will attempt to resolve the query on the server; below this threshold, it will resolve it on the client.

The minimum value for this property is 10. If a number less than 10 is used, then the value will silently be set to 10.

Connection string example: `Large Level=500`

Locale Identifier

This OLE DB property is used to set the locale ID (LCID) of preference for the client application.

Default: `NULL`.

Set: Only when connection is established.

The client application can modify the locale settings under which it runs by setting the Locale Identifier property when the connection is established. The locale will determine (among other things) how numbers, currency, and dates/times will be formatted. The LCID must be already installed through the Control Panel. If it is not, the attempt to set the LCID fails. By default, the `Locale Identifier` property is reported as `NULL`.

Pivot Table Services can use only one LCID for each process. If the first connection specifies an LCID and other connections are opened in the same process, each connection after the first connection must specify the same LCID as that of the first connection.

Refer to Microsoft platform documentation for how to obtain locale ID numbers.

Connection string example: `Locale Identifier=409`

Log File

This property sets or returns the name of a file used to log queries and commands.

Default: None.

Set: Only when connection is established.

If you set a value for this property, then it is taken as the name of a file to log queries and commands into. This can be very useful for debugging queries generated by a client program. Queries are logged whether successful or not. The specified file is opened for exclusive write; any concurrent attempt by another connection to open the same file for write access will fail. The format of the log file is as follows:

Process_name : Process_ID

Date

Time

Command type (either MDX, SQL, or DM)

Query text

Each field is separated by a tab character and records are terminated by a carriage return/line feed pair. If the command contains carriage returns and/or line feeds, you should parse the log by looking for patterns of process name, process ID, and date/time.

Note: If the log file exists when the connection is made, queries and commands are logged from the beginning of the file and any pre-existing contents are deleted.

Connection string example: `Log File=C:\Temp\Debug MDX.log`

MDX Compatibility

This property determines how placeholder members in ragged and unbalanced hierarchies are treated and how object names are generated.

Default: 0 (same meaning as 1). The default meaning may change in future versions.

Set: When connecting, and at any time during a connection.

Ragged (level-based) hierarchies are implemented in Analysis Services 2000 and Analysis Services 2005 either by hiding members in levels or by adding members to positions in the hierarchy. In a level-based ragged hierarchy, placeholder members are hidden to create the appearance of raggedness. In a parent-child hierarchy, members may be added to create the appearance of raggedness. This property determines whether placeholder members in a ragged or unbalanced hierarchy are visible or not.

Table B-7 describes possible values for this property.

NOTE In order to see the effect of nondefault values of the MDX Unique Name Style property, you also need to ensure that this property is set to a value of 2. Exposing placeholder members neutralizes the special name algorithms.

Table B-7 MDX Compatibility Values and Meanings

VALUE	DESCRIPTION
0	Default. For compatibility with earlier versions, this is the same as Value 1. The meaning of this default value is subject to change in future versions.
1	Placeholder members are exposed.
2	Placeholder members are not exposed.

Setting this property overrides the setting found in following server registry key:

```
HKLM\Software\Microsoft\OLAP Server\CurrentVersion\MDXCompatiblityValue
```

Connection string example: MDX Compatibility=2

TIP In Analysis Services 2000, changing this setting during a session only affects names generated for databases subsequently loaded (for example, by setting a new value for the ADO Connection's DefaultDatabase property). Unique names for the database currently being accessed will not change.

MDX Missing Member Mode

This property determines how Analysis Services 2005 deals with members referenced in MDX queries that do not exist in the cube to be queried.

Default: The value defined on the server for a dimension

Set: When connecting, but cannot be changed subsequently

For whatever reason, members may disappear from dimensions over the lifetime of a cube. In Analysis Services 2000, if a query references a member that subsequently disappears, then the entire query will fail, and in this way a minor ETL error can ruin hundreds of predefined reports. Analysis Services 2005 allows for more fault tolerance in this area through the MDX Missing Member Mode property on each dimension: Instead of the Analysis Services 2000 behavior, you can ignore any members in a query that have a valid dimension but an unrecognized name or key. The MDX Missing Member Mode connection string property allows you to override the server-defined behavior for all dimensions. Table B-8 describes the possible values for this property.

Connection String example: MDX Missing Member Mode=Error

Table B-8 MDX Missing Member Mode Values and Meanings

VALUE	DESCRIPTION
Default	Use the value defined in the MDX Missing Member property on each dimension on the server.
Ignore	Ignore missing members.
Error	Raise an error when an unrecognized member is detected.

MDX Unique Name Style

This property determines the algorithm used to generate unique names in OLAP metadata. (Note: This does not affect interpretation of names in any way.)

Default: 0 (means the same as 2).

Set: When connecting, and at any time during a connection.

Setting this property can cause Analysis Services to generate unique names using one of the algorithms listed in Table B-9.

NOTE In order to see the effect of values 1 or 3, you also need to ensure that the MDX Compatibility property is set to a value of 2.

In Analysis Services 2000, changing this setting during a session only affects names generated for databases subsequently loaded (for example, by setting a new value for the ADO Connection's DefaultDatabase property). Unique names for the database currently being accessed will not change.

Table B-9 MDX Unique Name Style Values and Meanings

VALUE	ALGORITHM
0	Default. For compatibility with earlier versions, this is the same as Value 2. The meaning of this default value is subject to change in future versions.
1	Key path algorithm: [Dimension].&[Key1].&[Key2]
2	Compatible with version 7.0, name path algorithm: [Dimension].[Member1].[Member2]
3	Compatible with SQL Server 2000 Analysis Services. The algorithm uses as stable a name as can be derived from the underlying dimension and level settings.

Setting this property overrides the setting found in following key:

`HKEY_CLASSES_ROOT\CLSID\{a07ccd00-8148-11d0-87bb-00c04fc33942}`

Connection string example: MDX Unique Name Style=3

Non Empty Threshold

This property controls which algorithm Analysis Services 2000 uses to remove empty tuples from a query axis.

Default: 5,000

Set: At connection.

Analysis Services 2000 can choose between two algorithms to remove empty tuples from a query axis when the Non Empty keywords are used. The first filters out empty tuples after all the data for a query has been retrieved, a process that is necessarily slow but completely reliable. The second is the same algorithm as is used by the NonEmptyCrossjoin function, which is much faster but cannot be used when cells in the query will have their values supplied by custom rollup formulas, calculated cells, calculated members on non-measures dimensions, or calculated measures that do not have their Non Empty Behavior property set. The Non Empty Threshold property sets the limit for the number of tuples on an axis above which Analysis Services will use the second algorithm if it can; below this limit, even if it can use the second algorithm, it will always use the first.

This property is useful when working with client tools (such as all versions of Excel pivot tables) that do not support the use of the NonEmptyCrossjoin function in the MDX they generate. If, for example, you have calculated measures that take a long time to evaluate and whose Non Empty Behavior property you can set, setting the Non Empty Threshold property to 1 will ensure that the second algorithm is always used whenever the Non Empty keywords are used on an axis. As a result, query performance is likely to benefit because when all regular measures for a tuple on an axis are empty, any calculated measures present in the query will not be evaluated for that tuple.

Connection string example: Non Empty Threshold=10

Real Time OLAP

This property causes queries on partitions listening for notifications to be run in real time, bypassing caching.

Default: False

Set: At connection time, or at any point in the session.

The proactive caching functionality of Analysis Services 2005 allows users to strike a balance between MOLAP storage, where query performance is good but data may be out of date, and real-time ROLAP storage, where query performance is poor but the data reflects the most recent changes. However, even when the database administrator has configured proactive caching to use one of the higher data latency settings (such as "Automatic MOLAP"), it may be that occasionally a user might need to run a query against the most recent data. The Real Time Olap connection string property allows the user to ensure that any queries against partitions listening for notifications completely bypass the MOLAP cache, and go directly to the relational source to ensure that the data retrieved is the most current.

Connection string example: `Real Time Olap=True`

Restricted Client

This property prevents clients from using local cube or local mining model functionality, or raising dialogs.

Default: 0

Set: At connection

This property is important when Pivot Table Services is used in a middle-tier scenario: When set to true (that is, any numeric value other than 0 or any string such as "Y" or "T" that can be converted to a numeric value other than 0), any attempt to use a statement such as CREATE CUBE, which results in the creation of a local object, will result in an error. This prevents MDX injection attacks that use such statements. Second, any statement that involves deep recursion, such as a series of nested DRILLDOWN statements, raises an error if this statement can potentially overflow the statement stack maintained by Pivot Table Services. Third, it prevents Pivot Table Services from raising dialogs.

Connection string example: `Restricted Client=1`

Roles

This property specifies the roles that a client application connects under.

Default: None.

Set: Only when session is established.

If specified, this property will contain a comma-delimited string of the role names under which the client application will connect to the server. The role names used need to be specified in the collection of database roles on that server. The user connecting to the server must be a member of these roles for the connection to succeed. This can be helpful for testing out the access of different roles. This is separate from using the User ID and Password connection properties, which may be required to authenticate you to the server as being a member of the stated role(s).

NOTE Connecting under more than one role may get confusing because permissions are as though the least restricted role is connected.

Role names are case-sensitive. You should not include spaces between the role names (although if the role names contain spaces, you must use them).

Connection string example: `Roles=VP Sales`

Safety Options

This property determines how safety and security for user-defined functions and actions are handled.

Default: `DBPROPVAL_MSMD_SAFETY_OPTIONS_DEFAULT`

Set: Only when session is established.

The value of the property determines whether "unsafe" libraries can be registered and loaded by Pivot Table Services or the server. If safety checking is enabled and an attempt is made to load an unsafe library or reference an unsafe user-defined function, Pivot Table Services will return the following error message: "User defined functions are not allowed by security settings for current connection."

Table B-10 lists the possible values for this property.

Table B-10   Safety Options Values and Meanings

VALUE	DESCRIPTION
0	For connections via an IIS server, this value is the same as 2. If the connection is to a local cube and the `CREATE CUBE` statement is used, this value is the same as 1; if `CREATE CUBE` is not used, it is the same as 2. For all other connections, this value is the same as 1.
1	This value enables all user-defined function libraries without verifying that they are safe for initialization and scripting, and also allows the `PASSTHROUGH` keyword to be used in `CREATE CUBE` statements.

(continued)

Table B-10   *(continued)*

VALUE	DESCRIPTION
2	This value ensures that all classes for a particular user-defined function library are checked to ensure that they are safe for initialization and scripting. If a function is not safe, then an attempt to access a cell calculated by it will result in an error with the text, "A user-defined function from interface X is not safe to be called." In addition, this value means that the PASSTHROUGH keyword cannot be used in CREATE CUBE statements, and command-line and HTML actions are removed from the actions schema as are any URL actions that do not start with http:// or https://.
3	This value prevents user-defined functions from being used during the session. (Note: The Excel and VBA function libraries are exempt from this prohibition.) The PASSTHROUGH keyword cannot be used in CREATE CUBE statements. All actions are removed from the actions schema.

Information about signing libraries as safe can be found at `http://msdn.microsoft.com/workshop/components/activex/signmark.asp`.

Connection string example: `Safety Options=3`

Secured Cell Value

This property determines the value returned for secured cells.

Default: 0 (Means same as 1). Meaning may change in future.

Set: Only when connection is established.

Depending on the value set through this property, a query that attempts to access a secured cell can return a specified error code and/or content for the `Value` and `Formatted Value` cell properties. The possible property values and results for proscribed cells are listed in Table B-11.

Table B-11   Secured Cell Value Settings and Meanings

VALUE	DESCRIPTION
0	Default. In Analysis Services 2000, this means the same as Value 1. The meaning of the default value may change in future versions.
1	OLE DB: HRESULT 5 NO_ERROR/ADO MD: no cell access error. Cell properties: Value holds nothing, Formatted Value holds "#NA".

Table B-11   *(continued)*

VALUE	DESCRIPTION
2	OLE DB: `HRESULT` holds an error/ADO MD: error raised accessing cell.
3	OLE DB: `HRESULT 5 NO_ERROR`/ADO MD: no cell access error. Cell properties: `Value` is `NULL`, `Formatted Value` is `NULL`.
4	OLE DB: `HRESULT 5 NO_ERROR`/ADO MD: no cell access error. Cell properties: `Value` is numerical zero (0), `Formatted Value` holds the value zero formatted according to the active cell `FORMAT_STRING`.
5	OLE DB: `HRESULT 5 NO_ERROR`/ADO MD: no cell access error. Cell properties: `Value` is the string "`#SEC`," `Formatted Value` is the string "`#SEC`".

This property interacts with the Default Isolation Mode setting of the query. If `Default Isolation Mode` is set to true and `Secured Cell Value` is set to 2 or 5, then in our experience, it is the same as value 3 in the preceding table. If the `Secured Cell Value` is set to 1 or 4, then the default isolation mode does not matter.

Connection string example: `Secured Cell Value=5`

Source_DSN

This property contains the OLE DB or ODBC connection string or ODBC data source name (DSN) for the relational database or server cube that will be used as the source for a local cube.

Default: None.

Set: Only when session is established.

This property is used only when creating a local cube. You must use this together with the `CreateCube` and `InsertInto` properties.

The value for this property is stored in the cube file and used every time a client opens the cube (in the case of a ROLAP cube) or whenever the cube is refreshed (in the case of a MOLAP cube). Different cubes in a cube file may have different values for `Source_DSN` (but the `Source_DSN_Suffix`, if any, are shared among them).

Connection string example (note the enclosing double quotes, and the specification of the server's initial catalog):

```
Source_DSN="Provider=SQLOLEDB;
Initial Catalog=Sales Data Mart;"
```

Source_DSN_Suffix

This property contains a string that is appended to the `Source_DSN` property value when creating or connecting to a local cube.

Default: None.

Set: Only when session is established.

This property holds connection information that is appended to the contents of the `Source_DSN` when a connection is established with a local cube. The primary purpose of this property is to separate out and contain information that should be provided each time the cube is opened, such as the username and password required to access the RDBMS that underpins a ROLAP cube, or when a MOLAP cube is refreshed. If you specify username and password in the `Source_DSN`, then they are stored in the cube definition and will be used every time the cube is opened. If you specify them in this property, then they must be supplied every time the cube is re-opened as well.

Connection string example (note that the contents are bounded by double quotes): `Source_DSN_Suffix="UserID=Adam;Password= 1Eval;"`

UseExistingFile

This property indicates whether an existing local cube file is to be overwritten or appended to when creating a local cube file.

Default: None.

Set: Only when connecting.

The function of this property depends on the existence and contents of the cube file being created. If you do not set a value for this property, when the data source is opened, any previous cube file is overwritten with the one cube specified in the `CreateCube` property. Table B-12 shows the interaction between the condition of the cube file and the value to which this property is set.

Manipulating this property will allow you to create and maintain multiple cubes in a single local cube file. Once a cube file contains a single cube, in order to add additional cubes to the file, you need to set this property to True.

Connection string example: `UseExistingFile=True`

Table B-12   Effect of UseExistingFile Setting

FILE CONDITION	CUBE CONDITION	EFFECT WHEN TRUE	EFFECT WHEN FALSE
Does not exist	–	Returns E_FAIL (OLE DB for OLAP) when you open a new data source.	New file and cube are created when the data source is opened.
Exists	Not in file	Cube is created in file.	Cube is created in file.
Exists	Exists in file	No changes made to cube.	Cube overwritten in file.

Intrinsic Cell and Member Properties

OLE DB for OLAP gives you the ability to treat the members and cells returned by queries as groups of related properties. This enables multiple related pieces of information to be returned to a client for both members and cells. If you do not request specific cell or member properties in a query, then a default set is returned. This appendix provides a reference to aid you in specifying the properties in MDX queries. (You may also wish to refer to the documentation for OLE DB for OLAP or ADO MD or ADOMD.NET for programmer-level information on how to extract and use the returned property information.)

When you are considering the use of member properties, it is important that you recognize that Microsoft Analysis Services does not make a syntactic distinction between intrinsic member properties and properties that you define (which might otherwise be called "member attributes" or "related attributes"). This means that you should avoid creating member properties whose names collide with those of the intrinsic member properties. In Microsoft's OLAP products, you do not have the ability to define custom cell properties, so this is not yet a consideration for cell properties.

The main purpose of the cell properties supported in Microsoft's OLAP/ Analysis Services is to assist in the rendering of cells. Client tools that look for these properties will be able to render results as these properties specify, whereas other clients will not. If you are interested in creating the functional equivalent of custom cell properties, you can always create additional calculated members that return their values and construct your front-end tool to look for them and interpret them accordingly.

Member Properties

A query specifies the member properties to return for a dimension in the axis specification that contains that dimension. This syntax is covered in Chapter 4. To summarize, if the axis is to be retrieved with only default member information, then the axis will be specified as follows:

```
{ set specification } on axis
```

If member properties are to be retrieved, then the axis specification will look like the following:

```
{ set specification } [DIMENSION] PROPERTIES property-name [, property-
name . . . ] on axis
```

To request a specific set of member properties for the dimensions in an axis, you follow the set specification with DIMENSION PROPERTIES (or just PROPERTIES) and then list the unique names of each property. You would separate multiple property names by commas, and after the last property name, place the on axis as usual. For example, a query that requests the customer's gender, occupation, and yearly income would look like this:

```
SELECT [Measures].[Internet Sales Amount] ON COLUMNS,
[Customer].[Customer Geography].[Full Name].MEMBERS
DIMENSION PROPERTIES
[Customer].[Customer Geography].[Gender],
[Customer].[Customer Geography].[Occupation],
[Customer].[Customer Geography].[Yearly Income] ON ROWS
FROM
[Adventure Works]
```

It is important to recognize that whereas the .Properties() function evaluates its property name on a cell-by-cell basis, each property name that you list in this example is bound to one and only one dimension level. If you have the same property name at two or more levels in the dimension, then you will want to qualify the name of the property with the unique name of the level (such as [Organization].[Region].[Manager] as opposed to [Organization] .[Area].[Manager]). All of the intrinsic properties are bound on a level-by-level basis.

The intrinsic dimension member properties as defined by OLE DB for OLAP are shown in Table C-1. The intrinsic properties supported for the members of a dimension and of a level by Analysis Services 2005 are listed in Table C-2.

Table C-1 Member Properties Specified as Part of OLE DB for OLAP

MICROSOFT EXTENSION	PROPERTY NAME	TYPE	MEANING
	MEMBER_CAPTION	DBTYPE_WSTR	Caption of the member.
	MEMBER_NAME	DBTYPE_WSTR	Name (not unique name) of the member.
	MEMBER_UNIQUE_ NAME	DBTYPE_WSTR	Unique name of the member.
	CATALOG_NAME	DBTYPE_WSTR	Name of the catalog containing the cube(s).
	CHILDREN_ CARDINALITY	DBTYPE_UI4	Estimated child cardinality.
	CUBE_NAME	DBTYPE_WSTR	Name of the cube.
	DESCRIPTION	DBTYPE_WSTR	Description associated with the dimension.
	DIMENSION_ UNIQUE_NAME	DBTYPE_WSTR	Unique name of the dimension.
	HIERARCHY_ UNIQUE_NAME	DBTYPE_WSTR	Unique name of the hierarchy.
	LEVEL_NUMBER	DBTYPE_UI4	Unique name of the member.
	LEVEL_UNIQUE_ NAME	DBTYPE_WSTR	Unique name of the member.
	MEMBER_GUID	DBTYPE_GUID	Unique name of the member.
	MEMBER_ORDINAL	DBTYPE_UI4	Unique name of the member.

(continued)

Table C-1 *(continued)*

MICROSOFT EXTENSION	PROPERTY NAME	TYPE	MEANING
	MEMBER_TYPE	DBTYPE_I4	Type code for the member. It will be one of the following: MDMEMBER_TYPE_REGULAR (1) for a regular member, MDMEMBER_TYPE_ALL (2) for an All member, MDMEMBER_TYPE_FORMULA (3) for a formula member, MDMEMBER_TYPE_MEASURE (4) for a measure, MDMEMBER_TYPE_UNKNOWN (5) for a member not categorized by one of the other codes. A member calculated by a custom member formula is categorized as a regular member, not as a formula.
	PARENT_COUNT	DBTYPE_UI4	Number of parents (0 or 1 in Microsoft's OLAP).
	PARENT_LEVEL	DBTYPE_UI4	Level of the parent (will be 0 even if no parent).
	SCHEMA_NAME	DBTYPE_WSTR	Name of the schema containing the member.
	PARENT_UNIQUE_NAME	DBTYPE_WSTR	Unique name of the member's parent (NULL if no parent member).

Table C-2 Intrinsic Member Properties (Supported for Every Member in Analysis Services 2005)

MICROSOFT EXTENSION	PROPERTY NAME	TYPE	MEANING
	NAME	DBTYPE_WSTR	Name (not unique name) of the member.
	ID	DBTYPE_UI4	Internal database ordering number for the member; sorting on this provides hierarchical database ordering.
	KEY	DBTYPE_WSTR	Member key value as defined in the member key column from the dimensional table.
*	KEY (x)	variable	KEYx returns the 0-based key ordinal of the key. The original data type is retained.
*	UNARY_OPERATOR	DBTYPE_WSTR	The unary operator used for rollup operations (for parent-child hierarchies).
*	CUSTOM_ROLLUP	DBTYPE_WSTR	The custom member formula associated with the member (not the formula for a calculated member).
*	CUSTOM_ROLLUP_ PROPERTIES	DBTYPE_WSTR	Custom member properties.
	MEMBER_CAPTION	DBTYPE_WSTR	The caption for the member.
	MEMBER_NAME	DBTYPE_WSTR	Name of the member.
	MEMBER_TYPE	DBTYPE_I4	The indicates the type of the member, which can be one of the following: MDMEMBER_TYPE_REGULAR MDMEMBER_TYPE_ALL MDMEMBER_TYPE__FORMULA MDMEMBER_TYPE_MEASURE MDMEMBER_TYPE_UNKNOWN

(continued)

Table C-2 *(continued)*

MICROSOFT EXTENSION	PROPERTY NAME	TYPE	MEANING
	MEMBER_UNIQUE_NAME	DBTYPE_WSTR	The member unique name of this member.
*	MEMBER_VALUE	DBTYPE_VARIANT	Value of member in original data type.
*	MEMBER_KEY	DBTYPE_VARIANT	Value of key in original data type.
*	PARENT_COUNT	DBTYPE_UI4	The number of parents.
*	PARENT_LEVEL	DBTYPE_UI4	The distance of the member's parent from the root level of the hierarchy. Root level of the hierarchy is 0.
*	PARENT_UNIQUE_NAME	DBTYPE_WSTR	Unique name of member's parent. A value of NULL is returned for members at the root level of a hierarchy.
*	SKIPPED_LEVELS	DBTYPE_UI4	Only applicable for a member which has skipped levels.
*	LCID<LCID>	DBTYPE_UI4	The translation of the member in locale's ID.
	UNIQUE_NAME	DBTYPE_WSTR	Same as MEMBER_UNIQUE_NAME.
	CAPTION	DBTYPE_WSTR	Same as MEMBER_CAPTION.

Because these are member properties and they are returned through the standard OLE DB for OLAP interface, they will all be returned through a column of type `Variant`. Names and unary operators are returned as Unicode strings (wide characters), and IDs are returned as 32-bit integers. A member key's type depends on its definition in the dimension.

Intrinsic properties are only bound at the lowest level within a query by default. For example, consider the following query:

```
SELECT [Measures].[Internet Sales Amount] ON COLUMNS,
Descendants(
[Customer].[Customer Geography].[Country].&[Australia],
[Customer].[Customer Geography].[State-Province].&[BC]&[CA])
DIMENSION PROPERTIES
[id] ON ROWS
FROM
[Adventure Works]
```

If you want to explicitly retrieve the ID for each level, then you need to use the following MDX query where you explicitly query the ID from all the levels:

```
SELECT [Measures].[Internet Sales Amount] ON COLUMNS,
Descendants(
[Customer].[Customer Geography].[Country].&[Australia],
[Customer].[Customer Geography].[State-Province].&[BC]&[CA],
   SELF_BEFORE_AFTER
   )
DIMENSION PROPERTIES
[Customer].[Customer Geography].[Country].[id]
,
[Customer].[Customer Geography].[State-Province].[id],
[Customer].[Customer Geography].[Full Name].[id]
ON ROWS
FROM
[Adventure Works]
```

The intrinsic properties listed in Table C-1 may be queried for at the scope of an axis. Because these are queried for on an axis scope, if the axis has more than one dimension, you will obtain whatever property you request for every dimension in the axis.

By "axis scope," we mean that you cannot ask for these by dimension or level. When you request them, they will be provided for every dimension that appears in the axis. The following query succeeds:

```
SELECT [Measures].[Internet Sales Amount] ON COLUMNS,
[Customer].[Customer Geography].[State-Province].members
DIMENSION PROPERTIES
MEMBER_UNIQUE_NAME
ON ROWS
FROM
[Adventure Works]
```

whereas this query fails:

```
SELECT [Measures].[Internet Sales Amount] ON COLUMNS,
[Customer].[Customer Geography].[State-Province].members
DIMENSION PROPERTIES
Customer.[Customer Geography].MEMBER_UNIQUE_NAME
ON ROWS
FROM
[Adventure Works]
```

When you specify member properties in a query that is to be returned as a multidimensional dataset, the member properties are returned in addition to the default properties: member unique name, caption, and so on. For a query that is to be returned as a "flattened" rowset, if you do not specify any member properties, then the (nonunique) names for members in each level of the query result will be returned. If the query does specify member properties for an axis, then only the properties that you request for the axis will be returned. When you request these axis properties in a query that is requested as a rowset, the rowset will contain one MEMBER_UNIQUE_NAME column and/or one MEMBER_CAPTION column per level that contributes a member to the results, as described in Chapter 15. Note that MEMBER_NAME is not a synonym for MEMBER_CAPTION in Analysis Services 2005; the caption may contain a different string and may depend on language settings for the connection.

You can mix requests for dimension- and level-scoped properties in the same query with axis-scoped dimension properties.

Analysis Services 2005 is depreciating certain intrinsic member properties, and some of the intrinsic properties defined in OLEDB for OLAP of the dimension member properties are not supported. The deprecated dimension member properties are Datamember, Catalog_Name, Custom_rollup, Expression, Member_GUID, Member_Ordinal, Schema_Name, and Skip.

Cell Properties

Any cell property to be returned by a query is specified in the last clause. If the query has a WHERE slicer clause, then the cell properties clause follows it. If the query does not, then the cell properties follow the FROM clause. The syntax of the cell properties clause is as follows:

```
CELL PROPERTIES property-name [, property-name . . . ]
```

The intrinsic properties supported for a cell are shown in Table C-3. Table C-4 shows the intrinsic cell properties supported in Analysis Services 2005.

Table C-3 Cell Properties Supported in OLE DB for OLAP

MICROSOFT EXTENSION	PROPERTY NAME	TYPE	MEANING
	BACK_COLOR	DBTYPE_UI4	Color value for background color.
	CELL_ORDINAL	DBTYPE_UI4	Ordinal number of cell in result set (for use as index value).
	FORMAT_STRING	DBTYPE_WSTR	Format string used to render value.
	FONT_FLAGS	DBTYPE_I4	Flags for font-rendering effects (bold, italic, strikethrough).
	FONT_NAME	DBTYPE_WSTR	Name of font to use when rendering cell value.
	FONT_SIZE	DBTYPE_UI2	Font size to render value with.
	FORE_COLOR	DBTYPE_UI4	Color value for foreground color.
	FORMATTED_VALUE	DBTYPE_WSTR	Formatted string of raw value for displaying formatted value.
	VALUE	*	Raw data value for the cell (returned in a Variant).

Table C-4 Intrinsic Cell Properties (Supported for Every Member in Analysis Services 2005)

MICROSOFT EXTENSION	PROPERTY NAME	TYPE	MEANING

*	ACTION_TYPE	DBTYPE_UI4	This indicates which types of actions exist on the cell. The various action types are
			
			`MDACTION_TYPE_DRILLTHROUGH`
			
			(Drill-through actions are not included for queries that contain set in the where clause.)
			
			`MDACTION_TYPE_URL`
			`MDACTION_TYPE_HTML`
			`MDACTION_TYPE_STATEMENT`
			`MDACTION_TYPE_DATASET`
			`MDACTION_TYPE_ROWSET`
			`MDACTION_TYPE_COMMANDLINE`
			`MDACTION_TYPE_PROPREITARY`
			`MDACTION_TYPE_REPORT`

	BACK_COLOR	DBTYPE_UI4	Background color.
	CELL_ORDINAL	DBTYPE_UI4	The ordinal of the cell in the result set.

	FONT_FLAGS	DBTYPE_UI4	This indicates the effects of the font. The value can be a bit mask of the following values:
			
			`MDFF_BOLD = 1`
			`MDFF_ITALIC = 2`
			`MDFF_UNDERLINE = 4`
			`MDFF_STRIKEOUT = 8`

	FONT_NAME	DBTYPE_WSTR	The font to be used to display the cell value or the formatted value of the cell.
	FONT_SIZE	DBTYPE_UI2	This is used to display the value or formatted value of the cell.
	FORE_COLOR	DBTYPE_UI4	This is used to display the value or formatted value of the cell.

	formatted_value	dbtype_ wstr50	This is the character string that represents a formatted display of the cell value.
*	FORMAT		Same as FORMAT_STRING.
*	FORMAT_STRING	DBTYPE_WSTR	The format string used for creating the formatted value.
*	language	DBTYPE_WSTR	Display the language property defined for the cell. The value is 0 if it is not defined.
*	Updateable	DBTYPE_I4	This indicates if the cell can be updated. The various values the cell can have for this property are MD_MASK_ENABLED= 0x00000000 MD_MASK_NOTENABLED= 0x10000000 CELL_UPDATEENABLE=MD_MASK_ ENABLE | 0x00000001—Cell can be updated in the cellset. CELL_UPDATE_ENABLED_WITH_ UPDATE=MD_MASK_ENABLED | 0x00000002—Cell can be updated with update statement. A cell update can fail if a leaf cell is updated that is not write-enabled. CELL_UPDATE_NOT_ENABLED_ FORMULA MD_MASK_NOT_ENABLED | 0x00000001—Cell cannot be updated because the cell has a calculated member among its coordinates; cell was retrieved with a set in the Where clause. (Note that a cell can be updated even though a formula affects or a calculated cell is on the value of a cell—for example, somewhere along the aggregation path. In this scenario, the final value of the cell may not be the updated value because the calculation affects the result.)

(continued)

Table C-4 *(continued)*

MICROSOFT EXTENSION	PROPERTY NAME	TYPE	MEANING
			`CELL_UPDATE_NOT_ENABLED_ NONSUM_MEASURE = MD_MASK_ NOT_ENABLED	0x00000002`—Non-sum measures (count, min, max, distinct count, semi-additive) cannot be updated.
			`CELL_UPDATE_NOT_ENABLED_ NACELL_VIRTUALCUBE = MD_ MASK_NOT_ENABLED	0x00000003`—Cannot be updated because the cell does not exist as the cell is at the intersection of a measure and a dimension member unrelated to the measure's measure group.
			`CELL_UPDATE_NOT_ENABLED_ SECURE = MD_MASK_NOT_ ENABLED	0x00000005`—Cell is secured and cannot be updated.
			`CELL_UPDATE_NOT_ENABLED_ CALCLEVEL = MD_MASK_ NOT_ENABLED	0x00000006`—Not used in Yukon.
			`CELL_UPDATE_NOT_ENABLED_ CANNOTUPDATE = MD_MASK_ NOT_ENABLED	0x00000007`—Cannot update for internal reason.
			`CELL_UPDATE_NOT_ENABLED_ INVALIDDIMENSIONTYPE = MD_MASK_NOT_ENABLED	0x00000009`—The cell cannot be updated because update is not supported in MM, indirect, or data mining dimensions.
	VALUE	`DBTYPE_ VARIANT`	Unformatted value of the cell.

By default (both for OLE DB for OLAP and Microsoft's OLAP products), if you do not explicitly request any cell properties in a query, the VALUE, FORMATTED_VALUE, and CELL_ORDINAL properties are returned for each cell. If you request any cell properties in a query, then only those that you request are returned. For example, if you are going to use the result of a query only to format a spreadsheet grid of numbers for display, then you may only want to query for the formatted values. If you are going to use the result of a query only to create a chart from the numerical values, then you may want to only query for the unformatted value.

The cell properties condition, description, disabled, calculation_pass_number, calculation_pass_depth, cell_evaluation_list, non_empty_behavior, solveorder, solve_order, and visible are not supported in Analysis Services 2005.

For example, the following query requests the formatted value plus font name, size, flags, and color information:

```
SELECT [Measures].[Internet Sales Amount] ON COLUMNS,
[Date].[Calendar].members ON ROWS
FROM
[Adventure Works]
CELL PROPERTIES [Formatted_Value], [Font_Name], [Font_Size],
[Font_Flags], [Fore_Color], [Back_Color]
```

No cell properties will be returned for an MDX query that is returned as a "flattened" rowset. Instead, the columns of the recordset/rowset that return cell values will return only values.

Format String Codes

Calculated members and cell calculations can specify the formatting applied to a cell value to transform it into a formatted value. The formatted value is a text string, whereas the raw value can be numeric or textual (and a numeric cell could represent a date or time serial number). This appendix lays out the codes specified by OLE DB for OLAP and used by Microsoft's OLAP, Analysis Services 2000, and Analysis Services 2005. The codes match the format arguments used by the Visual Basic `Format()` function.

Formatting Numeric Values

A format expression for numeric values can have from one to four sections, each section separated by semicolons. If the format argument contains one of the named numeric formats, only one section can be used. Table D-1 lists the section usage and interpretations of sections in format strings.

The following example has one section, and formats a number with two decimal places:

```
"#.00"
```

Table D-1 Format String Sections and Interpretations

SECTION USAGE	INTERPRETATION
One section	The format expression applies to all values.
Two sections	The first section applies to positive values and zeros, the second to negative values.
Three sections	The first section applies to positive values, the second to negative values, and the third to zeros.
Four sections	The first section applies to positive values, the second to negative values, the third to zeros, and the fourth to null values.

The following example has two sections. The first section defines the format for positive values and zeros, and the second section defines the format for negative values. The result is that negative numbers are displayed within parentheses:

```
"#,##0%;(#,##0%)"
```

If you include semicolons with nothing between them, the missing section is printed using the format of the positive value. For example, the following format displays positive and negative values using the format in the first section and displays "Zero" if the value is zero:

```
"$#,##0;;\Z\e\r\o"
```

Table D-2 describes the characters that can appear in the format string for number formats.

Table D-2 Formatting Code Characters and Interpretations

CHARACTER	DESCRIPTION
None	Displays the number with basic formatting (a decimal point if necessary).
0	Placeholder that displays either a digit or a zero, depending on whether the number would have a nonzero digit in that position. If the format expression has more zeros to either the right or left side of the decimal point than significant digits are in the number, leading or trailing zeros will be shown. If there are fewer zeros in the format expression than in significant digits to the right of the decimal point, the number will be rounded to as many decimal places as there are zeros to the right. If there are fewer zeros in the format expression to the left of the decimal point than there are digits to the left of the decimal point in the numerical value, then the extra digits in the number will be displayed.

Table D-2 *(continued)*

CHARACTER	DESCRIPTION
#	Placeholder that displays a digit or nothing. If the numerical value has a digit in the same position as the # in the format string, the digit will be displayed. Otherwise, nothing is displayed in that position.
.	Placeholder for the decimal in some locales. (In other locales, a comma is the placeholder for the decimal separator.) This placeholder is used with the # and 0 placeholders to determine how many digits are displayed to the left and right of the decimal separator. If a 0 appears as the first digit placeholder to the left of the decimal separator, then a fractional number (smaller than 1) will begin with 0 (for example, "0.5"). If the format expression contains only number signs (#) to the left of this symbol, numbers smaller than 1 begin with a decimal separator. Note: The actual character used as a decimal placeholder in the formatted output depends on your system and connection locale.
%	Placeholder for percentage representation. The numeric value is effectively multiplied by 100 (it has its decimal point shifted by two). The percent character (%) is inserted into the resulting string at the position where it appears in the format string.
,	Thousands separator in some locales. (In other locales, a period is used as a thousand separator.) The thousand separator separates thousands from hundreds within a number that has four or more places to the left of the decimal separator, and also millions from hundred thousands within a number that has seven or more places to the left of the decimal separator. Ordinary use of the thousand separator is specified if the format contains a thousand separator surrounded by the digit placeholders 0 or #. Two adjacent thousand separators, or a thousand separator immediately to the left of the decimal separator (whether or not a decimal is specified) means "scale the number by dividing it by 1,000, rounding as needed." For example, the format string "##0,," indicates that 100 million should be represented as 100, and numbers smaller than 1 million should be represented as 0. If two thousand separators are adjacent anywhere other than immediately to the left of the decimal separator, they indicate simply that a thousands separator should be used in formatting the numerical value. Note: The actual character used as the thousands separator in the formatted output depends on your system and connection locale.

(continued)

Table D-2   *(continued)*

CHARACTER	DESCRIPTION
E2 E1 e2 e1	Scientific format. If the format expression contains at least one digit placeholder (0 or #) to the right of E2, E1, e2, or e1, the number is displayed in scientific format and E or e is inserted between the number and its exponent. The number of digit placeholders to the right determines the number of digits in the exponent. Use E2 or e2 to place a minus sign next to negative exponents. Use E1 or e1 to place a minus sign next to negative exponents and a plus sign next to positive exponents.
– + $ ( )	Used to display one of these literal characters. To display any other character, precede it with a backslash (\) or enclose it in double quotation marks (" ").
\	Displays the next character in the format string. This can be used to display a character that has special meaning as a literal character. The backslash itself is not displayed. Using a backslash is the same as enclosing the next character in double quotation marks. To display a backslash, use two backslashes (\\). Examples of characters that cannot be displayed as literal characters are the numeric-formatting characters (#, 0, %, E, e, „ and .), the date- and time-formatting characters (a, c, d, h, m, n, p, q, s, t, w, y, /, and :), and the string-formatting characters (@, &, „ ., and !).
"string"	Displays the string inside the double quotation marks (" ").

In addition, the strings in Table D-3 may be used to identify predefined formats.

Table D-3   Predefined Format Code Strings

STRING	DESCRIPTION
Standard	Formats as a simple number (as if no format string was applied).
Currency	Formats as a currency value, using the locale in effect for currency symbol, thousands separator, and decimal separator. Provides two decimal places. Encloses the formatted number in parentheses if less than zero.
Percent	Formats as a percentage with two decimal places, and a negative sign if less than zero.

Date Values

Table D-4 describes the formatting characters that can appear in the format string for date/time formats. The numerical value is interpreted as a date serial number. If you need to convert a value of a different type (such as a time range measured in seconds only) into a date serial number, you can use the `TimeSerial()` VBA function inside a calculated member to do so, remembering that the three arguments for hours, minutes, and seconds that this function takes must each be in the range of -32,768 to 32,767.

Table D-4   Date/Time Format Codes and Interpretations

CHARACTER	DESCRIPTION
:	Time separator in some locales. (In other locales, another character may be used to represent the time separator.) The time separator separates hours, minutes, and seconds when time values are formatted. Note: The actual character used as the time separator in formatting a string is determined by your system and connection locale.
/	Date separator. (In some locales, other characters may be used to represent the date separator.) The date separator separates the day, month, and year when date values are formatted. Note: The actual character used as the date separator in formatting a string is determined by your system and connection locale.
c	Displays the date as ddddd and displays the time as ttttt, in that order. Displays only date information if the date serial number has no fractional part. Displays only time information if no integer portion is present.
d	Formats the day's number without a leading zero (1–31).
dd	Formats the day's number with a leading zero (01–31).
ddd	Formats the abbreviated day name (Sun–Sat).
dddd	Formats the full day name (Sunday–Saturday).
ddddd	Formats the complete date including day, month, and year, formatted according to your system's short date format setting. In MS-Windows, the default short date format is m/d/yy.
dddddd	Formats a complete date including day, month, and year, formatted according to the long date setting recognized by your system. In MS-Windows, the default long date format is mmmm dd, yyyy.

(continued)

Table D-4 *(continued)*

CHARACTER	DESCRIPTION
w	Formats the weekday as a number (Sunday = 1, Saturday = 7).
ww	Formats the week of the year as a number (1–54).
m	Formats the month as a number without a leading zero (1–12).
m immediately after h or hh	Formats the minute without a leading zero (0–59).
mm	Formats the month as a number with a leading zero (01–12).
mm immediately after h or hh	Formats the minute with a leading zero (00–59).
mmm	Formats the month as an abbreviation (Jan–Dec).
mmmm	Formats the month as a full month name (January–December).
q	Formats the quarter of the year as a number (1–4).
y	Formats the day of the year as a number (1–366).
yy	Formats the year as a two-digit number (00–99).
yyyy	Formats the year as a four-digit number (100–9999).
h	Formats the hour as a number without leading zeros (0–23).
hh	Formats the hour as a number with leading zeros (00–23).
n	Formats the minute as a number without leading zeros (0–59).
nn	Formats the minute as a number with leading zeros (00–59).
s	Formats the second as a number without leading zeros (0–59).
ss	Formats the second as a number with leading zeros (00–59).
ttttt	Formats a time as a complete time (including hour, minute, and second), formatted using the time separator defined by the time format recognized by your system. A leading zero is displayed if the leading zero option is selected and the time is earlier than 10:00 (for example 09:59), in either the a.m. or the p.m. cycle. For Windows, the default time format is h:mm:ss.

Table D-4 *(continued)*

CHARACTER	DESCRIPTION
AM/PM or am/pm	Formats the time using a 12-hour clock. Displays AM or am with any hour from midnight until noon; displays an uppercase PM or lowercase pm with any hour from noon until midnight.
A/P or a/p	Formats the time using a 12-hour clock. Displays an uppercase A or lowercase a with any time from midnight until noon; displays an uppercase P or lowercase p with any hour from noon until midnight.
AMPM or ampm	Formats the time using a 12-hour clock. Displays the AM string literal as defined by your system with any time from midnight until noon; displays the PM string literal as defined by your system with any time from noon until midnight. The case of the string displayed matches the string as defined by your system settings. For Windows, the default format is AM/PM.

In addition, the following strings in Table D-5 may be used to identify predefined formats.

Table D-5 Predefined Date/Time Format Code Strings

STRING	DESCRIPTION
Short Date	Formats the complete date including day, month, and year, formatted according to the locale's short date format setting.
Short Time	Formats a time as a complete time (including hour, minute, and second), formatted according to your system's short time format setting.
Medium Date	Formats the complete date including day, month, and year, formatted according to the locale's medium date format setting.
Medium Time	Formats a time as a complete time (including hour, minute, and second), formatted according to the locale's medium time format setting.
Long Date	Formats the complete date including day, month, and year, formatted according to the locale's long date format setting.
Long Time	Formats a time as a complete time (including hour, minute, and second), formatted according to the locale's long time format setting.

String Values

A format expression for strings can have one section or two sections separated by a semicolon (;). Table D-6 describes the sections and usage for string format strings.

The characters described in Table D-7 can appear in the format string for character strings.

For example, if the string value is "Flaxen," Table D-8 shows the results of four different string formats.

Table D-6 Sections in Format Strings for String Values

USAGE	RESULT
One section	The format applies to all string values.
Two sections	The first section applies to string data, whereas the second section applies to NULL values and zero-length strings ("").

Table D-7 Format String Codes for Strings and Interpretation

CHARACTER	DESCRIPTION
@	Placeholder for a single character. If the string has a character in the position where the @ appears in the format string, it displays the character. Otherwise, it displays a space in that position. Placeholders are filled from right to left (right-justifying the string) unless an exclamation point (!) is in the format string. Note: If the string expression being formatted has more characters than there are @ and & symbols in the format string, the remainder of the string expression will be placed at the end of the formatted string.
&	Character placeholder. It displays a character or nothing. If the string has a character in the position where the & appears, it displays the character. Otherwise, no character is displayed. Placeholders are filled from right to left (right-justifying the string) unless an exclamation point (!) is in the format string. Note: If the string expression being formatted has more characters than there are @ and & symbols in the format string, the remainder of the string expression will be placed at the end of the formatted string.
<	Forces the result string to be in all lowercase.
>	Forces the result string to be in all uppercase.
!	Forces left-to-right fill of placeholders. This creates left-justification for the string. (The default is to fill placeholders from right to left.)

Table D-8   Format String Examples for String Values

FORMAT STRING	RESULT
@	"Flaxen"
@@@\F\o\o@@	"FlaFooxen"
!@@@@@@@@	"Flaxen"
<	"flaxen"

Conditional Formatting

Since calculated members and Microsoft's cell calculations can apply across cells having different types and meanings (string, number, date serial-number), finding the right format string for a particular calculation or query may be difficult. Microsoft Analysis Services 2005 allows you to use MDX to construct the format string to apply to a particular cell (see "Assigning Cell Property Values to Subcubes" in Chapter 13); however, unlike other display information such as the font flag and color, Microsoft Analysis Services 2000 does not.

If you need to be able to apply more complex conditional formatting in Analysis Services 2000, you can work around this limitation by relying on the fact that calculated members and cells inherit the formatting from the members whose values they derive from. You can, for example, create calculated members that return the same values but have different formats for each of your conditions, and then use another calculated member to implement the conditional logic and return the appropriately formatted calculated member. The following query illustrates this by formatting [Measures].[Total] differently if its value is under 700,000:

```
WITH
MEMBER [Measures].[Totals Under 700,000] AS '[Measures].[Total]',
FORMAT_STRING='(#,#.##)'
MEMBER [Measures].[Totals Formatted Conditionally] AS
'iif([Measures].[Total]>700000, [Measures].[Total], [Measures].[Totals
Under 700,000])'
SELECT {[Measures].[Total], [Measures].[Totals Under 700,000],
[Measures].[Totals Formatted Conditionally]} on columns,
[Time].[ByMonth].[Month].MEMBERS on rows
FROM SALES
```

The obvious drawback of this is that if you have a lot of members that need conditional formatting, you need a lot of calculated members to support this. The alternative, if you are using Analysis Services 2000 Enterprise Edition, is to use calculated cells instead of calculated members:

```
WITH
CELL CALCULATION [Totals Under 700,000]
FOR '({[Measures].[Total]})'
AS 'CALCULATIONPASSVALUE([Measures].[Total],-1, RELATIVE)'
, CONDITION='CALCULATIONPASSVALUE([Measures].[Total],-1,
RELATIVE)<700000'
, FORMAT_STRING='(#,#.##)'
SELECT {[Measures].[Total]} on columns,
[Time].[ByMonth].[Month].MEMBERS on rows
FROM SALES
```

While this might seem to be a more appealing technique, note that calculated cells carry a sometimes significant performance overhead that you might not want to incur.

Index

unary operators
 calculation method, 338–339
 MDX Scripts, 393–395
 multiple dimension precedence, 352
 pass order, 376
UnaryOperator() function, Return
 clause support, 415, 625
UnaryOperatorColumn property,
 unary operator definitions, 338
Union() function
 hierarchical order, 181–182, 626
 member selections, 279
UniqueName() function, Return
 clause support, 415, 626
UnOrder() function, optimization
 methods, 480, 627
Unrestricted permission, stored
 procedures, 317
unweighted allocations
 calculations, 71
 MDX Scripts, 409
UPDATE CUBE statement
 data cell updates, 323
 data updates, 330–334
updates
 member definitions, 327–328
 UPDATE CUBE statement, 323
URL action, uses, 420
USE LIBRARY statement, stored
 procedures, 316
UseExistingFile property, local
 cubes, 521
user hierarchies, MDX Scripts, 386–387
user profiles, Username() function,
 270
user-defined attributes (UDAs)
 base dimension member selections,
  276–280
 calculation uses, 275–276
 IsUDA() function, 276
 retrieval query, 274–275
 versus attributes, 273–274
user-defined functions (UDFs), Analysis
 Services 2000, 283
Username() function, user profile
 security, 270, 628

V

VAL() function, MDX Script, 495, 628
ValidMeasure() function, 261, 629
value operators, 538–539
Var(), summary statistical operator,
 54–55, 629
variables, substitution, 59
Variance(), summary statistical
 operator, 54–55
VarP(), summary statistical operator,
 55, 629
VISIBLE flag, calculated members, 343
Visual Basic for Applications (VBA),
 date calculations, 183
Visual Studio 2005
 debugging .NET stored procedures, 299
 viewing/editing MDX Scripts, 366–367
Visual Stuido.NET, ADOMD.NET
 reference, 443
VisualTotals() function, report-
 based totals-to-parent, 197–199, 629

W

Web servers, commandline action
 security, 425
Weight rollup operator, Analysis
 Services 2005, 338
weighted averages, 73–74
WHERE clause, query execution stage,
 101–102
WHERE keyword, MDX queries, 3–4
whitespace
 code readability, 7
 comment placement, 17
WITH clause, named sets, 129
WITH keyword, 39–42
WITH CELL CALCULATION statement,
 346
WITH MEMBER section, 39–43
 statement, 344–345
WITH SET command, 57–58
 statement, 150
WithAttr() function, 278–279, 630
wizards
 Add Business Intelligence, 405
 Define Time Intelligence, 227